THREE

By Alan Watts

Behold the Spirit (1947, 1971)
The Wisdom of Insecurity (1949)
The Supreme Identity (1950, 1972)
The Way of Zen (1957)
Nature, Man, and Woman (1958)
This Is It (1960)
Psychotherapy East and West (1961)
The Joyous Cosmology (1962)
Beyond Theology (1974)
The Book (1966)
Does It Matter? (1970)
In My Own Way (1972)
The Art of Contemplation (1973)
Cloud-Hidden, Whereabouts Unknown (1973)
Tao: The Watercourse Way (1975)

THREE

BY ALAN WATTS

THE WAY OF ZEN

NATURE, MAN, AND WOMAN

PSYCHOTHERAPY EAST
AND WEST

Pantheon Books, New York

Library of Congress Cataloging in Publication Data

Watts, Alan Wilson, 1915–1973.
Three.

Includes bibliographies.
CONTENTS: The Way of Zen.—Nature, Man, and Woman.
—Psychotherapy East and West.
1. Zen Buddhism.   2. Religion—Philosophy.
3. Sex and religion.   4. Psychotherapy.   5. East and West.
I. Title.
BQ9265.4.W37   1977   200'.8   77-76500
ISBN 0-394-41904-9
Manufactured in the United States of America

The Way of Zen was first published in April 1957

Nature, Man, and Woman was first published in September 1958

Psychotherapy East and West was first published in October 1961

200.8
WAT
1/81

Contents

THE WAY OF ZEN

To
TIA, MARK, AND RICHARD
who will understand it all the better
for not being able to read it

CONTENTS

PREFACE

During the past twenty years there has been an extraordinary growth of interest in Zen Buddhism. Since the Second World War this interest has increased so much that it seems to be becoming a considerable force in the intellectual and artistic world of the West. It is connected, no doubt, with the prevalent enthusiasm for Japanese culture which is one of the constructive results of the late war, but which may amount to no more than a passing fashion. The deeper reason for this interest is that the viewpoint of Zen lies so close to the "growing edge" of Western thought.

The more alarming and destructive aspects of Western civilization should not blind us to the fact that at this very time it is also in one of its most creative periods. Ideas and insights of the greatest fascination are appearing in some of the newer fields of Western science–in psychology and psychotherapy, in logic and the philosophy of science, in semantics and communications theory. Some of these developments might be due to suggestive influences from Asian philosophy, but on the whole I am inclined to feel that there is more of a parallelism than a direct influence. We are, however, becoming aware of the parallelism, and it promises an exchange of views which should be extremely stimulating.

Western thought has changed so rapidly in this century that we are in a state of considerable confusion. Not only are there serious difficulties of communication between the intellectual and the general public, but the course of our thinking and of our very history has seriously undermined the common-sense assumptions which lie at the roots of our social conventions and institutions. Familiar concepts of space, time, and motion, of nature and natural law, of history and social change, and of human personality itself have dissolved, and we find ourselves adrift without landmarks in a universe which more and more resembles the Buddhist principle of the "Great Void." The various wisdoms of the West, religious, philosophical, and scientific, do not offer much guidance to the art of living in such a universe, and we find the prospects of making our way in so trackless an ocean of relativity rather frightening. For we are used to absolutes, to firm principles and laws to which we can cling for spiritual and psychological security.

This is why, I think, there is so much interest in a culturally productive way of life which, for some fifteen hundred years, has felt thoroughly at home in "the Void," and which not only feels no terror for it but rather a positive delight. To use its own words, the situation of Zen has always been—

> *Above, not a tile to cover the head;*
> *Below, not an inch of ground for the foot.*

Such language should not actually be so unfamiliar to us, were we truly prepared to accept the meaning of "the foxes have holes, and the birds of the air have nests; but the Son of Man hath not where to lay his head."

I am not in favor of "importing" Zen from the Far East, for it has become deeply involved with cultural institutions which are quite foreign to us. But there is no doubt that there are things which we can learn, or unlearn, from it and apply in our own way. It has the special merit of a mode of expressing itself which is as intelligible–or perhaps as baffling–to the intellectual as to the illiterate, offering possibilities of communication which we have not explored. It has a directness, verve, and humor, and a sense of both beauty and nonsense at once exasperating and delightful. But above all it has a way of being able to turn one's mind inside out, and dissolving what seemed to be the most oppressive human problems into questions like "Why is a mouse when it spins?" At its heart there is a strong but completely unsentimental compassion for human beings suffering and perishing from their very attempts to save themselves.

There are many excellent books about Zen, though some of the best are out of print or otherwise difficult to obtain. But as yet no one–not even Professor Suzuki–has given us a comprehensive account of the subject which includes its historical background and its relation to Chinese and Indian ways of thought. The three volumes of Suzuki's *Essays in Zen Buddhism* are an unsystematic collection of scholarly papers on various aspects of the subject, enormously useful for the advanced student but quite baffling to the general reader without an understanding of the general principles. His delightful *Introduction to Zen Buddhism* is rather narrow and specialized. It omits the essential information about the relation of Zen to Chinese Taoism and Indian Buddhism, and is in some respects rather more mystifying than it need be. His other works are studies of special aspects of Zen, all of which require general background and historical perspective.

R. H. Blyth's *Zen in English Literature and Oriental Classics* is one of the best introductions available, but it is published only in Japan and, again, lacks the background information. As a series of rambling and marvelously perceptive observations, it makes no attempt to give an orderly presentation of the subject. My own *Spirit of Zen* is a popularization of Suzuki's earlier works, and besides being very unscholarly it is in many respects out of date and misleading, whatever merits it may have in the way of lucidity and simplicity. Christmas Humphreys' *Zen Buddhism*, published only in England, is likewise a popularization of Suzuki and, once more, does not really begin to put Zen in its cultural context. It is written in a clear and sprightly fashion, but the author finds identities between Buddhism and Theosophy which I feel to be highly questionable. Other studies of Zen by both Western and Asian authors are of a more specialized character, or are discussions of Zen *à propos* of something else– psychology, art, or cultural history.

In default, then, of a fundamental, orderly, and comprehensive account of the subject, it is no wonder that Western impressions of Zen are somewhat confused, despite all the enthusiasm and interest which it has aroused. The problem, then, is to write such a book—and this I have tried to do since no one who understands the subject better than I seems willing or able to do so. Ideally, I suppose, such a work should be written by an accomplished and recognized Zen master. But at present no such person has sufficient command of English. Furthermore, when one speaks from within a tradition, and especially from within its institutional hierarchy, there is always apt to be a certain lack of perspective and grasp of the outsider's viewpoint. Again, one of the biggest obstacles to communication between Japanese Zen masters and Westerners is the absence of clarity as to difference of basic cultural premises. Both sides are so "set in their ways" that they are unaware of the limitations of their means of communication.

Perhaps, then, the most appropriate author of such a work would be a Westerner who had spent some years under a Japanese master, going through the whole course of Zen training. Now from the standpoint of Western "scientific scholarship" this would not do at all, for such a person would have become an "enthusiast" and "partisan" incapable of an objective and disinterested view. But, fortunately or unfortunately, Zen is above all an experience, nonverbal in character, which is simply inaccessible to the purely literary and scholarly approach. To know what Zen is, and especially what it is not, there is no alternative but to practice it, to experiment with it in the concrete so as to discover the meaning which underlies the words. Yet such Westerners as have undergone some of the special type of training followed in Rinzai Zen tend to become "cagey" and uncommunicative on the principle that

> *Those who know do not speak;*
> *Those who speak do not know.*

Although, however, they do not "put up," they do not completely "shut up." On the one hand, they would love to share their understanding with others. But on the other hand, they are convinced that words are ultimately futile, and are, furthermore, under an agreement not to discuss certain aspects of their training. They begin, therefore, to take the characteristically Asian attitude of "Come and find out for yourself." But the scientifically trained Westerner is, not without reason, a cautious and skeptical fellow who likes to know what he is "getting into." He is acutely conscious of the capacity of the mind for self-deception, for going into places where entrance is impossible without leaving one's critical perspective at the door. Asians tend so much to despise this attitude, and their Western devotees even more so, that they neglect to tell the scientific inquirer many things that are still well within the possibilities of human speech and intellectual understanding.

To write about Zen is, therefore, as problematic for the outside, "objective" observer as for the inside, "subjective" disciple. In varying situations I have found myself on both sides of the dilemma. I have associated and studied with the "objective observers" and am convinced that, for all their virtues, they invariably miss the point and eat the menu instead of the dinner. I have also been on the inside of a traditional hierarchy—not Zen—and am equally convinced that from this position one does not know what dinner is being eaten. In such a position one becomes technically "idiotic," which is to say, out of communication with those who do not belong to the same fold.

It is both dangerous and absurd for our world to be a group of communions mutually excommunicate. This is especially true of the great cultures of the East and the West, where the potentialities of communication are the richest, and the dangers of failure to communicate the worst. As one who has spent somewhat more than twenty years trying to interpret the East to the West, I have become increasingly certain that to interpret such a phenomenon as Zen there is a clear principle to be followed.

On the one hand, it is necessary to be sympathetic and to experiment personally with the way of life to the limit of one's possibilities. On the other hand, one must resist every temptation to "join the organization," to become involved with its institutional commitments. In this friendly neutral position one is apt to be disowned by both sides. But, at the worst, one's misrepresentations provoke them to express themselves more clearly. For the relationship between two positions becomes far more clear when there is a third with which to compare them. Thus even if this study of Zen does no more than express a standpoint which is neither Zen nor anything Western, it will at least provide that third point of reference.

However, there can be no doubt that the essential standpoint of Zen refuses to be organized, or to be made the exclusive possession of any institution. If there is anything in this world which transcends the relativities of cultural conditioning, it is Zen–by whatever name it may be called. This is an excellent reason for Zen's not being institutionalized, and for the fact that many of its ancient exponents were "universal individualists" who were never members of any Zen organization, and never sought the acknowledgment of any formal authority.

This, then, is my position with respect to Zen–and I feel I should be frank with the reader in a day when there is so much anxiety about people's credentials or "quantifications." I cannot represent myself as a Zenist, or even as a Buddhist, for this seems to me to be like trying to wrap up and label the sky. I cannot represent myself as a scientifically objective academician, for–with respect to Zen–this seems to me to be like studying birdsong in a collection of stuffed nightingales. I claim no rights to speak of Zen. I claim only the pleasure of having studied its literature and observed its art forms since I was hardly more than a boy, and of having had the delight of informal association with a number of Japanese and Chinese travelers of the same trackless way.

This book is intended both for the general reader and for the more serious student, and I trust that the former will be tolerant of the use of some technical terminology, a Chinese character appendix, and other critical apparatus most useful for those who wish to explore the subject more deeply. The book is divided into two parts, the first dealing with the background and history of Zen, and the second with its principles and practice. The sources of information are of three types. I have, firstly, used almost all the studies of Zen in European languages. Naturally, I have made considerable use of the works of Professor D. T. Suzuki, but at the same time I have tried not to rely upon them too heavily—not because of any defect in them, but because I think readers are entitled to something more, by way of a fresh viewpoint, than a mere summarization of his views.

Secondly, I have based the essential view of Zen here presented upon a careful study of the more important of its early Chinese records, with special reference to the *Hsin-hsin Ming,* the *T'an Ching* or *Sutra of the Sixth Patriarch,* the *Lin-chi Lu,* and the *Ku-tsun-hsü Yü-lu.* My own knowledge of T'ang dynasty Chinese is certainly not enough to deal with some of the finer points of this literature, but sufficient, I think, to get what I wanted, which was a clear view of the essential doctrine. In all this, my efforts have been greatly aided by colleagues and research associates at the American Academy of Asian Studies, and I wish in particular to express my thanks to Professors Sabro Hasegawa and Gi-ming Shien, to Dr. Paul and Dr. George Fung, Dr. Frederick Hong, Mr. Charles Yick, and to Mr. Kazumitsu Kato, priest of the Soto-Zen School.

Thirdly, my information is derived from a large number of personal encounters with teachers and students of Zen, spread over more than twenty years.

In the following pages the translations from the original texts are my own, unless otherwise indicated. For the convenience of those who read Chinese, I have supplied, following the Bibliography, an appendix of the original Chinese forms of the more important quotations and technical terms. I have found these almost essential for the more serious student, for even among the most highly qualified scholars there is still much uncertainty as to the proper translation of T'ang dynasty Zen texts. References to this appendix are by superscribed index letters in alphabetical order.

References to other works are by surname of the author and number, directing the reader to the Bibliography for full details. Scholarly readers will have to excuse me for not using the absurd diacritical marks in romanized Sanskrit words, since these are merely confusing to the general reader and unnecessary to the Sanskritist who will at once call to mind the Devanagiri script. As to the proper names of Zen masters and titles of Zen texts, these are given in the romanized forms of Mandarin or Japanese according to the country of origin, and technical terms are given in Mandarin unless used in the discussion of specifically Japanese Zen. For Mandarin one is almost compelled by general usage to adopt the Wade-Giles romanization, for which I have appended a table of pronunciation following this Preface, since it has so little relation to the actual sounds.

I am most grateful to Mr. R. H. Blyth for his kind permission to quote a number of his translations of *haiku* poems from his magnificent four-volume anthology, *Haiku,* published by the Hokuseido Press in Tokyo; to Professor Sabro Hasegawa for his generous help in preparing the jacket and providing illustrations; and to my daughter Joan for the photographs of Ryoanji.

In conclusion, I am most happy to express my thanks to the Bollingen Foundation for a three-year fellowship, during which much of the preliminary study was done for the writing of this book.

ALAN WATTS

Mill Valley, California
July 1956

THE PRONUNCIATION OF CHINESE WORDS

Consonants   Aspirated: Read *p', t', k', ch',* and *ts'* as in *p*in,
*t*ip, *k*ilt, *ch*in, and bi*ts*.

Unaspirated: Read *p, t, k, ch,* and *ts* (or *tz*) as
in *b*in, *d*ip, *g*ilt, *g*in, and bi*ds*.

hs or *sh,* as in *sh*oe.

j is nearly like an "unrolled" *r,* so that *jen* is
nearly the English *wren*.

Vowels   Usually Italian values,

a as in f*a*ther

e as in *ei*ght

eh as in broth*er*

i as in mach*i*ne and p*i*n

ih as in sh*ir*t

o as in s*o*ap

u as in g*oo*se

ü as in German *ü*ber

Diphthongs   *ai* as in l*i*ght

ao as in l*ou*d

ei as in w*ei*ght

ia as in Will*ia*m

ieh as in Kor*ea*

ou as in gr*ou*p

ua as in s*wa*n

ueh as in d*oer*

ui as in s*way*

uo as in *who*ah!

Combinations   *an* and *ang* as in b*un* and b*ung*

en and *eng* as in wood*en* and am*ong*

in and *ing* as in s*in* and s*ing*

un and *ung* with the *u* as in l*oo*k.

PART ONE

BACKGROUND AND HISTORY

One

THE PHILOSOPHY OF THE TAO

Zen Buddhism is a way and a view of life which does not belong to any of the formal categories of modern Western thought. It is not religion or philosophy; it is not a psychology or a type of science. It is an example of what is known in India and China as a "way of liberation," and is similar in this respect to Taoism, Vedanta, and Yoga. As will soon be obvious, a way of liberation can have no positive definition. It has to be suggested by saying what it is not, somewhat as a sculptor reveals an image by the act of removing pieces of stone from a block.

Historically, Zen may be regarded as the fulfillment of long traditions of Indian and Chinese culture, though it is actually much more Chinese than Indian, and, since the twelfth century, it has rooted itself deeply and most creatively in the culture of Japan. As the fruition of these great cultures, and as a unique and peculiarly instructive example of a way of liberation, Zen is one of the most precious gifts of Asia to the world.

The origins of Zen are as much Taoist as Buddhist, and, because its flavor is so peculiarly Chinese, it may be best to begin by inquiring into its Chinese ancestry—illustrating, at the same time, what is meant by a way of liberation by the example of Taoism.

Much of the difficulty and mystification which Zen presents to the Western student is the result of his unfamiliarity with Chinese ways of thinking—ways which differ startlingly from our own and which are, for that very reason, of special value to us in attaining a critical perspective upon our own ideas. The problem here is not simply one of mastering different ideas, differing from our own as, say, the theories of Kant differ from those of Descartes, or those of Calvinists from those of Catholics. The

3

problem is to appreciate differences in the basic premises of thought and in the very methods of thinking, and these are so often overlooked that our interpretations of Chinese philosophy are apt to be a projection of characteristically Western ideas into Chinese terminology. This is the inevitable disadvantage of studying Asian philosophy by the purely literary methods of Western scholarship, for words can be communicative only between those who share similar experiences.

This is not to go so far as to say that so rich and subtle a language as English is simply incapable of expressing Chinese ideas. On the contrary, it can say much more than has been believed possible by some Chinese and Japanese students of Zen and Taoism whose familiarity with English leaves something to be desired. The difficulty is not so much in the language as in the thought-patterns which have hitherto seemed inseparable from the academic and scientific way of approaching a subject. The unsuitability of these patterns for such subjects as Taoism and Zen is largely responsible for the impression that the "Oriental mind" is mysterious, irrational, and inscrutable. Furthermore, it need not be supposed that these matters are so peculiarly Chinese or Japanese that they have no point of contact with anything in our own culture. While it is true that none of the *formal* divisions of Western science and thought corresponds to a way of liberation, R. H. Blyth's marvelous study of *Zen in English Literature* has shown most clearly that the essential insights of Zen are universal.

The reason why Taoism and Zen present, at first sight, such a puzzle to the Western mind is that we have taken a restricted view of human knowledge. For us, almost all knowledge is what a Taoist would call *conventional* knowledge, because we do not feel that we really know anything unless we can represent it to ourselves in words, or in some other system of conventional signs such as the notations of mathematics or music. Such knowledge is called conventional because it is a matter of social agreement as to the codes of communication. Just as people speaking the same language have tacit agreements as to what words shall stand for what things, so the members of every society and every culture are united by bonds of communication resting upon all kinds of agreement as to the classification and valuation of actions and things.

Thus the task of education is to make children fit to live in a society by persuading them to learn and accept its codes–the rules and conventions of communication whereby the society holds itself together. There is first the spoken language. The child is taught to accept "tree" and not "boojum" as the agreed sign for *that* (pointing to the object). We have no difficulty in understanding that the word "tree" is a matter of convention. What is much less obvious is that convention also governs the delineation of the thing to which the word is assigned. For the child has to be taught not only what words are to stand for what things, but also the way in which his culture has tacitly agreed to divide things from each other, to mark out the boundaries within our daily experience. Thus scientific convention decides whether an eel shall be a fish or a snake, and grammatical convention determines what experiences shall be called objects and what shall be called events or actions. How arbitrary such conventions may be can be seen from the question, "What happens to my fist [noun-object] when I open my hand?" The object miraculously vanishes because an action was disguised by a part of speech usually assigned to a thing! In English the differences between things and actions are clearly, if not always logically, distinguished, but a great number of Chinese words do duty for both nouns and verbs–so that one who thinks in Chinese has little difficulty in seeing that objects are also events, that our world is a collection of processes rather than entities.

Besides language, the child has to accept many other forms of code. For the necessities of living together require agreement as to codes of law and ethics, of etiquette and art, of weights, measures, and numbers, and, above all, of role. We have difficulty in communicating with each other unless we can identify ourselves in terms of roles–father, teacher, worker, artist, "regular guy," gentleman, sportsman, and so forth. To the extent that we identify ourselves with these stereotypes and the rules of behavior associated with them, we ourselves feel that we *are* someone because our fellows have less difficulty in accepting us–that is, in identifying us and feeling that we are "under control." A meeting of two strangers at a party is always somewhat embarrassing when the host has not identified their roles in introducing them, for neither knows what rules of conversation and action should be observed.

Once again, it is easy to see the conventional character of roles. For a man who is a father may also be a doctor and an artist, as well as an employee and a brother. And it is obvious that even the sum total of these role labels will be far from supplying an adequate description of the man himself, even though it may place him in certain general classifications. But the conventions which govern human identity are more subtle and much less obvious than these. We learn, very thoroughly though far less explicitly, to identify ourselves with an equally conventional view of "myself." For the conventional "self" or "person" is composed mainly of a history consisting of selected memories, and beginning from the moment of parturition. According to convention, I am not simply what I am doing now. I am also what I have done, and my conventionally edited version of my past is made to seem almost more the real "me" than what I am at this moment. For what I *am* seems so fleeting and intangible, but what I *was* is fixed and final. It is the firm basis for predictions of what I will be in the future, and so it comes about that I am more closely identified with what no longer exists than with what actually is!

It is important to recognize that the memories and past events which make up a man's historical identity are no more than a selection. From the actual infinitude of events and experiences some have been picked out–abstracted–as significant, and this significance has of course been determined by conventional standards. For the very nature of conventional knowledge is that it is a system of abstractions. It consists of signs and symbols in which things and events are reduced to their general outlines, as the Chinese character *jen* ^{a} stands for "man" by being the utmost simplification and generalization of the human form.

The same is true of words other than ideographs. The English words "man," "fish," "star," "flower," "run," "grow," all denote classes of objects or events which may be recognized as members of their class by very simple attributes, abstracted from the total complexity of the things themselves.

Abstraction is thus almost a necessity for communication, since it enables us to represent our experiences with simple and rapidly made "grasps" of the mind. When we say that we can think only of one thing at a time, this is like saying that the Pacific Ocean cannot be swallowed at a gulp. It has to be taken in a cup, and downed bit by bit. Abstractions and conventional signs are like the cup; they reduce experience to units simple enough to be comprehended one at a time. In a similar way, curves are measured by reducing them to a sequence of tiny straight lines, or by thinking of them in terms of the squares which they cross when plotted on graph paper.

Other examples of the same process are the newspaper photograph and the transmission of television. In the former, a natural scene is reproduced in terms of light and heavy dots arranged in a screen or gridlike pattern so as to give the general impression of a black-and-white photograph when seen without a magnifying glass. Much as it may look like the original scene, it is only a reconstruction of the scene in terms of dots, somewhat as our conventional words and thoughts are reconstructions of experience in terms of abstract signs. Even more like the thought process, the television camera transmits a natural scene in terms of a linear series of impulses which may be passed along a wire.

Thus communication by conventional signs of this type gives

us an abstract, one-at-a-time translation of a universe in which things are happening altogether-at-once–a universe whose concrete reality always escapes perfect description in these abstract terms. The perfect description of a small particle of dust by these means would take everlasting time, since one would have to account for every point in its volume.

The linear, one-at-a-time character of speech and thought is particularly noticeable in all languages using alphabets, representing experience in long strings of letters. It is not easy to say why we must communicate with others (speak) and with ourselves (think) by this one-at-a-time method. Life itself does not proceed in this cumbersome, linear fashion, and our own organisms could hardly live for a moment if they had to control themselves by taking thought of every breath, every beat of the heart, and every neural impulse. But if we are to find some explanation for this characteristic of thought, the sense of sight offers a suggestive analogy. For we have two types of vision–central and peripheral, not unlike the spotlight and the floodlight. Central vision is used for accurate work like reading, in which our eyes are focused on one small area after another like spotlights. Peripheral vision is less conscious, less bright than the intense ray of the spotlight. We use it for seeing at night, and for taking "subconscious" notice of objects and movements not in the direct line of central vision. Unlike the spotlight, it can take in very many things at a time.

There is, then, an analogy–and perhaps more than mere analogy–between central vision and conscious, one-at-a-time thinking, and between peripheral vision and the rather mysterious process which enables us to regulate the incredible complexity of our bodies without thinking at all. It should be noted, further, that we *call* our bodies complex as a result of trying to understand them in terms of linear thought, of words and concepts. But the complexity is not so much in our bodies as in the task of trying to understand them by this means of thinking. It is like trying to make out the features of a large room with no other light than a single bright ray. It is as complicated as trying to drink water with a fork instead of a cup.

In this respect, the Chinese written language has a slight advantage over our own, and is perhaps symptomatic of a different way of thinking. It is still linear, still a series of abstractions taken in one at a time. But its written signs are a little closer to life than spelled words because they are essentially pictures, and, as a Chinese proverb puts it, "One showing is worth a hundred sayings." Compare, for example, the ease of showing someone how to tie a complex knot with the difficulty of telling him how to do it in words alone.

Now the general tendency of the Western mind is to feel that we do not really understand what we cannot represent, what we cannot communicate, by linear signs—by thinking. We are like the "wallflower" who cannot learn a dance unless someone draws him a diagram of the steps, who cannot "get it by the feel." For some reason we do not trust and do not fully use the "peripheral vision" of our minds. We learn music, for example, by restricting the whole range of tone and rhythm to a notation of fixed tonal and rhythmic intervals—a notation which is incapable of representing Oriental music. But the Oriental musician has a rough notation which he uses only as a reminder of a melody. He learns music, not by reading notes, but by listening to the performance of a teacher, getting the "feel" of it, and copying him, and this enables him to acquire rhythmic and tonal sophistications matched only by those Western jazz artists who use the same approach.

We are not suggesting that Westerners simply do not use the "peripheral mind." Being human, we use it all the time, and every artist, every workman, every athlete calls into play some special development of its powers. But it is not academically and philosophically respectable. We have hardly begun to realize its possibilities, and it seldom, if ever, occurs to us that one of its most important uses is for that "knowledge of reality" which we try to attain by the cumbersome calculations of theology, metaphysics, and logical inference.

When we turn to ancient Chinese society, we find two "philosophical" traditions playing complementary parts–Confucianism and Taoism. Generally speaking, the former concerns itself with the linguistic, ethical, legal, and ritual conventions which provide the society with its system of communication. Confucianism, in other words, preoccupies itself with conventional knowledge, and under its auspices children are brought up so that their originally wayward and whimsical natures are made to fit the Procrustean bed of the social order. The individual defines himself and his place in society in terms of the Confucian formulae.

Taoism, on the other hand, is generally a pursuit of older men, and especially of men who are retiring from active life in the community. Their retirement from society is a kind of outward symbol of an inward liberation from the bounds of conventional patterns of thought and conduct. For Taoism concerns itself with unconventional knowledge, with the understanding of life directly, instead of in the abstract, linear terms of representational thinking.

Confucianism presides, then, over the socially necessary task of forcing the original spontaneity of life into the rigid rules of convention–a task which involves not only conflict and pain, but also the loss of that peculiar naturalness and un-self-consciousness for which little children are so much loved, and which is sometimes regained by saints and sages. The function of Taoism is to undo the inevitable damage of this discipline, and not only to restore but also to develop the original spontaneity, which is termed *tzu-jan* [b] or "self-so-ness." For the spontaneity of a child is still childish, like everything else about him. His education fosters his rigidity but not his spontaneity. In certain natures, the conflict between social convention and repressed spontaneity is so violent that it manifests itself in crime, insanity, and neurosis, which are the prices we pay for the otherwise undoubted benefits of order.

But Taoism must on no account be understood as a revolution against convention, although it has sometimes been used as a pretext for revolution. Taoism is a way of liberation, which never comes by means of revolution, since it is notorious that most revolutions establish worse tyrannies than they destroy. To be free from convention is not to spurn it but not to be deceived by it. It is to be able to use it as an instrument instead of being used by it.

The West has no recognized institution corresponding to Taoism because our Hebrew-Christian spiritual tradition identifies the Absolute–God–with the moral and logical order of convention. This might almost be called a major cultural catastrophe, because it weights the social order with excessive authority, inviting just those revolutions against religion and tradition which have been so characteristic of Western history. It is one thing to feel oneself in conflict with socially sanctioned conventions, but quite another to feel at odds with the very root and ground of life, with the Absolute itself. The latter feeling nurtures a sense of guilt so preposterous that it must issue either in denying one's own nature or in rejecting God. Because the first of these alternatives is ultimately impossible–like chewing off one's own teeth–the second becomes inevitable, where such palliatives as the confessional are no longer effective. As is the nature of revolutions, the revolution against God gives place to the worse tyranny of the absolutist state–worse because it cannot even forgive, and because it recognizes nothing outside the powers of its jurisdiction. For while the latter was theoretically true of God, his earthly representative the Church was always prepared to admit that though the laws of God were immutable, no one could presume to name the limits of his mercy. When the throne of the Absolute is left vacant, the relative usurps it and commits the real idolatry, the real indignity against God–

the absolutizing of a concept, a conventional abstraction. But it is unlikely that the throne would have become vacant if, in a sense, it had not been so already—if the Western tradition had had some way of apprehending the Absolute directly, outside the terms of the conventional order.

Of course the very word "Absolute" suggests to us something abstract and conceptual, such as "Pure Being." Our very idea of "spirit" as opposed to "matter" seems to have more kinship with the abstract than the concrete. But with Taoism, as with other ways of liberation, the Absolute must never be confused with the abstract. On the other hand, if we say that the *Tao*,° as the ultimate Reality is called, is the concrete rather than the abstract, this may lead to still other confusions. For we are accustomed to associate the concrete with the material, the physiological, the biological, and the natural, as distinct from the supernatural. But from the Taoist and Buddhist standpoints these are still terms for conventional and abstract spheres of knowledge.

Biology and physiology, for example, are types of knowledge which represent the real world in terms of their own special abstract categories. They measure and classify that world in ways appropriate to the particular uses they want to make of it, somewhat as a surveyor deals with earth in terms of acres, a contractor in truckloads or tons, and a soil analyst in types of chemical structures. To say that the concrete reality of the human organism *is* physiological is like saying that the earth *is* so many tons or acres. And to say that this reality is natural is accurate enough if we mean spontaneous (*tzu-jan*) or *natura naturans* ("nature naturing"). But it is quite inaccurate if we mean *natura naturata* ("nature natured"), that is to say, nature classified, sorted into "natures" as when we ask, "What is the *nature* of this thing?" It is in this sense of the word that we must think of "scientific naturalism," a doctrine which has nothing in common with the naturalism of Taoism.

Thus to begin to understand what Taoism is about, we must at least be prepared to admit the possibility of some view of the world other than the conventional, some knowledge other than the contents of our surface consciousness, which can apprehend reality only in the form of one abstraction (or thought, the Chinese *nien* [d]) at a time. There is no real difficulty in this, for we will already admit that we "know" how to move our hands, how to make a decision, or how to breathe, even though we can hardly begin to explain how we do it in words. We know how to do it because we just do it! Taoism is an extension of this kind of knowledge, an extension which gives us a very different view of ourselves from that to which we are conventionally accustomed, and a view which liberates the human mind from its constricting identification with the abstract ego.

According to tradition, the originator of Taoism, Lao-tzu, was an older contemporary of Kung Fu-tzu, or Confucius, who died in 479 B.C.[1] Lao-tzu is said to have been the author of the *Tao Te Ching*, a short book of aphorisms, setting forth the principles of the Tao and its power or virtue (*Te* [e]). But traditional Chinese philosophy ascribes both Taoism and Confucianism to a still earlier source, to a work which lies at the very foundation of Chinese thought and culture, dating anywhere from 3000 to 1200 B.C. This is the *I Ching*, or *Book of Changes*.

The *I Ching* is ostensibly a book of divination. It consists of oracles based on sixty-four abstract figures, each of which is composed of six lines. The lines are of two kinds—divided (negative) and undivided (positive)—and the six-line figures, or hexagrams, are believed to have been based on the various ways in which a tortoise shell will crack when heated.[2] This refers to an ancient method of divination in which the soothsayer bored a hole in

[1] Modern scholarship has questioned both the date and the historicity of Lao-tzu, but it is hard to say whether this is really more than a manifestation of fashion, since there are periodic tendencies to cast doubts on the existence of great sages or to question the hoariness of their antiquity. One recalls similar doubts in connection with Jesus and the Buddha. There are some serious arguments for a later date, but it seems best to keep the traditional date until evidence to the contrary becomes more conclusive. See Fung Yu-lan (1), vol. 1, pp. 170–76.

[2] Fung Yu-lan (1), vol. 1, pp. 379–80.

the back of a tortoise shell, heated it, and then foretold the future from the cracks in the shell so formed, much as palmists use the lines on the hand. Naturally, these cracks were most complicated, and the sixty-four hexagrams are supposed to be a simplified classification of the various patterns of cracks. For many centuries now the tortoise shell has fallen into disuse, and instead the hexagram appropriate to the moment in which a question is asked of the oracle is determined by the random division of a set of fifty yarrow stalks.

But an expert in the *I Ching* need not necessarily use tortoise shells or yarrow stalks. He can "see" a hexagram in anything–in the chance arrangement of a bowl of flowers, in objects scattered upon a table, in the natural markings on a pebble. A modern psychologist will recognize in this something not unlike a Rorschach test, in which the psychological condition of a patient is diagnosed from the spontaneous images which he "sees" in a complex ink-blot. Could the patient interpret his own projections upon the ink-blot, he would have some useful information about himself for the guidance of his future conduct. In view of this, we cannot dismiss the divinatory art of the *I Ching* as mere superstition.

Indeed, an exponent of the *I Ching* might give us quite a tough argument about the relative merits of our ways for making important decisions. We feel that we decide rationally because we base our decisions on collecting relevant data about the matter in hand. We do not depend upon such irrelevant trifles as the chance tossing of a coin, or the patterns of tea leaves or cracks in a shell. Yet he might ask whether we really know what information is relevant, since our plans are constantly upset by utterly unforeseen incidents. He might ask how we know when we have collected enough information upon which to decide. If we were rigorously "scientific" in collecting information for our decisions, it would take us so long to collect the data that the time for action would have passed long before the work had been completed. So how do we know when we have enough? Does the information itself tell us that it is enough? On the contrary, we go through the motions of gathering the necessary information in a rational way, and then, just because of a hunch, or because we are tired of thinking, or because the time has come to decide, we act. He would ask whether this is not depending just as much upon "irrelevant trifles" as if we had been casting the yarrow stalks.

In other words, the "rigorously scientific" method of predicting the future can be applied only in special cases–where prompt action is not urgent, where the factors involved are largely mechanical, or in circumstances so restricted as to be trivial. By far the greater part of our important decisions depend upon "hunch"–in other words, upon the "peripheral vision" of the mind. Thus the reliability of our decisions rests ultimately upon our ability to "feel" the situation, upon the degree to which this "peripheral vision" has been developed.

Every exponent of the *I Ching* knows this. He knows that the book itself does not contain an exact science, but rather a useful tool which will work for him if he has a good "intuition," or if, as he would say, he is "in the Tao." Thus one does not consult the oracle without proper preparation, without going quietly and meticulously through the prescribed rituals in order to bring the mind into that calm state where the "intuition" is felt to act more effectively. It would seem, then, that if the origins of Taoism are to be found in the *I Ching*, they are not so much in the text of the book itself as in the way in which it was used and in the assumptions underlying it. For experience in making decisions by intuition might well show that this "peripheral" aspect of the mind works best when we do not try to interfere with it, when we trust it to work by itself–*tzu-jan*, spontaneously, "self-so."

Thus the basic principles of Taoism begin to unfold themselves. There is, first of all, the Tao–the indefinable, concrete "process" of the world, the Way of life. The Chinese word means originally a way or road, and sometimes "to speak," so that the first line of the *Tao Te Ching* contains a pun on the two meanings:

The Tao which can be spoken is not eternal Tao.[3][1]

But in trying at least to suggest what he means, Lao-tzu says:

> There was something vague before heaven and earth arose. How calm! How void! It stands alone, unchanging; it acts everywhere, untiring. It may be considered the mother of everything under heaven. I do not know its name, but call it by the word *Tao*. (25)

And again:

> *The Tao is something blurred and indistinct.*
> *How indistinct! How blurred!*
> *Yet within it are images.*
> *How blurred! How indistinct!*
> *Yet within it are things.*
> *How dim! How confused!*
> *Yet within it is mental power.*
> *Because this power is most true,*
> *Within it there is confidence.* (21)

"Mental power" is *ching*,[g] a word which combines the ideas of essential, subtle, psychic or spiritual, and skillful. For the point seems to be that as one's own head looks like nothing to the eyes yet is the source of intelligence, so the vague, void-seeming, and indefinable Tao is the intelligence which shapes the world with a skill beyond our understanding.

The important difference between the Tao and the usual idea of God is that whereas God produces the world by making (*wei*[h]), the Tao produces it by "not-making" (*wu-wei*[i])—which is approximately what we mean by "growing." For things made are separate parts put together, like machines, or things fashioned from without inwards, like sculptures. Whereas things grown divide themselves into parts, from within outwards. Because the nat-

---

[3] Duyvendak (1) suggests that *tao* did not have the meaning of "to speak" at this date, and so translates the passage, "The Way that may truly be regarded as the Way is other than a permanent way." It really comes to the same thing, for what Duyvendak means by a "permanent way" is a fixed concept of the Tao—i.e., a definition. Almost every other translator, and most of the Chinese commentators, take the second *tao* to mean "spoken."

ural universe works mainly according to the principles of growth, it would seem quite odd to the Chinese mind to ask how it was made. If the universe were made, there would of course be someone who knows *how* it is made–who could explain how it was put together bit by bit as a technician can explain in one-at-a-time words how to assemble a machine. But a universe which grows utterly excludes the possibility of knowing how it grows in the clumsy terms of thought and language, so that no Taoist would dream of asking whether the Tao knows how it produces the universe. For it operates according to spontaneity, not according to plan. Lao-tzu says:

The Tao's principle is spontaneity. (25) [j]

But spontaneity is not by any means a blind, disorderly urge, a mere power of caprice. A philosophy restricted to the alternatives of conventional language has no way of conceiving an intelligence which does not work according to plan, according to a (one-at-a-time) order of thought. Yet the concrete evidence of such an intelligence is right to hand in our own thoughtlessly organized bodies.[3a] For the Tao does not "know" how it produces the universe just as we do not "know" how we construct our brains. In the words of Lao-tzu's great successor, Chuang-tzu:

Things are produced around us, but no one knows the whence. They issue forth, but no one sees the portal. Men one and all value that part of knowledge which is known. They do not know how to avail themselves of the Unknown in order to reach knowledge. Is not this misguided? [4]

[3a] The above was written before I had seen the second volume of Joseph Needham's masterly *Science and Civilization in China,* where he discusses the organismic nature of the Chinese, and especially the Taoist, conception of the universe. See especially Section 13*f*, pp. 279 ff. Needham also draws attention to the essential differences between Hebrew-Christian and Chinese views of natural law, the former deriving from the "word" of a lawgiver, God, and the latter from a relationship of spontaneous processes working in an organismic pattern. See Section 18, *f* and *h*, esp. pp. 557–64 and 572–83.
[4] H. A. Giles (1), p. 345.

The conventional relationship of the knower to the known is often that of the controller to the controlled, and thus of lord to servant. Thus whereas God is the master of the universe, since "he knows about it all! He knows! He knows!," the relationship of the Tao to what it produces is quite otherwise.

> *The great Tao flows everywhere,*
> *to the left and to the right.*
> *All things depend upon it to exist,*
> *and it does not abandon them.*
> *To its accomplishments it lays no claim.*
> *It loves and nourishes all things,*
> *but does not lord it over them.* (34)

In the usual Western conception God is also self-knowing–transparent through and through to his own understanding, the image of what man would like to be: the conscious ruler and controller, the absolute dictator of his own mind and body. But in contrast with this, the Tao is through and through mysterious and dark (*hsüan* [k]). As a Zen Buddhist said of it in later times:

There is one thing: above, it supports Heaven; below, it upholds Earth. It is black like lacquer, always actively functioning.[5] [l]

Hsüan is, of course, a metaphorical darkness–not the darkness of night, of black as opposed to white, but the sheer inconceivability which confronts the mind when it tries to remember the time before birth, or to penetrate its own depths.

Western critics often poke fun at such nebulous views of the Absolute, deriding them as "misty and mystical" in contrast with their own robustly definite opinions. But as Lao-tzu said:

> *When the superior man hears of the Tao,*
> *he does his best to practice it.*
> *When the middling man hears of the Tao,*
> *he sometimes keeps it, and sometimes loses it.*

[5] T'ung-shan Liang-chieh. Dumoulin and Sasaki (1), p. 74.

When the inferior man hears of the Tao,
he will laugh aloud at it.
If he did not laugh, it would not be the Tao. (41)

For it is really impossible to appreciate what is meant by the Tao without becoming, in a rather special sense, stupid. So long as the conscious intellect is frantically trying to clutch the world in its net of abstractions, and to insist that life be bound and fitted to its rigid categories, the mood of Taoism will remain incomprehensible; and the intellect will wear itself out. The Tao is accessible only to the mind which can practice the simple and subtle art of *wu-wei*, which, after the Tao, is the second important principle of Taoism.

We saw that the *I Ching* had given the Chinese mind some experience in arriving at decisions spontaneously, decisions which are effective to the degree that one knows how to let one's mind alone, trusting it to work by itself. This is *wu-wei*, since *wu* means "not" or "non-" and *wei* means "action," "making," "doing," "striving," "straining," or "busyness." To return to the illustration of eyesight, the peripheral vision works most effectively–as in the dark–when we see out of the corners of the eyes, and do not look at things directly. Similarly, when we need to see the details of a distant object, such as a clock, the eyes must be relaxed, not staring, not *trying* to see. So, too, no amount of working with the muscles of the mouth and tongue will enable us to taste our food more acutely. The eyes and the tongue must be trusted to do the work by themselves.

But when we have learned to put excessive reliance upon central vision, upon the sharp spotlight of the eyes and mind, we cannot regain the powers of peripheral vision unless the sharp and staring kind of sight is first relaxed. The mental or psychological equivalent of this is the special kind of stupidity to which Lao-tzu and Chuang-tzu so often refer. It is not simply calmness of mind, but "non-graspingness" of mind. In Chuang-tzu's words, "The perfect man employs his mind as a mirror. It grasps nothing; it refuses nothing. It receives, but does not keep." One might almost say that it "fuzzes" itself a little to compensate for too harsh a clarity. Thus Lao-tzu says of himself:

> *Cut out cleverness and there are no anxieties!* . . .
> *People in general are so happy, as if enjoying a feast,*
> *Or as going up a tower in spring.*
> *I alone am tranquil, and have made no signs,*
> *Like a baby who is yet unable to smile;*
> *Forlorn as if I had no home to go to.*
> *Others all have more than enough,*
> *And I alone seem to be in want.*
> *Possibly mine is the mind of a fool,*
> *Which is so ignorant!*
> *The vulgar are bright,*
> *And I alone seem to be dull.*
> *The vulgar are discriminative,*
> *And I alone seem to be blunt.*
> *I am negligent as if being obscure;*
> *Drifting, as if being attached to nothing.*
> *The people in general all have something to do,*
> *And I alone seem to be impractical and awkward.*
> *I alone am different from others,*
> *But I value seeking sustenance from the Mother (Tao).* (20) [6]

In most Taoist writings there is a slight degree of exaggeration or overstatement of the point which is actually a kind of humor, a self-caricature. Thus Chuang-tzu writes on the same theme:

> The man of character (*te*) lives at home without exercising his mind and performs actions without worry. The notions of right and wrong and the praise and blame of others do not disturb him. When within the four seas all people can enjoy themselves, that is happiness for him. . . . Sorrowful in countenance, he looks like a baby who has lost his mother; appearing stupid, he goes about

[6] Save for the first line, I have followed Ch'u Ta-kao (1), p. 30.

like one who has lost his way. He has plenty of money to spend, but
does not know where it comes from. He drinks and eats just enough
and does not know where the food comes from. (3:13) [7]

Lao-tzu is still more forceful in his apparent condemnation of
conventional cleverness:

> Cut out sagacity; discard knowingness,
> and the people will benefit an hundredfold.
> Cut out "humanity"; discard righteousness,
> and the people will regain love of their fellows.
> Cut out cleverness; discard the utilitarian,
> and there will be no thieves and robbers. . . .
> Become unaffected; [8]
> Cherish sincerity;
> Belittle the personal;
> Reduce desires. (19)

The idea is not to reduce the human mind to a moronic
vacuity, but to bring into play its innate and spontaneous intelligence by using it without forcing it. It is fundamental to
both Taoist and Confucian thought that the natural man is to be
trusted, and from their standpoint it appears that the Western
mistrust of human nature—whether theological or technological—
is a kind of schizophrenia. It would be impossible, in their view,
to believe oneself innately evil without discrediting the very
belief, since all the notions of a perverted mind would be perverted notions. However religiously "emancipated," the technological mind shows that it has inherited the same division against
itself when it tries to subject the whole human order to the
control of conscious reason. It forgets that reason cannot be
trusted if the brain cannot be trusted, since the power of reason

---

[7] Lin Yutang (1), p. 129.
[8] "Unaffected" is an attempt to render *su*,[m] a character which refers originally to unbleached silk, or to the unpainted silk background of a picture.
"Humanity" refers to the central Confucian principle of *jen*,[n] which would
ordinarily mean "human-heartedness," though it is obvious that Lao-tzu
refers to its self-conscious and affected form.

depends upon organs that were grown by "unconscious intelligence."

The art of letting the mind alone is vividly described by another Taoist writer, Lieh-tzu (*c*. 398 B.C.), celebrated for his
mysterious power of being able to ride upon the wind. This,
no doubt, refers to the peculiar sensation of "walking on air"
which arises when the mind is first liberated. It is said that when
Professor D. T. Suzuki was once asked how it feels to have attained *satori*,° the Zen experience of "awakening," he answered,
"Just like ordinary everyday experience, except about two inches
off the ground!" Thus when asked to explain the art of riding
on the wind, Lieh-tzu gave the following account of his training
under his master Lao Shang:

> After I had served him . . . for the space of three years, my mind
> did not venture to reflect on right and wrong, my lips did not ven-
> ture to speak of profit and loss. Then, for the first time, my master
> bestowed one glance upon me—and that was all.
>
> At the end of five years a change had taken place; my mind was
> reflecting on right and wrong, and my lips were speaking of profit
> and loss. Then, for the first time, my master relaxed his countenance
> and smiled.
>
> At the end of seven years, there was another change. I let my
> mind reflect on what it would, but it no longer occupied itself with
> right and wrong. I let my lips utter whatsoever they pleased, but
> they no longer spoke of profit and loss. Then, at last, my master led
> me in to sit on the mat beside him.
>
> At the end of nine years, my mind gave free rein to its reflections,ᵖ
> my mouth free passage to its speech. Of right and wrong, profit and
> loss, I had no knowledge, either as touching myself or others.
> . . . Internal and external were blended into unity. After that,
> there was no distinction between eye and ear, ear and nose, nose
> and mouth: all were the same. My mind was frozen, my body in
> dissolution, my flesh and bones all melted together. I was wholly
> unconscious of what my body was resting on, or what was under
> my feet. I was borne this way and that on the wind, like dry chaff
> or leaves falling from a tree. In fact, I knew not whether the wind
> was riding on me or I on the wind.⁹

⁹ L. Giles (1), pp. 40–42. From *Lieh-tzu*, ii.

The state of consciousness described sounds not unlike being pleasantly drunk–though without the "morning after" effects of alcohol! Chuang-tzu noticed the similarity, for he wrote:

> A drunken man who falls out of a cart, though he may suffer, does not die. His bones are the same as other people's; but he meets the accident in a different way. His spirit is in a condition of security. He is not conscious of riding in the cart; neither is he conscious of falling out of it. Ideas of life, death, fear, etc., cannot penetrate his breast; and so he does not suffer from contact with objective existences. And if such security is to be got from wine, how much more is it to be got from Spontaneity. (19) [10]

Since Lao-tzu, Chuang-tzu, and Lieh-tzu were all conscious enough to write very intelligible books, it may be assumed that some of this language is, again, exaggerated or metaphorical. Their "unconsciousness" is not coma, but what the exponents of Zen later signified by *wu-hsin*,[q] literally "no-mind," which is to say un-self-consciousness. It is a state of wholeness in which the mind functions freely and easily, without the sensation of a second mind or ego standing over it with a club. If the ordinary man is one who has to walk by lifting his legs with his hands, the Taoist is one who has learned to let the legs walk by themselves.

Various passages in the Taoist writings suggest that "no-mindedness" is employing the whole mind as we use the eyes when we rest them upon various objects but make no special effort to take anything in. According to Chuang-tzu:

> The baby looks at things all day without winking; that is because his eyes are not focussed on any particular object. He goes without knowing where he is going, and stops without knowing what he is doing. He merges himself with the surroundings and moves along with it. These are the principles of mental hygiene. (23) [11]

And again:

[10] H. A. Giles (1), p. 232.
[11] Lin Yutang (1), p. 86.

If you regulate your body and unify your attention, the harmony of heaven will come upon you. If you integrate your awareness, and unify your thoughts, spirit will make its abode with you. *Te* (virtue) will clothe you, and the Tao will shelter you. Your eyes will be like those of a new-born calf, which seeks not the wherefore. (22)

Each of the other senses might similarly be used to illustrate the "non-active" functioning of the mind—listening without straining to hear, smelling without strong inhalation, tasting without screwing up the tongue, and touching without pressing the object. Each is a special instance of the mental function which works through all, and which Chinese designates with the peculiar word *hsin.*[r]

This term is so important for the understanding of Zen that some attempt must be made to say what Taoism and Chinese thought in general take it to mean.[12] We usually translate it as "mind" or "heart," but neither of these words is satisfactory. The original form of the ideograph.[s] seems to be a picture of the heart, or perhaps of the lungs or the liver, and when a Chinese speaks of the *hsin* he will often point to the center of his chest, slightly lower than the heart.

The difficulty with our translations is that "mind" is too intellectual, too cortical, and that "heart" in its current English usage is too emotional—even sentimental. Furthermore, *hsin* is not always used with quite the same sense. Sometimes it is used for an obstruction to be removed, as in *wu-hsin,* "no-mind." But sometimes it is used in a way that is almost synonymous

[12] The central Zen principle of "no-mind" or *wu-hsin* is already found in Chuang-tzu. Cf. *Chuang-tzu* (22):

> Body like dry bone,
> Mind like dead ashes;
> This is true knowledge,
> Not to strive after knowing the whence.
> In darkness, in obscurity,
> The mindless (wu-hsin) cannot plan;—
> What manner of man is that?

H. A. Giles (1), p. 281.

with the Tao. This is especially found in Zen literature, which abounds with such phrases as "original mind" (*pen hsin* [t]), "Buddha mind" (*fu hsin* [u]), or "faith in mind" (*hsin hsin* [v]). This apparent contradiction is resolved in the principle that "the true mind is no mind," which is to say that the *hsin* is true, is working properly, when it works as if it were not present. In the same way, the eyes are seeing properly when they do not see themselves, in terms of spots or blotches in the air.

All in all, it would seem that *hsin* means the totality of our psychic functioning, and, more specifically, the center of that functioning, which is associated with the central point of the upper body. The Japanese form of the word, *kokoro,* is used with even more subtleties of meaning, but for the present it is enough to realize that in translating it "mind" (a sufficiently vague word) we do not mean exclusively the intellectual or thinking mind, nor even the surface consciousness. The important point is that, according to both Taoism and Zen, the center of the mind's activity is not in the conscious thinking process, not in the ego.

When a man has learned to let his mind alone so that it functions in the integrated and spontaneous way that is natural to it, he begins to show the special kind of "virtue" or "power" called *te.* This is not virtue in the current sense of moral rectitude but in the older sense of effectiveness, as when one speaks of the healing virtues of a plant. *Te* is, furthermore, unaffected or spontaneous virtue which cannot be cultivated or imitated by any deliberate method. Lao-tzu says:

> *Superior* te *is not* te,
> *and thus has* te.
> *Inferior* te *does not let go of* te,
> *and thus is not* te.
> *Superior* te *is non-active* [wu-wei] *and aimless.*
> *Inferior* te *is active and has an aim.* (38)

The literal translation has a strength and depth which is lost in such paraphrases as "Superior virtue is not conscious of itself as virtue, and thus really is virtue. Inferior virtue cannot dispense with virtuosity, and thus is not virtue."

When the Confucians prescribed a virtue which depended upon the artificial observance of rules and precepts, the Taoists pointed out that such virtue was conventional and not genuine. Chuang-tzu made up the following imaginary dialogue between Confucius and Lao-tzu:

> "Tell me," said Lao-tzu, "in what consist charity and duty to one's neighbour?"
>
> "They consist," answered Confucius, "in a capacity for rejoicing in all things; in universal love, without the element of self. These are the characteristics of charity and duty to one's neighbour."
>
> "What stuff!" cried Lao-tzu. "Does not universal love contradict itself? Is not your elimination of self a positive manifestation of self? Sir, if you would cause the empire not to lose its source of nourishment,—there is the universe, its regularity is unceasing; there are the sun and moon, their brightness is unceasing; there are the stars, their groupings never change; there are the birds and beasts, they flock together without varying; there are trees and shrubs, they grow upwards without exception. Be like these: follow Tao, and you will be perfect. Why then these vain struggles after charity and duty to one's neighbour, as though beating a drum in search of a fugitive. Alas! Sir, you have brought much confusion into the mind of man." (13) [13]

The Taoist critique of conventional virtue applied not only in the moral sphere but also in the arts, crafts, and trades. According to Chuang-tzu:

> Ch'ui the artisan could draw circles with his hand better than with compasses. His fingers seemed to accommodate themselves so naturally to the thing he was working at, that it was unnecessary to fix his attention. His mental faculties thus remained One (i.e., integrated), and suffered no hindrance. To be unconscious of one's feet implies that the shoes are easy. To be unconscious of a waist implies that the girdle is easy. The intelligence being unconscious of positive and negative implies that the heart (*hsin*) is at ease. . . . And he who, beginning with ease, is never not at ease, is unconscious of the ease of ease. (19) [14]

[13] H. A. Giles (1), p. 167.
[14] H. A. Giles (1), p. 242.

Just as the artisan who had mastered *te* could do without the artificiality of the compass, so the painter, the musician, and the cook would have no need for the conventional classifications of their respective arts. Thus Lao-tzu said:

> *The five colours will blind a man's sight.*
> *The five sounds will deaden a man's hearing.*
> *The five tastes will spoil a man's palate.*
> *Chasing and hunting will drive a man wild.*
> *Things hard to get will do harm to a man's conduct.*
> *Therefore the sage makes provision for the stomach*
> *   and not for the eye.* (12) [15]

This must by no means be taken as an ascetic's hatred of sense experience, for the point is precisely that the eye's sensitivity to color is impaired by the fixed idea that there are just five true colors. There is an infinite continuity of shading, and breaking it down into divisions with names distracts the attention from its subtlety. This is why "the sage makes provision for the stomach and not for the eye," which is to say that he judges by the concrete content of the experience, and not by its conformity with purely theoretical standards.

In sum, then, *te* is the unthinkable ingenuity and creative power of man's spontaneous and natural functioning–a power which is blocked when one tries to master it in terms of formal methods and techniques. It is like the centipede's skill in using a hundred legs at once.

> *The centipede was happy, quite,*
> *Until a toad in fun*
> *Said, "Pray, which leg goes after which?"*
> *This worked his mind to such a pitch,*
> *He lay distracted in a ditch,*
> *Considering how to run.*

A profound regard for *te* underlies the entire higher culture of the Far East, so much so that it has been made the basic principle of every kind of art and craft. While it is true that these arts em-

[15] Ch'u Ta-kao (1), p. 22.

ploy what are, to us, highly difficult technical disciplines, it is always recognized that they are instrumental and secondary, and
that superior work has the quality of an accident. This is not
merely a masterful mimicry of the accidental, an assumed spontaneity in which the careful planning does not show. It lies at a
much deeper and more genuine level, for what the culture of
Taoism and Zen proposes is that one might become the kind
of person who, without intending it, is a source of marvelous
accidents.

Taoism is, then, the original Chinese way of liberation which
combined with Indian Mahayana Buddhism to produce Zen. It
is a liberation *from* convention and *of* the creative power of *te*.
Every attempt to describe and formulate it in words and one-at-
a-time thought symbols must, of necessity, distort it. The foregoing chapter has perforce made it seem one of the "vitalist" or
"naturalistic" philosophical alternatives. For Western philosophers are constantly bedeviled by the discovery that they *cannot*
think outside certain well-worn ruts–that, however hard they
may try, their "new" philosophies turn out to be restatements of
ancient positions, monist or pluralist, realist or nominalist, vitalist or mechanist. This is because these are the only alternatives
which the conventions of thought can present, and they cannot
discuss anything else without presenting it in their own terms.
When we try to represent a third dimension upon a two-
dimensional surface, it will of necessity seem to belong more or
less to the two alternatives of length and breadth. In the words
of Chuang-tzu:

> Were language adequate, it would take but a day fully to set forth
> Tao. Not being adequate, it takes that time to explain material ex-
> istences. Tao is something beyond material existences. It cannot be
> conveyed either by words or by silence. (25) [16]

[16] H. A. Giles (1), p. 351.

Two

THE ORIGINS OF BUDDHISM

Chinese civilization was at least two thousand years old when it first encountered Buddhism. Thus the new philosophy entered into a solidly established culture in which it could hardly become acceptable without major adaptations to the Chinese mentality, even though there were some resemblances between Taoism and Buddhism so strong that they have aroused speculation as to whether contacts between the two were much earlier than has been supposed. China absorbed Buddhism as it has absorbed so many other external influences—not only philosophies and ideas, but also alien populations and invaders. Undoubtedly this is due in some measure to the extraordinary stability and maturity which the Chinese have derived from Confucianism. Reasonable, unfanatical, humanistic, Confucianism is one of the most workable patterns of social convention that the world has known. Coupled with the "let well enough alone" attitude of Taoism, it nurtured a mellow and rather easygoing type of mentality which, when it absorbed Buddhism, did much to make it more "practical." That is to say, it made Buddhism a possible way of life for *human* beings, for people with families, with everyday work to do, and with normal instincts and passions.

It was a basic Confucian principle that "it is man who makes truth great, not truth which makes man great." For this reason, "humanness" or "human-heartedness" (*jen* [a]) was always felt to be superior to "righteousness" (*i* [b]), since man himself is greater than any idea which he may invent. There are times when men's passions are much more trustworthy than their principles. Since opposed principles, or ideologies, are irreconcilable, wars fought over principle will be wars of mutual annihilation. But wars fought for simple greed will be far less destructive, because the aggressor will be careful not to destroy what he is fighting to capture. Reasonable–that is, human–men will always be capable of compromise, but men who have dehumanized themselves by becoming the blind worshipers of an idea or an ideal are fanatics whose devotion to abstractions makes them the enemies of life.

Modified by such attitudes, Far Eastern Buddhism is much more palatable and "according to nature" than its Indian and Tibetan counterparts, with ideals of life which seem at times to be superhuman, more suited to angels than to men. Even so, all forms of Buddhism subscribe to the Middle Way between the extremes of angel (*deva*) and demon (*preta*), ascetic and sensualist, and claim that supreme "awakening" or Buddhahood can be attained only from the human state.

There are some serious difficulties in the way of giving an historically accurate account of Indian Buddhism, as of the whole philosophical tradition from which it arose. No student of Asian thought should be unaware of these difficulties, because they make it necessary to take almost every important pronounce-ment about ancient Indian thought with caution. Thus before attempting to describe Indian Buddhism, some of these difficulties should be mentioned.

The first, and most serious, is the problem of interpreting the Sanskrit and Pali texts in which ancient Indian literature is preserved. This is especially true of Sanskrit, the sacred language of India, and more particularly the form of Sanskrit used in the Vedic period. Both Western and Indian scholars are uncertain as to its exact interpretation, and all modern dictionaries rely heavily on a single source–the lexicon compiled by Böthlingk and Roth in the latter part of the last century, and now admitted to contain a great deal of guesswork. This seriously affects our understanding of the primary sources of Hinduism–the *Vedas* and *Upanishads*. The discovery of proper European equivalents for philosophical terms has been hindered by the fact that early lexicographers were all too ready to find correspondences with Western theological terms, since one of the primary objects of their studies was to assist the missionaries.[1]

The second is that it is extremely hard to know what was the original form of Buddhism. There are two sets of Buddhist scriptures: the Pali Canon of the Theravada or Southern School of Buddhism, which flourishes in Ceylon, Burma, and Thailand, and the Sanskrit-Tibetan-Chinese Canon of the Mahayana, or Northern School. There is a general consensus of scholars that the Pali Canon is, on the whole, the earlier of the two, and that the principal *sutras* (as the sacred texts are called) of the Mahayana Canon were all compiled after 100 B.C. However, the literary form of the Pali Canon does not suggest that it represents the actual words of Gautama the Buddha. If the *Upanishads* are characteristic of the style of discourse of an Indian teacher between 800 and 300 B.C., they bear little resemblance to the tediously repetitious and scholastic style of most Buddhist scriptures. There can be little doubt that the greater part of both Buddhist Canons is the work of the pandits of the Sangha, the Buddhist monastic order, for it shows every sign of being the reverential elaboration of an original doctrine. As with Russian icons, the original painting has been almost lost to sight in the overlay of jewels and gold.

The third is that the Hindu-Buddhist tradition has never had the historical sense of the Hebrew-Christian tradition, so that there are few, if any, marks to indicate the date of a given text. Scriptures were handed down by oral tradition for an indeterminable period of time before being committed to writing, and it is quite possible that historical references could have been changed to suit the times as the oral form was handed down. Furthermore, a Buddhist monk writing in A.D. 200 would have no compunction in attributing his own words to the Buddha if he felt sincerely that they were an expression, not of personal

[1] See Monier-Williams, *Sanskrit-English Dictionary*, p. ix. (Oxford, 1951.)

opinion, but of the supra-personal state of awakening to which he had attained. He would attribute the words to the Buddha as speaking in a spiritual rather than material body.

The danger of scholarship is always that, in extreme specialization, it may be unable to see the forest for the trees. But the problem of gaining some idea of the thought of India at the time of the Buddha, six centuries before Christ, is not to be solved by careful piece-work alone–necessary as this may be. There is, however, enough reliable information to suggest the grand and beautifully ordered form of Upanishadic Hinduism if we do not read it with our noses against the page.

Fundamental to the life and thought of India from the very earliest times is the great mythological theme of *atma-yajna*–the act of "self-sacrifice" whereby God gives birth to the world, and whereby men, following the divine pattern, reintegrate themselves with God. The act by which the world is created is the same act by which it is consummated–the giving up of one's life– as if the whole process of the universe were the type of game in which it is necessary to pass on the ball as soon as it is received. Thus the basic myth of Hinduism is that the world is God playing hide-and-seek with himself. As Prajapati, Vishnu, or Brahma, the Lord under many names creates the world by an act of self-dismemberment or self-forgetting, whereby the One becomes Many, and the single Actor plays innumerable parts. In the end, he comes again to himself only to begin the play once more–the One dying into the Many, and the Many dying into the One.

A thousand heads hath Purusha, a thousand eyes, a thousand feet.
On every side pervading earth he fills a space ten fingers wide.

This Purusha is all that yet hath been and all that is to be;
The lord of immortality that waxes greater still by food.

So mighty is his greatness; yea, greater than this is Purusha.
All creatures are one fourth of him, three-fourths eternal life in heaven. . . .

When the gods prepared the sacrifice with Purusha as their offering,
Its oil was spring, the holy gift was autumn; summer was the wood.

From that great general sacrifice the dripping fat was gathered up.
He formed the creatures of the air, and animals both wild and
tame. . . .

When they divided Purusha, how many portions did they make?
What do they call his mouth, his arms? What do they call his thighs
and feet?

The Brahman (caste) was his mouth, of both his arms was the Ra-
janya (Kshatriya caste) made.
His thighs became Vaishya, from his feet the Shudra was produced.

The moon was gendered from his mind, and from his eye the sun had
birth;
Indra and Agni from his mouth were born, and Vayu from his breath.

Forth from his navel came mid-air; the sky was fashioned from his
head;
Earth from his feet, and from his ear the regions. Thus they formed
the worlds.[2]

The thousand heads, eyes, and feet of the Purusha are the
members of men and other beings, for the point is that That
which knows in and through every individual is God himself,
the *atman* or Self of the world. Every life is a part or role in
which the mind of God is absorbed, somewhat as an actor absorbs
himself in being Hamlet and forgets that in real life he is Mr.
Smith. By the act of self-abandonment God becomes all beings,
yet at the same time does not cease to be God. "All creatures are
one fourth of him, three-fourths eternal life in heaven." For God
is divided in play, in make-believe, but remains undivided in
reality. So that when the play comes to an end, the individualized
consciousness awakes to find itself divine.

In the beginning this world was *Atman* (the Self), alone in the
form of Purusha. Looking about he saw nothing other than himself.

[2] *Rigveda* x. 90. The translation is from R. T. H. Griffith. Purusha is "the
Person," i.e., the original consciousness behind the world.

He said first, "I am." Thence came the word "I." Thus even now, when one is spoken to, he first answers simply, "It is I," and then tells whatever name he has.[3]

> On all sides That has hands and feet;
> On all sides eyes, heads, and faces;
> On all sides in the world it hears;
> All things it embraces.[4]

It is important to remember that this picture of the world as the play (*lila*) of God is mythological in form. If, at this stage, we were to translate it directly into philosophical statement it would be a crude type of pantheism, with which Hindu philosophy is generally and erroneously confused. Thus the idea of each man, each thing, as a part which the Purusha plays in the state of self-forgetting must not be confused with a logical or scientific statement of fact. The form of statement is poetic, not logical. In the words of the *Mundaka Upanishad*,

> Truly this *atman* (Self)—the poets say—travels on this earth from body to body. (ii. 7)

Hindu philosophy has not made the mistake of imagining that one can make an informative, factual, and positive statement about the ultimate reality. As the same *Upanishad* says,

> Where knowledge is without duality, without action, cause, or effect, unspeakable, incomparable, beyond description, what is that? It is impossible to say! (vi. 7)

Every positive statement about ultimate things must be made in the suggestive form of myth, of poetry. For in this realm the direct and indicative form of speech can say only "*Neti, neti*" ("No, no"), since what can be described and categorized must always belong to the conventional realm.

Hindu mythology elaborates the theme of the divine play on a fabulous scale, embracing not only colossal concepts of time and

[3] *Brihadaranyaka Upanishad* i. 4. 5.
[4] *Bhagavad-Gita* xiii. 13.

space, but also the widest extremes of pleasure and pain, virtue and depravity. The inmost Self of saint and sage is no less the veiled Godhead than the inmost Self of the debauchee, the coward, the lunatic, and the very demons. The opposites (*dvandva*) of light and darkness, good and evil, pleasure and pain, are the essential elements of the game, for although the Godhead is identified with Truth (*sat*), Consciousness (*chit*), and Bliss (*ananda*), the dark side of life has its integral part in the game just as every drama must have its villain, to disrupt the *status quo*, and as the cards must be shuffled, thrown into chaos, in order that there may be a significant development of the play. For Hindu thought there is no Problem of Evil. The conventional, relative world is necessarily a world of opposites. Light is inconceivable apart from darkness; order is meaningless without disorder; and, likewise, up without down, sound without silence, pleasure without pain. In the words of Ananda Coomaraswamy:

> For anyone who holds that "God made the world," the question, Why did He permit the existence in it of any evil, or of that Evil One in whom all evil is personified, is altogether meaningless; one might as well enquire why He did not make a world without dimensions or one without temporal succession.[5]

According to the myth, the divine play goes on through endless cycles of time, through periods of manifestation and withdrawal of the worlds measured in units of *kalpas*, the *kalpa* being a span of 4,320,000,000 years. From the human standpoint such a conception presents a terrifying monotony, since it goes on aimlessly for ever and ever. But from the divine standpoint it has all the fascination of the repetitious games of children, which go on and on because time has been forgotten and has reduced itself to a single wondrous instant.

The foregoing myth is not the expression of a formal philoso-

[5] Coomaraswamy (1), p. 77.

phy, but of an experience or state of consciousness which is called *moksha* or "liberation." On the whole it is safer to say that Indian philosophy is primarily this experience; it is only quite secondarily a system of ideas which attempt to translate the experience into conventional language. At root, then, the philosophy becomes intelligible only by sharing the experience which consists of the same type of nonconventional knowledge found in Taoism. It is also termed *atma-jnana* (Self-knowledge) or *atma-bodha* (Self-awakening), since it may be considered as the discovery of who or what I am, when I am no longer identified with any role or conventional definition of the person. Indian philosophy does not describe the content of this discovery except in mythological terms, using the phrase "I am Brahman" (*aham brahman*) or "That art thou" (*tat tvam asi*) to suggest that Self-knowledge is a realization of one's original identity with God.

But this does not imply what "claiming to be God" means in a Hebrew-Christian context, where mythical language is ordinarily confused with factual language so that there is no clear distinction between God as described in the terms of conventional thought and God as he is in reality. A Hindu does not say "I am Brahman" with the implication that he is personally in charge of the whole universe and informed as to every detail of its operation. On the one hand, he is not speaking of identity with God at the level of his superficial personality. On the other, his "God"–Brahman–is not in charge of the universe in a "personal" way; he does not know and act in the manner of a person since he does not know the universe in terms of conventional facts nor act upon it by means of deliberation, effort, and will. It may be of significance that the word "Brahman" is from the root *brih-*, "to grow," since his creative activity, like that of the Tao, is with the spontaneity proper to growth as distinct from the deliberation proper to making. Furthermore, though Brahman is said to "know" himself, this knowing is not a matter of information, a knowledge such as one has of objects distinct from a subject. In the words of Shankara,

For He is the Knower, and the Knower can know other things, but cannot make Himself the object of His own knowledge, in the same way that fire can burn other things, but cannot burn itself.[6]

To the Western mind the puzzle of Indian philosophy is that it has so much to say about what the *moksha* experience is not, and little, or nothing, to say about what it is. This is naturally bewildering, for if the experience is really without content, or if it is so lacking in relation to the things which we consider important, how is one to explain the immense esteem which it holds in the Indian scheme of life?

Even at the conventional level it is surely easy to see that knowing what is not so is often quite as important as knowing what is. Even when medicine can suggest no effective remedy for the common cold, there is some advantage in knowing the uselessness of certain popular nostrums. Furthermore, the function of negative knowledge is not unlike the uses of space–the empty page upon which words can be written, the empty jar into which liquid can be poured, the empty window through which light can be admitted, and the empty pipe through which water can flow. Obviously the value of emptiness lies in the movements it permits or in the substance which it mediates and contains. But the emptiness must come first. This is why Indian philosophy concentrates on negation, on liberating the mind from concepts of Truth. It proposes no *idea*, no description, of what is to fill the mind's void because the idea would exclude the fact–somewhat as a picture of the sun on the windowpane would shut out the true sun's light. Whereas the Hebrews would not permit an image of God in wood or stone, the Hindus will not permit an image of thought–unless it be so obviously mythological as not to be mistaken for the reality.

Therefore the practical discipline (*sadhana*) of the way of

[6] *Bashya* on *Kena Upanishad*, 9–11. "Cannot" may give the wrong implication since the word is ordinarily privative. The point is that, as light has no need to shine upon itself since it is luminous already, so there is no advantage to be gained and, indeed, no meaning in the notion of Brahman's being the object of his own knowledge.

liberation is a progressive disentanglement of one's Self (*atman*) from every identification. It is to realize that I am not this body, these sensations, these feelings, these thoughts, this consciousness. The basic reality of my life is not any conceivable object. Ultimately it is not even to be identified with any idea, as of God or *atman*. In the words of the *Mandukya Upanishad:*

> (It is) That which is conscious neither of the subjective nor of the objective, nor of both; which is neither simple consciousness, nor undifferentiated sentience, nor mere darkness. It is unseen, without relations, incomprehensible, uninferable, and indescribable—the essence of Self-consciousness, the ending of *maya*. (vii)

The *atman* is to our total consciousness what the head is to the sense of sight—neither light nor darkness, neither full nor empty, only an inconceivable beyond. In the moment when every last identification of the Self with some object or concept has ceased, in the state called *nirvikalpa* or "without conception," there flashes forth from its unknown depths the state of consciousness which is called divine, the knowledge of Brahman.

Translated into conventional and—let it be repeated—mythopoetic language, the knowledge of Brahman is represented as the discovery that this world which seemed to be Many is in truth One, that "all is Brahman" and that "all duality is falsely imagined." Taken as statements of fact, such utterances are logically meaningless and convey no information. Yet they seem to be the best possible expression in words of the experience itself, though it is as if in the moment of saying the "last word" the tongue were paralyzed by its own revelation, and compelled to babble nonsense or be silent.

Moksha is also understood as liberation from *maya*—one of the most important words in Indian philosophy, both Hindu and Buddhist. For the manifold world of facts and events is said to be *maya*, ordinarily understood as an illusion which veils the one underlying reality of Brahman. This gives the impression that *moksha* is a state of consciousness in which the whole varied world of nature vanishes from sight, merged in a boundless

ocean of vaguely luminous space. Such an impression should be
dismissed at once, for it implies a duality, an incompatibility,
between Brahman and *maya* which is against the whole principle
of Upanishadic philosophy. For Brahman is not One *as opposed
to* Many, not simple *as opposed* to complex. Brahman is without
duality (*advaita*), which is to say without any opposite since
Brahman is not in any class or, for that matter, outside any class.

Now classification is precisely *maya*. The word is derived
from the Sanskrit root *matr-*, "to measure, form, build, or lay
out a plan," the root from which we obtain such Greco-Latin
words as meter, matrix, material, and matter. The fundamental
process of measurement is division, whether by drawing a line
with the finger, by marking off or by enclosing circles with the
span of the hand or dividers, or by sorting grain or liquids into
measures (cups). Thus the Sanskrit root *dva-* from which we
get the word "divide" is also the root of the Latin *duo* (two)
and the English "dual."

To say, then, that the world of facts and events is *maya* is
to say that facts and events are terms of measurement rather
than realities of nature. We must, however, expand the concept
of measurement to include setting bounds of all kinds, whether
by descriptive classification or selective screening. It will thus
be easy to see that facts and events are as abstract as lines of
latitude or as feet and inches. Consider for a moment that it is
impossible to isolate a single fact, all by itself. Facts come in
pairs at the very least, for a single body is inconceivable apart
from a space in which it hangs. Definition, setting bounds, delineation—these are always acts of *division* and thus of duality,
for as soon as a boundary is defined it has two sides.

This point of view is somewhat startling, and even quite hard
to understand, for those long accustomed to think that things,
facts, and events are the very building-blocks of the world, the
most solid of solid realities. Yet a proper understanding of the
maya doctrine is one of the most essential prerequisites for the
study of Hinduism and Buddhism, and in trying to grasp its

meaning one must try to put aside the various "idealist" philosophies of the West with which it is so often confused—even by
modern Indian Vedantists. For the world is not an illusion of the
mind in the sense that—to the eyes of the liberated man (*jivan-
mukta*)—there is nothing to be seen but a trackless void. He sees
the world that we see; but he does not mark it off, measure it,
divide it in the same way. He does not look upon it as really or
concretely broken down into separate things and events. He
sees that the skin may just as well be regarded as what joins us to
our environment as what separates us from it. He sees, furthermore, that the skin will be considered as joining only if it has
first been considered as separating, or vice versa.

Thus his point of view is not monistic. He does not think that
all things are in reality One because, concretely speaking, there
never were any "things" to be considered One. To join is as
much *maya* as to separate. For this reason both Hindus and
Buddhists prefer to speak of reality as "nondual" rather than
"one," since the concept of one must always be in relation to
that of many. The doctrine of *maya* is therefore a doctrine of
relativity. It is saying that things, facts, and events are de-
lineated, not by nature, but by human description, and that the
way in which we describe (or divide) them is relative to our
varying points of view.

It is easy to see, for example, that an event called the First
World War can only rather arbitrarily be said to have begun
on August 4, 1914, and to have ended on November 11, 1918.
Historians can discover "actual" beginnings of the war long
before and "resumptions" of the same strife long after these
formal boundaries of the event. For events can divide and
merge like blobs of mercury according to the changing fashions
of historical description. The boundaries of events are conventional rather than natural, in the sense that a man's life is
said to have begun at the moment of parturition, rather than at
conception on the one hand or weaning on the other.

Similarly, it is easy to see the conventional character of things.

Ordinarily a human organism is counted as one thing, though from the physiological standpoint it is as many things as it has parts or organs, and from the sociological standpoint it is merely part of a larger thing called a group.

Certainly the world of nature abounds with surfaces and lines, with areas of density and vacuity, which we employ in marking out the boundaries of events and things. But here again, the *maya* doctrine asserts that these forms (*rupa*) have no "own-being" or "self-nature" (*svabhava*): they do not exist in their own right, but only in relation to one another, as a solid cannot be distinguished save in relation to a space. In this sense, the solid and the space, the sound and the silence, the existent and the nonexistent, the figure and the ground are inseparable, interdependent, or "mutually arising," and it is only by *maya* or conventional division that they may be considered apart from one another.

Indian philosophy also thinks of *rupa* or form as *maya* because it is impermanent. Indeed, when Hindu and Buddhist texts speak of the "empty" or "illusory" character of the visible world of nature–as distinct from the conventional world of things–they refer precisely to the impermanence of its forms. Form is flux, and thus *maya* in the slightly extended sense that it cannot be firmly marked down or grasped. Form is *maya* when the mind attempts to comprehend and control it in the fixed categories of thought, that is, by means of names (*nama*) and words. For these are precisely the nouns and verbs by means of which the abstract and conceptual categories of things and events are designated.

To serve their purpose, names and terms must of necessity be fixed and definite like all other units of measurement. But their use is–up to a point–so satisfactory that man is always in danger of confusing his measures with the world so measured, of identifying money with wealth, fixed convention with fluid reality. But to the degree that he identifies himself and his life with these rigid and hollow frames of definition, he condemns himself to the perpetual frustration of one trying to catch water in a sieve. Thus Indian philosophy speaks constantly of the un-wisdom of pursuing things, of striving for the permanence of particular entities and events, because it sees in all this nothing more than an infatuation with ghosts, with the abstract meas-ures of the mind (*manas*).[7]

Maya is, then, usually equated with *nama-rupa* or "name-and-form," with the mind's attempt to grasp the fluid forms of nature in its mesh of fixed classes. But when it is understood that form is ultimately void—in the special sense of ungraspable and im-measurable—the world of form is immediately seen as Brahman rather than *maya*. The formal world becomes the real world in the moment when it is no longer clutched, in the moment when its changeful fluidity is no longer resisted. Hence it is the very transitoriness of the world which is the sign of its divinity, of its actual identity with the indivisible and immeasurable infinity of Brahman.

This is why the Hindu-Buddhist insistence on the imper-manence of the world is not the pessimistic and nihilistic doc-trine which Western critics normally suppose it to be. Transitori-ness is depressing only to the mind which insists upon trying to grasp. But to the mind which lets go and moves with the flow of change, which becomes, in Zen Buddhist imagery, like a ball in a mountain stream, the sense of transience or emptiness becomes a kind of ecstasy. This is perhaps why, in both East and West, impermanence is so often the theme of the most profound and moving poetry—so much so that the splendor of change shines through even when the poet seems to resent it the most.

> *Tomorrow, and tomorrow, and tomorrow,*
> *Creeps in this petty pace from day to day*
> *To the last syllable of recorded time,*
> *And all our yesterdays have lighted fools*

[7] From the same root as *maya*, and from which also come our words "mensu-ration" (Lat., *mensura*), "mental" (Lat., *mens*), "dimension," and "man" himself, "the measure of all things." Cf. also the Latin *mensis* (month).

The way to dusty death. Out, out, brief candle!
Life's but a walking shadow, a poor player
That struts and frets his hour upon the stage
And then is heard no more: it is a tale
Told by an idiot, full of sound and fury,
Signifying nothing.

Stated thus–as R. H. Blyth observes–it seems not so bad after all.

In sum, then, the *maya* doctrine points out, firstly, the impossibility of grasping the actual world in the mind's net of words and concepts, and, secondly, the fluid character of those very forms which thought attempts to define. The world of facts and events is altogether *nama*, abstract names, and *rupa*, fluid form. It escapes both the comprehension of the philosopher and the grasp of the pleasure-seeker like water from a clutching fist. There is even something deceptive in the idea of Brahman as the eternal reality underlying the flux, and of the *atman* as the divine ground of human consciousness, for in so far as these are concepts they are as incapable of grasping the real as any other.

It is precisely this realization of the *total* elusiveness of the world which lies at the root of Buddhism. This is the special shift of emphasis which, more than anything else, distinguishes the doctrine of the Buddha from the teaching of the *Upanishads*, which is the *raison d'être* for the growth of Buddhism as a distinct movement in Indian life and thought.

For Gautama the "Awakened One" or Buddha (died *c.* 545 B.C.) lived at a time when the major *Upanishads* were already in existence, and their philosophy must be seen as the point of departure for his own teaching. It would be a serious mistake, however, to look upon the Buddha as the "founder" or "reformer" of a religion which came into being as some kind of organized revolt against Hinduism. For we are speaking of a time when there was no consciousness of "religions," when such terms as "Hindu-ism" or "Brahman-ism" would have meant nothing. There was simply a tradition, embodied in the orally transmitted doctrine of the *Vedas* and *Upanishads,* a tradition that was not specifically "religious" in that it involved a whole way of life and concerned everything from the methods of agriculture to the knowledge of the ultimate reality. The Buddha was acting in full accord with this tradition when he became a *rishi* or "forest sage," who had abandoned the life of the householder and divested himself of caste in order to follow a way of liberation. As with every other *rishi,* the method of his way of liberation had certain characteristic features, and his doctrine contained criticisms of men's failure to practice the tradition which they professed.

Furthermore, he was being entirely traditional in his abandonment of caste and in accepting a following of casteless and homeless students. For the Indian tradition, even more than the Chinese, specifically encourages the abandonment of the conventional life at a certain age, after the duties of family and citizenship have been fulfilled. Relinquishment of caste is the outward and visible sign of the realization that one's true state is "unclassified," that one's role or person is simply conventional, and that one's true nature is "no-thing" and "no-body."

This realization was the crux of the Buddha's experience of awakening (*bodhi*) which dawned upon him one night, as he sat under the celebrated Bo Tree at Gaya, after seven years of meditation in the forests. From the standpoint of Zen, this experience is the essential content of Buddhism, and the verbal doctrine is quite secondary to the wordless transmission of the experience itself from generation to generation. For seven years Gautama had struggled by the traditional means of *yoga* and *tapas,* contemplation and ascesis, to penetrate the cause of man's enslavement to *maya,* to find release from the vicious circle of clinging-to-life (*trishna*) which is like trying to make the hand grasp itself. All his efforts had been in vain. The eternal *atman,* the real Self, was not to be found. However much he concentrated upon his own mind to find its root and ground, he found only his own effort to concentrate. The evening before his awakening he simply "gave up," relaxed his ascetic diet, and ate some nourishing food.

Thereupon he felt at once that a profound change was coming over him. He sat beneath the tree, vowing never to rise until he had attained the supreme awakening, and–according to a tradition–sat all through the night until the first glimpse of the morning star suddenly provoked a state of perfect clarity and understanding. This was *anuttara samyak sambodhi*, "unexcelled, complete awakening," liberation from *maya* and from the everlasting Round of birth-and-death (*samsara*), which goes on and on for as long as a man tries in any way whatsoever to grasp at his own life.

Yet the actual content of this experience was never and could never be put into words. For words are the frames of *maya*, the meshes of its net, and the experience is of the water which slips through. Thus so far as words are concerned the most that may be said of this experience are the words attributed to the Buddha in the *Vajracchedika*:

> Just so, Subhuti, I obtained not the least thing from unexcelled, complete awakening, and for this very reason it is called "unexcelled, complete awakening." (22)

Thus from the standpoint of Zen the Buddha "never said a word," despite the volumes of scriptures attributed to him. For his real message remained always unspoken, and was such that, when words attempted to express it, they made it seem as if it were nothing at all. Yet it is the essential tradition of Zen that what cannot be conveyed by speech can nevertheless be passed on by "direct pointing," by some nonverbal means of communication without which the Buddhist experience could never have been handed down to future generations.

In its own (probably rather late) tradition, Zen maintains that the Buddha transmitted awakening to his chief disciple, Mahakasyapa, by holding up a flower and remaining silent. The Pali Canon, however, relates that immediately after his awakening the

Buddha went to the Deer Park at Benares, and set forth his doctrine to those who had formerly been his companions in the ascetic life, expressing it in the form of those Four Noble Truths which provide so convenient a summary of Buddhism.

These Four Truths are patterned on the traditional Vedic form of a physician's diagnosis and prescription: the identification of the disease, and of its cause, the pronouncement as to whether it may be cured, and the prescription for the remedy.

The First Truth is concerned with the problematic word *duhkha,* loosely translatable as "suffering," and which designates the great disease of the world for which the Buddha's method (*dharma*) is the cure.

> Birth is *duhkha,* decay is *duhkha,* sickness is *duhkha,* death is *duhkha,* so also are sorrow and grief. . . . To be bound with things which we dislike, and to be parted from things which we like, these also are *duhkha.* Not to get what one desires, this also is *duhkha.* In a word, this body, this fivefold aggregation based on clutching (*trishna*), this is *duhkha.*[8]

This, however, cannot quite be compressed into the sweeping assertion that "life is suffering." The point is rather that life as we usually live it is suffering—or, more exactly, is bedeviled by the peculiar frustration which comes from attempting the impossible. Perhaps, then, "frustration" is the best equivalent for *duhkha,* even though the word is the simple antonym of *sukha,* which means "pleasant" or "sweet." [9]

In another formulation of the Buddha's teaching *duhkha* is one of the three characteristics of being, or becoming (*bhava*), whereof the other two are *anitya,* impermanence, and *anatman,* absence of any Self. These two terms are of basic importance. The *anitya* doctrine is, again, not quite the simple assertion that the world is impermanent, but rather that the more one grasps at

[8] *Samyutta Nikaya,* 421.
[9] Or, if we were to translate *duhkha* as "sour," we might say that the Buddha's doctrine is that life is soured by man's grasping attitude towards it—as milk turns sour when kept too long.

the world, the more it changes. Reality in itself is neither permanent nor impermanent; it cannot be categorized. But when
one tries to hold on to it, change is everywhere apparent, since,
like one's own shadow, the faster one pursues it, the faster it
flees.

In the same way, the *anatman* doctrine is not quite the bald
assertion that there is no real Self (*atman*) at the basis of our
consciousness. The point is rather that there is no Self, or basic
reality, which may be grasped, either by direct experience or by
concepts. Apparently the Buddha felt that the doctrine of the
atman in the *Upanishads* lent itself too easily to a fatal misinterpretation. It became an object of belief, a desideratum, a
goal to be reached, something to which the mind could cling as
its one final abode of safety in the flux of life. The Buddha's
view was that a Self so grasped was no longer the true Self, but
only one more of the innumerable forms of *maya*. Thus *anatman*
might be expressed in the form, "The true Self is non-Self," since
any attempt to conceive the Self, believe in the Self, or seek for
the Self immediately thrusts it away.

The *Upanishads* distinguish between *atman*, the true, supra-
individual Self, and the *jivatman* or individual soul, and the
Buddha's *anatman* doctrine agrees with them in denying the
reality of the latter. It is fundamental to every school of Buddhism that there is no ego, no enduring entity which is the constant subject of our changing experiences. For the ego exists in
an abstract sense alone, being an abstraction from memory,
somewhat like the illusory circle of fire made by a whirling torch.
We can, for example, imagine the path of a bird through the
sky as a distinct line which it has taken. But this line is as
abstract as a line of latitude. In concrete reality, the bird left no
line, and, similarly, the past from which our ego is abstracted has
entirely disappeared. Thus any attempt to cling to the ego or to
make it an effective source of action is doomed to frustration.

The Second Noble Truth relates to the cause of frustration,
which is said to be *trishna*, clinging or grasping, based on *avidya*,

which is ignorance or unconsciousness. Now *avidya* is the formal opposite of awakening. It is the state of the mind when hypnotized or spellbound by *maya*, so that it mistakes the abstract world of things and events for the concrete world of reality. At a still deeper level it is lack of self-knowledge, lack of the realization that all grasping turns out to be the futile effort to grasp oneself, or rather, to make life catch hold of itself. For to one who has self-knowledge, there is no duality between himself and the external world. *Avidya* is "ignoring" the fact that subject and object are relational, like the two sides of a coin, so that when one pursues, the other retreats. This is why the egocentric attempt to dominate the world, to bring as much of the world as possible under the control of the ego, has only to proceed for a little while before it raises the difficulty of the ego's controlling itself.

This is really a simple problem of what we now call cybernetics, the science of control. Mechanically and logically it is easy to see that any system approaching perfect self-control is also approaching perfect self-frustration. Such a system is a vicious circle, and has the same logical structure as a statement which states something about itself, as for example, "I am lying," when it is implied that the statement is itself a lie. The statement circulates fatuously forever, since it is always true to the extent that it is false, and false to the extent that it is true. Expressed more concretely, I cannot throw a ball so long as I am holding on to it– so as to maintain perfect control of its movement.

Thus the desire for perfect control, of the environment and of oneself, is based on a profound mistrust of the controller. *Avidya* is the failure to see the basic self-contradiction of this position. From it therefore arises a futile grasping or controlling of life which is pure self-frustration, and the pattern of life which follows is the vicious circle which in Hinduism and Buddhism is called *samsara,* the Round of birth-and-death.[10]

10 The dynamic structure of the Round is called *pratitya-samutpada,* the twelvefold chain of "dependent origination," in which the twelve causal links give rise to one another mutually, constituting a closed circle without

The active principle of the Round is known as *karma* or "conditioned action," action, that is, arising from a motive and seeking a result—the type of action which always requires the necessity for further action. Man is involved in *karma* when he interferes with the world in such a way that he is compelled to go on interfering, when the solution of a problem creates still more problems to be solved, when the control of one thing creates the need to control several others. *Karma* is thus the fate of everyone who "tries to be God." He lays a trap for the world in which he himself gets caught.

Many Buddhists understand the Round of birth-and-death quite literally as a process of reincarnation, wherein the *karma* which shapes the individual does so again and again in life after life until, through insight and awakening, it is laid to rest. But in Zen, and in other schools of the Mahayana, it is often taken in a more figurative way, as that the process of rebirth is from moment to moment, so that one is being reborn so long as one identifies himself with a continuing ego which reincarnates itself afresh at each moment of time. Thus the validity and interest of the doctrine does not require acceptance of a special theory of survival. Its importance is rather that it exemplifies the whole problem of action in vicious circles and its resolution, and in this respect Buddhist philosophy should have a special interest for students of communication theory, cybernetics, logical philosophy, and similar matters.

The Third Noble Truth is concerned with the ending of self-frustration, of grasping, and of the whole viciously circular pattern of *karma* which generates the Round. The ending is called

beginning or end. Thus ignorance (*avidya*) gives rise to motivation (*samskara*), and this in series to consciousness (*vijnana*), name-and-form (*namarupa*), the six senses (*shadayatana*), sense stimulation (*sparsa*), sense experience (*vedana*), grasping (*trishna*), possessiveness (*upadana*), coming-to-be (*bhava*), birth (*jati*), and old-age-and-death (*jaramarana*), which again gives rise to *avidya*. The Buddha explained that *avidya* was put first on the list, not because it was the temporal beginning of the series, but for simple convenience of exposition. The whole series arises together, and its terms exist only in relation to one another.

nirvana, a word of such dubious etymology that a simple translation is exceedingly difficult. It has been variously connected
with Sanskrit roots which would make it mean the blowing out
of a flame, or simply blowing out (ex- or de-spiration), or with
the cessation of waves, turnings, or circlings (*vritti*) of the
mind.

The two latter interpretations seem, on the whole, to make
most sense. If *nirvana* is "de-spiration" it is the act of one who
has seen the futility of trying to hold his breath or life (*prana*)
indefinitely, since to hold the breath is to lose it. Thus *nirvana* is
the equivalent of *moksha*, release or liberation. Seen from one
side, it appears to be despair–the recognition that life utterly
defeats our efforts to control it, that all human striving is no more
than a vanishing hand clutching at clouds. Seen from the other
side, this despair bursts into joy and creative power, on the
principle that to lose one's life is to find it–to find freedom of
action unimpeded by self-frustration and the anxiety inherent
in trying to save and control the Self.

If *nirvana* is related to the cessation (*nir-*) of turnings (*vritti*),
the term is synonymous with the aim of *yoga*, defined in the
Yogasutra as *citta vritti nirodha*–the cessation of turnings of the
mind. These "turnings" are the thoughts whereby the mind
endeavors to grasp the world and itself. *Yoga* is the practice of
trying to stop these thoughts by thinking about them, until the
utter futility of the process is *felt* so vividly that it simply drops
away, and the mind discovers its natural and unconfused state.

It is obvious, however, that both etymologies give us the same
essential meaning. *Nirvana* is the way of life which ensues when
clutching at life has come to an end. In so far as all definition is
clutching, *nirvana* is necessarily indefinable. It is the natural,
"un-self-grasped" state of the mind; and here, of course, the
mind has no specific meaning, for what is not grasped is not
known in the conventional sense of knowledge. More popularly
and literally understood, *nirvana* is the disappearance of the

being from the Round of incarnations, not into a state of annihilation, but simply into a state escaping definition, and thus
immeasurable and infinite.

To attain *nirvana* is also to attain Buddhahood, awakening.
But this is not attainment in any ordinary sense, because no
acquisition and no motivation are involved. It is impossible to
desire *nirvana*, or to intend to reach it, for anything desirable
or conceivable as an object of action is, by definition, not *nirvana*.
Nirvana can only arise unintentionally, spontaneously, when the
impossibility of self-grasping has been thoroughly perceived. A
Buddha, therefore, is a man of no rank. He is not above, like
an angel; he is not below, like a demon. He does not appear anywhere in the six divisions of the Round, and it would be mistaken
to think of him as superior to the angels, for the law of the
Round is that what goes up must come down, and vice versa.
He has transcended all dualities whatsoever, and thus it would
mean nothing to him to think of himself as a superior person or a
spiritual success.

The Fourth Noble Truth describes the Eightfold Path of the
Buddha's *Dharma*, that is, the method or doctrine whereby self-
frustration is brought to an end. Each section of the path has a
name preceded by the word *samyak* (Pali, *samma*), which has
the meaning of "perfect" or "complete." The first two sections
have to do with thought; the following four have to do with action; and the final two have to do with contemplation or awareness. We therefore have:

1 *Samyag-drishti,* or complete view.
2 *Samyak-samkalpa,* or complete understanding.

3 *Samyag-vak,* or complete (i.e., truthful) speech.
4 *Samyak-karmanta,* or complete action.
5 *Samyagajiva,* or complete vocation.
6 *Samyag-vyayama,* or complete application.

7 *Samyak-smriti,* or complete recollectedness.
8 *Samyak-samadhi,* or complete contemplation.

Without discussing these sections in detail, it may simply be said that the first two are concerned with a proper understanding of the doctrine and of the human situation. In some ways the first section, "complete view," contains all the others, since the method of Buddhism is above all the practice of clear awareness, of seeing the world *yathabhutam*–just as it is. Such awareness is a lively attention to one's direct experience, to the world as immediately sensed, so as not to be misled by names and labels. *Samyak-samadhi*, the last section of the path, is the perfection of the first, signifying pure experience, pure awareness, wherein there is no longer the dualism of the knower and the known.

The sections dealing with action are often misunderstood because they have a deceptive similarity to a "system of morals." Buddhism does not share the Western view that there is a moral law, enjoined by God or by nature, which it is man's duty to obey. The Buddha's precepts of conduct–abstinence from taking life, taking what is not given, exploitation of the passions, lying, and intoxication–are voluntarily assumed rules of expediency, the intent of which is to remove the hindrances to clarity of awareness. Failure to observe the precepts produces "bad *karma*," not because *karma* is a law or moral retribution, but because all motivated and purposeful actions, whether conventionally good or bad, are *karma* in so far as they are directed to the grasping of life. Generally speaking, the conventionally "bad" actions are rather more grasping than the "good." But the higher stages of Buddhist practice are as much concerned with disentanglement from "good *karma*" as from "bad." Thus complete action is ultimately free, uncontrived, or spontaneous action, in exactly the same sense as the Taoist *wu-wei*.[11]

Smriti, recollectedness, and *samadhi*, contemplation, constitute the section dealing with the life of meditation, the inner, mental practice of the Buddha's way. Complete recollectedness is a constant awareness or watching of one's sensations, feelings, and

[11] Technically such action would be called *akarma,* unconditioned action, or *asamskrita,* uncontrived action.

thoughts–without purpose or comment. It is a total clarity and presence of mind, actively passive, wherein events come and go like reflections in a mirror: nothing is reflected except what *is*.

> In walking, standing, sitting, or lying down he understands that he is so doing, so that, however his body is engaged, he understands it just as it is. . . . In setting out or returning, in looking before or around, in bending or stretching his arm, . . . he acts with clear awareness.[12]

Through such awareness it is seen that the separation of the thinker from the thought, the knower from the known, the subject from the object, is purely abstract. There is not the mind on the one hand and its experiences on the other: there is just a process of experiencing in which there is nothing to be grasped, as an object, and no one, as a subject, to grasp it. Seen thus, the process of experiencing ceases to clutch at itself. Thought follows thought without interruption, that is, without any need to divide itself from itself, so as to become its own object.

> "Where there is an object, there thought arises." Is then the thought one thing, and the object another? No, what is the object, just that is the thought. If the object were one thing, and the thought another, then there would be a double state of thought. So the object itself is just thought. Can then thought review thought? No, thought cannot review thought. As the blade of a sword cannot cut itself, as a finger-tip cannot touch itself, so a thought cannot see itself.[13]

This nonduality of the mind, in which it is no longer divided against itself, is *samadhi,* and because of the disappearance of that fruitless threshing around of the mind to grasp itself, *samadhi* is a state of profound peace. This is not the stillness of total inactivity, for, once the mind returns to its natural state, *samadhi* persists at all times, in "walking, standing, sitting, and lying." But, from the earliest times, Buddhism has especially emphasized the practice of recollectedness and contemplation while sitting.

[12] *Majjhima Nikaya,* I. 56.
[13] *Sikshasamuccaya,* 234. In Conze (2), p. 163.

Most images of the Buddha show him in the posture of sitting meditation, in the particular attitude known as *padmasana,* the posture of the lotus, with the legs crossed and the feet resting, soles upward, upon the thighs.

Sitting meditation is not, as is often supposed, a spiritual "exercise," a practice followed for some ulterior object. From a Buddhist standpoint, it is simply the proper way to sit, and it seems perfectly natural to remain sitting so long as there is nothing else to be done, and so long as one is not consumed with nervous agitation. To the restless temperament of the West, sitting meditation may seem to be an unpleasant discipline, because we do not seem to be able to sit "just to sit" without qualms of conscience, without feeling that we ought to be doing something more important to justify our existence. To propitiate this restless conscience, sitting meditation must therefore be regarded as an exercise, a discipline with an ulterior motive. Yet at that very point it ceases to be meditation (*dhyana*) in the Buddhist sense, for where there is purpose, where there is seeking and grasping for results, there is no *dhyana.*

This word *dhyana* (Pali, *jhana*) is the original Sanskrit form of the Chinese *ch'an* [c] and the Japanese *zen,* and thus its meaning is of central importance for an understanding of Zen Buddhism. "Meditation" in the common sense of "thinking things over" or "musing" is a most misleading translation. But such alternatives as "trance" or "absorption" are even worse, since they suggest states of hypnotic fascination. The best solution seems to be to leave *dhyana* untranslated and add it to the English language as we have added Nirvana and Tao.[14]

[14] The Pali Canon (*Vinaya Pitaka,* III. 3–6, and *Majjhima Nikaya,* I. 349–52) lists eight types of *jhana*–the four *rupa-jhana* and the four *arupa-jhana* –the states of *jhana* with form and without form. The first four involve the progressive settling of conception (*vitakka*) and discursive thought (*vicara*) into a state of equanimity (*upekkha*) through the practice of *samadhi.* In other words, as the mind returns to its natural state of integrity and non-duality, it ceases to clutch at experience with the symbols of discursive thought. It simply perceives without words or concepts. Beyond this lie the four *arupa-jhana,* described as the spheres of Boundless Space, Boundless

As used in Buddhism, the term *dhyana* comprises both recollectedness (*smriti*) and *samadhi,* and can best be described as
the state of unified or one-pointed awareness. On the one hand,
it is one-pointed in the sense of being focused on the present,
since to clear awareness there is neither past nor future, but just
this one moment (*ekaksana*) which Western mystics have called
the Eternal Now. On the other hand, it is one-pointed in the
sense of being a state of consciousness without differentiation
of the knower, the knowing, and the known.

> A Tathagata (i.e., a Buddha) is a seer of what is to be seen, but
> he is not mindful (*na mannati,* or does not conceive) of the seen,
> the unseen, the seeable, or the seer. So too with the heard, the
> sensed, and the known: he does not think of them in these cate-
> gories.[15]

The difficulty of appreciating what *dhyana* means is that the
structure of our language does not permit us to use a transitive
verb without a subject and a predicate. When there is "knowing,"
grammatical convention requires that there must be someone
who knows and something which is known. We are so accustomed to this convention in speaking and thinking that we fail
to recognize that it is simply a convention, and that it does not
necessarily correspond to the actual experience of knowing. Thus
when we say, "A light flashed," it is somewhat easier to see
through the grammatical convention and to realize that the flashing is the light. But *dhyana* as the mental state of the liberated
or awakened man is naturally free from the confusion of conventional entities with reality. Our intellectual discomfort in trying
to conceive knowing without a distinct "someone" who knows
and a distinct "something" which is known, is like the discomfort of arriving at a formal dinner in pajamas. The error is conventional, not existential.

Consciousness, Nothingness, and Neither-Perception-nor-Nonperception,
which are stages of the mind's realization of its own nature. At the time of
his death, the Buddha is said to have entered into *parinirvana* (i.e., final
nirvana) from the fourth *rupa-jhana.*

[15] *Anguttara Nikaya,* II. 25.

Once again, therefore, we see how convention, how the *maya* of measurement and description, populates the world with those ghosts which we call entities and things. So hypnotic, so persuasive is the power of convention that we begin to feel these ghosts as realities, and make of them our loves, our ideals, our prized possessions. But the anxiety-laden problem of what will happen to me when I die is, after all, like asking what happens to my fist when I open my hand, or where my lap goes when I stand up. Perhaps, then, we are now able to understand the celebrated summary of the Buddha's doctrine given in the *Visuddhimagga*:

> *Suffering alone exists, none who suffer;*
> *The deed there is, but no doer thereof;*
> *Nirvana is, but no one seeking it;*
> *The Path there is, but none who travel it.* (16)

Three

MAHAYANA BUDDHISM

Because the teaching of the Buddha was a way of liberation, it had no other object than the experience of *nirvana*. The Buddha did not attempt to set forth a consistent philosophical system, trying to satisfy that intellectual curiosity about ultimate things which expects answers in words. When pressed for such answers, when questioned about the nature of *nirvana*, the origin of the world, and the reality of the Self, the Buddha maintained a "noble silence," and went on to say that such questions were irrelevant and did not lead to the actual experience of liberation.

It has often been said that the later development of Buddhism was due to the inability of the Indian mind to rest content with that silence, so that at last it had to indulge its overwhelming urge for "abstract metaphysical speculations" about the nature of reality. Such a view of the genesis of Mahayana Buddhism is, however, rather misleading. The vast body of Mahayana doctrine arose not so much to satisfy intellectual curiosity as to deal with the practical psychological problems encountered in following the Buddha's way. Certainly the treatment of these problems is highly scholastic, and the intellectual level of the Mahayana texts is very lofty. But the consistent aim is to bring about the experience of liberation, not to construct a philosophical system. In the words of Sir Arthur Berriedale Keith:

> The metaphysics of the Mahayana in the incoherence of its systems shows clearly enough the secondary interest attaching to it in the eyes of the monks, whose main interest was concentrated on the attainment of release; the Mahayana no less than the Hinayana is concerned vitally with this practical end, and its philosophy is of value merely in so far as it helps men to attain their aim.[1]

[1] Keith (1), p. 273.

There are, no doubt, respects in which Mahayana Buddhism is a concession both to intellectual curiosity and to a popular desire for short cuts to the goal. But at root it is the work of highly sensitive and perceptive minds studying their own inner workings. To anyone who is highly self-aware, the Buddhism of the Pali Canon leaves many practical problems unanswered. Its psychological insight goes little further than the construction of analytical catalogues of mental functions, and though its precepts are clear it is not always helpful in explaining their practical difficulties. Perhaps it is too sweeping a generalization, but one receives the impression that whereas the Pali Canon would unlock the door to *nirvana* by sheer effort, the Mahayana would jiggle the key until it turns smoothly. Thus the great concern of the Mahayana is the provision of "skillful means" (*upaya*) for making *nirvana* accessible to every type of mentality.

How and when the Mahayana doctrines arose is a matter of historical guesswork. The great Mahayana *sutras* are ostensibly the teachings of the Buddha and his immediate disciples, but their style is so different and their doctrine so much more subtle than that of the Pali Canon that scholars almost unanimously assign them to later dates. There is no evidence of their existence in the time of the great Buddhist emperor Asoka, grandson of Chandragupta Maurya, who was converted to Buddhism in 262 B.C. Asoka's rock inscriptions reflect no more than the social teachings of the Pali Canon, its insistence on *ahimsa* or nonviolence to both men and animals and its general precepts for the life of the laity. The principal Mahayana texts were being translated into Chinese by Kumarajiva shortly after A.D. 400, but our knowledge of Indian history during the intervening six hundred years from Asoka's death is so fragmentary, and the internal evidences of the *sutras* themselves so vague, that we can do little more than assign them to the four hundred years between 100 B.C. and A.D. 300. Even specific individuals associated with their development—Asvaghosha, Nagarjuna, Asanga, and Vasubandhu—can be dated only very approximately.

The traditional Mahayanist account of its own origin is that its teachings were delivered by the Buddha to his intimate disciples but their public revelation withheld until the world was ready for them. The principle of "delayed revelation" is a well-known expedient for permitting the growth of a tradition, for exploring the implications contained in the original seed. Apparent contradictions between earlier and later doctrines are explained by assigning them to different levels of truth, ranging from the most relative to the absolute, and of which the (probably quite late) Avatamsaka School distinguishes no less than five. However, the problem of the historical origins of the Mahayana is of no very direct importance for an understanding of Zen, which, as a Chinese rather than Indian form of Buddhism, came into being when Indian Mahayana was fully grown. We can pass on, therefore, to the central Mahayana doctrines from which Zen arose.

The Mahayana distinguishes itself from the Buddhism of the Pali Canon by terming the latter the Little (*hina*) Vehicle (*yana*) of liberation and itself the Great (*maha*) Vehicle–great because it comprises such a wealth of *upaya*, or methods for the realization of *nirvana*. These methods range from the sophisticated dialectic of Nagarjuna, whose object is to free the mind of all fixed conceptions, to the Sukhavati or Pure Land doctrine of liberation through faith in the power of Amitabha, the Buddha of Boundless Light, who is said to have attained his awakening many aeons before the time of Gautama. They include even the Tantric Buddhism of medieval India, wherein liberation may be realized through the repetition of sacred words and formulae called *dharani*, and through special types of *yoga* involving sexual intercourse with a *shakti* or "spiritual wife." [2]

[2] The alleged "obscenity" of *maithuna*, as this practice is called, is entirely in the minds of Christian missionaries. In fact, the relationship with the *shakti* was anything but promiscuous, and involved the mature and all-too-infrequent notion of a man and a woman undertaking their spiritual development in common. This included a sanctification of the sexual relationship which should logically have been part of the Catholic view of marriage as a sacrament. For a full treatment see S. B. Dasgupta, *An Introduction to Tantric Buddhism* (Calcutta, 1952), and Sir John Woodroffe, *Shakti and Shakta* (Madras and London, 1929).

A preliminary study of the Pali Canon will certainly give the impression that *nirvana* is to be realized only through rigorous effort and self-control, and that the aspirant should lay aside all other concerns for the pursuit of this ideal. Mahayanists may be perfectly correct in assuming that the Buddha intended this emphasis as an *upaya,* a skillful means of enabling one to realize, concretely and vividly, the absurd vicious circle of desiring not to desire, or of trying to get rid of selfishness by oneself. For this is certainly the conclusion to which the practice of the Buddha's doctrine led. It may be attributed to laziness and loss of nerve, but it seems more plausible to suggest that those who remained in the path of self-deliverance were merely unconscious of the paradox involved. For wherever the Mahayana continues to teach the way of liberation by one's own effort, it does so as an expedient for bringing the individual to a vivid awareness of his own futility.

Various indications suggest that one of the earliest notions of the Mahayana was the conception of the Bodhisattva, not simply as a potential Buddha, but as one who by renouncing *nirvana* was at a higher spiritual level than one who attained it and so withdrew from the world of birth-and-death. In the Pali Canon the disciples of the Buddha who attain *nirvana* are termed Arhans or "worthy ones," but in the Mahayana texts the ideal of the Arhan is accounted almost selfish. It is fit only for the *sravaka,* the "hearer" of the doctrine who has progressed only so far as to get a theoretical understanding. The Bodhisattva, however, is one who realizes that there is a profound contradiction in a *nirvana* attained by himself and for himself. From the popular standpoint, the Bodhisattva became a focus of devotion (*bhakti*), a savior of the world who had vowed not to enter the final *nirvana* until all other sentient beings had likewise attained it. For their sakes he consented to be born again and again into the Round of *samsara,* until, in the course of innumerable ages, even the grass and the dust had attained Buddhahood.

But from a deeper standpoint it became obvious that the idea of the Bodhisattva is implicit in the logic of Buddhism, that it flows naturally from the principle of not-grasping and from the doctrine of the unreality of the ego. For if *nirvana* is the state in which the attempt to grasp reality has wholly ceased, through the realization of its impossibility, it will obviously be absurd to think of *nirvana* itself as something to be grasped or attained. If, furthermore, the ego is merely a convention, it is nonsense to think of *nirvana* as a state to be attained by some being. As is said in the *Vajracchedika:*

> All Bodhisattva-heroes should cultivate their minds to think: all sentient beings of whatever class . . . are caused by me to attain the boundless liberation of *nirvana*. Yet when vast, innumerable, and immeasurable numbers of beings have thus been liberated, in truth no being has been liberated! Why is this, Subhuti? It is because no Bodhisattva who is truly a Bodhisattva holds to the idea of an ego, a personality, a being, or a separate individual. (3)

The corollary of this position is that if there is no *nirvana* which can be attained, and if, in reality, there are no individual entities, it will follow that our bondage in the Round is merely apparent, and that in fact we are already in *nirvana*—so that to seek *nirvana* is the folly of looking for what one has never lost. Naturally, then, the Bodhisattva makes no motion to depart from the Round of *samsara,* as if *nirvana* were somewhere else, for to do so would imply that *nirvana* is something that needs to be attained and that *samsara* is an actual reality. In the words of the *Lankavatara Sutra:*

> Those who, afraid of the sufferings arising from the discrimination of birth-and-death (*samsara*), seek for Nirvana, do not know that birth-and-death and Nirvana are not to be separated from one another; and, seeing that all things subject to discrimination have no reality, (they) imagine that Nirvana consists in the future annihilation of the senses and their fields. (II. 18) [3]

To strive, then, to blot out the conventional world of things and events is to admit that it exists in reality. Hence the Mahayanist

[3] In Suzuki (3), p. 55. The "fields" of the senses are the areas or aspects of the external world to which the particular sense organs are related.

principle that "what has never arisen does not have to be annihilated." [a]

These are not the idle speculations and sophistries of a system of subjective idealism or nihilism. They are answers to a practical problem which may be expressed thus: "If my grasping of life involves me in a vicious circle, how am I to learn not to grasp? How can I try to let go when trying is precisely not letting go?" Stated in another way, to try not to grasp is the same thing as to grasp, since its motivation is the same—my urgent desire to save myself from a difficulty. I cannot get rid of this desire, since it is one and the same desire as the desire to get rid of it! This is the familiar, everyday problem of the psychological "double-bind," of creating the problem by trying to solve it, of worrying because one worries, and of being afraid of fear.

Mahayana philosophy proposes a drastic but effective answer which is the theme of a class of literature called *Prajna-paramita*, or "wisdom for crossing to the other shore," a literature closely associated with the work of Nagarjuna (*c.* A.D. 200), who ranks with Shankara as one of the greatest minds of India. Stated baldly, the answer is that all grasping, even for *nirvana,* is futile—for there is nothing to be grasped. This is Nagarjuna's celebrated Sunyavada, his "Doctrine of the Void," otherwise known as the Madhyamika, the "middle way," because it refutes all metaphysical propositions by demonstrating their relativity. From the standpoint of academic philosophy, the *Prajna-paramita* and the doctrine of Nagarjuna are no doubt some form of nihilism or "absolute relativism." But this is not Nagarjuna's standpoint. The dialectic with which he demolishes every conception of reality is merely a device for breaking the vicious circle of grasping, and the terminus of his philosophy is not the abject despair of nihilism but the natural and uncontrived bliss (*ananda*) of liberation.

The Sunyavada takes its name from the term *sunya,* void, or *sunyata,* voidness, with which Nagarjuna described the nature of reality, or rather, of the *conceptions* of reality which the human mind can form. Conceptions here include not only metaphysical views but also ideals, religious beliefs, ultimate hopes and ambitions of every kind–everything which the mind of man seeks and grasps for his physical or spiritual security. Not only does the Sunyavada demolish the beliefs which one consciously adopts; it also seeks out the hidden and unconscious premises of thought and action, and submits them to the same treatment until the very depths of the mind are reduced to a total silence. Even the idea of *sunya* is itself to be voided.

> *It cannot be called void or not void,*
> *Or both or neither;*
> *But in order to point it out,*
> *It is called "the Void."* [4]

Stcherbatsky (1) is certainly right in thinking that the Sunyavada is best called a doctrine of relativity. For Nagarjuna's method is simply to show that all things are without "self-nature" (*svabhava*) or independent reality since they exist only in relation to other things. Nothing in the universe can stand by itself–no thing, no fact, no being, no event–and for this reason it is absurd to single anything out as the ideal to be grasped. For what is singled out exists only in relation to its own opposite, since what is is defined by what is not, pleasure is defined by pain, life is defined by death, and motion is defined by stillness. Obviously, the mind can form no idea of what "to be" means without the contrast of "not to be," since the ideas of being and non-being are abstractions from such simple experiences as that there is a penny in the right hand and no penny in the left.

From one point of view, the same relativity exists between *nirvana* and *samsara, bodhi* (awakening) and *klesa* (defilement). That is to say, the search for *nirvana* implies the existence and the problem of *samsara,* and the quest for awakening implies that one is in the state of defilement with delusion. To put it in another way: as soon as *nirvana* is made an object of desire, it be-

[4] *Madhyamika Shastra,* XV. 3.

comes an element of *samsara*. The real *nirvana* cannot be desired because it cannot be conceived. Thus the *Lankavatara Sutra* says:

> Again, Mahamati, what is meant by non-duality? It means that light and shade, long and short, black and white, are relative terms, Mahamati, and not independent of each other; as Nirvana and Samsara are, all things are not-two. There is no Nirvana except where is Samsara; there is no Samsara except where is Nirvana; for the condition of existence is not of a mutually exclusive character. Therefore it is said that all things are non-dual as are Nirvana and Samsara. (II. 28) [5]

But the equation *"Nirvana is samsara"* is true in another sense as well–namely, that what appears to us to be *samsara* is really *nirvana*, and that what appears to be the world of form (*rupa*) is really the void (*sunya*). Hence the famous saying:

> Form is not different from emptiness; emptiness is not different from form. Form is precisely emptiness; emptiness is precisely form.[6]

Once again, this is not to say that awakening will cause the world of form to vanish without trace, for *nirvana* is not to be sought as "the future annihilation of the senses and their fields." The *sutra* is saying that form is void just as it is, in all its prickly uniqueness.

The point of this equation is not to assert a metaphysical proposition but to assist the process of awakening. For awakening will not come to pass when one is trying to escape or change the everyday world of form, or to get away from the particular experience in which one finds oneself at this moment. Every such attempt is a manifestation of grasping. Even the grasping itself is not to be changed by force, for

> *bodhi* [awakening] is the five offenses, and the five offenses are *bodhi*. . . . If anyone regards *bodhi* as something to be attained, to be cultivated by discipline, he is guilty of the pride of self.[7]

[5] In Suzuki (3), p. 67.
[6] *Prajna-paramita-hridaya* Sutra (Chinese version).
[7] *Saptasatika-prajna-paramita* Sutra, 232, 234.

Some of these passages may suggest that the Bodhisattva may just as well be an easygoing, worldly fellow, who–because *samsara* is *nirvana* anyhow–can go on living just as he pleases. He may be thoroughly deluded, but since even delusion is *bodhi* there would be no point in trying to change it. There is often a deceptive resemblance between opposite extremes. Lunatics frequently resemble saints, and the unaffected modesty of the sage often lets him seem to be a very ordinary person. Yet there is no easy way of pointing out the difference, of saying what it is that the ordinary, worldly fellow does or does not do which makes him different from a Bodhisattva, or vice versa. The entire mystery of Zen lies in this problem, and we shall return to it at the proper time. It is enough to say here that the so-called "ordinary person" is only apparently natural, or perhaps that his real naturalness feels unnatural to him. In practice it is simply impossible to decide, intentionally, to stop seeking for *nirvana* and to lead an ordinary life, for as soon as one's "ordinary" life is intentional it is not natural.

It is for this reason that the insistence of the Mahayana texts on the unattainability of *nirvana* and *bodhi* is not something to be accepted theoretically, as a mere philosophical opinion. One has to know "in one's bones" that there is nothing to be grasped.

> Thereupon the thought came to some of the Gods in that assembly: What the fairies talk and murmur, that we understand though mumbled. What Subhuti has just told us, that we do not understand!
> Subhuti read their thoughts and said: There is nothing to understand, there is nothing to understand. For nothing in particular has been indicated, nothing in particular has been explained. . . . No one will grasp this perfection of wisdom as here explained. For no Dharma (doctrine) at all has been indicated, lit up, or communicated. So there will be no one who can grasp it.[8]

The point arrives, then, when it is clearly understood that all one's intentional acts–desires, ideals, stratagems–are in vain. In the whole universe, within and without, there is nothing whereon

[8] *Ashtasahasrika*, II. 38, 40. In Conze (2), pp. 177–78.

to lay any hold, and no one to lay any hold on anything. This has been discovered through clear awareness of everything that seemed to offer a solution or to constitute a reliable reality, through the intuitive wisdom called *prajna,* which sees into the relational character of everything. With the "eye of *prajna*" the human situation is seen for what it is—a quenching of thirst with salt water, a pursuit of goals which simply require the pursuit of other goals, a clutching of objects which the swift course of time renders as insubstantial as mist. The very one who pursues, who sees and knows and desires, the inner subject, has his existence only in relation to the ephemeral objects of his pursuit. He sees that his grasp upon the world is his strangle-hold about his own neck, the hold which is depriving him of the very life he so longs to attain. And there is no way out, no way of letting go, which he can take by effort, by a decision of the will. . . . But who is it that wants to get out?

There comes a moment when this consciousness of the inescapable trap in which we are at once the trapper and the trapped reaches a breaking point. One might almost say that it "matures" or "ripens," and suddenly there is what the *Lankavatara Sutra* calls a "turning about in the deepest seat of consciousness." In this moment all sense of constraint drops away, and the cocoon which the silkworm spun around himself opens to let him go forth winged as a moth. The peculiar anxiety which Kierkegaard has rightly seen to lie at the very roots of the ordinary man's soul is no longer there. Contrivances, ideals, ambitions, and self-propitiations are no longer necessary, since it is now possible to live spontaneously without trying to be spontaneous. Indeed, there is no alternative, since it is now seen that there never was any self to bring the self under its control.

Reduced to the bare essentials, such is the inner process which the Sunyavada is trying to set in motion with its philosophy of total negation. Thus the greater part of Nagarjuna's work was a carefully logical and systematic refutation of every philosoph-

ical position to be found in the India of his time.[9] Granting that
its object is an inner experience, Western students have always
had difficulty in understanding how such a purely negative point
of view could have any creative consequences. It must therefore
be repeated that the negations apply, not to reality itself, but to
our ideas of reality. The positive and creative content of the
Sunyavada is not in the philosophy itself, but in the new vision
of reality which is revealed when its work is done, and Nagarjuna
does not spoil this vision by trying to describe it.

The Mahayana does, however, have another term for reality
which is perhaps rather more indicative than *sunya*, the void. This
is the word *tathata*, which we may translate as "suchness," "thus-
ness," or "thatness." Similarly, the Buddhas are called Tathagatas–
they who go, or come, "thus." The Sanskrit word *tat* (our "that")
is probably based on a child's first efforts at speech, when it
points at something and says, "Ta" or "Da." Fathers flatter themselves by imagining that the child is calling them by name–
"Dada" or "Daddy." But perhaps the child is just expressing its
recognition of the world, and saying "That!" When we say just
"That" or "Thus," we are pointing to the realm of nonverbal
experience, to reality as we perceive it directly, for we are trying
to indicate what we see or feel rather than what we think or say.
Tathata therefore indicates the world just as it is, unscreened and
undivided by the symbols and definitions of thought. It points to
the concrete and actual as distinct from the abstract and conceptual. A Buddha is a Tathagata, a "thus-goer," because he is
awakened to this primary, nonconceptual world which no words
can convey, and does not confuse it with such ideas as being or
non-being, good or bad, past or future, here or there, moving or

[9] The reader who is interested in exploring Nagarjuna's philosophy more
deeply should refer to the magnificent work of Professor T. R. V. Murti,
The Central Philosophy of Buddhism. (See Bibliography.) Unhappily, there
are now available only fragmentary translations of Nagarjuna's writings in
English, unless he was indeed the author of the *Prajna-paramita* literature,
for which see Conze (2, 3).

still, permanent or impermanent. As the Bodhisattva Manjusri speaks of the Tathagata in the *Saptasatika:*

> Suchness (*tathata*) neither becomes nor ceases to become; thus do I see the Tathagata. Suchness does not stand at any point or place; thus do I see the Tathagata. Suchness is neither past, future, nor present; thus do I see the Tathagata. Suchness does not arise from the dual or the non-dual; thus do I see the Tathagata. Suchness is neither impure nor pure; thus do I see the Tathagata. Suchness neither arises nor comes to an end; thus do I see the Tathagata. (195) [10]

Because *tathata* is the true state of a Buddha and of all beings whatsoever, it is also referred to as our true or original nature, and thus our "Buddha nature." One of the cardinal doctrines of the Mahayana is that all beings are endowed with Buddha nature, and so have the possibility of becoming Buddhas. Because of the identity of Buddha nature and *tathata,* the term "Buddha" is frequently used of reality itself and not just of the awakened man. It so comes about that in the Mahayana a Buddha is often seen as a personification of reality, forming the basis of those popular cults in which the Buddhas seem to be worshiped as gods. I say "seem to be" because even Mahayana Buddhism has no real equivalent of Judaeo-Christian theism, with its strict identification of God with the moral principle. Furthermore, the various Buddhas who are so venerated—Amitabha, Vairocana, Amitayus, Ratnasambhava, etc.—are always personifications of one's own true nature.

Here, too, lies the basis of the Buddhism of faith, of the Sukhavati or Pure Land school, in which it is held that all efforts to become a Buddha are merely the false pride of the ego. All that is necessary is to repeat the formula *namo-amitabhaya* (literally, "the Name of Amitabha" or "Hail, Amitabha") in the faith that this alone is sufficient to bring about one's rebirth in the Pure

[10] "Suchness is neither past, future, nor present," for when it is seen that there is neither past nor future there is no more a present, since the idea of the present has meaning only in relation to past and future.

Land over which Amitabha presides. In this Pure Land all the obstacles which stand in the way of becoming a Buddha in this world are removed, so that rebirth in the Pure Land is virtually equivalent to becoming a Buddha. The repetition of the Name is held to be effective because, in ages past, Amitabha vowed that he would not enter into supreme Buddhahood unless rebirth in the Pure Land were assured for all beings who invoked his name. Because he subsequently entered the state of Buddhahood, the vow is effectively fulfilled.

Even Nagarjuna was in sympathy with this doctrine, for it is obviously a popular and more graphic way of saying that since one's own true nature is already the Buddha nature, one does not have to do anything to make it so. On the contrary, to seek to become Buddha is to deny that one is already Buddha–and this is the sole basis upon which Buddhahood can be realized! In short, to become a Buddha it is only necessary to have the faith that one is a Buddha already. Shinran, the great Japanese exponent of the Pure Land, went even so far as to say that it was only necessary to repeat the Name, for he saw that the attempt to make an act of faith was too artificial, and led one to doubt one's own faith.

Pure Land Buddhism is clearly an outgrowth of the Bodhisattva doctrine that the proper work of the liberated man is the liberation of all other beings by *upaya* or "skillful means." By *prajna* or intuitive wisdom he sees into the nature of reality, and this in turn awakens *karuna* or compassion for all who are still in the bonds of ignorance. At its deepest level *karuna* means something rather more than compassion for the ignorance of others. For we saw that the Bodhisattva's return into the world of *samsara* was based on the principle that *samsara* is in fact *nirvana*, and that "the void is precisely form." If *prajna* is to see that "form is void," *karuna* is to see that "the void is form." It is therefore an "affirmation" of the everyday world in its natural "suchness," and this is one of the features of the Mahayana most strongly emphasized in Zen. Indeed, it makes nonsense of the idea that Buddhism is always a philosophy of world-denial, in which the uniqueness of forms has no importance. It was because of *karuna* that Mahayana Buddhism became the principal inspiration of Chinese art in the Sung and Yüan dynasties, an art which stressed natural forms rather than religious symbols. For by *karuna* it is seen that the dissolution of forms into the void is in no way different from the particular characteristics of the forms themselves. The life of things is only conventionally separable from their death; in reality the dying is the living.

The perception that each single form, just as it is, is the void and that, further, the uniqueness of each form arises from the fact that it exists in relation to every other form is the basis of the Dharmadhatu ("Dharma realm") doctrine of the enormous *Avatamsaka Sutra*. This voluminous work is probably the final culmination of Indian Mahayana, and one of its central images is a vast network of gems or crystals, like a spider's web at dawn, in which each gem reflects all the others. This net of gems is the Dharmadhatu, the universe, the realm of innumerable *dharmas* or "thing-events."

Chinese commentators worked out a fourfold classification of the Dharmadhatu which became of considerable importance for Zen late in the T'ang dynasty. Their classification of the "Four Dharma Realms" [b] was as follows:

1. *Shih*,[c] the unique, individual "thing-events" of which the universe is composed.

2. *Li*,[d] the "principle" or ultimate reality underlying the multiplicity of things.

3. *Li shih wu ai*,[e] "between principle and thing no obstruction," which is to say that there is no incompatibility between *nirvana* and *samsara*, void and form. The attainment of the one does not involve the annihilation of the other.

4. *Shih shih wu ai*,[f] "between thing and thing no obstruction," which is to say that each "thing-event" involves every other, and that the highest insight is simply the perception of them in their natural "suchness." At this level every "thing-event" is seen

to be self-determinative, self-generating, or spontaneous, for to be quite naturally what it is, to be *tatha*–just "thus"–is to be free and without obstruction.

The doctrine of the Dharmadhatu is, approximately, that the proper harmony of the universe is realized when each "thing-event" is allowed to be freely and spontaneously itself, without interference. Stated more subjectively, it is saying, "Let everything be free to be just as it is. Do not separate yourself from the world and try to order it around." There is a subtle distinction between this and mere *laissez faire*, which may be suggested by the way in which we move our various limbs. Each one moves by itself, from within. To walk, we do not pick up our feet with our hands. The individual body is therefore a system of *shih shih wu ai*, and a Buddha realizes that the whole universe is his body, a marvelously interrelated harmony organized from within itself rather than by interference from outside.

Mahayana philosophy thinks of the Buddha's body as three-fold, as the *Trikaya* or "Triple Body." His body, considered either as the multitude of "thing-events" or as his particular human forms, is termed the *Nirmanakaya*, or "Body of Transformation." The particular human forms are such historic and prehistoric Buddhas as Gautama, Kasyapa, or Kanakamuni, and since these appear "in the flesh" the *Nirmanakaya* includes, in principle, the entire universe of form. There is next the *Sambhogakaya*, or "Body of Enjoyment." This is the sphere of *prajna*, wisdom, and *karuna*, compassion, the latter looking down to the world of form, and the former looking up to the realm of the void. *Sambhogakaya* might also be called the "Body of Realization" since it is in this "body" that a Buddha realizes that he is a Buddha. Finally there is the *Dharmakaya*, the "Dharma Body," which is the void, the *sunya* itself.

Nagarjuna did not discuss the way in which the void appears as form, the *Dharmakaya* as the *Nirmanakaya*, feeling, perhaps, that this would be completely unintelligible to those who had not actually realized awakening. For the Buddha himself had compared such inquiries to the foolishness of a man shot with an arrow, who would not permit it to be taken out of his flesh until he had been told all the details of his assailant's appearance, family, and motivations. Nevertheless, Nagarjuna's successors, the brothers Asanga and Vasubandhu (c. 280–360), who worked out the type of Mahayana philosophy generally known as Yoga-cara, made some attempt to discuss this particular problem.

According to the Yogacara the world of form is *cittamatra*– "mind only"–or *vijnaptimatra*–"representation only." This view seems to have a very close resemblance to Western philosophies of subjective idealism, in which the external and material world is regarded as a projection of the mind. However, there seem to be some differences between the two points of view. Here, as always, the Mahayana is not so much a theoretical and specula-tive construction as an account of an inner experience, and a means of awakening the experience in others. Furthermore, the word *citta* is not precisely equivalent to our "mind." Western thought tends to define mind by opposition to matter, and to consider matter not so much as "measure" as the solid stuff which is measured. Measure itself, abstraction, is for the West more of the nature of mind, since we tend to think of mind and spirit as more abstract than concrete.

But in Buddhist philosophy *citta* does not stand over against a conception of solid stuff. The world has never been considered in terms of a primary substance shaped into various forms by the action of mind or spirit. Such an image is not in the history of Buddhist thought, and thus the problem of how impalpable mind can influence solid matter has never arisen. Wherever we should speak of the material or physical or substantial world, Buddhism employs the term *rupa,* which is not so much our "matter" as "form." There is no "material substance" underlying *rupa* unless it be *citta* itself!

The difficulty of making equations and comparisons between Eastern and Western ideas is that the two worlds do not start with the same assumptions and premises. They do not have the same basic categorizations of experience. When, therefore, the world has never been divided into mind and matter, but rather into mind and form, the word "mind" cannot mean quite the same thing in both instances. The word "man," for example, does not have quite the same meaning when contrasted with "woman" as when contrasted with "animal."

A simplified, and somewhat rough, way of stating the difference is that Western idealists have begun to philosophize from a world consisting of mind (or spirit), form, and matter, whereas the Buddhists have begun to philosophize from a world of mind and form.

The Yogacara does not, therefore, discuss the relation of forms of matter to mind; it discusses the relation of forms to mind, and concludes that they are forms *of* mind. As a result, the term "mind" (*citta*) becomes logically meaningless. But because the main concern of Buddhism is with a realm of experience which is nonlogical and meaningless, in the sense that it does not symbolize or signify anything other than itself, there is no objection to "meaningless" terms.

From the logical standpoint the proposition "Everything is mind" says no more than that everything is everything. For if there is nothing which is not mind, the word belongs to no class, and has no limits, no definition. One might as well use "blah"– which is almost exactly what Buddhism does with the nonsense word *tathata*. For the function of these nonsense terms is to draw our attention to the fact that logic and meaning, with its inherent duality, is a property of thought and language but not of the actual world. The nonverbal, concrete world contains no classes and no symbols which signify or mean anything other than themselves. Consequently it contains no duality. For duality arises only when we classify, when we sort our experiences into mental boxes, since a box is no box without an inside and an outside.

Mental boxes are probably formed in our minds long before formal thought and language supply labels to identify them. We have begun to classify as soon as we notice differences, regularities and irregularities, as soon as we make associations of any kind. But–if the word "mental" means anything at all–this act of classification is certainly mental, for to notice differences and to associate them with one another is something more than simply to respond to sense contacts. Yet if classes are a product of the mind, of noticing, association, thought, and language, the world *considered simply as all classes of objects* is a product of the mind.

This is, I think, what the Yogacara means by the assertion that the world is mind-only (*cittamatram lokam*). It means that external and internal, before and after, heavy and light, pleasant and painful, moving and still are all ideas, or mental classifications. Their relation to the concrete world is the same as that of words. Thus the world that we know, when understood as the world as classified, is a product of the mind, and as the sound "water" is not actually water, the classified world is not the real world.

The problem of "what" the mind is can now be seen to be the same as the problem of "what" the real world is. It cannot be answered, for every "what" is a class, and we cannot classify the classifier. Is it not, then, merely absurd to speak of the mind, the *citta*, at all if there is no way of saying what it is? On the contrary, the mathematician Kurt Gödel has given us a rigorous proof of the fact that every logical system must contain a premise which it cannot define without contradicting itself.[11] The Yogacara takes *citta* as its premise and does not define it, since *citta* is here the equivalent of *sunya* and *tathata*. For the mind

> is beyond all philosophical views, is apart from discrimination, it is not attainable, nor is it ever born: I say there is nothing but Mind. It is not an existence, nor is it a non-existence; it is indeed beyond both existence and non-existence. . . . Out of Mind spring innumerable things, conditioned by discrimination (i.e., classifica-

[11] For a general account see E. Nagel and J. R. Newman, "Gödel's Proof," *Scientific American*, CXCVI. 6 (June, 1956), pp. 71–86.

tion) and habit-energy; these things people accept as an external world. . . . What appears to be external does not exist in reality; it is indeed Mind that is seen as multiplicity; the body, property, and abode–all these, I say, are nothing but Mind.[12]

Within this undefined continuum of *citta* the Yogacara describes eight kinds of *vijnana,* or "discriminating consciousness." There is a consciousness appropriate to each of the five senses; there is the sixth sense-consciousness (*mano-vijnana*), unifying the other five so that what is touched or heard may be related to what is seen; there is *manas,* center of the mind's discriminative and classifying activity; and finally there is the "store-consciousness" (*alaya-vijnana*), the supra-individual mind which contains the seeds of all possible forms.

The "store-consciousness" is almost equivalent to the *citta* itself, and is supra-individual because it stands prior to every differentiation. It is not to be conceived as a sort of ghostly gas permeating all beings, since space and extension are likewise here only in potentiality. In other words, the "store-consciousness" is that from which the formal world arises spontaneously or playfully (*vikridita*). For the Mahayana does not make the mistake of trying to account for the production of the world from the mind by a series of necessary causes. Whatever is linked by causal necessity is *of* the world of *maya,* not beyond it. Speaking somewhat poetically, the world illusion comes out of the Great Void for no reason, purposelessly, and just because there is no necessity for it to do so. For the "activity" of the Void is playful or *vikridita* because it is not motivated action (*karma*).

Thus, as the Yogacara describes it, the production of the formal world arises spontaneously from the "store-consciousness," flows up into the *manas,* where the primordial differentiations are

[12] *Lankavatara Sutra,* 154, 29–30, 32–33. In Suzuki (2), p. 242. I have cited the *Lankavatara* for both Madhyamika and Yogacara viewpoints, since either both schools have used the *sutra* or else it is a work of the latter incorporating views of the former. Since historical order is here a matter of conjecture, I have simply chosen sources which seem to express the ideas in question most effectively.

made, passes thence into the six sense-consciousnesses, which in turn produce the sense organs or "gates" (*ayatana*) through which it finally projects the classified external world.

The Buddhist *yoga* therefore consists in reversing the process, in stilling the discriminative activity of the mind, and letting the categories of *maya* fall back into potentiality so that the world may be seen in its unclassified "suchness." Here *karuna* awakens, and the Bodhisattva lets the projection arise again, having become consciously identified with the playful and purposeless character of the Void.

Four

THE RISE AND DEVELOPMENT OF ZEN

The qualities which distinguish Zen or Ch'an from other types of Buddhism are rather elusive when it comes to putting them in words, yet Zen has a definite and unmistakable "flavor." Although the name Zen is *dhyana,* or meditation, other schools of Buddhism emphasize meditation as much as, if not more than, Zen–and at times it seems as if the practice of formal meditation were not necessary to Zen at all. Nor is Zen peculiar in "having nothing to say," in insisting that the truth cannot be put into words, for this is already the Madhyamika as well as the teaching of Lao-tzu.

> *Those who know do not speak;*
> *Those who speak do not know.* (56)

Perhaps the special flavor of Zen is best described as a certain directness. In other schools of Buddhism, awakening or *bodhi* seems remote and almost superhuman, something to be reached only after many lives of patient effort. But in Zen there is always the feeling that awakening is something quite natural, something startlingly obvious, which may occur at any moment. If it involves a difficulty, it is just that it is much too simple. Zen is also direct in its way of teaching, for it points directly and openly to the truth, and does not trifle with symbolism.

Direct pointing (*chih-chih* [a]) is the open demonstration of Zen by nonsymbolic actions or words, which usually appear to the uninitiated as having to do with the most ordinary secular affairs, or to be completely crazy. In answer to a question about Buddhism, the master makes a casual remark about the weather, or performs some simple action which seems to have nothing to do with philosophical or spiritual matters. However, it is dif-

77

ficult to find many instances of this method before the middle of the T'ang dynasty, by which time Zen was already well established. But it is certainly consistent with the emphasis of the earlier masters on immediate awakening in the midst of everyday affairs.

No one has been able to find any trace of a specific Dhyana School in Indian Buddhism, though because of our lack of historical materials this is no evidence that it did not exist. If the characteristic note of Zen is immediate or instantaneous awakening (*tun wu* [b]) without passing through preparatory stages, there are certainly evidences of this principle in India. The *Lankavatara Sutra* states that there are both gradual and sudden (*yugapat*) ways of awakening, the former by purification of the tainted outflows or projections (*ashrava*) of the mind, and the latter by *paravritti*–an instantaneous "turning about" within the depths of consciousness whereby dualistic views are cast off. It is likened to a mirror immediately reflecting whatever forms and images appear before it.[1] There is, too, a clear connection between the idea of immediate awakening and the teaching of the *Vajracchedika,* or "Diamond Cutter Sutra," on the fact that to attain awakening is not to attain anything. In other words, if *nirvana* is actually here and now so that to seek it is to lose it, a realization through progressive stages is hardly appropriate. One would have to see into it in the present moment, directly.

Although its origins are probably later than those of Zen in China, there is also a tradition of this kind in Tantric Buddhism, and there is nothing to indicate that there was a reverse influence from Chinese Zen. Parallels to Zen sayings may be seen in a tenth-century Tantric work by Saraha:

If it [*the Truth*] *is already manifest, what's the use of meditation?*
And if it is hidden, one is just measuring darkness. (20)

[1] *Lankavatara Sutra,* II. 14, in Suzuki (3), pp. 49–51. According to tradition this was the favorite *sutra* of Bodhidharma, the semi-legendary founder of Zen in China. Its connection with Zen is fully discussed in Suzuki (2), pp. 44–63.

Mantras and tantras, meditation and concentration,
They are all a cause of self-deception.
Do not defile in contemplation thought that is pure in its own nature,
But abide in the bliss of yourself and cease those torments. (23)
Whatever you see, that is it,
In front, behind, in all the ten directions.
Even today let your master make an end of delusion! (28)
The nature of the sky is originally clear,
But by gazing and gazing the sight becomes obscured. (34) [2]

Tibetan Buddhism likewise comprises a tradition of the Short Path, considered as a swift and steep ascent to *nirvana* for those who have the necessary courage, though a doctrine more suggestive of the Zen emphasis on immediacy and naturalness is found in the "Six Precepts" of Tilopa:

> *No thought, no reflection, no analysis,*
> *No cultivation, no intention;*
> *Let it settle itself.*[3]

Immediate release without any special contrivance or intention is also implied in the Tantric idea of *sahaja*, the "easy" or "natural" state of the liberated sage.

This is not the place to discuss the real meaning of immediate awakening and naturalness, but these instances are cited to show that the tradition of a direct path existed outside China, suggest-

[2] *Saraha's Treasury of Songs,* translated by David Snellgrove in Conze (2), pp. 224–39.
[3] The original is:
   Mi-mno, mi-bsam, mi-dpyad-ching,
   Mi-bsgom, mi-sems, rang-babs-bzhag.
The translation is based upon an elucidation of the passage given me by Mr. Alex Wayman of the University of California. *Mi-mno* is approximately equivalent to the Zen terms *wu-hsin* or *wu-nien,* "no-mind" or "no-thought." *Bsam* is the equivalent of the Sanskrit *cintana,* i.e., discursive thinking about what has been heard, and *dpyad* of *mimamsa,* or "philosophical analysis." *Bsgom* is probably *bhavana* or the Chinese *hsiu,* "to cultivate," "to practice," or "intense concentration." *Sems* is *cetana* or *szu,* with the sense of intention or volition. *Rang-babs-bzhag* is literally "self-settle-establish," and "self-settle" would seem to be an almost exact equivalent of the Taoist *tzu-jan,* "self-so," "spontaneous," or "natural."

ing some original source in Indian Buddhism. An obvious reason for the lack of materials would be that a principle of this kind, so easily open to misinterpretation, might have been kept as a "secret doctrine," discussed openly only in later times. Zen tradition does indeed maintain that immediate awakening is not communicated by the *sutras*, but has been passed down directly from master to pupil. This does not necessarily imply anything so "esoteric" as an experience conveyed by telepathy, but something much less sensational. Thus when Hindu pandits insist that wisdom is not to be gained from the scriptures but only from a teacher or *guru*, it means that the actual texts–such as the *Yoga-sutra*–contain only the headings of the doctrine, and that its full explanation requires someone who has learned the oral tradition. To this it should hardly be necessary to add that since the tradition is primarily an experience, words can communicate it no more and no less than any other experience.

However, it is not really necessary to suppose that there was ever a specific Dhyana School in India. The creation of Zen would seem to be sufficiently explained by the exposure of Taoists and Confucians to the main principles of Mahayana Buddhism. Therefore the appearance of trends very close to Zen can be seen almost as soon as the great Mahayana *sutras* became available in China–that is to say, with the work of the great Indian scholar-monk Kumarajiva. Kumarajiva was translating the *sutras* in Ku-tsang and Ch'ang-an between 384 and 413, at which time one of his outstanding students was the young monk Seng-chao (384–414), who had started out in life as a copyist of the Confucian and Taoist texts.

Seng-chao had been converted to Buddhism as a result of reading the *Vimalakirti Sutra*–a text which has exercised considerable influence upon Zen. Although Seng-chao became a monk, this *sutra* is the story of a layman, Vimalakirti, who excelled all the Buddha's disciples in the depth of his understanding. He had surpassed all the other disciples and Bodhisattvas by answering a question as to the nature of the nondual reality with a "thunderous silence"–an example frequently followed by Zen masters. Vimalakirti "thunderingly silent" is, too, a favorite theme of Zen artists. But the main importance of this *sutra* for China and for Zen was the point that perfect awakening was consistent with the affairs of everyday life, and that, indeed, the highest attainment was to "enter into awakening without exterminating the defilements [*klesa*]."

There was an appeal here to both the Confucian and the Taoist mentality. The Confucian stress on the importance of family life would not easily sympathize with a rigorously monastic type of Buddhism. Though the Chinese Buddhist masters were normally monks, they had large numbers of advanced lay students, and Zen, in particular, has always attached great importance to the expression of Buddhism in formally secular terms–in arts of every type, in manual labor, and in appreciation of the natural universe. Confucian and Taoist alike would be especially agreeable to the idea of an awakening which did not involve the extermination of human passions, as *klesa* may also be translated. We have already noted the peculiar trust in human nature which both these philosophies professed. However, not exterminating the passions does not mean letting them flourish untamed. It means letting go of them rather than fighting them, neither repressing passion nor indulging it. For the Taoist is never violent, since he achieves his ends by noninterference (*wu-wei*), which is a kind of psychological *judo*.

Seng-chao's writings, as well as his commentary on the *Vimalakirti Sutra*, are full of Taoist quotations and phrases, for he seemed to be following the example of less important, though earlier, monks such as Hui-yüan (334–416) and Tao-an (312–385) in using "extension of the idea" (*ko-i *[c]) for explaining Buddhism through Taoist parallels. So much did this suggest an equivalence between the two traditions that by the end of the fifth century Liu Ch'iu could say:

From the K'un-lun mountains eastward the (Taoist) term "Great Oneness" is used. From Kashmir westward the (Buddhist) term *sambodhi* is used. Whether one looks longingly toward "non-being" (*wu*) or cultivates "emptiness" (*sunyata*), the principle involved is the same.[4]

Two of Seng-chao's doctrines would seem to have had some importance for the later development of Zen–his view of time and change, and his idea that "*prajna* is not knowledge." The chapter on "The Immutability of Things" in his *Book of Chao* is so original and so startlingly similar to the section on time in the first volume of Dogen's *Shobogenzo*, that the celebrated Japanese Zen philosopher can hardly have been unfamiliar with it.

Past things are in the past and do not go there from the present, and present things are in the present, and do not go there from the past. . . . Rivers which compete with one another to inundate the land do not flow. The "wandering air" that blows about is not moving. The sun and moon, revolving in their orbits, do not turn around.[5]

In the same way Dogen pointed out that firewood does not become ashes and life does not become death, just as the winter does not become the spring. Every moment of time is "self-contained and quiescent." [6]

Seng-chao also discussed the seeming paradox that *prajna* is a kind of ignorance. Because the ultimate reality has no qualities and is not a thing, it cannot become an object of knowledge. Therefore *prajna*, direct insight, knows the truth by not knowing.

Wisdom knows not, yet it illumines the deepest profundity. Spirit calculates not, yet it responds to the necessities of the given moment. Because it calculates not, spirit shines in lonely glory in what is beyond the world. Because it knows not, Wisdom illumines the

[4] Quoted by Fung Yu-lan (1), vol. 2, p. 240, from Seng-yu, *Ch'u San-tsang Chi-chi*, 9.
[5] Liebenthal (1), p. 49.
[6] The same idea was used even before Dogen by the Zen master Ma-tsu (*d.* 788): "So with former thoughts, later thoughts, and thoughts in between: the thoughts follow one another without being linked together. Each one is absolutely tranquil." *Ku-tsun-hsü Yü-lu*, 1. 4.

Mystery (*hsüan*) beyond mundane affairs. Yet though Wisdom lies outside affairs, it never lacks them. Though Spirit lies beyond the world, it stays ever within it.[7]

Here is one of the main links between Taoism and Zen, for the style and terminology of the *Book of Chao* is Taoist throughout though the subject matter is Buddhist. The sayings of the early Zen masters, such as Hui-neng, Shen-hui, and Huang-po, are full of these very ideas—that truly to know is not to know, that the awakened mind responds immediately, without calculation, and that there is no incompatibility between Buddhahood and the everyday life of the world.

Even closer to the standpoint of Zen was Seng-chao's fellow student Tao-sheng (360–434), the first clear and unequivocal exponent of the doctrine of instantaneous awakening. If *nirvana* is not to be found by grasping, there can be no question of approaching it by stages, by the slow process of the accumulation of knowledge. It must be realized in a single flash of insight, which is *tun wu*, or, in Japanese, *satori*, the familiar Zen term for sudden awakening. Hsieh Ling-yün [8] in his discussion of Tao-sheng's doctrine even suggests that instantaneous awakening is more appropriate to the Chinese mentality than to the Indian, and lends weight to Suzuki's description of Zen as the Chinese "revolution" against Indian Buddhism. Tao-sheng's doctrine, however unusual and startling, must have found considerable acceptance. It is mentioned again, more than a century later, in a work by Hui-yüan (523–592), who also associates it with the master Hui-tan who lived until about 627.

The importance of these early precursors of Zen is that they provide a clue to the historical beginnings of the movement if we cannot accept the traditional story that it arrived in China in 520, with the Indian monk Bodhidharma. Modern scholars such

[7] Liebenthal (1), pp. 71–72.
[8] 385–433. His *Discussion of Essentials* (*Pien Tsung Lun*) is our principal source of information about Tao-sheng's ideas. See Fung Yu-lan (1), vol. 2, pp. 274–84.

as Fung Yu-lan and Pelliot have cast serious doubts upon the truth of this tradition. They suggest that the Bodhidharma story was a pious invention of later times, when the Zen School needed historical authority for its claim to be a direct transmission of experience from the Buddha himself, outside the *sutras*. For Bodhidharma is represented as the twenty-eighth of a somewhat fanciful list of Indian Patriarchs, standing in a direct line of "apostolic succession" from Gautama.[9]

At this stage of the inquiry it is hard to say whether the views of these scholars are to be taken seriously, or whether they are but another instance of an academic fashion for casting doubt upon the historicity of religious founders. The traditional story which the Zen School gives of its own origin is that Bodhidharma arrived in Canton from India around the year 520, and proceeded to the court of the Emperor Wu of Liang, an enthusiastic patron of Buddhism. However, Bodhidharma's doctrine and his abrupt attitude did not appeal to the Emperor, so that he withdrew for some years to a monastery in the state of Wei, and spent his time "gazing at the wall" until at last he found a suitable disciple in Hui-k'o, who subsequently became the Second Patriarch of Zen in China.[10]

There is, of course, nothing improbable in the arrival of a great Buddhist master from India at this period. Kumarajiva had arrived shortly before 400, Bodhiruci just after 500, and Paramartha was at the court of Liang about the same time as Bodhidharma. Is it really surprising that there should be no surviving record of his existence until little more than a hundred years after his time? These were not the days of newspapers and "Who's Whos," and even in our own excessively documented times people with important contributions to our knowledge and culture

[9] Hu Shih (1) and T'ang Yung-t'ing have suggested that Bodhidharma was in China at the earlier date of 420 to 479. See also Fung Yu-lan (1), vol. 2, pp. 386–90, Pelliot (1), and Dumoulin (2).
[10] The traditional sources are Tao-hsüan's *Sung-kao Seng-chuan* (Taisho 2061), composed between 645 and 667, and Tao-yüan's *Ching Te Ch'uan Teng Lu* (Taisho 2076), written about 1004.

can remain unrecognized and unrecorded until years after their death. Here again, it seems that we may as well accept the story of Bodhidharma until there is some really overwhelming evidence against it, recognizing that the ideas of Seng-chao, Tao-sheng, and others could also have been tributaries to the stream of Zen.

One of the reasons for suspecting the Bodhidharma story is that Zen is so Chinese in style that an Indian origin seems improbable. Yet the very Taoistic Seng-chao was a pupil of Kumarajiva, as was Tao-sheng, and the writings attributed to Bodhidharma and his successors until Hui-neng (638–713) show the clear transition from an Indian to a Chinese view of *dhyana*.[11]

The absence of any record of a Dhyana School in Indian Buddhist literature, or of Bodhidharma in connection with it, is perhaps due to the fact that there was never any Dhyana or Zen School even in China until some two hundred years after Bodhidharma's time. On the other hand, there would have been an almost universal practice of *dhyana*–that is, or *ts'o-ch'an* [d] (Japanese, *za-zen*) or sitting meditation–among Buddhist monks, and the special instructors who supervised this practice were called *dhyana* masters, no matter what their school or sect. There were likewise *vinaya* masters, or instructors in monastic discipline, and *dharma* masters, or instructors in doctrine. Zen became a distinct school only as it promulgated a view of *dhyana* which differed sharply from the generally accepted practice.[12]

Zen tradition represents Bodhidharma as a fierce-looking fellow with a bushy beard and wide-open, penetrating eyes–in which, however, there is just the hint of a twinkle. A legend says that he once fell asleep in meditation and was so furious that he cut

[11] Works attributed to Bodhidharma will be found in Suzuki (1), vol. 1, pp. 165–70, and Senzaki and McCandless (1), pp. 73–84. The style is always Indian and lacks Taoist "flavor."

[12] Hui-neng's *Tan Ching*, for example, records several instances of the Sixth Patriarch's interviews with *dhyana* masters who obviously did not belong to his own "sudden school" of *dhyana*. Furthermore, it was not until the time of Po-chang (720–814), or even later, that the Zen School had monasteries of its own. See Dumoulin and Sasaki (1), p. 13.

off his eyelids, and falling to the ground they arose as the first tea plant. Tea has thereafter supplied Zen monks with a protection against sleep, and so clarifies and invigorates the mind that it has been said, "The taste of Zen [*ch'an*] and the taste of tea [*ch'a*] are the same." Another legend holds that Bodhidharma sat so long in meditation that his legs fell off. Hence the delightful symbolism of those Japanese Daruma dolls which represent Bodhidharma as a legless roly-poly so weighted inside that he always stands up again when pushed over. A popular Japanese poem says of the Daruma doll:

> Jinsei nana korobi
> Ya oki.
> *Such is life–*
> *Seven times down,*
> *Eight times up!*

Bodhidharma's alleged interview with the Emperor Wu of Liang is typical of his abrupt and direct manner. For the Emperor described all that he had done to promote the practice of Buddhism, and asked what merit he had gained thereby–taking the popular view that Buddhism is a gradual accumulation of merit through good deeds, leading to better and better circumstances in future lives, and finally to *nirvana*. But Bodhidharma replied, "No merit whatever!" This so undermined the Emperor's idea of Buddhism that he asked, "What, then, is the sacred doctrine's first principle?" Bodhidharma replied, "It's just empty; there's nothing sacred." "Who, then, are you," said the Emperor, "to stand before us?" "I don't know." [13] [6]

After this interview, so unsatisfactory from the Emperor's point of view, Bodhidharma retired to a monastery in Wei, where he is said to have spent nine years in a cave, "gazing at the wall" (*pi-kuan* [1]). Suzuki holds that this is not to be taken literally, and that the expression refers to Bodhidharma's inner state, his

[13] *Ch'uan Teng Lu*, 3.

exclusion of all grasping thoughts from his mind.[14] Thus Bodhidharma remained, until he was approached by the monk Shenkuang, afterwards Hui-k'o (486–593, maybe!), who was to become Bodhidharma's successor as the Second Patriarch.

Hui-k'o again and again asked Bodhidharma for instruction, but was always refused. Yet he continued to sit in meditation outside the cave, waiting patiently in the snow in the hope that Bodhidharma would at last relent. In desperation he finally cut off his left arm and presented it to Bodhidharma as a token of his agonized sincerity. At this Bodhidharma at last asked Hui-k'o what he wanted.

"I have no peace of mind [hsin]," said Hui-k'o. "Please pacify my mind."

"Bring out your mind here before me," replied Bodhidharma, "and I will pacify it!"

"But when I seek my own mind," said Hui-k'o, "I cannot find it."

"There!" snapped Bodhidharma, "I have pacified your mind!" [15] *g*

At this moment Hui-k'o had his awakening, his *tun-wu* or *satori*, so that this interchange purports to be the first instance of what became the characteristic Zen method of instruction—the *wen-ta* [h] (Japanese, *mondo*) or "question-and-answer," sometimes loosely called the "Zen story." The greater part of Zen literature consists of these anecdotes, many of them much more puzzling than this, and their aim is always to precipitate some type of sudden realization in the questioner's mind, or to test the depth of his insight. For this reason, such anecdotes cannot be "explained" without spoiling their effect. In some respects they are like jokes which do not produce their intended effect of laughter when the "punch line" requires further explanation. One must see the point immediately, or not at all.

[14] Suzuki (1), vol. 1, pp. 170–71.
[15] *Wu-men kuan,* 41.

It should, furthermore, be understood that the main character of these anecdotes is only rarely symbolic, and then, usually, in a rather secondary way, as when the dialogue contains allusions which are obvious to both parties. But such commentators as Gernet (3) are, I feel, mistaken in supposing that the main point is the communication of some Buddhist principle by means of a symbol. The *satori* which so frequently follows these interchanges is by no means a mere comprehension of the answer to a riddle. For whatever the Zen master says or does is a direct and spontaneous utterance of "suchness," of his Buddha nature, and what he gives is no symbol but the very thing. Zen communication is always "direct pointing," in line with the traditional four-phrase summary of Zen:

Outside teaching; apart from tradition.
Not founded on words and letters.
Pointing directly to the human mind.
Seeing into one's nature and attaining Buddhahood.[16] [4]

The successor to Hui-k'o is said to have been Seng-ts'an (*d.* 606), and the story of their initial interview is of the same form as between Hui-k'o and Bodhidharma, except that where Hui-k'o asked for "peace of mind," Seng-ts'an asked to be "cleansed of faults." To him there is attributed a celebrated poem called the *Hsin-hsin Ming*, the "Treatise on Faith in the Mind." [17] If Seng-ts'an was indeed its author, this poem is the first clear and comprehensive statement of Zen. Its Taoist flavor is apparent in the opening lines,

The perfect Tao is without difficulty,
Save that it avoids picking and choosing.

[16] In modern Chinese the first two characters mean something like "worldly" or "outside the fold." In the present context they are usually taken to mean that the truth of Zen cannot be expressed in any form of doctrine, or that a teacher can do no more than show how to get it for oneself. However, the marvelous ambiguity of Chinese might intentionally allow both meanings. Consider the predominantly "secular" form of Zen expression, and such sayings as "Wash out your mouth every time you say, 'Buddha!' "
[17] Translations will be found in Suzuki (1), vol. 1, p. 182, and a revision in Suzuki (6), p. 91. Another by Arthur Waley is in Conze (2) p. 295.

And again,

> Follow your nature and accord with the Tao;
> Saunter along and stop worrying.
> If your thoughts are tied you spoil what is genuine. . . .
> Don't be antagonistic to the world of the senses,
> For when you are not antagonistic to it,
> It turns out to be the same as complete Awakening.
> The wise person does not strive (wu-wei);
> The ignorant man ties himself up. . . .
> If you work on your mind with your mind,
> How can you avoid an immense confusion? [18] *j*

Not only is the poem full of such Taoist terms as *wu-wei* and *tzu-jan* (spontaneity), but its whole attitude is that of letting one's mind alone and trusting it to follow its own nature—in contrast to the more typically Indian attitude of bringing it under rigid control and shutting out the experience of the senses.

The Fourth Patriarch, following Seng-ts'an, is believed to have been Tao-hsin (579–651). When he came to Seng-ts'an he asked, "What is the method of liberation?"

"Who binds you?" replied Seng-ts'an.

"No one binds me."

"Why then," asked Seng-ts'an, "should you seek liberation?" [19] *k*

And this was Tao-hsin's *satori*. The *Ch'uan Teng Lu* records a fascinating encounter between Tao-hsin and the sage Fa-yung, who lived in a lonely temple on Mount Niu-t'ou, and was so holy that the birds used to bring him offerings of flowers. As the two men were talking, a wild animal roared close by, and Tao-hsin jumped. Fa-yung commented, "I see it is still with you!" —referring, of course, to the instinctive "passion" (*klesa*) of fright. Shortly afterwards, while he was for a moment unobserved, Tao-hsin wrote the Chinese character for "Buddha" on the rock where Fa-yung was accustomed to sit. When Fa-yung

[18] The last two lines carry the same point as Hui-k'o's interview with Bodhidharma.
[19] *Ch'uan Teng Lu*, 3.

returned to sit down again, he saw the sacred Name and hesitated to sit. "I see," said Tao-hsin, "it is still with you!" At this remark Fa-yung was fully awakened . . . and the birds never brought any more flowers.

The Fifth Patriarch—and here we begin to enter a more reliable chapter of history—was Hung-jan (601–675). At his first meeting with Hung-jan the Patriarch asked:

"What is your name [*hsing*]?"

"I have a nature [*hsing*]," replied Hung-jan punning, "but it's no usual nature."

"What is this name?" inquired the Patriarch, missing the pun.

"It's Buddha nature."

"You have no name, then?"

"That's because it's an empty nature." [20]

Hung-jan was apparently the first of the Patriarchs to have any large following, for it is said that he presided over a group of some five hundred monks in a monastery on the Yellow Plum Mountain (Wang-mei Shan) at the eastern end of modern Hupeh. He is, however, much overshadowed by his immediate successor, Hui-neng (637–713), whose life and teaching mark the definitive beginning of a truly Chinese Zen—of Zen as it flourished during what was later called "the epoch of Zen activity," the latter two hundred years of the T'ang dynasty, from about 700 to 906.

One must not overlook Hui-neng's contemporaries, for he lived at a time which was most creative for Chinese Buddhism as a whole. The great translator and traveler Hsüan-tsang had returned from India in 645, and was expounding the *vijnapti-matra* ("representation-only") doctrines of the Yogacara in Ch'ang-an. His former student Fa-tsang (643–712) was developing the important school of the Hua-yen (Japanese, Kegon) based on the *Avatamsaka Sutra,* and which later provided Zen with a formal philosophy. Nor must we forget that not so long before these two men, Chih-k'ai (538–597) had written his re-

[20] *Ch'uan Teng Lu,* 3.

markable treatise on the *Mahayana Method of Cessation and Contemplation*,[21] containing the fundamental teaching of the T'ien-t'ai School, which is in many ways close to Zen. Much of Chih-k'ai's treatise foreshadows in both content and terminology the doctrines of Hui-neng and some of his immediate successors.

Hui-neng is said to have had his first awakening when, almost as a boy, he happened to overhear someone reading the *Vajracchedika*. He set out almost at once for Hung-jan's monastery at Wang-mei to have his understanding confirmed and to receive further instruction. We should note (for future reference) that his original *satori* occurred spontaneously, without the benefit of a master, and that his biography represents him as an illiterate peasant from the neighborhood of Canton. Apparently Hung-jan immediately recognized the depth of his insight, but fearing that his humble origins might make him unacceptable in a community of scholarly monks, the Patriarch put him to work in the kitchen compound.

Some time later, the Patriarch announced that he was looking for a successor to whom he might transmit his office, together with the robe and begging bowl (said to have been handed down from the Buddha) which were its insignia. This honor was to be conferred upon the person who submitted the best poem, expressing his understanding of Buddhism. The chief monk of the community was then a certain Shen-hsiu, and all the others naturally assumed that the office would go to him and so made no attempt to compete.

Shen-hsiu, however, was in doubt as to his own understanding, and decided to submit his poem anonymously, claiming authorship only if the Patriarch approved of it. During the night, then, he posted the following lines in the corridor near the Patriarch's quarters:

> *The body is the Bodhi Tree;*
> *The mind like a bright mirror standing.*

[21] *Ta-ch'eng Chih-kuan Fa-men,* Taisho 1924.

Take care to wipe it all the time,
And allow no dust to cling.[l]

The following morning, the Patriarch read the poem and ordered incense to be burned before it, saying that all who put it into practice would be enabled to realize their true nature. But when Shen-hsiu came to him in private and claimed authorship, the Patriarch declared that his understanding was still far from perfect.

On the following day, another poem appeared beside the first:

There never was a Bodhi Tree,
Nor bright mirror standing.
Fundamentally, not one thing exists,
So where is the dust to cling? [m]

The Patriarch knew that only Hui-neng could have written this, but to avoid jealousy he rubbed out the poem with his shoe, and summoned Hui-neng to his room secretly, by night. Here he conferred the Patriarchate, the robe, and the bowl upon him, and told him to flee into the mountains until the hurt feelings of the other monks had subsided and the time was ripe for him to begin his public teaching.[22]

A comparison of the two poems shows at once the distinctive flavor of Hui-neng's Zen. Shen-hsiu's poem reflects what was apparently the general and popular view of *dhyana* practice in Chinese Buddhism. It was obviously understood as the discipline of sitting meditation (*ts'o-ch'an*), in which the mind was "purified" by an intense concentration which would cause all thoughts and attachments to cease. Taken rather literally, many Buddhist and Taoist texts would substantiate this view—that the highest

[22] *T'an-ching,* 1. The full title of the work which records the life and teaching of Hui-neng is the *Platform-Sutra of the Sixth Patriarch,* or *Liu-tsu T'an-ching,* Taisho 2008. For translations, see Bibliography under Wong Mou-lam and Rousselle.

state of consciousness is a consciousness empty of all contents, all ideas, feelings, and even sensations. Today in India this is a very prevalent notion of *samadhi*. But our own experience with Christianity should make this type of literalism, even in high circles, rather familiar.

Hui-neng's position was that a man with an empty consciousness was no better than "a block of wood or a lump of stone." He insisted that the whole idea of purifying the mind was irrelevant and confusing, because "our own nature is fundamentally clear and pure." In other words, there is no analogy between consciousness or mind and a mirror that can be wiped. The true mind is "no-mind" (*wu-hsin*), which is to say that it is not to be regarded as an object of thought or action, as if it were a thing to be grasped and controlled. The attempt to work on one's own mind is a vicious circle. To try to purify it is to be contaminated with purity. Obviously this is the Taoist philosophy of naturalness, according to which a person is not genuinely free, detached, or pure when his state is the result of an artificial discipline. He is just imitating purity, just "faking" clear awareness. Hence the unpleasant self-righteousness of those who are deliberately and methodically religious.

Hui-neng's teaching is that instead of trying to purify or empty the mind, one must simply let go of the mind—because the mind is nothing to be grasped. Letting go of the mind is also equivalent to letting go of the series of thoughts and impressions (*nien*) which come and go "in" the mind, neither repressing them, holding them, nor interfering with them.

> Thoughts come and go of themselves, for through the use of wisdom there is no blockage. This is the *samadhi* of *prajna*, and natural liberation. Such is the practice of "no-thought" [*wu-nien*]. But if you do not think of anything at all, and immediately command thoughts to cease, this is to be tied in a knot by a method, and is called an obtuse view. (2) *

Of the usual view of meditation practice he said:

> To concentrate on the mind and to contemplate it until it is still is a disease and not *dhyana*. To restrain the body by sitting up for a long time—of what benefit is this towards the Dharma? (8) [o]

And again:

> If you start concentrating the mind on stillness, you will merely produce an unreal stillness. . . . What does the word "meditation" [*ts'o-ch'an*] mean? In this school it means no barriers, no obstacles; it is beyond all objective situations whether good or bad. The word "sitting" [*ts'o*] means not to stir up thoughts in the mind. (5) [p]

In counteracting the false *dhyana* of mere empty-mindedness, Hui-neng compares the Great Void to space, and calls it great, not just because it is empty, but because it contains the sun, moon, and stars. True *dhyana* is to realize that one's own nature is like space, and that thoughts and sensations come and go in this "original mind" like birds through the sky, leaving no trace. Awakening, in his school, is "sudden" because it is for quick-witted rather than slow-witted people. The latter must of necessity understand gradually, or more exactly, after a long time, since the Sixth Patriarch's doctrine does not admit of stages or growth. To be awakened at all is to be awakened completely, for, having no parts or divisions, the Buddha nature is not realized bit by bit.

His final instructions to his disciples contain an interesting clue to the later development of the *mondo* or "question-answer" method of teaching:

> If, in questioning you, someone asks about being, answer with non-being. If he asks about non-being, answer with being. If he asks about the ordinary man, answer in terms of the sage. If he asks about the sage, answer in terms of the ordinary man. By this method of opposites mutually related there arises an understanding of the Middle Way. For every question that you are asked, respond in terms of its opposite. (10) [q]

Hui-neng died in 713, and with his death the institution of the Patriarchate ceased, for the genealogical tree of Zen put forth branches. Hui-neng's tradition passed to five disciples: Huai-jang (*d.* 775), Ch'ing-yüan (*d.* 740), Shen-hui (668–770), Hsüan-chüeh (665–713), and Hui-chung (677–744).[23] The spiritual descendants of Huai-jang and Hsing-ssu live on today as the two principal schools of Zen in Japan, the Rinzai and the Soto. In the two centuries following the death of Hui-neng the proliferation of lines of descent and schools of Zen is quite complex, and we need do no more than consider some of the more influential individuals.[24]

The writings and records of Hui-neng's successors continue to be concerned with naturalness. On the principle that "the true mind is no-mind," and that "our true nature is no (special) nature," it is likewise stressed that the true practice of Zen is no

[23] A state of total confusion prevails among writers on Zen as to the naming of the great T'ang masters. For example, Shen-hui's full name is Ho-tse Shen-hui, of which the Japanese pronunciation is Kataku Jinne. Shen-hui is his monastic name, and Ho-tse designates his locality. Japanese writers usually refer to him as Jinne, using the personal monastic name. On the other hand, Hsüan-chüeh is Yung-chia Hsüan-chüeh, in Japanese Yoka Genkaku. But the Japanese writers usually employ his locality name, Yoka! On the whole, Suzuki uses locality names and Fung Yu-lan monastic names. Suzuki sometimes gives the Japanese form, and sometimes the Chinese, but uses a somewhat different way of romanizing the Chinese than Fung (or rather Bodde, the translator). Lin-chi I-hsüan (Rinzai Gigen) appears in Suzuki mostly as Rinzai and sometimes as Lin-chi, but in Fung he is Yi-hsüan! Dumoulin and Sasaki make some attempt at consistency by using only the Japanese forms, but then it is impossible at first sight to distinguish Chinese from Japanese individuals. Thus anyone who studies Zen from other than the original sources is confronted with a situation which makes historical clarity extremely difficult. Suzuki has been so widely read that most Western students of Zen are familiar with his usage, however inconsistent, and I do not want to confuse them further by such an attempt at consistency as calling Hui-neng by his locality name, Ta-chien. All I can offer is an index giving all the names. To make matters worse, there is also much confusion with respect to dates. For Shen-hui, Fung gives 686–760, Gernet 668–760, and Dumoulin and Sasaki 668–770.
[24] This period is treated in detail in Dumoulin and Sasaki (1). Demiéville (2) has translated a Tun-huang ms. (Pelliot 4646) concerning a debate held at Lhasa *c.* 792–794 between a master of the Sudden Ch'an School and a group of Indian Buddhist scholars. The Ch'an master is identified only by the name "Mahayana" and there is apparently nothing to link him with the tradition descending from Hui-neng. His doctrine seems to be somewhat more quietistic than that of the Sixth Patriarch. The fact that the Indian scholars were astonished and repelled by his teaching suggests its purely Chinese origin.

practice, that is, the seeming paradox of being a Buddha without intending to be a Buddha. According to Shen-hui:

> If one has this knowledge, it is contemplation [*samadhi*] without contemplating, wisdom [*prajna*] without wisdom, practice without practicing. (4. 193)
>
> All cultivation of concentration is wrong-minded from the start. For how, by cultivating concentration, could one obtain concentration? (1. 117)
>
> If we speak of working with the mind, does this working consist in activity or inactivity of the mind? If it is inactivity, we should be no different from vulgar fools. But if you say that it is activity, it is then in the realm of grasping, and we are bound up by the passions [*klesa*]. What way, then, should we have of gaining deliverance? The *sravakas* cultivate emptiness, dwell in emptiness, and are bound by it. They cultivate concentration, dwell in concentration, and are bound by it. They cultivate tranquillity, dwell in tranquillity, and are bound by it. . . . If working with the mind is to discipline one's mind, how could this be called deliverance? (1. 118) [25]

In the same vein Hsüan-chüeh begins his celebrated poem, the *Song of Realizing the Tao (Cheng-tao Ke)*:

> *See you not that easygoing Man of Tao, who has abandoned learning and does not strive* [wu-wei]?
> *He neither avoids false thoughts nor seeks the true,*
> *For ignorance is in reality the Buddha nature,*
> *And this illusory, changeful, empty body is the Dharma body.*[26] r

The following story is told of Huai-jang, initiating into Zen his great successor Ma-tsu (d. 788), who was at the time practicing sitting meditation at the monastery of Ch'uan-fa.

"Your reverence," asked Huai-jang, "what is the objective of sitting in meditation?"

"The objective," answered Ma-tsu, "is to become a Buddha."

[25] *Shen-hui Ho-chang I-chi.* The Chinese text has been edited by Hu Shih, Shanghai, 1930.
[26] I.e., the Dharmakaya, for which see above, p. 71. Full translations of the *Cheng-tao Ke* (Japanese, *Shodoka*) will be found in Suzuki (6) and Senzaki and McCandless (1).

Thereupon Huai-jang picked up a floor-tile and began to polish it on a rock.

"What are you doing, master?" asked Ma-tsu.

"I am polishing it for a mirror," said Huai-jang.

"How could polishing a tile make a mirror?"

"How could sitting in meditation make a Buddha?" [27] [s]

Ma-tsu was the first Zen master celebrated for "strange words and extraordinary behavior," and is described as one who walked like a bull and glared like a tiger. When a monk asked him, "How do you get into harmony with the Tao?" Ma-tsu replied, "I am already out of harmony with the Tao!" He was the first to answer questions about Buddhism by hitting the questioner, or by giving a loud shout—"Ho!" [28] [t] Sometimes, however, he was more discursive, and one of his lectures takes up the problem of discipline thus:

> The Tao has nothing to do with discipline. If you say that it is attained by discipline, when the discipline is perfected it can again be lost (or, finishing the discipline turns out to be losing the Tao). . . . If you say that there is no discipline, this is to be the same as ordinary people. [29] [u]

Hsing-ssu's disciple Shih-t'ou (700–790), in the line of Soto Zen, was even more forthright:

> My teaching which has come down from the ancient Buddhas is not dependent on meditation (dhyana) or on diligent application of any kind. When you attain the insight as attained by the Buddha, you realize that mind is Buddha and Buddha is mind, that mind, Buddha, sentient beings, bodhi and klesa are of one and the same substance while they vary in names. [30]

His interesting name "Stone-head" is attributed to the fact that he lived on top of a large rock near the monastery of Heng-chou.

[27] Ch'uan Teng Lu, 5.
[28] Ku-tsun-hsü Yü-lu, 1. 6.
[29] Ibid., 1. 4.
[30] In Suzuki (6), p. 123.

With Ma-tsu's disciple Nan-ch'üan (748–834) and his successor Chao-chou (778–897), the teaching of Zen became peculiarly lively and disturbing. The *Wu-men kuan* (14) tells how Nan-ch'üan interrupted a dispute among his monks as to the ownership of a cat by threatening to cleave the animal with his spade if none of the monks could say a "good word"–that is, give an immediate expression of his Zen. There was dead silence, so the master cut the cat in two. Later in the day Nan-ch'üan recounted the incident to Chao-chou, who at once put his shoes on his head and left the room. "If you had been here," said Nan-ch'üan, "the cat would have been saved!"

Chao-chou is said to have had his awakening after the following incident with Nan-ch'üan:

Chao-chou asked, "What is the Tao?"

The master replied, "Your ordinary [i.e., natural] mind is the Tao."

"How can one return into accord with it?"

"By intending to accord you immediately deviate." *v*

"But without intention, how can one know the Tao?"

"The Tao," said the master, "belongs neither to knowing nor not knowing. Knowing is false understanding; not knowing is blind ignorance. If you really understand the Tao beyond doubt, it's like the empty sky. Why drag in right and wrong?" [31]

When Chao-chou was asked whether a dog has Buddha nature –which is certainly the usual Mahayana doctrine–he gave the one word "No!" (*Wu,*[w] Japanese, *Mu*).[32] When a monk asked him for instruction he merely inquired whether he had eaten his gruel, and then added, "Go wash your bowl!" [33] When asked about the spirit which remains when the body has decomposed, he remarked, "This morning it's windy again." [34]

Ma-tsu had another notable disciple in Po-chang (720–814),

[31] *Wu-men kuan,* 19.
[32] *Ibid.,* 1.
[33] *Ibid.,* 7.
[34] *Chao-chou Yü-lu,* in *Ku-tsun-hsü Yü-lu,* 3. 13.

who is said to have organized the first purely Zen community
of monks and to have laid down its regulations on the principle
that "a day of no working is a day of no eating." Since his time
a strong emphasis on manual work and some degree of self-
support has been characteristic of Zen communities. It might
be remarked here that these are not exactly monasteries in the
Western sense. They are rather training schools, from which one
is free to depart at any time without censure. Some members
remain monks for their whole lives; others become secular priests
in charge of small temples; still others may return into lay life.[35]
To Po-chang is attributed the famous definition of Zen, "When
hungry, eat; when tired, sleep." He is said to have had his *satori*
when Ma-tsu shouted at him and left him deaf for three days,
and to have been in the habit of pointing out the Zen life to his
disciples with the saying, "Don't cling; don't seek." For when
asked about seeking for the Buddha nature he answered, "It's
much like riding an ox in search of the ox."

Po-chang's student Huang-po (*d.* 850) is also of considerable
importance in this period. Not only was he the teacher of the
great Lin-chi, but he was also the author of the *Ch'uan Hsin Fa
Yao,* or "Treatise on the Essentials of the Doctrine of Mind."
The content of this work is essentially the same body of doctrine
as is found in Hui-neng, Shen-hui, and Ma-tsu, but it contains
some passages of remarkable clarity as well as some frank and
careful answers to questions at the end.

> By their very seeking for it [the Buddha nature] they produce the
> contrary effect of losing it, for that is using the Buddha to seek for
> the Buddha, and using mind to grasp mind. Even though they do
> their utmost for a full *kalpa,* they will not be able to attain to
> it. (1)
>   If those who study the Tao do not awake to this mind substance,

[35] The somewhat misleading word "monk" seems to be the inevitable translation of *seng,*[x] though *yun shui,*[y] "cloud and water," is a common and re-
vealingly picturesque term for the Zen student, who "drifts like a cloud and
flows like water." But I am at a loss to find a concise English expression for
this term.

they will create a mind over and above mind, seek the Buddha outside themselves and remain attached to forms, practices and performances—all of which is harmful and not the way to supreme knowledge. (3) [36]

Much of it is devoted to a clarification of what is meant by the Void, and by the terms "no-mind" (*wu-hsin*) and "no-thought" (*wu-nien*), all of which are carefully distinguished from literal blankness or nothingness. The use of Taoist language and ideas is found throughout the text:

> Fearing that none of you would understand, they [the Buddhas] gave it the name Tao, but you must not base any concept upon that name. So it is said that "when the fish is caught the trap is forgotten." (From Chuang-tzu.) When body and mind achieve spontaneity, the Tao is reached and universal mind can be understood. (29) . . . In former times, men's minds were sharp. Upon hearing a single sentence, they abandoned study and so came to be called "the sages who, abandoning learning, rest in spontaneity." In these days, people only seek to stuff themselves with knowledge and deductions, placing great reliance on written explanations and calling all this the practice. (30) [37]

It appears, however, that Huang-po's personal instruction of his disciples was not always so explanatory. Lin-chi (Japanese, Rinzai, *d.* 867) could never get a word out of him. Every time he attempted to ask a question Huang-po struck him, until in desperation he left the monastery and sought the advice of another master, Ta-yü, who scolded him for being so ungrateful for Huang-po's "grandmotherly kindness." This awakened Lin-chi, who again presented himself before Huang-po. This time, however, it was Lin-chi who did the striking, saying, "There is not much in Huang-po's Buddhism after all!" [38]

The record of Lin-chi's teaching, the *Lin-chi Lu* (Japanese, *Rinzai Roku*), shows a character of immense vitality and original-

---

[36] In Chu Ch'an (1), pp. 16 and 18. Another partial translation appears in Suzuki (6), pp. 132–40.
[37] In Chu Ch'an (1), pp. 42–43.
[38] *Ch'uan Teng Lu*, 12.

ity, lecturing his students in informal and often somewhat "racy" language. It is as if Lin-chi were using the whole strength of his personality to force the student into immediate awakening. Again and again he berates them for not having enough faith in themselves, for letting their minds "gallop around" in search of something which they have never lost, and which is "right before you at this very moment." Awakening for Lin-chi seems primarily a matter of "nerve"–the courage to "let go" without further delay in the unwavering faith that one's natural, spontaneous functioning is the Buddha mind. His approach to conceptual Buddhism, to the students' obsession with stages to be reached and goals to be attained, is ruthlessly iconoclastic.

> Why do I talk here? Only because you followers of the Tao go galloping around in search of the mind, and are unable to stop it. On the other hand, the ancients acted in a leisurely way, appropriate to circumstances (as they arose). O you followers of the Tao– when you get my point of view you will sit in judgment on top of the . . . Buddhas' heads. Those who have completed the ten stages will seem like underlings, and those who have arrived at Supreme Awakening will seem as if they had cangues around their necks. The Arhans and Pratyeka-buddhas are like a dirty privy. Bodhi and nirvana are like hitching-posts for a donkey.[39]

On the importance of the "natural" or "unaffected" (wu-shih [g]) life he is especially emphatic:

> There is no place in Buddhism for using effort. Just be ordinary and nothing special. Relieve your bowels, pass water, put on your clothes, and eat your food. When you're tired, go and lie down. Ignorant people may laugh at me, but the wise will understand. . . . As you go from place to place, if you regard each one as your own home, they will all be genuine, for when circumstances come you must not try to change them. Thus your usual habits of feeling, which make karma for the Five Hells, will of themselves become the Great Ocean of Liberation.[40]

And on creating karma through seeking liberation–

[39] Lin-chi Lu in Ku-tsun-hsü Yü-lu, 1. 4, pp. 5–6.
[40] Ibid., p. 7.

Outside the mind there is no Dharma, and inside also there is nothing to be grasped. What is it that you seek? You say on all sides that the Tao is to be practiced and put to the proof. Don't be mistaken! If there is anyone who can practice it, this is entirely *karma* making for birth-and-death. You talk about being perfectly disciplined in your six senses and in the ten thousand ways of conduct, but as I see it all this is creating *karma*. To seek the Buddha and to seek the Dharma is precisely making *karma* for the hells.[41 aa]

In Ma-tsu, Nan-ch'üan, Chao-chou, Huang-po, and Lin-chi we can see the "flavor" of Zen at its best. Taoist and Buddhist as it is in its original inspiration, it is also something more. It is so earthy, so matter-of-fact, and so direct. The difficulty of translating the records of these masters is that their style of Chinese is neither classical nor modern, but rather the colloquial speech of the T'ang dynasty. Its "naturalness" is less refined, less obviously beautiful than that of the Taoist sages and poets; it is almost rough and common. I say "almost" because the expression is not really correct. We are at a loss for parallels from other cultures for comparison, and the Western student can best catch its flavor through observing the works of art which it was subsequently to inspire. The best image might be a garden consisting of no more than an expanse of raked sand, as a ground for several unhewn rocks overgrown with lichens and moss, such as one may see today in the Zen temples of Kyoto. The media are the simplest imaginable; the effect is as if man had hardly touched it, as if it had been transported unchanged from the seashore; but in practice only the most sensitive and experienced artist can achieve it. This sounds, of course, as though "Zen flavor" were a studied and affected primitivism. Sometimes it is. But the genuine Zen flavor is when a man is almost miraculously natural without intending to be so. His Zen life is not to make himself but to *grow* that way.

Thus it should be obvious that the "naturalness" of these T'ang masters is not to be taken just literally, as if Zen were merely to

[41] *Ibid.*, p. 11.

glory in being a completely ordinary, vulgar fellow who scatters ideals to the wind and behaves as he pleases–for this would in itself be an affectation. The "naturalness" of Zen flourishes only when one has lost affectedness and self-consciousness of every description. But a spirit of this kind comes and goes like the wind, and is the most impossible thing to institutionalize and preserve.

Yet in the late T'ang dynasty the genius and vitality of Zen was such that it was coming to be the dominant form of Buddhism in China, though its relation to other schools was often very close. Tsung-mi (779–841) was simultaneously a Zen master and the Fifth Patriarch of the Hua-yen School, representing the philosophy of the *Avatamsaka Sutra*. This extremely subtle and mature form of Mahayana philosophy was employed by T'ung-shan (807–869) in developing the doctrine of the Five Ranks (*wu-wei* bb), concerning the fivefold relationship of the absolute (*cheng* cc) and the relative (*p'ien* dd), and was related by his student Ts'ao-shan (840–901) to the philosophy of the *I Ching*, the *Book of Changes*. Fa-yen (885–958) and Fen-yang (947–1024) were also influential masters who made a deep study of the Hua-yen, and to this day it constitutes as it were the intellectual aspect of Zen. On the other hand, such masters as Te-chao (891–972) and Yen-shou (904–975) maintained close relations with the T'ien-t'ai and Pure Land Schools.

In 845 there was a brief but vigorous persecution of Buddhism by the Taoist Emperor Wu-tsung. Temples and monasteries were destroyed, their lands confiscated, and the monks compelled to return to lay life. Fortunately, his enthusiasm for Taoist alchemy soon involved him in experiments with the "Elixir of Immortality," and from partaking of this concoction he shortly died. Zen had survived the persecution better than any other school, and now entered into a long era of imperial and popular favor. Hundreds of monks thronged its wealthy monastic institutions, and the fortunes of the school so prospered and its numbers so increased that the preservation of its spirit became a very serious problem.

Popularity almost invariably leads to a deterioration of quality, and as Zen became less of an informal spiritual movement and more of a settled institution, it underwent a curious change of character. It became necessary to "standardize" its methods and to find means for the masters to handle students in large numbers. There were also the special problems which arise for monastic communities when their membership increases, their traditions harden, and their novices tend more and more to be mere boys without natural vocation, sent for training by their pious families. The effect of this last factor upon the development of institutional Zen can hardly be underestimated. For the Zen community became less an association of mature men with spiritual interests, and more of an ecclesiastical boarding school for adolescent boys.

Under such circumstances the problem of discipline became paramount. The Zen masters were forced to concern themselves not only with the way of liberation from convention, but also with the instilling of convention, of ordinary manners and morals, in raw youths. The mature Western student who discovers an interest in Zen as a philosophy or as a way of liberation must be careful to keep this in mind, for otherwise he may be unpleasantly startled by monastic Zen as it exists today in Japan. He will find that Zen is a discipline enforced with the big stick. He will find that, although it is still an effective way of liberation at its "upper end," its main preoccupation is with a disciplinary regimen which "trains character" in the same way as the old-fashioned British public school or the Jesuit novitiate. But it does the job remarkably well. The "Zen type" is an extremely fine type—as types go—self-reliant, humorous, clean and orderly to a fault, energetic though unhurried, and "hard as nails" without lack of keen aesthetic sensibility. The general impression of these men is that they have the same sort of balance as the Daruma doll: they are not rigid, but no one can knock them down.

Still another crucial problem arises when a spiritual institution comes into prosperity and power—the very human problem of competition for office and of who has the right to be a master.

Concern for this problem is reflected in the writing of the *Ch'uan Teng Lu*, or "Record of the Transmission of the Lamp," by Tao-yüan in about 1004. For one of the main objects of this work was to establish a proper "apostolic succession" for the Zen tradition, so that no one could claim authority unless his *satori* had been approved by someone who had been approved . . . right back to the time of the Buddha himself.

Nothing, however, is more difficult than establishing proper qualifications in the imponderable realm of spiritual insight. Where the candidates are few the problem is not so grave, but where one master is responsible for some hundreds of students the process of teaching and testing requires standardization. Zen solved this problem with remarkable ingenuity, employing a means which not only provided a test of competence but–what was much more–a means of transmitting the Zen experience itself with a minimum of falsification.

This extraordinary invention was the system of the *kung-an* [ee] (Japanese, *koan*) or "Zen problem." Literally, this term means a "public document" or "case" in the sense of a decision creating a legal precedent. Thus the *koan* system involves "passing" a series of tests based on the *mondo* or anecdotes of the old masters. One of the beginning *koans* is Chao-chou's answer "*Wu*" or "No" to the question as to whether a dog has Buddha nature. The student is expected to show that he has experienced the meaning of the *koan* by a specific and usually nonverbal demonstration which he has to discover intuitively.[42]

The period of prosperity which came with the tenth and eleventh centuries was attended by a sense of "loss of spirit," which in turn gave rise to much study of the great T'ang masters. Their anecdotes were subsequently collected in such anthologies as the *Pi-yen Lu* (1125) and the *Wu-men kuan* (1229). The use of these anecdotes for the *koan* method was originated by Yüan-wu (1063–1135) and his disciple Ta-hui (1089–1163), in

[42] For a fuller description see below, p. 159. In its Japanese form *Koan*, the syllables are pronounced separately–*Ko-an*.

the tenth or eleventh generation of descent from Lin-chi. However, something which already began to resemble it was employed by Huang-lung (1002–1069) in order to cope with his particularly large following. He devised three test-questions known as "Huang-lung's Three Barriers"—

Question: Everybody has a place of birth. Where is your place of birth?
Answer: Early this morning I ate white rice gruel. Now I'm hungry again.

Question: How is my hand like the Buddha's hand?
Answer: Playing the lute under the moon.

Question: How is my foot like a donkey's foot?
Answer: When the white heron stands in the snow it has a different color.[43]

No doubt the answers given were the original replies to the questions, but later the problem becomes both the question and its answer, for the student is expected to see into the relationship between the two, which, to say the least, is none too obvious. For the moment, it is enough to say that every *koan* has a "point" which is some aspect of Zen experience, that its point is often concealed by being made very much more apparent than one would expect, and that *koans* are concerned not only with the primary awakening to the Void but also with its subsequent expression in life and thought.

The *koan* system was developed in the Lin-chi (Rinzai) School of Zen, but not without opposition. The Soto School felt that it was much too artificial. Whereas the *koan* advocates used this technique as a means for encouraging that overwhelming "feeling of doubt" (*i ching* [tt]) which they felt to be essential as a prerequisite for *satori,* the Soto School argued that it lent itself too easily to that very seeking for *satori* which thrusts it away, or —what is worse—induces an artificial *satori.* Adherents of the Rinzai School sometimes say that the intensity of the *satori* is

[43] *Jen-t'ien Yen-mu,* 2.

proportionate to the intensity of the feeling of doubt, of blind
seeking, which precedes it, but for Soto this suggests that such a
satori has a dualistic character, and is thus no more than an
artificial emotional reaction. Thus the Soto view was that proper
dhyana lay in motiveless action (*wu-wei*), in "sitting just to sit,"
or "walking just to walk." The two schools therefore came to be
known respectively as *k'an-hua* Zen (observing the anecdote Zen)
and *mo-chao* Zen (silently illumined Zen).

The Rinzai School of Zen was introduced into Japan in 1191 by
the Japanese T'ien-t'ai monk Eisai (1141–1215), who established
monasteries at Kyoto and Kamakura under imperial patronage.
The Soto School was introduced in 1227 by the extraordinary
genius Dogen (1200–1253), who established the great monastery
of Eiheiji, refusing, however, to accept imperial favors. It should
be noted that Zen arrived in Japan shortly after the beginning
of the Kamakura Era, when the military dictator Yoritomo and
his *samurai* followers had seized power from the hands of the
then somewhat decadent nobility. This historical coincidence
provided the military class, the *samurai,* with a type of Buddhism
which appealed to them strongly because of its practical and
earthy qualities and because of the directness and simplicity of
its approach. Thus there arose that peculiar way of life called
bushido, the Tao of the warrior, which is essentially the application of Zen to the arts of war. The association of the peace-loving
doctrine of the Buddha with the military arts has always been a
puzzle to Buddhists of other schools. It seems to involve the
complete divorce of awakening from morality. But one must face
the fact that, in its essence, the Buddhist experience is a liberation from conventions of every kind, including the moral conventions. On the other hand, Buddhism is not a revolt against convention, and in societies where the military caste is an integral
part of the conventional structure and the warrior's role an accepted necessity Buddhism will make it possible for him to fulfill
that role as a Buddhist. The medieval cult of chivalry should be
no less of a puzzle to the peace-loving Christian.

The contribution of Zen to Japanese culture has by no means been confined to *bushido*. It has entered into almost every aspect of the people's life–their architecture, poetry, painting, gardening, their athletics, crafts, and trades; it has penetrated the everyday language and thought of the most ordinary folk. For by the genius of such Zen monks as Dogen, Hakuin, and Bankei, by such poets as Ryokan and Basho, and by such a painter as Sesshu, Zen has been made extraordinarily accessible to the common mind.

Dogen, in particular, made an incalculable contribution to his native land. His immense work, the *Shobogenzo* ("Treasury of the Eye of the True Doctrine"), was written in the vernacular and covered every aspect of Buddhism from its formal discipline to its profoundest insights. His doctrine of time, change, and relativity is explained with the aid of the most provoking poetic images, and it is only regrettable that no one has yet had the time and talent to translate this work into English. Hakuin (1685–1768) reconstituted the *koan* system, and is said to have trained no less than eighty successors in Zen. Bankei (1622–1693) found a way of presenting Zen with such ease and simplicity that it seemed almost too good to be true. He spoke to large audiences of farmers and country folk, but no one "important" seems to have dared to follow him.[44]

Meanwhile, Zen continued to prosper in China until well into the Ming dynasty (1368–1643), when the divisions between the various schools of Buddhism began to fade, and the popularity of the Pure Land School with its "easy way" of invoking the Name of Amitabha began to be fused with *koan* practice and at last to absorb it. A few Zen communities seem to have survived to the present day, but, so far as I have been able to study

---

[44] Because my purpose is only to give enough of the history of Zen to serve as a background for its doctrine and practice, I am not entering into any full discussion of its history in Japan. The work of Dogen, Hakuin, Bankei, and others will be discussed in another context.

them, their emphasis inclines either to Soto or to the more "occultist" preoccupations of Tibetan Buddhism. In either case, their view of Zen seems to be involved with a somewhat complex and questionable doctrine of man's psychic anatomy, which would appear to derive from Taoist alchemical ideas.[45]

The history of Chinese Zen raises one problem of great fascination. Both Rinzai and Soto Zen as we find them in Japanese monasteries today put enormous emphasis on *za-zen* or sitting meditation, a practice which they follow for many hours of the day—attaching great importance to the correctness of posture and the way of breathing which it involves. To practice Zen is, to all intents and purposes, to practice *za-zen*, to which the Rinzai School adds *sanzen*, the periodic visits to the master (*roshi*) for presenting one's view of the *koan*. However, the *Shen-hui Ho-chang I-chi* records the following conversation between Shen-hui and a certain Ch'eng:

> The Master asked Dhyana Master Ch'eng: "What method must be practiced to see into one's own nature?"
>
> "It is first of all necessary to apply oneself to the practice of sitting cross-legged in *samadhi*. Once *samadhi* is obtained, one must, by means of *samadhi*, awaken *prajna* in oneself. By *prajna* one is able to see into one's own nature."
>
> (Shen-hui:) "When one practices *samadhi*, isn't this a deliberate activity of the mind?"
>
> (Ch'eng:) "Yes."
>
> (Shen-hui:) "Then this deliberate activity of the mind is an activity of restricted consciousness, and how can it bring seeing into one's own nature?"
>
> (Ch'eng:) "To see into one's own nature, it is necessary to practice *samadhi*. How could one see it otherwise?"
>
> (Shen-hui:) "All practice of *samadhi* is fundamentally a wrong view. How, by practicing *samadhi*, could one attain *samadhi*?"
> (1. 111)

[45] An example of this fusion may be seen in the *T'ai I Chin Hua Tsung Chih*, a treatise of the Ming or perhaps Ch'ing dynasty, for which see Wilhelm (1).

We have already mentioned the incident between Ma-tsu and Huai-jang, in which the latter compared sitting in meditation to polishing a tile for a mirror. On another occasion Huai-jang said:

> To train yourself in sitting meditation [*za-zen*] is to train yourself to be a sitting Buddha. If you train yourself in *za-zen*, (you should know that) Zen is neither sitting nor lying. If you train yourself to be a sitting Buddha, (you should know that) the Buddha is not a fixed form. Since the Dharma has no (fixed) abode, it is not a matter of making choices. If you (make yourself) a sitting Buddha this is precisely killing the Buddha. If you adhere to the sitting position, you will not attain the principle (of Zen).[46] *gg*

This seems to be the consistent doctrine of all the T'ang masters from Hui-neng to Lin-chi. Nowhere in their teachings have I been able to find any instruction in or recommendation of the type of *za-zen* which is today the principal occupation of Zen monks.[47] On the contrary, the practice is discussed time after time in the apparently negative fashion of the two quotations just cited.

It could be assumed that *za-zen* was so much the normal rule of the Zen monk's life that our sources do not bother to discuss it, and that their teachings are designed solely for advanced students who have so mastered *za-zen* that the time has come to go beyond it. This, however, does not agree too well with the references to the enormous clerical and lay audiences attending some of the discourses, since it would be somewhat fantastic to suppose that China was swarming with accomplished yogis. The discourses frequently begin by saying, in a rather brief and off-hand fashion, that these teachings are for those who are well

---

[46] *Ku-tsun-hsü Yü-lu*, 1. 1, p. 2.
[47] It is true that a text known as the *T'so-chan I*, or "Directions for Za-zen," is incorporated in the *Po-chang Ching-kuei*—the regulations for the Zen community attributed to Po-chang (720–814)—and that the regulations themselves prescribe times for meditation. However, we can find no edition of this work prior to 1265 (Suzuki), and it may even be as late as 1338 (Dumoulin). The existing version shows the influence of the Shingon sect, which is akin to Tibetan Lamaism and came to China during the eighth century.

trained in the Buddhist virtues. But this could mean no more than that they are for mature people who have mastered the ordinary social and moral conventions, and are therefore not in danger of using Buddhism as a pretext for rebellion against the common decencies.

Alternatively, it could be assumed that the type of za-zen under criticism is za-zen practiced for a purpose, to "get" Buddhahood, instead of "sitting just to sit." This would concur with the Soto objection to the Rinzai School with its method of cultivating the state of "great doubt" by means of the koan. While the Soto is not quite fair to the Rinzai in this respect, this would certainly be a plausible interpretation of the early masters' doctrine. However, there are several references to the idea that prolonged sitting is not much better than being dead. There is, of course, a proper place for sitting–along with standing, walking, and lying–but to imagine that sitting contains some special virtue is "attachment to form." Thus in the T'an-ching Hui-neng says:

> A living man who sits and does not lie down;
> A dead man who lies down and does not sit!
> After all these are just dirty skeletons. (8) [hh]

Even in Japanese Zen one occasionally encounters a Zen practice which lays no special emphasis upon za-zen, but rather stresses the use of one's ordinary work as the means of meditation. This was certainly true of Bankei,[48] and this principle underlies the common use of such arts as "tea ceremony," flute playing, brush drawing, archery, fencing, and ju-jutsu as ways of practicing Zen. Perhaps, then, the exaggeration of za-zen in later times is part and parcel of the conversion of the Zen monastery into a boys' training school. To have them sit still for hours on end under the watchful eyes of monitors with sticks is certainly a sure method of keeping them out of mischief.

[48] See Suzuki (10), pp. 176–80.

Yet however much *za-zen* may have been exaggerated in the Far East, a certain amount of "sitting just to sit" might well be the best thing in the world for the jittery minds and agitated bodies of Europeans and Americans–provided they do not use it as a method for turning themselves into Buddhas.

PART TWO

PRINCIPLES AND PRACTICE

One

"EMPTY AND MARVELOUS"

The opening words of the oldest Zen poem say that

> The perfect Way [Tao] is without difficulty,
> Save that it avoids picking and choosing.
> Only when you stop liking and disliking
> Will all be clearly understood.
> A split hair's difference,
> And heaven and earth are set apart!
> If you want to get the plain truth,
> Be not concerned with right and wrong.
> The conflict between right and wrong
> Is the sickness of the mind.[1] [a]

The point is not to make an effort to silence the feelings and cultivate bland indifference. It is to see through the universal illusion that what is pleasant or good may be wrested from what is painful or evil. It was a first principle in Taoism that

> When everyone recognizes beauty as beautiful,
>   there is already ugliness;
> When everyone recognizes goodness as good,
>   there is already evil.
> "To be" and "not to be" arise mutually;
> Difficult and easy are mutually realized;
> Long and short are mutually contrasted;
> High and low are mutually posited; . . .
> Before and after are in mutual sequence.[2]

To see this is to see that good without evil is like up without down, and that to make an ideal of pursuing the good is like try-

[1] Seng-ts'an, *Hsin-hsin Ming.*
[2] *Tao Te Ching,* 2.

ing to get rid of the left by turning constantly to the right. One is therefore compelled to go round in circles.[3]

The logic of this is so simple that one is tempted to think it over-simple. The temptation is all the stronger because it upsets the fondest illusion of the human mind, which is that in the course of time everything may be made better and better. For it is the general opinion that were this not possible the life of man would lack all meaning and incentive. The only alternative to a life of constant progress is felt to be a mere existence, static and dead, so joyless and inane that one might as well commit suicide. The very notion of this "only alternative" shows how firmly the mind is bound in a dualistic pattern, how hard it is to think in any other terms than good or bad, or a muddy mixture of the two.

Yet Zen is a liberation from this pattern, and its apparently dismal starting point is to understand the absurdity of choosing, of the whole feeling that life may be significantly improved by a constant selection of the "good." One must start by "getting the feel" of relativity, and by knowing that life is not a situation from which there is anything to be grasped or gained—as if it were something which one approaches from outside, like a pie or a barrel of beer. To succeed is always to fail—in the sense that the more one succeeds in anything, the greater is the need to go on succeeding. To eat is to survive to be hungry.

The illusion of significant improvement arises in moments of contrast, as when one turns from the left to the right on a hard bed. The position is "better" so long as the contrast remains, but before long the second position begins to feel like the first. So one acquires a more comfortable bed and, for a while, sleeps in peace. But the solution of the problem leaves a strange vacuum in one's consciousness, a vacuum soon filled by the sensation of another intolerable contrast, hitherto unnoticed, and just as urgent, just as frustrating as the problem of the hard bed. The vacuum arises

[3] Believe it or not, there is actually a politician in San Francisco who so detests the political Left Wing that he will not make a left turn with his car.

because the sensation of comfort can be maintained only in relation to the sensation of discomfort, just as an image is visible to the eye only by reason of a contrasting background. The good and the evil, the pleasant and the painful are so inseparable, so identical in their difference–like the two sides of a coin–that

Fair is foul, and foul is fair,

or, in the words of a poem in the *Zenrin Kushu:* [4]

> *To receive trouble is to receive good fortune;*
> *To receive agreement is to receive opposition.*[b]

Another puts it more vividly:

> *At dusk the cock announces dawn;*
> *At midnight, the bright sun.*[c]

Zen does not, for this reason, take the attitude that it is so futile to eat when hungry that one may as well starve, nor is it so inhuman as to say that when we itch we should not scratch. Disillusionment with the pursuit of the good does not involve the evil of stagnation as its necessary alternative, for the human situation is like that of "fleas on a hot griddle." None of the alternatives offer a solution, for the flea who falls must jump, and the flea who jumps must fall. Choosing is absurd because there is no choice.

To the dualistic mode of thought it will therefore seem that the standpoint of Zen is that of fatalism as opposed to free choice. When Mu-chou was asked, "We dress and eat every day, and how do we escape from having to put on clothes and eat food?" he answered, "We dress; we eat." "I don't understand," said the

---

[4] The *Zenrin Kushu* is an anthology of some five thousand two-line poems, compiled by Toyo Eicho (1429–1504). Its purpose was to provide Zen students with a source-book of verses from which to select couplets expressing the theme of a newly solved *koan*. Many masters require such a verse as soon as the proper answer to the *koan* has been given. The couplets have been drawn from a vast variety of Chinese sources–Buddhist, Taoist, classical literature, popular songs, etc.

monk. "If you don't understand, put on your clothes and eat your food." [5] [d] On being asked how to escape from the "heat," another master directed the questioner to the place where it is neither hot nor cold. When asked to explain himself he replied, "In summer we sweat; in winter we shiver." Or, as a poem puts it:

When cold, we gather round the hearth before the blazing fire;
When hot, we sit on the bank of the mountain stream in the bamboo grove.[6] [e]

And from this point of view one can

See the sun in the midst of the rain;
Scoop clear water from the heart of the fire.[f]

But the viewpoint is not fatalistic. It is not simply submission to the inevitability of sweating when it is hot, shivering when it is cold, eating when hungry, and sleeping when tired. Submission to fate implies someone who submits, someone who is the helpless puppet of circumstances, and for Zen there is no such person. The duality of subject and object, of the knower and the known, is seen to be just as relative, as mutual, as inseparable as every other. We do not sweat *because* it is hot; the sweating is the heat. It is just as true to say that the sun is light because of the eyes as to say that the eyes see light because of the sun. The viewpoint is unfamiliar because it is our settled convention to think that heat comes first and then, by causality, the body sweats. To put it the other way round is startling, like saying "cheese and bread" instead of "bread and cheese." Thus the *Zenrin Kushu* says:

Fire does not wait for the sun to be hot,
Nor the wind for the moon, to be cool.

This shocking and seemingly illogical reversal of common sense may perhaps be clarified by the favorite Zen image of "the moon in the water." The phenomenon moon-in-the-water is likened to

[5] *Mu-chou Lu,* in *Ku-tsun-hsü Yü-lu,* 2. 6.
[6] *Zenrin Ruishu,* 2.

human experience. The water is the subject, and the moon the object. When there is no water, there is no moon-in-the-water, and likewise when there is no moon. But when the moon rises the water does not wait to receive its image, and when even the tiniest drop of water is poured out the moon does not wait to cast its reflection. For the moon does not intend to cast its reflection, and the water does not receive its image on purpose. The event is caused as much by the water as by the moon, and as the water manifests the brightness of the moon, the moon manifests the clarity of the water. Another poem in the *Zenrin Kushu* says:

> *Trees show the bodily form of the wind;*
> *Waves give vital energy to the moon.*[9]

To put it less poetically–human experience is determined as much by the nature of the mind and the structure of its senses as by the external objects whose presence the mind reveals. Men feel themselves to be victims or puppets of their experience because they separate "themselves" from their minds, thinking that the nature of the mind-body is something involuntarily thrust upon "them." They think that they did not ask to be born, did not ask to be "given" a sensitive organism to be frustrated by alternating pleasure and pain. But Zen asks us to find out "who" it is that "has" this mind, and "who" it was that did not ask to be born before father and mother conceived us. Thence it appears that the entire sense of subjective isolation, of being the one who was "given" a mind and to whom experience happens, is an illusion of bad semantics–the hypnotic suggestion of repeated wrong thinking. For there is no "myself" apart from the mind-body which gives structure to my experience. It is likewise ridiculous to talk of this mind-body as something which was passively and involuntarily "given" a certain structure. It *is* that structure, and before the structure arose there was no mind-body.

Our problem is that the power of thought enables us to construct symbols of things apart from the things themselves. This includes the ability to make a symbol, an idea of ourselves apart from ourselves. Because the idea is so much more comprehensible than the reality, the symbol so much more stable than the fact, we learn to identify ourselves with our idea of ourselves. Hence the subjective feeling of a "self" which "has" a mind, of an inwardly isolated subject to whom experiences involuntarily happen. With its characteristic emphasis on the concrete, Zen points out that our precious "self" is just an idea, useful and legitimate enough if seen for what it is, but disastrous if identified with our real nature. The unnatural awkwardness of a certain type of self-consciousness comes into being when we are aware of conflict or contrast between the idea of ourselves, on the one hand, and the immediate, concrete feeling of ourselves, on the other.

When we are no longer identified with the idea of ourselves, the entire relationship between subject and object, knower and known, undergoes a sudden and revolutionary change. It becomes a real relationship, a mutuality in which the subject creates the object just as much as the object creates the subject. The knower no longer feels himself to be independent of the known; the experiencer no longer feels himself to stand apart from the experience. Consequently the whole notion of getting something "out" of life, of seeking something "from" experience, becomes absurd. To put it in another way, it becomes vividly clear that in concrete fact I have no other self than the totality of things of which I am aware. This is the Hua-yen (Kegon) doctrine of the net of jewels, of *shih shih wu ai* (Japanese, *ji ji mu ge*), in which every jewel contains the reflection of all the others.

The sense of subjective isolation is also based on a failure to see the relativity of voluntary and involuntary events. This relativity is easily felt by watching one's breath, for by a slight change of viewpoint it is as easy to feel that "I breathe" as that "It breathes me." We feel that our actions are voluntary when they follow a decision, and involuntary when they happen without decision. But if decision itself were voluntary, every decision would have to be preceded by a decision to decide—an infinite regression which fortunately does not occur. Oddly enough, if we had to decide to decide, we would not be free to decide. We are free to decide because decision "happens." We just decide without having the faintest understanding of how we do it. In fact, it is neither voluntary nor involuntary. To "get the feel" of this relativity is to find another extraordinary transformation of our experience as a whole, which may be described in either of two ways. I feel that I am deciding everything that happens, or, I feel that everything, including my decisions, is just happening spontaneously. For a decision–the freest of my actions–just happens like hiccups inside me or like a bird singing outside me.

Such a way of seeing things is vividly described by a modern Zen master, the late Sokei-an Sasaki:

> One day I wiped out all the notions from my mind. I gave up all desire. I discarded all the words with which I thought and stayed in quietude. I felt a little queer–as if I were being carried into something, or as if I were touching some power unknown to me . . . and Ztt! I entered. I lost the boundary of my physical body. I had my skin, of course, but I felt I was standing in the center of the cosmos. I spoke, but my words had lost their meaning. I saw people coming towards me, but all were the same man. All were myself! I had never known this world. I had believed that I was created, but now I must change my opinion: I was never created; I was the cosmos; no individual Mr. Sasaki existed.[7]

It would seem, then, that to get rid of the subjective distinction between "me" and "my experience"–through seeing that my idea of myself is not myself–is to discover the actual relationship between myself and the "outside" world. The individual, on the one hand, and the world, on the other, are simply the abstract limits or terms of a concrete reality which is "between" them, as the concrete coin is "between" the abstract, Euclidean surfaces of its two sides. Similarly, the reality of all "inseparable opposites"–life and death, good and evil, pleasure and pain, gain and loss–is that "between" for which we have no words.

[7] "The Transcendental World," Zen Notes, vol. 1, no. 5. First Zen Institute of America. New York, 1954.

Man's identification with his idea of himself gives him a specious and precarious sense of permanence. For this idea is relatively fixed, being based upon carefully selected memories of his past, memories which have a preserved and fixed character. Social convention encourages the fixity of the idea because the very usefulness of symbols depends upon their stability. Convention therefore encourages him to associate his idea of himself with equally abstract and symbolic roles and stereotypes, since these will help him to form an idea of himself which will be definite and intelligible. But to the degree that he identifies himself with the fixed idea, he becomes aware of "life" as something which flows past him—faster and faster as he grows older, as his idea becomes more rigid, more bolstered with memories. The more he attempts to clutch the world, the more he feels it as a process in motion.

On one occasion Ma-tsu and Po-chang were out for a walk, when they saw some wild geese flying past.

"What are they?" asked Ma-tsu.

"They're wild geese," said Po-chang.

"Where are they going?" demanded Ma-tsu.

Po-chang replied, "They've already flown away."

Suddenly Ma-tsu grabbed Po-chang by the nose and twisted it so that he cried out in pain.

"How," shouted Ma-tsu, "could they ever have flown away?"

This was the moment of Po-chang's awakening.[8]

The relativity of time and motion is one of the principal themes of Dogen's *Shobogenzo*, where he writes:

> If we watch the shore while we are sailing in a boat, we feel that the shore is moving. But if we look nearer to the boat itself, we know then that it is the boat which moves. When we regard the universe in confusion of body and mind, we often get the mistaken belief that our mind is constant. But if we actually practice (Zen) and come back to ourselves, we see that this was wrong.
>
> When firewood becomes ashes, it never returns to being firewood. But we should not take the view that what is latterly ashes was

[8] *Pi-yen Chi.*

formerly firewood. What we should understand is that, according to the doctrine of Buddhism, firewood stays at the position of firewood. . . . There are former and later stages, but these stages are clearly cut.

It is the same with life and death. Thus we say in Buddhism that the Un-born is also the Un-dying. Life is a position of time. Death is a position of time. They are like winter and spring, and in Buddhism we do not consider that winter *becomes* spring, or that spring *becomes* summer.[9]

Dogen is here trying to express the strange sense of timeless moments which arises when one is no longer trying to resist the flow of events, the peculiar stillness and self-sufficiency of the succeeding instants when the mind is, as it were, going along with them and not trying to arrest them. A similar view is expressed thus by Ma-tsu:

A *sutra* says, "It is only a group of elements which come together to make this body." When it arises, only these elements arise. When it ceases, only these elements cease. But when these elements arise, do not say, "I am arising," and when they cease, do not say, "I am ceasing." So, too, with our former thoughts, later thoughts, and intervening thoughts (or, experiences): the thoughts follow one another without being linked together. Each one is absolutely tranquil.[10] *h*

Buddhism has frequently compared the course of time to the apparent motion of a wave, wherein the actual water only moves up and down, creating the illusion of a "piece" of water moving over the surface. It is a similar illusion that there is a constant "self" moving through successive experiences, constituting a link between them in such a way that the youth becomes the man who becomes the graybeard who becomes the corpse.

Connected, then, with the pursuit of the good is the pursuit of the future, the illusion whereby we are unable to be happy without a "promising future" for the symbolic self. Progress towards

[9] *Shobogenzo*, fasc. 1. For this translation I am indebted to my colleague Professor Sabro Hasegawa.
[10] *Ku-tsun-hsü Yü-lu*, 1. 2. 4.

the good is therefore measured in terms of the prolongation of human life, forgetting that nothing is more relative than our sense of the length of time. A Zen poem says:

> *The morning glory which blooms for an hour*
> *Differs not at heart from the giant pine,*
> *Which lives for a thousand years.*

Subjectively, a gnat doubtless feels that its span of a few days is a reasonably long lifetime. A tortoise, with its span of several hundred years, would feel subjectively the same as the gnat. Not so long ago the life expectancy of the average man was about forty-five years. Today it is from sixty-five to seventy years, but subjectively the years are faster, and death, when it comes, is always all too soon. As Dogen said:

> *The flowers depart when we hate to lose them;*
> *The weeds arrive while we hate to watch them grow.*

This is perfectly natural, perfectly human, and no pulling and stretching of time will make it otherwise.

On the contrary, the measuring of worth and success in terms of time, and the insistent demand for assurances of a promising future, make it impossible to live freely both in the present and in the "promising" future when it arrives. For there is never anything but the present, and if one cannot live there, one cannot live anywhere. The *Shobogenzo* says:

When a fish swims, he swims on and on, and there is no end to the water. When a bird flies, he flies on and on, and there is no end to the sky. From the most ancient times there was never a fish who swam out of the water, nor a bird who flew out of the sky. Yet when the fish needs just a little water, he uses just a little; and when he needs lots, he uses lots. Thus the tips of their heads are always at the outer edge (of their space). If ever a bird flies beyond that edge, he dies, and so also with the fish. From the water the fish makes his life, and from the sky, the bird. But this life is made by the bird and the fish. At the same time, the bird and the fish are made by life. Thus there are the fish, the water, and life, and all three create each other.

Yet if there were a bird who first wanted to examine the size of the sky, or a fish who first wanted to examine the extent of the water—and then try to fly or to swim, they will never find their own ways in the sky or water.[11]

This is not a philosophy of not looking where one is going; it is a philosophy of not making where one is going so much more important than where one is that there will be no point in going.

The life of Zen begins, therefore, in a disillusion with the pursuit of goals which do not really exist—the good without the bad, the gratification of a self which is no more than an idea, and the morrow which never comes. For all these things are a deception of symbols pretending to be realities, and to seek after them is like walking straight into a wall upon which some painter has, by the convention of perspective, suggested an open passage. In short, Zen *begins* at the point where there is nothing further to seek, nothing to be gained. Zen is most emphatically not to be regarded as a system of self-improvement, or a way of becoming a Buddha. In the words of Lin-chi, "If a man seeks the Buddha, that man loses the Buddha."

For all ideas of self-improvement and of becoming or getting something in the future relate solely to our abstract image of ourselves. To follow them is to give ever more reality to that image. On the other hand, our true, nonconceptual self is already the Buddha, and needs no improvement. In the course of time it may grow, but one does not blame an egg for not being a chicken; still less does one criticize a pig for having a shorter neck than a giraffe. A *Zenrin* poem says:

In the landscape of spring there is neither high nor low;
The flowering branches grow naturally, some long, some short.[i]

When Ts'ui-wei was asked about the meaning of Buddhism, he answered: "Wait until there is no one around, and I will tell you." Some time later the monk approached him again, saying: "There is nobody here now. Please answer me." Ts'ui-wei led him out

11 *Shobogenzo*, fasc. 1. Read to the author by Sabro Hasegawa.

into the garden and went over to the bamboo grove, saying nothing. Still the monk did not understand, so at last Ts'ui-wei said: "Here is a tall bamboo; there is a short one!" [12] Or, as another *Zenrin* verse puts it:

> A long thing is the long Body of Buddha;
> A short thing is the short Body of Buddha.[j]

What is therefore to be gained from Zen is called *wu-shih* (Japanese, *buji*) or "nothing special," for as the Buddha says in the *Vajracchedika:*

> I obtained not the least thing from unexcelled, complete awakening, and for this very reason it is called "unexcelled, complete awakening." (22)

The expression *wu-shih* also has the sense of the perfectly natural and unaffected, in which there is no "fuss" or "business." The attainment of *satori* is often suggested by the old Chinese poem:

> Mount Lu in misty rain; the River Che at high tide.
> When I had not been there, no rest from the pain of longing!
> I went there and returned. . . . It was nothing special:
> Mount Lu in misty rain; the River Che at high tide.

According to the famous saying of Ch'ing-yüan:

> Before I had studied Zen for thirty years, I saw mountains as mountains, and waters as waters. When I arrived at a more intimate knowledge, I came to the point where I saw that mountains are not mountains, and waters are not waters. But now that I have got its very substance I am at rest. For it's just that I see mountains once again as mountains, and waters once again as waters.[13] [k]

The difficulty of Zen is, of course, to shift one's attention from the abstract to the concrete, from the symbolic self to one's true nature. So long as we merely talk about it, so long as we turn over ideas in our minds about "symbol" and "reality," or keep repeating, "I am not my idea of myself," this is still mere abstrac-

[12] *Ch'uan Teng Lu,* 15.
[13] *Ch'uan Teng Lu,* 22.

tion. Zen created the method (*upaya*) of "direct pointing" in order to escape from this vicious circle, in order to thrust the real immediately to our notice. When reading a difficult book it is of no help to think, "I *should* concentrate," for one thinks about concentration instead of what the book has to say. Likewise, in studying or practicing Zen it is of no help to think about Zen. To remain caught up in ideas and words about Zen is, as the old masters say, to "stink of Zen."

For this reason the masters talk about Zen as little as possible, and throw its concrete reality straight at us. This reality is the "suchness" (*tathata*) of our natural, nonverbal world. If we see this just as it is, there is nothing good, nothing bad, nothing inherently long or short, nothing subjective and nothing objective. There is no symbolic self to be forgotten, and no need for any idea of a concrete reality to be remembered.

A monk asked Chao-chou, "For what reason did the First Patriarch come from the West?" (This is a formal question, asking for the central point of Bodhidharma's teaching, i.e., of Zen itself.)

Chao-chou answered: "The cypress tree in the yard."

"Aren't you trying," said the monk, "to demonstrate it by means of an objective reality?"

"I *am* not!" retorted the master.

"For what reason, then, did the First Patriarch come from the West?"

"The cypress tree in the yard!" [14]

Notice how Chao-chou whips the monk out of his conceptualization about the answer. When T'ung-shan was asked, "What is the Buddha?" he answered, "Three pounds of flax!" Upon this Yüan-wu comments:

Various answers have been given by different masters to the question, "What is the Buddha?" . . . None, however, can excel T'ung-shan's "three pounds (*chin*) of flax" as regards its irrationality which cuts off all passage of speculation. Some comment that

[14] *Chao-chou Lu* in *Ku-tsun-hsü Yü-lu*, 3. 13.

T'ung-shan was weighing flax at the moment, hence the answer.
. . . Still others think that as the questioner was not conscious of
the fact that he himself was the Buddha, T'ung-shan answered him
in this indirect way. Such are all like corpses, for they are utterly
unable to comprehend the living truth. There are still others who
take the "three pounds of flax" as the Buddha. What wild and
fantastic remarks they make! [15]

The masters are resolute in cutting short all theorizing and
speculation about these answers. "Direct pointing" entirely fails
in its intention if it requires or stimulates any conceptual
comment.

Fa-yen asked the monk Hsüan-tzu why he had never asked him
any questions about Zen. The monk explained that he had already attained his understanding from another master. Pressed
by Fa-yen for an explanation, the monk said that when he had
asked his teacher, "What is the Buddha?" he had received the
answer, "Ping-ting T'ung-tzu comes for fire!"

"A good answer!" said Fa-yen. "But I'm sure you don't understand it."

"Ping-ting," explained the monk, "is the god of fire. For him to
be seeking for fire is like myself, seeking the Buddha. I'm the
Buddha already, and no asking is needed."

"Just as I thought!" laughed Fa-yen. "You didn't get it."

The monk was so offended that he left the monastery, but
later repented of himself and returned, humbly requesting instruction.

"You ask me," said Fa-yen.

"What is the Buddha?" inquired the monk.

"Ping-ting T'ung-tzu comes for fire!" [16]

The point of this *mondo* is perhaps best indicated by two
poems submitted by the Pure Land Buddhist Ippen Shonin to the
Zen master Hoto, translated by Suzuki from the *Sayings of Ippen*.
Ippen was one of those who studied Zen to find a *rapprochement*

[15] *Pi-yen Chi*, 12, in Suzuki (1), vol. 2, pp. 71–72.
[16] *Ch'uan Teng Lu*, 25.

between Zen and the Pure Land School, with its practice of repeating the Name of Amitabha. In Japanese, the formula is
"*Namu Amida Butsu!*" Ippen first presented this verse:

> *When the Name is uttered,*
> *Neither the Buddha nor the self*
> *There is:*
> Na-mu-a-mi-da-bu-tsu–
> *The voice alone is heard.*

Hoto, however, felt that this did not quite express the point, but
gave his approval when Ippen submitted a second verse:

> *When the Name is uttered,*
> *Neither the Buddha nor the self*
> *There is:*
> Na-mu-a-mi-da-bu-tsu,
> Na-mu-a-mi-da-bu-tsu! [17]

Po-chang had so many students that he had to open a second
monastery. To find a suitable person as its master, he called his
monks together and set a pitcher before them, saying:
"Without calling it a pitcher, tell me what it is."
The head monk said, "You couldn't call it a piece of wood."
At this the monastery cook kicked the pitcher over and walked
away. The cook was put in charge of the new monastery. [18] One
of Nan-ch'üan's lectures is worth quoting here:

> During the period (*kalpa*) before the world was manifested there
> were no names. The moment the Buddha arrives in the world there
> are names, and so we clutch hold of forms. In the great Tao there
> is absolutely nothing secular or sacred. If there are names, every-
> thing is classified in limits and bounds. Therefore the old man
> West of the River (i.e., Ma-tsu) said: "It is not mind; it is not
> Buddha; it is not a thing." [19] *l*

This, of course, reflects the doctrine of the *Tao Te Ching* that

---

[17] Suzuki (1), vol. 2, p. 263.
[18] *Wu-men kuan*, 40. However, as Wu-men comments, he fell right into
Po-chang's trap, because he exchanged an easy job for a difficult one!
[19] *Nan-ch'üan Yü-lu* in *Ku-tsun-hsü Yü-lu*, 3. 12.

The nameless is the origin of heaven and earth;
Naming is the mother of the ten thousand things. (1)

But Lao-tzu's "nameless" and Nan-ch'üan's "*kalpa* of the void" before the manifestation of the world are not prior to the conventional world of things in time. They are the "suchness" of the world just as it is now, and to which the Zen masters are directly pointing. Po-chang's cook was living wide awake in that world, and answered the master's problem in its concrete and nameless terms.

A monk asked Ts'ui-wei, "For what reason did the First Patriarch come from the West?"

Ts'ui-wei answered, "Pass me that chin-rest."

As soon as the monk passed it, Ts'ui-wei hit him with it.[20]

Another master was having tea with two of his students when he suddenly tossed his fan to one of them, saying, "What's this?" The student opened it and fanned himself. "Not bad," was his comment. "Now you," he went on, passing it to the other student, who at once closed the fan and scratched his neck with it. This done, he opened it again, placed a piece of cake on it, and offered it to the master. This was considered even better, for when there are no names the world is no longer "classified in limits and bounds."

There is, no doubt, some parallel between these demonstrations and the viewpoint of Korzybskian semantics. There is the same stress on the importance of avoiding confusion between words and signs, on the one hand, and the infinitely variable "unspeakable" world, on the other. Class demonstrations of semantic principles often resemble types of *mondo*. Professor Irving Lee, of Northwestern University, used to hold up a matchbox before his class, asking "What's this?" The students would usually drop squarely into the trap and say, "A matchbox!" At this Professor Lee would say, "No, no! It's *this*–" throwing the matchbox at the class, and adding, "*Matchbox* is a noise. Is *this* a noise?"

However, it would seem that Korzybski still thought of the

[20] *Pi-yen Lu*, 20. The chin-rest is the *ch'an-pan*, a board for supporting the chin during long meditation.

"unspeakable" world as a multiplicity of infinitely differentiated events. For Zen, the world of "suchness" is neither one nor many, neither uniform nor differentiated. A Zen master might hold up his hand–to someone insisting that there are real differences in the world–and say, "Without saying a word, point to the difference between my fingers." At once it is clear that "sameness" and "difference" are abstractions. The same would have to be said of all categorizations of the concrete world–even "concrete" itself –for such terms as "physical," "material," "objective," "real," and "existential" are extremely abstract symbols. Indeed, the more one tries to define them, the more meaningless they turn out to be.

The world of "suchness" is void and empty because it teases the mind out of thought, dumfounding the chatter of definition so that there is nothing left to be said. Yet it is obvious that we are not confronted with literal nothingness. It is true that, when pressed, every attempt to catch hold of our world leaves us empty-handed. Furthermore, when we try to be sure at least of ourselves, the knowing, catching subjects, we disappear. We cannot find any self apart from the mind, and we cannot find any mind apart from those very experiences which the mind– now vanished–was trying to grasp. In R. H. Blyth's arresting metaphor, when we were just about to swat the fly, the fly flew up and sat on the swatter. In terms of immediate perception, when we look for things there is nothing but mind, and when we look for mind there is nothing but things. For a moment we are paralyzed, because it seems that we have no basis for action, no ground under foot from which to take a jump. But this is the way it always was, and in the next moment we find ourselves as free to act, speak, and think as ever, yet in a strange and miraculous new world from which "self" and "other," "mind" and "things" have vanished. In the words of Te-shan:

> Only when you have no thing in your mind and no mind in things are you vacant and spiritual, empty and marvelous.[21] *m*

[21] *Lien-teng Hui-yao*, 22. This is Ruth Sasaki's elegant translation in Dumoulin and Sasaki (1), p. 48, where she points out that in this context "spiritual" connotes a state beyond expression in words.

The marvel can only be described as the peculiar sensation of freedom in action which arises when the world is no longer felt to be some sort of obstacle standing over against one. This is not freedom in the crude sense of "kicking over the traces" and behaving in wild caprice. It is the discovery of freedom in the most ordinary tasks, for when the sense of subjective isolation vanishes, the world is no longer felt as an intractable object.

Yün-men once said, "Our school lets you go any way you like. It kills and it brings to life—either way."

A monk then asked, "How does it kill?"

The master replied, "Winter goes and spring comes."

"How," asked the monk, "is it when winter goes and spring comes?"

The master said, "Shouldering a staff you wander this way and that, East or West, South or North, knocking at the wild stumps as you please." [22] *

The passing of the seasons is not passively suffered, but "happens" as freely as one wanders in the fields, knocking at old stumps with a stick. In the context of Christianity this might be interpreted as feeling that one has become omnipotent, that one is God, directing everything that happens. However, it must be remembered that in Taoist and Buddhist thought there is no conception of a God who deliberately and consciously governs the universe. Lao-tzu said of the Tao:

> *To its accomplishments it lays no claim.*
> *It loves and nourishes all things,*
> *but does not lord it over them.* (34)
> *The Tao, without doing anything* (wu-wei),
> *leaves nothing undone.* (37)

To use the imagery of a Tibetan poem, every action, every event comes of itself from the Void "as from the surface of a clear lake there leaps suddenly a fish." When this is seen to be as true of

[22] *Yün-men Kuang-lu*, in *Ku-tsun-hsü Yü-lu*, 4. 16.

the deliberate and the routine as of the surprising and the unforeseen, one can agree with the Zen poet P'ang-yun:

> *Miraculous power and marvelous activity—*
> *Drawing water and hewing wood!* [23] °

[23] *Ch'uan Teng Lu*, 8.

Two

"Sitting Quietly, Doing Nothing"

In both life and art the cultures of the Far East appreciate nothing more highly than spontaneity or naturalness (*tzu-jan*). This is the unmistakable tone of sincerity marking the action which is not studied and contrived. For a man rings like a cracked bell when he thinks and acts with a split mind—one part standing aside to interfere with the other, to control, to condemn, or to admire. But the mind, or the true nature, of man cannot actually be split. According to a *Zenrin* poem, it is

> *Like a sword that cuts, but cannot cut itself;*
> *Like an eye that sees, but cannot see itself.*[a]

The illusion of the split comes from the mind's attempt to be both itself and its idea of itself, from a fatal confusion of fact with symbol. To make an end of the illusion, the mind must stop trying to act upon itself, upon its stream of experiences, from the standpoint of the idea of itself which we call the ego. This is expressed in another *Zenrin* poem as

> *Sitting quietly, doing nothing,*
> *Spring comes, and the grass grows by itself.*[b]

This "by itself" is the mind's and the world's natural way of action, as when the eyes see by themselves, and the ears hear by themselves, and the mouth opens by itself without having to be forced apart by the fingers. As the *Zenrin* says again:

> *The blue mountains are of themselves blue mountains;*
> *The white clouds are of themselves white clouds.*[c]

In its stress upon naturalness, Zen is obviously the inheritor of Taoism, and its view of spontaneous action as "marvelous activity" (*miao-yung* [d]) is precisely what the Taoists meant by the word *te*–"virtue" with an overtone of magical power. But neither in Taoism nor in Zen does it have anything to do with magic in the merely sensational sense of performing superhuman "miracles." The "magical" or "marvelous" quality of spontaneous action is, on the contrary, that it is perfectly human, and yet shows no sign of being contrived.

Such a quality is peculiarly subtle (another meaning of *miao*), and extremely hard to put into words. The story is told of a Zen monk who wept upon hearing of the death of a close relative. When one of his fellow students objected that it was most unseemly for a monk to show such personal attachment he replied, "Don't be stupid! I'm weeping because I want to weep." The great Hakuin was deeply disturbed in his early study of Zen when he came across the story of the master Yen-t'ou, who was said to have screamed at the top of his voice when murdered by a robber.[1] Yet this doubt was dissolved at the moment of his *satori*, and in Zen circles his own death is felt to have been especially admirable for its display of human emotion. On the other hand, the abbot Kwaisen and his monks allowed themselves to be burned alive by the soldiers of Oda Nobunaga, sitting calmly in the posture of meditation. Such contradictory "naturalness" seems most mysterious, but perhaps the clue lies in the saying of Yün-men: "In walking, just walk. In sitting, just sit. Above all, don't wobble." For the essential quality of naturalness is the sincerity of the undivided mind which does not dither between alternatives. So when Yen-t'ou screamed, it was such a scream that it was heard for miles around.

But it would be quite wrong to suppose that this natural sincerity comes about by observing such a platitude as "Whatsoever thy hand findeth to do, do it with all thy might." When Yen-t'ou screamed, he was not screaming *in order* to be natural, nor did he first make up his mind to scream and then implement the decision with the full energy of his will. There is a total con-

[1] *Ch'uan Teng Lu*, 26.

tradition in planned naturalness and intentional sincerity. This is to overlay, not to discover, the "original mind." Thus to try to be natural is an affectation. To try not to try to be natural is also an affectation. As a *Zenrin* poem says:

> *You cannot get it by taking thought;*
> *You cannot seek it by not taking thought.*[e]

But this absurdly complex and frustrating predicament arises from a simple and elementary mistake in the use of the mind. When this is understood, there is no paradox and no difficulty. Obviously, the mistake arises in the attempt to split the mind against itself, but to understand this clearly we have to enter more deeply into the "cybernetics" of the mind, the basic pattern of its self-correcting action.

It is, of course, part of the very genius of the human mind that it can, as it were, stand aside from life and reflect upon it, that it can be aware of its own existence, and that it can criticize its own processes. For the mind has something resembling a "feed-back" system. This is a term used in communications engineering for one of the basic principles of "automation," of enabling machines to control themselves. Feed-back enables a machine to be informed of the effects of its own action in such a way as to be able to correct its action. Perhaps the most familiar example is the electrical thermostat which regulates the heating of a house. By setting an upper and a lower limit of desired temperature, a thermometer is so connected that it will switch the furnace on when the lower limit is reached, and off when the upper limit is reached. The temperature of the house is thus kept within the desired limits. The thermostat provides the furnace with a kind of sensitive organ—an extremely rudimentary analogy of human self-consciousness.[2]

[2] I do not wish to press the analogy between the human mind and servo-mechanisms to the point of saying that the mind-body is "nothing but" an extremely complicated mechanical automaton. I only want to go so far as to show that feed-back involves some problems which are similar to the problems of self-consciousness and self-control in man. Otherwise,

The proper adjustment of a feed-back system is always a complex mechanical problem. For the original machine, say, the furnace, is adjusted by the feed-back system, but this system in turn needs adjustment. Therefore to make a mechanical system more and more automatic will require the use of a series of feed-back systems–a second to correct the first, a third to correct the second, and so on. But there are obvious limits to such a series, for beyond a certain point the mechanism will be "frustrated" by its own complexity. For example, it might take so long for the information to pass through the series of control systems that it would arrive at the original machine too late to be useful. Similarly, when human beings think too carefully and minutely about an action to be taken, they cannot make up their minds in time to act. In other words, one cannot correct one's means of self-correction indefinitely. There must soon be a source of information at the end of the line which is the final authority. Failure to trust its authority will make it impossible to act, and the system will be paralyzed.

The system can be paralyzed in yet another way. Every feed-back system needs a margin of "lag" or error. If we try to make a thermostat absolutely accurate–that is, if we bring the upper and lower limits of temperature very close together in an attempt to hold the temperature at a constant 70 degrees–the whole system will break down. For to the extent that the upper and lower limits coincide, the signals for switching off and switching on will coincide! If 70 degrees is both the lower and upper limit the "go" sign will also be the "stop" sign; "yes" will imply "no" and "no" will imply "yes." Whereupon the mechanism will start "trembling," going on and off, on and off, until it shakes itself to pieces. The system is too sensitive and shows symptoms which are startlingly like human anxiety. For when a

mechanism and organism seem to me to be different in principle–that is, in their actual functioning–since the one is made and the other grown. The fact that one can translate some organic processes into mechanical terms no more implies that organism is mechanism than the translation of commerce into arithmetical terms implies that commerce *is* arithmetic.

human being is so self-conscious, so self-controlled that he cannot let go of himself, he dithers or wobbles between opposites. This is precisely what is meant in Zen by going round and round on "the wheel of birth-and-death," for the Buddhist *samsara* is the prototype of all vicious circles.[3]

Now human life consists primarily and originally in action–in living in the concrete world of "suchness." But we have the power to control action by reflection, that is, by thinking, by comparing the actual world with memories or "reflections." Memories are organized in terms of more or less abstract images–words, signs, simplified shapes, and other symbols which can be reviewed very rapidly one after another. From such memories, reflections, and symbols the mind constructs its idea of itself. This corresponds to the thermostat–the source of information about its own past action by which the system corrects itself. The mind-body must, of course, trust that information in order to act, for paralysis will soon result from trying to remember whether we have remembered everything accurately.

But to keep up the supply of information in the memory, the mind-body must continue to act "on its own." It must not cling too closely to its own record. There must be a "lag" or distance between the source of information and the source of action. This does *not* mean that the source of action must hesitate before it accepts the information. It means that it must not identify itself with the source of information. We saw that when the furnace responds too closely to the thermostat, it cannot go ahead without also trying to stop, or stop without also trying to go ahead. This is just what happens to the human being, to the mind, when the desire for certainty and security prompts identification between the mind and its own image of itself. It cannot let go of itself. It feels that it should not do what it is doing, and that it should do what it is not doing. It feels that it should not be what

[3] See the fascinating discussion of analogies between mechanical and logical contradictions and the psychoneuroses by Gregory Bateson in Reusch and Bateson, *Communication: the Social Matrix of Psychiatry*, esp. Chap. 8. (Norton; New York, 1950.)

it is, and be what it isn't. Furthermore, the effort to remain always "good" or "happy" is like trying to hold the thermostat to a constant 70 degrees by making the lower limit the same as the upper.

The identification of the mind with its own image is, therefore, paralyzing because the image is fixed–it is past and finished. But it is a fixed image of oneself in motion! To cling to it is thus to be in constant contradiction and conflict. Hence Yün-men's saying, "In walking, just walk. In sitting, just sit. Above all, don't wobble." In other words, the mind cannot act without giving up the impossible attempt to control itself beyond a certain point. It must let go of itself both in the sense of trusting its own memory and reflection, and in the sense of acting spontaneously, on its own into the unknown.

This is why Zen often seems to take the side of action as against reflection, and why it describes itself as "no-mind" (*wu-hsin*) or "no-thought" (*wu-nien*), and why the masters demonstrate Zen by giving instantaneous and unpremeditated answers to questions. When Yün-men was asked for the ultimate secret of Buddhism, he replied, "Dumpling!" In the words of the Japanese master Takuan:

> When a monk asks, "What is the Buddha?" the master may raise his fist; when he is asked, "What is the ultimate idea of Buddhism?" he may exclaim even before the questioner finishes his sentence, "A blossoming branch of the plum," or "The cypress-tree in the court-yard." The point is that the answering mind does not "stop" anywhere, but responds straightway without giving any thought to the felicity of an answer.[4]

This is allowing the mind to act on its own.

But reflection is also action, and Yün-men might also have said, "In acting, just act. In thinking, just think. Above all, don't wobble." In other words, if one is going to reflect, just reflect–but do not reflect about reflecting. Yet Zen would agree that reflection about reflection is also action–provided that in doing it we

[4] In Suzuki (7), p. 80.

do just that, and do not tend to drift off into the infinite regression of trying always to stand above or outside the level upon which we are acting. Thus Zen is also a liberation from the dualism of thought and action, for it thinks as it acts–with the same quality of abandon, commitment, or faith. The attitude of *wu-hsin* is by no means an anti-intellectualist exclusion of thinking. *Wu-hsin* is action on any level whatsoever, physical or psychic, without trying *at the same moment* to observe and check the action from outside. This attempt to act and think about the action simultaneously is precisely the identification of the mind with its idea of itself. It involves the same contradiction as the statement which states something about itself–"This statement is false."

The same is true of the relationship between feeling and action. For feeling blocks action, and blocks itself as a form of action, when it gets caught in this same tendency to observe or feel itself indefinitely–as when, in the midst of enjoying myself, I examine myself to see if I am getting the utmost out of the occasion. Not content with tasting the food, I am also trying to taste my tongue. Not content with feeling happy, I want to feel myself feeling happy–so as to be sure not to miss anything.

Whether trusting our memories or trusting the mind to act on its own, it comes to the same thing: ultimately we must act and think, live and die, from a source beyond all "our" knowledge and control. But this source is ourselves, and when we see that, it no longer stands over against us as a threatening object. No amount of care and hesitancy, no amount of introspection and searching of our motives, can make any ultimate difference to the fact that the mind is

Like an eye that sees, but cannot see itself.

In the end, the only alternative to a shuddering paralysis is to leap into action regardless of the consequences. Action in this spirit may be right or wrong with respect to conventional standards. But our decisions upon the conventional level must be supported by the conviction that whatever we do, and whatever "happens" to us, is ultimately "right." In other words, we must enter into it without "second thought," without the *arrière-pensée* of regret, hesitancy, doubt, or self-recrimination. Thus when Yün-men was asked, "What is the Tao?" he answered simply, "Walk on! (*ch'ü¹*)."

But to act "without second thought," without double-mindedness, is by no means a mere precept for our imitation. For we cannot realize this kind of action until it is clear beyond any shadow of doubt that it is actually impossible to do anything else. In the words of Huang-po:

> Men are afraid to forget their own minds, fearing to fall through the void with nothing on to which they can cling. They do not know that the void is not really the void but the real realm of the Dharma. . . . It cannot be looked for or sought, comprehended by wisdom or knowledge, explained in words, contacted materially (i.e., objectively) or reached by meritorious achievement. (14) [5]

Now this impossibility of "grasping the mind with the mind" is, when realized, the non-action (*wu-wei*), the "sitting quietly, doing nothing" whereby "spring comes, and the grass grows by itself." There is no necessity for the mind to try to let go of itself, or to try not to try. This introduces further artificialities. Yet, as a matter of psychological strategy, there is no need for trying to avoid artificialities. In the doctrine of the Japanese master Bankei (1622–1693) the mind which cannot grasp itself is called the "Unborn" (*fusho⁹*), the mind which does not arise or appear in the realm of symbolic knowledge.

> A layman asked, "I appreciate very much your instruction about the Unborn, but by force of habit second thoughts [*nien*] keep tending to arise, and being confused by them it is difficult to be in perfect accord with the Unborn. How am I to trust in it entirely?"
> Bankei said, "If you make an attempt to stop the second thoughts which arise, then the mind which does the stopping and the mind which is stopped become divided, and there is no occasion for

[5] In Chu Ch'an (1), p. 29.

peace of mind. So it is best for you simply to believe that originally there is no (possibility of control by) second thoughts. Yet
because of karmic affinity, through what you see and what you
hear these thoughts arise and vanish temporarily, but are without
substance." (2)

"Brushing off thoughts which arise is just like washing off blood
with blood. We remain impure because of being washed with
blood, even when the blood that was first there has gone—and if we
continue in this way the impurity never departs. This is from
ignorance of the mind's unborn, unvanishing, and unconfused nature. If we take second thought for an effective reality, we keep
going on and on around the wheel of birth-and-death. You should
realize that such thought is just a temporary mental construction,
and not try to hold or to reject it. Let it alone just as it occurs and
just as it ceases. It is like an image reflected in a mirror. The mirror
is clear and reflects anything which comes before it, and yet no
image sticks in the mirror. The Buddha mind (i.e., the real, unborn
mind) is ten thousand times more clear than a mirror, and more
inexpressibly marvelous. In its light all such thoughts vanish without trace. If you put your faith in this way of understanding, however strongly such thoughts may arise, they do no harm." (4) [6]

This is also the doctrine of Huang-po, who says again:

If it is held that there is something to be realized or attained apart
from mind, and, thereupon, mind is used to seek it, (that implies)
failure to understand that mind and the object of its search are one.
Mind cannot be used to seek something from mind for, even after
the passage of millions of kalpas, the day of success would never
come. (10) [7]

One must not forget the social context of Zen. It is primarily
a way of liberation for those who have mastered the disciplines
of social convention, of the conditioning of the individual by the
group. Zen is a medicine for the ill effects of this conditioning,
for the mental paralysis and anxiety which come from excessive
self-consciousness. It must be seen against the background of

[6] Bankei's *Daiho Shogen Kokushi Hogo.* Japanese text edited by Furata and
Suzuki. (Tokyo, 1943.) Translation read to the author by Professor
Hasegawa.
[7] In Chu Ch'an (1), p. 24.

societies regulated by the principles of Confucianism, with their heavy stress on propriety and punctilious ritual. In Japan, too, it must be seen in relation to the rigid schooling required in the training of the *samurai* caste, and the emotional strain to which the *samurai* were exposed in times of constant warfare. As a medicine for these conditions, it does not seek to overthrow the conventions themselves, but, on the contrary, takes them for granted—as is easily seen in such manifestations of Zen as the *cha-no-yu* or "tea ceremony" of Japan. Therefore Zen might be a very dangerous medicine in a social context where convention is weak, or, at the other extreme, where there is a spirit of open revolt against convention ready to exploit Zen for destructive purposes.

With this in mind, we can observe the freedom and natural-ness of Zen without loss of perspective. Social conditioning fosters the identification of the mind with a fixed idea of itself as the means of self-control, and as a result man thinks of himself as "I"—the ego. Thereupon the mental center of gravity shifts from the spontaneous or original mind to the ego image. Once this has happened, the very center of our psychic life is identified with the self-controlling mechanism. It then becomes almost impossible to see how "I" can let go of "myself," for I am pre-cisely my habitual effort to hold on to myself. I find myself totally incapable of any mental action which is not intentional, affected, and insincere. Therefore anything I do to give myself up, to let go, will be a disguised form of the habitual effort to hold on. I cannot be intentionally unintentional or purposely spontaneous. As soon as it becomes important for me to be spontaneous, the intention to be so is strengthened; I cannot get rid of it, and yet it is the one thing that stands in the way of its own fulfillment. It is as if someone had given me some medicine with the warning that it will not work if I think of a monkey while taking it.

While I am remembering to forget the monkey, I am in a "double-bind" situation where "to do" is "not to do," and vice versa. "Yes" implies "no," and "go" implies "stop." At this point Zen comes to me and asks, "If you cannot help remembering the monkey, are you doing it on purpose?" In other words, do I have an intention for being intentional, a purpose for being purposive? Suddenly I realize that my very intending is spontaneous, or that my controlling self–the ego–arises from my uncontrolled or natural self. At this moment all the machinations of the ego come to nought; it is annihilated in its own trap. I see that it is actually impossible not to be spontaneous. For what I cannot help doing I am doing spontaneously, but if I am at the same time trying to control it, I interpret it as a compulsion. As a Zen master said, "Nothing is left to you at this moment but to have a good laugh."

In this moment the whole quality of consciousness is changed, and I feel myself in a new world in which, however, it is obvious that I have always been living. As soon as I recognize that my voluntary and purposeful action happens spontaneously "by itself," just like breathing, hearing, and feeling, I am no longer caught in the contradiction of trying to be spontaneous. There is no real contradiction, since "trying" is "spontaneity." Seeing this, the compulsive, blocked, and "tied-up" feeling vanishes. It is just as if I had been absorbed in a tug-of-war between my two hands, and had forgotten that both were mine. No block to spontaneity remains when the trying is seen to be needless. As we saw, the discovery that both the voluntary and involuntary aspects of the mind are alike spontaneous makes an immediate end of the fixed dualism between the mind and the world, the knower and the known. The new world in which I find myself has an extraordinary transparency or freedom from barriers, making it seem that I have somehow become the empty space in which everything is happening.

Here, then, is the point of the oft-repeated assertion that "all beings are in *nirvana* from the very beginning," that "all dualism is falsely imagined," that "the ordinary mind is the Tao" and that there is therefore no meaning in trying to get into accord with it. In the words of the *Cheng-tao Ke:*

> *Like the empty sky it has no boundaries,*
> *Yet it is right in this place, ever profound and clear.*
> *When you seek to know it, you cannot see it.*
> *You cannot take hold of it,*
> *But you cannot lose it.*
> *In not being able to get it, you get it.*
> *When you are silent, it speaks;*
> *When you speak, it is silent.*
> *The great gate is wide open to bestow alms,*
> *And no crowd is blocking the way.* (34)ʰ

It was through seeing this that, in the moment of his *satori*, Hakuin cried out, "How wondrous! How wondrous! There is no birth-and-death from which one has to escape, nor is there any supreme knowledge after which one has to strive!"⁸ Or in the words of Hsiang-yen:

> *At one stroke I forgot all my knowledge!*
> *There's no use for artificial discipline,*
> *For, move as I will, I manifest the ancient Way.*⁹ ᶦ

Paradoxically, nothing is more artificial than the notion of artificiality. Try as one may, it is as impossible to go against the spontaneous Tao as to live in some other time than now, or some other place than here. When a monk asked Bankei what he thought of disciplining oneself to attain *satori*, the master said, "*Satori* stands in contrast to confusion. Since each person is the substance of Buddha, (in reality) there is not one point of confusion. What, then, is one going to achieve by *satori?*"¹⁰

Seeing, then, that there is no possibility of departing from the Tao, one is like Hsüan-chüeh's "easygoing" man who

---

⁸ *O"rategama*, in Suzuki (1), vol. 1, p. 239.
⁹ *Wu-teng Hui-yüan*, 9.
¹⁰ *Bankei Kokushi Seppo*. Read to the author by Professor Hasegawa.

Neither avoids false thoughts nor seeks the true,
For ignorance is in reality the Buddha nature,
And this illusory, changeful, empty body is the Dharmakaya.[11]

One stops trying to be spontaneous by seeing that it is unnecessary to try, and then and there it can happen. The Zen masters often bring out this state by the device of evading a question and then, as the questioner turns to go, calling him suddenly by name. As he naturally replies, "Yes?" the master exclaims, "There it is!"

To the Western reader it may seem that all this is a kind of pantheism, an attempt to wipe out conflicts by asserting that "everything is God." But from the standpoint of Zen this is a long way short of true naturalness since it involves the use of the artificial concept–"everything is God" or "everything is the Tao." Zen annihilates this concept by showing that it is as unnecessary as every other. One does not realize the spontaneous life by depending on the repetition of thoughts or affirmations. One realizes it by seeing that no such devices are necessary. Zen describes all means and methods for realizing the Tao as "legs on a snake"–utterly irrelevant attachments.

To the logician it will of course seem that the point at which we have arrived is pure nonsense–as, in a way, it is. From the Buddhist point of view, reality itself has no meaning since it is not a sign, pointing to something beyond itself. To arrive at reality–at "suchness"–is to go beyond *karma*, beyond consequential action, and to enter a life which is completely aimless. Yet to Zen and Taoism alike this is the very life of the universe, which is complete at every moment and does not need to justify itself by aiming at something beyond. In the words of a *Zenrin* poem:

If you don't believe, just look at September, look at October!
The yellow leaves falling, falling, to fill both mountain and river.[j]

To see this is to be like the two friends of whom another *Zenrin* poem says:

[11] *Cheng-tao Ke, 1.*

Meeting, they laugh and laugh—
The forest grove, the many fallen leaves! ᵏ

To the Taoist mentality, the aimless, empty life does not suggest anything depressing. On the contrary, it suggests the freedom of clouds and mountain streams, wandering nowhere, of flowers in impenetrable canyons, beautiful for no one to see, and of the ocean surf forever washing the sand, to no end.

Furthermore, the Zen experience is more of a conclusion than a premise. It is never to be used as the first step in a line of ethical or metaphysical reasoning, since conclusions draw to it rather than from it. Like the Beatific Vision of Christianity, it is a "which than which there is no whicher"–the true end of man–not a thing to be used for some other end. Philosophers do not easily recognize that there is a point where thinking–like boiling an egg–must come to a stop. To try to formulate the Zen experience as a proposition–"everything is the Tao"–and then to analyze it and draw conclusions from it is to miss it completely. Like the Crucifixion, it is "to the Jews [the moralists] a stumblingblock and to the Greeks [the logicians] foolishness." To say that "everything is the Tao" almost gets the point, but just at the moment of getting it, the words crumble into nonsense. For we are here at a limit at which words break down because they always imply a meaning beyond themselves–and here there is no meaning beyond.

Zen does not make the mistake of using the experience "all things are of one Suchness" as the premise for an ethic of universal brotherhood. On the contrary, Yüan-wu says:

> If you are a real man, you may by all means drive off with the farmer's ox, or grab the food from a starving man.[12] ˡ

This is only to say that Zen lies beyond the ethical standpoint, whose sanctions must be found, not in reality itself, but in the mutual agreement of human beings. When we attempt to universalize or absolutize it, the ethical standpoint makes it im-

[12] Comment on *Pi-yen Lu*, 3.

possible to exist, for we cannot live for a day without destroying the life of some other creature.

If Zen is regarded as having the same function as a religion in the West, we shall naturally want to find some logical connection between its central experience and the improvement of human relations. But this is actually putting the cart before the horse. The point is rather that some such experience or way of life as this is the object of improved human relations. In the culture of the Far East the problems of human relations are the sphere of Confucianism rather than Zen, but since the Sung dynasty (959–1278) Zen has consistently fostered Confucianism and was the main source of the introduction of its principles into Japan. It saw their importance for creating the type of cultural matrix in which Zen could flourish without coming into conflict with social order, because the Confucian ethic is admittedly human and relative, not divine and absolute.

Although profoundly "inconsequential," the Zen experience has consequences in the sense that it may be applied in any direction, to any conceivable human activity, and that wherever it is so applied it lends an unmistakable quality to the work. The characteristic notes of the spontaneous life are *mo chih ch'u* [m] or "going ahead without hesitation," *wu-wei*, which may here be understood as purposelessness, and *wu-shih*, lack of affectation or simplicity.

While the Zen experience does not imply any specific course of action, since it has no purpose, no motivation, it turns unhesitatingly to anything that presents itself to be done. *Mo chih ch'u* is the mind functioning without blocks, without "wobbling" between alternatives, and much of Zen training consists in confronting the student with dilemmas which he is expected to handle without stopping to deliberate and "choose." The response to the situation must follow with the immediacy of sound issuing from the hands when they are clapped, or sparks from a flint when struck. The student unaccustomed to this type of response will at first be confused, but as he gains faith in his "original" or spontaneous mind he will not only respond with ease, but the responses themselves will acquire a startling appropriateness. This is something like the professional comedian's gift of unprepared wit which is equal to any situation.

The master may begin a conversation with the student by asking a series of very ordinary questions about trivial matters, to which the student responds with perfect spontaneity. But suddenly he will say, "When the bath-water flows down the drain, does it turn clockwise or counter-clockwise?" As the student stops at the unexpectedness of the question, and perhaps tries to remember which way it goes, the master shouts, "Don't think! Act! This way–" and whirls his hand in the air. Or, perhaps less helpfully, he may say, "So far you've answered my questions quite naturally and easily, but where's your difficulty now?"

The student, likewise, is free to challenge the master, and one can imagine that in the days when Zen training was less formal the members of Zen communities must have had enormous fun laying traps for each other. To some extent this type of relationship still exists, despite the great solemnity of the *sanzen* interview in which the *koan* is given and answered. The late Kozuki Roshi was entertaining two American monks at tea when he casually asked, "And what do you gentlemen know about Zen?" One of the monks flung his closed fan straight at the master's face. All in the same instant the master inclined his head slightly to one side, the fan shot straight through the paper *shoji* behind him, and he burst into a ripple of laughter.

Suzuki has translated a long letter from the Zen master Takuan on the relationship of Zen to the art of fencing, and this is certainly the best literary source of what Zen means by *mo chih ch'u*, by "going straight ahead without stopping." [13] Both Takuan and Bankei stressed the fact that the "original" or "unborn" mind is constantly working miracles even in the most ordinary person. Even though a tree has innumerable leaves, the mind takes them

[13] Suzuki (7), pp. 73–87. Excerpts from this letter also appear in Suzuki (1), vol. 3, pp. 318–19.

in all at once without being "stopped" by any one of them. Explaining this to a visiting monk, Bankei said, "To prove that your mind is the Buddha mind, notice how all that I say here goes into you without missing a single thing, even though I don't try to push it into you." [14] When heckled by an aggressive Nichiren monk who kept insisting that he couldn't understand a word, Bankei asked him to come closer. The monk stepped forward. "Closer still," said Bankei. The monk came forward again. "How well," said Bankei, "you understand me!" [15] In other words, our natural organism performs the most marvelously complex activities without the least hesitation or deliberation. Conscious thought is itself founded upon its whole system of spontaneous functioning, for which reason there is really no alternative to trusting oneself completely to its working. Oneself *is* its working.

Zen is not merely a cult of impulsive action. The point of *mo chih ch'u* is not to eliminate reflective thought but to eliminate "blocking" in both action and thought, so that the response of the mind is always like a ball in a mountain stream—"one thought after another without hesitation." There is something similar to this in the psychoanalytic practice of free association, employed as a technique to get rid of obstacles to the free flow of thought from the "unconscious." For there is a tendency to confuse "blocking"—a purely obstructive mechanism—with thinking out an answer, but the difference between the two is easily noticed in such a purely "thinking out" process as adding a column of figures. Many people find that at certain combinations of numbers, such as 8 and 5 or 7 and 6, a feeling of resistance comes up which halts the process. Because it is always annoying and disconcerting, one tends also to block at blocking, so that the state turns into the kind of wobbling dither characteristic of the snarled feed-back system. The simplest cure is to feel free to block, so that one does not block at blocking. When one feels

[14] *Bankei Kokushi Seppo.* Read to the author by Professor Hasegawa.
[15] In Suzuki (10), p. 123.

free to block, the blocking automatically eliminates itself. It is like riding a bicycle. When one starts falling to the left, one does not resist the fall (i.e., the block) by turning to the right. One turns the wheel to the left–and the balance is restored. The principle here is, of course, the same as getting out of the contradiction of "trying to be spontaneous" through accepting the "trying" as "spontaneous," through not resisting the block.

"Blocking" is perhaps the best translation of the Zen term *nien* [n] as it occurs in the phrase *wu-nien,* "no-thought" or, better, "no second thought." Takuan points out that this is the real meaning of "attachment" in Buddhism, as when it is said that a Buddha is free from worldly attachments. It does not mean that he is a "stone Buddha" with no feelings, no emotions, and no sensations of hunger or pain. It means that he does not block at anything. Thus it is typical of Zen that its style of action has the strongest feeling of commitment, of "follow-through." It enters into everything wholeheartedly and freely without having to keep an eye on itself. It does not confuse spirituality with thinking about God while one is peeling potatoes. Zen spirituality is just to peel the potatoes. In the words of Lin-chi:

> When it's time to get dressed, put on your clothes. When you must walk, then walk. When you must sit, then sit. Don't have a single thought in your mind about seeking for Buddhahood. . . . You talk about being perfectly disciplined in your six senses and in all your actions, but in my view all this is making *karma.* To seek the Buddha (nature) and to seek the Dharma is at once to make *karma* which leads to the hells. To seek (to be) Bodhisattvas is also making *karma,* and likewise studying the *sutras* and commentaries. Buddhas and Patriarchs are people without such artificialities. . . . It is said everywhere that there is a Tao which must be cultivated and a Dharma which must be realized. What Dharma do you say must be realized, and what Tao cultivated? What do you lack in the way you are functioning right now? What will you add to where you are? [16] [o]

As another *Zenrin* poem says:

[16] *Lin-chi Lu* in *Ku-tsun-hsü Yü-lu,* 1. 4. 6, 11–12, 12.

There's nothing equal to wearing clothes and eating food.
Outside this there are neither Buddhas nor Patriarchs.ᵖ

This is the quality of *wu-shih,* of naturalness without any
contrivances or means for being natural, such as thoughts of
Zen, of the Tao, or of the Buddha. One does not exclude such
thoughts; they simply fall away when seen to be unnecessary.
"He does not linger where the Buddha is, and where there is no
Buddha he passes right on." [17]
For as the *Zenrin* says again:

To be conscious of the original mind, the original nature—
Just this is the great disease of Zen! q

As "the fish swims in the water but is unmindful of the water, the
bird flies in the wind but knows not of the wind," so the true life
of Zen has no need to "raise waves when no wind is blowing," to
drag in religion or spirituality as something over and above life
itself. This is why the sage Fa-yung received no more offerings
of flowers from the birds after he had had his interview with the
Fourth Patriarch, for his holiness no longer "stood out like a sore
thumb." Of such a man the *Zenrin* says:

Entering the forest he moves not the grass;
Entering the water he makes not a ripple.ʳ

No one notices him because he does not notice himself.

It is often said that to be clinging to oneself is like having a
thorn in the skin, and that Buddhism is a second thorn to extract
the first. When it is out, both thorns are thrown away. But in the
moment when Buddhism, when philosophy or religion, becomes
another way of clinging to oneself through seeking a spiritual
security, the two thorns become one—and how is it to be taken
out? This, as Bankei said, is "wiping off blood with blood."
Therefore in Zen there is neither self nor Buddha to which one
can cling, no good to gain and no evil to be avoided, no thoughts

[17] *Shih Niu T'u,* 8.

to be eradicated and no mind to be purified, no body to perish and no soul to be saved. At one blow this entire framework of abstractions is shattered to fragments. As the *Zenrin* says:

> *To save life it must be destroyed.*
> *When utterly destroyed, one dwells for the first time in peace.*
>
> *One word settles heaven and earth;*
> *One sword levels the whole world.*

Of this "one sword" Lin-chi said:

> If a man cultivates the Tao, the Tao will not work—on all sides evil conditions will head up competitively. But when the sword of wisdom [*prajna*] comes out there's not one thing left.[18]

The "sword of *prajna*" which cuts away abstraction is that "direct pointing" whereby Zen avoids the entanglements of religiosity and goes straight to the heart. Thus when the Governor of Lang asked Yao-shan, "What is the Tao?" the master pointed upwards to the sky and downwards to a water jug beside him. Asked for an explanation, he replied: "A cloud in the sky and water in the jug."

[18] In *Ku-tsun-hsü Yü-lu,* 1. 4. 13.

Three

ZA-ZEN AND THE KOAN

There is a saying in Zen that "original realization is marvelous practice" (Japanese, *honsho myoshu* ᵃ). The meaning is that no distinction is to be made between the realization of awakening (*satori*) and the cultivation of Zen in meditation and action. Whereas it might be supposed that the practice of Zen is a means to the end of awakening, this is not so. For the practice of Zen is not the true practice so long as it has an end in view, and when it has no end in view it is awakening–the aimless, self-sufficient life of the "eternal now." To practice with an end in view is to have one eye on the practice and the other on the end, which is lack of concentration, lack of sincerity. To put it in another way: one does not practice Zen to become a Buddha; one practices it because one is a Buddha from the beginning–and this "original realization" is the starting point of the Zen life. Original realization is the "body" (*t'i* ᵇ) and the marvelous practice the "use" (*yung* ᶜ), and the two correspond respectively to *prajna*, wisdom, and *karuna*, the compassionate activity of the awakened Bodhisattva in the world of birth-and-death.

In the two preceding chapters we discussed the original realization. In this and the one that follows we turn to the practice or activity which flows from it–firstly, to the life of meditation and, secondly, to the life of everyday work and recreation. We have seen that–whatever may have been the practice of the T'ang masters–the modern Zen communities, both Soto and Rinzai, attach the highest importance to meditation or "sitting Zen" (*za-zen*). It may seem both strange and unreasonable that strong and intelligent men should simply sit still for hours on end. The Western mentality feels that such things are not only unnatural but a great waste of valuable time, however useful as

154

a discipline for inculcating patience and fortitude. Although the West has its own contemplative tradition in the Catholic Church, the life of "sitting and looking" has lost its appeal, for no religion is valued which does not "improve the world," and it is hard to see how the world can be improved by keeping still. Yet it should be obvious that action without wisdom, without clear awareness of the world as it really is, can never improve anything. Furthermore, as muddy water is best cleared by leaving it alone, it could be argued that those who sit quietly and do nothing are making one of the best possible contributions to a world in turmoil.

There is, indeed, nothing unnatural in long periods of quiet sitting. Cats do it; even dogs and other more nervous animals do it. So-called primitive peoples do it–American Indians, and peasants of almost all nations. The art is most difficult for those who have developed the sensitive intellect to such a point that they cannot help making predictions about the future, and so must be kept in a constant whirl of activity to forestall them. But it would seem that to be incapable of sitting and watching with the mind completely at rest is to be incapable of experiencing the world in which we live to the full. For one does not know the world simply in thinking about it and doing about it. One must first experience it more directly, and prolong the experience without jumping to conclusions.

The relevance of za-zen to Zen is obvious when it is remembered that Zen is seeing reality directly, in its "suchness." To see the world as it is concretely, undivided by categories and abstractions, one must certainly look at it with a mind which is not thinking–which is to say, forming symbols–about it. Za-zen is not, therefore, sitting with a blank mind which excludes all the impressions of the inner and outer senses. It is not "concentration" in the usual sense of restricting the attention to a single sense object, such as a point of light or the tip of one's nose. It is simply a quiet awareness, without comment, of whatever happens to be here and now. This awareness is attended by the most vivid sensation of "nondifference" between oneself and the external world, between the mind and its contents–the various sounds, sights, and other impressions of the surrounding environment. Naturally, this sensation does not arise by trying to acquire it; it just comes by itself when one is sitting and watching without any purpose in mind–even the purpose of getting rid of purpose.

In the *sodo* or *zendo*, monks' hall or meditation hall, of a Zen community there is, of course, nothing particularly distracting in the external surroundings. There is a long room with wide platforms down either side where the monks both sleep and meditate. The platforms are covered with *tatami*, thick floor-mats of straw, and the monks sit in two rows facing one another across the room. The silence which prevails is deepened rather than broken by occasional sounds that float up from a near-by village, by the intermittent ringing of soft-toned bells from other parts of the monastery, and by the chatter of birds in the trees. Other than this there is only the feel of the cold, clear mountain air and the "woody" smell of a special kind of incense.

Much importance is attached to the physical posture of *za-zen*. The monks sit on firmly padded cushions with legs crossed and feet soles-upward upon the thighs. The hands rest upon the lap, the left over the right, with palms upward and thumbs touching one another. The body is held erect, though not stiffly, and the eyes are left open so that their gaze falls upon the floor a few feet ahead. The breathing is regulated so as to be slow without strain, with the stress upon the out-breath, and its impulse from the belly rather than the chest. This has the effect of shifting the body's center of gravity to the abdomen so that the whole posture has a sense of firmness, of being part of the ground upon which one is sitting. The slow, easy breathing from the belly works upon the consciousness like bellows, and gives it a still, bright clarity. The beginner is advised to accustom himself to the stillness by doing nothing more than counting his breaths from one to ten, over and over again, until the sensation of sitting without comment becomes effortless and natural.

While the monks are thus seated, two attendants walk slowly back and forth along the floor between the platforms, each carrying a *keisaku* or "warning" stick, round at one end and flattened at the other–a symbol of the Bodhisattva Manjusri's sword of *prajna*. As soon as they see a monk going to sleep, or sitting in an incorrect posture, they stop before him, bow ceremoniously, and beat him on the shoulders. It is said that this is not "punishment" but an "invigorating massage" to take the stiffness out of the shoulder muscles and bring the mind back to a state of alertness. However, monks with whom I have discussed this practice seem to have the same wryly humorous attitude about it which one associates with the usual corporal disciplines of boys' boarding schools. Furthermore, the *sodo* regulations say, "At the time of morning service, the dozing ones are to be severely dealt with the *keisaku*." [1]

At intervals, the sitting posture is interrupted, and the monks fall into ranks for a swift march around the floor between the platforms to keep themselves from sluggishness. The periods of za-zen are also interrupted for work in the monastery grounds, cleaning the premises, services in the main shrine or "Buddha hall," and other duties–as well as for meals and short hours of sleep. At certain times of year za-zen is kept up almost continuously from 3:30 a.m. until 10 p.m., and these long periods are called *sesshin*, or "collecting the mind." Every aspect of the monks' lives is conducted according to a precise, though not ostentatious, ritual which gives the atmosphere of the *sodo* a slightly military air. The rituals are signaled and accompanied by about a dozen different kinds of bells, clappers, and wooden gongs, struck in various rhythms to announce the times for za-zen, meals, services, lectures, or *sanzen* interviews with the master.

[1] In Suzuki (5), p. 99. The regulations also say, "When submitting to the *keisaku*, courteously fold your hands and bow; do not permit any egoistic thoughts to assert themselves and cherish anger." The point seems to be that the *keisaku* has two uses–one for shoulder massage and another, however politely worded, for punishment. It is of interest that Bankei abolished this practice in his own community, on the ground that a man is no less a Buddha when asleep than when awake.

The ritualistic or ceremonious style is so characteristic of Zen that it may need some explanation in a culture which has come to associate it with affectation or superstition. In Buddhism the four principal activities of man–walking, standing, sitting, and lying–are called the four "dignities," since they are the postures assumed by the Buddha nature in its human (*nirmanakaya*) body. The ritualistic style of conducting one's everyday activities is therefore a celebration of the fact that "the ordinary man is a Buddha," and is, furthermore, a style that comes almost naturally to a person who is doing everything with total presence of mind. Thus if in something so simple and trivial as lighting a cigarette one is fully aware, seeing the flame, the curling smoke, and the regulation of the breath as the most important things in the universe, it will seem to an observer that the action has a ritualistic style.

This attitude of "acting as a Buddha" is particularly stressed in the Soto School, where both *za-zen* and the round of daily activities are not at all seen as means to an end but as the actual realization of Buddhahood. As Dogen says in the *Shobogenzo:*

> Without looking forward to tomorrow every moment, you must think only of this day and this hour. Because tomorrow is difficult and unfixed and difficult to know, you must think of following the Buddhist way while you live today. . . . You must concentrate on Zen practice without wasting time, thinking that there is only this day and this hour. After that it becomes truly easy. You must forget about the good and bad of your nature, the strength or weakness of your power.[2]

In *za-zen* there must be no thought either of aiming at *satori* or of avoiding birth-and-death, no striving for anything in future time.

> If life comes, this is life. If death comes, this is death. There is no reason for your being under their control. Don't put any hope in them. This life and death are the life of the Buddha. If you try to throw them away in denial, you lose the life of the Buddha.[3]

[2] *Zuimonki* chapter. In Masunaga (1), p. 42.
[3] *Shoji* chapter. *Ibid.*, p. 44.

The "three worlds" of past, present, and future are not, as is commonly supposed, stretched out to inaccessible distances.

> The so-called past is the top of the heart; the present is the top of the fist; and the future is the back of the brain.[4]

All time is here in this body, which is the body of Buddha. The past exists in its memory and the future in its anticipation, and both of these are now, for when the world is inspected directly and clearly past and future times are nowhere to be found.

This is also the teaching of Bankei:

> You are primarily Buddhas; you are not going to be Buddhas for the first time. There is not an iota of a thing to be called error in your inborn mind. . . . If you have the least desire to be better than you actually are, if you hurry up to the slightest degree in search of something, you are already going against the Unborn.[5]

Such a view of Zen practice is therefore somewhat difficult to reconcile with the discipline which now prevails in the Rinzai School, and which consists in "passing" a graduated series of approximately fifty koan problems. Many of the Rinzai masters are most emphatic about the necessity of arousing a most intense spirit of seeking—a compelling sense of "doubt" whereby it becomes almost impossible to forget the koan one is trying to solve. Naturally, this leads to a good deal of comparison between the degrees of attainment of various individuals, and a very definite and formal recognition is attached to final "graduation" from the process.

Since the formal details of the koan discipline are one of the few actual secrets remaining in the Buddhist world, it is difficult to appraise it fairly if one has not undergone the training. On the other hand, if one has undergone it one is obliged not to talk about it—save in vague generalities. The Rinzai School has always forbidden the publication of formally acceptable answers to the various koan because the whole point of the discipline is to dis-

[4] *Kenbutsu* chapter. *Ibid.*, p. 45.
[5] In Suzuki (10), pp. 177–78.

cover them for oneself, by intuition. To know the answers without having so discovered them would be like studying the map without taking the journey. Lacking the actual shock of recognition, the bare answers seem flat and disappointing, and obviously no competent master would be deceived by anyone who gave them without genuine feeling.

There is no reason, however, why the process should actually involve all the silliness about "grades of attainment," about who has "passed" and who has not, or about who is or is not a "genuine" Buddha by these formal standards. All well-established religious institutions are beset by this kind of nonsense, and they generally boil down to a kind of aestheticism, an excessive passion for the cultivation of a special "style" whose refinements distinguish the sheep from the goats. By such standards the liturgical aesthete can distinguish Roman from Anglican Catholic priests, confusing the mannerisms of traditional atmosphere with the supernatural marks of true or false participation in the apostolic succession. Sometimes, however, the cultivation of a traditional style may be rather admirable, as when a school of craftsmen or artists hands down from generation to generation certain trade secrets or technical refinements whereby objects of peculiar beauty are manufactured. Even so, this very easily becomes a rather affected and self-conscious discipline, and at that moment all its "Zen" is lost.

The *koan* system as it exists today is largely the work of Hakuin (1685–1768), a formidable and immensely versatile master, who gave it a systematic organization so that the complete course of Zen study in the Rinzai School is divided into six stages. There are, first, five groups of *koan* [d]:

1. *Hosshin*, or *Dharmakaya koan*, whereby one "enters into the frontier gate of Zen."

2. *Kikan*, or "cunning barrier" *koan*, having to do with the active expression of the state realized in the first group.

3. *Gonsen*, or "investigation of words" *koan*, presumably having to do with the expression of Zen understanding in speech.

4. *Nanto*, or "hard to penetrate" *koan.*

5. *Goi*, or "Five Ranks" *koan*, based on the five relationships of "lord" and "servant" or of "principle" (*li*) and "thing-event" (*shih*), wherein Zen is related to the Hua-yen or *Avatamsaka* philosophy.

The sixth stage is a study of the Buddhist precepts and the regulations of the monk's life (*vinaya*) in the light of Zen understanding.[6]

Normally, this course of training takes about thirty years. By no means all Zen monks complete the whole training. This is required only of those who are to receive their master's *inka* or "seal of approval" so that they themselves may become masters (*roshi*), thoroughly versed in all the "skillful means" (*upaya*) for teaching Zen to others. Like so many other things of this kind, the system is as good as one makes it, and its graduates are both tall Buddhas and short Buddhas. It should not be assumed that a person who has passed a *koan*, or even many *koan*, is necessarily a "transformed" human being whose character and way of life are radically different from what they were before. Nor should it be assumed that *satori* is a single, sudden leap from the common consciousness to "complete, unexcelled awakening" (*anuttara samyak sambodhi*). *Satori* really designates the sudden and intuitive way of seeing into anything, whether it be remembering a forgotten name or seeing into the deepest principles of Buddhism. One seeks and seeks, but cannot find. One then gives up, and the answer comes by itself. Thus there may be many occasions of *satori* in the course of training, great *satori* and little *satori*, and the solution of many of the *koan* depends upon nothing more sensational than a kind of "knack" for understanding the Zen style of handling Buddhist principles.

Western ideas of Buddhist attainments are all too often distorted by the "mysterious East" approach, and by the sensational fantasies so widely circulated in theosophical writings during the

[6] This outline is based on information given in a conference at the American Academy of Asian Studies by Ruth Sasaki.

decades just before and after the turn of the century. Such fantasies were based not upon a first-hand study of Buddhism but on literal readings of mythological passages in the *sutras*, where the Buddhas and Bodhisattvas are embellished with innumerable miraculous and superhuman attributes. Thus there must be no confusion between Zen masters and theosophical "mahatmas"– the glamorous "Masters of Wisdom" who live in the mountain fastnesses of Tibet and practice the arts of occultism. Zen masters are quite human. They get sick and die; they know joy and sorrow; they have bad tempers or other little "weaknesses" of character just like anyone else, and they are not above falling in love and entering into a fully human relationship with the opposite sex. The perfection of Zen is to be perfectly and simply human. The difference of the adept in Zen from the ordinary run of men is that the latter are, in one way or another, at odds with their own humanity, and are attempting to be angels or demons.[7] A *doka* poem by Ikkyu says:

> We eat, excrete, sleep, and get up;
> This is our world.
> All we have to do after that–
> Is to die.[8]

Koan training involves typically Asian concepts of the relation between master and pupil which are quite unlike ours. For in Asian cultures this is a peculiarly sacred relationship in which the master is held to become responsible for the *karma* of the

---

[7] One can hardly exaggerate the importance of the great Buddhist symbol of the *bhavachakra*, the Wheel Becoming. The angels and demons occupy the highest and lowest positions, the positions of perfect happiness and perfect frustration. These positions lie on the opposite sides of a circle because they lead to each other. They represent not so much literal beings as our own ideals and terrors, since the Wheel is actually a map of the human mind. The human position lies in the middle, i.e., at the left of the Wheel, and it is only from this position that one may become a Buddha. Human birth is therefore regarded as unusually fortunate, but this is not to be confused with the physical event, for one is not actually "born into the human world" until one has fully accepted one's humanity.

[8] Translated by R. H. Blyth in "Ikkyu's Doka," *The Young East*, vol. 2, no. 7. (Tokyo, 1953.)

pupil. The pupil, in turn, is expected to accord absolute obedience and authority to the master, and to hold him in almost higher respect than his own father–and in Asian countries this is saying a great deal. To a young Zen monk the *roshi* therefore stands as a symbol of the utmost patriarchal authority, and he usually plays the role to perfection–being normally a man advanced in years, fierce and "tigerish" in aspect, and, when formally robed and seated for the *sanzen* interview, a person of supreme presence and dignity. In this role he constitutes a living symbol of everything that makes one afraid of being spontaneous, everything that prompts the most painful and awkward self-consciousness. He assumes this role as an *upaya,* a skillful device, for challenging the student to find enough "nerve" to be perfectly natural in the presence of this formidable archetype. If he can do this, he is a free man whom no one on earth can embarrass. It must be borne in mind, too, that in Japanese culture the adolescent and the youth are peculiarly susceptible to ridicule, which is freely used as a means of conforming the young to social convention.

To the normal Asian concept of the master-pupil relationship, Zen adds something of its own in the sense that it leaves the formation of the relationship entirely to the initiative of the pupil. The basic position of Zen is that it has nothing to say, nothing to teach. The truth of Buddhism is so self-evident, so obvious that it is, if anything, concealed by explaining it. Therefore the master does not "help" the student in any way, since helping would actually be hindering. On the contrary, he goes out of his way to put obstacles and barriers in the student's path. Thus Wu-men's comments on the various *koan* in the *Wu-men kuan* are intentionally misleading, the *koan* as a whole are called "wisteria vines" or "entanglements," and particular groups "cunning barriers" (*kikan*) and "hard to penetrate" (*nanto*). This is like encouraging the growth of a hedge by pruning, for obviously the basic intention is to help, but the Zen student does not really know Zen unless he finds it out for himself. The Chinese proverb

"What comes in through the gate is not family treasure" is understood in Zen to mean that what someone else tells you is not your own knowledge. *Satori*, as Wu-men explained, comes only after one has exhausted one's thinking, only when one is convinced that the mind cannot grasp itself. In the words of another of Ikkyu's *doka:*

> *A mind to search elsewhere*
> *For the Buddha,*
> *Is foolishness*
> *In the very centre of foolishness.*

For

> *My self of long ago,*
> *In nature non-existent;*
> *Nowhere to go when dead,*
> *Nothing at all.*[9]

The preliminary *hosshin* type of *koan* begins, therefore, to obstruct the student by sending him off in the direction exactly opposite to that in which he should look. Only it does it rather cleverly, so as to conceal the stratagem. Everyone knows that the Buddha nature is "within" oneself and is not to be sought outside, so that no student would be fooled by being told to seek it by going to India or by reading a certain *sutra*. On the contrary, he is told to look for it in himself! Worse still, he is encouraged to seek it with the whole energy of his being, never giving up his quest by day or night, whether actually in *za-zen* or whether working or eating. He is encouraged, in fact, to make a total fool of himself, to whirl round and round like a dog trying to catch up with its own tail.

Thus normal first *koan* are Hui-neng's "Original Face," Chao-chou's "*Wu*," or Hakuin's "One Hand." At the first *sanzen* interview, the *roshi* instructs the reluctantly accepted student to discover his "original face" or "aspect," that is, his basic nature, as it

[9] R. H. Blyth, *ibid.*, vol. 3, no. 9, p. 14, and vol. 2, no. 2, p. 7.

was before his father and mother conceived him. He is told to return when he has discovered it, and to give some proof of discovery. In the meantime he is under no circumstance to discuss the problem with others or to seek their help. Joining the other monks in the *sodo*, the *jikijitsu* or "head monk" will probably instruct him in the rudiments of *za-zen*, showing him how to sit, and perhaps encouraging him to return to the *roshi* for *sanzen* as soon as possible, and to lose no opportunity for getting the proper view of his *koan*. Pondering the problem of his "original face," he therefore tries and tries to imagine what he was before he was born, or, for that matter, what he now is at the very center of his being, what is the basic reality of his existence apart from his extension in time and space.

He soon discovers that the *roshi* has no patience whatever with philosophical or other wordy answers. For the *roshi* wants to be "shown." He wants something concrete, some solid proof. The student therefore begins to produce such "specimens of reality" as lumps of rock, leaves and branches, shouts, gestures of the hands–anything and everything he can imagine. But all is resolutely rejected until the student, unable to imagine anything more, is brought to his wits' end–at which point he is of course beginning to get on the right track. He "knows that he doesn't know."

When the beginning *koan* is Chao-chou's "*Wu*," the student is asked to find out why Chao-chou answered "*Wu*" or "None" to the question, "Does a dog have the Buddha nature?" The *roshi* asks to be shown this "nothing." A Chinese proverb says that "A single hand does not make a clap," *e* and therefore Hakuin asked, "What is the sound of one hand?" Can you hear what is not making a noise? Can you get any sound out of this one object which has nothing to hit? Can you get any "knowledge" of your own real nature? What an idiotic question!

By such means the student is at last brought to a point of feeling completely stupid–as if he were encased in a huge block of ice, unable to move or think. He just knows nothing; the whole world, including himself, is an enormous mass of pure doubt. Everything he hears, touches, or sees is as incomprehensible as "nothing" or "the sound of one hand." At *sanzen* he is perfectly dumb. He walks or sits all day in a "vivid daze," conscious of everything going on around him, responding mechanically to circumstances, but totally baffled by everything.

After some time in this state there comes a moment when the block of ice suddenly collapses, when this vast lump of unintelligibility comes instantly alive. The problem of who or what it is becomes transparently absurd–a question which, from the beginning, meant nothing whatever. There is no one left to ask himself the question or to answer it. Yet at the same time this transparent meaninglessness can laugh and talk, eat and drink, run up and down, look at the earth and sky, and all this without any sense of there being a problem, a sort of psychological knot, in the midst of it. There is no knot because the "mind seeking to know the mind" or the "self seeking to control the self" has been defeated out of existence and exposed for the abstraction which it always was. And when that tense knot vanishes there is no more sensation of a hard core of selfhood standing over against the rest of the world. In this state, the *roshi* needs only a single look at the student to know that he is now ready to begin his Zen training in earnest.

It is not quite the paradox which it seems to say that Zen training can begin only when it has been finished. For this is simply the basic Mahayana principle that *prajna* leads to *karuna,* that awakening is not truly attained unless it also implies the life of the Bodhisattva, the manifestation of the "marvelous use" of the Void for the benefit of all sentient beings.

At this point the *roshi* begins to present the student with *koan* which ask for impossible feats of action or judgment, such as:

"Take the four divisions of Tokyo out of your sleeve."

"Stop that ship on the distant ocean."

"Stop the booming of the distant bell."

"A girl is crossing the street. Is she the younger or the older sister?"

Such *koan* are rather more obviously "tricky" than the basic introductory problems, and show the student that what are dilemmas for thought present no barriers to action. A paper handkerchief easily becomes the four divisions of Tokyo, and the student solves the problem of the younger or older sister by mincing across the room like a girl. For in her absolute "suchness" the girl is just *that;* she is only relatively "sister," "older," or "younger." One can perhaps understand why a man who had practiced *za-zen* for eight years told R. H. Blyth that "Zen is just a trick of words," for on the principle of extracting a thorn with a thorn Zen is extricating people from the tangle in which they find themselves from confusing words and ideas with reality.

The continued practice of *za-zen* now provides the student with a clear, unobstructed mind into which he can toss the *koan* like a pebble into a pool and simply watch to see what his mind does with it. As he concludes each *koan,* the *roshi* usually requires that he present a verse from the *Zenrin Kushu* which expresses the point of the *koan* just solved. Other books are also used, and the late Sokei-an Sasaki, working in the United States, found that an admirable manual for this purpose was *Alice in Wonderland!* As the work goes on, crucial *koan* alternate with subsidiary *koan* which explore the implications of the former, and give the student a thorough working acquaintance with every theme in the Buddhist view of the universe, presenting the whole body of understanding in such a way that he knows it in his bones and nerves. By such means he learns to respond with it instantly and unwaveringly in the situations of everyday life.

The final group of *koan* are concerned with the "Five Ranks" (*go-i*)—a schematic view of the relations between relative knowledge and absolute knowledge, thing-events (*shih*) and underlying principle (*li*). The originator of the scheme was T'ung-shan (807–869), but it arises from the contacts of Zen with the Hua-yen (Japanese, Kegon) School, and the doctrine of the Five Ranks is closely related to that of the fourfold *Dharmadhatu*.[10] The Ranks are often represented in terms of the relative positions of lord and servant or host and guest, standing respectively for the underlying principle and the thing-events. Thus we have:

1. The lord looks down at the servant.
2. The servant looks up at the lord.
3. The lord.
4. The servant.
5. The lord and the servant converse together.

Suffice it to say that the first four correspond to the four *Dharmadhatu* of the Hua-yen School, though the relationship is somewhat complex, and the fifth to "naturalness." In other words, one may regard the universe, the *Dharmadhatu*, from a number of equally valid points of view–as many, as one, as both one and many, and as neither one nor many. But the final position of Zen is that it does not take any special viewpoint, and yet is free to take every viewpoint according to the circumstances. In the words of Lin-chi:

> Sometimes I take away the man (i.e., the subject) but do not take away the circumstances (i.e., the object). Sometimes I take away the circumstances but do not take away the man. Sometimes I take away both the man and the circumstances. Sometimes I take away neither the man nor the circumstances.[11] *f*

And sometimes, he might have added, I just do nothing special (*wu-shih*).[12]

Koan training comes to its conclusion in the stage of perfect naturalness of freedom in both the absolute and the relative

[10] For details, see above, pp. 160f.
[11] In *Ku-tsun-hsü Yü-lu*, 1. 4, pp. 3–4.
[12] A detailed but extremely confusing account of the Five Ranks will be found in Dumoulin and Sasaki (1), pp. 25–29.

worlds, but because this freedom is not opposed to the conventional order, but is rather a freedom which "upholds the world" (*lokasamgraha*), the final phase of study is the relationship of Zen to the rules of social and monastic life. As Yun-men once asked, "In such a wide world, why answer the bell and put on ceremonial robes?"[13] Another master's answer in quite a different context applies well here–"If there is any reason for it you may cut off my head!" For the moral act is significantly moral only when it is free, without the compulsion of a reason or necessity. This is also the deepest meaning of the Christian doctrine of free will, for to act "in union with God" is to act, not from the constraint of fear or pride, nor from hope of reward, but with the baseless love of the "unmoved mover."

To say that the *koan* system has certain dangers or drawbacks is only to say that anything can be misused. It is a highly sophisticated and even institutionalized technique, and therefore lends itself to affectation and artificiality. But so does any technique, even when so untechnical as Bankei's method of no method. This, too, can become a fetish. Yet it is important to be mindful of the points at which the drawbacks are most likely to arise, and it would seem that in *koan* training there are two.

The first is to insist that the *koan* is the "only way" to a genuine realization of Zen. Of course, one may beg the question by saying that Zen, over and above the experience of awakening, is precisely the style of handling Buddhism which the *koan* embody. But in this case the Soto School is not Zen, and no Zen is to be found anywhere in the world outside the particular tradition of the Rinzai branch. So defined, Zen has no universality and becomes as exotic and culturally conditioned as No drama or the practice of Chinese calligraphy. From the standpoint of the West, such Zen will appeal only to fanciers of "Nipponery," to romanticists who like to play at being Japanese. Not that there is anything inherently "bad" in such romanticism, for there are no such things as "pure" cultures, and the borrowing of other

[13] *Wu-men kuan*, 16.

people's styles always adds to the variety and spice of life. But Zen is so much more than a cultural refinement.

The second, and more serious, drawback can arise from the opposition of *satori* to the intense "feeling of doubt" which some *koan* exponents so deliberately encourage. For this is to foster a dualistic *satori*. To say that the depth of the *satori* is proportional to the intensity of seeking and striving which precede it is to confuse *satori* with its purely emotional adjuncts. In other words, if one wants to feel exhilaratingly light-footed, it is always possible to go around for some time with lead in one's shoes—and then take them off. The sense of relief will certainly be proportional to the length of time such shoes have been worn, and to the weight of the lead. This is equivalent to the old trick of religious revivalists who give their followers a tremendous emotional uplift by first implanting an acute sense of sin, and then relieving it through faith in Jesus. But such "uplifts" do not last, and it was of such a *satori* that Yün-feng said, "That monk who has any *satori* goes right into hell like a flying arrow." [14]

Awakening almost necessarily involves a sense of relief because it brings to an end the habitual psychological cramp of trying to grasp the mind with the mind, which in turn generates the ego with all its conflicts and defenses. In time, the sense of relief wears off—but not the awakening, unless one has confused it with the sense of relief and has attempted to exploit it by indulging in ecstasy. Awakening is thus only incidentally pleasant or ecstatic, only at first an experience of intense emotional release. But in itself it is just the ending of an artificial and absurd use of the mind. Above and beyond that it is *wu-shih*—nothing special—since the ultimate content of awakening is never a particular object of knowledge or experience. The Buddhist doctrine of the "Four Invisibles" is that the Void (*sunya*) is to a Buddha as water to a fish, air to a man, and the nature of things to the deluded—beyond conception.

[14] *Ku-tsun-hsü Yü-lu*, 41.

It should be obvious that what we are, most substantially and fundamentally, will never be a distinct object of knowledge. Whatever we can know–life and death, light and darkness, solid and empty–will be the relative aspects of something as inconceivable as the color of space. Awakening is not to know what this reality is. As a *Zenrin* poem says:

> *As butterflies come to the newly planted flowers,*
> *Bodhidharma says, "I know not."* [9]

Awakening is to know what reality is not. It is to cease identifying oneself with any object of knowledge whatsoever. Just as every assertion about the basic substance or energy of reality must be meaningless, any assertion as to what "I am" at the very roots of my being must also be the height of folly. Delusion is the false metaphysical premise at the root of common sense; it is the average man's unconscious ontology and epistemology, his tacit assumption that he is a "something." The assumption that "I am nothing" would, of course, be equally wrong since something and nothing, being and non-being, are related concepts, and belong equally to the "known."

One method of muscular relaxation is to begin by increasing tension in the muscles so as to have a clear feeling of what *not* to do.[15] In this sense there is some point in using the initial *koan* as a means of intensifying the mind's absurd effort to grasp itself. But to identify *satori* with the consequent feeling of relief, with the *sense* of relaxation, is quite misleading, for the *satori* is the letting go and not the feeling of it. The conscious aspect of the Zen life is not, therefore, *satori*–not the "original mind"–but everything one is left free to do and to see and feel when the cramp in the mind has been released.

From this standpoint Bankei's simple trust in the "Unborn mind" and even Shinran's view of *Nembutsu* are also entrances to *satori*. To "let go" it is not always necessary to wear out the

[15] See Edmund Jacobson, *Progressive Relaxation*. (Chicago, 1938.)

attempt to grasp until it becomes intolerable. As against this violent way there is also a *judo*–a "gentle way," the way of seeing that the mind, the basic reality, remains spontaneous and ungrasped whether one tries to grasp it or not. One's own doing or not doing drop away by sheer irrelevance. To think that one must grasp or not grasp, let go or not let go, is only to foster the illusion that the ego is real, and that its machinations are an effective obstacle to the Tao. Beside the spontaneous functioning of the "Unborn mind" these efforts or non-efforts are strictly null. In the more imagistic language of Shinran, one has only to hear of the "saving vow" of Amitabha and to say his Name, the *Nembutsu*, even just once without concern as to whether one has faith or not, or as to whether one is desireless or not. All such concern is the pride of the ego. In the words of the Shin-shu mystic Kichibei:

> When all the idea of self-power based upon moral values and disciplinary measures is purged, there is nothing left in you that will declare itself to be the hearer, and just because of this you do not miss anything you hear.[16]

So long as one thinks about listening, one cannot hear clearly, and so long as one thinks about trying or not trying to let go of oneself, one cannot let go. Yet whether one thinks about listening or not, the ears are hearing just the same, and nothing can stop the sound from reaching them.

The advantage of the *koan* method is perhaps that, for general purposes, the other way is too subtle, and too easily subject to misinterpretation—especially by monks who might all too readily use it as an excuse for loafing around the monastery while living off the donations of the devout laity. This is almost certainly why the emphasis of the T'ang masters on "not-seeking" gave way to the more energetic use of the *koan* as a means of exhausting the strength of the egoistic will. Bankei's Zen without method or means offers no basis for a school or institution, since the monks

16 In Suzuki (10), p. 130.

may just as well go their way and take up farming or fishing. As a result no external sign of Zen is left; there is no longer any finger pointing at the moon of Truth—and this is necessary for the Bodhisattva's task of delivering all beings, even though it runs the risk of mistaking the finger for the moon.

Four

ZEN IN THE ARTS

Happily, it is possible for us not only to hear about Zen but also to see it. Since "one showing is worth a hundred sayings," the expression of Zen in the arts gives us one of the most direct ways of understanding it. This is the more so because the art forms which Zen has created are not symbolic in the same way as other types of Buddhist art, or as is "religious" art as a whole. The favorite subjects of Zen artists, whether painters or poets, are what we should call natural, concrete, and secular things. Even when they turn to the Buddha, or to the Patriarchs and masters of Zen, they depict them in a peculiarly down-to-earth and human way. Furthermore, the arts of Zen are not merely or primarily representational. Even in painting, the work of art is considered not only as representing nature but as being itself a work of nature. For the very technique involves the art of artlessness, or what Sabro Hasegawa has called the "controlled accident," so that paintings are formed as naturally as the rocks and grasses which they depict.

This does not mean that the art forms of Zen are left to mere chance, as if one were to dip a snake in ink and let it wiggle around on a sheet of paper. The point is rather that for Zen there is no duality, no conflict between the natural element of chance and the human element of control. The constructive powers of the human mind are no more artificial than the formative actions of plants or bees, so that from the standpoint of Zen it is no contradiction to say that artistic technique is discipline in spontaneity and spontaneity in discipline.

The art forms of the Western world arise from spiritual and philosophical traditions in which spirit is divided from nature, and comes down from heaven to work upon it as an intelligent energy upon an inert and recalcitrant stuff. Thus Malraux speaks always of the artist "conquering" his medium as our explorers and scientists also speak of conquering mountains or conquering space. To Chinese and Japanese ears these are grotesque expressions. For when you climb it is the mountain as much as your own legs which lifts you upwards, and when you paint it is the brush, ink, and paper which determine the result as much as your own hand.

Taoism, Confucianism, and Zen are expressions of a mentality which feels completely at home in this universe, and which sees man as an integral part of his environment. Human intelligence is not an imprisoned spirit from afar but an aspect of the whole intricately balanced organism of the natural world, whose principles were first explored in the *Book of Changes*. Heaven and earth are alike members of this organism, and nature is as much our father as our mother, since the Tao by which it works is originally manifested in the *yang* and the *yin*–the male and female, positive and negative principles which, in dynamic balance, maintain the order of the world. The insight which lies at the root of Far Eastern culture is that opposites are relational and so fundamentally harmonious. Conflict is always comparatively superficial, for there can be no ultimate conflict when the pairs of opposites are mutually interdependent. Thus our stark divisions of spirit and nature, subject and object, good and evil, artist and medium are quite foreign to this culture.

In a universe whose fundamental principle is relativity rather than warfare there is no purpose because there is no victory to be won, no end to be attained. For every end, as the word itself shows, is an extreme, an opposite, and exists only in relation to its other end. Because the world is not going anywhere there is no hurry. One may as well "take it easy" like nature itself, and in the Chinese language the "changes" of nature and "ease" are the same word, *i.*[a] This is a first principle in the study of Zen and of any Far Eastern art: hurry, and all that it involves, is fatal. For there is no goal to be attained. The moment a goal is conceived it becomes impossible to practice the discipline of the art, to master the very rigor of its technique. Under the watchful and critical eye of a master one may practice the writing of Chinese characters for days and days, months and months. But he watches as a gardener watches the growth of a tree, and wants his student to have the attitude of the tree—the attitude of purposeless growth in which there are no short cuts because every stage of the way is both beginning and end. Thus the most accomplished master no more congratulates himself upon "arriving" than the most fumbling beginner.

Paradoxical as it may seem, the purposeful life has no content, no point. It hurries on and on, and misses everything. Not hurrying, the purposeless life misses nothing, for it is only when there is no goal and no rush that the human senses are fully open to receive the world. Absence of hurry also involves a certain lack of interference with the natural course of events, especially when it is felt that the natural course follows principles which are not foreign to human intelligence. For, as we have seen, the Taoist mentality makes, or forces, nothing but "grows" everything. When human reason is seen to be an expression of the same spontaneous balance of *yang* and *yin* as the natural universe, man's action upon his environment is not felt as a conflict, an action from outside. Thus the difference between forcing and growing cannot be expressed in terms of specific directions as to what should or should not be done, for the difference lies primarily in the quality and feeling of the action. The difficulty of describing these things for Western ears is that people in a hurry cannot feel.

The expression of this whole attitude in the arts is perhaps best approached through painting and poetry. Although it may seem that the arts of Zen are confined to the more refined expressions of culture, it should be remembered that almost every profession and craft is known in Japan as a *do*, that is, a Tao or Way, not unlike what used to be known in the West as a "mystery." To some extent, every *do* was at one time a lay method of learning the principles which are embodied in Taoism, Zen, and Confucianism, even as modern Masonry is a survival from times when the craft of the mason was a means of initiation into a spiritual tradition. Even in modern Osaka some of the older merchants follow a *do* or way of commerce based upon *shingaku*–a system of psychology closely related to Zen.

After the persecution of Chinese Buddhism in 845, Zen was for some time not only the dominant form of Buddhism but also the most powerful spiritual influence in the growth of Chinese culture. This influence was at its height during the Southern Sung dynasty (1127–1279), and during this time the Zen monasteries became leading centers of Chinese scholarship. Lay scholars, Confucian and Taoist alike, visited them for periods of study, and Zen monks in turn familiarized themselves with Chinese classical studies. Since writing and poetry were among the chief preoccupations of Chinese scholars, and since the Chinese way of painting is closely akin to writing, the roles of scholar, artist, and poet were not widely separated. The Chinese gentleman-scholar was not a specialist, and it was quite against the nature of the Zen monk to confine his interests and activities to purely "religious" affairs. The result was a tremendous cross-fertilization of philosophical, scholarly, poetic, and artistic pursuits in which the Zen and Taoist feeling for "naturalness" became the dominant note. It was during this same period that Eisai and Dogen came from Japan to return with Zen to their own country, to be followed by an incessant stream of Japanese scholar-monks eager to take home not only Zen but every other aspect of Chinese culture. Shiploads of monks, amounting almost to floating monasteries, plied between China and Japan, carrying not only *sutras* and Chinese classical books, but also tea, silk, pottery, incense, paintings, drugs, musical instruments, and every refinement of Chinese culture–not to mention Chinese artists and craftsmen.

Closest to the feeling of Zen was a calligraphic style of painting, done with black ink on paper or silk–usually a painting and poem in one. Chinese black ink is capable of a great variety of tones, varied by the amount of water, and the ink itself is found in an enormous number of qualities and "colors" of black. The ink comes in a solid stick, and is prepared by pouring a little water into a flat stone dish, upon which the stick is rubbed until the liquid is of the required density. Writing or painting is done with a sharply pointed brush set in a bamboo stem–a brush which is held upright without resting the wrist on the paper, and whose soft hairs give its strokes a great versatility. Since the touch of the brush is so light and fluid, and since it must move continuously over the absorbent paper if the ink is to flow out regularly, its control requires a free movement of the hand and arm as if one were dancing rather than writing on paper. In short, it is a perfect instrument for the expression of unhesitating spontaneity, and a single stroke is enough to "give away" one's character to an experienced observer.

Sumi-e, as the Japanese call this style of painting, may have been perfected as early as the T'ang dynasty by the almost legendary masters Wu Tao-tzu (*c.* 700–760) and Wang-wei (*c.* 698–759). However, the authenticity of works ascribed to them is doubtful, though they may be as early as the ninth century and include a painting so fully characteristic of Zen as the impressionistic waterfall attributed to Wang-wei–a thundering stream of sheer power, suggested by a few slightly curved sweeps of the brush between two masses of rock. The great formative age of this style was undoubtedly the Sung dynasty (959–1279), and is represented by such painters as Hsia-kuei, Ma-yüan, Mu-ch'i, and Liang-k'ai.

The Sung masters were pre-eminently landscape painters, crea-tors of a tradition of "nature painting" which has hardly been surpassed anywhere in the world. For it shows us the life of na-ture–of mountains, waters, mists, rocks, trees, and birds–as felt by Taoism and Zen. It is a world to which man belongs but which he does not dominate; it is sufficient to itself, for it was not "made for" anyone and has no purpose of its own. As Hsüan-chüeh said:

Over the river, the shining moon; in the pine trees, sighing wind;
All night long so tranquil—why? And for whom? [1] [b]

Sung landscapes are by no means as fantastic and stylized as
Western critics often suggest, for to travel in similar territory, in
mountainous, misty country, is to see them at every turn of the
road, and it is a simple matter for the photographer to take pictures which look exactly like Chinese paintings. One of the most
striking features of the Sung landscape, as of *sumi-e* as a whole,
is the relative emptiness of the picture—an emptiness which appears, however, to be part of the painting and not just unpainted
background. By filling in just one corner, the artist makes the
whole area of the picture alive. Ma-yüan, in particular, was a
master of this technique, which amounts almost to "painting by
not painting," or what Zen sometimes calls "playing the string-
less lute." The secret lies in knowing how to balance form with
emptiness and, above all, in knowing when one has "said"
enough. For Zen spoils neither the aesthetic shock nor the *satori*
shock by filling in, by explanation, second thoughts, and intellectual commentary. Furthermore, the figure so integrally related
to its empty space gives the feeling of the "marvelous Void"
from which the event suddenly appears.

Equally impressive is the mastery of the brush, of strokes
ranging from delicate elegance to rough vitality, from minutely
detailed trees to bold outlines and masses given texture by the
"controlled accidents" of stray brush hairs and uneven inking
of the paper. Zen artists have preserved this technique to the
present day in the so-called *zenga* style of Chinese characters,
circles, bamboo branches, birds, or human figures drawn with
these uninhibited, powerful brush strokes which keep on moving
even when the painting is finished. After Mu-ch'i, perhaps the
greatest master of the rough brush was the Japanese monk Sesshu
(1421–1506), whose formidable technique included the most refined screens of pine trees and birds, mountain landscapes remi-

[1] *Cheng-tao Ke, 24.*

niscent of Hsia-kuei, and almost violently alive landscapes for which he used not only the brush but fistfuls of inked straw to get the right texture of "flying hair lines."

The Western eye is immediately struck by the absence of symmetry in these paintings, by the consistent avoidance of regular and geometrical shapes, whether straight or curved. For the characteristic brush line is jagged, gnarled, irregularly twisting, dashing, or sweeping–always spontaneous rather than predictable. Even when the Zen monk or artist draws a solitary circle–one of the most common themes of *zenga*–it is not only slightly eccentric and out of shape, but the very texture of the line is full of life and verve with the incidental splashes and gaps of the "rough brush." For the abstract or "perfect" circle becomes concrete and natural–a living circle–and, in the same way, rocks and trees, clouds and waters appear to the Chinese eye as most like themselves when most unlike the intelligible forms of the geometer and architect.

Western science has made nature intelligible in terms of its symmetries and regularities, analyzing its most wayward forms into components of a regular and measurable shape. As a result we tend to see nature and to deal with it as an "order" from which the element of spontaneity has been "screened out." But this order is *maya*, and the "true suchness" of things has nothing in common with the purely conceptual aridities of perfect squares, circles, or triangles–except by spontaneous accident. Yet this is why the Western mind is dismayed when ordered conceptions of the universe break down, and when the basic behavior of the physical world is found to be a "principle of uncertainty." We find such a world meaningless and inhuman, but familiarity with Chinese and Japanese art forms might lead us to an altogether new appreciation of this world in its living, and finally unavoidable, reality.

Mu-ch'i and Liang-k'ai did many paintings of the Zen Patriarchs and masters, whom they represented for the most part as abandoned lunatics, scowling, shouting, loafing around, or roaring with laughter at drifting leaves. As favorite themes they adopted, as Zen figures, the two crazy hermits Han-shan and Shih-te, and the enormously rotund folk-god Pu-tai, to complete a marvelous assortment of happy tramps and rogues to exemplify the splendid nonsense and emptiness of the Zen life. Zen and–to some extent–Taoism seem to be the only spiritual traditions which feel secure enough to lampoon themselves, or to feel sufficiently un-self-conscious to laugh not only about their religion but in the midst of it. In these lunatic figures the Zen artists portray something slightly more than a parody of their own *wu-shin* or "mindless" way of life, for as "genius is to madness close allied" there is a suggestive parallel between the meaningless babble of the happy lunatic and the purposeless life of the Zen sage. In the words of a *Zenrin* poem:

> *The wild geese do not intend to cast their reflection;*
> *The water has no mind to receive their image.*

Thus the aimless life is the constant theme of Zen art of every kind, expressing the artist's own inner state of going nowhere in a timeless moment. All men have these moments occasionally, and it is just then that they catch those vivid glimpses of the world which cast such a glow over the intervening wastes of memory– the smell of burning leaves on a morning of autumn haze, a flight of sunlit pigeons against a thundercloud, the sound of an unseen waterfall at dusk, or the single cry of some unidentified bird in the depths of a forest. In the art of Zen every landscape, every sketch of bamboo in the wind or of lonely rocks, is an echo of such moments.

Where the mood of the moment is solitary and quiet it is called *sabi.*[c] When the artist is feeling depressed or sad, and in this peculiar emptiness of feeling catches a glimpse of something rather ordinary and unpretentious in its incredible "suchness," the mood is called *wabi.*[d] When the moment evokes a more intense, nostalgic sadness, connected with autumn and the vanishing away of the world, it is called *aware.*[e] And when the vision is the sudden perception of something mysterious and strange, hinting at an unknown never to be discovered, the mood is called *yugen.* These extremely untranslatable Japanese words denote the four basic moods of *furyu,* that is, of the general atmosphere of Zen "taste" in its perception of the aimless moments of life.

Inspired by the Sung masters, the Japanese produced a whole cluster of superb *sumi* painters whose work ranks today among the most prized treasures of the nation's art—Muso Kokushi (1275–1351), Cho Densu (*d.* 1431), Shubun (1414–1465), Soga Jasoku (*d.* 1483), Sesshu (1421–1506), Miyamoto Musashi (1582–1645), and many others. Notable paintings were also made by the great Zen monks Hakuin and Sengai (1750–1837), the latter showing a flair for abstract painting so startlingly suggestive of the twentieth century that it is easy to understand the interest of so many contemporary painters in Zen.

Toward the beginning of the seventeenth century, Japanese artists developed a still more suggestive and "offhand" style of *sumi-e* called *haiga* as an illustrative accompaniment to *haiku* poems. These were derived from *zenga,* the informal paintings of the Zen monks accompanying verses from the *Zenrin Kushu* and sayings from the various *mondo* and the *sutras. Zenga* and *haiga* represent the most "extreme" form of *sumi* painting—the most spontaneous, artless, and rough, replete with all those "controlled accidents" of the brush in which they exemplify the marvelous meaninglessness of nature itself.

From the earliest times the Zen masters had shown a partiality for short, gnomic poems—at once laconic and direct like their answers to questions about Buddhism. Many of these, like those we have quoted from the *Zenrin Kushu,* contained overt references to Zen and its principles. However, just as T'ung-shan's "Three pounds of flax!" was an answer full of Zen but not about Zen, so the most expressive Zen poetry is that which "says nothing," which, in other words, is not philosophy or commentary *about* life. A monk asked Feng-hsüeh, "When speech and silence

are both inadmissible, how can one pass without error?" The
master replied:

> *I always remember Kiangsu in March—*
> *The cry of the partridge, the mass of fragrant flowers!* [2] [h]

Here again, as in painting, is the expression of a live moment in
its pure "suchness"–though it is a pity to have to say so–and the
masters frequently quoted classical Chinese poetry in this way,
using couplets or quatrains which pointed, and said no more.

The practice of taking couplets from the old Chinese poems for
use as songs was also favored in literary circles, and at the beginning of the eleventh century Fujiwara Kinto compiled an anthology of such excerpts, together with short Japanese *waka* poems,
under the title *Roeishu*, the *Collection of Clear Songs*. Such a use
of poetry obviously expresses the same type of artistic vision as
we find in the paintings of Ma-yüan and Mu-ch'i, the same use
of empty space brought to life with a few strokes of the brush. In
poetry the empty space is the surrounding silence which a two-
line poem requires–a silence of the mind in which one does not
"think about" the poem but actually feels the sensation which it
evokes–all the more strongly for having said so little.

By the seventeenth century the Japanese had brought this
"wordless" poetry to perfection in the *haiku*, the poem of just
seventeen syllables which drops the subject almost as it takes it
up. To non-Japanese people *haiku* are apt to seem no more than
beginnings or even titles for poems, and in translation it is impossible to convey the effect of their sound and rhythm. However, translation can usually convey the image–and this is the
important point. Of course there are many *haiku* which seem as
stilted as the Japanese paintings on cheap lacquer trays for ex-
port. But the non-Japanese listener must remember that a good
haiku is a pebble thrown into the pool of the listener's mind,
evoking associations out of the richness of his own memory. It

[2] *Wu-men Kuan*, 24.

invites the listener to participate instead of leaving him dumb with admiration while the poet shows off.

The development of the *haiku* was largely the work of Basho (1643–1694), whose feeling for Zen wanted to express itself in a type of poetry altogether in the spirit of *wu-shih*–"nothing special." "To write *haiku*," he said, "get a three-foot child"–for Basho's poems have the same inspired objectivity as a child's expression of wonder, and return us to that same feeling of the world as when it first met our astonished eyes.

> Kimi hi take
> Yoki mono miseru
> Yukimaroge!

> *You light the fire;*
> *I'll show you something nice,–*
> *A great ball of snow!* [3]

Basho wrote his *haiku* in the simplest type of Japanese speech, naturally avoiding literary and "highbrow" language, so creating a style which made it possible for ordinary people to be poets. Bankei, his contemporary, did just the same thing for Zen, for as one of Ikkyu's *doka* poems says:

> *Whatever runs counter*
> *To the mind and will of ordinary people*
> *Hinders the Law of Men*
> *And the Law of Buddha.* [4]

This is in the spirit of Nan-ch'üan's saying, "The ordinary mind is the Tao" where "ordinary" means "simply human" rather than "merely vulgar." It was thus that the seventeenth century saw an

---

[3] This and all the following translations of *haiku* are the work of R. H. Blyth, and come for the most part from his superb work, the four-volume *Haiku*, which is without any question the best treatment of the subject in English. Blyth has the additional advantage of some experience in Zen training, and as a result his grasp of Chinese and Japanese literature is unusually perceptive. See Blyth (2) in the Bibliography.

[4] R. H. Blyth in "Ikkyu's Doka," *The Young East*, vol. 2, no. 7. (Tokyo, 1953.)

extraordinary popularization of the Zen atmosphere in Japan, reaching down from the monks and *samurai* to farmers and artisans.

The true feeling of *haiku* is "given away" in one of Basho's poems which, however, says just too much to be true *haiku:*

> *How admirable,*
> *He who thinks not, "Life is fleeting,"*
> *When he sees the lightning!*

For the *haiku* sees things in their "suchness," without comment–a view of the world which the Japanese call *sono-mama,* "Just as it is," or "Just so."

> *Weeds in the rice-field,*
> *Cut and left lying just so–*
> *Fertilizer!*

In Zen a man has no mind apart from what he knows and sees, and this is almost expressed by Gochiku in the *haiku:*

> *The long night;*
> *The sound of the water*
> *Says what I think.*

And still more directly–

> *The stars on the pond;*
> *Again the winter shower*
> *Ruffles the water.*

Haiku and *waka* poems convey perhaps more easily than painting the subtle differences between the four moods of *sabi, wabi, aware,* and *yugen.* The quiet, thrilling loneliness of *sabi* is obvious in

> *On a withered branch*
> *A crow is perched,*
> *In the autumn evening.*

But it is less obvious and therefore deeper in

With the evening breeze,
The water laps against
The heron's legs.

In the dark forest
A berry drops:
The sound of the water.

Sabi is, however, loneliness in the sense of Buddhist detachment, of seeing all things as happening "by themselves" in miraculous spontaneity. With this goes that sense of deep, illimitable quietude which descends with a long fall of snow, swallowing all sounds in layer upon layer of softness.

Sleet falling;
Fathomless, infinite
Loneliness.

Wabi, the unexpected recognition of the faithful "suchness" of very ordinary things, especially when the gloom of the future has momentarily checked our ambitiousness, is perhaps the mood of

A brushwood gate,
And for a lock–
This snail.

The woodpecker
Keeps on in the same place:
Day is closing.

Winter desolation;
In the rain-water tub,
Sparrows are walking.

Aware is not quite grief, and not quite nostalgia in the usual sense of longing for the return of a beloved past. *Aware* is the echo of what has passed and of what was loved, giving them a resonance such as a great cathedral gives to a choir, so that they would be the poorer without it.

No one lives at the Barrier of Fuha;
The wooden penthouse is fallen away;
All that remains
Is the autumn wind.

The evening haze;
Thinking of past things,
How far-off they are!

Aware is the moment of crisis between seeing the transience of the world with sorrow and regret, and seeing it as the very form of the Great Void.

The stream hides itself
In the grasses
Of departing autumn.

Leaves falling,
Lie on one another;
The rain beats on the rain.

That moment of transition is just about to "cross over" in the *haiku* written by Issa upon the death of his child:

This dewdrop world—
It may be a dewdrop,
And yet—and yet—

Since *yugen* signifies a kind of mystery, it is the most baffling of all to describe, and the poems must speak for themselves.

The sea darkens;
The voices of the wild ducks
Are faintly white.

The skylark:
Its voice alone fell,
Leaving nothing behind.

In the dense mist,
What is being shouted
Between hill and boat?

> A *trout leaps;*
> *Clouds are moving*
> *In the bed of the stream.*

Or an example of *yugen* in the *Zenrin* poems:

> *Wind subsiding, the flowers still fall;*
> *Bird crying, the mountain silence deepens.*[4]

Because Zen training had involved a constant use of these Chinese couplets since at least the end of the fifteenth century, the emergence of *haiku* is hardly surprising. The influence is self-evident in this "*yugen*-in-reverse" *haiku* by Moritake. The *Zenrin* says:

> *The shattered mirror will reflect no more;*
> *The fallen flower will hardly rise to the branch.*[j]

And Moritake–

> *A fallen flower*
> *Returning to the branch?*
> *It was a butterfly.*

The association of Zen with poetry must inevitably bring up the name of the Soto Zen monk and hermit Ryokan (1758–1831). So often one thinks of the saint as a man whose sincerity provokes the enmity of the world, but Ryokan holds the distinction of being the saint whom everyone loved–perhaps because he was natural, again as a child, rather than good. It is easy to form the impression that the Japanese love of nature is predominantly sentimental, dwelling on those aspects of nature which are "nice" and "pretty"–butterflies, cherry blossoms, the autumn moon, chrysanthemums, and old pine trees.[5] But Ryokan is also the poet of lice, fleas, and being utterly soaked with cold rain.

---

[5] An impression especially sickening to the poetic mood of the middle twentieth century. It comes, however, from a level of *haiku* and other art forms which corresponds to our own greeting-card verse and confectionery-box

On rainy days
The monk Ryokan
Feels sorry for himself.

And his view of "nature" is all of a piece:

The sound of the scouring
Of the saucepan blends
With the tree-frogs' voices.

In some ways Ryokan is a Japanese St. Francis, though much less obviously religious. He is a wandering fool, un-self-consciously playing games with children, living in a lonely hut in the forest where the roof leaks and the wall is hung with poems in his marvelously illegible, spidery handwriting, so prized by Japanese calligraphers. He thinks of the lice on his chest as insects in the grass, and expresses the most natural human feelings–sadness, loneliness, bewilderment, or pity–without a trace of shame or pride. Even when robbed he is still rich, for

The thief
Left it behind–
The moon at the window.

And when there is no money,

The wind brings
Fallen leaves enough
To make a fire.

When life is empty, with respect to the past, and aimless, with respect to the future, the vacuum is filled by the present–normally reduced to a hairline, a split second in which there is no time

art. But consider the almost surrealistic imagery of the following from the Zenrin:

On Mount Wu-t'ai the clouds are steaming rice;
Before the ancient Buddha hall, dogs piss at heaven.

And there are many *haiku* such as this from Issa:

The mouth
That cracked a flea
Said, "Namu Amida Butsu!"

for anything to happen. The sense of an infinitely expanded present is nowhere stronger than in *cha-no-yu,* the art of tea. Strictly, the term means something like "Tea with hot water," and through this one art Zen has exercised an incalculable influence on Japanese life, since the *chajin,* or "man of tea," is an arbiter of taste in the many subsidiary arts which *cha-no-yu* involves–architecture, gardening, ceramics, metalwork, lacquer, and the arrangement of flowers (*ikebana*).

Since *cha-no-yu* has become a conventional accomplishment for young ladies, it has been made the subject of a great deal of sentimental nonsense–associated with brocaded young dolls in moonlit rooms, nervously trying to imitate the most stilted feelings about porcelain and cherry blossom. But in the austere purity of, say, the Soshu Sen School the art of tea is a genuine expression of Zen which requires, if necessary, no further apparatus than a bowl, tea, and hot water. If there is not even that, *chado*–"the way of tea"–can be practiced anywhere and with anything, since it is really the same as Zen.

If Christianity is wine and Islam coffee, Buddhism is most certainly tea. Its quietening, clarifying, and slightly bitter taste gives it almost the same taste as awakening itself, though the bitterness corresponds to the pleasing roughness of "natural texture," and the "middle path" between sweet and sour. Long before the development of *cha-no-yu,* tea was used by Zen monks as a stimulant for meditation, and in this context it was drunk in a mood of unhurried awareness which naturally lent itself to a ritualistic type of action. In summer it refreshed and in winter warmed those wandering hermit-monks who liked to build grass and bamboo huts in the mountain forests, or by rock-filled streams in the gorges. The totally undistracting emptiness and simplicity of the Taoist or Zen hermitage has set the style not only for the special type of house for *cha-no-yu* but for Japanese domestic architecture as a whole.[6]

[6] An influence combined with a native style which can still be seen at the ancient Shinto shrine of Ise–a style which strongly suggests the cultures of the southern Pacific islands.

The monastic "tea ceremony" was introduced into Japan by Eisai, and though its form is different from the present *cha-no-yu*, it was nonetheless its origin, and appears to have been adopted for lay use during the fifteenth century. From this the *cha-no-yu* proper was perfected by Sen-no-Rikyu (1518–1591), and from him descend the three main schools of tea now flourishing. Ceremonial tea is not the ordinary leaf tea which is steeped in hot water; it is finely powdered green tea, mixed with hot water by means of a bamboo whisk until it becomes what a Chinese writer called "the froth of the liquid jade." *Cha-no-yu* is most appreciated when confined to a small group, or just two companions, and was especially loved by the old-time *samurai*–as today by harassed businessmen–as a frank escape from the turmoil of the world.[7]

Ideally, the house for *cha-no-yu* is a small hut set apart from the main dwelling in its own garden. The hut is floored with *tatami*, or straw mats, enclosing a fire-pit; the roof is usually thatched with rice straw; and the walls, as in all Japanese homes, are paper *shoji* supported by uprights of wood with a natural finish. One side of the room is occupied by an alcove, or *tokonoma*, the position for a single hanging scroll of painting or calligraphy, together with a rock, a spray of flowers, or some other object of art.

The atmosphere, though formal, is strangely relaxed, and the guests feel free to talk or watch in silence as they wish. The host takes his time to prepare a charcoal fire, and with a bamboo dipper pours water into a squat kettle of soft brown iron. In the same formal but completely unhurried manner, he brings in the other utensils–a plate with a few cakes, the tea bowl and caddy, the whisk, and a larger bowl for leavings. During these preparations a casual conversation continues, and soon the water in the kettle begins to simmer and sigh, so that the guests fall silent to listen. After a while, the host serves tea to the guests one by one

[7] Since it is frequently my pleasure to be invited for *cha-no-yu* by Sabro Hasegawa, who has a remarkable intuition for issuing these invitations at the most hectic moments, I can testify that I know no better form of psychotherapy.

from the same bowl, taking it from the caddy with a strip of bamboo bent into a spoon, pouring water from the kettle with the long-handled dipper, whipping it into a froth with the whisk, and laying the bowl before the first guest with its most interesting side towards him.

The bowls used for *cha-no-yu* are normally dull-colored and roughly finished, often unglazed at the base, and on the sides the glaze has usually been allowed to run–an original fortunate mistake which has been seen to offer endless opportunities for the "controlled accident." Specially favored are Korean rice bowls of the cheapest quality, a peasant ware of crude texture from which the tea masters have selected unintentional masterpieces of form. The tea caddy is often of tarnished silver or infinitely deep black lacquer, though sometimes old pottery medicine jars are used–purely functional articles which were again picked out by the masters for their unaffected beauty. A celebrated caddy once smashed to pieces was mended with gold cement, and became the much more treasured for the haphazard network of thin gold lines which then covered its surface. After the tea has been drunk, the guests may ask to inspect all the utensils which have been used, since every one of them has been made or chosen with the utmost care, and often brought out for the occasion because of some feature that would particularly appeal to one of the guests.

Every appurtenance of the *cha-no-yu* has been selected in accordance with canons of taste over which the most sensitive men in Japan have brooded for centuries. Though the choice is usually intuitive, careful measurement of the objects reveals interesting and unexpected proportions–works of spontaneous geometry as remarkable as the spiral shell of the nautilus or the structure of the snow crystal. Architects, painters, gardeners, and craftsmen of all kinds have worked in consultation with the *cha-no-yu* masters, like an orchestra with its conductor, so that their "Zen taste" has passed on into the objects made by the same craftsmen for everyday use. This applies most particularly to ordinary, functional things–kitchen implements, *shoji* paper, soup bowls, common teapots and cups, floor mats, baskets, utilitarian bottles and jars, textiles for everyday clothing, and a hundred other simple artifacts in which the Japanese show their good taste to best advantage.

The "Zen" of the *cha-no-yu* comes out all the more for the purely secular character of the ritual, which has no liturgical character like the Catholic Mass or the elaborate ceremonies of Shingon Buddhism. Though the guests avoid political, financial, or business matters in their conversation, there is sometimes non-argumentative discussion of philosophical matters, though the preferred topics are artistic and natural. It must be remembered that Japanese people take to such subjects as readily and un-self-consciously as we talk of sports or travel, and that their discussion of natural beauty is not the affectation it might be in our own culture. Furthermore, they do not feel in the least guilty about this admitted "escape" from the so-called "realities" of business and worldly competition. Escape from these concerns is as natural and necessary as sleep, and they feel neither compunction nor awkwardness in belonging for a while to the Taoist world of carefree hermits, wandering through the mountains like wind-blown clouds, with nothing to do but cultivate a row of vegetables, gaze at the drifting mist, and listen to the waterfalls. A few, perhaps, find the secret of bringing the two worlds together, of seeing the "hard realities" of human life to be the same aimless working of the Tao as the patterns of branches against the sky. In the words of Hung Tzu-ch'eng:

> If the mind is not overlaid with wind and waves, you will always be living among blue mountains and green trees. If your true nature has the creative force of Nature itself, wherever you may go, you will see fishes leaping and geese flying.[8]

The style of garden which goes with Zen and *cha-no-yu* is not, of course, one of those ornate imitation landscapes with bronze cranes and miniature pagodas. The intention of the best Japanese

[8] *Ts'ai-ken T'an*, 291. Hung's book of "vegetable-root talk" is a collection of wandering observations by a sixteenth-century poet whose philosophy was a blend of Taoism, Zen, and Confucianism.

gardens is not to make a realistic illusion of landscape, but simply to suggest the general atmosphere of "mountain and water" in a small space, so arranging the design of the garden that it seems to have been helped rather than governed by the hand of man. The Zen gardener has no mind to impose his own intention upon natural forms, but is careful rather to follow the "intentionless intention" of the forms themselves, even though this involves the utmost care and skill. In fact the gardener never ceases to prune, clip, weed, and train his plants, but he does so in the spirit of being part of the garden himself rather than a directing agent standing outside. He is not interfering with nature because he is nature, and he cultivates as if not cultivating. Thus the garden is at once highly artificial and extremely natural!

This spirit is seen at its best in the great sand and rock gardens of Kyoto, of which the most famous example is the garden of Ryoanji. It consists of five groups of rocks laid upon a rectangle of raked sand, backed by a low stone wall, and surrounded by trees. It suggests a wild beach, or perhaps a seascape with rocky islands, but its unbelievable simplicity evokes a serenity and clarity of feeling so powerful that it can be caught even from a photograph. The major art which contributes to such gardens is *bonseki,* which may well be called the "growing" of rocks. It requires difficult expeditions to the seashore, to mountains and rivers, in search of rock forms which wind and water have shaped into asymmetrical, living contours. These are carted to the garden site, and placed so as to look as if they had grown where they stand, so as to be related to the surrounding space or to the area of sand in the same way as figure to background in Sung paintings. Because the rock must look as if it had always been in the same position, it must have the air of moss-covered antiquity, and, rather than try to plant moss on the rock, the rock is first set for some years in a place where the moss will grow by itself, and thereafter is moved to its final position. Rocks picked out by the sensitive eye of the *bonseki* artist are ranked among Japan's

most precious national treasures, but, except to move them, they
are untouched by the human hand.

The Zen monks liked also to cultivate gardens which took advantage of an existing natural setting–to arrange rocks and plants
along the edges of a stream, creating a more informal atmosphere
suggesting a mountain canyon adjoining the monastery buildings.
They were always sparing and reserved in their use of color, as
were the Sung painters before them, since masses of flowers in
sharply varying colors are seldom found in the state of nature.
Though not symmetrical, the Japanese garden has a clearly
perceptible form; unlike so many English and American flower
gardens, they do not resemble a daub in oil colors, and this delight in the form of plants carries over into the art of flower
arrangement inside the house, accentuating the shapes of single
sprays and leaves rather than bunched colors.

Every one of the arts which have been discussed involves a
technical training which follows the same essential principles as
training in Zen. The best account of this training thus far available in a Western language is Eugen Herrigel's *Zen in the Art
of Archery*, which is the author's story of his own experience
under a master of the Japanese bow. To this should be added the
already mentioned letter on Zen and swordsmanship (*kendo*) by
the seventeenth-century master Takuan, translated by Suzuki in
his *Zen Buddhism and Its Influence on Japanese Culture*.

The major problem of each of these disciplines is to bring the
student to the point from which he can really begin. Herrigel
spent almost five years trying to find the right way of releasing
the bowstring, for it had to be done "unintentionally," in the same
way as a ripe fruit bursts its skin. His problem was to resolve
the paradox of practicing relentlessly without ever "trying," and
to let go of the taut string intentionally without intention. His
master at one and the same time urged him to keep on working
and working, but also to stop making an effort. For the art cannot be learned unless the arrow "shoots itself," unless the string
is released *wu-hsin* and *wu-nien*, without "mind" and without

blocking, or "choice." After all those years of practice there came a day when it just happened–how, or why, Herrigel never understood.

The same is true in learning to use the brush for writing or painting. The brush must draw by itself. This cannot happen if one does not practice constantly. But neither can it happen if one makes an effort. Similarly, in swordsmanship one must not first decide upon a certain thrust and then attempt to make it, since by that time it will be too late. Decision and action must be simultaneous. This was the point of Dogen's image of firewood and ashes, for to say that firewood does not "become" ashes is to say that it has no intention to be ash before it is actually ash– and then it is no longer firewood. Dogen insisted that the two states were "clearly cut," and in the same way Herrigel's master did not want him to "mix" the two states of stretching and releasing the bow. He instructed him to draw it to the point of fullest tension and stop there without any purpose, any intention in mind as to what to do next. Likewise, in Dogen's view of za-zen one must be sitting "just to sit" and there must not be any intention to have satori.

The sudden visions of nature which form the substance of haiku arise in the same way, for they are never there when one looks for them. The artificial haiku always feels like a piece of life which has been deliberately broken off or wrenched away from the universe, whereas the genuine haiku has dropped off all by itself, and has the whole universe inside it.

Artists and craftsmen of the Far East have, indeed, measured, analyzed, and classified the techniques of the masters to such a degree that by deliberate imitation they can come close to "deceiving, if it were possible, even the elect." By all quantitative standards the work so contrived is indistinguishable from its models, just as bowmen and swordsmen trained by quite other methods can equal the feats of Zen-inspired samurai. But, so far as Zen is concerned, the end results have nothing to do with it. For, as we have seen all along, Zen has no goal; it is a traveling without point, with nowhere to go. To travel is to be alive, but to get somewhere is to be dead, for as our own proverb says, "To travel well is better than to arrive."

A world which increasingly consists of destinations without journeys between them, a world which values only "getting somewhere" as fast as possible, becomes a world without substance. One can get anywhere and everywhere, and yet the more this is possible, the less is anywhere and everywhere worth getting to. For points of arrival are too abstract, too Euclidean to be enjoyed, and it is all very much like eating the precise ends of a banana without getting what lies in between. The point, therefore, of these arts is the doing of them rather than the accomplishments. But, more than this, the real joy of them lies in what turns up unintentionally in the course of practice, just as the joy of travel is not nearly so much in getting where one wants to go as in the unsought surprises which occur on the journey.

Planned surprises are as much of a contradiction as intentional *satori*, and whoever aims at *satori* is after all like a person who sends himself Christmas presents for fear that others will forget him. One must simply face the fact that Zen is all that side of life which is completely beyond our control, and which will not come to us by any amount of forcing or wangling or cunning–stratagems which produce only fakes of the real thing. But the last word of Zen is not an absolute dualism–the rather barren world of controlled action on the one side, and the spontaneous world of uncontrolled surprise on the other. For who controls the controller?

Because Zen does not involve an ultimate dualism between the controller and the controlled, the mind and the body, the spiritual and the material, there is always a certain "physiological" aspect to its techniques. Whether Zen is practiced through *za-zen* or *cha-no-yu* or *kendo*, great importance is attached to the way of breathing. Not only is breathing one of the two fundamental rhythms of the body; it is also the process in which control and spontaneity, voluntary and involuntary action, find their most obvious identity. Long before the origins of the Zen School, both Indian *yoga* and Chinese Taoism practiced "watching the breath," with a view to *letting*–not forcing–it to become as slow and silent as possible. Physiologically and psychologically, the relationship between breathing and "insight" is not yet altogether clear. But if we look at man as process rather than entity, rhythm rather than structure, it is obvious that breathing is something which he does–and thus *is*–constantly. Therefore grasping air with the lungs goes hand-in-hand with grasping at life.

So-called "normal" breathing is fitful and anxious. The air is always being held and not fully released, for the individual seems incapable of "letting" it run its full course through the lungs. He breathes compulsively rather than freely. The technique therefore begins by encouraging a full release of the breath–easing it out as if the body were being emptied of air by a great leaden ball sinking through the chest and abdomen, and settling down into the ground. The returning in-breath is then allowed to follow as a simple reflex action. The air is not actively inhaled; it is just allowed to come–and then, when the lungs are comfortably filled, it is allowed to go out once more, the image of the leaden ball giving it the sense of "falling" out as distinct from being pushed out.

One might go as far as to say that this way of breathing is Zen itself in its physiological aspect. Yet, as with every other aspect of Zen, it is hindered by striving for it, and for this reason beginners in the breathing technique often develop the peculiar anxiety of feeling unable to breathe unless keeping up a conscious control. But just as there is no need to try to be in accord with the Tao, to try to see, or to try to hear, so it must be remembered that the breath will always take care of itself. This is not a breathing "exercise" so much as a "watching and letting" of the breath, and it is always a serious mistake to undertake it in the spirit of a compulsive discipline to be "practiced" with a goal in mind.

This way of breathing is not for special times alone. Like Zen itself, it is for all circumstances whatsoever, and in this way, as in others, every human activity can become a form of *za-zen*. The application of Zen in activity is not restricted to the formal arts, and, on the other hand, does not absolutely require the specific "sitting technique" of *za-zen* proper. The late Dr. Kunihiko Hashida, a lifelong student of Zen and editor of the works of Dogen, never used formal *za-zen*. But his "Zen practice" was precisely his study of physics, and to suggest his attitude he used to say that his lifework was "to science" rather than "to study science."

In its own way, each one of the arts which Zen has inspired gives vivid expression to the sudden or instantaneous quality of its view of the world. The momentariness of *sumi* paintings and *haiku,* and the total presence of mind required in *cha-no-yu* and *kendo,* bring out the real reason why Zen has always called itself the way of instantaneous awakening. It is not just that *satori* comes quickly and unexpectedly, all of a sudden, for mere speed has nothing to do with it. The reason is that Zen is a liberation from time. For if we open our eyes and see clearly, it becomes obvious that there is no other time than this instant, and that the past and the future are abstractions without any concrete reality.

Until this has become clear, it seems that our life is all past and future, and that the present is nothing more than the infinitesimal hairline which divides them. From this comes the sensation of "having no time," of a world which hurries by so rapidly that it is gone before we can enjoy it. But through "awakening to the instant" one sees that this is the reverse of the truth: it is rather the past and future which are the fleeting illusions, and the present which is eternally real. We discover that the linear succession of time is a convention of our single-track verbal thinking, of a consciousness which interprets the world by grasping little pieces of it, calling them things and events. But every such grasp of the mind excludes the rest of the world, so that this type of consciousness can get an approximate vision of the whole only through a series of grasps, one after another. Yet the super-ficiality of this consciousness is seen in the fact that it cannot and does not regulate even the human organism. For if it had to con-trol the heartbeat, the breath, the operation of the nerves, glands, muscles, and sense organs, it would be rushing wildly around the body taking care of one thing after another, with no time to do anything else. Happily, it is not in charge, and the organism is regulated by the timeless "original mind," which deals with life in its totality and so can do ever so many "things" at once.

However, it is not as if the superficial consciousness were one thing, and the "original mind" another, for the former is a specialized activity of the latter. Thus the superficial conscious-ness can awaken to the eternal present if it stops grasping. But this does not come to pass by trying to concentrate on the present –an effort which succeeds only in making the moment seem ever more elusive and fleeting, ever more impossible to bring into focus. Awareness of the "eternal now" comes about by the same principle as the clarity of hearing and seeing and the proper freedom of the breath. Clear sight has nothing to do with trying to see; it is just the realization that the eyes will take in every detail all by themselves, for so long as they are open one can hardly prevent the light from reaching them. In the same way, there is no difficulty in being fully aware of the eternal present as soon as it is seen that one cannot possibly be aware of any-thing else–that in concrete fact there *is* no past or future. Making an effort to concentrate on the instantaneous moment implies at once that there are other moments. But they are nowhere to be found, and in truth one rests as easily in the eternal present as the eyes and ears respond to light and sound.

Now this eternal present is the "timeless," unhurried flowing of the Tao–

> Such a tide as, moving, seems to sleep,
> Too full for sound or foam.

As Nan-ch'üan said, to try to accord with it is to deviate from it, though in fact one cannot deviate and there is no one to deviate.

So, too, one cannot get away from the eternal present by trying to attend to it, and this very fact shows that, apart from this present, there is no distinct self that watches and knows it–which is why Hui-k'o could not find his mind when Bodhidharma asked him to produce it. However puzzling this may be, and however many philosophical problems it may raise, one clear look is enough to show its unavoidable truth. There is only this *now*. It does not come from anywhere; it is not going anywhere. It is not permanent, but it is not impermanent. Though moving, it is always still. When we try to catch it, it seems to run away, and yet it is always here and there is no escape from it. And when we turn round to find the self which knows this moment, we find that it has vanished like the past. Therefore the Sixth Patriarch says in the *T'an-ching:*

> In this moment there is nothing which comes to be. In this moment there is nothing which ceases to be. Thus there is no birth-and-death to be brought to an end. Wherefore the absolute tranquillity (of *nirvana*) is this present moment. Though it is at this moment, there is no limit to this moment, and herein is eternal delight. (7) *k*

Yet, when it comes to it, this moment can be called "present" only in relation to past and future, or to someone to whom it is present. But when there is neither past nor future, and no one to whom this moment is present, what is it? When Fa-ch'ang was dying, a squirrel screeched on the roof. "It's just this," he said, "and nothing else."

BIBLIOGRAPHY

The Bibliography is divided into two parts: (1) The principal original sources consulted in the preparation of this book. The Japanese pronunciations are in round brackets. References are to the Japanese edition of the complete Chinese Tripitaka, the *Taisho Daizokyo* in 85 volumes (Tokyo, 1924–1932), and to Nanjio's *Catalogue of the Chinese Translation of the Buddhist Tripitaka* (Oxford, 1883; repr., Tokyo, 1929). (2) A general bibliography of works on Zen in European languages, together with some other works on Indian and Chinese philosophy to which reference has been made in this book. To the best of my knowledge, this section includes every important book or scholarly article on Zen published until the present time, July, 1956.

1. PRINCIPAL SOURCES

Cheng-tao Ke (Shodoka) 證道歌
Song of the Realization of the Way.
Yung-chia Hsüan-chüeh (Yoka Genkaku), 665–713.
Taisho 2014.
Trans. Suzuki (6), Senzaki & McCandless (1).

Ching-te Ch'uan-teng Lu (Keitoku Dento Roku) 景德傳燈錄
Record of the Transmission of the Lamp.
Tao-yüan (Dogen), *c.* 1004.
Taisho 2076. Nanjio 1524.

Daiho Shogen Kokushi Hogo 大法正眼國師法語
Sermons of the National Teacher Daiho Shogen (i.e., Bankei).
Bankei Zenji, 1622–1693.
Ed. Suzuki and Furata. Daito Shuppansha, Tokyo, 1943.

Hsin-hsin Ming (Shinjinmei) 信心銘
Treatise on Faith in the Mind.

Seng-ts'an (Sosan), *d.* 606.
Taisho 2010.
Trans. Suzuki (1), vol. 1, and (6), and Waley in Conze (2).

Ku-tsun-hsü Yü-lu (*Kosonshuku Goroku*) 古尊宿語錄
Recorded Sayings of the Ancient Worthies.
Tse (Seki), Sung dynasty.
Fu-hsüeh Shu-chü, Shanghai, n.d. Also in *Dainihon Zoku-
zokyo,* Kyoto, 1905–1912.

Lin-chi Lu (*Rinzai Roku*) 臨濟錄
Record of Lin-chi.
Lin-chi I-hsüan (Rinzai Gigen), *d.* 867.
Taisho 1985. Also in *Ku-tsun-hsü Yü-lu,* fasc. 1.

Liu-tsu T'an-ching (*Rokuso Dangyo*) 六祖壇經
Platform Sutra of the Sixth Patriarch.
Ta-chien Hui-neng (Daikan Eno), 638–713.
Taisho 2008. Nanjio 1525.
Trans. Wong Mou-lam (1) and Rousselle (1).

Pi-yen Lu (*Hekigan Roku*) 碧巖錄
Record of the Green Rock.
Yuan-wu K'o-ch'in (Engo Kokugon), 1063–1135.
Taisho 2003.

Shen-hui Ho-chang I-chi (*Jinne Osho Ishu*) 神會和尚遺集
Collected Traditions of Shen-hui.
Ho-tse Shen-hui (Kataku Jinne), 668–770.
Tun-huang MS, Pelliot 3047 and 3488.
Ed. Hu Shih. Oriental Book Co., Shanghai, 1930.
Trans. Gernet (1).

Shobo Genzo 正法眼藏
The Eye Treasury of the True Dharma.
Dogen Zenji, 1200–1253.
Ed. Kunihiko Hashida. Sankibo Busshorin, Tokyo, 1939.
  Also in *Dogen Zenji Zenshu,* pp. 3–472. Shinjusha,
  Tokyo, 1940.

Wu-men Kuan (*Mumon Kan*) 無門關
The Barrier Without Gate.
Wu-men Hui-k'ai (Mumon Ekai), 1184–1260.
Taisho 2005.
Trans. Senzaki & Reps (1), Ogata (1), and Dumoulin (1).

2. WORKS IN EUROPEAN LANGUAGES

ANESAKI, M. *History of Japanese Religion*. Kegan Paul, London, 1930.

BENOIT, H. *The Supreme Doctrine*. Pantheon, New York, and Routledge, London, 1955.

BLYTH, R. H. (1) *Zen in English Literature and Oriental Classics*. Hokuseido, Tokyo, 1948.
(2) *Haiku*. 4 vols. Hokuseido, Tokyo, 1949–1952.
(3) *Buddhist Sermons on Christian Texts*. Kokudosha, Tokyo, 1952.
(4) "Ikkyu's Doka," *The Young East*, vols. II. 2 to III. 9. Tokyo, 1952–1954.

CHAPIN, H. B. "The Ch'an Master Pu-tai," *Journal of the American Oriental Society*, vol. LIII, pp. 47–52.

CHU CH'AN (BLOFELD, J.) (1) *The Huang Po Doctrine of Universal Mind*. Buddhist Society, London, 1947.
(2) *The Path to Sudden Attainment*. Buddhist Society, London, 1948.

CH'U TA-KAO *Tao Te Ching*. Buddhist Society, London, 1937.

CONZE, E. (1) *Buddhism: Its Essence and Development*. Cassirer, Oxford, 1953.
(2) *Buddhist Texts Through the Ages*. Edited in conjunction with I. B. Horner, D. Snellgrove, and A. Waley. Cassirer, Oxford, 1954.
(3) *Selected Sayings from the Perfection of Wisdom*. Buddhist Society, London, 1955.

COOMARASWAMY, A. K. "Who Is Satan and Where Is Hell?" *The Review of Religion*, vol. XII. 1, pp. 76–87. New York, 1947.

DEMIÉVILLE, P. (1) *Hobogirin*. 4 fasc. Edited in conjunction with S. Levi and J. Takakusu. Maison Franco-Japonaise, Tokyo, 1928–1931.

(2) *Le Concile de Lhasa*. vol. I. Imprimerie Nationale de France, Paris, 1952.

DUMOULIN, H. (1) "Das Wu-men-kuan oder 'Der Pass ohne Tor,'" *Monumenta Serica*, vol. VIII. 1943.

(2) "Bodhidharma und die Anfänge des Ch'an Buddhismus," *Monumenta Nipponica*, vol. VII. 1951.

DUMOULIN, H., & SASAKI, R. F. *The Development of Chinese Zen after the Sixth Patriarch*. First Zen Institute, New York, 1953.

DUYVENDAK, J. J. L. *Tao Te Ching*. Murray, London, 1954.

ELIOT, SIR C. *Japanese Buddhism*. Arnold, London, 1935.

FIRST ZEN INSTITUTE OF AMERICA. (1) *Cat's Yawn*, 1940–1941. Published in one vol., First Zen Institute, New York, 1947.

(2) *Zen Notes*. First Zen Institute, New York, since January, 1954.

FUNG YU-LAN (1) *A History of Chinese Philosophy*. 2 vols. Tr. Derk Bodde. Princeton, 1953.

(2) *The Spirit of Chinese Philosophy*. Tr. E. R. Hughes. Kegan Paul, London, 1947.

GATENBY, E. V. *The Cloud Men of Yamato*. Murray, London, 1929.

GERNET, J. (1) "Entretiens du Maître de Dhyana Chen-houei du Ho-tsö," *Publications de l'École Française d'Extrême-Orient*, vol. XXXI. 1949.

(2) "Biographie du Maître Chen-houei du Ho-tsö," *Journal Asiatique*, 1951.

(3) "Entretiens du Maître Ling-yeou du Kouei-chan," *Bulletin de l'École Française d'Extrême-Orient*, vol. XLV. 1. 1951.

GILES, H. A. *Chuang-tzu*. Kelly & Walsh, Shanghai, 1926.

GILES, L. *Taoist Teachings*. Translations from Lieh-tzu. Murray, London, 1925.

GROSSE, E. *Die Ostasiatische Tuschmalerei*. Cassirer, Berlin, 1923.

HARRISON, E. J. *The Fighting Spirit of Japan.* Unwin, London, 1913.

HERRIGEL, E. *Zen in the Art of Archery.* Pantheon, New York, 1953.

HUMPHREYS, C. *Zen Buddhism.* Heinemann, London, 1949.

HU SHIH (1) "The Development of Zen Buddhism in China," *Chinese Political and Social Review,* vol. XV. 4. 1932. (2) "Ch'an (Zen) Buddhism in China, Its History and Method," *Philosophy East and West,* vol. III. 1. Honolulu, 1953.

KEITH, SIR A. B. *Buddhist Philosophy in India and Ceylon.* Oxford, 1923.

LIEBENTHAL, W. "The Book of Chao," *Monumenta Serica,* Monog., XIII. Peking, 1948.

LIN YUTANG *The Wisdom of Lao-tse.* Modern Library, New York, 1948.

LINSSEN, R. *Essais sur le Bouddhisme en général et sur le Zen en particulier.* 2 vols. Editions Etre Libre, Brussels, 1954.

MASUNAGA, R. "The Standpoint of Dogen and His Treatise on Time," *Religion East and West,* vol. I. University of Tokyo, 1955.

MURTI, T. R. V. *The Central Philosophy of Buddhism.* Allen & Unwin, London, 1955.

NEEDHAM, J. *Science and Civilization in China.* 2 vols. (5 vols. to follow). Cambridge University Press, 1954 and 1956.

NUKARIYA, K. *The Religion of the Samurai.* Luzac, London, 1913.

OGATA, S. *Guide to Zen Practice.* A partial translation of the *Mu-mon Kan.* Bukkasha, Kyoto, 1934.

OHASAMA, S., & FAUST, A. *Zen, der lebendige Buddhismus in Japan.* Gotha, 1925.

OKAKURA, K. *The Book of Tea.* Foulis, Edinburgh, 1919.

PELLIOT, P. "Notes sur quelques artistes des Six Dynasties et des T'ang," *T'oung Pao,* vol. XXII. 1923.

ROUSSELLE, E. "Liu-tsu T'an-ching," *Sinica,* vols. V, VI, & XI. 1930, 1931, 1936.

SASAKI, T. *Zen: With Special Reference to Soto Zen.* Soto Sect Headquarters, Tokyo, 1955.

SENGAI *India-Ink Drawings.* Oakland Museum, Oakland, 1956.

SENZAKI, N. *Zen Meditation.* Bukkasha, Kyoto, 1936.

SENZAKI, N., & MCCANDLESS, R. *Buddhism and Zen.* Philosophical Library, New York, 1953.

SENZAKI, N., & REPS, P. (1) *The Gateless Gate.* A translation of the *Mu-mon Kan.* Murray, Los Angeles, 1934.

(2) *101 Zen Stories.* McKay, Philadelphia, n.d.

SIREN, O. "Zen Buddhism and Its Relation to Art," *Theosophical Path.* Point Loma, Calif., October, 1934.

SOGEN ASAHINA *Zen.* Sakane, Tokyo, 1954.

SOROKIN, P. (ed). *Forms and Techniques of Altruistic and Spiritual Growth.* Beacon Press, Boston, 1954.

SOYEN SHAKU *Sermons of a Buddhist Abbot.* Open Court, Chicago, 1906.

STCHERBATSKY, TH. *The Conception of Buddhist Nirvana.* Leningrad, 1927.

STEINILBER-OBERLIN, E., & MATSUO, K. *The Buddhist Sects of Japan.* Allen & Unwin, London, 1938.

SUZUKI, D. T. (1) *Essays in Zen Buddhism.* 3 vols. Luzac, London, 1927, 1933, 1934. Repr., Rider, London, 1949, 1950, 1951.

(2) *Studies in the Lankavatara Sutra.* Routledge, London, 1930.

(3) *The Lankavatara Sutra.* Routledge, London, 1932. Repr., 1956.

(4) *Introduction to Zen Buddhism.* Kyoto, 1934. Repr., Philosophical Library, New York, 1949.

(5) *Training of the Zen Buddhist Monk.* Eastern Buddhist Society, Kyoto, 1934.

(6) *Manual of Zen Buddhism.* Kyoto, 1935. Repr., Rider, London, 1950.

(7) *Zen Buddhism and Its Influence on Japanese Culture.* Eastern Buddhist Society, Kyoto, 1938. (Shortly to be reprinted in the Bollingen Series.)

(8) *The Essence of Buddhism.* Buddhist Society, London, 1947.

(9) *The Zen Doctrine of No-Mind.* Rider, London, 1949.

(10) *Living by Zen.* Rider, London, 1950.

(11) *Studies in Zen.* Rider, London, 1955.

(12) "Professor Rudolph Otto on Zen Buddhism," *Eastern Buddhist,* vol. III, pp. 93–116.

(13) "Zen Buddhism on Immortality. An Extract from the Hekiganshu," *Eastern Buddhist,* vol. III, pp. 213–23.

(14) "The Recovery of a Lost MS on the History of Zen in China," *Eastern Buddhist,* vol. IV, pp. 199–298.

(15) "Ignorance and World Fellowship," *Faiths and Fellowship.* Watkins, London, 1937.

(16) "Buddhist Symbolism," *Symbols and Values.* Harper, New York, 1954.

(17) "Zen and Pragmatism," *Philosophy East and West,* vol. IV. 2. Honolulu, 1954.

(18) "The Awakening of a New Consciousness in Zen," *Eranos-Jahrbuch,* vol. XXIII. Rhein-Verlag, Zürich, 1955.

TAKAKUSU, J. *Essentials of Buddhist Philosophy.* University of Hawaii, Honolulu, 1947.

WALEY, A. *Zen Buddhism and Its Relation to Art.* Luzac, London, 1922.

WATTS, A. W. (1) *The Spirit of Zen.* Murray, London, 1936. 2nd ed., 1955.

(2) *Zen Buddhism.* Buddhist Society, London, 1947.

(3) *Zen.* (Same as above, but enlarged.) Delkin, Stanford, 1948.

(4) *The Way of Liberation in Zen Buddhism.* American Academy of Asian Studies, San Francisco, 1955.

(5) "The Problem of Faith and Works in Buddhism," *Review of Religion,* vol. V. 4. New York, May, 1941.

WENTZ, W. Y. E. *Tibetan Yoga and Secret Doctrines.* Oxford, 1935.

WILHELM, R. (1) *The Secret of the Golden Flower.* A translation of the *T'ai I Chin Hua Tsung Chih,* with commentary by C. G. Jung. Kegan Paul, London, 1931.

(2) *The I Ching or Book of Changes.* 2 vols. Tr. Cary Baynes. Pantheon, New York, 1950.

WONG MOU-LAM *The Sutra of Wei Lang (Hui-neng).* Luzac, London, 1944.

CHINESE NOTES

Read horizontally, from left to right

I. 1. THE PHILOSOPHY OF THE TAO

[a] 人 [b] 自然 [c] 道 [d] 念 [e] 德

[f] 道可道非常道 [g] 精 [h] 爲

[i] 無爲 [j] 道法自然 [k] 玄

[l] 有一物上拄天下拄地。黑似漆。常在動用中。 [m] 素

[n] 仁 [o] 悟 [p] 横心之所念 [q] 無心

[r] 心 [s] 忢 [t] 本心 [u] 佛心 [v] 信心

I. 2. THE ORIGINS OF BUDDHISM

[a] 仁 [b] 義 [c] 禪

I. 3. MAHAYANA BUDDHISM

[a] 不生不滅 [b] 四法界

事 理 理事無礙

事事無礙

I. 4. THE RISE AND DEVELOPMENT OF ZEN

直指　頓悟　格義　坐禪

帝問如何是聖諦第一義、

師曰廓然無聖、帝曰對朕

者誰、師曰不識。　壁觀

二祖云、弟子心未安、乞師安

心。磨云、將心來爲汝安。祖

云、覓心了不可得。磨云、爲汝

安心竟。　問答

教外別傳、

不立文字、

212

直指人心、
見性成佛。

至道無難、唯嫌揀擇。
任性合道、逍遙絕惱、
繫念乖真。勿惡六塵、
六塵不惡、還同正覺、
智者無爲、愚人自縛。
將心用心、豈非大錯。

來禮師曰、乞與解脫法門。
師曰、誰縛汝、曰無人縛、師
曰、何更求解脫乎。

身是菩提樹、心如明鏡臺、
時時勤拂拭、莫使惹塵埃。

[m]菩提本無樹、心鏡亦非臺。
本來無一物、何處惹塵埃。
[n]來去自由通用無滯即是
般若三昧自在解脱名無
念行。若百物不思當令念
絶即是法縛即名邊見。
[o]住心觀淨是病非禪、長坐
拘身於理何益。
[p]起心著淨却生淨妄。何名
坐禪此法門中無障無礙
外於一切善惡境界、心念
不起名爲坐。
[q]若有人問汝義問有將無對。

問無將有對、問凡以聖對、
問聖以凡對。二道相因生
中道義、汝一問一對。
「君不見絕學無爲道人、
不除妄想不求真、
無明實性即佛性、
幻化空身即法身。」
往問曰、大德坐禪圖什麼、
一曰、圖作佛、師乃取一塼
於彼庵前石上磨。一曰、師
作什麼。師曰、磨作鏡。一曰、
磨塼豈得成鏡耶。師曰坐
禪豈成佛耶。 「喝」

道不屬修若言修得修
成還壞即同聲聞若言不
修即同凡　泉云、平常心是
道。趙州云、還可趣向否。泉云、
擬向即乖。　無　僧　雲水
無事　山僧與麼說意在什
麼處、祇為道流一切馳求
心不能歇、止他古人閒機
境、道流取山僧見處坐斷
報化佛頭十地滿心猶如
客作兒等妙二覺擔枷
鎖漢羅漢辟支猶如廁穢
菩提涅槃如繫驢橛。

佛法無用功處、祇是平常無
事屙屎送尿著 衣喫飯困
來即臥愚人笑 我 智乃知。
你且隨處作主立處皆眞境
來回換不得、縱有從來習氣
五無間業自爲解脱大海。
心外無法內亦不可得、求什
麼物你諸方言道有修有證、
莫錯設有修得者皆是生死
業、你言六度萬行齊修我
見皆是造業、求佛求法即是
造地獄業。^{bb}五位 ^{cc}正 ^{dd}偏
^{ee}公案 ^{ff}疑 情 ^{gg}汝學坐禪爲

學坐佛若學坐禪禪非坐臥、
若學坐佛佛非定相於無住
法不應取捨汝若坐佛即是
殺佛若執坐相非達其理。
[hh]生來坐不臥、
死去臥不坐、
元是臭骨頭。

II. 1. "EMPTY AND MARVELOUS"

[a]至道無難、唯嫌揀擇、
但莫憎愛、洞然明白、
毫釐有差 天地懸隔、
欲得現前、莫存順逆、
違順相爭、是爲心病。

^b受災如受福、受降如受敵。

^c黃昏雞報曉、半夜日頭明。

^d問終日著衣喫飯如何免得著衣喫飯、師云著衣喫飯、進云、不會、師云、不會即著衣喫飯。

^e寒即圍爐向猛火、
熱即竹林溪畔坐。

^f雨中看杲日、火裏酌清泉。

^g樹呈風體態、波弄月精神。

^h經云但以眾法合成此身、起時唯法起、滅時唯法滅、此法起時不言我起、滅時

不言我滅、前念後念中念
念念不相待念念寂滅。
[i]春色無高下、花枝自短長。
[j]長者長法身、短者短法身。
[k]老僧三十年前未參禪時、
見山是山、見水是水及至
後來親見知識、有箇入處、
見山不是山、見水不是水。
而今得箇體歇處、依然見
山秖是山、見水秖是水。
[l]空劫之時無一切名字、佛
纔出世來便有名字、所以
取相、大道一切實無凡聖、

220

苦有名字皆屬限量。所以江
西老宿云、不是心不是佛不
是物。汝但無事於心無心
於事則虛而靈空而妙。

宗門七縱八橫殺活臨時。僧
便問、如何是殺。師云、冬去春
來。僧云、冬去春來時如何。師
云、橫擔拄杖。東西南北、一
任打野榿。

神通並妙用、運水及搬柴。

II. 2. "SITTING QUIETLY, DOING NOTHING"

如刀能割不自割、
如眼能看不自看。

^b兀然無事坐、春來草自生。
^c青山自青山、白雲自白雲。
^d妙用 ^e不可以有心得、
　　　　不可以無心求。
^f去 ^g不生 ^h若虛空勿涯岸
不離當処常湛然、覓即知君
不可見、取不得、捨不得、不可
得中、只麼得、默時説、説時默、
大施門開無擁塞。
ⁱ一撃忘所知、更不假修治、
動容揚古路。
^j不信只看八九月、
紛紛黃葉滿山川。

相見呵呵笑、園林落葉多。
若是本分人、須是有驅耕
夫之牛、奪飢人之食底手腳。
驀直去　念　任運著衣裳、
要行即行、要坐即坐、無一念
心希求佛果。你諸方言道有
修有證、莫錯　設有修得者皆
是生死業　你言六度萬行齊
修我見皆是造業、求佛求法
即是造地獄業、求菩薩亦是
造業、看經看教亦是造業、佛
與祖師是無事人。諸方說有
道可修有法可證、何法修何

道、你今用處欠少什麼物、
修補何處。

ᵖ爭如著衣喫飲、
此外更無佛祖。

�ۛ識得本心本性、
正是宗門大病。

ʳ入林不動草、入水不立波。

ˢ護生須是殺、殺盡始安居。

ᵗ一句定乾坤、一劍平天下。

ᵘ若人修道道不行、萬般邪境
競頭生、智劍出來無一物。

II. 3. ZA-ZEN AND THE KO-AN

[a]本証妙修 [b]體 [c]用 [d]法身。
機關、言詮、難透、五位。
[e]孤掌難鳴 [f]有時奪人不
奪境、有時奪境不奪人有
時人境俱奪、有時人境俱
不奪。
[g]移花兼蝶到達磨道不知。

II. 4. THE ARTS OF ZEN

[a]易 [b]江月照松風吹、
永夜清宵何所爲。
[c]寂 [d]侘 [e]哀 [f]幽玄 [g]風流
[h]風穴和尚因僧問、語默流離

225

微如何通不犯，穴云、
　　長憶江南三月裏、
　　鷓鴣啼處百花香。
風定花猶落、鳥鳴山更幽。
破鏡不重照、落花難上枝。
無有生相刹那無有滅相、
更無生滅可滅是則寂滅
現前當現前時亦無現前
之量乃為常樂。

INDEX

Proper names of persons are printed in capitals, and, in the case of Chinese Zen masters, the Japanese pronunciation follows the Chinese in parentheses. Titles of works are printed in italics.

NATURE, MAN,
AND WOMAN

To the beloved company of the stars, the moon, and the sun;
to ocean, air, and the silence of space;
to jungle, glacier, and desert,
soft earth, clear water, and fire on my hearth.
To a certain waterfall in a high forest;
to night rain upon the roof and the wide leaves,
grass in the wind, tumult of sparrows in a bush,
and eyes which give light to the day.

Contents

Preface

AS I LOOK AROUND MY LIBRARY I AM OFTEN
strangely troubled by the way in which my books fit so
snugly into categories. Most of my books have to do with
philosophy, psychology, and religion, and they represent
points of view from every great culture of the world.
Yet with an absolutely oppressive monotony they fit themselves into the stale dualities of philosophical and theological argument, varied from time to time with sensible and
uninspiring compromises. Volume after volume is so easily
identified as supernaturalist or naturalist, vitalist or mechanist, metaphysical or positivist, spiritualist or materialist,
and the compromise volumes are usually so watered down
as to be compilations of platitudes and sentimentalities.

Underlying all these dualities there seems to be a basic
division of opinion about those two great poles of human
thought, spirit and nature. Some people stand plainly "for"
one and "against" the other. Some stand mainly for one but
give the other a subordinate role. Others attempt to bring
the two together, though human thinking moves in such
firm ruts that it usually turns out that they have settled
inadvertently for one or the other. It is doubtless foolhardy
for any philosopher to claim that he has broken loose from
these ruts and at the same time said anything meaningful.
Discussion is so much a matter of juggling with categories
that to start breaking up the categories is usually to break
up the discussion.

But this is not just a matter of categories, logic, and phil-

osophical argument. The opposition of spirit and nature
is also a matter of life and feeling. Ever since I began to
study these matters I have been puzzled by the way in
which exponents of the life of the spirit do not seem to be
at home in nature and in their bodies, for even when they
do not identify the natural with the evil they damn it with
faint praise. So often I have sympathized with bold pagan
rebellion against this bodiless spirituality, and yet never
joined it because the final word of this "gather ye rosebuds
while ye may" philosophy is always despair—or some
fatuous utopianism which, because it is only a matter of
time, comes to the same thing. For the congenitally sick,
the victims of accident, the impoverished, and the dying
this philosophy has no message.

But is the alternative to joy in the body delight in the
discarnate spirit? I have been realizing more and more
that partisans to opposed philosophies share the same
premises, which are usually unconscious. Furthermore,
these premises are transmitted by such social institutions
as the structure of language and the learning of roles, influencing us in ways of which we are hardly aware. Thus
the conventional saint and the conventional sinner, the
ascetic and the sensualist, the metaphysician and the materialist may have so much in common that their opposition is quite trivial. Like alternating heat and cold, they
may be symptoms of the same fever.

Unconscious premises of this kind come to light when
we try to understand cultures very far removed from our
own. They too have their hidden assumptions, but when
we compare these cultures with our own the basic differences must at last become obvious. This is peculiarly true
of the cultures of the Far East, because they are high civilizations which arose in isolation from the West, developing patterns of thought and language startlingly different

from those of the Indo-European strain. Thus the value of the study of Chinese language and thought is not simply that we ought to be able to communicate with the Chinese people, important as this is. It is rather that Chinese studies tell us so much about ourselves, for the very reason that of all the advanced cultures of the world this is the most unlike our own in its ways of thinking.

Thus it was always such a delight to me that Chinese philosophy would never quite fit into the ruts of Western, and even Indian, thought, and this was pre-eminently true of the problem of spirit and nature. For there were no categories of Chinese thought corresponding to spirit and nature as we understand them. Here was a culture in which the conflict between spirit and nature hardly existed, a culture where the most "naturalistic" painting and poetry were precisely the most "spiritual" of its art forms.

This book is not, however, a formal account of the Chinese philosophy of nature. I have discussed this at length in my previous book, *The Way of Zen,* and it has been marvellously illuminated by Joseph Needham in his *Science and Civilization in China.* My object here is not to expound and compare philosophical systems; it is to reflect upon a great human problem in the light of the Chinese view of nature, especially as it was expressed by Lao-tzu and Chuang-tzu. The urgency of the problem of man's relation to nature and the general intent of this book are, I think, sufficiently discussed in the Introduction which follows. Here I have also explained why the problem of man's relation to nature raises the problem of man's relation to woman—a matter about which the spiritually-minded members of our own culture have been significantly squeamish.

Because this book is one in which I am frankly "thinking out loud," I would like to repeat some remarks from the

Preface to my *Supreme Identity*. "I am not one who believes that it is any necessary virtue in the philosopher to spend his life defending a consistent position. It is surely a kind of spiritual pride to refrain from 'thinking out loud,' and to be unwilling to let a thesis appear in print until you are prepared to champion it to the death. Philosophy, like science, is a social function, for a man cannot think rightly alone, and the philosopher must publish his thought as much to learn from criticism as to contribute to the sum of wisdom. If, then, I sometimes make statements in an authoritative and dogmatic manner, it is for the sake of clarity rather than from the desire to pose as an oracle."

There is the prevalent belief in the West that intellectual and philosophical pursuits are unessential ornaments of culture of far less value than active and technological accomplishments. This attitude is in great danger of being confused with the Eastern view that real knowledge is nonverbal and beyond the reach of concepts. But our actions are almost invariably directed by a philosophy of ends and values, and to the extent that this is unconscious it is liable to be bad philosophy with disastrous active consequences. The so-called "nonintellectuality" of the East lies as far above thought as mere activism lies below it. Such knowledge cannot be reached by making one's concepts unconscious under the impression that one is sacrificing the intellect. Distorting premises can be abandoned only by those who go down to the roots of their thinking and find out what they are.

ALAN WATTS

Mill Valley, California
February, 1958

Introduction

A FLOOR OF MANY-COLORED PEBBLES LIES
beneath clear water, with fish at first noticed only by
their shadows, hanging motionless or flashing through the
liquid, ever-changing net of sunlight. We can watch it for
hours, taken clear out of time and our own urgent history,
by a scene which has been going on just like this for
perhaps two million years. At times, it catches us right
below the heart with an ache of nostalgia and delight compounded, when it seems that this is, after all, the world
of sane, enduring reality from which we are somehow in
exile.

But the feeling does not last because we *know* better.
We know that the fish swim in constant fear of their lives,
that they hang motionless so as not to be seen, and dart into
motion because they are just nerves, startled into a jump
by the tiniest ghost of an alarm. We know that the "love
of nature" is a sentimental fascination with surfaces—that
the gulls do not float in the sky for delight but in watchful
hunger for fish, that the golden bees do not dream in the
lilies but call as routinely for honey as collection agents
for rent, and that the squirrels romping, as it seems, freely
and joyously through the branches, are just frustrated little
balls of appetite and fear. We know that the peaceful
rationality, the relaxed culture, and the easy normality of
civilized human life are a crust of habit repressing emotions too violent or poignant for most of us to stand—the
first resting place which life has found in its arduous climb

1

from the primordial, natural world of relentless struggle and terror.

But we *think* we know, for this robustly realistic, tough-guy picture is as much a re-creation of the natural world in our own image as the most romantic and escapist of country ecstasies. Our view of nature is largely a matter of changing intellectual and literary fashions, for it has become a world strangely alien to us. This estrangement is intensified in a time and a culture wherein it is widely believed that we must depart from the principles which have hitherto governed the evolution of life. For it is felt that the future organization of the world can no longer be left to the complex and subtle processes of natural balance from which life and man himself arose. When the process brought forth human intelligence, it introduced an entirely new principle of order. From now on, it is claimed, the organization of life cannot *happen;* it must be *controlled,* however intricate the task. In this task the human intellect will no longer be able to rely upon the innate and natural "wisdom" of the organism which produced it. It will have to stand alone, relying strictly upon its own resources. Whether he likes it or not, man—or rather the conscious intelligence of man—must henceforth rule the world.

This is an astonishing jump to conclusions for a being who knows so little about himself, and who will even admit that such sciences of the intelligence as psychology and neurology are not beyond the stage of preliminary dabbling. For if we do not know even how we manage to be conscious and intelligent, it is most rash to assume that we know what the role of conscious intelligence will be, and still more that it is competent to order the world. [It is this very ignorance of and, indeed, estrangement from ourselves which explains our feeling of isolation from nature.] We are, as it were, cut asunder into a confined

"I" is seperated from its environment

center of attentiveness, which is "I," and a vast organic complexity which we know only in terms of indescribable and disquieting feelings, or abstract biological technicalities: and this is "myself." Throughout his history, the type of man molded by the Western cultures has been peculiarly estranged from himself, and thus from the natural environment in which his organism inheres. Christian philosophy, which knows so much about the nature of God, has so little to say about the nature of man, for beside its precise and voluminous definitions of the Holy Trinity stand the vaguest and briefest descriptions of the human soul and spirit. The body, grudgingly admitted to be good because it is God's handiwork, has in practice been viewed as territory captured by the Devil, and the study of human nature has been mostly the study of its foibles. In this respect the psychologists have faithfully followed the theologians.

For the scientist, despite his theoretical naturalism, tends to regard nature, human and otherwise, as a world to be conquered and reordered, to be made subject to the technology of the rational intellect, which has somehow disowned and shaken off its roots in the very organism it now presumes to improve. In practice, the technical, rational consciousness is as alien to the natural man as was the supernatural soul. For both alike, nature and the natural man is an object, studied always by a technique which makes it external and therefore different from the subjective observer. For when no knowledge is held to be respectable which is not objective knowledge, what we know will always seem to be *not* ourselves, not the subject. Thus we have the feeling of knowing things only from the outside, never from within, of being confronted eternally with a world of impenetrable surfaces within surfaces within surfaces. No wonder, then, that our ideas of what nature is like on the inside are guesses at the mercy of fashion.

In some ways, however, the temper of scientific thought is far less managing and imperious than it was at the beginning of this century, if only because greater knowledge brings with it an awareness of ignorance. At the same time, even from the most coldly intellectual point of view, it becomes clearer and clearer that we do not live in a divided world. The harsh divisions of spirit and nature, mind and body, subject and object, controller and controlled are seen more and more to be awkward conventions of language. These are misleading and clumsy terms for describing a world in which all events seem to be mutually interdependent—an immense complexity of subtly balanced relationships which, like an endless knot, has no loose end from which it can be untangled and put in supposed order.

It is not that spirit has been reduced to nature, or to what "nature" used to mean, or that the mind has been reduced to the body. We have less and less use for words which denote stuffs, entities, and substances, for mind and matter have together disappeared into *process*. Things have become events, and we think of them in terms of pattern, configuration, or structure, no longer finding any meaning in the question, "Of what stuff is this pattern made?" But the important point is that a world of interdependent relationships, where things are intelligible only in terms of each other, is a seamless unity. In such a world it is impossible to consider man apart from nature, as an exiled spirit which controls this world by having its roots in another. Man is himself a loop in the endless knot, and as he pulls in one direction he finds that he is pulled from another and cannot find the origin of the impulse. For the mold of his thoughts prevents him. He has an idea of himself, the subject, and of nature, the object. If he cannot find the source of the impulse in either, he is confused. He cannot settle for voluntarism and he cannot settle for determinism. But the confusion lies in the tangle of his thoughts rather than the convolutions of the knot.

Yet in the present atmosphere of Western thought the realization of man's total involvement with nature is perhaps depressing. It is humiliating for a culture which always used to think of man as nature's head and lord. Even now, despite ever louder voices of warning, the culture still revels in technical power. Contrary to its avowed philosophy of living for the future, its perspective is really no longer than the day after tomorrow, for it exploits the resources of the earth and the energies of radioactivity with only the most fragmentary knowledge of the complex relationships so disturbed. The apparently depressing thing is not merely that the universe is not to be pushed heedlessly around, but that the very state of mind in which we attempt to do so is an illusion. For if man is one with nature in a seamless unity, his beneficent ideals must after all be rationalizations of the great primordial forces of lust and terror, of blind striving for survival, which we believe to be the basic impulses of nature.

But before we decide to be depressed we could learn to know nature from the inside. The discovery of our total involvement is momentous, so that the understanding of the character and inner working of the endless knot is the most important of all philosophical inquiries. As already suggested, we might find out that our notions of blind primordial urges are pure mythology. Might it not be that they are fashions in anthropomorphic thinking which have simply swung to the opposite pole from the older notion that the primordial impulse was the will of a personal and beneficent God? The very ideas of impulses, forces, motivations, and urges may be nothing more than abstract intellectual ghosts as impalpable as the mysterious "it" in the sentence, "It is raining." The same grammatic convention which requires subjects for verbs may be the sole reason for urges and drives behind actions. Yet such a line of thought may be even more disturbing, since it suggests a universe of life which has no motive at all—not even survival—and surely an absolutely purposeless world would be the most depressing of all possibilities.

But the idea of a purposeless world is horrifying because it is incomplete. Purpose is a pre-eminently human attribute. To say that the world has no purpose is to say that it is not human, or, as the *Tao Tê Ching* puts it:

> *Heaven and earth are not human-hearted* [jen].

But it continues:

> *The sage is not human-hearted.* v

For what is not human appears to be inhuman only when man sets himself over against nature, for then the inhumanity of nature seems to deny man, and its purposelessness to deny his purposes. But to say that nature is not human and has no purpose is not to say what it has instead. The human body as a whole is not a hand, but it does not for this reason deny the hand.

It is obviously the purest anthropomorphism to assume that the absence of a human quality in bird, cloud, or star is the presence of a total blank, or to assume that what is not conscious is merely unconscious. Nature is not necessarily arranged in accordance with the system of mutually exclusive alternatives which characterize our language and logic. Furthermore, may it not be that when we speak of nature as blind, and of matter-energy as unintelligent, we are simply projecting upon them the blankness which we feel when we try to know our own consciousness as an object, when we try to see our own eyes or taste our own tongues?

There is much to suggest that when human beings acquired the powers of conscious attention and rational thought they became so fascinated with these new tools that they forgot all else, like chickens hypnotized with their beaks to a chalk line. Our total sensitivity became identified with these partial functions so that we lost the ability to feel nature from the inside, and, more, to feel the seamless unity of ourselves and the world. Our philosophy of action falls into the alternatives of voluntarism and determinism, freedom and fate, because we have no sense of the wholeness of the endless knot and of the identity of its actions and ours. As Freud said:

> Originally the ego includes everything, later it detaches from itself the external world. The ego-feeling we are aware of now is thus only a shrunken vestige of a far more extensive feeling—a feeling which embraced the universe and expressed an inseparable connection of the ego with the external world.[1]

If this be true, we must not think of the hungers and fears of the plants and beasts in terms of our own exclusively egocentric style of awareness, for which the fate of the separated ego is the all-consuming interest because it is felt to be all that we are. Our difficulty is not that we have developed conscious attention but that we have lost the wider style of feeling which should be its background, the feeling which would let us know what nature is from the inside. Perhaps some intimation of this lost feeling underlies our perennial nostalgia for the "natural life," and the myth of a golden age from which we have fallen.

[1] Freud (1), p. 13.

There may be no reason to believe that a return to the lost feeling will cost us the sacrifice of the individualized consciousness, for the two are not incompatible. We can see an individual leaf in all its clarity without losing sight of its relation to the tree. The difference between ourselves and the animals is possibly that they have only the most rudimentary form of the individualized consciousness but a high degree of sensitivity to the endless knot of nature. If so, the extreme insecurity of their lives is by no means as intolerable as it would be for us.[2] Without some such compensation, it is hard to see how forms of life other than man could have found the game of life worth the candle for so many millions of years.

In coming to an understanding of nature in which man is to be something more than a frustrated outsider one of our most valuable sources of insight is the Taoist tradition of Chinese philosophy, with its outgrowths in Zen Buddhism and Neo-Confucianism. In the second volume of his *Science and Civilization in China* Joseph Needham has indicated many points at which the Chinese philosophy of nature is of the utmost relevance to the inquiries of modern science and philosophy, and some of these need to be explored. The standpoint of Taoism is of special interest and value because it is a form of naturalism entirely different from our own mechanistic and vitalistic naturalisms, avoiding their antimetaphysical bias and their simplist reductions of nature to systems of abstraction which have absolutely nothing in common with what the Chinese mean by nature.

[2] Do the rapid and "nervous" motions with which animals avoid danger indicate that they are actually afraid? Human city-dwellers are just as agile in dodging traffic and negotiating superhighways, yet carry on all the darting and twisting required with relative unconcern. And what about the numberless neural adjustments whose lightning action keeps us from falling when we walk or run, from choking when we eat, and from being concussed when we play ball games?

Furthermore, the Taoist philosophy of nature is much more than a theoretical system—indeed, it is hardly this at all. It is primarily a way of life in which the original sense of the seamless unity of nature is restored without the loss of individual consciousness. It involves a new style of human action in relation to the environment, a new attitude to technical skills whereby man seems to interfere artificially with the natural world. It requires a fundamental revision of the very roots of our common sense, especially with respect to such matters as the instinct for survival, the pursuit of the good and the pleasurable to the elimination of the evil and painful, and of the function of effort and discipline, or will power, in creative action.

For our purposes, however, the best way of exploring the Chinese philosophy of nature is not to embark upon a systematic and historical account of Taoism.[3] It is better to introduce it as one goes along in a general discussion of the relation of man to nature which will also clarify the Western attitude to the problem.

Of central importance in any such discussion are the actual means whereby awareness of the seamless unity may be discovered, since this whole inquiry is in the realm of feeling rather than thought, and is in the spirit of poetry rather than formal, intellective philosophy. But the so-called means of discovery are apparently problematic and paradoxical since the lost awareness is found by "no means." Actions of the will or ego can only strengthen its divided mode of consciousness, and at first sight this is extremely frustrating for one who knows no other way of action. Yet we are familiar enough with the insincerity and contradiction of trying to be natural, the more so when it is most urgent that we should act naturally and without

[3] Which would in any case be a rather un-Taoistic procedure, although it has been admirably done by Holmes Welch in his recent *Parting of the Way*, for which see Welch (1).

self-consciousness. The Taoist idea of naturalness goes far beyond the merely normal, or the simply unostentatious way of behaving. It is the concrete realization that all our experiences and actions are movements of the Tao, the way of nature, the endless knot, including the very experience of being an individual, a knowing subject.

The Chinese phrase which is ordinarily translated as "nature" is *tzu-jan*, literally "of itself so," and thus a better equivalent might be "spontaneity." This is almost Aristotle's idea of God as the unmoved mover, for nature in both whole and part is not regarded as being moved by any external agency. Every movement in the endless knot is a movement of the knot, acting as a total organism, though the parts, or loops, of the knot are not looked upon as passive entities moved by the whole. For they are parts only figuratively divided from the whole for purposes of recognition and discussion; in reality, the loops are the knot, differences within identity like the two sides of a coin, neither of which can be removed without removing the other.[4] Thus all art and artifice, all human action, is felt to be the same as natural or spontaneous action—a world-feeling marvellously expressed in Chinese poetry and landscape painting, whose technique involves the fascinating discipline of the "controlled accident," of doing exactly the right thing without force or self-conscious intention.

The techniques of Far Eastern art are, however, somewhat exotic to serve as illustrations for Western people of the application of this philosophy of nature. Yet the specific application of the philosophy should be discussed, and, for a number of reasons, it has seemed that the most

[4] An even better illustration might be the Möbius strip, a paper tape formed into a ring with a single twist. It clearly has two faces, and yet they are identical.

suitable subject for this discussion is the relationship of man and woman, especially in its sexual phase. For one thing, there is an obvious symbolic correlation between man's attitude to nature and man's attitude to woman. However fanciful this symbolism may sometimes be, it has in fact had an enormous influence upon sexual love in both Eastern and Western cultures. For another, sexual love is a troubled and problematic relationship in cultures where there is a strong sense of man's separation from nature, especially when the realm of nature is felt to be inferior or contaminated with evil. Needless to say, the Christian, and particularly the Anglo-Saxon, cultures are preoccupied with sexuality in ways that strike outsiders as peculiarly odd, and we ourselves are well aware that we have "sex on the brain" to an extraordinary degree. We are not going to solve this preoccupation by trying to forget about it, which has been the advice of our moralists for two thousand years. Nor will it yield to treatment at a narrowly medical or psychiatric level, as if it were a purely biological affair.

Above all, sexual love is the most intense and dramatic of the common ways in which a human being comes into union and conscious relationship with something outside himself. It is, furthermore, the most vivid of man's customary expressions of his organic spontaneity, the most positive and creative occasion of his being transported by something beyond his conscious will. We need hardly wonder, then, that cultures in which the individual feels isolated from nature are also cultures wherein men feel squeamish about the sexual relationship, often regarding it as degrading and evil—especially for those dedicated to the life of the spirit.

The disordered sexuality of the Western (and some other) cultures is surely due to the fact that the sexual relationship has never been seriously integrated with and illumined by a philosophy of life. It has had no effective contact with the realm of spiritual experience. It has never even achieved the dignity of an art, as in the Indian *Kamasutra,* and would thus seem to rank in our estimation far below cookery. Theoretically, the Christian sacrament of Holy Matrimony is supposed to sanctify the relationship, but in practice it does so only by indirection and by prohibitions. We have dubbed the relationship "animal," and animal we have for the most part let it remain. Matrimony has not so much ennobled it as fenced it in, trusting naïvely that "true love" would somehow find a way to make the relationship whole and holy. And this might indeed have come to pass, without introducing any studied techniques, given the presence of certain other conditions. It might have come to pass of itself, spontaneously, if the culture had known anything of real spontaneity. But this was, and is, impossible when human personality is centered exclusively in the ego, which in its turn is set over against nature as the dissociated soul or mind. Generally speaking, the style of philosophy which we have followed and the type of spiritual experience which we have cultivated have not lent themselves to a constructive application to sexuality.

> It is good for a man not to touch a woman. . . . I say therefore to the unmarried and widows, "It is good for them if they abide even as I." But if they cannot contain, let them marry; for it is better to marry than to burn. . . . But and if thou marry, thou hast not sinned; and if a virgin marry, she hath not sinned. Nevertheless such shall have trouble in the flesh [or, perhaps better, with the flesh]. . . . But this I say, brethren, the time is short: it remaineth, that both they that have wives be as though they had none. . . . I would have you without preoccupation. He that is unmar-

ried careth for the things that belong to the Lord, how he may please the Lord. But he that is married careth for the things that are of the world, how he may please his wife.[5]

This grudging toleration of sexuality as an unbearable pressure which, sometimes and under strict conditions, has to be released puts it on the level of an urge to stool, of a regrettable vestige of animality, happily to be left behind in the Kingdom of Heaven. As such it has no positive relation whatsoever to the life of the spirit.

But fortunately for the growth of Christian spirituality, St. Paul gave these words as advice and not as a commandment. For they are offset, in the sacred scriptures, with the Song of Songs, which has thus far been interpreted allegorically in terms of "the spiritual marriage betwixt Christ and his Church," or between Christ and the soul. As we shall see, there are potentialities in the Christian heritage not only for the development of sexual love in matrimony as a means to the contemplative life, but also for resolving the basic rift between spirit and nature which has so troubled the Christian cultures of the West.

The approved academic method of studying the sexual implications of the Taoist philosophy of nature would, presumably, be to investigate the erotic customs and literature of the Far East. But in place of such a difficult and time-consuming task there is a simple and practical short cut: to understand the basic principles of the philosophy and apply them directly to the problem. Other than this, there is no clear way of approach, for in the Far East the influence of Taoist philosophy upon the mass culture has always been indirect. Actual followers of the philosophy, as distinct from the organized Taoist religion, which is a very different affair, have been relatively few. Documents do

[5] St. Paul in 1 Corinthians, 7.

indeed exist about Taoist sexual practices, but they savor
more of the psychophysiological theories of the Taoist
religion than of the nature philosophy of Lao-tzu and
Chuang-tzu. Even so, the general tenor of these documents
is approximately what one would imagine the sexual application of the Taoist philosophy to be. Furthermore, even
at the mass level, sexual love in the Far Eastern cultures
appears to be far less problematic than with us, for there
is no doubt that the Taoist feeling of the naturalness of
the human state has, however indirectly, had a wide influence upon the everyday life of the people.

Other Asian traditions than the Taoist have much to
contribute to both aspects of our inquiry. Various trends of
Hindu philosophy, which seem, however, to be submerged
in modern times, illuminate the theme with a marvellous
symbology which has been interpreted with such deep insight in the works of Heinrich Zimmer. As to the crucial
problem of realizing or feeling the seamless unity of nature, nowhere is there anything more direct, simple, and
concrete than the approach of Zen Buddhism—the way of
life which has contributed so much to the profound nature
philosophy of the Japanese.

It is tragic that at a time when these universally human
insights nurtured in Asia "speak to our condition" so ap-
propriately, the Asian peoples themselves are associated in
our minds with rampant nationalisms which we are feeling
as a serious political threat. Unhappily, it is probably far
more serious than we have yet recognized. But is it of any
use to point out that they have learned these political
philosophies, by reaction, from us, and that, in their differing ways, Gandhi, Nehru, Nasser, Mao Tse-tung, and
the other leaders of Asian nationalism are to a large degree
Western in both personality and doctrine? Almost every
one of them is a product of an educational system estab-

lished by Western colonialism, and their political philosophies and ambitions are remote indeed from the principles of statecraft set forward in the *Tao Tê Ching*.

Less and less has the "wisdom of the East" anything to do with modern Asia, with the geographical and political boundaries of the world which such terms as East and West, Asia, Europe, and America, now represent. More and more "the East" as a source of wisdom stands for something not geographical but inward, for a perennial philosophy which, in varying forms, has been the possession of traditional, nonhistorical cultures in all parts of the world. For the spiritual contrast of East and West is really a contrast between two styles of culture, two radically different categories of social institutions, which never really corresponded to the contrast of Europe and Asia as geographical divisions.

We might call these two types of culture progressive and historical on the one hand, and traditional and nonhistorical on the other. For the philosophy of the first is that human society is on the move, that the political state is a biological organism whose destiny is to grow and expand. Examining the record of its past, the progressive society reconstructs it as history, that is, as a significant series of events which constitute a destiny, a motion toward specific temporal goals for the society as a whole. The fabricators of such histories easily forget that their selection of "significant" events from the record is subjectively determined—largely by the need to justify the immediate political steps which they have in mind. History exists as a force because it is created or invented here and now.

On the other hand, traditional societies are nonhistorical in that they do not imagine themselves to be in linear motion toward temporal goals. Their records are not histories but simple chronicles which delineate no pattern in human events other than a kind of cycling like the rotation of the seasons. Their political philosophy is to maintain the balance of nature upon which the human community depends, and which is expressed in public rites celebrating the timeless correspondences between the social order and the order of the universe.

Thus the focus of interest in the traditional society is not the future but the present, "the still point of the turning world." All their artifacts are made for the immediate material advantage of the thing itself, rather than for abstract monetary profit, or for such purely psychological by-products as prestige or success. Such artifacts are therefore made unhurriedly through and through; they are not fine surfaces slapped together, with every imaginable short cut on the inside. On the other hand, the progressive workman has his eye on the clock—on the play which is to come when the work is over, on the leisure society which is to follow the completion of the Five-Year Plan. He therefore rushes to complete artifacts which, for that very reason, are not worth playing with when playtime comes. Like a spoiled child, he soon tires of his toys (which is exactly what most of his products are),[6] and is wooed back to work by the prospect of ever more sensational (as distinct from material) gimmicks to come.

For it is strictly incorrect to think of the progressive cultures as materialistic, if the materialist is one who loves concrete materials. No modern city looks as if it were made by people who love material. The truth is rather that progressive man hates material and does everything possible to obliterate its resistances, its spatial and temporal limits. Increasingly his world consists of end-points, of destinations and goals with the times and spaces between them

[6] The Cadillac or Thunderbird automobile of this date being essentially a toy rocket-ship rather than a convenient means of transportation.

eliminated by jet propulsion. Consequently there is little material satisfaction in reaching the goal, since a life full of goals or end-points is like trying to abate one's hunger by eating merely the two precise ends of a banana. The concrete reality of the banana is, on the contrary, all that lies between the two ends, the journey as it were, all that jet propulsion cuts out. Furthermore, when the time and space between destinations are cut out, all destinations tend to become ever more similar. The more rapidly we can travel to Hawaii or Japan or Sicily, the more rapidly the resort is, as tourists say, "spoiled," which means that it is increasingly like Los Angeles, Chicago, or London.

Once again, we see that the goals of progressive men are actually psychological and spiritual, the sensations, kicks, and boosts for which material realities are merely the unfortunately necessary occasions. His hatred of materiality is the continuing expression of the basic rift between his ego and nature. In the sexual sphere the goal is not so much the concrete personality of the woman as the orgasm which she provokes, and provokes not so much as an integral woman as an aggregation of stylized lips, busts, and buttocks—woman in the abstract rather than this or that particular woman. As de Rougemont has pointed out so clearly in his *Love in the Western World*,[7] such love is not the love of woman but the love of being in love, expressing a dualistic, dissociated, spirit-loving and matter-hating attitude to life. But no less short-circuited and antinatural is the conception of love which makes future procreation its sole end, especially because what, in this conception, is to be procreated is another *soul*,

---

[7] De Rougemont (1). At a later point it will be necessary to take issue with some of the historical aspects of this remarkable work, which has managed to foist upon historical Christianity a doctrine of love which is really a modern and novel development of Christianity that would probably have horrified the Patristic age.

willy-nilly attached to a body which it will never be really permissible to enjoy. Here, too, we see the essential continuity of the Western attitude from historical Christianity to modern "paganism."

Underlying this continuity is the fact that, as one might say, both God and the Devil subscribe to the same philosophy since both inhabit a cosmology where spirit stands against nature. Furthermore, the architects of this cosmology were unaware of the mutual interdependence, or correlativity, of opposites, which is the principal reason why they did not perceive the inner identity of spirit and nature, subject and object, and why they did not notice the hidden compact between God and the Devil to reproduce one another. They did not notice it even when, as the conceptions of the two became fully elaborated, they sometimes exchanged characters so that the image of God became diabolical and the image of the Devil divine. For as the image of God was composed of goodness piled on goodness, power piled on power, it became insufferable and monstrous. But in conceiving the image of the Devil there were no laws to be kept, and the creative imagination could run riot, emptying all its repressed and sensuous contents. Hence the persistent allure of Satanism and the fascination of evil.

When the mutual interdependence of the opposites is not seen, it becomes possible to dream of a state of affairs in which life exists without death, good without evil, pleasure without pain, and light without darkness. The subject, the soul, can be set free from the concrete limitations of the object, the body. Thus in the Christian doctrine of the resurrection of the body, the body is usually considered to be so transformed by the spirit that it is no longer in any real sense a body. It is rather a fantasy-body from which all the really earthy qualities have been taken away—weightless, sexless, and ageless. The idea that the good can be wrested from the evil, that life can be delivered permanently from death, is the seed-thought of the progressive and historical cultures. Since their appearance, history seems to have taken a sudden leap forward, and, in a few centuries, the conditions of human life have been under radical and ever faster change, though hitherto they had remained relatively constant for millennia.

However, it is not so much that history has taken a sudden leap forward as that, with the progressive cultures, history has come into being. The partisans of historical culture seem to congratulate themselves on having escaped from cyclic into linear time, from a static into a dynamic and "on-going" world order—failing to see that nothing is so cyclic as a vicious circle. A world where one can go more and more easily and rapidly to places that are less and less worth visiting, and produce an ever-growing volume of ever-less-nourishing food, is, to cite only the mildest examples, a vicious circle. The essence of a vicious circle is that one is pursuing, or running away from, a terminus which is inseparable from its opposite, and that so long as this is unrecognized the chase gets faster and faster. The sudden outburst of history in the last five hundred years might strike one as more of a cancer than an orderly growth.

The foregoing might well seem the prelude to a doctrine of revolution. But it is nothing of the kind. Nothing is further from our intent than to advocate a return to the traditional style of culture and an abandonment of the progressive. The fallacy of all traditionalist or "back-to-nature" romanticisms is that they are themselves progressive, looking to a future state of affairs which is better than the present. Just as the ego can do nothing to overcome its own isolated mode of consciousness, the community can do nothing *in order* to deliver itself from the progressive fallacy, for this would be the contradiction of affected naturalness. The "goal" of a traditional culture is not the future but the present. That is to say, it lays its material and practical plans for food and shelter in the days and years to come, but no more. It does not aim at the psychological enjoyment which the future meals will bring. In a word, it does not pursue happiness.

Furthermore, the wiser members of such cultures do not even seek enjoyment from the present moment. For in the instant that one grasps the moment to get something from it, it seems to disappear. The reason is perhaps that enjoyment is a function of nerves rather than muscles, and that nerves receive automatically and passively, whereas muscles grasp actively. Enjoyment is always gratuitous and can come no other way than of itself, spontaneously. To try to force it is, furthermore, to try to experience the future before it has arrived, to seek the psychological *result* of attending to the present experience and thus short-circuiting or cutting out the experience itself. Obviously, however, the person who attempts to get something from his present experience feels divided from it. He is the subject and it is the object. He does not see that he *is* that experience, and that trying to get something from it is merely self-pursuit.

Ordinarily we think of self-consciousness as the subject's awareness of itself. We would be far less confused if we saw that it is the subject-object's awareness of itself. For the knower is what he knows in somewhat the same way as the seemingly two surfaces of the Möbius strip are one. Pushing the analogy a little further, conscious experiencing

Wut?

seems to be a field which, like the strip, twists back upon itself:

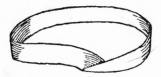

It is not, then, that I know both other things and myself. It is rather that the total field I-know-this knows itself.

While this problem of our awareness of the present will receive fuller attention at a later point, it is necessary at least to see the principle of it here so that we may understand the illusion of making an attempt to get something from life in the sense of a good, happy, or pleasant psychological state. For the point is not, in our accustomed egocentric mode of thinking, that it would be good to return to our original integrity with nature. The point is that it is simply impossible to get away from it, however vividly we may imagine that we have done so. Similarly, it is impossible to experience the future and not to experience the present. But trying to realize this is another attempt to experience the future. Some logician may object that this is a merely tautological statement which has no consequence, and he will be right. But we are not looking for a consequence. We are no longer saying "So what?" to everything, as if the only importance of our present experience were in what it is leading to, as if we should constantly interrupt a dancer, saying, "Now just where are you going, and what, exactly, is the meaning of all these movements?"

There is, indeed, a place for commentary, for interpretations of nature and predictions of its future course. But we need to know what we are talking about, which requires a primary background of contemplation and inward silence, of watching without questions and jumping to conclusions. May we go back, then, to the floor of pebbles beneath the water and the fish in the sunlight's rippling net . . . and watch?

I: MAN AND NATURE

1: Urbanism and Paganism

WHEN CHRISTIANS FIRST DISTINGUISHED
themselves from pagans, the word "pagan" meant "coun-
try-dweller." For the first centers of Christianity in the
Roman Empire were the great cities—Antioch, Corinth,
Ephesus, Alexandria, and Rome itself. Furthermore, during the centuries in which Christianity was born and
spread throughout the Empire, the growing mercantile
wealth of Rome was attracting population to the cities, so
that as early as 37 B.C. the government of the Emperor
Augustus showed concern for the decline of agriculture.
The *Georgics* of Vergil were a direct expression of this
concern—poems written at the behest of the government
in praise of the rural life:

> *O fortunatos nimium, sua si bona norint*
> *Agricolas!*

Blest, aye, blest to excess, knew they how goodly the portion
Earth giveth her farmers!

That Christianity grew up in the cities, at a time when,
as today, the big city was the center of economic and
cultural attraction, is a circumstance which must have had
a deep influence upon the whole character of the religion.
For Christianity as a whole has a decidedly urban style,
and this is true not only of Roman Catholicism but also of
Protestantism, which first arose in the burgher cities of
Western Europe. In evangelizing the West, the main dif-

ficulty which Christianity encountered was, for as long as fifteen hundred years, the competition of the tenacious nature religions of the peasantry.

Perhaps it is easiest to express the effect of these circumstances upon Christianity in the form of a personal impression, not, I believe, at all peculiar to myself. For as long as I can remember, I have been puzzled by the fact that I can feel like a Christian only when I am indoors. As soon as I get into the open air, I feel entirely out of relation with everything that goes on in a church—including both the worship and the theology. It is not as if I disliked being in church. On the contrary, I spent much of my boyhood in the precincts of one of Europe's most noble cathedrals, and I have never recovered from its spell. Romanesque and Gothic architecture, Gregorian chant, medieval glass and illuminated manuscripts, the smell of frankincense or of the mere must of ancient stone, and, above all, the ritual of the Mass—these are as magical for me as for the most ardent Catholic romanticist. Nor am I insensible to the profundities and splendors of Christian philosophy and theology, and I am well aware that early training implanted in me the bitter-sweetness of a Christian conscience. But all this is in a watertight compartment, or rather, in a closed sanctuary where the light of the open sky comes only through the symbolic jewelry of stained-glass windows.

It is often said that the aesthetic atmosphere of Christianity is a mere irrelevance. The Christian life is not what one feels, but what one wills, usually in the teeth of one's feelings. The contemplative mystic would say that to know God is precisely not to feel him; it is to know him by the love of the will in a "cloud of unknowing," in the dark night of the spirit where, to sense and feeling, God is ut-

terly absent. Therefore he who knows Christianity in
terms largely of its aesthetic glamour knows it not at all.

> *Illuminated missals—spires—*
> *Wide screens and decorated quires—*
> *All these I loved, and on my knees*
> *I thanked myself for knowing these*
> *And watched the morning sunlight pass*
> *Through richly stained Victorian glass*
> *And in the colour-shafted air*
> *I, kneeling, thought the Lord was there.*
> *Now, lying in the gathering mist,*
> *I know that Lord did not exist.*[1]

Yet this denial of feeling, while heroic, manly, and robust,
is yet another symptom of what I am trying to express—
of the fact that the Christian world, as we know it, is only
a half-world in which the feeling and the symbolically
feminine is unassimilated. Feeling, as a means of judgment
and knowledge, is misleading to those who do not know
how to use it, through lack of exercise and cultivation.
Furthermore, in a milieu where feeling is underestimated
or disregarded, its expressions are all the more revealing
of the underlying state of mind.

It has, then, been my impression that there is a deep
and quite extraordinary incompatibility between the atmosphere of Christianity and the atmosphere of the natural world. It has seemed well-nigh impossible to relate
God the Father, Jesus Christ, the angels, and the saints to
the universe in which I actually live. Looking at trees and
rocks, at the sky with its clouds or stars, at the sea, or at a
naked human body, I find myself in a world where this

[1] John Betjeman, "Before the Anaesthetic or A Real Fright," in *Selected Poems.* John Murray, London, 1948.

religion simply does not fit. Indeed, it is a characteristically Christian attitude to confirm this impression, since "my kingdom is not of this world." Yet if God made this world, how is it possible to feel so powerful a difference of style between the God of church and altar, for all his splendor, and the world of the open sky? No one would dream of attributing a landscape by Sesshu to Constable, or a symphony by Hindemith to Haydn. In the same way, I have found it a basic impossibility to associate the author of the Christian religion with the author of the physical universe. This is not a judgment as to the relative merits of the two styles; it is only to say that they are not by the same hand, and that they do not mix well together.

This has, of course, been felt before, and there is an argument to explain it. It is said that whereas the beauty and the style of the physical world is natural, the beauty of Christianity is supernatural. The nearest thing in the physical world to supernatural beauty is the beauty of the human being, and more especially of the human mind. Christianity suggests the urban rather than rural atmosphere because in the former we are surrounded by works of the mind. While it is true that all creatures under the sky are the works of God, man, and even the works of man, are far higher works of God than anything else. They reveal more of the character of God than the sun, moon, and stars, for what we sometimes call the artificial is nearer to the supernatural than to the natural.

It is easy, this argument would continue, to love the aesthetic surfaces of nature, so long as we do not have to contend with the ruthless heartlessness, the cold struggle for life, which underlies it. But it is in man alone that there have arisen ethical and moral ideas which, as it were, give nature a feeling heart—and this, again, goes to show that God is reflected in nature nowhere so clearly as in man. It is true that we sometimes need to seek relief from the hideousness of crowds and cities in the solitudes of nature, but this is only because the worst is the corruption of the best. The evil of man far exceeds the evil of the spider or the shark, but only because the goodness of man immeasurably exceeds the goodness of a spring landscape. One has only to consider how cold and desolate the fairest face of nature can seem to a man left utterly alone, willing to exchange the whole sum of natural beauty for a single human face.

Making a still stronger point, the argument could go on to say that however poor the fit between Christianity and nature, nowhere is there a religion so perfectly in accord with human nature. By and large, the naturalistic religions hold out for man no greater hope than a philosophic acceptance of the inevitable, a noble but sorrowful resignation to the truth that nature is beyond good and evil, and that death is the necessary counterpart of life, as pain of pleasure. But this sacrifices the most human thing about man—his eternal, childlike hope that somehow, someday, the deepest yearnings of his heart will come true. Who is so proud and unfeeling that he will not admit that he would not be deliriously happy if, by some strange magic, these deep and ingrained longings could be fulfilled? If there were everlasting life beyond death after all? If there were eternal reunion with the people we have loved? If, forever and ever, there were the vision and the union of hearts with a God whose beatitude exceeds immeasurably the most intense joy that we have known—somehow including all the variety of form and color, uniqueness and individuality, that we value so much upon earth? Christianity alone, it would be argued, has the audacity to affirm this basic hope which the wisdom of the world represses, and so is the only fundamentally joyous religion. For it gambles, recklessly, upon the scheme of things turning out to be the best that we hope for, challenging man to put the whole might of his faith in the idea that his nature, at its most human, is made in the image of the ultimate reality, God. . . . And, it might be added, if we lose the gamble, we shall never know that we have lost.

This is not, perhaps, the most profound version of the final ideal at which Christianity aims. It is, however, representative. For in discussing the attitude of Christianity to nature, I am not exploring as yet the deepest resources of the Christian tradition. I am trying to state the attitude of Christianity as it has been held by large numbers of intelligent people, and thus as it has been an influential force in Western culture. The individual Christian will sometimes protest in reading the following pages that this or that is not how he understands Christianity, and he may feel in particular that the presentation is theologically immature. But I have found that when Christian theologians become subtle and mystical, and sometimes when pressed in conversation to say what they *really* mean, it becomes increasingly difficult to tell the difference between Christianity and, say, Vedanta. Here, however, we are discussing the characteristics which make Christianity unique, and the majority of intelligent Christians who take their religion in a partisan way do indeed insist upon its uniqueness—even when their knowledge of other traditions is rudimentary. We are discussing, above all, the atmosphere, the quality of feeling, which Christianity involves, and which is so influential upon the culture. So powerful is the sway of this feeling quality that, in practice, the individual often yields to it even when his intellectual grasp of the faith is extremely mature. And the appeal of Christianity is to very human and very powerful feelings—the love of man for his own kind, the bedrock of nostalgia for home and one's own people, coupled with the fascination of the heroic, the challenge to believe in the possibility of an ultimate victory over evil and pain. In the face of this appeal, the non-Christian may be tempted to feel like a spoilsport or a skeleton at the banquet.

But the premise of the argument is just that, in his heart of hearts, man *does* feel alien from nature, and that his very deepest longing is for an eternity of joy, to the exclusion of sadness and suffering. As even Nietzsche said in *Zarathustra:*

> *All joys want eternity,*
> *Want deep, profound eternity.*

Yet to hold that these are ultimate and universal facts of human nature and feeling is to reveal a form of self-awareness which is still close to the surface, and a readiness to confuse what one feels as a result of social conditioning with what one feels absolutely and necessarily. The more a person knows of himself, the more he will hesitate to define his nature and to assert what he must necessarily feel, and the more he will be astounded at his capacity to feel in unsuspected and unpredictable ways. Still more will this be so if he learns to explore, or feel deeply into, his negative states of feeling—his loneliness, sorrow, grief, depression, or fear—without trying to escape from them.

In many so-called primitive cultures it is a requirement of tribal initiation to spend a lengthy period alone in the forests or mountains, a period of coming to terms with the solitude and nonhumanity of nature so as to discover who, or what, one really is—a discovery hardly possible while the community is telling you what you are, or ought to be. He may discover, for instance, that loneliness is the masked fear of an unknown which is himself, and that the

alien-looking aspect of nature is a projection upon the
forests of his fear of stepping outside habitual and conditioned patterns of feeling. There is much evidence to show
that for anyone who passes through the barrier of loneliness, the sense of individual isolation bursts, almost by
dint of its own intensity, into the "all-feeling" of identity
with the universe. One may pooh-pooh this as "nature
mysticism" or "pantheism," but it should be obvious that a
feeling of this kind corresponds better with a universe of
mutually interdependent processes and relations than with
a universe of distinct, blocklike entities.

The more deeply we understand the play of our feelings,
the more, too, we realize their ambivalence—the strange
polarity of joy and sorrow, love and hate, humility and
pride, elation and depression. We find that our feelings are
not fixed, unrelated states, but slowly or rapidly swinging
motions such that a perpetuity of joy would be as meaningless as the notion of swinging only to the right. In other
words, just because it is static, a perpetual feeling is not a
feeling, so that the conception of the perpetually good is a
verbal abstraction which can neither be imagined, felt, nor
actually desired. Such an idea can, once more, be taken
seriously only by those who have not thoroughly explored
the nature of feeling, who are unrelated to the natural
realities of the very humanity which they hold to be God's
image.

We begin, then, to discern the reasons why Christianity
as we have known it differs so profoundly in style from
the natural universe. To a large extent it is a construction
of ideas or concepts playing together on their own, without
adequate relation to that world of nature which ideas
represent. It is true, of course, that in mathematics and
physics we find purely conceptual constructions and ideas
for which we can discover no sensuous image, such as

curved space or quanta. But, in physics at least, these ideas are related to the physical world by testing their use in predicting the course of events. Furthermore, the physicist does not maintain that such ideas necessarily represent any concrete reality. He sees them rather as tools, like compasses, rulers, or numbers, which enable us to handle and measure that reality—tools which are not found but invented.

May it not be, then, that many of the central ideas of Christianity are creative inventions, like the cities in which they were nurtured? This would of course be true of any religion or philosophy to the extent that it is a system of ideas, especially of ideas that cannot be verified by an appeal to experience. But Christianity differs sharply at this point from other traditions, such as Buddhism and the Vedanta. In the latter, ideas play a very secondary part, for the real center of these traditions is an ineffable experience, which is to say an experience which is concrete and nonverbal, not an idea at all. In Christianity, however, the stress is upon belief rather than experience, and immense importance has always been attached to an acceptance of the correct formulation of a dogma, doctrine, or rite. Early in its history Christianity rejected *gnosis*, or direct experience of God, in favor of *pistis*, or the trust of the will in certain revealed propositions about God.

Spirit, then, is distinguished from nature as the abstract from the concrete, and the things of the spirit are identified with the things of the mind—with the world of words and thought-symbols—which are then seen, not as representing the concrete world, but as underlying it. For "in the beginning was the Word," God the Son conceived as the Divine Idea after whose pattern the universe was made. Thus the realm of concepts acquires not only an independent life of its own, but a life more real and more fundamental than that of nonverbal nature. Ideas do not represent nature, but nature represents ideas in the clogging vesture of material stuff. Hence what is impossible and unimaginable in nature is possible in idea—as that the positive may be separated permanently from polarity with the negative, and joy from interdependence with sorrow. In short, purely verbal possibility is considered as having a higher reality than physical possibility. It is hard not to feel that this is the power of thought running away with itself and getting out of hand, and defending itself against the charge of nonsense by asserting that its own reality is primordial, and nature but its clumsy copy.

Things are separable in words which are inseparable in nature because words are counters and classifiers which can be arranged in any order. The word "being" is formally separate from the word "nothing," as "pleasure" from "pain." But in nature being and nothing, or solid and space, constitute a relationship as inseparable as back and front. In the same way, the formally static character of our words for feelings conceals the fact (or better, the event) that our feelings are directions rather than states, and that in the realm of direction there is no North without South.

In the great Asian traditions, however, spirit—as Brahman or Tao—is less easily confused with the abstract. Spirit is found in the direct experience of the concrete, natural world in what Buddhists would call its "suchness" (*tathata*), that is, in its nonverbal and nonconceptual state. This is not, however, what we mean by the world in its material or physical state, for, as we shall see, the word "material" stands for the world as "metered" or measured —the nonverbal world represented in terms of distinct facts, things, and events, which, like feet and inches, are human inventions for handling and describing the world. There is no word for *what* the world is in its natural, nonverbal state. For the question "What is it?" is really asking, "In what class is it?" Now it should be obvious that classification is, again, a human invention, and that the natural world is not given to us in a classified form, in cans with labels. When we ask what anything is in its natural state, the only answer can be to point to it directly, suggesting that the questioner observe it with a silent mind.

Silent observation of this kind is exactly what is meant here by feeling (as distinct from particular feelings), the attitude and approach whereby nature must be explored if we are to recover our original sense of integrity with the natural world. In Taoism and Zen this attitude is called *kuan*, or "wordless contemplation." Just as one must sometimes be silent in order to hear what others have to say, so thought itself must be silent if it is to think about anything other than itself. We need hardly be surprised if, in default of this silence, our minds begin to be haunted by words about words about words. It is a short step from this to the fantasy that the word is prior to nature itself, when, in fact, it is only prior to the *classification* of nature—to the sorting of nature into things and events. For it is things, not the natural world itself, which are created by the word. But, for lack of mental silence, the two are confused.

The spell of words is by no means an enchantment to which only the intellectual is disposed. The most simple-minded people are as easily its prey, and it would seem that, at all levels of society, the cultures in which Christianity has arisen have been peculiarly confused by the powerful instrument of language. It has run away with them like a new gadget with a child, so that excessive verbal communication is really the characteristic disease of the West. We are simply unable to stop it, for when we are not talking to others we are compulsively thinking,

that is, talking subvocally to ourselves. Communication
has become a nervous habit, and cultures strike us as
mysterious and baffling which do not at once tell all, or,
worse, expect us to understand certain things without being told. I shall never forget the Japanese artist Hasegawa
yelling in exasperation at the endless request for explanations from his Western students, "What's the matter with
you! Can't you *feel?*"

For one type of culture, then, the "truth about nature"
is the verbal explanation or reconstruction of the world,
considered as a system of law which precedes and underlies it as the plan in the mind of the architect comes before
the building of a house. But for another type it is nature
itself, experienced directly in mental silence, which in
Zen Buddhism is called *wu-nien* or "no-thought." [2] Thus in
the cultures of the Far East we rarely find the discrepancy
between religion and nature so characteristic of the West.
On the contrary, the finest Buddhist and Taoist art of
China and Japan is not, as one might suppose, concerned
with formally religious themes, but landscape painting,
and studies of birds, trees, rocks, and plants. Furthermore,
Zen is applied directly to the technique of gardening, and
to a style of architecture which deliberately integrates the
house with its natural surroundings—which simultaneously encloses man and admits nature. These, rather than
Buddha images, express the knowledge of ultimate reality.

And here we might mention a curious and apparently
trivial symptom of the rift, not only between Christianity
and nature, but also between Christianity and the natu-

[2] But this is not what we should call "thoughtlessness" or mere empty-
mindedness. For thoughts are themselves in and of nature, and *kuan,* or
wordless contemplation, can persist even in the midst of thinking. *Kuan*
is therefore an absence of "mental mitosis," of the mind constantly trying to split itself, trying simultaneously to act and reflect, to think and to
think about thinking, and so setting up the infinite regression or vicious
circle of "words about words about words."

ralistic art forms of the Far East. Strangely enough, it is almost impossible to represent the central symbol of Christianity, the Cross or Crucifixion, in the Chinese style of painting. It has been tried many times, but never succeeds, for the symmetrical form of the Cross completely destroys the rhythm of a Chinese painting if it is made the principal image in the picture. Chinese Christians have tried to solve the problem by painting rustic Crosses with bark, twigs, and moss still on the wood. But those two straight beams simply jar with the rest of the painting, and, without destroying the symbol of the Cross, the artist cannot follow his natural tendency to bend the straight lines irregularly. For he follows nature in loving forms that are flowing, jagged, and unsymmetrical—forms eminently suited to his media, the soft brush and black ink. But in the art forms of Christianity, such as the Byzantine and Gothic, we find a love for the architectural and the courtly. God is conceived in the image of a throned monarch, and the rituals of the Church are patterned after the court ceremonials of the Greco-Roman emperors. Likewise, in the ancient Hebrew religion, the Ark of the Covenant was essentially a throne, hidden in the inner sanctuary of the Holy of Holies, which was built in the form of a perfect cube—symbol of completeness and perfection.

Yet from the standpoint of Chinese philosophy and aesthetics, this symmetrical and architectonic perfection is rigid and lifeless. Such forms are found but rarely in nature, and thus when the Chinese artist starts to paint the rigid Cross he finds himself in conflict, for what he really wants to paint is a living tree. Furthermore, he thinks of the power behind nature, not in the image of a monarch, but as the Tao—the way, course, or flow of nature—and finds images for it in water and wind, in the air and sky, as well as in the processes of growth. There was no sense that the Tao had any inclination to obtrude itself or to

shine in glory like a monarch, but rather to work hidden
and unknown, making it appear that all its achievements
were the work of others. In the words of Lao-tzu:

> *The great Tao flows everywhere,*
> *to the left and to the right.*
> *All things depend upon it to exist,*
> *and it does not abandon them.*
> *To its accomplishments it lays no claim.*
> *It loves and nourishes all things,*
> *but does not lord it over them.* xxxiv

On the other hand:

> His eyes were as a flame of fire, and on his head were
> many crowns; and he had a name written, that no man
> knew, but he himself. And he was clothed with a vesture
> dipped in blood: and his name is called the Word of God.
> . . . And out of his mouth goeth a sharp sword, that with it
> he should smite the nations: and he shall rule them with
> a rod of iron; and he treadeth the winepress of the fierceness
> and wrath of Almighty God. And he hath on his vesture and
> on his thigh a name written: KING OF KINGS, AND LORD OF
> LORDS.[3]

Magnificent as this is, the style is utterly different from
the Taoist conception of the monarch, who is to

> *Blunt his sharpness;*
> *Get rid of his separateness;*
> *Soften his brilliance;*
> *Be even with the dust.*
> *This is called the profound identity.*[4] lvi

For,

> *The ruler who wants to be above the people must speak*
> *of himself as below them.*

[3] Revelation 19, 12–16.
[4] That is, the profound (or mysterious) identity of man and nature.

If he wants to be ahead of the people, he must keep
        himself behind them.
Thus when the sage is above, the people do not feel
        him as a burden;
When he is ahead, the people do not feel him as a
        hindrance. lxvi

The king takes his pattern from the Tao, not the Tao from
the king. And the Tao is always anonymous and unknown,
and the incessant changefulness and flowing impermanence of nature is seen as a symbol of the fact that the Tao
can never be grasped or conceived in any fixed form.

The architectonic and artificial style of Christianity is
nowhere clearer than in the idea of God as the *maker* of
the world, and thus of the world itself as an artifact which
has been constructed in accordance with a plan, and which
has, therefore, a purpose and an explanation. But the mode
of action of the Tao is called *wu-wei,* translatable both as
"nonstriving" and "nonmaking." For from the standpoint of
Taoist philosophy natural forms are not made but *grown,*
and there is a radical difference between the organic and
the mechanical. Things which are made, such as houses,
furniture, and machines, are an assemblage of parts put
together, or shaped, like sculpture, from the outside inwards. But things which grow shape themselves from
within outwards. They are not assemblages of originally
distinct parts; they partition themselves, elaborating their
own structure from the whole to the parts, from the simple
to the complex.

It is fascinating to watch the formation of nature's most
unnatural-looking object—the crystal. For it does not appear in the solution piece by piece but altogether at once,
as if it were a projected image gradually coming into
focus upon a screen. Similarly, the lines of force in a mag-
netic field do not appear serially, as in drawing, but con-

stellate themselves in the iron filings as if a thousand hands were drawing them simultaneously—all in perfect co-ordination. Even when such an object as a plant-stem grows linearly, it does not do so by mere addition, as one builds a wall of bricks or pours concrete. The whole form expands from within, and this direction—from within—is exactly the meaning of the Chinese term for "nature," *tzu-jan* or spontaneity.

The form of Christianity differs from the form of nature because in the Church and in its spiritual atmosphere we are in a universe that has been *made*. Outside the Church we are in a universe that has *grown*. Thus the God who made the world stands outside it as the carpenter stands outside his artifacts, but the Tao which grows the world is within it. Christian doctrine admits, in theory, that God is immanent, but in practice it is his transcendence, his otherness, which is always stressed. We are permitted to think of him as within things and within the world only on the strict condition that we maintain an infinite qualitative distance between God and the creature which he inhabits. Even on the inside he is outside, as the architect is still really outside the house which he builds, even when he goes in to decorate the interior.

Conceiving, then, man and the universe as made, the Western and Christian mind endeavors to interpret them mechanically—and this is at once its genius and its blindness. It is an *idée fixe* that the universe consists of distinct things or entities, which are precisely the structural parts of artifacts. Man himself is a part, brought from outside into the total assemblage of nature as a part is added to a building. Furthermore, the workings of the natural universe are understood in terms of logical laws—the mechanical order of things viewed as a linear series of causes and effects, under the limitations of a consciousness which takes them in and symbolizes them one at a time, piece by piece. Earth and sky are measured by approximating the wayward and whimsical shapes of nature to the abstract circles, triangles, and straight lines of Euclid. It appears that nature is a mechanism because such a mentality can grasp only as much of nature as it can fit into some mechanical or mathematical analogy. Thus it never really sees nature. It sees only the pattern of geometrical forms which it has managed to project upon it.

Unhappily, this mechanical cast of thought turns back upon God himself, for although Christianity wants above all to insist that God is personal and living, his nature as conceived in practice lacks the most important attribute of personality. God is actually conceived as a set of principles —principles of morality and reason, of science and art. His love tempered with justice is likewise principled, since it is willed love rather than felt love, the masculine Logos rather than the feminine Eros. The missing attribute is perhaps best called *inwardness*—in the archaic rather than modern and sentimental sense of "having a heart." For as living organisms grow from within outwards, and do not fashion themselves by standing outside themselves like architects or mechanics, they move according to inner spontaneity rather than objective principle. Inwardness is therefore mysterious and inscrutable but not chaotic and capricious. It does not work according to law, but the "laws of nature" are somewhat clumsily abstracted from its behavior—*ex post facto*. They are the mechanical analogy of living and spontaneous order, the triangle standing for the mountain.

Once when my children asked me what God is, I replied that God is the deepest inside of everything. We were eating grapes, and they asked whether God was inside the grapes. When I answered, "Yes," they said, "Let's cut one

open and see." Cutting the grape, I said, "That's funny, I
don't think we have found the real inside. We've found
just another outside. Let's try again." So I cut one of the
halves and put the other in one of the children's mouths.
"Oh dear," I exclaimed, "we seem to have just some more
outsides!" Again I gave one quarter to one of the children
and split the other. "Well, all I see is still another outside,"
I said, eating one eighth part myself. But just as I was
about to cut the other, my little girl ran for her bag and
cried, "Look! Here is the inside of my bag, but God isn't
there." "No," I answered, "that isn't the inside of your bag.
That's the inside-outside, but God is the inside-inside, and
I don't think we'll ever get at it."

For the truly inward can never become an object. Because of the inwardness of our life-process we do not
know, or rather, cannot tell, how or why we live, even
though it is our own inmost selves which are doing the
living. Yet, in the West at least, we do not actually recognize that we are doing it, for to the extent that we do not
consciously control or understand the formation of our
nervous systems, we feel that someone or something else—
perhaps God—is doing it. We feel strange to our own in-
sides, so that even the mystic feels that his inner experience of God is the experience of something wholly other.
But this is because the beat of his heart also feels "other,"
pulsing with an involuntary life which appears to be its
own rather than ours. We have learned to identify ourselves only with the narrow and superficial area of the
conscious and the voluntary.

Thus it is in the image of this superficial self that we
conceive God, though with its capacities vastly enlarged.
God is the "other" conscious Self who designs and operates
both our own inner processes and all the workings of nature. By his omniscience he attends consciously to every

thing at once, and by his omnipotence makes it subject to his will. At first sight this is a fascinating and marvellous conception—an infinitely conscious mind, concentrated simultaneously on every galaxy and every atom with the entirety of its attention. Yet on second thought the conception is more monstrous than marvellous—a kind of intellectual elephantiasis, being simply a colossal magnification and multiplication of the conscious, analytical mode of knowledge. For God is conceived in the image of a severed consciousness, without inwardness, since he knows not only all things but himself as well through and through. He is completely transparent to his own conscious understanding; his subjectivity is totally objective, and for this very reason he lacks an inside. This is perhaps what Western man would himself like to be—a person in total control of himself, analyzed to the ultimate depths of his own unconscious, understood and explained to the last atom of his brain, and to this extent completely mechanized. When every last element of inwardness has become an object of knowledge, the person is, however, reduced to a rattling shell.

Equally monstrous is the notion of absolute omnipotence when considered as perfect self-control, which is actually tantamount to a state of total paralysis. For control is a degree of inhibition, and a system which is perfectly inhibited is completely frozen. Of course, when we say that a pianist or a dancer has perfect control we refer to a certain combination of control and spontaneity. The artist has established an area of control within which he can abandon himself to spontaneity without restraint. We should rather think of God as the one whose spontaneity is so perfect that it needs no control, whose inside is so harmonious that it requires no conscious scrutiny. But this is not the regal God of ecclesiastical imagery, presiding

44   MAN AND NATURE

over a cosmos which is a beneficent despotism run by en-
lightened force.

Fortunately, there is another strain in Christianity,
though it is seen more fully in Eastern Orthodoxy than in
the West. This is the view that the creation is God's
kenosis, or "self-emptying." The incarnation of God the
Son in Jesus is seen as the historical image of the whole
production of the universe.

> Let this mind be in you which was also in Christ Jesus,
> who, being in the form of God, thought not equality with
> God a thing to be grasped, but made himself of no reputa-
> tion, and took upon himself the form of a servant, and was
> made in the likeness of men. And being found in fashion as
> a man, he humbled himself, and became obedient unto
> death.[5]

The world, too, as the creation of God the Son, the Divine
Word, is seen as God's self-abandonment and self-concealment, so that nature is not so much governed from without
as enlivened from within. The "love which moves the sun
and other stars" is seen as an interior force, which is God
forever giving himself away. There is likewise a strain in
both Catholic and Protestant teaching which regards the
humility and self-abasement of God in Christ as a deeper
revelation of the divine heart than all the imagery of royal
pomp and power. Yet this is offset by the thought that the
"one full, perfect, and sufficient sacrifice" is historically
past, and that now the risen Christ reigns in glory at the
right hand of the Father, whence he shall come to judge
the living and the dead by fire. Again, a subtle theological
insight can reconcile the two motifs. It can see the regal

[5] Philippians 2, 5–8. (Following the AV except in v. 6.) The kenotic
theory of the creation, as distinct from the Incarnation, is perhaps something of a minority view in the Orthodox Church, prevailing mostly
among Hesychast mystics.

imagery as a symbol of the purely inward, spiritual, and unseen glory of humility and love. It can point out that the fire of judgment is the burning pride and anxiety in the hearts of those who will not yield to love and faith. Yet if this be so, the imagery is frankly misleading, and because imagery is far more powerful than rational speech, it would be better to drop it or change it than to explain it away. For it is the imagery rather than the actual doctrine which creates the persuasive feeling of a religion, and to regard it as relatively trivial is merely to be insensitive to the influence which it holds, not only upon those who believe it literally but also upon those who live within its atmosphere—however allegorically they may understand it.[6]

Returning, then, to the personal impression which I mentioned at the start, the imagery of Christianity and the atmosphere of the Church seem utterly foreign to the world beyond its walls. But the reason is that when I leave the Church and the city behind and go out under the sky, when I am with the birds, for all their voraciousness, with the clouds, for all their thunders, and with the oceans, for all their tempests and submerged monsters—I cannot feel Christianly because I am in a world which grows from within. I am simply incapable of feeling its life as coming from above, from beyond the stars, even recognizing this to be a figure of speech. More exactly, I cannot feel that its life comes from Another, from one who is qualitatively

---

[6] A history of Christian theology and apologetics might be written from the standpoint that their development has arisen largely from the embarrassment of Biblical imagery, and the constant necessity of explaining it away. The writings of the early Fathers, almost as a matter of course, treat much of the Old Testament allegorically in order to rationalize the crude behavior of the Lord God in early Hebrew imagery, which Origen called "puerile." And to this day the apologist has to keep on pointing out that it is not necessary to think of God as a white-haired old gentleman on a throne, nor of heaven as a golden city above the sky.

and spiritually external to all that lives and grows. On the contrary, I feel this whole world to be moved from the inside, and from an inside so deep that it is my inside as well, more truly I than my surface consciousness. My sense of kinship with this world is not only with its obviously sympathetic and beautiful aspects, but also with the horrendous and strange. For I have found that the monstrous and inhuman aspects of fish and insects and reptiles are not so much in them as in me. They are external embodiments of my natural creeps and shudders at the thought of pain and death.

To some extent the conflict between spirit and nature is based on the association of death and decay with evil, as if they were not originally part of the divine plan. It is easy, of course, to show that life is life-death rather than life as opposed to death, but rationalizations do not alter a revulsion so deeply embedded. Yet the problem of death is surely not to be solved by the abolition of death, which is almost analogous to chopping off the head to cure headache. The problem lies in our revulsion, and especially in our unwillingness to feel revulsion—as if it were a weakness of which we should be ashamed.

But, once again, the association of God with being and life to the exclusion of nonbeing and death, and the attempt to triumph over death by the miracle of resurrection, is the failure to see that these pairs are not alternatives but correlatives. To be or not to be is *not* the question, for pure being and pure nonbeing are alike conceptual ghosts. But as soon as the "inner identity" of these correlatives is felt, as well as that which lies between man and nature, the knower and the known, death seems simply to be a return to that unknown inwardness out of which we were born. This is not to say that death, biologically speaking, is reversed birth. It is rather that the truly inward source of one's life was never born, but has always remained inside, somewhat as the life remains in the tree, though the fruits may come and go. Outwardly, I am one apple among many. Inwardly, I am the tree.[7]

Possibly this is what Jesus meant when he said, "I am the vine; you are the branches." For Christianity is not necessarily against nature, and within its tradition lie the seeds of a flowering which may someday change its atmosphere profoundly. The rigid Cross may blossom like the Rod of Jesse, and among its thorns bear flowers, because, as an ancient hymn suggests, the Cross is really a tree.

> *Crux fidelis, inter omnes*
> *Arbor una nobilis;*
> *Nulla silva talem profert*
> *Fronde, flore, germine.*
> *Dulce lignum, dulces clavos,*
> *Dulce pondus sustinet.*

Faithful Cross, the one Tree noble above all; no forest affords the like of this in leaf, or flower, or seed. Sweet the wood, sweet the nails, and sweet the weight it bears.

This is what must happen if the Chinese artist is to be able to paint the Crucifixion. Certainly this does not mean the mere symbolic substitution of a tree for the stiff wooden beams. Nor does it mean a prettification of the symbol to conceal the agony and blood. It would simply be the outward sign that Western man had discovered the God of nature instead of the God of abstraction, and that the Crucifixion is not just a distant and isolated historical

[7] This is of course speaking poetically—not fancifully but analogically. Obviously the "life" in the tree is not what we mean when we think of "life" as related to "death." It is the "inner identity" of the two which cannot be expressed outwardly because words, as classifiers, restrict us to talking about classes in which things either are or are not.

event but the inner life of a world, which, when seen from beyond the narrowly individual point of view, is sacrificial to its core. For the fact that life is ever related to death, living by the sacrifice of life, shows only that this "merely natural" world is the very incarnation of "This is my Body which is given for you, and this is my Blood which is shed for you." Prophetically, then, the hymn continues:

> *Flecte ramos, arbor alta,*
> *Tensa laxa viscera,*
> *Et rigor lentescat ille,*
> *Quem dedit nativitas;*
> *Et superni membra Regis*
> *Tende miti stipite.*

Bend thy boughs, O lofty Tree; loosen thy taut sinews, soften thy native hardness, and upon a gentle stem spread out the members of the heavenly King.

But the taut sinews have not yet relaxed, and this is because nature is still feared as the beguiler and temptress, the Spider Mother, the abyss of universal flux which is always threatening to swallow the human person. Nature is seen as the wilderness encroaching upon the garden and the ocean washing away the shore—blind, disorganized, almost cancerous proliferation, against which every human work must be defended with perpetual vigilance. Chief of these works is the personality, the conscious ego, which needs an ark of salvation against the waters of the unconscious and its vast currents of "animal" lust and fear.

Christian reason as distinct from feeling knows, however, that nature is in process of redemption and that its dark and destructive aspects work only under the permission and control of the will of God. Limitless in power, the divine order is in no danger from nature. But the human order, with its awesome gift of freedom, is secure

against nature only so long as it patterns itself upon the
divine. As soon as the human turns away from the divine,
nature becomes, like the devils, an instrument of the wrath
of God. Thus when a post-Christian technological society
sees nature only as a vast randomness upon which man
must relentlessly impose his order, the Christian finds himself in a position to point out that nature will always be
the enemy to the man who has lost God. He will remind
us of the saints who could live unharmed among wild
beasts and who had power to command the forces of
nature miraculously.

Yet at root this is a conception of universal unity which
is an imperium, depending ultimately upon the force of
divine omnipotence, a cosmology whose order is political
rather than organic. It is true that as Christianity matures
the force of omnipotence is seen more and more as the persuasive force of love, just as in well-established states it
becomes possible to abolish capital punishment and send
criminals to psychiatric hospitals instead of prisons. Yet
even in the most beneficent state, force remains the ultimate authority however well hidden. This is because, politically conceived, people are *others,* that is to say, alien
wills and isolated consciousnesses upon which order has to
be imposed from without.

Political order is, then, different in principle from organic order, wherein the parts constitute a whole by nature as distinct from force or persuasion. In organic order
the whole is primary, and the parts arise mutually within
it. But in political order the whole is contrived. There is
no "body politic" since political societies are put together
rather than grown. Similarly, neither the universe nor the
Church can be considered the Body of Christ while they
are also considered as the Kingdom of God. The two conceptions are profoundly contradictory. There is no com-

mon measure between the order of the Vine and the order of the City. But, once again, it is clear that a political conception of the universe and, furthermore, a political conception of human society go hand in hand with a fractured and disorganized view of the world, with a mentality so fascinated by speech and thought that it has lost the power to feel the interval, the reality lying between terms. The terms, the Euclidean points, ends, and boundaries, are everything and the content nothing.

2: Science and Nature

A KING OF ANCIENT INDIA, OPPRESSED BY
the roughness of the earth upon soft human feet, proposed
that his whole territory should be carpeted with skins.
However, one of his wise men pointed out that the same
result could be achieved far more simply by taking a single skin and cutting off small pieces to bind beneath the
feet. These were the first sandals. To a Hindu the point
of this story is not its obvious illustration of technical ingenuity. It is a parable of two different attitudes to the
world, attitudes which correspond approximately to those
of the progressive and traditional types of culture. Only
in this case the more technically skillful solution represents the traditional culture, in which it is felt that it is
easier for man to adapt himself to nature than to adapt
nature to himself. This is why science and technology, as
we know them, did not arise in Asia.

Westerners generally feel that Asian indifference to the
technical control of nature is either tropical laziness or
the lack of a social conscience. It is easy to believe that
religions which concern themselves with inward rather
than outward solutions to suffering encourage callousness
toward hunger, injustice, and disease. It is easy to say that
they are aristocrats' methods of exploiting the poor. But it
is, perhaps, not so easy to see that the poor are also being
exploited when they are persuaded to desire more and
more possessions, and led to confuse happiness with progressive acquisition. The power to change nature or to

perform miracles conceals the truth that suffering is relative, and that the fact that nature abhors a vacuum is
above all true of troubles.

The Western experiment in changing the face of nature
by science and technology has its roots in the political
cosmology of Christianity. For Christian apologists are
indeed justified in pointing out that science has arisen pre-
eminently in the context of the Hebrew-Christian tradition,
notwithstanding the constant conflicts between the two.
There can be conflict between Christianity and science for
the very reason that both are speaking the same language
and dealing with the same universe—the universe of facts.
The claim of Christianity to be unique is bound up with
its insistence on the truth of certain historical facts. To
other spiritual traditions historical facts are of minor
importance, but to Christianity it has always been "of the
essence" that Jesus Christ did in fact rise physically from
the dead, that he was, biologically speaking, born of a virgin, and that even God has the kind of objective and intractable reality which we associate with "hard facts."
The Christian who does not feel this to be so will also
insist less upon the uniqueness of his religion. However,
the temper of most current theology, both Catholic and
Protestant, is to re-emphasize the historicity of the Biblical
narrative. Even among theological liberals who have their
doubts about miracles, this trend takes the curious form
of arguing that the historical and narrative style of Christianity, however unhistorical in certain respects, nevertheless reveals that history is the unfolding of God's purposes.

Christianity is also unique in that the historical facts
upon which it insists are miracles, betokening a state of
mind for which the transformation of the physical world
is of immense importance, for "if Christ be not risen from
the dead, then is your faith vain." Other traditions contain

miraculous elements aplenty, but they are always treated as incidental signs, corroborating the divine authority of the performer. They are never the heart of the matter. But nothing is more important for Christianity than the subservience of nature to the commands of Christ, culminating in his victory over the hardest and most certain of all natural facts—death itself.

However post-Christian and secular the present culture of the West may seem to be, it is still the culture uniquely preoccupied with miracles—that is to say, with the transformation of that world which is felt to be objective and external to the ego. Concurrently, an unparalleled cultural imperialism has taken the place of religious proselytism, and the progressive course of history toward the establishment of the Kingdom of God is seen in terms of the expansion of technological power, the increasing "spiritualization" of the physical world through the abolition of its finite limitations.

All this has its roots in the political cosmology of the Hebrew-Christian tradition, which, until very recently, was also the cosmology of Western science and in some respects still remains so. For, as we have seen, a political universe is one in which separate things, facts, and events are governed by the force of law. However much ideas of the laws of nature may have changed, there is no doubt that the idea of natural law first arose from the supposition that the world obeyed the commandments of a ruler conceived in the image of an earthly king.

Yet the notion of natural law is not fully accounted for by a primitive analogy between the world and a political kingship. There must also be taken into consideration a mode of thought apart from which such an analogy would hardly suggest itself. So far as one can see, this mode of thought arises from an accidental confusion which could easily occur in the development of language in particular and of abstract thought in general.

It is commonly felt that the mind can think only of one thing at a time, and language, in so far as it is the main instrument of thought, confirms this impression by being a linear series of signs read or sounded one at a time. The sense of this common feeling is presumably that conscious thought is focused attention, and that such concentration of our awareness is difficult or impossible when the field of attention is too complex. Attention therefore requires selection. The field of awareness must be divided into relatively simple unities or wholes, so structured that their parts can be taken in at one glance. This may be done both by breaking the whole field down into component parts of the required simplicity, and by so screening out certain details of the whole that it is reduced to a single easily comprehensible form. It is thus that we actually see or hear infinitely more than we attend to or think about, and although we respond and adjust ourselves with extraordinary intelligence to much that we never notice, we feel in better control of a situation to the degree that we can bring it under conscious scrutiny.

Now the simplified units of attention thus selected from the total field of awareness are what we call things and events, or facts. This does not ordinarily occur to us because we naïvely suppose that things are what we see in the first place, prior to the act of conscious attention. Obviously the eye as such does not see things: it sees the total visual field in all its infinite detail. Things appear to the mind when, by conscious attention, the field is broken down into easily thinkable unities. Yet we tend to consider this an act of discovery. Studying the visual or tactile field, intelligence arrives at the conclusion that there are actually things in the external world—a conclusion which appears to be verified by acting upon that assumption. This is to say, in other words, that by attending to the sensed world with the aid of these concentrated and simplified "grasps" or "glances" of the mind, we are able to predict its behavior and find our way around it.

Yet the conclusion does not actually follow. We are also able to predict events and manage the external world by breaking down distances into feet and inches, weights into pounds and ounces, and motions into minutes and seconds. But do we actually suppose that twelve inches of wood are twelve separate bits of wood? We do not. We know that "breaking" wood into inches or pounds is done abstractly and not concretely. It is not, however, so easy to see that breaking the field of awareness into things and events is also done abstractly, and that things are the measuring units of thought just as pounds are the measuring units of weighing. But this begins to be apparent when we realize that any one thing may, by analysis, be broken down into any number of component things, or may in its turn be regarded as the component part of some larger thing.

The real difficulty of understanding this point is that whereas inches are divisions on a ruler which do not themselves appear on the wooden board to be measured, the delineation of things seems to follow divisions and boundaries actually given in nature. For example, the thing called the human body is divided from other things in its environment by the clearly discernible surface of the skin. The point, though, is that the skin *divides* the body from the rest of the world as one thing from others in thought but not in nature. In nature the skin is as much a joiner as a divider, being, as it were, the bridge whereby the inner organs have contact with air, warmth, and light.

Just because concentrated attention is exclusive, selective, and divisive it is much easier for it to notice differences than unities. Visual attention notices things as figures against a contrasting background, and our thought about such things emphasizes the difference between figure and ground. The outline of the figure or the "inline" of the ground divides the two from each other. Yet we do not so easily notice the union or inseparability of figure and ground, or solid and space. This is easily seen when we ask what would become of the figure or the solid without any surrounding ground or space. Conversely, we might ask what would become of the surrounding space if unoccupied by any solids. The answer is surely that it would no longer be space, for space is a "surrounding function" and there would be nothing to surround. It is important to note that this mutuality or inseparability of figure and ground is not only logical and grammatical but also sensuous.[1]

Figure-and-ground, then, constitute a relationship—an inseparable relationship of unity-in-diversity. But when human beings become preoccupied with concentrated attentiveness, with a type of thought which is analytic, divisive, and selective, they cease to notice the mutuality of contrasting "things" and the "identity" of differences. Similarly, when we ask what we really mean by a fact or a thing, we realize that because facts are divisions or selections of experience there can never be less than two! One solitary fact or thing cannot exist by itself, since it would be infinite—without delineating limits, without anything other. Now this essential duality and multiplicity of facts should be the clearest evidence of their interdependence and inseparability.

[1] The naïve idea that there is first of all empty space and then things filling it underlies the classical problem of how the world came out of nothing. Now the problem has to be rephrased, "How did something-and-nothing come out of . . . what?"

What it comes to, then, is that the fundamental realities of nature are not, as thought construes them, separate things. The world is not a collection of objects assembled or added together so as to *come* into relationship with each other. The fundamental realities are the relations or "fields of force" in which facts are the terms or limits— somewhat as hot and cold are the upper and lower terms (that is, termini or ends) of the field of temperature, and scalp and soles the upper and lower limits of the body. Scalp and soles are obviously surfaces *of* the body, and though a person may be scalped, a scalp is never found *sui generis*, coming into being all on its own. But, save through the use of rather unsatisfactory analogies, words and thought forms cannot embrace this world. "Relations" rather than "things" as the basic constituents of nature sound impossibly tenuous and abstract, unless it can dawn upon us that relations are what we are actually sensing and feeling. We know nothing more concrete.

But the dawning of this realization becomes still more remote when we proceed from the primary act of abstraction, selective attention, to the secondary, the signifying of thoughts with words. Because words other than proper names are classifiers, they will aggravate the impression that the world is a disjointed multiplicity. For when we say *what* anything is we identify it with a class. There is no other way of saying what this or that is than to classify it. But that is simply to divide it from everything else, to stress its differentiating characteristics as the most important. Thus it comes to be felt that an identity is a matter of separation, that, for instance, my identity is firstly in my role or class, and secondly in the special ways in which I differ from other members of my class. If, then, I am identified by my differences, my boundaries, my divisions from all else, I experience selfhood as a sense of separation. Thereupon I fail to notice, to feel identified with, the concrete unity which underlies these selected and abstracted marks of difference. Marks of difference are then felt as forms of separation and dissociation rather than relationship. In this situation I feel the world as something to which I must *form* a relation rather than with which I *have* a relation.

A political cosmology presupposes, then, this fractured way of experiencing the world. God is not, as in Hindu cosmology, the underlying identity of the differences, but one of the differences—albeit the ruling difference. Man is related to God as to another distinct person, as subject to king or as son to father. The individual is, from the beginning and out of nothing, created separate and must bring himself or be brought into conformity with the divine will.

Furthermore, because the world consists of things, and because things are defined by their classes, and their classes are ordered and marked by words, it appears that Logos, that word-and-thought actually *underlies* the world. "And God *said*, Let there be light." "By the word of the Lord were the heavens made, and all the hosts of them by the breath of his mouth." When it is not recognized that thought orders the world, it is supposed that thought discovers an order which is already there—a type of order which is, furthermore, expressible in terms of word-and-thought.

Here, then, is the genesis of two of the most important historical premises of Western science. The first is that there is a law of nature, an order of things and events awaiting our discovery, and that this order can be formulated in thought, that is, in words or in some type of notation. The second is that the law of nature is universal, a premise deriving from monotheism, from the idea of one God ruling the whole world.

Science is, moreover, an extreme instance of the entire method of attention which we have been discussing. It is an awareness of nature based upon the selective, analytic, and abstractive way of focusing attention. It understands the world by reducing it as minutely as possible to intelligible things. This it does by a "universal calculus," that is, by translating the formlessness of nature into structures made up of simple and manageable units, as a surveyor measures a "shapeless" piece of land by approximating its areas as minutely as possible to such simple abstract figures as triangles, squares, and circles. By this method all oddities and irregularities are progressively screened out until at last it appears that God himself is the supreme geometer. We say, "How astonishing it is that natural structures conform so precisely to geometrical laws!"— forgetting that by ignoring their irregularities we have forced them to do so. But this we have been able to do by analysis, by the ever minuter division of the world into parts which approximate the supreme simplicity of mathematical points.

Alternatively, this way of regularizing the world may be illustrated by the method of the matrix. Superimpose a transparent sheet of finely squared graph paper upon some complex natural image. The "formless" image can then be described with approximate precision in terms of the highly formal arrangement of squares. Seen through such a screen, the path of an object moving at random can be "plotted" in terms of so many squares up or down, left or right. Reduced to these terms, we can by statistical averages predict the approximate trend of its future motion— and then suppose that the object itself is *obeying* statistical laws. The object, however, is doing nothing of the kind. The statistical laws are being "obeyed" by our regularized model of the object's behavior.

In the twentieth century scientists are increasingly aware of the fact that the laws of nature are not discovered but invented, and the whole notion that nature is obeying or following some innate pattern or order is being supplanted by the idea that these patterns are not determinative but descriptive. This is a fundamental revolution in the philosophy of science which has hardly reached the general public and which has still but barely affected some of the special sciences. The scientist was first discovering the laws of God, in the faith that the workings of the world could be reformulated into the terms of the word, the reason, and the law which they were obeying. As the hypothesis of God made no difference to the accuracy of his predictions, he began to leave it out and to consider the world as a machine, something which followed laws with no lawgiver. Lastly, the hypothesis of pre-existing and determinative laws became unnecessary. They were seen simply as human tools, like knives, with which nature is chopped up into digestible portions.

There are signs, however, that this is but one phase of a still more radical change in the outlook of science. For we may ask whether scientific method must confine itself to the analytic and abstractive mode of attention in studying nature. Until not so long ago the main preoccupation of almost every scientific discipline was classification—a minute, rigorous, and exhaustive identification of species, whether of birds or fish, chemicals or bacilli, organs or diseases, crystals or stars. Obviously this approach encouraged an atomistic and disintegrated view of nature, the disadvantages of which begin to appear when, on the basis of this view, science becomes technology and men start to extend their control of the world. For they begin to discover that nature cannot wisely be controlled in the same way in which it has been studied—piecemeal. Nature is through and through relational, and interference at one point has interminable and unforeseeable effects. The analytic study of these interrelations produces an ever-growing accumulation of extremely complicated information, so vast and so complex as to be unwieldy for many practical purposes, especially when quick decisions are needed.

Consequently the progress of technology begins to have the opposite of its intended effect. Instead of simplifying human tasks, it makes them more complicated. No one dares move without consulting an expert. The expert in his turn cannot hope to have mastered more than a small section of the ceaselessly expanding volume of information. But whereas formal scientific knowledge is departmentalized, the world is not, so that the mastery of a single department of knowledge is often as frustrating as a closetful of left shoes. This is not only a problem of dealing with such formally "scientific" questions as endocrinology, soil chemistry, or nuclear fall-out. In a society whose means of production and communication are highly technological, the most ordinary matters of politics, economics, and law become so involved that the individual citizen feels paralyzed. The growth of bureaucracy and totalitarianism has, then, far less to do with sinister influences than with the mere mechanics of control in an impossibly complex system of interrelations.

Yet if this were the whole story scientific knowledge would already have reached the point of total self-strangulation. That it has done so only in some degree is because the scientist actually understands interrelations by other means than analysis and step-by-step thinking. In practice he relies heavily upon intuition—upon a process of intelligence whose steps are unconscious, which does not appear to work in the painfully linear, one-thing-at-a-time fashion of thought, and which can therefore grasp whole fields of related detail simultaneously.

For the notion that the interrelatedness of nature is complex and highly detailed is merely the result of translating it into the linear units of thought. Despite its rigor and despite its initial successes, this is an extremely clumsy mode of intelligence. Just as it is a highly complicated task to drink water with a fork instead of a glass, so the complexity of nature is not innate but a consequence of the instruments used to handle it. There is nothing complex about walking, breathing, and circulating one's blood. Living organisms have developed these functions without thinking about them at all. The circulation of the blood becomes complex only when stated in physiological terms, that is, when understood by means of a conceptual model constructed of the kind of simple units which conscious attention requires. The natural world seems a marvel of complexity, requiring a vastly intricate intelligence to create and govern it, just because we have represented it to ourselves in the clumsy "notation" of thought. In a somewhat similar way, multiplication and division are processes of the most frustrating complexity for those working with Roman or Egyptian numerals. But with Arabic numerals they are relatively simple, and with an abacus simpler still.

Understanding nature by means of thought is like trying to make out the contours of an enormous cave with the aid of a small flashlight casting a bright but very thin beam. The path of the light and the series of "spots" over which it has passed must be retained in memory, and from this record the general appearance of the cave must laboriously be reconstructed.

In practice, then, the scientist must perforce use his intuition for grasping the wholes of nature, though he does not trust it. He must always stop to check intuitive insight with the thin bright beam of analytic thought. For intuition can so easily be wrong, just as the "organic intelligence" which regulates the body without thought cannot always be relied upon to avoid the "mistakes" of congenital deformity or cancer, nor to control instincts which, under special circumstances, lead directly to destruction. Thus it is natural enough and "healthy" enough to want to reproduce the species, but the reproductive urge cannot be relied upon to keep a watch on the environment and automatically check itself when the food supply is insufficient. Hence the only way of correcting the errors of intuition or unconscious intelligence seems to be by the laborious work of analysis and experiment. But this involves an interference with the natural order from the start, and the wisdom of this interference cannot be known until its work is well advanced!

Therefore the scientist has to ask himself whether the "mistakes" of nature are really mistakes. Does a species destroy itself in the interests of the natural order as a whole—in the sense that if it did not do so, life would be intolerable for all, including itself? Are "errors" of congenital disease, or of epidemics or pestilence, necessary for maintaining a balance of life? Will correction of these errors give rise in the long run to far more serious problems than one has solved? And will the solution of *those* problems in turn create ever more fantastic difficulties? Must unconscious intelligence every so often be wrong lest, if it were always right, the species would be too successful and again upset the balance?

On the other hand, he may ask whether the birth of conscious analysis is not itself an act of unconscious intelligence. Is conscious interference with nature actually quite natural, in the sense that it is still working in the interests of the natural order as a whole, even if it is going to involve the elimination of man? Or may it be that in pushing conscious analysis just as far as we can we shall discover means of enabling the unconscious intelligence to be far more effective?

The difficulty with all these questions is that we can hardly find out the answers until it is too late to make use of them. What, furthermore, will be the test of doing the right thing? What, in other words, is the "good" of the natural order as a whole? The usual answer to the problem of what is good for any or all species is simply survival. Science is mainly interested in prediction because it assumes that the chief good of humanity is to continue into the future. This is likewise the test of almost all practical action: it has "survival-value." Accepting this premise, that the good of life lies in its indefinite perpetuation through time, and assuming that such perpetuation must be pleasant for it to go on at all, the test of whether we have done wisely is that we are still here, and seem likely to remain for as long as we can foresee.

But on this assumption the human race had survived, and seemed likely to go on surviving, for perhaps more than a million years before the arrival of modern technology. We must, on this premise, assume that it had acted wisely thus far. We may argue that its life was not highly pleasant, but it is difficult to know what this means. The race was certainly pleased to go on living, for it did so. On the other hand, after a bare two centuries of industrial technology the prospects of human survival are being quite seriously questioned. It is not unlikely that we may eat or blow ourselves off the planet.

Yet surely the ideal of survival is completely inane.

Studying human and animal psychology, it does indeed seem that "self-preservation is the first law of nature," though it is possible that this is an anthropomorphism, a projection into nature of a peculiarly human attitude. If survival is the test of wisdom, the significance of life is merely time: we go on in order to keep going on. Our attitude to experience seems to be one of perpetual hunger, for even when we are satisfied and delighted to be alive we keep calling for more. The cry "Encore!" is the highest mark of approval. Obviously, this is because no moment of life is a true fulfillment. Even in satisfaction there remains a gnawing emptiness which nothing save an infinity of time can fill, for "all joys want eternity."

But the hunger for time is the direct result of our specialization in narrowed attention, of the mode of consciousness which takes the world in serially, one thought and one thing at a time. Each experience is for this reason partial, fractured, and incomplete, and no amount of these fragments ever add up to a whole experience, a true fulfillment. By and large they attain only to the weariness of satiation. The impression that all nature, like ourselves, hungers endlessly for survival is, then, the necessary result of the way in which we study it. The answer is predetermined by the character of the question. Nature seems to be a series of unsatisfactory moments ever demanding more because those are the terms in which we perceive it. We understand it by cutting it to pieces, assume that it is in itself this heap of fragments, and conclude that it is a system of endless incompleteness which can seek fulfillment only through everlasting addition.

Thought and science are therefore raising problems which their terms of study can never answer, many of which are doubtless problems only for thought. The trisection of an angle is similarly an insoluble problem only for compass and straight-edge construction, and Achilles cannot overtake the tortoise so long as their progress is considered piecemeal, endlessly halving the distance between them. However, as it is not Achilles but the method of measurement which fails to catch up with the tortoise, so it is not man but his method of thought which fails to find fulfillment in experience. This is by no means to say that science and analytic thought are useless and destructive tools, but rather that the people who use them must be greater than their tools. To be an effective scientist one must be more than a scientist, and a philosopher must be more than a thinker. For the analytic measurement of nature tells us nothing if we cannot see nature in any other way.

Thus the scientist *as* scientist does not see nature at all— or rather he sees it only by means of an instrument of measurement, as if trees became visible to the carpenter only as he sawed them into planks or marked them out with his ruler. More importantly, man as ego does not see nature at all. For man as ego is man identifying himself or his mind, his total awareness, with the narrowed and exclusive style of attention which we call consciousness.[2] Thus the radical change which may yet overcome modern science will be the recognition of itself as a secondary form of perception, related to a primary and more basic form. This involves a good deal more than the scientist's recognition that there are other modes of knowledge than his own—for example, the religious—all of which are valid in their own spheres. For this merely puts the scientist as a man of religion in one compartment, and the scientist

[2] Trigant Burrow (1) coined the useful terms "ditention" and "cotention" for the intensive and extensive modes of awareness. His whole discussion of the relation between the psychoneuroses and ditentive thought and feeling is most provocative.

as scientist in another. But we have seen that the most important scientific insights, or intuitions, come precisely through the somewhat reluctant use of a nonthinking mode of awareness.

It is therefore becoming generally realized that for the most creative research, men of science must be trusted and encouraged to let their minds wander unsystematically without any pressure for results. The visitor to such an inspired foundation as the Institute for Advanced Studies at Princeton will see some of the world's greatest mathematicians just sitting at their desks with their heads in their hands, or staring blankly out of the window, apparently financed munificently to do nothing but "goof off." Yet as R. G. H. Siu has shown in his *Tao of Science*, this is precisely the Taoist principle of "using no-knowledge to attain knowledge," the Western discovery of the creative power of *wu-nien*, or "no-thought," and *kuan*, or contemplation without strained attention. As an experienced director of research he has cogently argued that such a mode of awareness is essential when research is expected to bring forth new concepts, and to be something more than the verification of old ones.[3] At present this mode is mistrusted and rigorously checked by analysis, but it is highly possible that the unreliability of scientific intuition is due to lack of use, and to the constant distraction of the mind by selective attention both in scientific and everyday consciousness.

Now the recovery of our extensive and inclusive type of awareness is completely different from the acquisition of a

[3] The whole work, Siu (1), may be read as an expansion of themes discussed in the present chapter. Unfortunately, it did not come to my attention until I had almost finished writing this book. It gives a very wide application of Chinese thought to the problems of science, though for the Western reader it is rather too vague in describing the character of the necessary mental attitude.

moral virtue, to be urged upon society by persuasion and propaganda and cultivated by discipline and practice. As we know, such idealisms are notorious for their failure. Furthermore, moral and spiritual idealisms with all their efforts and disciplines aimed at the future are forms of the very mode of awareness which is giving us the trouble. For they perceive good and bad, ideal and real, separatively and fail to see that "goodness" is necessarily a "bad" man's ideal, that courage is the goal of cowards, and that peace is sought only by the disturbed. As Lao-tzu put it:

> When the great Tao is lost,
> we have "human-heartedness" and "righteousness."
> When "wisdom" and "sagacity" arise,
> we have great hypocrites.
> When the six family relations are not in harmony,
> we have "filial devotion."
> When the nation is confused and disordered,
> we have "loyal ministers." xviii

As "you cannot make a silk purse from a sow's ear," no amount of effort will turn turmoil into peace. For, as another Taoist saying puts it, "When the wrong man uses the right means, the right means work in the wrong way."

Thought, with its serial, one-at-a-time way of looking at things, is ever looking to the future to solve problems which can be handled only in the present—but not in the fragmentary present of fixed and pointed attention. The solution has to be found, as Krishnamurti has said, in the problem and not away from it. In other words, the "bad" man's disturbing emotions and urgent desires have to be seen as they are—or, better, the moment in which they arise has to be seen as it is, without narrowing attention upon any aspect of it. And just here, instead of straining toward a future in which one hopes to be different, the mind opens and admits a whole experience in which and by which the problem of what is the "good" of life is answered. In the words of Goethe's *Fragment on Nature:*

At each moment she starts upon a long, long journey and at each moment reaches her end. . . . All is eternally present in her, for she knows neither past nor future. For her the present is eternity.

3: The Art of Feeling

THE WORDS WHICH ONE MIGHT BE TEMPTED to use for a silent and wide-open mind are mostly terms of abuse—thoughtless, mindless, unthinking, empty-headed, and vague. Perhaps this is some measure of an innate fear of releasing the chronic cramp of consciousness by which we grasp the facts of life and manage the world. It is only to be expected that the idea of an awareness which is something other than sharp and selective fills us with considerable disquiet. We are perfectly sure that it would mean going back to the supposedly confused sensitivity of infants and animals, that we should be unable to distinguish up from down, and that we should certainly be run over by a car the first time we went out on the street.

Narrowed, serial consciousness, the memory-stored stream of impressions, is the means by which we have the sense of ego. It enables us to feel that behind thought there is a thinker and behind knowledge a knower—an individual who stands aside from the changing panorama of experience to order and control it as best he may. If the ego were to disappear, or rather, to be seen as a useful fiction, there would no longer be the duality of subject and object, experiencer and experience. There would simply be a continuous, self-moving stream of experiencing, without the sense either of an active subject who controls it or of a passive subject who suffers it. The thinker would be seen to be no more than the series of thoughts, and the feeler no more than the feelings. As Hume said in the *Treatise of Human Nature:*

> For my part, when I enter most intimately into what I call *myself,* I always stumble on some particular perception or other, of heat or cold, light or shade, love or hatred, pain or pleasure. I never can catch *myself* at any time without a perception, and never can observe any thing but the perception. . . . [We are] nothing but a bundle or collection of different perceptions, which succeed each other with an inconceivable rapidity, and are in a perpetual flux and movement.[1]

Now this is just what we fear—the loss of human identity and integrity in a transient stream of atoms. Hume, arguing against the notion of the self as a metaphysical or mental substance, had of course no alternative conception other than the "bundle or collection" of intrinsically separate perceptions, for he was translating his experience into the disjointed terms of linear thought. He maintained that all our impressions are "different, and distinguishable, and separable from each other, and may be separately consider'd, and may exist separately, and have no need of any thing to support their existence." Having seen the fiction of the separate ego-substance, he failed to see the fiction of separate things or perceptions which the ego, as a mode of awareness, abstracts from nature. As we have seen, inherently separate things can be ordered only mechanically or politically, so that without a real ego in which impressions are integrated and ordered, human experience is delivered over to mechanism or chaos.

If the world of nature is neither things seen by an ego nor things, some of which are sensations, bundled mechanically together, but a field of "organic" relations,

[1] Hume (1), p. 252.

there is no need to fear that disorder is the only alternative to political order or to mechanism. The stream of human experience would then be ordered neither by a transcendental ego nor by a transcendental God but by itself. Yet this is what we usually mean by a mechanical or automatic order, since the machine is what "goes by itself." We have seen, however, that there is a profound difference of operation betwen organism and mechanism. An organism can be represented in terms of a mechanical model just as "formless" shapes can be approximated by geometric models and as the movements of the stars can be translated into the figures in an almanac. But as the celestial bodies are other than and infinitely more than numerical relations and schedules, organisms and natural forms must never be confused with their mechanical representations.

Once again, because the order of thought is a linear, bit-by-bit series, it can approximate but never comprehend a system of relations in which everything is happening simultaneously. It would be as if our narrowed consciousness had to take charge of all the operations of the body so that, unless it took thought of them, the glands and nerves and arteries could not do their work. As language, both written and spoken, so eloquently shows, the order of thought must be strung out in a line. But nature is not strung out in a line. Nature is, at the very least, a volume, and at most an infinitely dimensioned field. We need, then, another conception of natural order than the logical, than the order of the Logos or word based on bit-by-bit awareness.

· As Needham has shown, Chinese philosophy provides this in the Neo-Confucian (and Buddhist) conception of *li*, for which there has been no better English equivalent than "principle." *Li* is the universal principle of order, but in this case the principle or principles cannot be stated in terms of law (*tse*). The root meaning of *li* is the markings in jade, the grain in wood, or the fiber in muscle. The root meaning of *tse* is the writing of imperial laws upon sacrificial caldrons.[2] Now the markings in jade are "formless." That is to say, they are unsymmetrical, fluid, and intricate patterns which appeal highly to the Chinese sense of beauty. Thus when it is said that the Tao has "no shape"[3] we are not to imagine a uniform blank so much as a pattern without clearly discernible features, in other words, just exactly what the Chinese painter admires in rocks and clouds, and what he sometimes conveys in the texture of black ink applied with bold strokes of a rather dry brush. In the words of the *Huai Nan Tzu:*

> The Tao of Heaven operates mysteriously and secretly; it has no fixed shape; it follows no definite rules (*tse*); it is so great that you can never come to the end of it; it is so deep that you can never fathom it.[4]

At the same time the order of the Tao is not so inscrutable that man can see it only as confusion. When the artist handles his material, perfection consists in knowing how to follow its nature, how to follow the grain in carving wood, and how to employ the sound-textures of various musical instruments. The nature of the material is precisely *li*. He discovers it, however, not by logical analysis but by *kuan*,[5] to which we have already referred as "silent

[2] For the characters see Mathews' *Chinese-English Dictionary* 3864 (*li*) and 6746 (*tse*). For the original forms, see Karlgren's *Grammata Serica* 978 and 906. Since the Romanized forms of Chinese words give little clue to the actual written term, we shall hereinafter identify Chinese terms with their numbers in the Mathews *Dictionary*, e.g., M 3864.

[3] *Yung*, M 7560.

[4] *Huai Nan Tzu*, 9. Tr. Needham (1), vol. 2, p. 561.

[5] M 3575.

contemplation," or looking at nature without *thinking* in the sense of narrowed attention. Speaking of the hexagram *kuan* in the *Book of Changes,* Wang Pi writes:

> The general meaning of the *tao* of "Kuan" is that one should not govern by means of punishments and legal pressure, but by looking forth one should exert one's influence so as to change all things. Spiritual power can no man see. We do not see Heaven command the four seasons, and yet they never swerve from their course. So also we do not see the sage ordering people about, and yet they obey and spontaneously serve him.[6]

The point is that things are brought into order through regarding them from a viewpoint unrestricted by the ego, since their *li* or pattern cannot be observed while looking and thinking piecemeal, nor when regarding them as objects apart from oneself, the subject. The Chinese character for *kuan* shows the radical sign for "seeing" beside a bird which is probably a heron, and although Needham feels that it may originally have had something to do with watching the flight of birds for omens, I am inclined to think that the root idea was taken from the way in which a heron stands stock-still at the edge of a pool, gazing into the water. It does not seem to be looking *for* fish, and yet the moment a fish moves it dives. *Kuan* is, then, simply to observe silently, openly, and without seeking any particular result. It signifies a mode of observation in which there is no duality of seer and seen: there is simply the seeing. Watching thus, the heron is all pool.

In some respects this is what we mean by *feeling,* as when one learns to dance by watching and "getting the feel of it" rather than following a diagram of the steps. Similarly the bowler in cricket or the pitcher in baseball

° Tr. Needham (1), vol. 2, pp. 561–62.

develops his skill by "feel" rather than by studying precise technical directions. So, too, it is by feeling that the musician distinguishes the styles of composers, that the wine taster identifies vintages, that the painter determines compositional proportions, that the farmer foretells the weather, and that the potter throws and shapes his clay. Up to a point these arts have communicable rules, but there is always something indefinable which distinguishes true mastery. As the wheelwright says in the *Chuang-tzu:*

> Let me take an illustration from my own trade. In making a wheel, if you work too slowly, you can't make it firm; if you work too fast, the spokes won't fit in. You must go neither too slowly nor too fast. There must be co-ordination of mind and hand. Words cannot explain what it is, but there is some mysterious art herein. I cannot teach it to my son; nor can he learn it from me. Consequently, though seventy years of age, I am still making wheels in my old age.[7]

Analytically studied, these skills appear at first sight to be the result of "unconscious thinking," the brain acting as an extremely complex electronic computer which delivers its results to the consciousness. In other words, they are the consequence of a thinking process which differs merely in quantity from conscious thought: it is faster and more complex. But this tells us not so much about what the brain does as about the way in which it has been studied and the model to which it has been approximated. The brain may be represented in terms of quantitative measurement, but it does not follow that it works in these terms. On the contrary, it does not work in terms at all, and for this reason can respond intelligently to relations which can be termed only approximately, slowly, and laboriously.

[7] H. A. Giles (1), p. 171.

But if we pursue the question, "How, then, does feeling work?" recognizing that an answer in terms is no answer, we shall have to say that it works as it feels from the inside, in the same way that we feel how to move our legs. We easily forget that this is a more intimate knowledge of our nature than objective description, which is of necessity superficial, being knowledge of surfaces. Thus it is of relatively little use to the scientist to know, in terms, how his brain operates, for in practice he gets his best results when he resorts to feeling or intuition, when his research is a kind of puttering without any specific result in mind. He must, of course, have a knowledge of terms which will enable him to recognize a result when he sees it. But these enable him to communicate the result to himself and to others; they do not supply the result any more than the dictionary and the rules of prosody supply the poet with poetry. *Kuan* as feeling without seeking, or open awareness, is therefore as essential to the scientist, for all his analytic rigor, as to the poet. The attitude is marvellously described by Lin Ching-hsi in his *Poetical Remains of the Old Gentleman of Chi Mountain* as follows:

> Scholars of old time said that the mind is originally empty, and only because of this can it respond [resonate] [8] to natural things without prejudices (lit. traces, *chi*,[9] left behind to influence later vision). Only the empty mind can respond to the things of Nature. Though everything resonates with the mind, the mind should be as if it had never resonated, and things should not remain in it. But once the mind has received (impressions of) natural things, they

[8] *Ying*, M 7477. Needham points out that this is the technical term for "resonance," an idea basic to the Chinese philosophy of the relations between events, derived from the *Book of Changes*. Cf. Eckhart, "If my eye is to discern color, it must itself be free from color."
[9] M 502. Also "effects" or "searching out."

tend to remain and not to disappear, thus leaving traces in the mind. It should be like a river gorge with swans flying overhead; the river has no desire to retain the swan, yet the swan's passage is traced out by its shadow without any omission. Take another example. All things, whether beautiful or ugly, are reflected perfectly in a mirror; it never refuses to show anything, nor retains anything afterwards.[10]

Kuan is no more a mind that is merely empty than *li*, the pattern of the Tao, is a featureless blank. Indeed, *kuan* is not so much a mind empty of contents as a mind empty of mind. It is mind or "experiencing" at work without the sense of the seeking and staring subject, for the sensation of the ego is the sensation of a kind of effort of consciousness, of a confusion of nerves with muscles. But as glaring and staring do not clarify the eyesight, and as straining to hear does not sharpen the ears, mental "trying" does not enhance understanding. Nevertheless the mind is constantly making efforts to fight off the sense of boredom or depression, to stop being afraid, to get the most out of a pleasure, or to compel itself to be loving, attentive, patient, or happy. On being told that this is wrong, the mind will even make efforts not to make efforts. This can come to an end only as it is clearly seen that all these efforts are as futile as trying to leap into the air and fly, as struggling to sleep, or as forcing an erection of the sexual member. Everyone is familiar with the contradiction of trying to recollect a forgotten name, and though it happens again and again, we never seem to trust the memory to supply the information spontaneously. Yet this is one of the most common forms of what is known in Zen Buddhism as *satori* —the effortless, spontaneous, and sudden dawning of a

[10] *Chi Shan Chi,* 4. Tr. Needham (1), vol. 2, p. 89.

realization. The difficulty is of course that the mind strains itself by force of habit, and that until it loses the habit it must be watched—gently—all the time.[11]

In saying that the ego is a sensation of mental strain, we must not overlook the fact that the words "ego" and "I" are sometimes used simply to denote *this* organism as distinct from its soul or from one of its psychological functions. In this sense, of course, "I" does not necessarily denote a state of strain or a psychological excrescence. But the sensation of the ego as a part function of the whole organism, or rather, as an inner entity which owns and inhabits the organism, is the result of an excess of activity in the use of the senses and of certain muscles. This is the habit of using more energy than is necessary to think, see, hear, or make decisions. Thus even when lying flat on the floor most people will continue to make totally needless muscular efforts to retain their position, almost as if they were afraid of the organism losing its shape and dissolving into a jelly. All this arises from anxiety acquired in learning control and co-ordination, for under social pressure

[11] The habitual straining of the mind can be relaxed temporarily by the use of certain drugs, such as alcohol, mescalin, and lysergic acid. Whereas alcohol dulls the clarity of awareness, mescalin and lysergic acid do not. Consequently these two, and sometimes also nitrous oxide and carbon dioxide, will induce states of consciousness in which the individual feels his relational identity with the whole realm of nature. Although these states appear to be similar to those realized through more "natural" means, they differ in the sense that being able to swim with a life jacket differs from swimming unaided. From personal, though limited, experimentation with a research group working with lysergic acid, I would judge that the state of consciousness induced is confused with a mystical state because of similarities of language used in describing the two. The experience is multidimensional, as if everything were inside, or implied, everything else, requiring a description which is paradoxical from the standpoint of ordinary logic. But whereas the drug gives a vision of nature which is infinitely complex, the mystical state is clarifying, and gives a vision which is as infinitely simple. The drug seems to give the intelligence a kaleidoscopic quality which "patterns" the perception of relations in accordance with its own peculiar structure.

the child tries to speed up his neural skills by sheer muscle-power.

For all that has been said, we are so convinced of the necessity of mental strain that the dropping of the habit will hardly be acceptable until certain theoretical objections are answered. The "mental strain" deplored by conventional psychology is, of course, highly excessive strain, but it is not generally recognized that there is a contradiction in mental strain as such and in any degree. The two principal objections are, I think, firstly, that an absence of strain would encourage a view of the world characterized by mystical and pantheistic vagueness which is both demoralizing and uncritical; and, secondly, that since mental strain is essential to any self-control, its absence will result in being completely swept away by one's feelings.

In theological circles "pantheism" has long been a definitively damning label, and those who like their religious and philosophical opinions to be robust and definite are also inclined to use the word "mysticism" with the same kind of opprobrium. They associate it with "mist," with vagueness, with clouding of issues and blurring of distinctions. Therefore from this standpoint nothing could be more ghastly than "mystical pantheism" or "pantheistic nature mysticism," which is just what the attitude of *kuan* appears to produce. However much the contrary may be pointed out, such people continue to insist that Taoist and Buddhist mysticism reduces the interesting and significant distinctions of the world to a miasma of uniform oneness.[12]

[12] In my *Supreme Identity* I put forward a view of the Vedanta which very carefully explained its difference from pantheism and from all those types of "acosmistic" mysticsm which seem to idealize the complete disappearance of the natural world from consciousness. Nevertheless, it was criticized by Reinhold Niebuhr in *The Nation* for advocating exactly those views which it opposed, an interesting example of the fact that Christian polemicists spend a good deal of energy attacking points of view which exist only in their own minds.

I am God, you are God, everything is God, and God is a boundless and featureless sea of dimly conscious tapioca pudding. The mystic is thus a feeble-minded fellow who finds in this boring "undifferentiated aesthetic continuum" (Northrop) a source of enthusiasm, because, somehow or other, it unifies the conflicts and evils of the world into a transcendental Goodness.

While this is obviously an ignorant caricature, there is something to be said in defense of philosophical vagueness. Strangely assorted people join forces in making fun of it—Logical Positivists and Catholic Neo-Thomists, Dialectical Materialists and Protestant Neo-Orthodoxists, Behaviorists and Fundamentalists. Despite intense differences of opinion among themselves, they belong to a psychological type which takes special glee in having one's philosophy of life clear-cut, hard, and rigid. They range from the kind of scientist who likes to lick his tongue around the notion of "brute" facts to the kind of religionist who fondles a system of "unequivocal dogma." There is doubtless a deep sense of security in being able to say, "The clear and authoritative teaching of the Church is . . . ," or to feel that one has mastered a logical method which can tear other opinions, and especially metaphysical opinions, to shreds. Attitudes of this kind usually go together with a somewhat aggressive and hostile type of personality which employs sharp definition like the edge of a sword. There is more in this than a metaphor, for, as we have seen, the laws and hypotheses of science are not so much discoveries as instruments, like knives and hammers, for bending nature to one's will. So there is a type of personality which approaches the world with an entire armory of sharp and hard instruments, by means of which it slices and sorts the universe into precise and sterile categories which will not interfere with one's peace of mind.

There is a place in life for a sharp knife, but there is a still more important place for other kinds of contact with the world. Man is not to be an intellectual porcupine, meeting his environment with a surface of spikes. Man meets the world outside with a soft skin, with a delicate eyeball and eardrum, and finds communion with it through a warm, melting, vaguely defined, and caressing touch whereby the world is not set at a distance like an enemy to be shot, but embraced to become one flesh, like a beloved wife. After all, the whole possibility of clear knowledge depends upon sensitive organs which, as it were, bring the outside world into our bodies, and give us knowledge of that world precisely in the form of our own bodily states.

Hence the importance of opinions, of instruments of the mind, which are vague, misty, and melting rather than clear-cut. They provide possibilties of communication, of actual contact and relationship with nature more intimate than anything to be found by preserving at all costs the "distance of objectivity." As Chinese and Japanese painters have so well understood, there are landscapes which are best viewed through half-closed eyes, mountains which are most alluring when partially veiled in mist, and waters which are most profound when the horizon is lost, and they are merged with the sky.

> *Through the evening mist a lone goose is flying;*
> *Of one tone are wide waters and sky.*

Or consider Po Chü-i's lines on "Walking at Night in Fine Rain," translated, I think, by Arthur Waley:

> *Autumn clouds, vague and obscure;*
> *The evening, lonely and chill.*
> *I felt the dampness on my garments,*
> *But saw no spot, and heard no sound of rain.*

Or Lin Yutang's version of Chia Tao's "Searching for the Hermit in Vain":

> *I asked the boy beneath the pines.*
> *He said, "The Master's gone alone*
> *Herb-picking somewhere on the mount,*
> *Cloud-hidden, whereabouts unknown."*

Images of a rather similar mood are strung together by Seami when he tries to suggest what the Japanese mean by *yugen*, a subtle order of beauty whose origin is dark and obscure: "To watch the sun sink behind a flower-clad hill, to wander on and on in a huge forest with no thought of return, to stand on the shore and gaze after a boat that goes hid by far-off islands, to ponder on the journey of wild geese seen and lost among the clouds." [13] But there is a kind of brash mental healthiness ever ready to rush in and clean up the mystery, to find out just precisely where the wild geese have gone, what herbs the master is picking and where, and that sees the true face of a landscape only in the harsh light of the noonday sun. It is just this attitude which every traditional culture finds utterly insufferable in Western man, not just because it is tactless and unrefined, but because it is blind. It cannot tell the difference between the surface and the depth. It seeks the depth by cutting into the surface. But the depth is known only when it reveals itself, and ever withdraws from the probing mind. In the words of Chuang-tzu:

> Things are produced around us, but no one knows the whence. They issue forth, but no one sees the portal. Men one and all value that part of knowledge which is known. They do not know how to avail themselves of the unknown in order to reach knowledge. Is not this misguided? [14]

[13] Waley (1), pp. 21–22.
[14] H. A. Giles (1), p. 345.

We fail so easily to see the difference between fear of the unknown and respect for the unknown, thinking that those who do not hasten in with bright lights and knives are deterred by a holy and superstitious fear. Respect for the unknown is the attitude of those who, instead of raping nature, woo her until she gives herself. But what she gives, even then, is not the cold clarity of the surface but the warm inwardness of the body—a mysteriousness which is not merely a negation, a blank absence of knowledge, but that positive substance which we call wonderfull.

"The highest that man can attain in these matters," said Goethe, "is wonder; if the primary phenomenon causes this, let him be satisfied; more it cannot bring; and he should forbear to seek for anything further behind it: here is the limit. But the sight of a prime phenomenon is generally not enough for people. They think they must go still further; and are thus like children, who, after peeping into a mirror, turn it round directly to see what is on the other side." [15]

For as Whitehead said:

When you understand all about the sun and all about the atmosphere and all about the rotation of the earth, you may still miss the radiance of the sunset. There is no substitute for the direct perception [kuan] of the concrete achievement of a thing in its actuality. [16]

This is, surely, a true materialism, or perhaps it would be better to say a true substantialism, since matter is really cognate to "meter" and properly designates not the reality of nature but nature in terms of measures. And "substance" in this sense would not be the gross notion of "stuff," but what is conveyed by the Chinese *t'i* [17]—the wholeness, the

[15] Eckermann (1). February 18th, 1829.
[16] Whitehead (1), p. 248.
[17] *M* 6246.

Gestalt, the complete field of relations, which escapes every linear description.

The natural world therefore reveals its content, its fullness of wonder, when respect hinders us from investigating it in such a way as to shatter it to abstractions. If I *must* cross every skyline to find out what is beyond, I shall never appreciate the true depth of sky seen between trees upon the ridge of a hill. If I must map the canyons and count the trees, I shall never enter into the sound of a hidden waterfall. If I must explore and investigate every trail, that path which vanishes into the forest far up on the mountainside will be found at last to lead merely back to the suburbs. To the mind which pursues every road to its end, every road leads nowhere. To abstain is not to postpone the cold disillusionment of the true facts but to see that one arrives by staying rather than going, that to be forever looking beyond is to remain blind to what is here.

To know nature, the Tao, and the "substance" of things, we must know it as, in the archaic sense, a man "knows" a woman—in the warm vagueness of immediate contact. As the *Cloud of Unknowing* says of God, "By love he may be gotten and holden, but by thought never." This implies, too, that it is also mistaken to think of it as *actually* vague, like mist or diffused light or tapioca pudding. The image of vagueness implies that to know nature, outside ourselves as within, we must abandon every idea, every thought and opinion, of what it is—and look. If we must have some idea of it, it must be the most vague imaginable, which is why, even for Westerners, such formless conceptions as the Tao are to be preferred to the idea of God, with its all too definite associations.

The danger of the "pantheistic" and mystical attitude to nature is, of course, that it may become exclusive and one-sided, though there seem to be few historical instances of this. There is no real reason why it should become so, for its advantage is precisely that it gives us a formless background against which the forms of everyday, practical problems may be seen more clearly. When our idea of the background, of God, is highly formal, practical conduct is as tortuous as trying to write upon a printed page. Issues cannot be seen clearly because it is not seen that matters of right and wrong are like the rules of grammar—conventions of communication. By grounding right and wrong in the Absolute, in the background, not only do the rules become too rigid, but they are also sanctioned by too weighty an authority. As a Chinese proverb says, "Do not swat a fly upon your friend's head with a hatchet." By grounding the rules of action in God, the West has not succeeded in fostering any unusual degree of morality. On the contrary, it has invited just those violent ideological revolutions against intolerable authority which are so characteristic of its history. The same would apply to a rigid scientific dogma as to what is natural and what is not.

In practice a mysticism which avoids all rigid formulations of both nature and God has usually been favorable to the growth of science.[18] For its attitude is empirical, emphasizing concrete experience rather than theoretical construction or belief, and its frame of mind is contemplative and receptive. It is unfavorable to science to the degree that science confuses abstract models with nature, and to the degree that science, as technology, interferes with nature myopically, or upon the basis of prescientific views of man from which it has not recovered. Furthermore, it provides a basis for action which is not a cumbersome linear and legal view either of God's will or of laws of nature based on an accumulation of *past* experiment.

[18] On which see Needham (1), vol. 2, pp. 89–98.

The attitude of *kuan* is peculiarly sensitive to the conditions of the immediate moment in all their changeful interrelatedness, and, as we have seen, one of the difficulties of scientific knowledge is that its linear complexity makes it hard to apply to swift decisions, especially when "circumstances alter cases." Thus in discussing the secrets of successful drama Seami wrote:

> If you look deeply into the ultimate essentials of this art, you will find that what is called "the flower" [of *yugen*] has no separate existence. Were it not for the spectator who reads into the performance a thousand excellences, there would be no "flower" at all. The Sutra says, "Good and ill are one; villainy and honesty are of like kind." Indeed, what standard have we whereby to discern good from bad? We can only take what suits the need of the moment and call it "good." [19]

Such an attitude would be short-sighted indeed if it were based on the linear and punctive view of the moment, where each "thing" is not seen in its relation to the whole.[20] For example, those whom we hate most violently are often those we love most deeply, and if we are insensitive to this interrelation we may confuse the part feeling with the whole, and destroy someone we love or marry someone we are going to hate.

---

[19] Waley (1), p. 22.

[20] An excellent example of sensitivity to the moment is found in the application of Zen to *kendo*, or swordsmanship. No amount of drilled-in rules or reflexes can prepare the swordsman for the infinity of different attacks which he may have to face, especially when confronted with more than one opponent. He is taught, therefore, never to make any specific preparation for attack nor to expect it from any particular direction. Otherwise, to meet an unusual attack he will have to retreat from one stance before being able to adopt another. He must be able to spring immediately from a relaxed center of rest to the direction required. This relaxed openness of sensitivity in every direction is precisely *kuan*, or, as it is more commonly called in Zen, *mushin*, which is to say no "mind," no strain of the mind to watch for a particular result.

This brings us, then, to the second theoretical objection: that the mental strain of the controlling ego is necessary if we are not to be carried away by naturally undisciplined feelings and emotions. The objection is, once again, based on a political instead of an organic view of human nature. Human psychology is seen as composed of separate parts, functions, or faculties, as if the Lord God had made him by grafting the soul of an angel to the body of an animal. Man is then conceived as a collection of powers, urges, and appetites to be governed by the ego-soul. It is obvious at once that this view has had a profound influence upon modern psychology, which, though advising the ego to govern with kindness rather than violence, still treats it as the responsible boss.

But if we think of the total course of a man's experience, inner and outer, together with its unconscious psychophysical bases, as a system regulated organically, the principle of control must be entirely different.

> Joy and anger, sorrow and happiness, caution and remorse, come upon us by turns, with ever-changing mood. They come like music from hollows (in wood, when played upon by the wind), or like mushrooms from the damp. Daily and nightly they alternate within us, but we cannot tell whence they spring. . . .
>
> But for these emotions I should not be. But for me, they would have no scope. So far we can go; but we do not know what it is that brings them into play. If there is really a governor [tsai, M 6655], we find no evidence of its being. One could believe that it might be active, but we do not see its form. It would have to have feeling without form.
>
> The hundred bones, the nine orifices, and the six internal organs are all complete in their places. Which of them should one prefer? Do we like them all equally, or some more than others? Are they all the servants [of another]?

88   MAN AND NATURE

Are these servants unable to govern one another mutually, or do they take the parts of ruler and servant alternately? [21]

Taking up this theme in his commentary on Chuang-tzu, Kuo Hsiang says:

The hands and feet differ in their duties; the five internal organs differ in their functions. They never associate with one another, yet the hundred parts (of the body) are held together by them in a common unity. This is the way in which they associate through non-association. They never (deliberately) cooperate, and yet, both internally and externally, all complete one another. This is the way in which they cooperate through non-cooperation. [22]

In other words, all parts of the organism regulate themselves spontaneously (tzu-jan), and their order is confused when the changing panorama of feelings seems to be confronted by a controlling ego, which attempts to retain the positive (yang) and to reject the negative (yin).

According to Taoist philosophy, it is just this attempt to regulate the psyche from outside and to wrest the positive from the negative which is at the root of all social and moral confusion. What needs, then, to be controlled is not so much the spontaneous flow of human passions as the ego which exploits them—in other words, the controller itself. This has likewise been evident to such highly perceptive Christians as St. Augustine and Martin Luther, who realized so keenly that mere self-control was in no sense a remedy for the ills of man since it was precisely in the self that evil had taken its root. But they never abandoned the political idea of control, since their solution was to have the self empowered and regenerated by the grace of God—the ego of the universe. They did not see that the difficulty lay, not in the good or ill will of the controller,

[21] Chuang-tzu, ii. Cf. H. A. Giles (1), p. 14, Lin Yutang (2), p. 235, and Needham (1), vol. 2, p. 52.
[22] Chuang-tzu Chu, iii, 25. Tr. Bodde in Fung Yu-lan (1), vol. 2, p. 211.

but in the whole rationale of control which they were attempting to use. They did not realize that the problem for God was the same as the problem for the human ego. For even God's universe had spawned the Devil, who arises not so much from his own independent malice as from God's "arrogance" in assuming omnipotent kingship and identifying himself with unalloyed goodness. The Devil is God's unconsciously produced shadow. Naturally, God is not allowed to be responsible for the origin of evil, for the connection between the two lies in the unconscious. Man says, "I didn't mean to hurt you, but my temper got the better of me. I shall try to control it in future." And God says, "I didn't mean there to be any evil, but my angel Lucifer brought it up of his own free will. In the future I will shut him up safely in hell." [23]

A problem of evil arises as soon as there is a problem of good, that is, as soon as there is any thought of what may be done to make the present situation "better," under whatever nomenclature the idea may be concealed. Taoist philosophy may easily be misunderstood as saying that it is better to let an organic system regulate itself than to meddle in it from without, and better to recognize that good and evil are correlative than to wrest the one from the other. And yet Chuang-tzu says plainly:

> Those who would have right without its correlative, wrong; or good government without its correlative, misrule, —they do not apprehend the great principles of the universe nor the conditions to which all creation is subject. One might as well talk of the existence of heaven without that of earth, or of the negative principle without the positive, which is clearly absurd. Such people, if they do not yield to argument, must be either fools or knaves.[24] *xvii*

[23] For a fuller discussion of this theme see Jung (1), and Watts (2), ch. 2.
[24] H. A. Giles (1), pp. 207–8.

Yet, if this be true, must there not be fools and knaves as the correlatives of sages and saints, and does not the fallacy attacked simply reappear in the attack?

If the positive and the negative, the good and the evil, are indeed correlative, no course of action can be recommended, including even the course of inaction. Nothing will make anything better which will not also make it worse. But this is exactly the predicament of the human ego as Taoist philosophy sees it. It is always wanting to control its situation so as to improve it, but neither action nor, with the motive of improvement, inaction will succeed. Recognizing the trap in which it finds itself, the mind has no alternative but to surrender that "straining after the good" which constitutes the ego. It does not surrender cunningly, with the thought that this will make things better. It surrenders unconditionally—not because it is good to do nothing, but because nothing can be done. All at once there descends upon it, quite spontaneously, a profound and completely uncontrived stillness—a quietude that envelops the world like the first fall of heavy snow, or like a windless afternoon in the mountains, where silence makes itself known in the undisturbed hum of insects in the grass.

In this stillness there is no sense of passivity, of submitting to necessity, for there is no longer any differentiation between the mind and its experience. All acts, one's own and others', seem to be happening freely from a single source. Life keeps moving on, and yet remains profoundly rooted in the present, seeking no result, for the present has spread out from its constriction in an elusive pin-point of strained consciousness to an all-embracing eternity. Feelings both positive and negative come and go without turmoil, for they seem to be simply observed, though there is no one observing. They pass trackless like birds in the sky, and build up no resistances which have to be dissipated in reckless action.

Clearly this state is, in retrospect, "better" than the seeking and staring strain of the mind which came before. But its goodness is of another order. Because it came unsought, it is not the kind of goodness which is in relation to evil, not the fantasy of peace which is conceived in the midst of turmoil. Furthermore, since nothing is done to retain it, it is not in relation to the memory of the former state, which otherwise would move one to fortify and protect it against change. For now there is no one left to build the fortifications. Memories rise and fall like other feelings, ordered perhaps better than before, but no longer congealing around an ego to build its illusion of continued identity.

From this standpoint it can be seen that intelligence is not a separate, ordering faculty of the mind, but a characteristic of the whole organism-environment relationship, the field of forces wherein lies the reality of a human being. For as Macneile Dixon said in his *Human Situation*, "Tangible and visible things are but the poles, or terminations of these fields of unperceived energy. Matter, if it exists at all in any sense, is a sleeping partner in the firm of Nature." Between subject and object, organism and environment, *yang* and *yin*, is the balancing or homeostatic relationship called Tao—intelligent not because it has an ego but because it has *li*, organic pattern. The spontaneous flow of feeling, rising and falling in its mood, is an essential part of this balancing process, and is not, then, to be regarded as the disordered play of blind passions. Thus it is said that Lieh-tzu attained the Tao by "letting the events of the heart go just as they liked." [25] As a good sailor gives

[25] *Lieh-tzu*, 2. L. Giles (1), p. 41, translates this passage, "my mind (*hsin*) gave free rein to its reflections (*nien*)," but this is rather too

himself to the motion of a ship and does not fight it with
his stomach muscles, the man of Tao gives himself to the
motion of his moods.

Surprisingly, perhaps, this is not at all the same thing
as is ordinarily meant by "giving in to one's feelings"—always a symptom of resistance rather than "give." For when
we think about our feelings we tend to represent them as
fixed states. Such words as anger, depression, fear, grief,
anxiety, and guilt suggest uniform states which tend to
persist if no action is taken to change or release them. As
fever was once considered a disease instead of a natural
healing process, we still think of negative feelings as dis-
orders of the mind which need to be cured. But what
needs to be cured is the inner resistance to those feelings
which moves us to dissipate them in precipitate action. To
resist the feeling is to be unable to contain it long enough
for it to work itself out. Anger, for example, is not a fixed
state but a motion, and unless compressed by resistance
into unusual violence, like boiling water in a sealed vessel,
it will adjust itself spontaneously. For anger is not a separate, autonomous demon rushing up from time to time
from his quarters in the unconscious. Anger is simply a
direction or pattern of psychic action. There is thus no
anger; there is only acting angrily, or feeling angrily.
Anger is feeling in motion to some other "state," for as
Lao-tzu said:

> A swishing wind does not outlast the morning; pelting
> rain does not outlast the day. Who makes these things but
> heaven and earth? If heaven and earth cannot maintain
> them for long, how can man? *xxiii*

intellectual since *hsin* (M 2735) is not so much the thinking mind as
the totality of psychic functioning, conscious and unconscious, and *nien*
(M 4716) is not so much cortical thought as any event of psychic experience.

To give free rein to the course of feeling is therefore to observe it without interference, recognizing that because feeling is motion it is not to be understood in terms which imply not only static states but judgments of good and bad. Watched without naming, feelings become simply neuromuscular tensions and changes, palpitations and pressures, tinglings and twitchings, of enormous subtlety and interest. This is, however, not quite the same thing as the psychotherapeutic gambit of "accepting" negative feelings *in order* to change them, that is, with the intention of effecting a shift of the whole tone of feeling in the direction of the positive and "good." "Acceptance" of this kind still implies the ego, standing apart from the immediate feeling or experience, and waiting for it to change—however patiently and submissively.

So long as the sense of the observing subject remains, there is the effort, however indirect, to control feeling from the outside, which is resistance setting up turmoil in the stream. Resistance disappears and the balancing process comes into full effect not by intention on the part of the subject, but only as it is seen that the feeling of being the subject, the ego, is itself part of the stream of experience and does not stand outside it in a controlling position. In the words of Chuang-tzu:

> Only the truly intelligent understand this principle of the identity of all things. They do not view things as apprehended by themselves, subjectively, but transfer themselves into the position of the things viewed. And viewing them thus they are able to comprehend them, nay, to master them.[26]

However, the point might be expressed more exactly by saying that the subject is treated not as an object but as the inseparable pole or term of a subject-object identity.

[26] *Chuang-tzu,* 2. Tr. H. A. Giles (1), p. 20.

The dividedness of the knower and the known becomes, without being simply obliterated, the plainest sign of their inner unity.

This is, indeed, the crucial point of the whole unitive philosophy of nature as it is set forward in Taoism and Buddhism, and which distinguishes it from a merely monistic pantheism. Distinct and unique events, whether external objects or the internal subject, are seen to be "one with nature" by virtue of their very distinctness, and not at all by absorption into a featureless uniformity. Once again, it is the mutual distinction of figure and ground, subject and object, and not their merging which reveals their inner identity. A Zen master was asked, "I have heard that there is one thing which cannot be named. It has not been born; it will not die when the body dies. When the universe burns up it will not be affected. What is that one thing?" The master answered, "A sesame bun."

In addition, then, to the mood of *yugen*, of mysterious and pregnant vagueness, which haunts Far Eastern painting, there is also an immensely forceful delineation of the unique event—the single bird, the spray of bamboo, the solitary tree, the lonely rock. Hence the sudden awakening to this "inner identity" which in Zen is called *satori* is usually precipitated by, or bound up with, some such simple fact as the sound of a berry falling in the forest or the sight of a piece of crumpled paper in the street. There is thus a double meaning in Suzuki's translation of the poem:

> *Oh, this one rare occurrence,*
> *For which would I not be glad to give ten thou-*
> *sand pieces of gold!*
> *A hat is on my head, a bundle round my loins;*
> *And on my staff the refreshing breeze and the*
> *full moon I carry!*

For the "one rare occurrence" is at once the *satori* experience and the unique event to which it is attached—one implying all, moment implying eternity. But to *state* the implication is, in a way, to say too much, especially if it were taken to mean that the perception of the particular ought to make us think about the universal. On the contrary, the universality of the unique event and the eternity of the moment come to be seen only as the straining of the mind is released and the present event, whatever it may be, is regarded without the slightest attempt to get anything from it. However, this attempt is so habitual that it can hardly be stopped, so that whenever anyone tries to accept the moment just as it is he becomes aware only of the frustration of himself trying to do so. This seems to present an unbreakable vicious circle—unless he realizes that the moment which he was trying to accept has now moved on and is presenting itself to him as his own sensation of strain! If he feels it to be voluntary, there is no problem in accepting it, for it is his own immediate act. If he feels it to be involuntary, he must perforce accept it, for he can do no other. Either way, the strain is accepted and it dissolves. But this is also the discovery of the inner identity of the voluntary and the involuntary, the subjective and the objective. For when the object, the moment to be accepted, presented itself as the sensation of the strain of trying to accept, this was the subject, the ego itself. In the words of the Zen master P'u-yen, "Nothing is left to you at this moment but to burst out into a loud laugh. You have accomplished a final turning and in very truth know that 'when a cow in Kuai-chou grazes the herbage, a horse in I-chou finds its stomach filled.'"[27]

In sum, then, the realization that nature is ordered organically rather than politically, that it is a field of relationships rather than a collection of things, requires an

[27] Suzuki (3), p. 80.

appropriate mode of human awareness. The habitual ego-centric mode in which man identifies himself with a subject facing a world of alien objects does not fit the physical situation. So long as it remains, our inward feeling is at variance with reality. Based on this feeling, our efforts to control ourselves and the surrounding world become viciously circular entanglements of ever-growing complexity. More and more the individual feels himself frustrated and impotent in the midst of a mechanical world order which has become an irresistible "march of progress" toward ends of its own. Therapies for the frustrated individual, whether religious or psychological, merely complicate the problem in so far as they assume that the separate ego is the very reality toward which their ministrations are directed. For, as Trigant Burrow saw, the source of the trouble is social rather than individual: that is to say, the ego is a social convention foisted upon human consciousness by conditioning. The root of mental disorder is not therefore a malfunctioning peculiar to this or that ego; it is rather that the ego-feeling as such is an error of perception. To placate it is only to enable it to go on confusing the mind with a mode of awareness which, because it clashes with the natural order, breeds the vast family of psychological frustrations and illnesses.

An organic natural order has its proper correspondence in a mode of consciousness which is a total feeling or experiencing. Where feeling is broken up into the feeler and the feeling, the knower and the known, what lies between the two is not relationship but mere juxtaposition. Identified with one of its terms alone, consciousness feels "out on a limb" facing an alien world which it controls only to find it more and more uncontrollable, and which it exploits only to find it more and more ungratifying.

4: The World as Ecstasy

DEEPLY INVOLVED WITH OUR WHOLE ES-
trangement from nature is the embarrassment of "having" a body. It is perhaps an egg-and-hen question as to
whether we resent the body because we think we are
spirits, or *vice versa*. But we are accustomed to feeling
that our bodies are vehicles in which we are compelled
to live, vehicles which are at once all too much ourselves
and yet utterly foreign. Responding only most imperfectly
to the will and resisting the comprehension of the intellect, the body seems to be thrust upon us like an indispensable wife with whom it is impossible to live. We love
it most dearly, and yet must spend most of our time working to support it. Its five senses, delicate and vibrant, communicate the whole delight and glory of the world at the
price of being equally receptive to its agony and horror.
For the body is sensitive because it is soft, pliant, and impressionable, but it lives in a universe which is for the
most part rock and fire. When young we let our consciousness expand with joy through all the innumerable passages
of its nerves, but as time goes on we begin to withdraw,
and beg the surgeon to "fix" it like a wayward machine,
to cut away the pieces which rot and ache, and to dope the
jangling senses which so inconsiderately retain their alertness while all else deteriorates. Modestly and graciously
posed, the naked form of man or woman is revered as the
height of beauty, yet this same form can turn in an instant
lascivious or grotesque, disgusting or uncouth, by the slight-

est change of posture or activity—so easily, indeed, that for most of the time we conceal it from sight with clothing, beneath which it grows pallid and potatoish like the white slugs that live under rocks.

The body is so alien to the mind that even when it is at its best it is not so much loved as exploited, and for the remainder of the time we do what we may to put it in a state of comfort where it may be forgotten, where its limitations will not encumber the play of emotion and thought. But contrive as we will to transcend this physical vehicle, the clarity of consciousness goes hand in hand with the sensitivity of nerves and thus with inevitable exposure to revulsion and pain. This is so much so that the hardness and painfulness of things become the measure of their reality. What does not resist us becomes dreamlike and impalpable, but in the shock of pain we *know* that we are alive and awake, and thus come to think of the real as that which conflicts most abruptly with the whole nature of sensitivity. One has thus never heard of soft facts, only of hard. Yet it is just because there are such soft facts as eyeballs and finger-tips that the hard are manifested.

But to the extent that the measure of reality is felt to be the degree of resistance and pain which the environment offers to our nerves, the body becomes above all else the instrument of our suffering. It negates our will; it decays before we have lost the capacity for disgust; its possession exposes us to all the twenty-one measurable degrees of agony by the cruelty of human torture, by accident, or by disease. Those who are fortunate enough to escape the worst that can happen are nevertheless tormented with imaginations of what might be, and their skins tingle and their stomachs turn in sympathy and horror at the fate of others.

It is little wonder, then, that we seek detachment from

the body, wanting to convince ourselves that the real "I" is not this quaking mass of tissue with all its repulsive possibilities for pain and corruption. It is little wonder that we expect religions, philosophies, and other forms of wisdom to show us above all else a way of deliverance from suffering, from the plight of being a soft body in a world of hard reality. Sometimes therefore it seems that the answer is to match hardness with hardness, to identify ourselves with a spirit which has principles but no feelings, to despise and mortify the body, and to withdraw into the comfortably fleshless world of abstract thought or psychic fantasy. To match the hardness of facts we then identify our minds with such symbols of fixity, entity, and power as the ego, the will, and the immortal soul, believing ourselves to belong in our inmost being to a realm of spirit beyond both the hardness of fact and the weakness of flesh. This is, as it were, a shrinking of consciousness from its environment of pain, gathering itself back and back into a knot around its own center.

Yet it is just in this shrinking and hardening that consciousness not only loses its true strength but also aggravates its plight. For the withdrawal from suffering is also suffering, such that the restricted and enclosed consciousness of the ego is really a spasm of fear. As a man with a stomach wound craves water, which it is fatal to drink, the mind's chronic withdrawal from suffering renders it just that much more vulnerable. Fully expanded, consciousness feels an identity with the whole world, but contracted it is the more inescapably attached to a single minute and perishable organism.

This is not to say that it is fatal for nerves and muscles to draw back from a sharp spike or some other occasion of pain, for did they not do so the organism would swiftly cease to exist. The withdrawal I am speaking of here is much deeper: it is a withdrawal from withdrawal, an unwillingness to be capable of feeling pain, unwillingness to squirm and shrink when the occasion of pain arises. Subtle as this distinction may be, it is of immense importance, though it may seem at first that pain and the unwillingness to react painfully are the same thing. But it must be obvious that unless the organism can feel pain, it cannot withdraw from danger, so that the unwillingness to be able to be hurt is in fact suicidal, whereas the simple retreat from an occasion of pain is not. It is true that we want to have our cake and eat it: we want to be sensitive and alive, but not sensitive to suffering. But this puts us in a contradiction of the specially intolerable type known as a "double bind."

The "double bind" is a situation wherein all the alternatives offered are forbidden. A witness in court is put in a double bind when the attorney asks him, "Have you stopped beating your wife? Answer yes or no!" Either answer will convict him of beating her. So also when suffering arises we want to escape both from its objective occasion and from its subjective reactions. But when escape from the former is impossible, so is escape from the latter. We *must* suffer—that is, we must react in the only way that is open to us, which would naturally be to writhe, shriek, or weep. Now the double bind comes in when we forbid ourselves this reaction, either in actual suffering or in the imagination of suffering to come. We revolt at the prospect of our own orgiastic reactions to pain because they are in flat contradiction with our socially conditioned image of ourselves. Such reactions are a fearful admission of the identity of consciousness with the organism, of the lack of a detached, powerful, and transcending will which is the essential core of the personality.

Hence the sadist and torturer takes his most unholy delight not just in watching the bodily convulsions of his victim, but in "breaking the spirit" which resists them. Yet if there were no resisting spirit his savagery would be rendered something like slashing at water with a sword, and he would find himself confronted with a total weakness that offered neither challenge nor interest. But it is exactly this weakness which is the mind's real and unsuspected strength. In Lao-tzu's words:

> Man when living is soft and tender; when dead he is hard and tough. All animals and plants are tender and fragile; when dead they become withered and dry. Therefore it is said: the hard and the tough are parts of death; the soft and tender are parts of life. This is the reason why the soldiers when they are too tough cannot carry the day; the tree when it is too tough will break. The position of the strong and great is low, and the position of the weak and tender is high.[1] *lxxvi*

There appear, then, to be two unexpected consequences of unreservedly permitting the organism its natural, orgiastic response to pain, of which one is the ability to endure pain and its anticipation by reason of a far greater amount of "give" in the system. The other is that this, in turn, cuts down the total shock of suffering upon the organism, which furthermore reduces the intensity of the reactions. In other words, the toughening of the spirit against suffering and the shrinking of consciousness from the orgiastic reactions which it involves are a socially inculcated error of behavior, making the human situation far worse than it need be. Moreover, this shrinking of consciousness from our reactions to suffering is at root the same psychological mechanism as the straining of consciousness to get the most from our reactions to pleasure,

[1] In Ch'u Ta-kao (1), p. 89.

and both make up the sensation of the separate, indwelling ego.

This is surely the reason why so many spiritual traditions insist that the way to liberation from egocentricity is through suffering. Yet this is so often misunderstood as "practice suffering," as toughening oneself against suffering by increasing doses of mortification to harden the body and soul. Interpreted in this way, the spiritual discipline of suffering becomes a way of death and insensitivity, of final withdrawal from life into a "spiritual" world which is totally removed from nature. It is to correct this error that Mahayana Buddhism maintains that "nirvana and samsara are not different," that the state of liberation is not away from the state of nature, and that the liberated Bodhisattva returns indefinitely into the "round of birth-and-death" out of his compassion for all sentient beings. For the same reason Buddhist doctrine denies the reality of a separate ego, saying:

> *Suffering alone exists, none who suffer;*
> *The deed there is, but no doer thereof;*
> *Nirvana is, but no one seeking it;*
> *Path there is, but none who travel it.*[2]

And again, unexpectedly, the dissolution of the egocentric contraction (*sankocha*) of consciousness by no means reduces the personality to a flabby nonentity. On the contrary, the organism is at its greatest strength in realizing the fullest possible relation to its environment—a relation which is hardly felt at all when the individualized consciousness tries to preserve itself by separation from the body and from all that it experiences. "Whosoever would save his soul shall lose it," and we should understand this "save" as "salvage," as enclosing and isolating. Conversely,

[2] *Visuddhimagga*, 16.

we should understand that the soul or personality lives just to the degree that it does not withdraw, that it does not shrink from the full implications of being one with the body and with the whole realm of natural experience. For although this seems to suggest the absorption of man into the flux of nature, the integrity of personality is far better preserved by the faith of self-giving than the shattering anxiety of self-preservation.

We saw that the shrinking of consciousness from suffering and the straining of consciousness to seek gratification are at root the same. In each case the way of dissolution is also the same, and involves first of all the recognition that consciousness, in so far as it feels itself to be the ego, cannot stop its own shrinking, its revulsion from the orgiastic response to pain. It must therefore be understood that this revulsion is itself part and parcel of the orgiastic response, and not, as we are led to believe, a means of escape from it. This is, in other words, the recognition that all our psychological defenses against suffering are useless. The more we defend, the more we suffer, and defending is itself suffering. Although we cannot help putting up the psychological defense, it dissolves when it is seen that the defense is all of a piece with what we are defending ourselves against. The entire movement is the convulsion *of* suffering which does not lead *away* from suffering. Continued as a means to get rid of suffering, it merely intensifies it. But continued because this is simply the natural response to which, if we do not deceive ourselves, we *must* give in, the whole experience of suffering undergoes a startling change.

It becomes what in Indian philosophy is called *ananda,* ordinarily translated "bliss." *Ananda* is attributed to Brahman, the ultimate Reality beyond all dualities, together with *sat,* truth, and *chit,* awareness. Yet we usually consider bliss to be an extremely dualistic state of mind—an extreme of happiness or pleasure, opposed to an equal extreme of misery or pain. There would seem to be a serious contradiction in making anything so relative as bliss one of the attributes of the Absolute. For if bliss is realized in contrast with abject misery as light is known in contrast with darkness, how is it possible to contemplate a bliss which is nondual and eternal?

It must first be understood that Indian philosophy uses a convention of terminology similar to the trick of perspective, of representing a three-dimensional object upon a two-dimensional surface. Any line drawn upon a flat surface will be more or less horizontal or perpendicular, spanning the height and the width of the area. But by the convention of perspective, slanting lines which approach a vanishing point are understood to represent the third dimension of depth. As the flat surface has but two dimensions, so our ordinary thought and language has a rigidly dualistic logic, in terms of which it makes no sense to speak of that which "neither is nor is not," nor of a bliss which transcends both pleasure and pain. But just as one can suggest three dimensions in terms of two, dualistic language can suggest an experience beyond duality. The very word "nondual" (*advaita*) is, formally speaking, the opposite of "dual" (*dvaita*), as bliss is the opposite of misery. But Indian philosophy uses *advaita* and *ananda* in a context where they refer to another dimension of experience, as lines that are more or less high or wide are taken to signify depth. Furthermore, this other dimension of experience is understood to be of a higher order of reality than the dualistic dimension, where life and death, pleasure and pain stand utterly apart.

What we feel is to an enormous and unsuspected degree dependent on what we think, and the basic contrasts of thought ordinarily strike us as the basic contrasts of the natural world. We therefore take it for granted that we *feel* an immense difference between pleasure and pain. But it is obvious in some of the milder forms of these sensations that the pleasure or the pain lies not so much in the feeling itself as in its context. There is no appreciable physiological difference between shudders of delight and shudders of fear, nor between the thrills of rapturous music and the thrills of terrifying melodrama. Likewise, intensities of joy and grief produce the same "heartbreak" feeling which is expressed in weeping, and to fall deeply in love is to enter a state where delight and anguish are at times so interwoven as to be indistinguishable. But the context of the feeling changes its interpretation, depending on whether the circumstances which arouse it are for us or against us. Similarly, one and the same verbal sound changes its meaning according to the setting, as in Thomas Hood's

> *They went and told the sexton,*
> *And the sexton tolled the bell.*

It is easy enough to see the sensational or physiological identity of these feelings in some of the milder forms of physical pleasure and pain, and even in some of the strong forms of moral pleasure and pain. But it is exceedingly difficult to see it when these sensations become more acute. Nevertheless, there are special circumstances of heightened feeling, such as religious devotion and sexual passion, in which far more poignant types of pleasure and pain lose their distinction. Ordinarily, such ascetic disciplines as self-flagellation, wearing hair shirts, and kneeling on chains are adopted to do violence to the desire for pleasure. Yet it is possible that asceticism is a way of genuine spiritual insight because it leads eventually, however unintentionally, to the realization that in the ardor of devotion pleasure and pain are a single ecstasy. Consider, for example, Bernini's celebrated effigy of St. Theresa of Ávila in rapture, pierced by the dart of the divine love. The face is equally expressive of ravishment or torture, and the smile of the angel wielding the dart is accordingly compassionate or cruel.

Perverse and abnormal as they are usually regarded, we should also consider the phenomena of sadism and masochism—better designated by the single term algolagnia, or "lustful pain." Merely to dismiss these phenomena as perverse and unnatural is to say no more than that they do not fit into a preconceived notion of order. The very fact that they are human possibilities shows that they are extensions of ordinary feelings, revealing depths of our nature which are usually left unexplored. Distasteful as they may be, this should not prevent us from trying to discover whether they throw any light on the problem of suffering.

The sadist is really a vicarious masochist, for in inflicting pain he identifies himself emotionally with his victim, and gives a sexual interpretation to his victim's reactions to pain. For masochism or algolagnia is the association of the orgiastic convulsions of pain with sexual ecstasy, and involves far more than that the two types of reaction look somewhat alike to an external observer. The masochist finds in pain of certain types a positive stimulant to sexual orgasm, and as the intensity of his feeling increases he is able to delight in harsher and harsher degrees of pain. The standard Freudian explanation is that the masochist so associates sexual pleasure with guilt that he cannot permit himself this pleasure unless he is also being punished. This seems to me to be doubtful and, like so much Freudian reasoning, unnecessarily complex, stretching facts to fit theories at all costs. For masochism is found in cultures where sexuality and sin are not allied to anything like the degree to which they are wedded in the Christian West.[3] It would be simpler and more reasonable to say that the masochist intensifies or stimulates sexual reactions by inducing similar reactions arising from pain. To this it should be added that the masochist's desire to be subjugated or humiliated is allied to the fact that all sexual ecstasy, male or female, has a quality of self-abandonment, of surrender to a force greater than the ego.

A still more notable instance of the pleasure-pain identity has come to light in the work of the British obstetrician Grantley Dick Reid in his remarkably successful techniques of natural childbirth. Labor pains may ordinarily reach a degree of extreme severity so as to reach almost the highest level of pain which the organism can experience. The interest of Reid's technique is that it focuses the mother's attention on the feeling of the uterine contraction itself, dissociating it from socially implanted ideas of how it is supposed to feel. So long as she regards it as a pain she will resist it, but if she can approach it simply as a tension she can be shown how to go with it and relax into it—a technique which is learned through prenatal exercises. By thus abandoning herself without reserve to the spontaneous contractions of the uterus, she can experience childbirth as an extremely strong physical ecstasy rather than a torture.

Now it may appear that all these types of pleasure-pain are induced hypnotically, through the circumstances of religious devotion, sexual passion, or the physician's authoritative suggestions. To some extent this is perhaps true, although it might be better to call it a counterhypnotism,

[3] There is some evidence to show that deliberate masochism was first introduced into the West from Arabian culture—a culture notably free from sexual squeamishness. See Havelock Ellis (1), Part II, p. 130, quoting Eulenburg, *Sadismus und Masochismus*.

counter, that is, to the immense force of social suggestion which has taught us since babyhood how we ought to interpret our sensations and feelings. Surely the child learns much of how he should experience his sensations of pain from the attitudes of sympathy, horror, or disgust displayed by his parents. In these attitudes the child sees sympathetic resistances to pain which he learns to make for himself.

On the other hand, circumstances of religious ardor, sexual passion, or medical assurance create an atmosphere in which the organism can permit its own spontaneous reactions to the full. Under these conditions the organism is no longer split into the natural animal and the controlling ego. The whole being is one with its own spontaneity and feels free to let go with the utmost abandon. The same conditions are induced by such religious exercises as the dervish dance or the chanting of *mantrams*, the rites of the Penitentes or the glossolalia (tongue-blabbering) of Pentecostal preachers. But the frantic, explosive, and even dangerous character of some of these abandonments to spontaneity is largely the result of its normal restraint. In a culture where sex is calculated, religion decorous, dancing polite, music refined or sentimental, and yielding to pain shameful, many people have never experienced full spontaneity. Little or nothing is known of its integrating, cathartic, and purifying consequences, let alone of the fact that it may not only be creatively controlled, but also become a constant way of life. Under such circumstances the cultivation of spontaneity is left to the "social underground" of Negro revivals, jam sessions, or rock-and-roll parties. We cannot even conceive that Coomaraswamy's description of the sage as living "a perpetual uncalculated life in the present" [4] could mean anything but total disorder.

[4] A. K. Coomaraswamy (1), p. 134.

The point here, however, is that when the organism's natural reactions to pain are permitted without restraint, pain goes beyond pleasure and pain to ecstasy, which is really the proper equivalent of *ananda*. We begin here to find an approach to the mystery of human suffering which is adequate to the immense inevitability of the problem. This is not to say that our efforts to reduce the amount of pain in the world should be given up, but only that at best they are pitifully insufficient. The same insufficiency affects all the ordinary religious and philosophical rationalizations, wherein suffering is somehow explained away as a temporary means in the fulfillment of a divine plan or as a penalty for sin or as an illusion of the finite mind. One feels almost instinctively that some of these answers are an affront to the *dignity* of suffering and to its overwhelming reality for every single form of life. For as we look back and forward into the history of the universe we find little evidence and little assurance of orderly comfort as anything but a rarity. Life has been and looks as if it will be for the most part convulsive and catastrophic, maintaining itself by slaying and eating itself.[5] The problem of suffering will therefore continue to have a kind of awesome holiness so long as life depends in any way upon the pain of even a single creature.

One must respect the Indian ideal of *ahimsa* or "harmlessness" and the Buddhist monk's reduction of killing and causing pain to the utmost minimum. But in effect this abstinence is no more than a gesture which, when we really come down to it, is a retreat from the problem. Again, the answer to the problem of suffering is not away from the

[5] It is curious to speculate upon the consequences of civilized man's refusal to be eaten by other forms of life, to return his body for the fertilization of the soil from which he took it. This is a significant symptom of his alienation from nature, and may be a by no means negligible deprivation of the earth's resources.

problem but in it. The inevitability of pain will not be met by deadening sensitivity but by increasing it, by exploring and feeling out the manner in which the natural organism itself wants to react and which its innate wisdom has provided. The physician attending the deathbed will have to use the same means as the physician attending childbed, creating an atmosphere in which the physical or moral revulsions to death and its pains are fully permitted and encouraged. The feelings of a suffering being must be allowed to move unblocked as nature directs them, subject only to the external control of destructive action.

We begin to see, then, that the *answer* to suffering is the organism's *response* to it, its innate tendency to transmute unavoidable pain into ecstasy. This is the insight which underlies the cosmological myth of Hinduism, where the world in all the fullness of its delight and horror is seen as the ecstasy of God, perpetually incarnating himself by an act of self-abandonment in the myriad forms of creatures. This is why Shiva, the divine prototype of all suffering and destruction, is *Nataraja,* the "Lord of the Dance." For the everlasting, agonizing dissolution and renewal of life is the dance of Shiva, always ecstatic because it is without inner conflict, because in other words it is nondual— without the resistance of a controller external to the controlled, without any other principle of motion than its own *sahaja,* or spontaneity.

Left thus to itself, the spontaneity of the organism encounters no obstacle to its continued movement, which, like flowing water, perpetually finds out the course of least resistance, for as Lao-tzu said:

> The highest goodness is like water. Water is beneficent to all things but does not contend. It stays in [lowly] places which others despise. Therefore it is near Tao.[6] *viii*

6 Ch'u Ta-kao (1), p. 18.

Because it does not block itself, the course of feeling acquires a sensation of freedom or "voidness," represented in Buddhist and Taoist terminology as *wu-hsin*—that is, "egolessness" or "no-mindness"—no feeler in conflict with feeling. In sorrow as in joy, in pain as in pleasure, the natural reactions follow one another without hindrance "like a ball in a mountain stream."

Suffering and death—all that dark and destructive side of nature for which Shiva stands—are therefore problematic for the ego rather than the organism. The organism accepts them through ecstasy, but the ego is rigid and unyielding and finds them problematic because they affront its pride. For, as Trigant Burrow has shown, the ego is the social image or role with which the mind is shamed into identifying itself, since we are taught to act the part which society wants us to play—the part of a reliable and predictable center of action which resists spontaneous change. But in extreme suffering and in death this part cannot be played, and as a result they become associated with all the shame and fear with which, as children, we were forced into becoming acceptable egos. Death and agony are therefore dreaded as loss of status, and their struggles are desperate attempts to maintain the assumed patterns of action and feeling. Yet in some traditional societies the individual prepares for death by abandoning status before he dies, that is, by relinquishing his role or caste and becoming, with full social approval, a "nobody." In practice, however, this is often frustrated by the fact that being "nobody" becomes a new kind of status—the formal role of "holy man" or *sanyassin*, the conventionally ecclesiastical monk.

The fear of spontaneity from which this arises is based not only on the confusion of the natural and biological type of order with the political, with legal and enforced order.

It arises also from failure to see that the socially problematic spontaneity of little children is as yet unco-ordinated and "embryonic." We then make the mistake of socializing children, not by developing their spontaneity, but by developing a system of resistances and fears which, as it were, splits the organism into a spontaneous center and an inhibiting center. Thus it is rare indeed to find an integrated person capable of self-controlling spontaneity, which sounds like a contradiction in terms. It is as if we were teaching our children to walk by lifting up their feet with their own hands instead of moving their legs from within. We do not see that before spontaneity can control itself it must be able to function. The legs must have full freedom of movement before they can acquire the discipline of walking and running or dancing. For disciplined motion is the control of relaxed motion. Similarly, disciplined action and feeling is the direction of relaxed action and feeling to prearranged ends. The pianist must therefore acquire relaxation and freedom in his arms and fingers before he can execute complex musical figures, but much abominable technique has been acquired by forcing the fingers to perform piano exercises without preliminary relaxation.[7]

Spontaneity is, after all, total sincerity—the whole being involved in the act without the slightest reservation—and as a rule the civilized adult is goaded into it only by abject despair, intolerable suffering, or imminent death. Hence the proverb, "Man's extremity is God's opportunity." Thus a modern Hindu sage has remarked that the first thing he has to teach Westerners who come to him is how to cry, which also goes to show that our spontaneity is

[7] See L. Bonpensiere (1). It is true that Beethoven fingered certain passages in his sonatas in such a way that they could be played only with a feeling of strain and conflict, but this is merely the exception that proves the rule. He wanted these passages to express conflict musically.

inhibited not only by the ego-complex as such but also by the Anglo-Saxon conception of masculinity. So far from being a form of strength, the masculine rigidity and toughness which we affect is nothing more than an emotional paralysis. It is assumed not because we are in control of our feelings but because we fear them, along with everything in our nature that is symbolically feminine and yielding. But a man who is emotionally paralyzed cannot be male, that is, he cannot be male in relation to female, for if he is to relate himself to a woman there must be something of the woman in his nature.

He who knows the masculine and yet keeps to the feminine
Will become a channel drawing all the world towards it;
Being a channel for the world, he will not be severed from
*   the eternal virtue,*
And then he can return again to the state of infancy (i.e.,
*   to spontaneity).*[8] xxviii

Childlikeness, or artless simplicity, is the ideal of the artist no less than of the sage, for it is to perform the work of art or of life without the least trace of affectation, of being in two minds. But the way to the child is through the woman, through yielding to spontaneity, through giving in to just what one is, moment by moment, in the ceaselessly changing course of nature. It is to this "just what one is" that the Hindu adage *Tat tvam asi*—"That art thou"—refers, and *That* is the eternal, nondual Brahman. To the degree, however, that this way is not one of anxiety-ridden self-control, it is equally removed from the exhibitionism of the arty libertine whose display of "being himself" is designed to shock and draw attention. His vices are as hypocritical as a Pharisee's virtues. I remember an *avant-garde* party at which a number of young men

[8] Ch'u Ta-kao (1), p. 38.

wandering around stark naked were more fully clothed than
anyone else in the room, failing to realize that nakedness
is a state that we cannot avoid. For our clothes, our skins,
our personalities, our virtues and our vices are as transparent as space. We cannot lay claim to them, and there
is no one to lay the claim, since the self is as transparent
as its garments.

Empty and nihilistic as it may sound, this recognition
of total nakedness and transparency is a joy beyond all telling, for what is empty is not reality itself but all that seems
to block its light.

> Old P'ang requires nothing in the world:
> All is empty with him, even a seat he has not,
> For absolute Emptiness reigns in his household;
> How empty indeed it is with no treasures!
> When the sun is risen, he walks through Emptiness,
> When the sun sets, he sleeps in Emptiness;
> Sitting in Emptiness he sings his empty songs,
> And his empty songs reverberate through Emptiness.[9]

To name or symbolize the joyous content of this emptiness
is always to say too much, to put, as they say in Zen, legs
upon the snake. For in Buddhist philosophy emptiness
(sunyata) denotes the most solid and basic reality, though
it is called empty because it never becomes an *object* of
knowledge. This is because, being common to all related
terms—figure and ground, solid and space, motion and rest
—it is never seen in contrast with anything else and thus
is never seen as an object. It may be called the fundamental reality or substance of the world only by analogy,
for strictly speaking reality is known by contrast with
unreality, and substance or stuff by contrast with shape
or with empty space. However, it may be realized by the

* P'ang Chü-shih, ninth-century Zen master. In Suzuki (1), vol. 2, p. 297.

intuitive wisdom which Buddhists call *prajna*, for, as we have seen, it is really obvious that all related terms have an "inner identity" which, not being one of the terms, is in the true sense of the word "interminable"—unable to be described or imagined. For *prajna* is the mode of knowledge which is direct, which is not knowledge *in terms* of words, symbols, images, and logical classes with their inevitable duality of inside and outside.

The "emptiness" of the universe also signifies the fact that the outlines, forms, and boundaries to which we attach all terms are in constant change, and in this sense its reality cannot be fixed or limited. It is called empty because it cannot be grasped, for even

> *the hills are shadows,*
> *And they flow from form to form,*
> *And nothing stands.*

Yet all man's resistance to Shiva, to change, suffering, dissolution, and death, is a resistance to being transparent, even though the resistance itself is as a phantom hand clutching at clouds. Suffering is ultimately ecstasy because it pries loose our strangling grasp upon ourselves and melts "this all too solid flesh." For the everlasting renewal and dissolution of the world is the most emphatic and inescapable revelation of the fact that "form is emptiness, and emptiness itself is form," and that the agonized ego is a ring of defense around nothing. The transience from which we seek liberation is the very liberator.

There are no means or methods for understanding this, for every such device is artfulness, is ultimately an attempt to become something, to be more than this melting moment which the utmost tension of the will cannot hold. Belief in an unchanging God, an immortal soul, or even in a deathless nirvana as something to be gained is all part of this artfulness, as is equally the sterile certainty and aggressive cocksureness of atheism and scientific materialism. There is no way to where we are, and whoever seeks one finds only a slick wall of granite without passage or foothold. Yogas, prayers, therapies, and spiritual exercises are at root only elaborate postponements of the recognition that there is nothing to be grasped and no way to grasp it.

This is not to say that there is no God or to deny the possibility that there is some form of personal continuity beyond death. It is rather to say that a God to be grasped or believed in is no God, and that a continuity to be wished for is only a continuity of bondage. Death presents itself to us as the possibility of sleep without waking, or at most as the possibility of waking up as someone else altogether —just as we did when we were born. Depressing or frightening as it may appear at first sight, the thought of sleep without waking—ever—is strangely fruitful, since it works

To tease us out of thought, as doth eternity.

Such a contemplation of death renders the hard core of "I-ness" already insubstantial, the more so as we go into it thoroughly and see that sleep without waking is not to be confused with the fantasy of being shut up forever in darkness. It is the disappearance even of darkness, reducing the imagination to impotence and thought to silence. At this point we ordinarily busy our brains with other matters, but the fascination of the certainty of death can sometimes hold us wonder-struck until the moment of a curious illumination in which we see that what dies is not consciousness but memory. Consciousness recurs in every newborn creature, and wherever it recurs it is "I." And in so far as it is only *this* "I," it struggles again and again in hundreds of millions of beings against the dissolution which would set it free. To see this is to feel the most peculiar solidarity—almost identity—with other creatures, and to begin to understand the meaning of compassion.

In the intense joy which attends the full realization that we are momentary and transparent, and that nothing can be grasped, there is no question of an icy detachment from the world. A man who had realized this very fully once wrote to me, "I am now becoming as deeply attached as I can be to as many people and things as possible." For after the *pralaya* in which all the manifested worlds are dissolved, Brahma once again precipitates himself into the myriad forms of life and consciousness, and after he has realized nirvana, the Bodhisattva returns into the interminable round of birth-and-death.

Even beyond the ultimate limits there extends a passageway
Whereby he comes back among the six realms of existence. . . .
Like a gem he stands out even in the mud;
Like pure gold he shines even in the furnace.[10]

In attachment there is pain, and in pain deliverance, so that at this point attachment itself offers no obstacle, and the liberated one is at last free to love with all his might and to suffer with all his heart. This is not because he has learned the trick of splitting himself into higher and lower selves so that he can watch himself with inward indifference, but rather because he has found the meeting-point of the limit of wisdom and the limit of foolishness. The Bodhisattva is the fool who has become wise by persisting in his folly.

The well-intentioned reverence of innumerable believers has, of course, set the Buddhas, the sages, the liberated ones upon the summit of spiritual success, though by this

[10] Tzu-te Hui. In Suzuki (2), pp. 150–51.

means they have piously postponed their own awakening. For the realm of liberation is absolutely incommensurable with the relativities of higher and lower, better and worse, gain and loss, since these are all the transparent and empty advantages and disadvantages of the ego. Though not strictly accurate, it is less misleading to think of liberation as the depth of spiritual failure—where one cannot even lay claim to vices, let alone virtues. For in seeing fully into his own empty momentariness, the Bodhisattva knows a despair beyond suicide, the *absolute* despair which is the etymological meaning of nirvana. It is complete disillusion from every hope of safety, or rest, or gain, suicide itself being no escape since "I" awakens once more in every being that is born. It is the recognition of final defeat for all the artfulness of the ego, which, in this disillusion, expires— finding only emptiness in its most frantic resistance to emptiness, suffering in escape from suffering, and nothing but clinging in its efforts to let go. But here he finds in his own dissolving the same emptiness from which there blazes the whole host of sun, moon, and stars.

5: The World as Non-Sense

THAT OUR LIFE IS A DISSOLVING MOMENT IN which there is nothing to grasp and no one to grasp it is the negative way of saying something which may also be said positively. But the positive way is not quite so effective and forceful, and lends itself more easily to misunderstanding. The sense that there is something to be grasped rests upon the seeming duality of the ego and its experience. But the reason why there is nothing to be grasped is that this duality is only seeming, so that the attempt to cling is like trying to bite the teeth with the teeth, or to clutch the hand with the hand. The corollary of this realization is that subject and object, oneself and the world, are a unity or, to be precise, a "nonduality" since the word "unity" may be taken to exclude diversity.

The sense of the vast gulf between the ego and the world disappears, and one's subjective, inner life seems no longer to be separate from everything else, from one's total experience of the stream of nature. It becomes simply obvious that "everything is the Tao"—an integrated, harmonious, and universal process from which it is absolutely impossible to deviate. This sensation is marvellous, to put it mildly, though there is no logical reason why it should be so, unless it is just through release from the chronic feeling of having to "face" reality. For here one does not face life any more; one simply is it.

But things are not usually felt to be marvellous unless they are full of consequence, unless they lead to definitive changes in practical life. When this sensation first dawns upon people, as it often does quite unexpectedly, they are apt to expect all kinds of results from it, which is why it vanishes as swiftly as it comes. They expect it to change their characters, to make them better, stronger, wiser, and happier. For they believe that they have grasped something immensely valuable, and go bouncing around as if they had inherited a fortune.

A Zen master was once asked, "What is the most valuable thing in the world?" He answered, "The head of a dead cat!" "Why?" "Because no one can put a price on it." The realization of the unity of the world is like this dead cat's head. It is the most priceless, the most inconsequential thing of all. It has no results, no implications, and no logical meaning. One cannot get anything out of it because it is impossible to take up a position outside it from which to reach in and grasp. The whole notion of gain, whether it be the gain of wealth or the gain of knowledge and virtue, is like stopping the pangs of hunger by gobbling oneself up from the toes. Yet we do it anyhow, for it really makes no difference whether it is one's own toes or roast duck: the satisfaction is always momentary. As the *Upanishads* say, "*Annam Brahman*—food is Brahman. I, the food, eat the eater of food!" [1] We are all eating ourselves like the serpent Ouroboros, and the only real disappointment comes from expecting to get something from it. This is why the Buddha said to his disciple Subhuti, "I gained absolutely nothing from unsurpassed and perfect Awakening." On the other hand, when there is no expectation, no looking for a result, and nothing gained but this "head of a dead cat," there is quite suddenly and gratuitously, quite miraculously and unreasonably, more than one ever had sought.

This is not a matter of renunciation and repressing desire

[1] *Taittiriya Upanishad, iii,* 10, 6.

—those traps which the clever and cunning lay for God. One cannot renounce life for the same reason that one cannot gain from it. As is said in the *Cheng-tao Ke:*

> *You cannot take hold of it,*
> *But you cannot lose it.*
> *In not being able to get it, you get it.*
> *When you are silent, it speaks;*
> *When you speak, it is silent.* xxxiv

For although it is often said that to seek the Tao is to lose it, since seeking puts a gap between the seeker and the sought, this is not quite true, as becomes evident when we try compulsively not to seek, not to wish, not to cling. The truth, however, is that one cannot deviate from the Tao even by seeking for it. There simply is no wrong attitude to the Tao because, again, there is no point outside it from which to take an attitude. The seeming separation of the subjective self is just as much an expression of the Tao as the clear outline of a leaf.

Such assertions will naturally be irritating to sensible and practical minds—this excitement about something which does not necessarily make any difference to anything, this perfectly meaningless idea of a harmony from which it is impossible to deviate. But the whole point of this "dead cat's head" philosophy is just that it is inconsequential, that, like nature itself, it is a kind of sublime nonsense, an expression of ecstasy, an end in itself without purpose or goal.

Restless, probing, and grasping minds are completely frustrated by such pointlessness, since for them only that has meaning which, like a word, points to something beyond itself. Therefore in so far as the world seems meaningful to them they have reduced it to a collection of signs like a dictionary. In their world flowers have scent and color *in*

order to attract bees, and chameleons change their skin-
tone with the intent of concealing themselves. Or, if what
they are projecting upon nature is not mind but machinery,
bees are attracted to flowers because they have scent and
color, and chameleons survive because they have skin which
changes its tone. They do not see the world of color and
scented bee-visited flowers growing—without the abstract
and divisive "because." Instead of interrelated patterns
wherein all the parts grow simultaneously together, they
see conglomerations of "billiard ball" things, strung together by the temporal sequence of cause and effect. In
such a world things are what they are only in relation to
what was and what will be, but in the goalless world of
the Tao, things are what they are in relation to each other's
presence.

Perhaps we may now begin to see why men have an almost universal tendency to seek relief from their own kind
among the trees and plants, the mountains and waters.
There is an easy and rather cheap sophistication in mock-
ing the love of nature, but there is always something profound and essential in the universal theme of poetry, however hackneyed. For hundreds of years the great poets of
East and West have given expression to this basically human love of "communing with nature," a phrase which in
present-day intellectual circles seems to have acquired a
slightly ridiculous tone. Presumably it is regarded as one
of those "escapes from reality" so much condemned by
those who restrict reality to what one reads about in the
newspapers.

But perhaps the reason for this love of nonhuman nature
is that communion with it restores us to a level of our own
human nature at which we are still sane, free from hum-
bug, and untouched by anxieties about the meaning and
purpose of our lives. For what we call "nature" is free from

a certain kind of scheming and self-importance. The birds and beasts indeed pursue their business of eating and breeding with the utmost devotion. But they do not justify it; they do not pretend that it serves higher ends, or that it makes a significant contribution to the progress of the world.

This is not meant to sound unkind to human beings, because the point is not so simple as that the birds are right and we are wrong. The point is that rapport with the marvellously purposeless world of nature gives us new eyes for ourselves—eyes in which our very self-importance is not condemned, but seen as something quite other than what it imagines itself to be. In this light all the weirdly abstract and pompous pursuits of men are suddenly transformed into natural marvels of the same order as the immense beaks of the toucans and hornbills, the fabulous tails of the birds of paradise, the towering necks of the giraffes, and the vividly polychromed posteriors of the baboons. Seen thus, neither as something to be condemned nor in its accustomed aspect of serious worth, the self-importance of man dissolves in laughter. His insistent purposefulness and his extraordinary preoccupation with abstractions are, while perfectly natural, overdone—like the vast bodies of the dinosaurs. As means of survival and adaptation they have been overplayed, producing a species too cunning and too practical for its own good, and which for this very reason stands in need of the "dead cat's head" philosophy. For this is the philosophy which, like nature, has no purpose or consequence other than itself.

Yet by indirection, surprisingly and artlessly, this philosophy arrives at an immensely heightened perception of the significance of the world. Perhaps "significance" is the wrong word, for seen thus the world does not point to a meaning beyond itself. It is like pure music—music when it is not a support for words, when it is not imitating natural sounds, and when, we might almost say, it does not represent feeling but *is* feeling. It is like the poetry of incantation and spellbinding where the words themselves are the meaning—

> *The silver is white, red is the gold;*
> *The robes they lay in fold.*
> *The bailey beareth the bell away;*
> *The lily, the rose, the rose I lay.*

People who turn with incomprehension from a nonobjective painting will nevertheless gaze with delight at a landscape where the artist has represented clouds and rocks which themselves represent nothing, paying unconscious tribute to the wonder of natural nonsense. For it is not as if these forms moved us by their approximation to the intelligible shapes of the geometer or by their resemblance to other things; the clouds are no less beautiful when not reminding us of mountains and cities in the sky. The rush of waterfalls and the babbling of streams are not loved for their resemblance to speech; the irregularly scattered stars do not excite us because of the formal constellations which have been traced out between them; and it is for no symmetry or suggestion of pictures that we delight in the patterns of foam, of the veins in rock, or of the black branches of trees in wintertime.

Seen in this light, the bewildering complexity of nature is a dance with no destination other than the figures now in performance, figures improvised not in response to an overruling law but mutually to each other. Even the cities lose their calculated practicality and become pumping ganglia in a network of arteries spread over the earth, sucking their corpuscles in at dawn and spitting them out at sunset. Caught up in the illusion of time and teleology, the dance and the ecstatic rhythm of the process is hidden and is seen instead as a frenzied pursuit, fighting its way through delays and obstacles. But when the final futility of the pursuit is recognized, the mind comes to rest and notices the rhythm, becoming aware that the timeless intent of the process is fulfilled at each instant.

There are occasions when this vision of the world takes us by surprise, the mind having slipped unconsciously into a receptive attitude. It is like the oft-recurring tale of coming upon an unexpected door in a familiar wall, a door that leads into an enchanted garden, or a cleft in a rock that gives entrance to a cavern of jewels. Yet when one comes back to the place again, looking for the entrance, it is no longer to be found. It was in just this way that late one afternoon my own garden became suddenly transfigured— for about half an hour, just at the beginning of twilight. The sky was in some way transparent, its blue quiet and clear, but more inwardly luminous than ever at high noon. The leaves of the trees and shrubs assumed qualities of green that were incandescent, and their clusterings were no longer shapeless daubs, but arabesques of marvellous complexity and clarity. The interlacing of branches against the sky suggested filigree or tracery, not in the sense of artificiality, but of distinctness and rhythm. Flowers—I remember especially the fuchsias—were suddenly the lightest carvings of ivory and coral.

It is as if the impressions of a restless and seeking mind are blurred by the speed at which they are overpassed, so that the rhythmic clarity of forms is unnoticed, and colors are seen flat without inner light. Furthermore, it is characteristic of almost all these openings of vision that every detail of the world appears to be in order, not as on a parade ground but as perfectly interconnected with everything else so that nothing is irrelevant, nothing inessential.

This, perhaps more than anything, explains the logically nonsensical feeling that everything is "right," or in harmony with the Tao, just as it is. And this applies equally to impressions that would ordinarily be thought simply messy, like garbage in a gutter or a spilled ash-tray on the carpet . . . or the head of a dead cat.

In the Western world it is second nature for us to assume that all creative action requires the incentive of inadequacy and discontent. It seems obvious that if we felt fulfilled at each instant and no longer regarded time as a path of pursuit, we should just sit down in the sun, pull large Mexican hats over our eyes, and put bottles of tequila at our elbows. Even if this were true it might not be so great a disaster as we imagine, for there is no doubt that our extreme busyness is as much nervous fidgets as industry, and that a certain amount of ordinary laziness would lend our culture the pleasant mellowness which it singularly lacks. However, it does not seem to occur to us that action goaded by a sense of inadequacy will be creative only in a limited sense. It will express the emptiness from which it springs rather than fullness, hunger rather than strength. Thus when our love for others is based simply on mutual need it becomes strangling—a kind of vampirism in which we say, all too expressively, "I love you so much I could eat you!" It is from such desiring that parental devotion becomes smother-love and marriage holy deadlock.

Modern theologians have used the Greek words *eros* and *agape* to distinguish between hungering love and generous love, ascribing the latter, however, to God alone. The fallen nature of man can only hunger, because sin is a descent from the fullness of Being to Nothingness. Lacking divine grace, man can act only from the natural incentive of need, and this assumption persists as a matter of common sense even when it is no longer believed that there is a God creating the world out of his infinite fullness. We assume, furthermore, that the whole realm of nature acts from hunger alone, for in Christianity it was understood that nature fell together with Adam, its head. And the notion that nature acts only from necessity accords perfectly with the mechanism which displaces theism.

But if the Fall was the loss of our sense of integrity with nature, the supposedly hunger-driven quality of natural action is a projection upon the world of our own state. If we are to abandon Newtonian mechanics in the physical sphere we must also do so in the psychological and moral. In the same measure that the atoms are not billiard balls struck into motion by others, our actions are not entities forced into operation by distinct motives and drives. Actions appear to be forced by other things to the degree that the agent identifies himself with a single part of the situation in which the actions occur, such as the will as distinct from the passions, or the mind as distinct from the body. But if he identifies himself with his passions and with his body, he will not seem to be moved by them. If he can go further and see that he is not simply his body but the whole of his body-environment relationship, he will not even feel forced to act by the environment. The effect appears to be controlled passively by its cause only in so far as it is considered to be distinct from the cause. But if cause and effect are just the terms of a single act, there is neither controller nor controlled. Thus the feeling that action has to spring from necessity comes from thinking that the self is the center of consciousness as distinct from the periphery.

The question "Why should one act?" has meaning only so long as motivation seems necessary to action. But if action or process rather than inert substance is what constitutes the world, it is absurd to seek an external reason for action. There is really no alternative to action, and this is not to say that we *must* act, since this would imply the reality of the inert, substantial "we" reluctantly activated from outside. The point is that, motivated or not, we *are* action. But when action is felt to be motivated, it expresses the hungering emptiness of the ego, the inertness of entity rather than the liveliness of act. When, however, man is not pursuing something outside himself, he is action expressing its own fullness, whether weeping for sorrow or jumping for joy.

In Indian philosophy *karma* signifies both motivated or purposeful action and cause and effect, and *karma* is the type of action which holds man in bondage. Goal-seeking, it reaches no goal, but ever perpetuates the need for goals. Solving problems, it ever creates more problems to solve. *Karma* is therefore significant action because, like the sign, it points beyond itself to a meaning, to the motive from which it sprang or the end which it seeks. It is action creating the *necessity* for further action. On the other hand, *sahaja* is spontaneous and inconsequential action characteristic of the *jivan-mukta,* the liberated one, who lives and moves in the same way as nature—babbling like streams, gesticulating like trees in the wind, wandering like clouds, or just existing like rocks on the sand. His life has the quality of what the Japanese call *fura-fura*—the flapping of a cloth in the breeze or the motion of an empty gourd in a bubbling river. "The wind bloweth where it listeth, and thou hearest the voice thereof, but canst not tell whence it cometh nor whither it goeth." No more can the wind itself.

This is why there is a universal likening of sages to lunatics, since in their subtly differing ways neither make any sense nor accept the world's practical scale of values.

His door stands closed, and the wise ones do not know him. His inner life is hidden, and he moves outside the ruts of the recognized virtues. Carrying a gourd, he enters the marketplace; making his way with a staff, he returns home. Even in the liquor shop and the fish market everyone is transformed into a Buddha.

Bare-chested and bare-footed, he goes into the dust of this world.
Smeared with mud and daubed with ashes, he wears a broad grin.
He has no need of the secret powers of the gods,
For by his direct command the dead trees blossom with flowers.[2]

For as the nonsense of the madman is a babble of words for its own fascination, the nonsense of nature and of the sage is the perception that the ultimate meaninglessness of the world contains the same hidden joy as its transience and emptiness. If we seek the meaning in the past, the chain of cause and effect vanishes like the wake of a ship. If we seek it in the future, it fades out like the beam of a searchlight in the night sky. If we seek it in the present, it is as elusive as flying spray, and there is nothing to grasp. But when only the seeking remains and we seek to know what *this* is, it suddenly turns into the mountains and waters, the sky and the stars, sufficient to themselves with no one left to seek anything from them.

❀   ❀   ❀

From all that has been said until now it may seem that our philosophy of nature has reached a point of complete self-contradiction. For if what it comes to is that there is no real division between man and nature, it follows that

---

[2] *Shih Niu T'ou,* x. Comment on the last of the *Ten Oxherding Pictures* which illustrate the stages of realization in Zen Buddhism.

there is nothing artificial from which the natural can be distinguished. As Goethe said again in the *Fragment on Nature:*

> The most unnatural also is nature. Who sees her not on all sides sees her truly nowhere. . . . Even in resisting her laws one obeys them; and one works with her even in desiring to work against her.

If this be true it would seem to render null all that has been said about the mechanical and unnatural character of the monotheistic God and of the linear and political views of the world order shared by Christianity and, until recently, by the philosophy of science. It would also seem to be pointless to prefer one mode of consciousness to another, to consider the open attentiveness of *kuan* more natural than the straining and staring attitude of egocentricity. If even the self-conscious artificialities and conceits of urban and industrial civilization are no more unnatural than the pretentious tail feathers of the peacock, this amounts to saying that in the natural life anything and everything "goes." As we said, there is no possibility of deviation from the Tao.

However, at the very least there is this much difference between such a position as this and, say, Christianity or a legalistic science: that they make a distinction between man and nature which this philosophy does not. It is granted that the making of this distinction is no less within the realm of nature than not making it. Both positions are therefore in some sense "right," if this is what we mean by natural, in the sense, perhaps, of a libertarian saying to a totalitarian, "I disagree entirely with what you say, but I will defend to the death your *right* to say it." As in an ideal democracy the exercise of freedom involves the right to vote for restrictions on freedom, so man's participation in nature involves the right and the freedom to feel that he stands above nature. As by democratic process the people may freely renounce freedom, one may likewise be naturally unnatural. Whereas the totalitarian may then assert that freedom has been abolished, the libertarian will point out that this is true only to the extent that he freely asserts it. Even under tyranny "a people gets what government it deserves," because it always retains the power, that is, the freedom to govern itself. In the same way it is possible for this philosophy to assert quite meaningfully that it is perfectly natural to believe that man is apart from nature and yet to disagree with the belief.

But if a people votes freely for certain restrictions on its freedom, it should never forget that freedom remains the background and authority for law. Similarly, the ultimate point of this philosophy is that as a people can never abandon its freedom and responsibility absolutely, a human being cannot absolutely abandon his naturalness and, likewise, should never forget it. To put it in another way, naturalness is a self-determining spontaneity (*tzu-jan*) which we retain even in the most awkward rigidity and affectation of attitude. But the "we" which retains this spontaneity is not the self-restriction called "ego"; it is the natural man, the organism-environment relationship.

Thus if political health consists in realizing that legal restraint is freely self-imposed by the people, philosophical health consists in realizing that our true self is the natural man, the spontaneous Tao, from which we never deviate. In psychological terms this realization is a total self-acceptance standing, like political freedom, as the constant background of every thought, feeling, and action—however restricted. Such acceptance of oneself is the condition of that underlying integrity, sincerity, and peace of heart which, in the sage, endures beneath every disturbance. It is, in short, a deeply inward consent to be just exactly what we are and to feel just exactly what we are feeling at every moment, even before what we are has been changed, however slightly, by accepting it. It is the recognition that "all things are lawful for me," even if "not all are expedient," but probably in a far wider sense than St. Paul ever intended. Stated boldly, if crudely, it is the insight that whatever we are just now, that is now what we should ideally be. This is the sense of the Zen Buddhist saying, "Your ordinary mind is the Tao," the "ordinary mind" being the present, given state of consciousness, whatever its nature. For enlightenment, or accord with the Tao, remains unrealized so long as it is considered as a specific state to be attained, and for which there are tests and standards of success. It is much rather freedom to be the failure that one is.

Unlikely as it may seem, this outrageous and nonmoral freedom is the basis of all mental and spiritual wholeness, provided, I was about to say, that it seeks no result. But so full an acceptance includes also this seeking, along with just anything that one happens to be doing or feeling. The apparently extreme passivity of this acceptance is, however, creative because it permits one to be all of a piece, to be good, bad, indifferent, or merely confused, with a whole heart. To act or grow creatively we must begin from where we are, but we cannot begin at all if we are not "all here" without reservation or regret. Lacking self-acceptance, we are always at odds with our point of departure, always doubting the ground on which we stand, always so divided against ourselves that we cannot act with sincerity. Apart from self-acceptance as the groundwork of thought and action, every attempt at spiritual or moral discipline is the fruitless struggle of a mind that is split asunder and insincere. It is the freedom which is the essential basis of self-restraint.

In the West we have always admitted in theory that truly moral acts must be expressions of freedom. Yet we have never allowed this freedom, never permitted ourselves to be everything that we are, to see that fundamentally all the gains and losses, rights and wrongs of our lives are as natural and "perfect" as the peaks and valleys of a mountain range. For in identifying God, the Absolute, with a goodness excluding evil we make it impossible for us to accept ourselves radically: what is not in accord with the will of God is at variance with Being itself and must not under any circumstances be accepted. Our freedom is therefore set about with such catastrophic rewards and punishments that it is not freedom at all, but resembles rather the totalitarian state in which one *may* vote against the government but always at the risk of being sent to a concentration camp. Instead of self-acceptance, the groundwork of our thought and action has therefore been metaphysical anxiety, the terror of being ultimately wrong and rotten to the core.

It is for this reason that the formal Catholic and Protestant orthodoxies have always been strictly exoteric doctrines, identifying the Absolute with the relativities of good and evil. Theologians are wont to say that if the distinctions between good and evil are not valid eternally they are not truly valid and important distinctions. But this actually amounts to saying that what is finite and relative is not important—a strange view for those who also insist that there is a real finite creation distinct from God and an object of his love. Not to be able to distinguish the absolutely important from the relatively important without thinking the latter unimportant is surely to adopt a most primitive scale of values.

Conversely, there is always the risk that a fundamental self-acceptance will render a person insensitive to the importance of moral values, but this is only to say that without risk there is no freedom. The fear that self-acceptance necessarily annihilates ethical judgment is groundless, for we are perfectly able to distinguish between up and down at any point on the earth's surface, realizing at the same time that there is no up and down in the larger framework of the cosmos. Self-acceptance is therefore the spiritual and psychological equivalent of space, of a freedom which does not annihilate distinctions but makes them possible.

> The capacity of the mind is great, like the emptiness of space. . . . The marvelous nature of the ordinary person is fundamentally empty and has no fixed character. Such is the truly sky-like quality of one's natural self. . . . The emptiness of universal space can contain the myriad things of every shape and form—the sun, moon, and stars, the mountains and rivers, the great earth with its springs, streams, and waterfalls, grass, trees, and dense forests, its sinners and saints, and the ways of good and evil. . . . All these are in the void, and the ordinary person's nature is void in just this way.[3]

But the healing and liberating force of self-acceptance is so contrary to the expectations of our pedestrian common sense that its power seems almost uncanny even to the psychotherapist who watches it happen again and again. For it is just this which restores the integrity and responsibility of the sick mind, liberating it from every radical compulsion to be what it is not. Nevertheless, this emergence of law from liberty, of cosmos from the void, and of energy from passivity is always so miraculously unexpected and improbable that it does not ordinarily come about except by some stratagem which enables us to permit ourselves this freedom in such a way that the right hand does not know what the left is doing. Thus we can bring ourselves

[3] Hui-neng, eighth-century Zen master, in the *Tan-ching, ii.*

to self-acceptance vicariously, through the agency of a liberalized God who is infinitely loving and forgiving, so that
it is *he* who accepts us totally, and not, at least directly, we
ourselves. Or it may be that we can accord ourselves the
right to self-acceptance only when we have paid for it by
going through some disciplinary mill or spiritual obstacle-
course, whereafter our acceptance of ourselves is rein-
forced by the collective authority of fellow initiates, representing some hallowed tradition.[4] Such are the ways of
placating the fear of freedom which society must almost
inevitably implant from our childhood. For lacking dis-
crimination between the hierarchies of value and truth, the
child may say that two and two are five if he is told the
higher mathematical truth that they are not always and
necessarily four.

Growth in philosophical understanding, or just plain
wisdom, is always a matter of being able to distinguish between levels of truth and frames of reference, at the same
time being able to see one's own life in its intimate relation
to these differing and ever more universal levels. Above all,
there is the level beyond levels, the boundless frame of
universal nature, which, however impossible to describe, is
the self-determining and spontaneous ground of our being
and our freedom. The degree of our freedom and self-
determination varies with the level which we realize to be
our self—the source from which we act. As our sense of
self is narrow, the more we feel our existence as restraint.

---

[4] In the course of such preliminary disciplines the neophyte may sometimes acquire various skills and powers or subtle traits of character and
manner which are subsequently understood as the signs of his liberation.
This is, however, a confusion of freedom with success in particular skills.
Thus an initiate who, in his preliminary training, learned to stand pain
without flinching may be unable to run a farm or build a house as well
as any ordinary neurotic. His response to pain may in fact prove nothing
more than that he has learned the trick of self-hypnosis, or managed to
lose his sensitivity.

"And therefore," said Ruysbroeck, "we must all found our lives upon a fathomless abyss"—so to discover that what we are is not what we are bound to be, but what we are free to be. For when we stand with our nature, seeing that there is nowhere to stand against it, we are at last able to move unmoved.

II: MAN AND WOMAN

6: Spirituality and Sexuality

THE DIVISION OF LIFE INTO THE HIGHER
and lower categories of spirit and nature usually goes hand
in hand with a symbolism in which spirit is male and nature
female. The resemblance was perhaps suggested by the
rains falling from heaven to fertilize the earth, the plant-
ing of seed in the ground, and the ripening of the fruit by
the warmth of the sun. To a considerable extent ancient
man reasoned in terms of such correspondences, and made
sense of his world by seeing analogies between one natural
process and another, analogies which were understood to
be actual relationships. The art of astrology, for example,
is the most complete monument to this way of reasoning,
based as it is upon the correspondences between the mac-
rocosm and the microcosm, the order of the stars and the
order of terrestrial affairs. In the words of the Hermetic
Emerald Tablet:

> *Heaven above, heaven below;*
> *Stars above, stars below.*
> *All that is over, under shall show.*
> *Happy who the riddle readeth!*

Unfortunately for those who search for consistent systems in ancient cosmology, it was always possible to read
the correspondences as well as the very orders of heaven
and earth in different ways. Heaven might be male and
earth female, but then it was equally possible to think of
space and the sky as an all-embracing womb in which the

139

universe had been brought to birth, for such is apparently the sense of the Egyptian sky goddess Nut. It is easy, however, for us to dismiss such ways of thinking as mere projection, as a confusion of objective nature with fantasies which it evokes from the human mind. Yet after all our own science is likewise a projection, though what it reads into nature is not a loosely knit system of poetic images but the highly exact and consistent structure of mathematics. Both are products of the human mind, and mathematics in particular may be developed indefinitely in the abstract as a pure creation of thought without reference to any external experience. But mathematics *works* because of its immense inner consistency and precision, serving thus as an admirable tool for measuring nature to suit the purposes which *we* have in mind. However, not all cultures have the same purposes, so that other ways of "reading" the world may serve equally well for ends which are as legitimate as ours, for there are no laws by which these ends may be judged apart from the very readings of the world which serve them.

Indeed, the world is not unlike a vast, shapeless Rorschach blot which we read according to our inner disposition, in such a way that our interpretations say far more about ourselves than about the blot. But whereas the psychologist has tried to develop a science to judge and compare the various interpretations of the Rorschach Test, there is as yet no supracultural science, no "metascience," whereby we can assess our differing interpretations of the cosmic Rorschach blot. Cultural anthropology, the nearest thing to this, suffers the defect of being thoroughly embedded in the conventions of Western science, of one particular way of interpreting the blot.

The importance of the correspondence between spirit and man and nature and woman is that it projects upon the world a disposition in which the members of several cultures, including our own, are still involved. It is a disposition in which the split between man and nature is related to a problematic attitude to sex, though like egg and hen it is doubtful which came first. It is perhaps best to treat them as arising mutually, each being symptomatic of the other.

The historical reasons for our problematic attitude to sexuality are so obscure that there are numerous contradictory theories to explain it. It seems useless, therefore, to try to decide between them in the present state of our knowledge. The problem may be discussed more profitably just by taking the attitude as given, and by considering its consequences and alternatives. The fact is that in some unknown way the female sex has become associated with the earthy aspect of human nature and with sexuality as such. The male sex could conceivably have been put in the same position, and there is no conclusive evidence that women are more desirous and provocative of sexual activity than men, or *vice versa*. These are almost certainly matters of cultural conditioning which do not explain how the culture itself came to be as it is. It seems plausible that the association of women with sexuality as such is a male point of view arising in cultures where the male is dominant, but this in turn may be not so much a cause of the attitude as one of its concurrent symptoms. It is, however, very possible that the attitude to women is rather more accidental than the attitude to sexuality, for we know that the male and the female alike can feel the sexual relationship to be a seduction, a danger, and a problem. But *why* they do so at any time may no longer be the reason for their having first done so, so that knowledge of historical causes may not of itself provide any solution to the problem.

Thus to say that man's relation to nature is in some sense parallel to his relation to woman is to speak symbolically.

The real parallel is the relation of the human being, male or female, to the sexual division of the species and to all that it involves. When, therefore, we shall speak loosely of the *reasons* for certain sexual attitudes, we shall not be speaking of fundamental historical causes, for these are, strictly speaking, prehistoric—not necessarily so much in point of time as in extent of knowledge. We shall be speaking of the reasons as they exist today, either as matters of open knowledge or as forms of unconscious conditioning. There is no clear evidence that we are unconsciously conditioned by events from the remote historical past, and we must therefore be most cautious in using the insights of psychoanalysis for reconstructing the history of cultures. Certainly we can trace the historical effects of Christian, Buddhist, or Hindu doctrines upon our sexual attitudes, but what lies behind these doctrines and the attitudes from which they arose remains conjectural and dim. Furthermore, it is always possible to argue not that we are conditioned *by* the past, but that we use the past to condition ourselves in the present, and for reasons which are not historical but deeply inward and unknown. For example, a physiologist does not need to call upon the whole history of living creatures to explain why a person is hungry. He explains it from the present state of the organism.[1]

Let us then say that in the Christian and post-Christian West we simply find ourselves in a culture where nature is called Mother Nature, where God is exclusively male, and where one of the common meanings of Woman or Women with the capital *W* is simply sex, whereas Man with the

---

[1] It is of interest that in the academic world only the more or less "effete" disciplines are studied by the historical method. Beginning courses in religion, philosophy, or "culture" are usually historical, but the history of mathematics, chemistry, or medicine is the concern of a few specialists only. The ordinary student begins at once to learn them from their *present* rudiments.

capital *M* means humanity in general. As part and parcel of this situation, as distinct from its historical explanation, we find that in the Indo-European language system the words *matter, materia,* and *meter* as well as *mother,* and its Latin and Greek forms *mater* and μήτηρ, are derived alike from the Sanskrit root *mā-* (*mātr-*), from which, in Sanskrit itself, come both *mātā* (mother) and *māyā* (the phenomenal world of nature). The meaning of the common root *mā-* is "to measure," thus giving *māyā* the sense of the world-as-measured, that is, as divided up into things, events, and categories. In contrast stands the world unmeasured, the infinite and undivided (*advaita*) Brahman, the supreme spiritual reality. While it can be pointed out that the Devil is *also* male, since as the angel Lucifer he is a pure spirit, it must be noted that his popular form is simply that of the god Pan— the lusty spirit of earth and fertility, the genius of natural beauty. Hell, his domain, lies downward in the heart of the earth, where all is dark, inward, and unconscious as distinct from the bright heavens above. The catalogue of popular images, figures of speech, and customs which associate spirit with the divine, the good, and the male and nature with the material, evil, sexual, and female could go on indefinitely.

But the heart of the matter begins to reveal itself when, considering nature in the Chinese sense of spontaneity (*tzu-jan*), we begin to realize that the opposition of spirit to both nature and sexuality is the opposition of the conscious will, of the ego, to that which it cannot control. If sexual abstinence is, as in so many spiritual traditions, the condition of enhanced consciousness, it is because consciousness as we know it is an act of restraint. The point comes out clearly in St. Augustine's discussion of the spontaneity of the sexual member:

Justly, too, these members themselves, being moved and restrained not at our will, but by a certain independent autocracy, so to speak, are called "shameful." Their condition was different before sin . . . because not yet did lust move those members without the will's consent. . . . But when [our first parents] were stripped of grace, that their disobedience might be punished by fit retribution, there began to be in the movement of their bodily members a shameless novelty which made nakedness indecent.[2]

This is clearly the reaction of one for whom the soul, the will, the spiritual part of man, is identified with that form of consciousness which we have seen to be a partial and exclusive mode of attention. It is the mode of attention which grasps and orders the world by seeing it as one-at-a-time things, excluding and ignoring the rest. For it is this which involves that straining of the mind which is also the sensation of willing and of being a separate, exclusive ego.

Shame is thus the accompaniment of the failure of concentrated attention and will which manifests itself not only in the spontaneity of sexual excitement, but also in crying, trembling, blushing, blanching, and so many other socially "shameful" reactions.[3] These reactions are ordinarily avoided by concentrating the attention elsewhere and so avoiding the shameful response, and thus the ascetic disciplinarian will overcome lust, not by pitting the will against it directly, but by attending resolutely to other matters.

Obviously, the sexual function is one of the most powerful manifestations of biological spontaneity, and thus more

---

[2] *De Civitate Dei*, xiv, 17. Tr. Dods (1), vol. 2, p. 33.

[3] Note the "double bind" involved in blushing. One blushes because of shame and is in turn ashamed to blush, and is thus left with no alternative but to be "covered with confusion." This is a mild example of the way in which, as Gregory Bateson (1) has shown, double-bind situations lead to the more serious "confusion" of insanity, and especially schizophrenia.

especially difficult for the will to control. The immediate reasons for controlling it vary from the belief that it saps virility, through proprietary rights upon women, to its association with a complex love relationship with one woman alone, to mention only a few. But these seem to be secondary to the fact that sexual restraint is a principal test of the strength of the ego, along with resistance to pain and regulation of the wanderings of thought and feeling. Such restraints are the very substance of individual consciousness, of the sensation that feeling and action are directed from within a limited center of the organism, and that consciousness is not the mere witness of activity but the responsible agent. Yet this is something quite different from the spontaneous self-control of, say, the circulation of blood, where the control is carried out by the organism as a whole, unconsciously. For willed control brings about a sense of duality within the organism, of consciousness in conflict with appetite.

But this mode of control is a peculiar example of the proverb that nothing fails like success. For the more consciousness is individualized by the success of the will, the more everything outside the individual seems to be a threat—including not only the external world but also the "external" and uncontrolled spontaneity of one's own body, which, for example, continues to age, die, and corrupt against one's desire. Every success in control therefore demands a further success, so that the process cannot stop short of omnipotence. But this, save perhaps in some inconceivably distant future, is impossible. Hence there arises the desire to protect the ego from alien spontaneity by withdrawal from the natural world into a realm of pure consciousness or spirit.

Now withdrawal requires the inner detachment of consciousness, which is felt to be bound to nature so long as it desires it, or rather, so long as it identifies itself with the bodily organism's natural appetites. Thus it must not only control them but also cease to enjoy them. It makes little difference whether the realm of spirit be pure and formless, as in many types of mysticism, or whether it be a world of transfigured and spiritualized matter, as in Christianity. The point is that in either case will and consciousness triumph, attaining omnipotence either in their own right or by the grace of union with an omnipotent God whose whole nature is that of a self- and all-controlling will.[4]

On some such lines as these we must explain the ancient and widely prevalent conflict between spirituality and sexuality, the belief, found in East and West alike, that sexual abstinence and freedom from lust are essential prerequisites for man's proper and ultimate development. Presumably, we are free to define man's ultimate goal as we will, even if what we desire is the stimulus of eternal conflict or the repose of bodily insensitivity. But if we think of spirituality less in terms of what it avoids and more in terms of what it

[4] Yet it is curious that both nature mysticism and supernatural mysticism can arrive at experiences which are almost indistinguishable. For it would seem that the latter, in struggling not only with external nature but also with its own wayward will and desire, reaches a point of *impasse* where it discovers the perversion or selfishness of the will in the very will to struggle. It is then forced to "give itself up" to a higher power which has been conceived as the supernatural will of God. But in fact the power to which it surrenders may be the very different "omnipotence" of natural spontaneity. Thus, even when trained in a tradition of supernaturalism, the mystic may return after his experience into the world bereft of all disgust for nature. On the contrary, he is often endowed with a completely artless and childlike love for every kind of creature. In his eyes the same old world is already transfigured with the "glory of God," though to his less fortunate coreligionists it is as sinful and corrupt as ever. Cf. Dame Julian's *Revelations of the Divine Love*: "See! I am God: see! I am in all thing; see! I do all thing: see! I lift never mine hands off my works, nor ever shall, without end: see! I lead all thing to the end I ordained it to from without beginning, by the same Might, Wisdom and Love whereby I made it. How should anything be amiss?" (xi). "Sin is behovable (i.e., permissible), but all shall be well, and all shall be well, and all manner of thing shall be well" (xxvii).

is positively, and if we may think of it as including an intense awareness of the inner identity of subject and object, man and the universe, there is no reason whatsoever why it should require the rejection of sexuality. On the contrary, this most intimate of relationships of the self with another would naturally become one of the chief spheres of spiritual insight and growth.

This is in no way to say that the monastic and celibate life is an aberration, for man is not absolutely obliged to have sexual relations, nor even to eat or to live. As under certain circumstances a voluntary death or fast is perfectly justifiable, so also is sexual abstinence—in order, for example, that the force of the libido may be expended in other directions. The common mistake of the religious celibate has been to suppose that the highest spiritual life absolutely demands the renunciation of sexuality, as if the knowledge of God were an alternative to the knowledge of woman, or to any other form of experience.

Indeed, the life of total chastity is often undertaken as a monogamous marriage of the soul with God, as an all-consuming love of creature for Creator in which love for a mortal woman would be a fatal distraction. In this context sexuality is often renounced, not because it is evil, but because it is a precious and beautiful possession *offered* to God in sacrifice. But this raises the question as to whether renunciation as such is sacrifice in the proper sense of an act which "makes holy" (*sacer-facere*) the thing offered. For if sexuality is a relationship and an activity, can it be offered when neither the relationship nor the activity exists? Does a dancer offer her dancing to God by ceasing to dance? An offering can cease to exist, for its original owner, if given away to another for his use. But sacrifice is only accidentally associated with the cessation, death, or mutilation of the offering because it was once supposed that, say, burning bulls on an altar was the only way of transporting them to heaven.

The offering of sexuality to God is in all probability a survival of the idea that a woman's body, and its sexual enjoyment, is the property of her husband, to whom she is bound to reserve herself even if he does not actually lie with her. By analogy, the body of the celibate becomes the property of God, dedicated to him alone. But this is not only a confusion of God with what is after all only his symbol, the tribal father, but also the likening of the Creator-creature relationship to a strictly barbarous conception of marriage. Obviously, the possession of a body is not a relationship to a person; one is related to the person only in being related to the organism of another in its total functioning. For the human being is not a thing but a process, not an object but a life.

The offering may be defended by saying that God uses the sexual energy of his human spouses in other ways, diverting them into prayer or into acts of charity. With this there can be no quarrel—provided that it does not exclude the possibility that God may use them for sexual activity itself as an aspect of life no whit less holy than prayer or feeding the poor. Historically, the supernaturalists have admitted this only with great reluctance—outside the Semitic-Islamic traditions, which have largely escaped sexual squeamishness. But the literature of the spiritual life is overwhelmingly preoccupied with the sinful aspects of sex. It has almost nothing to say, positively, about what holy sex might be, save that it must be reserved to a single life partner and consummated for the purpose of procreation in one particular physical attitude alone!

That matrimony may be an estate as holy as virginity is something which the Christian tradition admits theoretically, as a consequence of its Hebrew background.[5] But the force of Hebraic insistence on the goodness of things physical has had little effect on the actual feeling and practice of the Church. For from the earliest times the Church Fathers virtually equated sex with sin by identifying all sexual feeling and desire with the evil of lust. At the same time they could maintain, as against the Gnostics and Manichaeans, that the mere physical apparatus and mechanics of sex were, as God's creation, inherently pure. Speaking, then, of "ideal" sexuality as it might have been before the Fall, St. Augustine wrote:

> Those members, like the rest, would be moved by the command of his will, and the husband would be mingled with the loins of the wife without the seductive stimulus of passion, with calmness of mind and with no corruption of the innocence of the body. . . . Because the wild heat of passion would not activate those parts of the body, but, as would be proper, a voluntary control would employ them. Thus it would then have been possible to inject the semen into the womb through the female genitalia as innocently as the menstrual flow is now ejected.[6]

The general tenor and attitude of supernaturalism to sexuality is unmistakable: it is overwhelmingly negative, and to all intents and purposes the attitude is not the least modified by separating sexual mechanics from sexual feelings, a separation which in any case destroys the integrity of mind and body. Practically, if not theoretically, the basis of this attitude is the feeling that God and nature are simply

[5] Protestantism, with its greater interest in Biblical Christianity, is therefore more Hebraic in its attitude to sexuality than Catholicism, as witness Luther and Milton. But if it has to some extent liberalized sexual restraints, it has had as little notion as Catholicism of a positive sexual holiness.

[6] *De Civitate Dei,* xiv, 26.

incompatible. They may not have been so originally, but then nature was nothing like the nature we experience to-day. If we are to believe St. Augustine, it was something as lacking in spontaneity as artificial insemination.

Now the practical effect of a philosophy in which God and nature are incompatible is somewhat unexpected. For when the knowledge and love of God is considered to exclude other goals and other creatures, God is actually put on a par with his creatures. The knowledge of God and the knowledge of creatures can exclude one another only if they are of the same kind. One must choose between yellow and blue, as two of the kind color, but there is no need to choose between yellow and round, since what is round can also be yellow. If God is universal, the knowledge of God should include all other knowledge as the sense of sight includes all the differing objects of vision. But if the eye should attempt to see sight, it will turn in upon itself and see nothing.

Indeed, the celibate life is more appropriate to "worldly" vocations than spiritual, for while it is possible to be both a sage and a physician or artist, the exigencies of a professional or creative vocation so often suggest the Latin tag, *Aut libri aut liberi*—either books or children. But the vocation to sanctity should hardly be a specialization on the same level as writing, medicine, or mathematics, for God himself—the "object" of sanctity—is no specialist. Were he so, the universe would consist of nothing but formally religious creations—clergymen, bibles, churches, monasteries, rosaries, prayer-books, and angels.

Sanctity or sagehood as an exclusive vocation is, once again, symptomatic of an exclusive mode of consciousness in general and of the spiritual consciousness in particular. Its basic assumption is that God and nature are in competition and that man must choose between them. Its standpoint is radically dualistic, and thus it is strange indeed to find it in traditions which otherwise abjure dualism. This is a basic inconsistency, and its appearance is strangest of all in the nondualistic traditions of Indian Vedanta and Buddhism. But the confusion out of which it arises is highly instructive.

As we have seen, the relegation of sexuality and nature to the forces of evil grows out of the belief that strength and clarity of consciousness depend upon cultivating a one-pointed and exclusive mode of attention. This is, in other words, a type of attention which *ignores* the background in fastening upon the figure, and which grasps the world serially, one thing at a time. Yet this is exactly the meaning of the Hindu-Buddhist term *avidya,* ignorance, or "ignore-ance," the basic *unconsciousness* as a result of which it appears that the universe is a collection of *separate* things and events. A Buddha or "awakened one" is precisely the man who has overcome this unconsciousness and is no more bewitched by *sakaya-drishti,* the "vision of separateness." In other words, he sees each "part" of nature without ignoring its relation to the whole, without being deceived by the illusion of *māyā* which, as we also saw, is based on the idea of "measurement" (*mā-, mātr-*), the dividing of the world into classes, into countable things and events. So divided, the world appears to be dual (*dvaita*), but to the unobstructed vision of the sage it is in truth undivided or non-dual (*advaita*) and in this state identical with Brahman, the immeasurable and infinite reality.

Considered as a collection of separate things, the world is thus a creation of thought. *Maya,* or measuring and classifying, is an operation of the mind, and as such is the "mother" (*mata*) of a strictly abstract conception of nature, illusory in the sense that nature is so divided only in one's mind. *Maya* is illusory in an evil sense only when the vision of the world as divided is not subordinate to the vision of the world as undivided, when, in other words, the cleverness of the measuring mind does not become too much of a good thing and is "unable to see the forest for the trees."

But the general trend of Indian thought was to fall into the very trap which it should have avoided: it confused the abstract world of *maya* with the concrete world of nature, of direct experience, and then sought liberation from nature in terms of a state of consciousness bereft of all sense experience. It interpreted *maya* as an illusion of the senses rather than of thought projecting itself through the senses. In various forms of *yoga* it cultivated prolonged exclusive concentration upon a single point—*avidya!*—in order to exclude sense experience from consciousness, regarding it as the supreme obstacle to spiritual insight. Above all, sense experience implied "woman," not only as a highly attractive experience, but also as the "source" of birth into the natural world, and thus the very incarnation of *maya,* the Cosmic Seductress.

Thus the identification of *maya* with nature and with woman is the classic example of deception by *maya,* of confusing the world projected by the mind with the real world. Yet although *maya* is figuratively the "mother" of the projected world, projection is rather a male function than a female. As usual, however, man projects his seed into the woman and then accuses her of seducing him. As Adam said, "This woman whom thou gavest me, she tempted me and I did eat."

It was in this way that much of Indian philosophy became in practice the archetype of all world-denying dualisms, and in seeking liberation from sense experience became twice over the victim of *maya.* For in struggling for release from *maya* as the concrete world of nature, it confirmed itself more and more deeply in the very illusion that what our minds project upon the world is what we actually see. It forgot that the senses are innocent and that self-deception is the work of thought and imagination.[7]

Confusions of this kind obscure the ways in which both sexuality and sensuality may become *maya* in its proper sense, that is, when the mind seeks more from nature than she can offer, when isolated aspects of nature are pursued in the attempt to force from them a life of joy without sorrow, or pleasure without pain. Thus the desire for sexual experience is *maya* when it is "on the brain," when it is a purely willful and imaginative craving to which the organism responds reluctantly, or not at all. Idealized and fashionable conceptions of feminine beauty are *maya* when, as is often the case, they have little relation to the actual conformations of women. Love, as de Rougemont points out, is *maya* when it is being in love with being in love, rather than a relationship with a particular woman. *Maya* is indeed Woman in the abstract.

Now sexuality is in this sense abstract whenever it is exploited or forced, when it is a deliberate, self-conscious, and yet compulsive pursuit of ecstasy, making up for the stark absence of ecstasy in all other spheres of life. Ecstasy, or transcending oneself, is the natural accompaniment of a full relationship in which we experience the "inner identity" between ourselves and the world. But when that re-

---

[7] This misinterpretation of *maya* was largely corrected in Mahayana Buddhism, especially in its Chinese form. Thus the *Lankavatara Sutra*, ii, 18, states that nirvana or release from *maya* is not to be understood as "the future annihilation of the senses and their fields." So, too, the Chinese Zen master Seng-ts'an says explicitly:

> Do not be antagonistic to the world of the senses,
> For when you are not antagonistic to it,
> It turns out to be the same as complete Awakening.

Likewise Kuo-an in his comments upon the *Ten Oxherding Pictures* says, "Things oppress us not because of an objective world, but because of a self-deceiving mind."

lationship is hidden and the individual feels himself to be a restricted island of consciousness, his emotional experience is largely one of restriction, and it is as arid as the abstract *persona* which he believes himself to be. But the sexual act remains the one easy outlet from his predicament, the one brief interval in which he transcends himself and yields consciously to the spontaneity of his organism. More and more, then, this act is expected to compensate for defective spontaneity in all other directions, and is therefore abstracted or set apart from other experiences as *the* great delight.

Such abstract sexuality is thus the certain result of a forced and studied style of personality, and of confusing spirituality with mere will power—a confusion which remains even when one is *willing* one's will over to God. The individual ascetic may indeed succeed in sublimating his desire for sexual ecstasy into some other form, but he remains part of a society, a culture, upon which his attitude to sex has a powerful influence. By associating sex with evil he makes *the* great delight an even greater fascination for the other members of his society, and thereby unknowingly assists the growth of all the refinements of civilized lust. Considered from the standpoint of society as a whole, puritanism is as much a method of exploiting sex by titillation as black underwear, since it promotes the same shocking and exciting contrast between the naked flesh and the black of clerical propriety. It would not be unreasonable to regard puritanism, like masochism, as an extreme form of sexual "decadence."

The culture of Victorian England offers a striking example of this religious prurience, since it was by no means so sexless and staid as has often been supposed, but was, on the contrary, a culture of the most elegant lasciviousness. Extreme modesty and prudishness in the home so heightened the fascination of sex that prostitution, even for the upper classes, flourished on a far greater scale than in our own relatively liberal times. Fashionable and respectable boarding schools combined a total repression of overt sexuality with a proportionably flagrant indulgence in flagellomania. Fashions in clothing did everything to reveal and accentuate the feminine outline in the very act of covering it from neck to toe in veritable strait jackets of tweed, flannel, and boned corsetry. Even the chairs, tables, and household ornaments were suggestively bulged and curved—the chairs wide-shouldered and then waisted at the back, the seat broad, and the legs so obviously thighs or calves that squeamish housewives made the resemblance all the stronger by fitting them with skirts. For when sexuality is repressed in its direct manifestation, it irradiates other spheres of life to scatter on every side symbols and suggestions of its all the more urgent presence.

From the standpoint of cultural anthropology this backhanded manner of embellishing sexuality may be just one of many legitimate variants of the art of sex. For so sensitive a creature as man, art is natural. He does not care to masticate raw beef with hands and teeth, nor to make love with the same "natural" unconcern as that with which he sneezes, nor to live in homes thrown together anyhow to keep out the wet and cold. Therefore there is almost always an art of love, whether it be as directly concerned with the sexual act as the Indian *Kamasutra,* or a preoccupation with the long preliminaries of wooing to which the sexual act itself is merely the final swift climax. Puritanism is simply one of these variants—that is, if we look at it as a natural phenomenon and do not take it at its own valuation of itself. It is another case of serving nature in trying to work against her, of an extreme of human artifice being no less natural than the supposedly freakish creatures of the wild. It is simply damming a stream to increase its force, but doing so unintentionally or unconsciously. Thus it has often been noted that periods of license and periods of puritanism alternate, the latter creating an excitement that can no longer be contained, and the former a lassitude that requires reinvigoration. The more normal means of keeping the stream at an even strength is modesty rather than prudery, the heightening of sexual fascination by aesthetic concealment as distinct from moral condemnation.[8]

But if puritanism and cultivated licentiousness are not fundamental deviations from nature, they are simply the opposite poles of one and the same attitude—that, right or wrong, sexual pleasure is *the* great delight.[9] This attitude, like the cultivation of the ego, is indeed one of the innumerable possibilities of the freedom of our nature, but because it abstracts sexuality from the rest of life (or *attempts* to do so), it hardly begins to realize its possibilities. Abstract sexuality is partial—a function of dissociated brains instead of total organisms—and for this reason is a singular confusion of the natural world with the *maya* of intellectual divisions and categories. For when sexuality is set apart as

[8] Thus the Chinese and Japanese, who do not suffer from sexual guilt, have a strong sense of sexual shame, and have difficulty in appreciating our ready representation of the nude in art. Writing from Europe in 1900, a mandarin said, "The pictures in the palace set apart for them would not please the cultured mind of my venerable brother. The female form is represented nude or half nude. This would obtain fault from our propriety. . . . They have statues of plaster, and some of marble, in the public gardens and in this palace, most of them naked. In the winter's ice it makes me want to cover them. The artists do not know the attraction of rich flowing drapery." Hwuy-ung, *A Chinaman's Opinion of Us and His Own Country*. London, 1927.

[9] Thus a recent summary of the compendia of Catholic moral theology, Jone's *Moral Theology* (Newman Press, 1952), devotes 44 pages to a discussion of the various categories of sin, of which 32, in fine print, are occupied with sexual sins—showing their relative importance with respect to murder, greed, cruelty, lying, and self-righteousness.

a specially good or specially evil compartment of life, it no longer works in full relation to everything else. In other words, it loses universality. It becomes a part doing duty for the whole—the idolatry of a creature worshipped in place of God, and an idolatry committed as much by the ascetic as the libertine.

So long, then, as sexuality remains this abstract *maya* it remains a "demonic" and unspiritualized force, unspiritual in the sense that it is divorced from the universal and concrete reality of nature. For we are trying to wrest it from subordination to the total pattern of organism-environment relationship which, in Chinese philosophy, is *li*—the ordering principle of the Tao. But the universalization of sex involves far more than Freud's recognition that art, religion, and politics are expressions of sublimated libido. We must also see that sexual relations are religious, social, metaphysical, and artistic. Thus the "sexual problem" cannot be solved simply at the sexual level, for which reason our whole discussion makes it subordinate to the problem of man and nature. Sexuality will remain a problem so long as it continues to be the isolated area in which the individual transcends himself and experiences spontaneity. He must first allow himself to be spontaneous in the whole play of inner feeling and of sensory response to the everyday world. Only as the senses in general can learn to accept without grasping, or to be conscious without straining, can the special sensations of sex be free from the grasping of abstract lust and its inseparable twin, the inhibition of abstract or "spiritual" disgust.

It is in this way alone that the problem can be taken out of the fruitlessly alternating dualism in which we have set it. In this dualism sexuality is now good and now bad, now lustful and now prudish, now compellingly grasped and now guiltily inhibited. For when sexual activity is sought in the abstract its disappointments are proportionate to its exaggerated expectations, associating themselves with the swift transition from extreme excitement to lassitude which accompanies detumescence. The aftermath of intercourse, which should be a state of fulfilled tranquillity, is for the prude the depression of guilt and for the libertine the depression of ennui. The reason is that both are grasping at the sensation of intense lust which immediately precedes the orgasm, making it a goal rather than a gift, and so experienced it is an elation which swings over to depression, its opposite *maya*. But when the mounting excitement is accepted rather than grasped, it becomes a full realization of spontaneity, and the resulting orgasm is not its sudden end but the bursting in upon us of peace.

It will by now be clear that a truly natural sexuality is by no means a spontaneity in the sense of promiscuity breaking loose from restraint. No more is it the colorlessly "healthy" sexuality of mere animal release from biological tension. To the degree that we do not yet know what man is, we do not yet know what human sexuality is. We do not know what man is so long as we know him piecemeal, categorically, as the separate individual, the agglomeration of blocklike instincts and passions and sensations regarded one by one under the fixed stare of an exclusive consciousness. What man is, and what human sexuality is, will come to be known only as we lay ourselves open to experience with the full sensitivity of feeling which does not grasp.

The experience of sexual love is therefore no longer to be sought as the repetition of a familiar ecstasy, prejudiced by the expectation of what we already know. It will be the exploration of our relationship with an ever-changing, ever unknown partner, unknown because he or she is not in truth the abstract role or person, the set of conditioned reflexes which society has imposed, the stereotyped male or female which education has led us to expect. All these are *maya*, and the love of these is the endlessly frustrating love of fantasy. What is not *maya* is mystery, what cannot be described or measured, and it is in this sense—symbolized by the veil of modesty—that woman is always a mystery to man, and man to woman. It is in this sense that we must understand van der Leeuw's remarkable saying that "the mystery of life is not a problem to be solved, but a reality to be experienced."

7: Sacred and Profane Love

IT IS ALWAYS INSTRUCTIVE TO GO BACK TO the original meanings of words to discover not only what new senses they have gained, but also what old senses they have lost. The word "profane," for example, did not at first signify the blasphemous or irreligious, but an area or court before (*pro*) the entrance to a temple (*fanum*). It was thus the proper place of worship for the common people as distinct from the initiates, though here again the "common" is not the crude but the communal—the people living in society. By contrast, the sacred was not the merely religious but what lay outside or beyond the community, what was—again in an ancient sense—*extraordinary* or outside the social order.

But we seem to have lost sight of the fact that there can be a position outside the communal and conventional order which is not subversive, a position free from rule but not against it. Almost invariably we confuse this position with its opposite—that which lies below order, and which is chaos rather than freedom. It is part of the same confusion that speaking with "authority" has come to mean speaking for the government, the Church, or tradition, or with the backing of well-documented footnotes. Yet it was not thus that Jesus was described as "speaking as one having authority, and not as the Scribes." The point was that he spoke with inner conviction, which must again be distinguished from the dogmatism of inner uncertainty. The "original" has likewise come to mean the novel or even eccentric, but the deeper senses of authority and originality are to be the author and origin of one's own deeds as a free agent. The socially conditioned *persona* or role-playing ego is, however, never a free agent. Man is free to the extent that he realizes his genuine self to be the author and origin of nature.

Yet here again our accustomed confusion of levels makes this indistinguishable from the lunatic boast "I myself am God!" Out of this confusion the Western Church rejected the insight of Eckhart in saying:

> God must be very I, I very God, so consummately one that this he and this I are one "is," in this is-ness working one work eternally; but so long as this he and this I, to wit, God and the soul, are not one single here, one single now, the I cannot work with nor be one with that he.[1]

For the root of the confusion is that the Christian tradition of the West has lacked what we have called "inwardness." Its official position has always been profane, conventional, and exoteric without knowing it to be so. Thus it has confused the profane with the sacred, the relative with the absolute, the social sphere of law and order with the divine nature. The social order has therefore been enforced with sanctions which are too strong, and its laws have been made absolute imperatives. We have already seen this in the notion that the love of God and the love of nature can be considered alternatives, like mutually exclusive creatures and things. But when God, the Absolute, is thus dragged down into the realm of creatures and made to compete with them, the order of creatures, of society and convention, is blasted. For when the ear is singing, all other sounds are lost.

This is why Christian officialdom is itself the cause of

[1] Tr. Evans (1), vol. 1, p. 247.

the very secularism and shallow relativism which it so much condemns. For the secular revolution of the Renaissance and the Enlightenment and all that followed was a parody of the "mystery" which the Church had neglected. This was the strictly inner or sacred doctrine that in God, in reality, all men are free and equal, or, to put it in another way, that in God there are no classes or distinctions, no respect of persons. For the initiate into this mystery has

> put on the new man, which is renewed in knowledge after the image of him that created him: where there is neither Greek nor Jew, circumcision nor uncircumcision, Barbarian, Scythian, bond nor free; but Christ is all, and in all.[2]

A state Church, which is to say a profane Church, could not possibly admit or cherish such a doctrine, and thus when it was dragged out of neglect it became a pretext for revolution, and the Church could not claim it, saying, "Come, this is nothing new. We have known it all the time and are now ready to explain it to you correctly."

Instead, the Church virtually disowned its inner meaning, retreated into an ever more rigid identification of God with law, and abandoned the position beyond good and evil and beyond distinctions to the secularists. But here it became the position *below* good and evil. Standards were not transcended but rejected, and equality in the sight of God became the assumption that all men are equally inferior. Freedom became mere individualism, and the classless society a dull uniformity. Art became monotonous eccentricity, and craft monotonous mass production. These are sweeping generalizations to which there have been happy exceptions, but the consistent trend of the so-called modern or progressive spirit has been toward an obliteration of social distinctions which is, in effect, a dis-

[2] Colossians 3, 10–11.

organization of society. For the organic is always differentiated, in function if not in worth.

One of the most extreme forms of this parody is the attitude of so many Freudians which reduces all creative activity—art, philosophy, religion, and literature—to a manifestation of oral or anal eroticism, or infantile incestuousness, with the cynical implication that all men are thereby equally guilty. The transparent feeling of this attitude is not that these libidinous foundations are natural and pure, but that poets and sages can be debunked by being reduced to a level which, to these psychologists themselves, is still obscene. This resembles nothing so much as the "police psychology" which assumes that all men, the policemen included, are criminals and holds it over their heads. In such instances it comes out very clearly that this parody of the doctrine of equality is the tragic and destructive resentment of creativity by the underprivileged or unloved.

These are not, however, the people of *low* status: they are the people of *no* status, bred in profusion by a society which confuses the moral law with the divine nature. For such a society cannot give any status to what is low—to the gambler, courtesan, drunkard, beggar, sexual deviant, or tramp. In a system of absolutist morals such people have no place at all. They are unacceptable to God since there are no longer allowed to be any *least* in the Kingdom of Heaven, and his sun may no longer shine upon the unjust unless they consent to reform. But the unjust are not only special classes of people; unjust or unadjusted elements exist in every member of society as the ignored aspects of nature which do not fit in with *maya*, the conventional order. They are, in a technical sense, obscene or "off-scene" [3]

[3] On second thought I forget the source of the article in which I came across this suggestive but probably dubious derivation of the word. Ac-

because they do not come into the picture; they have no outward role or part in the social drama. Nevertheless, they are as essential to it as the stagehands behind the scenes, the faces behind the masks, and the bodies beneath the costumes.

But when the conventional order and the divine nature are confused, the unjust and the obscene become metaphysically sinful—absolutely intolerable to God. And what is intolerable to God becomes, in another way, intolerable to man. He cannot support a situation in which the ignored and obscene parts of his nature are brought out onto the stage and condemned. His only defense is to accuse the accusers, to unmask and unfrock everyone, saying, "Look, you are *really* just like me!" Yet this in its own way is just as much a mistake as the confusion which provoked it. The off-scene is not the *reality* behind the outward drama: it is also part of the illusion, for what is to be off-scene is determined by the selection of what is to be on-scene; what is ignored is relative to what is noticed. Herein is the error of supposing that repressed sexual forces are the realities behind cultural achievements, for the relationship between them is one of mutuality and not of subordination. While the evil is defined by the choice of the good, it is not the reality determining the choice.

Thus when the sacred idea of equality is profaned it turns out to be the parody that in reality, in God, all men are alike in their obscenity. What it should have meant

cording to the Oxford English Dictionary the etymology of "obscene" is unknown, whereas Webster derives it from *obs-caenum*, with *caenum* meaning "filth," though such a combination would ordinarily have appeared in English as "occene." However, the sense of "off-scene" is consistent with an alternative derivation from *ob-scaenum* (Greek, σκαιός), designating the left-hand, sinister, and inauspicious. For both the off-scene and the sinister have to do with the indispensable underside or dark aspect of things. Inauspicious as it may be, the left must always accompany the right.

is that in reality all men are alike in their essential inno-
cence—that the division of their natures into the good and
the evil, the on-scene and off-scene, is (in another original
sense of a word) *arbitrary* or a decision of an independent
spectator, none other than our old friend the isolated, observing ego. But to the eye of God there is no distinction
of on-scene and off-scene, and all men are just as they are,
as the Buddhists would say, of "one suchness." When the
curtain falls and all the actors come out in front with the
author and the director *as themselves* and no longer in
their roles, the hero and the villain, the men on-scene and
the men off-scene are alike applauded.

Therefore judge nothing before the time, until the Lord
come, who both will bring to light the hidden things of
darkness, and will make manifest the counsels of the hearts:
and then shall every man have praise of God.[4]

At times, however, the audience will be moved to boo.
But they will not boo the villain because he *was* the villain;
they will boo him, at the end of the play, if he did not act
true to character. They will boo if what should have stayed
off-scene has kept coming on-scene, or *vice versa*. In other
words, there is nothing wrong with the obscene so long as it

---

[4] 1 Corinthians 4, 5. St. Paul is often so quotable in senses that are
probably out of context and which would doubtless have horrified him.
However, I would like to see someone make a case for the idea that the
Apostles really did hand down an inner tradition to the Church, and that
through all these centuries the Church has managed to guard it from the
public eye. If so, it has remained far more secret and "esoteric" than in
any of the other great spiritual traditions of the world, so much so that
its existence is highly doubtful. For in the West the *philosophia perennis*
has always been an individual matter, often condemned and sometimes
barely tolerated by the official hierarchy. It would, however, be much
easier to make a case of this kind for the Eastern Orthodox Church than
for the Roman Catholic. On the other hand, a true esotericism is not a
matter of "secret information," formally withheld from public knowledge.
It is secret in the sense of ineffable, that is, a mode of knowledge which
cannot be described because it does not fall into any class.

remains off the scene and stays in its place. But in a moral absolutism it *has* no place—perhaps because the audience does not know that the play is a play. The social drama and its conventions are confused with reality.

The proper distinction of the sacred from the profane, and of the profane from the obscene, is of the utmost importance for a philosophy of love as between man and woman. Failure to see the difference between the sacred and the profane is one of the main reasons why the Christian tradition has no adequate idea of sacred love. For sacred love is not the love of God as an alternative to the love of creatures. Sacred love is not matrimony, though it may sometimes exist between the married. Nor is sacred love the "grand passion" in its popular and romantic sense. Just as we have a parody of equality before God in modern secularism, we have also a parody of sacred love which has arisen in much the same way.

It is common knowledge that the institution of marriage came to the West as a highly formal familial arrangement, a character which in some Latin countries it still retains. The founding of the branch of a family was by no means a matter of private choice, but a momentous decision involving many people. It was therefore arranged, not by the young couple, but by grandfathers and grandmothers, and stabilized by legal contracts which the modern version of the institution still involves. Whether the couple "loved" each other, or might come to do so, was a thing of minor importance. The marriage represented a familial alliance, and was governed by political, social, and—however "primitive"—eugenic considerations. In cultures where this form of marriage still exists, concubinage and other forms of extramarital sexuality flourish as a matter of course *for men,* even when tolerated rather than provided for by law. In general, such extramarital relations are off-scene, existing by a social agreement which is tacit but not explicit. Marriage was therefore a profane institution—a matter of communal convention as between people who were playing social roles. Therefore those who were above role, or, as in India, above caste, did not marry or at least abandoned marriage when the time came for their liberation from *maya*.

Now, Christianity arose in the West as an exceedingly strange mixture of social and religious ideas from many different sources. It comprised legal and social ideas of marriage that were mainly Jewish with notions of moral and spiritual chastity that were Greek or Essene, and probably garbled and remote influences from India. The resulting confusion was so involved that it may assist us to unravel it if we simply list the main factors that came into play:

1. The Jewish idea that the physical universe is inherently good.
2. The Orphic and garbled Indian idea that the physical universe is evil.
3. The Jewish institution of marriage as a property and familial arrangement.
4. The Jewish idea of the holiness of procreation, the duty of population increase, and the sin of sowing the human seed unprocreatively.
5. The Orphic-Essene-Indian idea of withdrawal from the flesh through nonprocreation, and thus of the greater holiness of virginity.
6. The Jewish idea of the sin of adultery as an infringement of property rights.
7. The generally Greco-Indian tradition that the holy or sacred person stands apart from social involvement.
8. The Jewish idea that the social conventions are the laws of God.

9. Jesus' own idea that women, too, have some rights since
   they are at least equal with men in having souls.

It is no wonder that an attempt to combine these ideas
plunged the relations between men and women into a
fearsome mess, though it may perhaps have been worth
while if only for the last idea involved—the recognition
that "women are people."

But to appreciate the full extent of the confusion we
must consider the fact that Indian ideas had reached the
West in an extremely popularized and literal form, a form
which they had of course assumed in India itself in the first
place. The main feature of this distortion was the confusion
of *maya* with evil on the one hand and with the natural
universe on the other. This involved the further confusion
of the virgin or sacred person with the totally abstinent,
the person withdrawn not only from society but also from
nature. But the original meaning of a *parthenos* or virgin
was a woman who did not submit to arranged marriage,
taking, instead, a partner of her own choice. She became
an "unmarried mother" not because she was vicious or
promiscuous, but because she was a person in her own
right.

Now the early Church combined all these diverse factors
by preserving the legal, familial marriage, restricting it to
one wife, and virtually outlawing divorce out of respect for
women's rights. Consistently, the next step would have
been to extend the tacit recognition of off-scene sexuality
to women, but instead it merely forbade it to men. Jesus
attacked divorce because a divorced woman was like mer-
chandise returned to the seller as unfit for use, as a result
of which she lost social status altogether. The important
point, however, was that the type of marriage which the
Church monogamized and protected against divorce, and

from which it excluded concubinage, was the familial *arranged* marriage.[5] Sexual love in any other sense than illicit and sinful lust is a matter which the New Testament totally ignores.[6]

In short, the Church combined the Jewish insistence on procreation and the Greco-Indian ideal of sexual abstinence in a form of marriage which would effect the greatest possible restriction of sexual feeling. In this way the profane institution of marriage was identified, or rather confused, with the sacred state of chastity, which was in turn mistaken for joyless sexuality or, preferably, abstinent virginity. As St. Paul said, "Let those with wives be as though they had none." The outcome, the sacrament of Holy Matrimony, was supposed to be the sanctification of the profane by the sacred by analogy with the union of the Word with the flesh in the Incarnation. But because

[5] "The girl is not consulted about her espousals, for she awaits the judgment of her parents, inasmuch as a girl's modesty will not allow her to choose a husband." St. Ambrose, *De Abraham,* i, *ad fin.* St. Basil, *Ep. ad Amphilocium,* ii, says that a marriage without paternal sanction is fornication, and under the laws of Constantius and Constans it was a capital offense.

[6] However, the celebrated text of Matthew 5, 28, imputing adultery to so much as looking on a woman to lust after her should be taken in context. The whole passage from verse 17 to the end is an ironical discussion of the legal righteousness of the Pharisees. Jesus shows the shallowness and absurdity of legal righteousness by taking it to an extreme. He begins with what to any but the most simple-minded literalist would be the obvious jest that the very punctuation marks and calligraphic ornaments of the law are now to be sacrosanct. He then arranges various types of anger and abuse in descending order of gravity, but assigns penalties for them in the reverse order. For unreasonable anger, the magistrate's court is assigned; for saying "Raca" or "silly idiot," the high court; and for saying "You fool," hellfire itself. But in Matthew 23, 17, Jesus uses the selfsame expression, "You fools" ($\mu\omega\rho\circ\iota$), in speaking to the followers of the Pharisees. In the verse in question he satirizes the property law against adultery by extending it to a similar extreme, and then goes on to recommend the excision of the lustful eye. The passage can be taken at its face value only on the assumption that Jesus was totally lacking in humor.

the Word and the Spirit, as conceived, were really antithetical to the flesh, and the sacred *opposed* to the profane, the coming together of the two was not a union but
an enslavement. Similarly, as the male stood for the spirit
and the female for the flesh, the wife had no choice of her
partner and must be subservient to her husband.

This was obviously a conception of marriage which could
not last, but it was some time before it was modified by the
exercise of mutual choice by the two partners. As the
Church became identified with the state and as its early
zeal flagged, Holy Matrimony was in practice modified in
many ways, mainly through reversion to polygyny, concubinage, and prostitution.[7] But the factor which transformed the Christian conception of marriage more than
anything else was the emergence in the early Middle Ages
of the cult of courtly love, which is the historical basis of
what we now know as the romantic conception of love and
marriage.

Historians are not in clear agreement as to the origins
and nature of this extraordinary movement, but the weight
of opinion is that the Catharist heresy, from which it arose,
was a form of the Persian religion of Manichaeism, of
which vestiges remained in Western Europe from the
days of the Roman Empire, or which was reintroduced by
returning crusaders. Now, Manichaeism was a syncretist
movement and seems to have been one of the principal car-
riers of distorted Indian ideas to the West. These included
an extreme dualism of spirit and nature reminiscent of the
Samkhya philosophy, and a conception of love as "pure desire" which is strangely similar to forms of the Indian cult
of Tantra, in which the arousal and transmutation of sexual desire was employed as a type of yoga. The spiritual
ideal of Manichaeism was the liberation of the world of

[7] G. R. Taylor (1), pp. 19–50.

light from the world of darkness, and thus the deliverance of the human spirit from its fleshly prison.

The conception of "pure desire" as well as the dualist distortion of the *maya* doctrine had, indeed, reached the West before the appearance of Catharism, for we find St. John Chrysostom, St. Gregory of Nazianzus, and St. Jerome condemning the spread among Christians of taking to themselves *agapetae* or *virgines subintroductae*. This was the practice of forming a love relationship with virgin Christian girls which went as far as caressing and sleeping with them, and perhaps involved *coitus reservatus*, but avoided actual emission of the seed. By this means sexual desire was not "dissipated" in orgasm but was restrained and built up into passion. To put it in another way, its restraint at the sexual center caused it to irradiate the whole organism, transmuting the atmosphere of sexual feeling into every phase of the relationship between the partners. In such a way sexual attraction was personalized. It became a desire not just for "woman," but for the particular woman whose whole body and whose day-to-day associations with her lover had become "perfumed" with restrained and irradiated lust. In this way, too, the beloved became idealized; she became more than mere woman; she became a goddess, image of the divine.

Repressed for a time by the official Church, the practice appeared again in Europe in the twelfth century, now in the form of Catharism and courtly love. But here the women involved were not only or chiefly virgins, but married women, often the wives of feudal princes, with whom young knights formed the bond of *donnoi*. This was apparently an "ideal" or "sexually pure" love relationship wherein sexual feeling was transmuted into all the attentions and gallantries which became expected of a *gentleman* toward a lady. These relationships formed the themes of troubadour poetry, the chief wellspring of all later European secular poetry, as well as the entire basis of the Western notion of ideal or romantic love.

Historians disagree as to whether these relationships were genuinely "ideal" or simply a cloak for refined adultery and fornication, the latter impression being founded on the many references in the poetic literature to caressing and embracing the naked body of the beloved lady. At the same time, there are equally frequent references to the absolute necessity of avoiding actual sexual intercourse, for as one of the poets said, "He knows nothing of *donnoi* who wants fully to possess his lady." Although, then, there is no direct evidence for the fact, the very ambiguity of the references suggests that the relationship often extended to *coitus reservatus* or, to use the Persian word, *karezza*—the prolonged sexual union without orgasm on the part of the male.

But whether *karezza* was employed or not, it is clear that courtly love introduced a contemplative as distinct from an active mode of sexuality—a distinction parallel to the religious differentiation between the contemplative and active lives. For the ideal of the troubadour was at least to gaze upon and worship the unveiled form of his lady. In this respect the troubadours had grasped one of the elements of sacred love, that is, of a love relationship consistent with and patterned after the contemplative life. It is important to remember that the contemplative life is not to be confused with the merely cloistered life, which, however, sometimes includes it. Essentially the contemplative life is the summit of spiritual insight—the vision or *theoria* of God—a realization permeating all one's ordinary and practical activities. In just the same way, the troubadour wished to contemplate his lady and have his whole life permeated by the atmosphere of her presence.

Although courtly love was adopted by individual members of the clergy and the *donnoi* relationship was often blessed with ecclesiastical rites, the cult was in the end subject to the most ruthless persecution which the Church has ever sponsored, prior to the Reformation. The Dominican campaign against the Cathars or Albigenses involved also an attempt to substitute the Virgin Mary for the idealized woman of courtly devotion. But the persecution never eradicated the process which changed Christian matrimony into the ideal of a fulfillment of romantic love—an ideal which, in later times, the Church itself adopted. Thus modern Catholic theories of Christian marriage differ so radically from the conceptions of the Patristic age just because they have absorbed so much from the philosophy of courtly love. This, rather than the few hints of the idea in the Gospels and St. Paul, is the real root of the modern Christian doctrine of married love. Few modern Catholic theologians regard matrimony as the mere restriction of sexual relations to one woman for the purpose of procreating Christian children. The emphasis has now passed to the idea of loving a woman as a person, as *this* woman rather than "woman," for in such a way marital love becomes analogous to God's own love, conceived as his eternal faithfulness to each and every individual person.

There is no doubt that this modern view of Holy Matrimony is a tremendous improvement upon what was originally nothing more than a rigid restriction of the arranged marriage and a total condemnation of sexual feeling. But it is still a parody of sacred love, and arises from the Church's inability to distinguish the profane from the sacred by making the two mutually exclusive, which is to say, of the same kind.[8]

---

[8] There are other instructive examples of the confusion. Thus the term "person," originally the *per-sona* or megaphone-mask indicating the as-

One of the best apologists for the modern ideal of Holy Matrimony is the Catholic-minded Protestant Denis de Rougemont, whose important work *Love in the Western World* is at the same time a marvellous clarification and a profound misunderstanding of the differences between sacred and profane love. The gist of his thesis is that mature sexual love is total devotion to the entirety of another human being—as distinct from bodily lust or passion, which he describes as being in love with being in love, passion in particular being an infatuation with the subjective feelings aroused by postponing sexual intercourse with an idealized woman. But he is surely mistaken in thinking that passion, as cultivated by the troubadours, stands alongside pure eroticism or "pagan love" in opposition to his own ideal of matrimony. For he sees both of the former as an attitude to woman in which she is merely the pretext for an ecstasy, whether it be self-frustrating passion or self-indulging lust. Yet the problem is not so simple, for it is precisely from courtly love that modern Christianity has obtained the idea that, in Holy Matrimony, sexual love may be completely fused with personal love.

We must repeat that in its early centuries Christianity had no conception of the hallowing of sexual feeling. Sexual intercourse between a married couple was pure to the

sumed role of the player in classical drama, is used to designate the basic spiritual reality of the human being and God alike. The human being is said to have spiritual dignity because he is a person, as God is three Persons. But a person is strictly what one is as a mask or role, at the social and conventional level. The word which should have been used for the ego is used for the self (*atman*) or spirit (*pneuma*), which in other traditions is supra-individual. Hence the Christian identification of the spirit with the ego, and the inability to see that man is more than ego, that his true and basic selfhood is divine. Another instance appears in the celibacy of the *secular* priesthood, indicating a confusion of the sacerdotal *caste* (profane) with the casteless (sacred) contemplatives —the monks and hermits who have abandoned worldly (or social) estate (or class). As we have seen, matters are made worse by the confusion of abandoning estate or status with abandoning nature.

extent that it was a brief physical exchange for procreation. The wife was loved and cherished inasmuch as, having an immortal soul, she was, after all, as good as another *man*. To lust after one's wife was little short of adultery. It was, then, from Manichaeans and Cathars that Christians learned the art of personalizing sexual desire, that is, of delaying the haste of lust so that sexual feeling would attach itself not merely to the subpersonal organs and limbs of the woman but to her total personality. The modern view of Holy Matrimony is therefore a middle position between the early Christian and the courtly, allowing sufficient passion, or delay of lust, to personalize the relationship and, unlike the Cathars, permitting the male orgasm so as to produce children and to prevent passion from becoming an end in itself. But the historical roots of this view are not purely Christian.

Even so, this conception of matrimony is far short of realizing what the sexual relationship may be at the sacred level. This is evident in the fact that de Rougemont identifies the sacred element in matrimony with fidelity to the legal or profane contract between the partners. As he sees it, the whole dignity and responsibility of being a person is realized in strength of will—in being able to stand by one's *word,* in the irrevocable decision of the couple to make their contractual pledge stand firm against all nonverbal, natural, fleshly, or emotional considerations. This is, he confesses, an absurdity against all practical reason, but such is precisely the divine absurdity of Christianity, of which Tertullian said, *Credo quia absurdum est*— "I believe because it is absurd."

> Forgoing any rationalist or hedonist form of apology, I propose to speak only of a troth that is observed *by virtue of the absurd*—that is to say, simply because it has been pledged—and by virtue of being an absolute which will up-

hold the husband and wife as persons. . . . I maintain that fidelity thus understood is the best means we have of becoming persons. The person is manifested in the making. What is person within each of us is an entity built up like a work of art—built up thanks to constructiveness and in the same conditions as we construct things. . . . Neither passion nor the heretical faith out of which it sprang could have inspired the belief that the control of Nature should be the aim of our lives.[9]

Here in a nutshell is the whole story of the identification of the absolute, the personal, and the divine with artifice in opposition to nature. In its original meaning the *persona*, the mask, is indeed a construct, a *maya* in its proper sense. But for this very reason it should have been distinguished from the divine and the absolute. For the divine, the real, is not the construct; it is the natural, nonverbal, and indescribable order (*li*) from which construction emerges and to which it is subordinate. To set the principle of artifice and construction outside and against nature is to tear the universe apart in such a way that the rift can only be healed upon the terms of the total submission of nature to the will and its legal violence. Such a view of the divinity of the law and the word issues in a conception of the marriage contract where man is made for the Sabbath, not the Sabbath for man. For man is held to acquire personality or spiritual dignity by submitting himself irrevocably to an absolute law. Faithfulness is thereby confused with complete mistrust of oneself, for on these terms the human organism is to be trusted only in so far as it binds itself to a law—a law which it has itself invented, and whose order and structure is far inferior to his own.

It was for this reason that Confucius made *jen* or "human-

[9] De Rougemont (1), pp. 307–8.

heartedness" a far higher virtue than *i* or "righteousness,"
and declined to give the former any clear definition. For
man cannot define or legalize his own nature. He may attempt to do so only at the cost of identifying himself with
an abstract and incomplete image of himself—that is, with
a mechanical principle which is qualitatively inferior to a
man. Thus Confucius felt that in the long run human passions and feelings were more trustworthy than human
principles of right and wrong, that the natural man was
more of a man than the conceptual man, the constructed
person. Principles were excellent, and indeed necessary,
so long as they were tempered with human-heartedness
and the sense of proportion or humor that goes with it.
War, for example, is less destructive when fought for greed
than for the justification of ideological principles, since
greed will not destroy what it wishes to possess, whereas
the vindication of principle is an abstract goal which is
perfectly ruthless in regard to the humane values of life,
limb, and property.

Zealots and fanatics of all kinds revolt at Confucian rea-
sonableness, with its spirit of compromise and mellow humor, feeling it to be ignoble and tame, lacking the heroism
and fire of irrevocable commitment to principle—and this
is precisely the attitude of Chinese Communism in its
present attempt to destroy the Confucian tradition.[10] But
from the Confucian standpoint the zealotry of irrevocable
commitment to principle is not only a silly bravado and a
striking of heroic attitudes; it is also a total insensitivity to
inner feeling and to the subtle intelligence of the natural
order. "The superior man," said Confucius in the *Analects*,
"goes through life without any one preconceived course of

[10] See Arthur F. Wright, "Struggle *versus* Harmony: Symbols of Com-
peting Values in Modern China," in Bryson, *et al.*, *Symbols and Values*,
pp. 589–602. Harper, New York, 1954.

action or any taboo. He merely decides for the moment what is the right thing to do." [11]

From our standpoint such a precept is the recommendation of caprice and disorder, for we feel that unless the artifice of law is held over our heads like a club we shall revert to our "basic" and "natural" depravity, as if this is what we really are under the "veneer" of civilization. This is not, however, what we are really, naturally, and basically. It is what we are off-scene, which, as we saw, is no more real than what we are on-scene. Unseemly disorderliness is, in fact, the last thing of which anyone would accuse followers of the Confucian and Taoist philosophies, since they have formed the foundations of one of the most stable societies in the world.

It will now be clear that we must discover the character of sacred love by analogy with the sacred or contemplative life in its other aspects. But it had first to be clear that the sacred is not in competition with the profane as if it were something of the same kind. In other words, the sacred is not in the conceptual and conventional order of things, and thus neither fights with them, avoids them, nor struggles to dominate them. It has no need to do so, for it is the superior order out of which they proceed and to which they are always eventually subordinate—and this is why every attempted escape from sexuality transforms itself into prurience. "Tao is that from which one cannot for a single instant depart. That from which one may depart is not Tao." [12]

In the life of spontaneity human consciousness shifts from the attitude of strained, willful attention to *kuan*, the attitude of open attention or contemplation. This at-

[11] Cf. de Rougemont (1), p. 308: "The pledge exchanged in marriage is the very type of a *serious* act, because it is a pledge given once and for all. The irrevocable alone is serious!"
[12] *Chung-yung, i.*

titude forms the basis of a more "feminine" and receptive
approach to love, an attitude which for that very reason
is more considerate of women. It will have been obvious
that most of the attitudes hitherto discussed are one-sidedly
and ridiculously male. Save among the practitioners of
karezza, they know nothing of the female orgasm, which,
for purposes of simple procreation, is almost irrelevant.
They are thus exclusively concerned with the rights and
wrongs of male pleasure in sex, and, furthermore, of a
male approach which is one-sidedly aggressive, domineer-
ing, and grasping. In short, they are attempts to make rules
for sexuality by people who knew extremely little about it.

The idea of equality in the sacred sphere has often been
taken to mean the disappearance of sexuality, since St.
Paul said that in Christ there is neither male nor female,
and Jesus said that in heaven there is neither marriage nor
giving in marriage. But the latter remark is only to say
that heaven, the sacred sphere, stands above the social
institutions of the profane sphere. Conversely, the secular
notion of sexual equality is one that merely permits women
to behave like men, and the two parodies, the Churchly
and the secular, are equally sexless rather than sexually
equal. Sexual equality should properly mean sexual fulfillment, the woman realizing her masculinity through man,
and the man realizing his femininity through woman. For
the "pure" male and the "pure" female have nothing in
common and no means of communication with each other.
They are cultural stereotypes and affectations. What a
real man or woman is always remains inconceivable, since
their reality lies in nature, not in the verbal world of concepts.

Sexual equality therefore implies a sexual life which is
free from, but not against, the profane definitions of man
and woman. It implies that they do not need to play roles

in loving each other, but enter into a relationship for which we may borrow words which St. Augustine used in another context, "Love—and do what you will." Given the open and mutually considerate attitude of attention to each other, they are in a situation where, without restraint, "anything goes."

Role-playing is so automatic that we seldom notice how deeply it pervades our lives, and readily confuse its attitudes with our own natural and genuine inclinations. This is so much so that the love relationship is often far more of an "act" than anything else. Love itself is frequently an assumed emotion which we believe we ought to feel. Its presence is supposed to be identifiable by certain known symptoms which men and women learn to expect in each other, and which we are very clever at imitating in such a way that the right hand does not know what the left is doing. Lovers are expected to be jealous of one another. The man is supposed to act protectively and the woman a little helplessly. The man is supposed to take the initiative in expressing love and the woman to wait longingly for his attentions. Certain types of feature, voice, and figure are supposed to be peculiarly lovable or sex-appealing, and the intimacies of sexual intercourse are governed by rituals in which the man is active and the woman passive, and in which the verbal and symbolic communications of love adhere to an extremely limited pattern.

Nor is this all, for roles lie within roles like the layers of an onion. The man playing husband to wife may also be playing son to mother, or the woman daughter to father. Or the normal role-playing may be dropped deliberately so as to assume the role of "naturalness," "sincerity," or "emancipatedness." Lustfulness itself may be subconsciously cultivated so that the man may assure himself that he is really male and gets from women the socially ex-

SACRED AND PROFANE LOVE 181

pected thrills and excitements. More than often we make love to prove that we are lovable, which is to say that we *can* identify ourselves with a role which is conventionally acceptable.

Anyone who becomes conscious of role-playing will swiftly discover that just about *all* his attitudes are roles, that he cannot find out what he is genuinely, and is therefore at a loss what to do to express himself sincerely. Thereupon he is self-conscious and blocked in his relationships, finding himself in the double-bind predicament where every road is closed. This leaves him in a state of complete paralysis if he persists in thinking that there is some "right" course of action and some particular set of feelings which constitute his real self. Where he expected to find the specific truth about himself he found freedom, but mistook it for mere nothingness. For human freedom does indeed comprise an order, yet because it is the nonlinear order of *li* and of the Tao, it cannot be classified; it cannot be identified with any particular role. Therefore at this point of the double bind he must wait, and see what happens of itself, spontaneously. He will find that the sensation that every road is barred abruptly switches into the sensation that every road is open. He can play all roles, just as in Hindu mythology the true self is pictured as the godhead acting all the parts of the multitude of finite creatures.

Strictly speaking, it is not quite true that one must *wait* for something to happen spontaneously. For the heart is beating, the breath is moving, and all the senses are perceiving. A whole world of experience is coming to the organism of itself, without the slightest forcing. This spontaneous arrival of experience is not actually passive; it is already spontaneous *action*. When it is watched and felt to be action in this sense, it flows naturally into further action. But blocking takes place if this action is ignored and its apparent passivity interpreted as "nothing happening." It is true that it may not be what was expected to happen, but then the expected is always liable to be forced rather than spontaneous. The constant action of spontaneous experiencing which, considered as an act, is the organism's creation of its world and the world's creation of the organism, is the basis and style of action from which love and its expressions arise. In this open and ungrasping mode of awareness the beloved, the other, is not possessed but is rather received into oneself with all the richness and splendor of the unpremeditated surprise.

In almost every culture love is an intimacy between two particular people in which conventions that govern other relationships are set aside. In this respect it already suggests, even if only symbolically, the sacred rather than the profane, and the lovers' removal of clothes in one another's presence is already a sign of taking off the personal mask and stepping out of role. Only a society which is seriously ignorant of the sacred could regard the taboo, the secrecy of love, as a cloak hiding an unfortunate but necessary reversion to animality. But this is just what would be expected in a culture which conceives of spirit as other than nature, and which tries to dominate the order of nature with the order of the word. To such a mentality the identification of sexuality with the sacred is a far more serious threat than the most crass and brutish bawdiness. Its censorship can tolerate sexuality so long as it is a matter of "dirty" jokes, or so long as it is kept at the merely physiological level of medical language, so long, in other words, as it is kept as far as possible from the sacred. The association of sexuality with the sacred conjures up the most superstitious fears and fantasies, including the suspicion that it must have something to do with Satanism and the weird practices of black magic and the left-hand path!

But if the union of lovers is already a symbolic transition from the profane to the sacred, from role to reality, it is a relationship peculiarly fitted for the actual realization of liberation from *maya*. Yet this can happen only if the minds and senses of the participants are in the state of open attention whereby nature is received in its unknown reality, since closed or strained attention can perceive only its projection of the known. Here is the ideal sphere for the type of awareness which Freud considered essential for psychoanalysis.

> For as soon as attention is deliberately concentrated in a certain degree, one begins to select from the material before one; one point will be fixed in the mind with particular clearness and some other consequently disregarded, and in this selection one's expectations or one's inclinations will be followed. This is just what must not be done, however; if one's expectations are followed in this selection there is danger of never finding anything but what is already known, and if one follows one's inclinations anything which is to be perceived will most certainly be falsified.[13]

It is commonly thought that, of all people, lovers behold one another in the most unrealistic light, and that in their encounter is but the mutual projection of extravagant ideals. But may it not be that nature has allowed them to see for the first time what a human being is, and that the subsequent disillusion is not the fading of dream into reality but the strangling of reality with an all too eager embrace?

[13] Freud (2), p. 324.

8: Consummation

LOVE BRINGS THE REAL, AND NOT JUST THE ideal, vision of what others are because it is a glimpse of what we are bodily. For what is ordinarily called the body is an abstraction. It is the conventional fiction of an object seen apart from its relation to the universe, without which it has no reality whatsoever. But the mysterious and unsought uprising of love is the experience of complete relationship with another, transforming our vision not only of the beloved but of the whole world. And so it remains until the relationship is itself abstracted by the anxiety of the grasping mind to be guarded from the rest of life as a possession.

The bodily and the physical is not to be mistaken for the world of atomic and discrete entities, and bodily union must not be confined to things so obviously visible as the juncture of Siamese twins. We need to recognize the physical reality of relationship between organisms as having as much "substance" as the organisms themselves, if not more. Thus however defective its doctrine of marriage in many respects, the Christian Church is perfectly correct in saying that husband and wife are one flesh. It is similarly correct to think of the members of the Church as the *Body* of Christ, especially if the Church is considered to be the process of realizing that the whole universe is the Body of Christ—which is what the doctrine of the Incarnation really implies.[1]

[1] Thus St. Cyril of Alexandria in *Epist. ad Rom.*, vi, says that in a sense the flesh of Christ "contained all nature, just as when Adam incurred

This makes it the more strange that conventional spirituality rejects the bodily union of man and woman as the most fleshly, animal, and degrading phase of human activity—a rejection showing the extent of its faulty perception and its misinterpretation of the natural world. It rejects the most concrete and creative form of man's relation to the world outside his organism, because it is through the love of a woman that he can say not only of her but also of all that is other, "This is my body."

Despite the Christian intuition of the world as the Body of Christ, the natural universe has been considered apart from and even opposed to God because it has not been experienced as one body. Considered as nothing more than a multiplicity of transient bodies, it appears that the natural world is finite and contingent upon something other than itself. No part of it remains, no part of it *is* being but only *has* being, and if the whole is only the sum of the parts, the whole cannot exist of itself. But all this comes from the failure to see that individual bodies are only the terms, the end-points, of relationships—in short, that the world is a system of inseparable relationships and not a mere juxtaposition of things. The verbal, piecemeal, and analytic mode of perception has blinded us to the fact that things and events do not exist apart from each other. The world is a whole greater than the sum of its parts because the parts are not merely summed—thrown together —but related. The whole is a pattern which remains, while the parts come and go, just as the human body is a dynamic pattern which persists despite the rapid birth and death of all its individual cells. The pattern does not, of course, exist disembodiedly apart from individual forms, but exists precisely through their coming and going—just as it is

condemnation the whole of nature contracted the disease of his curse in him."

through the structured motion and vibration of its electrons that a rock has solidity.

The naïve philosophical thinking upon which Western theology was founded assumed that what moved did not fully exist, since true existence must be stable and static. We see now that being and motion, mass and energy, are inseparable, and need no longer assume that what moves and changes is a defective form of reality. We can see that the eternal *is* the transient, for the changing panorama of sense experience is not just a sum of appearing and disappearings things: it is stable pattern or relationship manifested as and by transient forms. Our difficulty is that human consciousness has not adjusted itself to a relational and integrated view of nature. We must see that consciousness is neither an isolated soul nor the mere function of a single nervous system, but of that totality of interrelated stars and galaxies which makes a nervous system possible. We must come to *feel* what we know to be true in theory, to have a sense of ourselves compatible with what we know about the inseparability of the parts of nature.

In this light it will be clear that consciousness is no mere phosphorescent scum upon the foundations of fire and rock—a late addition to a world which is essentially unfeeling and mineral. Consciousness is rather the unfolding, the "e-volution," of what has always been hidden in the heart of the primordial universe of stars. For a universe in which consciousness is no more than a statistical probability is still a universe in which consciousness is implicit. It is in the living organism that the whole world feels: it is only by virtue of eyes that the stars themselves are light. Relationship is a kind of identity. The stars and human eyes are not mutually alien objects brought into relation by mere confrontation. Suns, stars, and planets provide the conditions in which and from which organisms can arise. Their peculiar structure *implies* organisms in such a way that, were there no organisms, the structure of the universe would be entirely different, and so that organisms, in their turn, imply a universe of just this structure. It is only the time lag and the immense complexity of the relations between stars and men which make it difficult to see that they imply one another just as much as man and woman, or the two poles of the earth.

The failure to realize the mutuality and bodily unity of man and the world underlies both the sensual and the ascetic attitudes. Trying to grasp the pleasure of the senses and to make their enjoyment the goal of life is already an attitude in which man feels divided from his experience, and sees it as something to be exploited and pursued. But the pleasure so gained is always fragmentary and frustrating, so that by way of reaction the ascetic gives up the pursuit, but not the sense of division which is the real root of the difficulty. He accentuates dividedness by pitting his will against the flesh, by siding with the abstract against the concrete, and so aggravates the very feeling from which the pursuit of pleasure arose. Ascetic spirituality is a symptom of the very disease which it intends to cure. Sensuality and conventional spirituality are not truly opposed; their conflict is a mock battle staged, unconsciously, by partisans to a single "conspiracy." [2]

Ascetic and sensualist alike confuse nature and "the body" with the abstract world of separate entities. Identifying themselves with the isolated individual, they feel inwardly incomplete. The sensualist tries to compensate

[2] See the marvellous discussion in L. L. Whyte (1), ch. 3, where the author attempts a physiological and historical analysis of the origins of the conflict. A current instance of this mock battle is the alliance of organized crime with conservative church groups to maintain the legal suppression of certain types of vice.

for his insufficiency by extracting pleasure, or complete-ness, from the world which appears to stand apart from him as something lacking. The ascetic, with an attitude of "sour grapes," makes a virtue of the lack. Both have failed to distinguish between pleasure and the pursuit of pleas-ure, between appetite or desire and the exploitation of desire, and to see that pleasure grasped is no pleasure. For pleasure is a grace and is not obedient to the com-mands of the will. In other words, it is brought about by the relationship between man and his world. Like mys-tical insight itself, it must always come unsought, which is to say that relationship can be experienced fully only by mind and senses which are open and not attempting to be clutching muscles. There is obviously nothing degrad-ing in sensuous pleasure which comes "of itself," without craving. But in fact there is no other kind of pleasure, and the error of the sensualist is not so much that he is doing something evil as that he is attempting the impossible. Naturally, it is possible to exercise the muscles in pur-suing something that may, or may not, give pleasure; but pleasure cannot be given unless the senses are in a state of accepting rather than taking, and for this reason they must not be, as it were, paralyzed and rigidified by the anxiety to get something out of the object.

All this is peculiarly true of love and of the sexual com-munion between man and woman. This is why it has such a strongly spiritual and mystical character when spon-taneous, and why it is so degrading and frustrating when forced. It is for this reason that sexual love is so prob-lematic in cultures where the human being is strongly iden-tified with the abstract separate entity. The experience neither lives up to expectations nor fulfills the relationship between man and woman. At the same time it is, frag-mentarily, gratifying enough to be pursued ever more relentlessly for the release which it seems to promise. Sex is therefore the virtual religion of very many people, the end to which they accord more devotion than any other. To the conventionally religious mind this worship of sex is a dangerous and positively sinful substitute for the worship of God. But this is because sex, or any other pleasure, as ordinarily pursued is never a true fulfillment. For this very reason it is *not* God, but not at all because it is "merely physical." The rift between God and nature would vanish if we knew how to experience nature, because what keeps them apart is not a difference of substance but a split in the mind.

But, as we have seen, the problems of sexuality cannot be solved at their own level. The full splendor of sexual experience does not reveal itself without a new mode of attention to the world in general. On the other hand, the sexual relationship is a setting in which the full opening of attention may rather easily be realized because it is so immediately rewarding. It is the most common and dramatic instance of union between oneself and the other. But to serve as a means of initiation to the "one body" of the universe, it requires what we have called a contemplative approach. This is not love "without desire" in the sense of love without delight, but love which is not contrived or willfully provoked as an escape from the habitual empty feeling of an isolated ego.

It is not quite correct to say that such a relationship goes far beyond the "merely sexual," for it would be better to say that sexual contact irradiates every aspect of the encounter, spreading its warmth into work and conversation outside the bounds of actual "love-making." Sexuality is not a separate compartment of human life; it is a radiance pervading every human relationship, but assuming a particular intensity at certain points. Conversely, we might say that sexuality is a special mode or degree of the total intercourse of man and nature. Its delight is an intimation of the ordinarily repressed delight which inheres in life itself, in our fundamental but normally unrealized identity with the world.

A relationship of this kind cannot adequately be discussed, as in manuals of sexual hygiene, as a matter of techniques. It is true that in Taoism and Tantric Buddhism there are what appear to be techniques or "practices" of sexual relationship, but these are, like sacraments, the "outward and visible signs of an inward and spiritual grace." Their use is the consequence rather than the cause of a certain inner attitude, since they suggest themselves almost naturally to partners who take their love as it comes, contemplatively, and are in no hurry to grasp anything from it. Sexual yoga needs to be freed from a misunderstanding attached to all forms of yoga, of spiritual "practice" or "exercise," since these ill-chosen words suggest that yoga is a method for the progressive achievement of certain results—and this is exactly what it is not.[3] Yoga means "union," that is, the realization of man's inner identity with Brahman or Tao, and strictly speaking this is not an end to which there are methods or means since it cannot be made an object of desire. The attempt to achieve it invariably thrusts it away. Yoga "practices" are therefore sacramental expressions or "celebrations" of this union, in rather the same sense that Catholics celebrate the Mass as an expression of Christ's "full, perfect, and *sufficient* sacrifice." Means are irrelevant to what is already sufficient. Thus contemplation or meditation which seeks a result is neither contemplation nor meditation, for the simple reason that contemplation (*kuan*) is consciousness without seeking. Naturally, such consciousness is concen-

[3] See the excellent discussion of this point in Guénon (1), pp. 261–67.

trated, but it is not "practicing concentration"; it is concentrated in whatever happens to be its "eternal now."

Sexual yoga or, as it is technically called, *maithuna* is a common theme of Hindu sculpture, though it has been suggested that its origins are Chinese, arriving in India as the backwash of the spread of Buddhism. Westerners, including missionaries and Theosophists and Indians under their influence, have rather naturally spread the idea that these images are pornographic, and that sexual yoga represents a perverse and depraved degeneration of Eastern spirituality. Such a reaction is only to be expected from spectators to whom the idea of spiritualized sexuality is completely unfamiliar. But such serious and responsible scholars as Woodroffe (1), S. B. Dasgupta (1), and Coomaraswamy (1) have made it plain not only that such images have no pornographic intention, but also that what they represent is at once a metaphysical doctrine and a sacrament at least as sacred as Christian matrimony. For the *maithuna* figures have nothing to do with promiscuous ritual orgies. On the one hand, they are emblems of the eternal union of spirit and nature; on the other, they represent the consummation of contemplative love between mutually dedicated partners.[4]

4 Woodroffe (1), p. 578, states that the partners are normally husband and wife, though in special circumstances, valid in a polygynous culture, the woman is a permanent wife-in-religion chosen because of spiritual compatibility with the man. The notion that sexual yoga is involved with "black magic" is one of the many distortions of Asian philosophy circulated by Theosophy—a Westernized version of Hindu-Buddhist teachings carrying over essentially Christian notions of evil. The Theosophists were in the first place misled by the fact that practitioners of sexual yoga adhered to the "left-hand path," a nomenclature to which they attached the purely Western associations of "sinister." But in Indian symbolism the right- and left-hand paths do not depart in opposite directions: they converge upon the same point like the two halves of a circle. The right-hand path seeks liberation by detachment from the world, and the left-hand by total acceptance of the world; the right is the—symbolically—male way, and the left the female, so that

The general idea of Tantric *maithuna,* as of its Taoist counterpart, is that sexual love may be transformed into a type of worship in which the partners are, for each other, incarnations of the divine. Perhaps this statement must be somewhat modified with respect to Buddhism and Taoism, to which the notion of worship is really foreign, and one must substitute the contemplation of nature in its true state. The embrace of *maithuna* involves also a transmutation of the sexual energy which it arouses, and this is described symbolically as sending it upwards from the loins to the head. Yoga, as is well known, involves a peculiar symbolism of human anatomy in which the spinal column is seen as a figure of the Tree of Life, with its roots in the nether world and its branches, or its flower, in the heavens beneath the "firmament" of the skull. The base of the spinal-tree is the seat of *kundalini,* the Serpent Power, which is an image of the divine life-energy incarnate in nature and asleep under the illusion of *maya.* Yoga consists in awakening the Serpent and allowing it to ascend the tree to the heavens, wherefrom it passes liberated through the "sun-door" at the apex of the skull. Thus when the Serpent is at the base of the spinal-tree it manifests its power as sexual energy; when it is at the crown it manifests itself as spiritual energy.

According to Tantric symbolism, the energy of the *kundalini* is aroused but simply dissipated in ordinary

in the left man finds liberation through nature and through woman. Hence the discipline is called *sahaja,* the natural or spontaneous way. It must furthermore be remembered that Theosophical attitudes reflected the nineteenth-century prudishness of middle-class England and America. A similar confusion was the Theosophical invention of a "lodge" of *"dugpas"* or black magicians, based on what was at the time mere hearsay about the now well-known Drug-pa Sect of Tibetan Buddhism. On the complex metaphysical symbolism of *maithuna* or *yab-yum* (Tibet) figures, see S. B. Dasgupta (1), pp. 98–134. The correspondence is not always strictly that of spirit and nature, but also of wisdom (*prajna*) and activity (*upaya*), voidness (*sunyata*) and compassion (*karuna*).

sexual activity. It can, however, be transmuted in a prolonged embrace in which the male orgasm is reserved and
the sexual energy diverted into contemplation of the divine
as incarnate in the woman.[5] The partners are therefore
seated in the cross-legged posture of meditation, the
woman clasping the man's waist with her thighs and her
arms about his neck. Such a position is clearly unsuitable
for motion, the point being that the partners should remain still and so prolong the embrace that the exchange
between them would be passive and receptive rather than
active. Nothing is *done* to excite the sexual energy; it is
simply allowed to follow its own course without being
"grasped" or exploited by the imagination and the will.
In the meantime the mind and senses are not given up
to fantasy, but remain simply open to "what is," without
—as we should say in current slang—trying to make something of it.

In trying to understand anything of this kind, the modern Westerner must be careful not to confuse the symbology of the *kundalini* and the ascension of the sexual
force with any physiological situation. Indeed, anatomical
symbolisms of this kind are so strange to us that they
hinder rather than help our comprehension of the real
intent. Furthermore, almost all ancient sexual ideas are
bound up with notions of the semen and its properties
which we no longer share, and thus we do not regard it as
a vital fluid to be conserved like blood. Our physiology does
not support the idea that the male orgasm is a debilitating
leakage of strength, and therefore the mere avoidance of
the orgasm will have little significance in any modern application of sexual yoga.

[5] The Taoist practice permits the orgasm in due course, and the female
orgasm was felt to nourish and strengthen the male force. See Needham
(1), vol. 2, pp. 149–50.

The importance of these ancient ideas to us lies not so much in their technicalities as in their psychological intent. They express an attitude to sexuality which, if absorbed by us today, could contribute more than anything else to the healing of the confusion and frustration of our marital and sexual relations. It remains, then, to separate the underlying sexual philosophy of Tantra and Taoism from symbolic and ritual elements which have no meaning for us, and to see whether it can be applied in terms of our own culture.

To clarify the basic intent of sexual yoga we must study its practice in context with the underlying principles of Buddhist and Taoist philosophy. For Buddhism the basic principle is to have one's consciousness undisturbed by *trishna,* or grasping desire, in such a way that the senses do not receive a distorted and fragmentary vision of the world. For Taoism the principle differs only in terminology: it is *wu-wei,* or noninterference with the Tao or course of nature, which is the organic and spontaneous functioning of man-in-relation-to-his-environment. Both involve the contemplative or open-sensed attitude to experience, the Buddhist *dhyana* (in Japanese, *zen*) and the Taoist *kuan.* In their respective yogas, both practice "watching over the breath" because the rhythm of breathing determines the total disposition of the organism. Now, their attitude to breathing is one of the main keys to understanding their attitude to sexuality.

According to some accounts, perfect mastery of the breath is attained when its rhythm comes to a total stop —without loss of life. This is obviously a literalistic caricature, based on a crude version of the meaning of *nirvana* —"breathed out." Actually, "watching over the breath" consists in letting the breath come and go as it wants, without forcing it or clutching at it. In due course its rhythm automatically slows down, and it flows in and out so smoothly that all rasping and hissing ceases *as if* it had stopped. This is both a symbol of and a positive aid to letting one's whole life come and go without grasping, since the way a person breathes is indicative of the way he lives.

In the sexual sphere the stopping of the male orgasm is just as much of a literalism as the stopping of breath; the point in both instances is not to stop but not to grasp. As contemplation of the breathing process automatically slows it down, sexual contemplation naturally delays the orgasm. For there is no value in prolonged and motionless intercourse as such; the point is to allow the sexual process to become spontaneous, and this cannot happen without the prior disappearance of the ego—of the forcing of sexual pleasure. Thus the orgasm is spontaneous (*tzu-jan*) when it happens of itself and in its own time, and when the rest of the body moves *in response* to it. Active or forced sexual intercourse is the deliberate imitation of movements which should ordinarily come about of themselves. Given the open attitude of mind and senses, sexual love in this spirit is a revelation. Long before the male orgasm begins, the sexual impulse manifests itself as what can only be described, psychologically, as a melting warmth between the partners so that they seem veritably to flow into each other. To put it in another way, "physical lust" transforms itself into the most considerate and tender form of love imaginable.

A valuable attempt to work out something of this kind for modern conditions has been made by von Urban (1), but for these purposes his approach is too much at the level of sexual hygiene and too preoccupied with technical directions that are somewhat inelastic and compulsive. Furthermore, just as the Tantric discussions are overlaid with their elaborate anatomical symbolism, von Urban has introduced some highly speculative ideas about electrical exchanges between sexual partners which resemble the "orgone" theories of Reich (1). But mechanistic symbolisms of mysterious "forces" and "fluids," to account for the intense feeling of interchange between the partners, are unnecessary in a philosophy of nature which gives due weight to the fact that organisms exist only by relation to each other and to their environment. Sexual love in the contemplative spirit simply provides the conditions in which we can be aware of our mutual interdependence and "oneness."

The point is so important that it can bear repetition: contemplative love—like contemplative meditation—is only quite secondarily a matter of technique. For it has no specific aim; there is nothing particular that has to be made to happen. It is simply that a man and a woman are together exploring their spontaneous feeling—without any preconceived idea of what it ought to be, since the sphere of contemplation is not what should be but what *is*. In a world of clocks and schedules the one really important technical item is the provision of adequate time. Yet this is not so much clock time as psychological time, the attitude of letting things happen in their own time, and of an ungrasping and unhurrying interchange of the senses with their objects. In default of this attitude the greater part of sexual experience in our culture falls far short of its possibilities.[6] The encounter is brief, the fe-

---

[6] Kinsey (1), p. 580, states that "for perhaps three-quarters of all males, orgasm is reached within two minutes after the initiation of the sexual relation, and for a not inconsiderable number of males the climax may be reached within less than a minute or even within ten or twenty seconds after coital entrance." He goes on to point out that this seems natural enough if man be compared with other mammals, but that unfortunately this makes it difficult for most women to experience the orgasm. He feels, therefore, that it is "demanding that the male be quite abnormal in his ability to prolong sexual activity without ejaculation if

male orgasm relatively rare, and the male orgasm precipitate or "forced" by premature motion. By contrast, the contemplative and inactive mode of intercourse makes it possible to prolong the interchange almost indefinitely, and to delay the male orgasm without discomfort or the necessity of diverting full attention from the situation. Furthermore, when the man has become accustomed to this approach, it is possible also for him to engage in active intercourse for a very much longer period, so affording the greatest possible stimulation for the woman.[7]

One of the first phases of contemplative love is the discovery of the depth and satisfaction of very simple contacts which are ordinarily called "preliminaries" to sexual activity. But in a relationship which has no goal other than itself, nothing is merely preliminary. One finds out what it can mean simply to look at the other person, to touch hands, or to listen to the voice. If these contacts are not regarded as leading to something else, but rather allowed to come to one's consciousness as if the source of activity lay in them and not in the will, they become sensations of immense subtlety and richness. Received thus, the ex-

he is required to match the female partner." It has been pointed out by Ford and Beach (1), pp. 30–31, that we have little evidence to show the extent of the female orgasm among mammals, but that it is supposedly rare or absent among the primates. However, the considerable physical differences between man and the higher mammals require caution in using these species to determine what is "natural" for man. Kinsey's statistical estimates, so often questioned, may be compared with those of Dickinson and Beam (1), quoted by Ford and Beach, p. 32, giving the duration of intercourse of a sample of 362 American couples as less than 10 minutes for 74 per cent and less than 20 minutes for 91 per cent.

[7] *Karezza*, or intercourse without the male orgasm (*coitus reservatus*), is also possible in this way, though there is considerable difference of opinion as to its psychological healthiness, especially when used frequently as a means of contraception. Possible psychological dangers are perhaps diminished by the great satisfaction of sexual contact alone in the contemplative mood. However the "spirituality" of *karezza* is connected with unverified notions about the sublimation of the semen and the loss of psychic "power" involved in its ejaculation.

ternal world acquires a liveliness which one ordinarily associates only with one's own bodily activity, and from this comes the sensation that one's body somehow includes the external world.

It was through the practice of *za-zen* or "sitting meditation" in this particular attitude that Japanese Zen Buddhists discovered the possibilities of such arts as the tea ceremony (*cha-no-yu*), wherein the most intense aesthetic delight is found in the simplest social association of drinking tea with a few friends. For the art developed into a contemplation of the unexpected beauty in the "primitive" and unpretentious utensils employed, and in the natural simplicity of the surroundings—the unchiselled mountain rocks in the garden, the texture of paper walls, and the grain of rough wooden beams. Obviously, the cultivation of this viewpoint can lead to an infinitely refined snobbery when it is done with an eye to oneself doing it—when, in other words, the point becomes not the objects of contemplation but the "exercise" of contemplating. For this reason, lovers who begin to relate themselves to each other in this way need not feel that they are practicing a skill in which there are certain standards of excellence which they *ought* to attain. It is simply absurd for them to sit down and *restrain* themselves just to looking at each other, while fighting off the intense desire to fall into each other's arms. The point is to discover the wonder of simple contacts, not the duty of it, for which reason it may be better at first to explore this type of relationship after intercourse than before.

The fact remains, however, that if they let themselves come gradually and gently into contact, they create a situation in which their senses can really work, so that when they have discovered what it can mean just to touch hands, the intimacy of a kiss or even of lips in near proximity re-

gains the "electric" quality which it had at the first meeting. In other words, they find out what the kiss *really* involves, just as profound love reveals what other people
really are: beings in relation, not in isolation.

If we say that from such contacts the movement toward
sexual intercourse grows of itself, it may be supposed that
this is no more than what ordinarily happens. Intimacy
just leads to passion; it certainly does not have to be willed.
But there is all the difference in the world between gobbling and actually tasting food when one is hungry. It is
not merely that appetite needs restraint; it needs awareness—awareness of the total process of the organism-environment moving into action of itself. As the lead and response of good dancers appears to be almost simultaneous,
as if they were a single entity, there comes a moment when
more intimate sexual contact occurs with an extraordinary
mutuality. The man does not lead and the woman follow;
the man-and-woman relationship acts of itself. The feeling
of this mutuality is entirely distinct from that of a man
initiating sexual contact with a perfectly willing woman.
His "advance" and her "response" seems to be the *same*
movement.

At a particular but unpredetermined moment they may,
for example, take off their clothes as if the hands of each
belonged to the other. The gesture is neither awkward nor
bold; it is the simultaneous expression of a unity beneath
the masks of social roles and proprieties by the revelation
and contact of the intimate and off-scene aspects of their
bodies. Now, these aspects are ordinarily guarded because
of their extreme sensitivity, or awareness of relationship.
Only the eyes are as sensitive, and in ordinary social intercourse prolonged eye-contact is avoided because of its
embarrassing intimacy—embarrassing because it creates
a sense of relationship belying and overpassing the sepa-

rative roles which we take so much trouble to maintain. For the sensitive organs of the body which we call most intimate and private are not, as might be supposed, the most central to the ego. On the contrary, they are those which most surpass the ego because their sensitivity brings the greatest contact with the outside world, the greatest intimacy with what is formally "other."

The psychic counterpart of this bodily and sensuous intimacy is a similar openness of attention to each other's thoughts—a form of communion which can be as sexually "charged" as physical contact. This is the feeling that one can express one's thoughts to the other just as they are, since there is not the slightest compulsion to assume a pretended character. This is perhaps the rarest and most difficult aspect of any human relationship, since in ordinary social converse the spontaneous arising of thought is more carefully hidden than anything else. Between unconscious and humorless people who do not know and accept their own limitations it is almost impossible, for the things which we criticize most readily in others are usually those of which we are least conscious in ourselves. Yet this is quite the most important part of a deep sexual relationship, and it is in some way understood even when thoughts are left unsaid.[8]

[8] Obviously, we are speaking here of a very special relationship which is seldom to be found in the ordinary marriage contracted between emotionally immature and socially rigid people, when the more mature partner should express his or her mind only with the utmost consideration for the other. Complete self-expression is really a form of self-indulgence in circumstances where it cannot be received. While it may sometimes be "good" for another person to be frank with them, husbands and wives should be the last people to take on programs of mutual improvement. It may be cynical, but it is good-naturedly and humanly so, to assume that one's spouse is going to remain just as he or she is, and that one is going to have to live with these limitations. If they are going to change at all, this is the only way to begin. For this is already an act of deep acceptance of the other person, which may become mutual by a kind of psychic osmosis.

It is significant that we commonly say that those with whom we can express ourselves most spontaneously are those with whom we can most fully be ourselves. For this already implies that the full and real self is not the willing and deliberating function but the spontaneous. In the same way that our most sensitive organs are guarded because they transcend and break the bonds of the ego, the flow of thought and feeling—though called one's "inner self"— is the most spontaneous and role-free activity of all. The more inward and central the form of activity, the less it partakes of the mask of the ego. To unveil the flow of thought can therefore be an even greater sexual intimacy than physical nakedness.

In contemplative love we do not speak of the sexual "act," since this puts intercourse into its own special dissociated compartment, where it becomes what Albert Jay Nock called very properly and humorously the "culbatising exercise." Perhaps one of the subordinate reasons why sex is a matter for laughter is that there is something ridiculous in "doing" it with set purpose and deliberation —even when described with so picturesque a phrase as the Chinese "flowery combat." Without wanting to make rules for this freest of all human associations, it is certainly best to approach it inactively. For when the couple are so close to each other that the sexual parts are touching, it is only necessary to remain quietly and unhurriedly still, so that in time the woman can absorb the man's member into herself without being actively penetrated.[9]

[9] Von Urban (1) does not recommend the cross-legged "Tantric" posture, which is naturally difficult for those not used to sitting in this way. Instead, he suggests lying at right angles to each other, the woman on her back with one leg between the man's thighs and the other resting on his hip. In this way the contact is purely genital and the whole relationship between the two "pours through" this center. While this is an excellent way of beginning, there is no need to make it a fixed rule, though there is an extraordinary intensity in letting the whole feeling-

It is at this juncture that simple waiting with open attention is most rewarding. If no attempt is made to induce the orgasm by bodily motion, the interpenetration of the sexual centers becomes a channel of the most vivid psychic interchange. While neither partner is working to make anything happen, both surrender themselves completely to whatever the process itself may feel like doing. The sense of identity with the other becomes peculiarly intense, though it is rather as if a new identity were formed between them with a life of its own. This life—one might say this Tao—lifts them out of themselves so that they feel carried together upon a stream of vitality which can only be called cosmic, because it is no longer what "you" and "I" are doing. Although the man does nothing either to excite or withhold the orgasm, it becomes possible to let this interchange continue for an hour or more, during which the female orgasm may occur several times with a very slight amount of active stimulation, depending upon the degree of her receptivity to the experience as a process taking charge of her.

In due course, both partners feel relieved of all anxiety as to whether orgasm will or will not happen, which makes it possible for them to give themselves up to whatever forms of sexual play may suggest themselves, however active or even violent. We say "suggest themselves" because this is a matter of immediate feeling rather than learned technique—a response to the marvellously overwhelming urge to turn themselves inside out for each other. Or it may happen that they prefer simply to remain still and let the process unfold itself at the level of pure feeling, which usually tends to be the deeper and more psychically satisfying way.

relationship pass through the sexual centers alone. The "absorption" of the male member depends, of course, upon the sufficient secretion of vaginal moisture.

Feelings which at the height of intercourse are often taken for the extremity of lust—that question-begging word—are simply the *ananda*, the ecstasy of bliss, which accompanies the experience of relationship as distinct from isolated selfhood. "Abandon" expresses the mood better than "lust," because the two individuals give themselves up to the process or relationship between them, and this abandonment of wills can become so intense that it feels like the desire to give up life itself—to die into the other person. De Rougemont (1) maintains—I think wrongly—that this "death wish" distinguishes mere passion or *eros* from divine love or *agape*. He feels that the former, being a purely creaturely love, seeks the nonbeing which was its origin, and that the latter is the love of the Creator which seeks life because its origin is pure Being. This entirely neglects the Christian mystery of Death and Resurrection, which is the Christian version of the more widely held truth that death and life are not opposed, but mutually arising aspects of a Whole—so that life emerges from plunging into death, and death from plunging into life. But the death wish in love is figurative, the giving up of life being a poetic image for the mystical, self-transcending quality of sexual transport. Death in the same figurative sense, as "dying to oneself," is commonly used in mystical literature for the process whereby the individual becomes divine. It is no more literal than the "death" of a grain of corn planted in the soil, or of a caterpillar sleeping in its chrysalis.

The mood of intense sexual delight is not, however, always quite so overwhelming as a desire to "die." The sense of "abandon" or of being carried out of oneself may equally find expression in gaiety, and this is peculiarly true when the experience brings a strong sense of fulfillment. Rare as such gaiety may be in cultures where there is a tie between sex and guilt, the release from self brings laughter in love-making as much as in mysticism, for we must remember that it was Dante who described the song of the angels in heaven as "the laughter of the universe." "Love," said Coventry Patmore, "raises the spirit above the sphere of reverence and worship into one of laughter and dalliance." This is above all true when the partners are not *working* at their love to be sure that they attain a "real experience." The grasping approach to sexuality destroys its gaiety before anything else, blocking up its deepest and most secret fountain. For there is really no other reason for creation than pure joy.

It is no matter for timing by the clock how long this play should continue. Let it be repeated again, its timeless quality is not attained by endurance or even duration, but by absence of purpose and hurry. The final release of orgasm, neither sought nor restrained, is simply allowed to "come," as even the popular expression suggests from our intuitive knowledge that it is not a deed but a gift and a grace. When this experience bursts in upon fully opened feelings it is no mere "sneeze in the loins" relieving physical tension: it is an explosion whose outermost sparks are the stars.

This may seem irreverent, or just claiming too much, to those who are unwilling to feel it completely, refusing to see anything mystical or divine in the moment of life's origin. Yet it is just in treating this moment as a bestial convulsion that we reveal our vast separation from life. It is just at this extreme point that we must find the physical and the spiritual to be one, for otherwise our mysticism is sentimental or sterile-pure and our sexuality just vulgar. Without—in its true sense—the lustiness of sex, religion is joyless and abstract; without the self-abandonment of religion, sex is a mechanical masturbation.

The height of sexual love, coming upon us of itself, is one

of the most total experiences of relationship to the other of which we are capable, but prejudice and insensitivity have prevented us from seeing that in any other circumstances such delight would be called mystical ecstasy. For what lovers feel for each other in this moment is no other than adoration in its full religious sense, and its climax is almost literally the pouring of their lives into each other. Such adoration, which is due only to God, would indeed be idolatrous were it not that in that moment love takes away illusion and shows the beloved for what he or she in truth is—not the socially pretended person but the naturally divine.

Mystical vision, as has always been recognized, does not remain at the peak of ecstasy. As in love, its ecstasy leads into clarity and peace. The aftermath of love is an anticlimax only when the climax has been taken and not received. But when the whole experience was received the aftermath finds one in a marvellously changed and yet unchanged world, and here we are speaking of spirituality and sexuality in the same breath. For the mind and senses do not now have to open themselves; they find themselves naturally opened, and it appears that the divine world is no other than the everyday world. Just as they come and just as they are, the simplest sights and sounds are sufficient, and do not have to be brushed aside in the mind's eagerness to find something more significant. One is thereby initiated from the world of clock time to the world of real time, in which events come and go of themselves in unforced succession—timed by themselves and not by the mind. As the accomplished singer does not *sing* a song but lets it sing itself with his voice—since otherwise he will lose the rhythm and strain the tone— the course of life is here seen to happen of itself, in a continuum where the active and the passive, the inward and the outward are the same. Here we have at last found the true place of man in nature which underlies the imagery of the Chinese poem:

> *Let us live*
> *Among the white clouds and scarlet woodlands,*
> *Singing together*
> *Songs of the Great Peace.*[10]

[10] *Teiwa shu, ii.* Tr. Ruth Sasaki, in *Zen Notes,* III, 10. New York, 1956.

Bibliographical References

This is neither a bibliography of the subject of this book nor a list of works read in its preparation, but simply a reference list of sources mentioned or quoted.

BATESON, G., with JACKSON, D. D., HALEY, J., and WEAKLAND, J. H. "Towards a Theory of Schizophrenia," *Behavioral Science*, vol. I, 4. October, 1956. Pp. 251–64.

BONPENSIERE, L. *New Pathways in Piano Technique*. Philosophical Library, New York, 1953.

BURROW, T. *Science and Man's Behavior*. Philosophical Library, New York, 1953.

CH'U TA-KAO. *Tao Te Ching*. The Buddhist Society, London, 1937.

COOMARASWAMY, A. K. *The Dance of Shiva*. Noonday Press, New York, 1957.

DASGUPTA, S. B. *An Introduction to Tantric Buddhism*. University of Calcutta Press, 1950.

DE ROUGEMONT, D. *Love in the Western World*. Pantheon Books, New York, 1956.

DICKINSON, R. L., and BEAM, L. *A Thousand Marriages*. Williams and Wilkins, Baltimore, 1931.

DODS, M. *The City of God* (St. Augustine). 2 vols. Clark, Edinburgh, 1872.

ECKERMANN, J. P. *Conversations of Goethe*. J. M. Dent, London, 1930.

ELLIS, H. *Studies in the Psychology of Sex*. 2-vol. ed. Random House, New York, 1942.

EVANS, C. de B. *Meister Eckhart*. 2 vols. Watkins, London, 1924.

FORD, C. S., and BEACH, F. A. *Patterns of Sexual Behavior*. Harper, New York, 1951.

FREUD, S. (1) *Civilization and Its Discontents*. Hogarth Press, London, 1949.

(2) *Collected Papers*. Vol. 2. Hogarth Press, London, 1924.

FUNG YU-LAN. *History of Chinese Philosophy*. 2 vols. Princeton University Press, 1953.

GILES, H. A. *Chuang-tzu*. Kelly and Walsh, Shanghai, 1926.

GILES, L. *Taoist Teachings*. Translations from Lieh-tzu. John Murray, London, 1925.

GUÉNON, R. *Introduction to the Study of the Hindu Doctrines*. Luzac, London, 1945.

HUME, D. *Treatise of Human Nature*. Oxford University Press, 1946.

JUNG, C. G. *Answer to Job*. Routledge, London, 1954.

KINSEY, A. C., POMEROY, W. B., and MARTIN, C. E. *Sexual Behavior in the Human Male*. Saunders, Philadelphia and London, 1948.

LIN YUTANG. (1) *My Country and My People*. Halcyon House, New York, 1938.

(2) *The Wisdom of Lao-tse*. Modern Library, New York, 1948.

NEEDHAM, J. *Science and Civilization in China*. Vol. 2. Cambridge University Press, 1956.

NORTHROP, F. S. C. *The Meeting of East and West*. Macmillan, New York, 1946.

REICH, W. *The Function of the Orgasm*. Orgone Institute Press, New York, 1948.

SIU, R. G. H. *The Tao of Science*. John Wiley, New York, 1957.

SUZUKI, D. T. (1) *Essays in Zen Buddhism*. Vol. 2. London and Kyoto, 1933. Repr., Rider, London, 1950.

(2) *Manual of Zen Buddhism*. Kyoto, 1935. Repr., Rider, London, 1950.

(3) *Training of the Zen Buddhist Monk*. Eastern Buddhist Society, Kyoto, 1934.

TAYLOR, G. R. *Sex in History*. Thames and Hudson, London, 1954.

VATSYAYANA. *Le Kama Soutra* (*Kamasutra*). J. Fort, Paris, n. d.

VON URBAN, R. *Sex Perfection and Marital Happiness*. Dial Press, New York, 1955.

WALEY, A. *The Nō Plays of Japan*. Allen and Unwin, London, 1950.

WATTS, A. W. (1) *The Supreme Identity*. Noonday Press, New York, 1957.

(2) *Myth and Ritual in Christianity*. Thames and Hudson, London, and Vanguard, New York, 1954.

WELCH, H. *The Parting of the Way*. Beacon Press, Boston, 1957.
WHITEHEAD, A. N. *Science and the Modern World*. Cambridge University Press, 1933.
WHYTE, L. L. *The Next Development in Man*. Henry Holt, New York, 1948.
WOODROFFE, Sir J. *Shakti and Shakta*. Luzac, London, 1929.
ZIMMER, H. (1) *Myths and Symbols in Indian Art and Civilization*. Pantheon Books (Bollingen Series), New York, 1946.
(2) *Philosophies of India*. Pantheon Books (Bollingen Series), New York, 1951.
(3) *The Art of Indian Asia*. 2 vols. Pantheon Books (Bollingen Series), New York, 1955.

Psychotherapy
East and West

FOR JANO

CONTENTS

Preface

THE subject of this book has been "in the air" for at least thirty years, and during this time there has been an ever-growing discussion of this or that parallel between Western psychotherapy and Eastern philosophy. But thus far no one has attempted, comprehensively, to find some basic design common to the methods and objectives of psychotherapy, on the one hand, and the disciplines of Buddhism, Vedanta, Yoga, and Taoism, on the other. The latter are not, perhaps, psychotherapies in the strict sense, but there is enough resemblance to make the comparison important.

The discussion seems to have begun in the early 1930's, following such works as Richard Wilhelm's translation of a Chinese text, *The Secret of the Golden Flower,* with a long psychological commentary by C. G. Jung (1929), G. R. Heyer's *Der Organismus der Seele* (1932), and Geraldine Coster's *Yoga and Western Psychology* (1934). I have been deeply interested in this fruitful interchange between East and West almost from its beginnings. I also made some contribution to it in a rather immature book called *The Legacy of Asia and Western Man* (1937), and a little later in *The Meaning of Happiness* (1940), which bore the subtitle "The Quest for Freedom of the Spirit in Modern Psychology and in the Wisdom of the East." At that time, almost the only form of psychotherapy which was thus "oriented" was the Jungian. But subsequent developments both in psychotherapy and in our knowledge of Eastern thought have made it possible for us to make much wider and more suggestive comparisons. The same period has also seen an astonishing growth of Western interest in Eastern ways of life, particularly in Zen Buddhism, and the latest contribution to this interchange is the collaboration of Erich Fromm and D. T. Suzuki in *Zen Buddhism and Psychoanalysis* (1960).

My purpose in writing this book is not, however, to sum up or review the development of this discussion. It is rather to give it a new turn. Before the writing began, I saw that there were two main ways of handling the subject. Since I have read almost everything that has been written about it, I saw that I could weave all this material into a kind of critical history of psychiatric interest in Eastern thought, combined with a point-by-point comparison of all the major forms of psychotherapy and all the principal techniques of the Eastern disciplines. But this would have produced an unwieldy volume of rather academic interest; furthermore, such formal studies are not my forte, and I leave them very gladly to those who have the necessary patience and industry. The other way was to describe what I feel to be the most fruitful way in which Eastern and Western psychotherapies can fertilize one another. For not only have they much to learn from each other, but also it seems to me that the comparison brings out hidden and highly important aspects of both. I decided, therefore, to write not a compendium of sober conclusions, but a provocative essay which may jolt both parties to the discussion. For I feel that both are fumbling in the dark, though not without some light. Wonderful as I have found them, I do not

believe that the Eastern disciplines are the last word in
sacrosanct and immemorial wisdom such that the world
must come and sit humbly at the feet of their masters.
Nor do I feel that there is a gospel according to Freud,
or to Jung, in which the great psychological truths are
forever fixed. The aim of this book is not to say the last
word on the subject, but to provoke thought and experiment.

My chosen approach to the subject does, however,
have the disadvantage of not being able to give adequate
mention to all the people who have influenced my thinking,
or sufficient recognition to all who have contributed to
the discussion. Conversations that were held and books
that were read long ago become so much a part of the
stream of one's own thinking that it is impossible, sometimes, to say which ideas are one's own and which are
borrowed. This book does not therefore make explicit
what may have come from my early reading of such speculative and adventurous therapists as Trigant Burrow,
Georg Groddeck, and my friend Eric Graham Howe. It
does not specify what I have gained over the years from
discussion of its main theme with Professor Frederic
Spiegelberg, of Stanford University, or with Dr. Lillian
Baker and the late Dr. Charles G. Taylor, both Jungian
analysts. Nor does it acknowledge the contributions which
have been made to the subject by Medard Boss, Hubert
Benoit, Henry Dicks, and Lili Abegg, in Europe; by Shoma
Morita, Takehisa Kora, and Akihisa Kondo in Japan; or by
Karen Horney, Harold Kellman, Joseph Campbell, Mar-
garet Rioch, and many others in the United States.

But the reader will quickly recognize, in the book's
underlying philosophy of the universe as organic and

transactional, my debt to A. N. Whitehead, Joseph Needham, L. L. Whyte, A. F. Bentley, and the Gestalt psychologists. If he has read my other books, he will also see
the more recent influence of what I must call, to distinguish them from the neo-Freudians like Horney and
Fromm, the "meta-Freudians" Norman O. Brown and
Herbert Marcuse. He will also note my increasing respect
for the "communication psychology" of Gregory Bateson
and his associates, particularly Jay Haley, which goes
hand in hand with my growing preference for discussing
these matters in a language that is more scientific and
less metaphysical.

He will find, therefore, that I place more weight upon
the connection of the Eastern disciplines with forms of
psychotherapy whose philosophy is social, interpersonal,
and communicational than with those which stress "the
unconscious" and its archetypal images. Even though
the discussion of this interchange between East and West
has so largely been carried on by those who follow the
latter trend, I cannot help feeling that it is becoming
more and more of a backwater in the development of
Western psychiatry, despite the debt which we shall always owe to Freud. Psychoanalysis in particular and
"depth psychology" in general seem to me to be increasingly out of touch with all that has been going on in the
sciences of human behavior during the last thirty years,
and many of us are wondering seriously how long it will
be possible for psychology, the study of an alleged psyche,
to remain a department of science.

In addition to the influences mentioned above, this
book has not been prepared without a great deal of
discussion with persons actively engaged in psychother-

apy. During the past few years I have had the privilege of conducting seminars upon its subject and of being a guest lecturer at many medical schools, hospitals, and psychiatric institutes—including the Yale Medical School, the Langley-Porter Clinic of the University of California, the C. G. Jung Institute in Zürich, the Washington School of Psychiatry, the Palo Alto Veterans' Hospital, the Stanford Medical School, and many state psychiatric hospitals. My thanks are due to all those responsible for these opportunities.

ALAN WATTS

San Francisco, 1960

Psychotherapy East and West

I

Psychotherapy
and Liberation

IF we look deeply into such ways of life as Buddhism
and Taoism, Vedanta and Yoga, we do not find either
philosophy or religion as these are understood in the West.
We find something more nearly resembling psychotherapy. This may seem surprising, for we think of the latter
as a form of science, somewhat practical and materialistic
in attitude, and of the former as extremely esoteric religions concerned with regions of the spirit almost entirely
out of this world. This is because the combination of our
unfamiliarity with Eastern cultures and their sophistication gives them an aura of mystery into which we project
fantasies of our own making. Yet the basic aim of these
ways of life is something of quite astonishing simplicity,
beside which all the complications of reincarnation and
psychic powers, of superhuman mahatmas, and of schools
for occult technology, are a smoke screen in which the
credulous inquirer can lose himself indefinitely. In fair-
ness it should be added that the credulous inquirer may be
Asian as well as Western, though the former has seldom
the peculiarly highbrow credulity of the Western fancier
of esotericism. The smoke is beginning to clear, but for
a long time its density has hidden the really important

contributions of the Eastern mind to psychological knowledge.

The main resemblance between these Eastern ways of life and Western psychotherapy is in the concern of both with bringing about changes of consciousness, changes in our ways of feeling our own existence and our relation to human society and the natural world. The psychotherapist has, for the most part, been interested in changing the consciousness of peculiarly disturbed individuals. The disciplines of Buddhism and Taoism are, however, concerned with changing the consciousness of normal, socially adjusted people. But it is increasingly apparent to psychotherapists that the normal state of consciousness in our culture is both the context and the breeding ground of mental disease. A complex of societies of vast material wealth bent on mutual destruction is anything but a condition of social health.

Nevertheless, the parallel between psychotherapy and, as I have called them (1), the Eastern "ways of liberation" is not exact, and one of the most important differences is suggested by the prefix *psycho-*. Historically, Western psychology has directed itself to the study of the psyche or mind as a clinical entity, whereas Eastern cultures have not categorized mind and matter, soul and body, in the same way as the Western. But Western psychology has to some extent so outgrown its historical origins as to become dissatisfied with the very term "psychological" as describing a major field of human behavior. It is not that it has become possible, as Freud himself once hoped, to reduce psychology to neurology and mind to body. It is not that for the entity "mind" we can substitute the entity "nervous system." It is rather that psychology cannot stand aloof from the whole revolution in scientific description which has been going on in this twentieth century, a revolution in which conceptions of entities and "stuffs," whether mental or material, have become obsolete. Whether it is describing chemical changes or biological forms, nuclear structures or human behavior, the language of modern science is simply concerned with changing patterns of relationship.

Perhaps this revolution has affected physics and biology far more deeply than psychology and as yet the theoretical ideas of psychoanalysis remain untouched. The common speech and the common sense of even educated society has been so little affected that it is still hard to convey in some nonmathematical language what has happened. It seems an affront to common sense that we can describe the world as patterns of relationship without needing to ask what "stuff" these patterns are "made of." For when the scientist investigates matter or stuff, he describes what he finds in terms of structured pattern. When one comes to think of it, what other terms could he use? The sensation of stuff arises only when we are confronted with patterns so confused or so closely knit that we cannot make them out. To the naked eye a distant galaxy looks like a solid star and a piece of steel like a continuous and impenetrable mass of matter. But when we change the level of magnification, the galaxy assumes the clear structure of a spiral nebula and the piece of steel turns out to be a system of electrical impulses whirling in relatively vast spaces. The idea of stuff expresses no more than the experience of coming to a limit at which our senses or our instruments are not fine enough to make out the pattern.

Something of the same kind happens when the scientist investigates any unit of pattern so distinct to the naked eye that it has been considered a separate entity. He finds that the more carefully he observes and describes it, the more he is *also* describing the environment in which it moves and other patterns to which it seems inseparably related. As Teilhard de Chardin has so well expressed it (2), the isolation of individual, atomic patterns "is merely an intellectual dodge."

> Considered in its physical, concrete reality, the stuff [*sic*] of the universe cannot divide itself but, as a kind of gigantic "atom," it forms in its totality . . . the only real indivisible. . . . The farther and more deeply we penetrate into matter, by means of increasingly powerful methods, the more we are confounded by the interdependence of its parts. . . . It is impossible to cut into this network, to isolate a portion without it becoming frayed and unravelled at all its edges.

In place of the inarticulate cohesion of mere stuff we find the articulate cohesion of inseparably interconnected patterns.

The effect of this upon the study of human behavior is that it becomes impossible to separate psychological patterns from patterns that are sociological, biological, or ecological. Departments of knowledge based upon what now appear to be crude and primitive divisions of nature begin to coalesce into such awkwardly named hybrids as neuropsychiatry, sociobiology, biophysics, and geopolitics. At a certain depth of specialization the divisions of scientific knowledge begin to run together because they are far enough advanced to see that the world itself runs together, however clear-cut its parts may have seemed to be. Hence the ever-increasing discussion of the need for a "unified science" and for a descriptive language common to all departments of science. Hence, too, the growing importance of the very science of description, of communication, of the patterns of signs and signals which represents and elucidates the pattern of the world.

Although the ancient cultures of Asia never attained the rigorously exact physical knowledge of the modern West, they grasped in principle many things which are only now occurring to us (3). Hinduism and Buddhism are impossible to classify as religions, philosophies, sciences, or even mythologies, or again as amalgamations of all four, because departmentalization is foreign to them even in so basic a form as the separation of the spiritual and the material. Hinduism, like Islam and Judaism, is really a whole culture, though the same cannot be said of Buddhism. Buddhism, in common with such aspects of Hinduism as Vedanta and Yoga, and with Taoism in China, is not a culture but a critique of culture, and enduring nonviolent revolution or "loyal opposition" to the culture with which it is involved. This gives these ways of liberation something in common with psychotherapy beyond the interest in changing states of consciousness. For the task of the psychotherapist is to bring about a reconciliation between individual feeling and social norms without, however, sacrificing the integrity of the individual. He tries to help the individual to be himself and to go it alone without giving unnecessary offense to his community, to be in the world (of social convention) but not of the world. A Chinese Buddhist text describes the sage in words that strongly suggest Riesman's "inner-directed" or Maslow's "self-actualizing" personality:

He walks always by himself, goes about always by himself;
Every perfect one saunters along one and the same
  passage of Nirvana;
His tone is classical, his spirit is transparent, his
  airs are naturally elevated,
His features are rather gaunt, his bones are firm, he
  pays no attention to others. (4)

From Freud onward, psychotherapy has been concerned with the violence done to the human organism and its functions by social repression. Whenever the therapist stands with society, he will interpret his work as adjusting the individual and coaxing his "unconscious drives" into social respectability. But such "official psychotherapy" lacks integrity and becomes the obedient tool of armies, bureaucracies, churches, corporations, and all agencies that require individual brainwashing. On the other hand, the therapist who is really interested in helping the individual is forced into social criticism. This does not mean that he has to engage directly in political revolution; it means that he has to help the individual in liberating himself from various forms of social conditioning, which includes liberation from hating this conditioning—hatred being a form of bondage to its object. But from this point of view the troubles and symptoms from which the patient seeks relief, and the unconscious factors behind them, cease to be merely psychological. They lie in the whole pattern of his relationships with other people and, more particularly, in the social institutions by which these relationships are governed: the rules of communication employed by the culture or group. These include the conventions of language and law, of ethics and aesthetics, of status, role, and identity, and of cosmology, philosophy, and religion. For this whole social complex is what provides the individual's conception of himself, his state of consciousness, his very feeling of existence. What is more, it provides the human organism's idea of its individuality, which can take a number of quite different forms.

Seeing this, the psychotherapist must realize that his science, or art, is misnamed, for he is dealing with something far more extensive than a psyche and its private troubles. This is just what so many psychotherapists are recognizing and what, at the same time, makes the Eastern ways of liberation so pertinent to their work. For they are dealing with people whose distress arises from what may be termed *maya*, to use the Hindu-Buddhist word whose exact meaning is not merely "illusion" but the entire world-conception of a culture, considered as illusion in the strict etymological sense of a play (Latin, *ludere*.) The aim of a way of liberation is not the destruction of *maya* but seeing it for what it is, or seeing through it. Play is not to be taken seriously, or, in other words, ideas of the world and of oneself which are social conventions and institutions are not to be confused with reality. The rules of communication are not necessarily the rules of the universe, and man is not the role or identity which society thrusts upon him. For when a man no longer confuses himself with the definition of himself that others have given him, he is at once universal and unique. He is universal by virtue of the inseparability of his organism from the cosmos. He is unique in that he is just *this* organism and not any stereotype of role, class, or identity assumed for the convenience of social communication.

There are many reasons why distress comes from con-

fusing this social *maya* with reality. There is direct conflict between what the individual organism is and what
others say it is and expect it to be. The rules of social
communication often contain contradictions which lead
to impossible dilemmas in thought, feeling, and action.
Or it may be that confusion of oneself with a limiting
and impoverished view of one's role or identity creates
feelings of isolation, loneliness, and alienation. The mul-
titudinous differences between individuals and their social contexts lead to as many ways of seeking relief from
these conflicts. Some seek it in the psychoses and neuroses
which lead to psychiatric treatment, but for the most
part release is sought in the socially permissible orgies
of mass entertainment, religious fanaticism, chronic sexual titillation, alcoholism, war—the whole sad list of
tedious and barbarous escapes.

Naturally, then, it is being said that the need for psychotherapy goes far beyond that of those who are clini-
cally psychotic or neurotic, and for many years now
increasing numbers of people have been receiving psychotherapy who would formerly have sought counsel from
a minister of religion or a sympathetic friend. But no one
has yet discovered how to apply psychotherapy on a mass
basis. Trained therapists exist in a ratio of about one to
eight thousand of the population, and the techniques of
psychotherapy are lengthy and expensive. Its growing
popularity is due in large measure to the prestige of
science and thus of the therapist as a scientific rather
than religious soul-doctor. Yet I know of few reputable
psychiatrists who will not admit, at least in private, that
their profession is still far from being a science. To begin
with, there is no generally accepted theory or even ter-

minology of the science, but rather a multiplicity of conflicting theories and divergent techniques. Our knowledge of neurology, if this should prove to be the basis
of psychiatry, is as yet extremely limited. To make things
worse, there is still no clear evidence that psychotherapy
is anything more than a hit-or-miss placebo, and, save
in the case of psychotic symptoms that can be controlled
by certain drugs, there is no sure way of distinguishing
its "cures" from spontaneous remission. And some of its
techniques, including lobotomy and shock treatment, are
nothing but measures of sheer desperation.

Nevertheless, the profession is on the whole a patient
and devoted fraternity, receptive to all manner of new
ideas and experiments. Even if it does not know what
sense to make of it, an enormous amount of detailed
information has been collected, and there is a growing
realization that, to make any progress, psychiatry must
ally itself more closely with neurology and biology on
one side and with sociology and anthropology on the
other. We must ask, then, to what other milieu in our
society we can look for anything to be done about the
distress of the individual in his conflict with social institutions which are self-contradictory, obsolete, or need-
lessly restricting—including, it must be repeated, the
current notion of the individual himself, of the skin-
encapsulated ego.

That many people now consult the psychotherapist
rather than the minister is not due simply to the fact that
science has greater prestige than religion. Many Protestant and Jewish theological seminaries include courses
of instruction in "pastoral psychiatry," comprising periods
of internship in mental hospitals. Furthermore, religion

has been so liberalized that in all metropolitan and many rural areas one has not far to go to find a minister who will listen to no matter what individual difficulty with the greatest sympathy and generosity, and often with considerable intelligence. But what hinders the minister in resolving conflicts between the individual and social institutions is precisely his own role. He represents a church, a community, and almost without exception religious communities work to establish social institutions and not to see through them. This is not to say that most religious groups abstain from social criticism, since this would be very far from true. Most religious groups oppose *some* social institutions quite vigorously, but at the same time they inculcate others without understanding their conventional nature. For those which they inculcate they claim the authority of the will of God or the laws of nature, thus making it extremely difficult for their members to see that social institutions are simply rules of communication which have no more universal validity than, say, the rules of a particular grammar. Furthermore, however sympathetic the minister of religion may be, in the back of his mind there is almost always the desire to bring the individual back into the fold of his church.

The Jewish and Christian idea of salvation means precisely membership in a community, the Communion of Saints. Ideally and theoretically the church as the Body of Christ is the entire universe, and because in Christ "there is neither Greek nor Jew, bond nor free," membership in Christ *could* mean liberation from *maya* and its categories. It could mean that one's conventional definition and classification is not one's real self, that "I live, yet no longer I; but Christ lives in me." But in practice it means nothing of the kind, and, for that matter, one hears little even of the theory. In practice it means accepting the religion or bondage of the Christian subgroup, taking its particular system of conventions and definitions to be the most serious realities. Now one of the most important Christian conventions is the view of man as what I have called the "skin-encapsulated ego," the separate soul and its fleshly vehicle together constituting a personality which is unique and ultimately valuable in the sight of God. This view is undoubtedly the historical basis of the Western style of individuality, giving us the sensation of ourselves as isolated islands of consciousness confronted with objective experiences which are quite "other." We have developed this sensation to a particularly acute degree. But the system of conventions which inculcates this sensation *also* requires this definitively isolated ego to act as the member of a body and to submit without reserve to the social pattern of the church. The tension so generated, however interesting at times, is in the long run as unworkable as any other flat self-contradiction. It is a perfectly ideal context for breeding psychosis. Yet, as we shall see, it would also be an ideal context for therapy if responsible religious leaders were aware of the contradiction and did not take it seriously. In other words, the minister might become an extraordinarily helpful person if he could see through his own religion. But his training and his economic situation do not encourage him to do so, and therefore the psychotherapist is in a more advantageous position.

Thus far, then, we have seen that psychotherapy and the ways of liberation have two interests in common:

first, the transformation of consciousness, of the inner feeling of one's own existence; and second, the release of the individual from forms of conditioning imposed upon him by social institutions. What are the useful means of exploring these resemblances so as to help the therapist in his work? Should he take practical instruction in Yoga, or spend time in a Japanese Zen monastery—adding yet more years of training to medical school, psychiatric residency, or training analysis? I do not feel that this is the point at all. It is rather that even a theoretical knowledge of other cultures helps us to understand our own, because we can attain some clarity and objectivity about our own social institutions by comparing them with others. It helps us to distinguish between social fictions, on the one hand, and natural patterns and relationships, on the other. If, then, there are in other cultures disciplines having something in common with psychotherapy, a theoretical knowledge of their methods, objectives, and principles may enable the psychotherapist to get a better perspective upon what he himself is doing.

This he needs rather urgently. For we have seen that at the present time psychology and psychiatry are in a state of great theoretical confusion. It may sound strange to say that most of this confusion is due to unconscious factors, for is it not the particular business of these sciences to understand "the unconscious"? But the unconscious factors bearing upon psychotherapy go far beyond the traumas of infancy and the repressions of anger and sexuality. For example, the psychotherapist carries on his work with an almost wholly unexamined "philosophical unconscious." He tends to be ignorant, by reason of his highly specialized training, not only of the contemporary philosophy of science, but also of the hidden metaphysical premises which underlie all the main forms of psychological theory. Unconscious metaphysics tend to be bad metaphysics. What, then, if the metaphysical presuppositions of psychoanalysis are invalid, or if its theory depends on discredited anthropological ideas of the nineteenth century? Throughout his writings Jung insists again and again that he speaks as a scientist and physician and not as a metaphysician. "Our psychology," he writes, "is . . . a science of mere phenomena without any metaphysical implications." It "treats all metaphysical claims and assertions as mental phenomena, and regards them as statements about the mind and its structure that derive ultimately from certain unconscious dispositions" (5). But this is a whopping metaphysical assumption in itself. The difficulty is that man can hardly think or act at all without some kind of metaphysical premise, some basic axiom which he can neither verify nor fully define. Such axioms are like the rules of games: some give ground for interesting and fruitful plays and some do not, but it is always important to understand as clearly as possible what the rules are. Thus the rules of tick tack toe are not so fruitful as those of chess, and what if the axioms of psychoanalysis resemble the former instead of the latter? Would this not put the science back to the level of mathematics when geometry was only Euclidean?

Unconscious factors in psychotherapy include also the social and ecological contexts of patient and therapist alike, and these tend to be ignored in a situation where two people are closeted together in private. As Norman O. Brown has put it:

There is a certain loss of insight in the tendency of psychoanalysis to isolate the individual from culture. Once we recognize the limitations of talk from the couch, or rather, once we recognize that talk from the couch is still an activity in culture, it becomes plain that there is nothing for the psychoanalyst to analyze except these cultural projections— the world of slums and telegrams and newspapers—and thus psychoanalysis fulfils itself only when it becomes historical and cultural analysis. (6)

Is not this a way of saying that what needs to be analyzed or clarified in an individual's behavior is the way in which it reflects the contradictions and confusions of the culture?

Now cultural patterns come to light and hidden metaphysical assumptions become clear only to the degree that we can step outside the cultural or metaphysical systems in which we are involved by comparing them with others. There are those who argue that this is simply impossible, that our impressions of other cultures are always hopelessly distorted by our own conditioning. But this is almost a cultural solipsism, and is equivalent to saying that we can never really be in communication with another person. If this be true, all study of foreign languages and institutions, and even all discourse with other individuals, is nothing but extending the pattern of one's own ignorance. As a metaphysical assumption there is no way of disproving it, but it offers nothing in the way of a fruitful development.

The positive aspect of liberation as it is understood in the Eastern ways is precisely freedom of play. Its negative aspect is criticism of premises and rules of the "social game" which restrict this freedom and do not allow what we have called fruitful development. The Buddhist *nirvana* is defined as release from *samsara,* literally the Round of Birth and Death, that is, from life lived in a vicious circle, as an endlessly repetitious attempt to solve a false problem. *Samsara* is therefore comparable to attempts to square the circle, trisect the angle, or construct a mechanism of perpetual motion. A puzzle which has no solution forces one to go over the same ground again and again until it appears that the question which it poses is nonsense. This is why the neurotic person keeps repeating his behavior patterns—always unsuccessfully because he is trying to solve a false problem, to make sense of a self-contradiction. If he cannot see that the problem itself is nonsense, he may simply retreat into psychosis, into the paralysis of being unable to act at all. Alternatively, the "psychotic break" may also be an illegitimate burst into free play out of sheer desperation, not realizing that the problem is impossible not because of overwhelming difficulty, but because it is meaningless.

If, then, there is to be fruitful development in the science of psychotherapy, as well as in the lives of those whom it intends to help, it must be released from the unconscious blocks, unexamined assumptions, and unrealized nonsense problems which lie in its social context. Again, one of the most powerful instruments for this purpose is intercultural comparison, especially with highly complex cultures like the Chinese and Indian which have grown up in relative isolation from our own, and especially with attempts that have been made within those cultures to find liberation from their own patterns. It is hard to imagine anything more constructive to the psychotherapist than the opportunity which this affords. But to make use of it he must overcome the habitual notion that he has nothing to learn from "prescientific" disciplines, for in the case of psychotherapy this may be a matter of the pot calling the kettle black. In any event, there is no question here of his adopting Buddhist or Taoist practices in the sense of becoming converted to a religion. If the Westerner is to understand and employ the Eastern ways of liberation at all, it is of the utmost importance that he keep his scientific wits about him; otherwise there is the morass of esoteric romanticism which awaits the unwary.

But today, past the middle of the twentieth century, there is no longer much of a problem in advocating a hearing for Eastern ideas. The existing interest in them is already considerable, and they are rapidly influencing our thinking by their own force, even though there remains a need for much interpretation, clarification, and assimilation. Nor can we commend their study to psychotherapists as if this were something altogether new. It is now thirty years since Jung wrote:

> When I began my life-work in the practice of psychiatry and psychotherapy, I was completely ignorant of Chinese philosophy, and it is only later that my professional experiences have shown me that in my technique I had been unconsciously led along that secret way which for centuries has been the preoccupation of the best minds of the East. (7)

An equivalence between Jung's analytical psychology and the ways of liberation must be accepted with some reservations, but it is important that he felt it to exist. Though the interest began with Jung and his school, suspect among other schools for its alleged "mysticism," it has gone far beyond, so much so that it would be a fair undertaking to document the discussions of Eastern ideas which have appeared in psychological books and journals during the past few years.[1]

The level at which Eastern thought and its insights may be of value to Western psychology has been admirably stated by Gardner Murphy, a psychologist who, incidentally, can hardly be suspected of the taint of Jung's "mysticism." He writes:

> If, moreover, we are serious about understanding all we can of personality, its integration and disintegration, we must understand the meaning of depersonalization, those experiences in which individual self-awareness is abrogated and the individual melts into an awareness which is no longer anchored upon selfhood. Such experiences are described by Hinduism in terms of the ultimate unification of the individual with the atman, the super-individual cosmic entity which transcends both selfhood and materiality. . . . Some men desire such experiences; others dread them. Our problem here is not their desirability, but the light which they throw on the relativity of our present-day psychology of personality. . . . Some other mode of personality configuration, in which self-awareness is less emphasized or even lacking, may prove to be the general (or the fundamental). (8)

It is of course a common misapprehension that the change of personal consciousness effected in the Eastern ways of liberation is "depersonalization" in the sense of regression to a primitive or infantile type of awareness. Indeed, Freud designated the longing for return to the

---

[1] Under the heading of "Contributions from Related Fields," the recent *American Handbook of Psychiatry* (Basic Books, New York, 1959) contains full articles by Eilhard von Domarus on Oriental "religions" and by Avrum Ben-Avi on Zen Buddhism.

oceanic consciousness of the womb as the *nirvana*-principle, and his followers have persistently confused all ideas of transcending the ego with mere loss of "ego strength." This attitude flows, perhaps, from the imperialism of Western Europe in the nineteenth century, when it became convenient to regard Indians and Chinese as backward and benighted heathens desperately in need of improvement by colonization.

It cannot be stressed too strongly that liberation does not involve the loss or destruction of such conventional concepts as the ego; it means seeing through them—in the same way that we can use the idea of the equator without confusing it with a physical mark upon the surface of the earth. Instead of falling below the ego, liberation surpasses it. Writing without apparent knowledge of Buddhism or Vedanta, A. F. Bentley put it thus:

> Let no quibble of skepticism be raised over this questioning of the existence of the individual. Should he find reason for holding that he does not exist in the sense indicated, there will in that fact be no derogation from the reality of what does exist. On the contrary, there will be increased recognition of reality. For the individual can be banished only by showing a plus of existence, not by alleging a minus. If the individual falls it will be because the real life of men, when it is widely enough investigated, proves too rich for him, not because it proves too poverty-stricken. (9)

One has only to look at the lively and varied features and the wide-awake eyes of Chinese and Japanese paintings of the great Zen masters to see that the ideal of personality here shown is anything but the collective nonentity or the weakling ego dissolving back into the womb.

Our mistake has been to suppose that the individual is

honored and his uniqueness enhanced by emphasizing his separation from the surrounding world, or his eternal difference in essence from his Creator. As well honor the hand by lopping it from the arm! But when Spinoza said that "the more we know of particular things, the more we know of God," he was anticipating our discovery that the richer and more articulate our picture of man and of the world becomes, the more we are aware of its relativity and of the interconnection of all its patterns in an undivided whole. The psychotherapist is perfectly in accord with the ways of liberation in describing the goal of therapy as individuation (Jung), self-actualization (Maslow), functional autonomy (Allport), or creative selfhood (Adler), but every plant that is to come to its full fruition must be embedded in the soil, so that as its stem ascends the whole earth reaches up to the sun.

II

Society and Sanity

THOUGH it cannot as yet be shown that a society is a body of people in the same way that a man is a body of cells, it is clear that any social group is something more than the sum of its members. People do not live in mere juxtaposition. To sum is to collect things together in a one-to-one correspondence with a series of numbers, and the relationship between 1 and 2 and 3 and 4 is so simple that it does not begin to resemble the relationship of people living together. A society is people living together in a certain pattern of behavior—a pattern which makes such physical traces as roads and the structure of towns, codes of law and language, tools and artifacts, all of which lay down "channels" determining the future behavior of the group. Moreover, a society is not "made up" of people in the same way that a house is composed of bricks, or even in the same way that an army is gathered together by recruitment. Strictly speaking, society is not so much a thing as a process of action which is really indistinguishable from human beings and animals, and from life itself. That no human organism exists without male and female parents is already society.

As a pattern of behavior, society is above all a system of people in communication maintained by *consistent* action. To keep the system going, what is done has to be consistent with what has been done. The pattern is recognizable as a pattern because it goes ahead with reference to its own past; it is just this that establishes what we call order and identity, a situation in which trees do not suddenly turn into rabbits and in which one man does not suddenly behave like another so that we do not know who he is. "Who" is consistent behavior. System, pattern, coherence, order, agreement, identity, consistency are all in a way synonymous. But in a pattern so mobile and volatile as human society, maintaining consistency of action and communication is not easy. It requires the most elaborate agreements as to what the pattern is, or, to put it in another way, as to what are the rules, the consistencies, of the system. Without agreement as to the rules of playing together there is no game. Without agreement as to the use of words, signs, and gestures there is no communication.

The maintenance of society would be simple enough if human beings were content just to survive. In this case they would be simply animals, and it would be enough to eat, sleep, and reproduce. But if these are their basic needs, human beings go about getting them in the most complicated way imaginable. If what must be done to survive is work, it would seem that the main concern of human beings is to play, yet at the same time pretending that most of such play is work. When one comes to think of it, the boundary between work and play is vague and changeable. Both are work in the sense that they expend energy; but if work is what *must* be done to survive, may we not ask, "But is it really necessary to survive? Is not survival, the continuation of the consistent pattern of the organism, a form of play?" We must be careful of the anthropomorphism which asserts that animals hunt and eat *in order* to survive, or that a sunflower turns *in order* to keep its face to the sun. There is no scientific reason to suppose that there are such things as instincts for survival or for pleasure. When we say that an organism *likes* to go on living, or that it goes on living because it likes it, what evidence is there for this "like" except that it does in fact go on living—until it doesn't? Similarly, to say that we always choose what we prefer says no more than that we always choose what we choose. If there is a basic urge to live, there must also, as Freud thought, be a basic urge to die. But language and thought are cleaner without these ghostly instincts, urges, and necessities. As Wittgenstein says, "A necessity for one thing to happen because another has happened does not exist. There is only *logical* necessity" (10).

An enduring organism is simply one that is consistent with its environment. Its climate and its food agree with it; its pattern assimilates them, eliminating what does not agree, and this consistent motion, this transformation of food and air into the pattern of the organism, is what we call its existence. There is no mysterious necessity for this to continue or discontinue. To say that the organism *needs* food is only to say that it *is* food. To say that it eats *because* it is hungry is only to say that it eats when it is ready to eat. To say that it dies because it cannot find food is only another way of saying that its death is the same thing as its ceasing to be consistent with the environment. The so-called causal explanation of an event is only the description of the same event in other words. To quote Wittgenstein again, "At the basis of the whole modern view of the world lies the illusion that the so-called laws of nature are the explanations of natural phenomena" (11).

More complex organisms, such as human beings, are more complex consistencies, more complex transformations of the environment. Not only are they patterns of transforming food, but their agreement or consistency with the environment changes nuclear vibrations into sound and light, weight and color, taste and smell, temperature and texture, until finally they generate elaborate patterns of signs and symbols of great interior consistency. When these mesh with the environment it becomes possible to describe the world in terms of sign patterns. The world is thus transformed into thought in the same way that food was transformed into body. The agreement or consistency of body pattern or thought pattern with the pattern of the world goes on as long as it goes on. To say *why* it starts or stops is only to describe particular consistencies or inconsistencies.

To say that there is no necessity for things to happen as they do is perhaps another way of saying that the world is play. But this idea is an affront to common sense because the basic rule of human societies is that one *must* be consistent. If you want to belong to our society, you must play our game—or, simply, *if* we are going to be consistent, we *must* be consistent. The conclusion is substituted for the premise. But this is understandable because, as we have seen, human society is so complex and volatile that consistency is difficult to maintain. Children keep slipping out of the patterns of behavior that we try to impose upon them, and for this and similar reasons our social conventions have to be maintained by force. The first rule of the game, put in another way, is that the game must continue, that the survival of the society is necessary. But we must not lose sight of the fact that the consistencies or regularities of nature are patterns that do occur, not patterns that must occur. Natural events do not obey commandments in the same way that human beings obey the law.[1]

Or put in still other words, the first rule of the game is that this game is *serious*, i.e., is not a game. This might be called the primordial "repression." By this I do not mean that it is an event at the temporal beginnings of human life, but rather that it may be our most deeply ingrained social attitude. But just as soon as we feel that certain things, such as survival, are serious necessities, life becomes problematic in a very special sense quite different from, say, the problems of chess or of science. Life and problem become the same; the human situation becomes a predicament for which there is no solution. Man then behaves as a self-frustrating organism, and this behavior can be seen in many different ways. For example, one of our greatest assets for survival is our sense of time, our marvellously sensitive memory which enables us to predict the future from the pattern of the past. Yet awareness of time ceases to be an asset when concern for the future makes it almost impossible to live fully in the present, or when increasing knowledge of the future makes it increasingly certain that, beyond a brief span, we have no future. If, too, man's growing sensitivity requires that he become more and more aware of himself as an individual, if social

[1] In his superb essay on "Human Law and the Laws of Nature" in Vol. 2 of *Science and Civilization in China*, Joseph Needham has shown that, largely because of Taoist influence, Chinese thought has never confused the order of nature with the order of law. As a way of liberation Taoism of course brings to light the manner in which men project their social institutions upon the structure of the universe.

institutions are designed more and more to foster the unique person, we are not only in great danger of over-population but we are also betting and concentrating upon man in his most vulnerable and impermanent form.[2]

This self-frustrating activity is *samsara,* the vicious circle from which the ways of liberation propose release. Release depends upon becoming aware of that primordial repression which is responsible for the feeling that life is a problem, that it is serious, that it *must* go on. It has to be seen that the problem we are trying to solve is absurd. But this means far more than mere resignation to fate, far more than the stoic despair of recognizing that human life is a losing battle with the chaos of nature. That would amount only to seeing that the problem has no solution. We should then simply withdraw from it and sit aloof in a kind of collective psychosis. The point is not that the problem has no solution, but that it is so meaningless that it need not be felt as a problem. To quote Wittgenstein again:

> For an answer which cannot be expressed the question too cannot be expressed. *The riddle* does not exist. If a question can be put at all, then it *can* also be answered. ... For doubt can only exist where there is a question; a question only where there is an answer, and this only where something can be *said.* We feel that even if *all possible* scientific questions be answered, the problems of life have still not been touched at all. Of course there is then no question left, and just this is the answer. The solution of the problem of life is seen in the vanishing of this problem. (Is not this the reason why men

[2] This is perhaps comparable to a shift in the level of magnification so as to observe the individual members of a colony of microorganisms instead of its over-all behavior.

to whom after long doubting the sense of life became clear, could not then say wherein this sense consisted?) (12)

When a psychiatrist asked a Zen master how he dealt with neurotic people he replied, "I trap them!" "And just how do you trap them?" "I get them where they can't ask any more questions!"

But the idea that human life need not be felt as a problem is so unfamiliar and seemingly implausible that we must go more deeply into the social origins of the problematic feeling. In the first place, the opposition of human order to natural chaos is false. To say that there is no natural necessity is *not* to say that there is no natural order, no pattern or consistency in the physical world. After all, man himself is part of the physical world, and so is his logic. But it should not be hard to see that the kind of order which we call logical or causal necessity is a subtype of order, a kind of order which appears in the world but is not characteristic of it as a whole. Similarly, the order of the rational integers 1, 2, 3, etc., is in the world, but mathematics would be a poor tool for describing the world if it were confined to simple arithmetic. We could say that the order of probability describes the world better than the order of causality. This is the same sort of truth as that a man with a saw can cut wood better than a man with a stone ax. The world is to us as we have means of assimilating it: patterns of thought-language in whose terms we can describe it. Yet these patterns are physical events, just as much as those which they describe. The point is surely that the world has no *fixed* order. We could almost say that the world is ordering itself ever more subtly both by means of and as the behaviors of living organisms.

We saw that primitive organisms consist with their environments by the transformation of food, etc., into the patterns of their bodies. This can be put the other way around by saying that environments consist with organisms by being of such a nature that this is possible. Ecologists speak of the evolution of the environment as well as the evolution of the organism. As Dewey and Bentley (13), Angyal (14), Brunswik (15), and many others have suggested, organism/environment is a unified pattern of behavior somewhat like a field in physics—not an interaction but a transaction. As Gardner Murphy has put it:

> We cannot define the situation operationally except in relation to the specific organism which is involved; we cannot define the organism operationally . . . except in reference to the situation. Each serves to define the other. (16)

To define operationally is to say what happens, to describe behavior, and as soon as we do this we find that we are talking about transactions. We cannot describe movements without describing the area or space in which they occur; we would not know that a given star or galaxy was moving except by comparing its position with others around it. Likewise, when we describe the world as completely as we can, we find that we are describing the form of man, for the scientific description of the world is actually a description of experiments, of what *men do* when they investigate the world. Conversely, when we describe the form of man as completely as we can—his physical structure, as well as his behavior in speech and action—we find that we are describing the world. There is no way of separating them except by not looking too carefully, that is, by ignorance.

The human behavior that we call perception, thought, speech, and action is a consistency of organism and environment of the same kind as eating. What happens when we touch and feel a rock? Speaking very crudely, the rock comes in touch with a multitude of nerve ends in our fingers, and any nerve in the whole pattern of ends which touches the rock "lights up." Imagine an enormous grid of electric light bulbs connected with a tightly packed grid of push buttons. If I open my hand and with its whole surface push down a group of buttons, the bulbs will light up in a pattern approximately resembling my hand. The shape of the hand is "translated" into the pattern of buttons and bulbs. Similarly, the feeling of a rock is what happens in the "grid" of the nervous system when it translates a contact with the rock. But we have at our disposal "grids" far more complex than this—not only optical and auditory, but also linguistic and mathematical. These, too, are patterns into whose terms the world is translated in the same way as the rock is translated into nerve patterns. Such a grid, for example, is the system of co-ordinates, three of space and one of time, in which we feel that the world is happening even though there are no actual lines of height, width, and depth filling all space, and though the earth does not go *tick-tock* when it revolves. Such a grid is also the whole system of classes, or verbal pigeonholes, into which we sort the world as things or events, still or moving; light or dark; animal, vegetable, or mineral; bird, beast, or flower; past, present, or future.

It is obvious, then, that when we are talking about the order and structure of the world, we are talking about the order of our grids. "Laws, like the law of causation, etc., treat of the network and not of what the network describes" (17). In other words, what we call the regularities of nature are the regularities of our grids. For regularity cannot be noticed except by comparing one process with another—e.g., the rotation of the earth about the sun with the strictly measured rotation of the clock. (The clock, with its evenly spaced seconds and minutes, is here the grid.) In the same way, what appear to be necessities of nature as a whole may be no more than necessities of grammar or mathematics. When anyone says that an unsupported body which is heavier than air *necessarily* falls to the ground, the necessity is not in nature but in the rules of definition. If it did not fall to the ground, it would not fit what we mean by "heavier than air." Consider the way in which a great deal of mathematical thinking is actually done. The mathematician does not ask whether his constructions are applicable, whether they correspond to any constructions in the natural world. He simply goes ahead and *invents* mathematical forms, asking only that they be consistent with themselves, with their own postulates. But every now and then it subsequently turns out that these forms can be correlated, like clocks, with other natural processes.

The puzzling thing is that some of the "grids" which we invent work, and some do not. In the same way, some animal behaviors seem to fit the environment and some do not. Those of ants, for example, have remained stable for millions of years, but the huge fangs of the saber-toothed tiger, the vast bulk of the saurians, and the great nose horns of the titanotheres were experimental failures. It would perhaps be more exact to say that they worked for a while, but not for as long as the experiments of other species. But what seems to happen in most of these cases is that the organism/environment relationship "splits": the organism's attack upon or defense against the environment becomes too strong, so isolating it from its source of life. Or it may be that the organism is too conservative for a swiftly changing environment, which is really the same situation: the pattern is too rigid, too insistent on survival, and thus again isolated. Or it may be that the organism, considered as a field in itself, is in self-contradiction: the weight of the nose horn is too much for the muscles. Turning to the human species, we may wonder whether such a split is taking place in the development of the over-isolated consciousness of the individual.

If this be so, we must be careful of a false step in reasoning. We must not say to the individual, "Watch out! If you want to survive you must *do* something about it!" Any action along these lines will simply make things worse; it will simply confirm the individual in his feeling of separation. It will become, like the nose horn, a survival mechanism frustrating survival. But if it is not up to the individual to do something, what is there to be said or done, and to whom and by whom?

Is it entirely unreasonable to suppose that the situation may correct itself, that the "field pattern" man/universe may be intelligent enough to do so? If this happens, or is happening, it will at first appear that individuals are initiating the changes on their own. But as the required change takes place, the individuals involved will simultaneously undergo a change of consciousness revealing the illusion of their isolation. May not something of the same kind be happening when a research worker, thinking that he has made an independent discovery, learns to his astonishment that several other people hit upon it at about the same time? As scientists sometimes say, the *field* of research had developed to the point where this particular discovery might naturally break out at several places.[3]

If we turn now to the social institution of language, or the "grid of words," we can easily see the ways in which it may be splitting organism from environment, and aspects of the environment from one another. Languages with such parts of speech as nouns and verbs obviously translate what is going on in the world into particular things (nouns) and events (verbs), and these in turn "have" properties (adjectives and adverbs) more or less separable from them. All such languages represent the world as if it were an assemblage of distinct bits and particles. The defect of such grids is that they screen out or ignore (or repress) interrelations. This is why it is so difficult to find the words to describe such fields as the organism/environment. Thus when the human body is analyzed and its organs are attached to nouns, we are at once in danger of the mechanical, overspecialized type of medicine and surgery which interferes at one point heedless of a disturbance of balance which may have unforeseen "effects" throughout the system. What *else* must the surgeon do if he has to remove a cancerous thyroid? Similar dangers arise in almost every sphere of human activity.

Let us suppose that social group A has an enemy group B. The fact that B periodically attacks A keeps the members of A on their toes and "prunes" its population. But

---

[3] I, for example, as an "independent philosopher" could not possibly be saying what I am if I were really independent. "My" ideas are inseparable from what Northrop Frye calls "the order of words," i.e., the total pattern of literature and discourse now being unfolded throughout the world.

group A considers its own side good and B's side bad, and because good and bad are irreconcilable the actual service which B does for A is ignored. The time comes when A mobilizes its forces and either exterminates B or makes it incapable of further attack. A is then in danger of breeding itself out of existence, or of debilitation through lack of "tonus." An inadequate system of classification has made it too difficult to understand that there can be an enemy/friend and a war/collaboration. Obviously there is a similar relationship between virtue and vice. It has been pointed out so often, but society finds it too treasonable to take it seriously. As Lao-tzu said, "When everyone recognizes goodness to be good, there is already evil. Thus to be and not to be arise mutually" (18). It is that simple, but it just cannot be admitted! It is true that social action may get rid of such particular evils as judicial torture, child labor, or leprosy, but after a brief lapse of time the general feeling of being alive remains the same. In other words, the freezing and the boiling of our emotions remain the same whether the scale lies between o and 100 centigrade or 32 and 212 Fahrenheit. At the same time, a contest between virtue and vice may remain as important as the contest between group A and group B. To see this, however, is to understand that the contest is a game.

All classification seems to require a division of the world. As soon as there is a class, there is what is inside it and what is outside it. In and out, yes and no, are explicitly exclusive of one another. They are formally opposed, like group A and its enemy group B, good and bad, virtue and vice. The separation between them seems to be as clear-cut as that between a solid and a space, a figure and its background. The separation, the difference, is therefore what we notice; it fits the notation of language, and because it is noted and explicit it is conscious and unrepressed. But there is also something unnoticed and ignored, which does not fit the notation of the language, and which because it is unnoted and implicit is unconscious and repressed. This is that the inside and the outside of the class go together and cannot do without each other. "To be and not to be arise mutually." Beneath the contest lies friendship; beneath the serious lies the playful; beneath the separation of the individual and the world lies the field pattern. In this pattern every push from within is at the same time a pull from without, every explosion an implosion, every outline an inline, arising mutually and simultaneously so that it is always impossible to say from which side of a boundary any movement begins. The individual no more acts *upon* the world than the world upon the individual. The cause and the effect turn out to be integral parts of the same event.

Wrestling as we are with languages whose forms resist and screen out insights of this kind, it is understandable that at present this view is only hypothetical in the behavioral sciences however well verified it may be in the physical. This is perhaps due in part to the fact that it is much easier to describe pure process and pattern in mathematics than in words, with their subjects, verbs, and predicates, their agents and acts. But we have not as yet gone very far in the mathematical description of living behavior. Yet it is not so hard to imagine a language which might describe all that man "is" and does as *doing*. After all, we can speak of a group of homes as housing without feeling impelled to ask, "*What* is it that is housing?" I do not think that such a language would be impoverished, any more than the sciences are impoverished through having given up such mysterious entities as the ether, the humors, phlogiston, or the planetary spheres. On the contrary, a language would be greatly enriched by making it easier for us to understand relationships which our present languages conceal. Described simply as pattern in motion, the mystery of what acts and what is acted upon, of how the cause issues in the effect, would be as easy as seeing the relationship between the concave and convex sides of a curve. Which side comes first?

The difficulty, however, is not so much in finding the language as in overcoming social resistance. Would it really do to find out that our game is not serious, that enemies are friends, and that the good thrives on the evil? Society as we know it seems to be a tacit conspiracy to keep this hushed up for fear that the contest will otherwise cease. If these opposites are not kept fiercely separate and antagonistic, what motivation will there be for the creative struggle between them? If man does not feel himself at war with nature, will there be any further impetus to technological progress? Imagine how the Christian conscience would react to the idea that, behind the scenes, God and the Devil were the closest friends but had taken opposite sides in order to stage a great cosmic game. Yet this is rather much how things stood when the Book of Job was written, for here Satan is simply the counsel for the prosecution in the court of Heaven, as faithful a servant of the court as the *advocatus diaboli* at the Vatican.[4]

The problem is, of course, that if men are patterns of

---

[4] I find it, likewise, difficult to read the stories of the Last Supper without getting the impression that Jesus *commanded* Judas to betray him.

action and not agents, and if the individual and the world act with each other, mutually, so that action does not originate in either, who is to be blamed when things go wrong? Can the police then come around asking, "Who started this?" The convention of the individual as the responsible, independent agent is basic to almost all our social and legal structures. Acceptance of this role or identity is the chief criterion of sanity, and we feel that if anyone is reducible to actions or behaviors with nobody doing them, he must be no more than a soulless mechanism. Indeed, there is at first glimpse an element of terror in this universe of pure activity; there seems to be no point from which to make a decision, to begin anything. It is not at all unlikely that some kind of slip into this way of feeling things may sometimes touch off a psychotic break, for the individual might well feel that he had lost control of everything and could no longer trust himself or others to behave consistently. But supposing one understood in the first place that this is the way things are anyhow, the experience itself would be far less unnerving. In practice it happens that just as soon as one gets used to this feeling and is not afraid of it, it is possible to go on behaving as rationally as ever—but with a remarkable sense of lightness.

Setting aside, for the time being, the moral and ethical implications of this view of man, it seems to have the same sort of advantage over the ordinary view that the Copernican solar system has over the Ptolemaic. It is so much simpler, even though it means giving up the central position of the earth. This is, moreover, the kind of simplicity which is fruitful rather than diminishing: it leads to further possibilities of play, greater richness of articulation. On the other hand, the ordinary conventional view seems increasingly to fail in what it purports to achieve.

One of the best accounts of the social and conventional character of the ego is in the work of George Herbert Mead (19). He points out that the difference between the social and the biological theories of the origin of individual self-consciousness corresponds to the difference between evolutionary and contract theories of the origin of the state. In the latter, discredited, view the social community is formed by deliberate contract between self-conscious persons. He reasons, however, that the individual cannot become an object to himself by himself, and in any case no animate individuals have ever existed by themselves.

> The view that mind [i.e., the ego] is a congenital biological endowment of the individual organism does not really enable us to explain its nature and origin at all: neither what sort of biological endowment it is, nor how organisms at a certain level of evolutionary progress come to possess it. (20)

He goes on to show that the "I," the biological individual, can become conscious of itself only in terms of the "me," but that this latter is a view of itself given to it by other people.

> The individual enters as such into his own experience only as an object, not as a subject; and he can enter as an object only on the basis of social relations and interactions, only by means of his experiential transactions with other individuals in an organized social environment . . . only by taking the attitudes of others towards himself—is he able to become an object to himself. (21)

As a result the mind or psychological structure of the individual cannot be identified with some entity inside his skin.

> If mind is socially constituted, then the field or locus of any given individual mind must extend as far as the social activity or apparatus of social relations which constitutes it extends; and hence that field cannot be bounded by the skin of the individual organism to which it belongs. (22)

And that is just the paradox of the situation: society gives us the idea that the mind or ego[5] is inside the skin and that it acts on its own apart from society.

Here, then, is a major contradiction in the rules of the social game. The members of the game are to play *as if* they were independent agents, but they are not to *know* that they are just playing as if! It is explicit in the rules that the individual is self-determining, but implicit that he is so only by virtue of the rules. Furthermore, while he is defined as an independent agent, he must not be so independent as not to submit to the rules which define him. Thus he is defined as an agent in order to be held responsible to the group for "his" actions. The rules of the game confer independence and take it away at the same time, without revealing the contradiction.

This is exactly the predicament which Gregory Bateson (23) calls the "double-bind," where the individual is called upon to take two mutually exclusive courses of action and at the same time is prevented from being able

---

[5] Mead himself does not use the term "ego" in quite this sense, for he associates it with the "I" rather than the "me." But since he is also associating the "I" with the organism, this seems quite inconsistent, for the ego is almost invariably considered as something *in* the organism like the chauffeur in a car, or a little man inside the head who thinks thoughts and sees sights. It is just this ego feeling that is the social construct.

to comment on the paradox. You are damned if you do and damned if you don't, and you mustn't realize it. Bateson has suggested that the individual who finds himself in a family situation which imposes the double-bind upon him in an acute form is liable to schizophrenia.[6] For if he cannot comment on the contradiction, what can he do but withdraw from the field? Yet society does not allow withdrawal; the individual *must* play the game. As Thoreau said, wherever you may seek solitude men will ferret you out "and compel you to belong to their desperate company of oddfellows." Thus in order to withdraw the individual must imply that *he* is not withdrawing, that his withdrawal is happening, and that he cannot help himself. In other words, he must "lose his mind" and become insane.

But as "genius is to madness close allied," the schizophrenic withdrawal is a caricature of liberation, including even the "lamasery" of the insane asylum or the peculiarly exempt status of the old-fashioned village idiot. As the terminology of Zen Buddhism implies, the liberated man also has "no mind" (*wu-hsin*) and does not feel himself to be an agent, a doer of deeds. So also it is said in the *Bhagavad-Gita*:

> The man who is united with the Divine and knows the truth thinks "I do nothing at all," for in seeing, hearing, touching, smelling, tasting, walking, sleeping, breathing; in speaking, emitting, grasping, opening and closing the eyes he holds that only the senses are occupied with the objects of the senses. (24)

[6] While he has assembled a good deal of evidence in support of this suggestion, he does not claim to have proved it. Other research is suggesting that schizophrenia may be explained chemically as a toxic condition, but the two points of view do not necessarily exclude each other. The stress induced by the double-bind situation could have something to do with generating the toxin.

But in liberation this comes to pass not through an un-conscious compulsion but through insight, through under-standing and breaking the double-bind which society imposes. One does not then get into the position of not being able to play the game; one can play it all the better for seeing that it is a game.

The schizophrenic withdrawal affects a minority, and occurs in circumstances where the double-bind imposed by society in general is compounded by special types of double-bind peculiar to a special family situation.[7] The rest of us are in differing degrees of neurosis, tolerable to the extent to which we can forget the contradiction thrust upon us, to which we can "forget ourselves" by absorption in hobbies, mystery novels, social service, tele-vision, business, and warfare. Thus it is hard to avoid the conclusion that we are accepting a definition of sanity which is insane, and that as a result our common human problems are so persistently insoluble that they add up to the perennial and universal "predicament of man," which is attributed to nature, to the Devil, or to God himself.

If what has been said up to this point is intelligible, it is only partly so; otherwise the reader would have been liberated forthwith! As I have suggested, there are un-avoidable verbal difficulties even in describing the para-dox we are in, let alone in describing the actual field pattern in which human life takes place. The trouble is that we are describing the difficulty with the very language structure that gets us into it. It has to say, "We are describing," and, "Gets us into it," confirming at every

[7] As when a mother requires her child to love her and yet withdraws from expressions of affection.

step the reality of the agent-entity presumed to stand behind the activity, or to be enduring it when it is understood to be coming from some other source. Common sense balks at the notion of action without agent just as it balks at the idea of pattern without substance, whether material or mental. But $1 + 2 = 3$ and $x - y = z$ are intelligible statements of relation without our having to ask what any of the symbols stand for, whether things or events, solids or spaces.

Thus the whole difficulty of both psychotherapy and liberation is that the problems which they address lie in the social institutions in whose terms we think and act. No co-operation can be expected from an individual ego which is itself the social institution at the root of the trouble. But these institutions are observable; we do not have to ask, "By whom?" They are observable *here*, for as William James pointed out, "The word 'I' . . . is primarily a noun of position like 'this' and 'here'" (25). If they are observable they are subject to comment, and it is the ability to comment upon it that breaks the double-bind. On the one hand, social institutions like the grid of language create, or better, translate the world in their terms, so that the world—life itself—appears to be self-contradictory if the terms are self-contradictory. On the other hand, social institutions do not create the world *ex nihilo*. They are in and of the pattern of nature which they in turn represent or misrepresent.

The pattern of nature can only be *stated* in terms of a language; but it can be *shown* in terms of, say, sense perceptions. For a society whose number system is only "1, 2, 3, many," it cannot be a fact that we have ten fingers, and yet all the fingers are visible. People who *know*, for whom it is a fact, that they are egos or that the sun goes around the earth can be shown that their facts are wrong by being persuaded to act consistently upon them. If you know that the earth is flat, sail consistently in one direction until you fall off the edge. Similarly, if you know that you are an independent agent, do something quite independently, be deliberately spontaneous, and show me this agent.

That there is a pattern of nature can be shown; *what* it is can be stated, and we can never be certain that what we have stated is finally correct because there is nothing about which we can act consistently *forever*. But when we are employing institutions in whose terms we cannot act consistently, we may be sure either that they are self-contradictory or that they do not fit the pattern of nature. Self-contradictions which are not observed and patterns of nature which the language screens out are, in psychological terms, unconscious and repressed. Social institutions are then in conflict with the actual pattern of man-in-the-world, and this comes out as distress in the individual organism, which *cannot* be inconsistent with itself or with nature without ceasing to exist. Freud was therefore right as far as he went in tracing neurosis to the conflict between sexual feeling and the peculiar sexual mores of Western cultures. But he was only scratching the surface. For one thing, his view of the sexual "instinct" itself was heavily conditioned by those very mores. As Philip Rieff has said:

> Not only did Freud employ sexuality to deflate the pride of civilized man, he further defined it pejoratively by those qualities which make the sexual instinct intractable to a civilized sensibility. . . . While urging, for the sake of our mental health, that we dispense with such childish fantasies

of purity as are epitomized in the belief that Mother (or Father) was too nice to have done those nasty things, Freud at the same time comes to the tacit understanding that sex really is nasty, an ignoble slavery to nature. (26)

For another, Freud's interpretation of the id and its libido as blind and brutish urges was simply a reflection of the current philosophy that the world is basically "mere" energy, a sort of crude volatile stuff, rather than organic pattern—which is, after all, another name for intelligence.

But what our social institutions repress is not just the sexual love, the mutuality, of man and woman, but also the still deeper love of organism and environment, of Yes and No, and of all those so-called opposites represented in the Taoist symbol of the *yang-yin,* the black and white fishes in eternal intercourse. It is hardly stretching a metaphor to use the word "love" for intimate relationships beyond those between human organisms. In those states of consciousness called "mystical" we have, I believe, a sudden slip into an inverse or obverse of the view of the world given in our divisive language forms. Where this slip is not, as in schizophrenia, a tortured withdrawal from conflict, the change of consciousness again and again brings the overwhelming impression that the world is a system of love. Everything fits into place in an indescribable harmony—indescribable because paradoxical in the terms which our language provides.

Now our language forms, our grids of thought, are by no means wholly wrong. The differences and divisions in the world which they note are surely there to be seen. There are indeed some mere ghosts of language, but in the main the categories of language seem to be valid and indeed essential to any description of the world whatsoever—as far as they go. But a given language cannot properly express what is implicit in it—the unity of differences, the logical inseparability of light and darkness, Yes and No. The question is whether these logical implications correspond to physical relations. The whole trend of modern science seems to be establishing the fact that, for the most part, they do. Things must be seen together with the form of the space between them. As Ernst Cassirer said as long ago as 1923:

> The new physical view proceeds neither from the assumption of a "space in itself," nor of "matter" nor of "force in itself"—it no longer recognizes space, force and matter as physical objects separated from each other, but . . . only the unity of certain *functional relations,* which are differently designated according to the system of reference in which we express them. (27)

While we must be careful not to overstress analogies between physics and human behavior, there must certainly be general principles in common between them. Compare what Cassirer said with Gardner Murphy:

> I have believed for a long time that human nature is a reciprocity of what is inside the skin and what is outside; that it is definitely not "rolled up inside us" but our way of being one with our fellows and our world. I call this field theory. (28)

The ways of liberation are of course concerned with making this so-called mystical consciousness the normal everyday consciousness. But I am more and more persuaded that what happens in their disciplines, regardless of the language in which it is described, is nothing either supernatural or metaphysical in the usual sense. It has nothing to do with a perception of something else than the physical world. On the contrary, it is the clear perception of this world as a field, a perception which is not just theoretical but which is also felt as clearly as we feel, say, that "I" am a thinker behind and apart from my thoughts, or that the stars are absolutely separate from space and from each other. In this view the differences of the world are not isolated objects encountering one another in conflict, but expressions of polarity. Opposites and differences have something between them, like the two faces of a coin; they do not meet as total strangers. When this relativity of things is seen very strongly, its appropriate affect is love rather than hate or fear.

Surely this is the way of seeing things that is required for effective psychotherapy. Disturbed individuals are, as it were, points in the social field where contradictions in the field break out. It will not do at all to confirm the contradictions from which they are suffering, for the psychiatrist to be the official representative of a sick system of institutions. The society of men with men and the larger ecological society of men with nature, however explicitly a contest, is implicitly a field—an agreement, a relativity, a game. The rules of the game are conventions, which again mean agreements. It is fine for us to agree that we are different from each other, provided we do not ignore the fact that we *agreed* to differ. We did not differ to agree, to create society by deliberate contract between originally independent parties. Furthermore, even if there is to be a battle, there must be a field of battle; when the contestants really notice this they will have a war dance instead of a war.

III

The Ways of Liberation

Iғ it is true that psychotherapy has not been seen clearly in its social context, it is also true of the Eastern ways of liberation as they have been studied and explained in the West. Almost all the modern literature on Buddhism, Vedanta, and Taoism treats of these subjects in a void with the barest minimum of reference to the larger background of Indian or Chinese culture. One gathers, therefore, that these disciplines are exportable units like bales of rice or tea, and that Buddhism can be "taken up" anywhere at any time like baseball. It has also seemed to the West that Christianity can be exported in the same way, that it will "work" in any culture, and, if not, so much the worse for that culture. At the same time let it be said that, at least in the higher civilizations, there are no such things as "pure" cultures uncontaminated by exotic influences. Buddhism did in fact travel from India to the very different cultures of China, Tibet, Thailand, and Japan in a way that Hinduism, as a total culture, could never have travelled. But wherever there was not some parallel institution, such as Taoism in China, it was difficult to assimilate and understand. In other words, it becomes intelligible—and applicable in our own terms—when we can see its relation to the culture from which it comes. In this way we can borrow things from other cultures, but always to the extent that they suit our own needs.

One of the blessings of easy communication between the great cultures of the world is that partisanship in religion or philosophy is ceasing to be intellectually respectable. Pure religions are as rare as pure cultures, and it is mentally crippling to suppose that there must be a number of fixed bodies of doctrine among which one must choose, where choice means accepting the system entirely or not at all. Highly organized religions always try to force such a choice because they need devoted members for their continuance. Those who rove freely through the various traditions, accepting what they can use and rejecting what they cannot, are condemned as undisciplined syncretists. But the use of one's reason is not a lack of discipline, nor is there any important religion which is not itself a syncretism, a "growing up together" of ideas and practices of diverse origin. Time will indeed give any religious syncretism an organic unity of its own, but also a rigidity which needs to be shaken. But one of the consequences of taking Buddhism or Vedanta out of its own cultural context is, as we have seen, the supposition that it is a religion in the same sense as Christianity and with the same social function.

Thus it strikes the uninformed Westerner that Buddhism could be an alternative to Christianity: a body of metaphysical, cosmological, psychological, and moral doctrine to be believed and simply substituted for what one has believed before. It also seems that the actual practice of these ways of liberation is almost entirely a matter of one's private life. They seem to be solitary explorations of man's inner consciousness, presumed to be the same everywhere, and thus as applicable in California as in Bengal— the more so because they do not require membership in a church. Yet if the main function of a way of liberation is to release the individual from his "hypnosis" by certain social institutions, what is needed in California will not be quite the same as what is needed in Bengal, for the institutions differ. Like different diseases, they require different medicines.

Yet very few modern authorities on Buddhism or Vedanta seem to realize that social institutions constitute the *maya*, the illusion, from which they offer release. It is almost invariably assumed that *nirvana* or *moksha* means release from the physical organism and the physical universe, an accomplishment involving powers of mind over matter that would give their possessor the omnipotence of a god. Aside, however, from some competent extrasensory perception and some imaginative use of hypnosis, no such powers have been demonstrated, though we shall have more to say about the therapeutic use of trickery.[1] Some discussions of liberation suggest that what is involved is not so much objective as subjective release from the physical world. In other words, it is assumed that our normal perception of the spatially and temporally extended world, and of the sense organs which transact with it, is a type of hypnotic illusion, and that anyone who acquires perfect concentration can see for himself that the spatiotemporal world is nothing but imagination. From what we know of the hypnotic state and its induction by concentration, it might be easy enough to produce the impression that this is so. If the operator can make himself invisible to the subject, why cannot he make the whole

[1] To some this may seem a bold statement, but it has always struck me as important that demonstrations of occult powers are almost invariably trivial in their achievements, e.g., cracking teacups at a distance, causing vases to fall off shelves, and alleged teleportations of small objects.

universe invisible? But I do not believe that the ways of liberation amount to anything so trivial as substituting one hypnotic state for another. We know that our perception of the world is relative to our neurological structure and the ways in which social conditioning has taught us to see. Because the latter can to some extent be changed, it means something to say that it is imaginary. But is the structure of the organism imaginary? No one can prove that it is unless he can demonstrate that it can change itself radically by other than surgical means.

All my experience of those who are proficient in the ways of liberation indicates that feats of magic or neurotechnology are quite beside the point. I have known one Zen master quite intimately, as a personal friend, and have met and talked with many others, as well as a considerable number of yogis and swamis both honest and phony. Furthermore, I have reliable friends who have studied and practiced with Zen and Yoga teachers far more extensively than I, and I have found no evidence whatsoever for any sensational achievements of this kind. If they have achieved anything at all it is of a far humbler nature and in quite a different direction, and something which strikes me as actually more impressive.

It is not within the scope of this book to present a fully documented argument for the idea that liberation is from the *maya* of social institutions and not of the physical world. Some evidence will be given, but I have not myself arrived at this idea by a rigorous examination of documents. It is simply a hypothesis which, to me, makes far better sense of Buddhism and Vedanta, Yoga and Taoism, than any other interpretation. The documents are often ambiguous, for what we mean by the real or physical world is obviously determined by social institutions. When Buddhist texts state that all things (*dharma*) are falsely imagined and without reality of their own (*svabhava*) this can mean (a) that the concrete physical universe does not exist, or (b) that things are relative: they have no self-existence because no one thing can be designated without relation to others, and furthermore because "thing" is a unit of description—not a natural entity. If the former interpretation is correct, the Buddhist *nirvana* will be an utterly blank state of consciousness; if the latter, it will be a transformed view of the physical world, seeing that world in its full relativity. Can there be any reasonable doubt that the latter is intended?[2]

If, then, the *maya* or unreality lies not in the physical world but in the concepts or thought forms by which it is described, it is clear that *maya* refers to social institutions —to language and logic and their constructs—and to the way in which they modify our feeling of the world. This becomes even clearer when we look at the relation of the Indian ways of liberation to the social structure and popular cosmology of the ancient Aryan culture. The commu-

[2] Buddhism is of course a matrix of many different schools with formally divergent points of view, and in their strictly popular forms some of these schools are certainly religions and not ways of liberation. When, therefore, I use the word "Buddhism" without further qualification it should be understood that I am referring to the Madhyamika school of Nagarjuna, described by T. R. V. Murti (29) as the central philosophy of Buddhism. With regard to the reality of the world, Murti writes: "The Absolute is not one reality set against another, the empirical. The Absolute looked at through thought-forms (vikalpa) is phenomenon (samsara or samvrta, literally covered). The latter, freed of the superimposed thought-forms (nirvikalpa, nisprapanca), is the Absolute. The difference is epistemic (subjective), and not ontological. Nagarjuna therefore declares that there is not the least difference between the world and the absolutely real. Transcendent to thought, the Absolute, however, is thoroughly immanent in experience." Cf. Wittgenstein, "Not *how* the world is, is the mystical, but *that* it is. . . . There is indeed the inexpressible. This *shows* itself; it is the mystical" (30).

nity is divided into four basic castes—Brahman (priestly), Kshatriya (military), Vaishya (mercantile), and Sudra (laboring)—in terms of which the role and identity of every individual is defined. An individual outside caste has no legal identity, and is thus regarded as a human animal rather than a human person. The four castes are, furthermore, the general classification of roles temporarily assumed by something beyond man and, indeed, beyond all classification. This is the Brahman, or Godhead, which is one and the same as the Atman, the essential Self playing each individual role. In this ancient Indian cosmology the creation of the world is thus a dramatic manifestation. The Godhead is playing at being finite; the One is pretending to be many, but in the process, in assuming each individual role, the One has so to speak forgotten Itself and so has become involved in unconsciousness or ignorance (*avidya*).

So long as this ignorance prevails, the individualized form of the Godhead, the soul or *jivatman*, is constantly reborn into the world, rising or falling in fortune and station according to its deeds and their consequences (*karma*). There are various levels above and below the human through which the individual soul may pass in the course of its reincarnations—the angelic, the titanic, the animal, the purgatories, and the realm of frustrated ghosts. Until it awakens to full self-knowledge, the individual soul may undergo reincarnation for amazingly long periods of time, touching the highest possibilities of pleasure and the lowest depths of pain, going round and round upon the wheel of *samsara* for thousands and millions of years.

If we go back in imagination to an India entirely uninfluenced by Western ideas, and especially those of Western

science, it is easy to see that this cosmology would have
been something much more than a belief. It would have
seemed to be a matter of fact which everyone *knew* to be
true. It was taken for granted, and was also vouched for by
the authority of the most learned men of the time, an
authority just as impressive then as scientific authority is
today. Without the distraction of some persuasive alternative one can know that such a cosmology is true just as
one can know that the sun goes around the earth—or just
as one can know that the following figure is a bear climb-
ing a tree, without being able to see the bear:

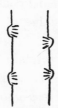

Or is it simply a trunk with burls on it?

To the degree, then, that this cosmology was a matter
of ingrained common sense, it would have been as difficult
for the average Hindu to see the world otherwise as it is
for us to imagine what a physicist means by curved space,
or to believe him when he says that matter is not solid.

All the ways of liberation offered release from the endless cycle of reincarnation—Vedanta and Yoga through the
awakening of the true Self, and Buddhism through the
realization that the process of life is not happening to any
subject, so that there no longer remains anyone to be reincarnated. They agreed, in other words, that the individual
soul with its continued reincarnation from life to life and
even moment to moment is *maya,* a playful illusion. Yet all

popular accounts of these doctrines, both Western and Asian, state that so long as the individual remains unliberated he will in fact continue to be reincarnated. Despite the Buddhist *anatman* doctrine of the unreality of the substantial ego, the *Milindapanha* records Nagasena's complex efforts to convince the Greek king Menander that reincarnation can occur, without any actual soul, until at last *nirvana* is attained. The vast majority of Asian Hindus and Buddhists continue to believe that reincarnation is a fact, and most Westerners adopting Vedanta or Buddhism adopt belief in reincarnation at the same time. Western Buddhists even find this belief consoling, in flat contradiction to the avowed objective of attaining release from rebirth.

It is, however, logical to retain the belief in reincarnation as a fact if one also believes that *maya* is the physical world as distinct from ideas *about* the physical world. That is to say, one will continue to believe in this Indian cosmology until one realizes that it is a social institution. I wish, therefore, to commend what to many students of these doctrines may seem to be a startling thesis: that Buddhists and Vedantists who understand their own doctrines profoundly, who are in fact liberated, do not believe in reincarnation in any literal sense. Their liberation involved, among other things, the realization that the Hindu cosmology was a myth and not a fact. It was, and remains, a liberation from being taken in by social institutions; it is not liberation from being alive. It is consistent with this view that, in India, liberation went hand in hand with renunciation of caste; the individual ceased to identify himself with his socially defined identity, his role. He underlined this ritually by abandoning family responsibilities when his sons were able to assume them, by discarding clothes, or, as in the case of the Buddhists, by donning the ocher robes which marked the criminal outcaste, and by retiring to the forests and mountains. Mahayana Buddhism later introduced the final and logical refinement— the Bodhisattva who returns to society and adopts its conventions without "attachment," who in other words *plays* the social game instead of taking it seriously.

If this thesis is true, why was it not stated openly, and why have the majority of Buddhists and Vedantists been allowed to go on thinking of the reincarnation cosmology as a fact? There are two reasons. First, liberation is not revolution. It is not going out of one's way to disturb the social order by casting doubt upon the conventional ideas by which people hold together. Furthermore, society is always insecure and thus hostile to anyone who challenges its conventions directly. To disabuse oneself of accepted mythologies without becoming the victim of other people's anxiety requires considerable tact. Second, the whole technique of liberation requires that the individual shall find out the truth for himself. Simply to tell it is not convincing. Instead, he must be asked to experiment, to act consistently upon assumptions which he holds to be true until he finds out otherwise. The *guru* or teacher of liberation must therefore use all his skill to persuade the student to act upon his own delusions, for the latter will always resist any undermining of the props of his security. He teaches, not by explanation, but by pointing out new ways of acting upon the student's false assumptions until the student convinces himself that they are false.

Herein, I feel, is the proper explanation of the esotericism of the ways of liberation. The initiate is one who knows that certain social institutions are self-contradictory or in actual conflict with the form of nature. But he knows also that these institutions have the strongest emotions invested in them. They are the rules of communication whereby people understand one another, and they have been beaten into the behavior patterns of impressionable children with the full force of social anxiety. At the same time, those who are taken in by such institutions are suffering from them—suffering from the very ideas which they believe to be vital to sanity and survival. There is therefore no way of disabusing the sufferer directly, by telling him that his cherished disease is a disease. If he is to be helped at all, he must be *tricked* into insight. If I am to help someone else to see that a false problem is false, I must pretend that I am taking his problem seriously. What I am actually taking seriously is his suffering, but he must be led to believe that it is what he considers as his problem.

Such trickery is basic to medicine and psychotherapy alike. It has been said that the good doctor is one who keeps the patient amused while nature works the cure. This is not always true, but it is a sound general principle. It is easier to wait for a natural change when one is given the impression that something is being done to bring it about. What is being done is the trick; the relaxed and rested waiting is the actual cure, but the anxiety which attends a disease makes direct and deliberate relaxation almost impossible. Patients lose confidence in their doctors to the extent that the trickery is exposed, and therefore the art of medicine progresses by the invention of new and ever more impenetrable tricks.

Let us suppose then that someone who is suffering from a social institution imagines that he is suffering because of an actual conflict in life, in the very structure of the physical world—that nature threatens his presumably physical ego. The healer must then appear to be a magician, a master of the physical world. He must do whatever is necessary to convince the sufferer that he can solve what seems to the latter to be a physical problem, for there is no other way of convincing him to do what is necessary for acting consistently upon his false assumption. He must above all convince the sufferer that he, the *guru*, has mastered the imaginary problem, that *his* ego is not disturbed by pain or death or worldly passions. Moreover, because the disease was engendered by social authority, the *guru* must appear to have equal or superior social authority to the parents, relatives, and instructors of the patient. In all this the Eastern ways of liberation have been astonishingly ingenious; their masters, whom society would have felt to be utterly subversive, have convinced society that they are its very pillars. It is thus that the *guru* who has a bad temper, or who likes to smoke or drink sake, gives the impression that he indulges in these "little vices" deliberately —in order to remain in his bodily manifestation, for if he were consistently unattached to the physical world he would cease to appear in it.

Stated thus baldly the technique will naturally seem to be dishonest. But this is a conscious and deliberate dishonesty to counter an unconscious and otherwise ineradicable self-deception on the homoeopathic principle of *similia similibus curantur*—likes are cured by likes. Set a thief to catch a thief. Speaking of mutual recognition between those who are liberated, a Zen Buddhist text says:

> *When two thieves meet they need no introduction:*
> *They recognize each other without question.* (31)

Of course the *guru* is human like everyone else. His advantage, his liberation, lies in the fact that he is not in conflict with himself for being so; he is not in the double-bind of pretending that he is an independent agent without knowing that he is pretending, of imagining that he is an ego or subject which can somehow manage to be permanently "one up" on its correlative object—the changing panorama of experiences, sensations, feelings, emotions, and thoughts. The *guru* accepts himself; more exactly, he does not think of himself as something other than his behavior patterns, as something which performs them. On the other hand, social conditioning as we know it depends entirely on persuading people *not* to accept themselves, and necessary as this stratagem, this "as if," may be for training the young, it is a fiction of limited use. The more it succeeds, the more it fails. Civilization attained at the price of inculcating this fiction permanently is necessarily self-destructive, and by comparison with such disaster the *guru's* "dishonesty" is a positive virtue.

A Japanese coastal village was once threatened by a tidal wave, but the wave was sighted in advance, far out on the horizon, by a lone farmer in the rice fields on the hillside above the village. At once he set fire to the fields, and the villagers who came swarming up to save their crops were saved from the flood. His crime of arson is like the trickery of the *guru*, the doctor, or the psychotherapist in persuading people to try to solve a false problem by acting consistently upon its premises.

This apparently unorthodox account of the basic method of the ways of liberation is required, I feel, to explain a number of problems. However various their doctrines and however different their formal techniques, all seem to culminate in the same state or mode of consciousness in which the duality of the ego and the world is overcome. Call it "cosmic consciousness" or "mystical experience," or what you will, it seems to me to be the felt realization of the physical world as a field. But because language is divisive rather than relational, not only is the feeling hard to describe but our attempted descriptions may also seem to be opposed. Buddhism emphasizes the unreality of the ego, whereas Vedanta emphasizes the unity of the field. Thus in describing liberation the former seems to be saying simply that the egocentric viewpoint evaporates, and the latter that we discover our true self to be the Self of the universe. However pundits may argue the fine points, it comes to the same thing in practical experience.

There is, then, nothing occult or supernatural in this state of consciousness, and yet the traditional methods for attaining it are complex, divergent, obscure, and, for the most part, extremely arduous. Confronted with such a tangle, one asks what is common to these methods, what is their essential ingredient, and if this can be found the result will be a practical and theoretical simplification of the whole problem. To do this we must look for a simplified and yet adequate way of describing what happens between the *guru* or Zen master and his student within the social context of their transaction. What we find is something very like a contest in *judo*: the expert does not attack; he waits for the attack, he lets the student pose the problem. Then, when the attack comes, he does not oppose it; he rolls with it and carries it to its logical conclusion, which is the downfall of the false social premise of the student's question.

Admittedly there may be many *gurus* who do not fully

realize that this is what they are doing, just as there are many physicians who do not realize that some of their medications are placebos. Successful psychotherapy is carried out by Freudian psychoanalysis, by Rogers' nondirective counselling, and by Jung's analytical psychology. The theories and methods differ and diverge, but there may be some hidden and essential factor in common. Yet there is good reason to believe that some teachers of the ways of liberation know perfectly well what they are doing, that they are fully aware of their merciful trickery and also of the fact that the release attained is not from physical reincarnation but from confused thinking and feeling.

Some evidence for this point of view must, however, be presented if we are to be sure that psychotherapy and the ways of liberation have common ground. We must start from the well-recognized fact that all the ways of liberation, Buddhism, Vedanta, Yoga, and Taoism,[3] assert that our ordinary egocentric consciousness is a limited and impoverished consciousness without foundation in "reality." Whether its basis is physical or social, biological or cultural, remains to be seen, but there is no doubt that release from this particular limitation is the aim of all four ways. In every case the method involves some form of meditation which may take the form of concentrated attention upon some particular object, problem, or aspect of consciousness, or simply of the relaxed and detached observation of whatever comes into mind. It may take the form of trying to suppress all verbal thinking, or the form of a dialectic in which the most rigorous thinking is

[3] Perhaps I should also include Islamic Sufism and aspects of Jainism, but these are subjects which I have not studied to anything like the same extent.

carried to its full conclusions. It may be an attempt to be directly aware of the perceiving self, or it may follow out the idea that the self is not anything that can be known, not the body, not the sensations, not the thoughts, not even consciousness. In some instances the student is simply asked to find out, exhaustively and relentlessly, *why* he wants liberation, or *who* it is that wants to be liberated. Methods vary not only among the differing schools and teachers, but also in accordance with the needs and temperaments of their disciples.

Some schools insist that a *guru* who is himself liberated is absolutely essential to the task; others say only that this makes things much easier, but that it is not impossible for the student to play the game upon himself. There is a similar division of opinion about psychotherapy. But in fact there is always a *guru* in some sense, even if it be only a friend who has given one the idea, or perhaps a book that one has read. The bondage that arises from a social relationship has to be released through social relationship. Both are functions of relationship—as is life itself.

Is it actually understood in Asia that liberation is from social rather than physical or metaphysical conditions? My own questioning of Zen Buddhist teachers on this point leaves no doubt about it. I have not found one that believes in reincarnation as a physical fact, still less one who lays claims to any literally miraculous powers over the physical world. All such matters are understood symbolically. What about the mysterious "masters of Tibet" to whom so much has been attributed in the way of occult knowledge about the superphysical worlds? While there is much purely literary and scholastic information about the texts of Tibetan Buddhism, very few Westerners have actually prac-

ticed its disciplines on the spot. An exception is Mme.
Alexandra David-Neel, a remarkable Frenchwoman who
has recently written an equally remarkable book to try to
explain as much as possible of the fundamental doctrine
of her teachers. She writes:

> If [the student] cannot refuse to play a role in the comedy
> or drama of the world, at least he understands that it is all a
> game. . . . They teach him to look . . . at the incessant work-
> ing of his mind and the physical activity displayed by the
> body. He ought to succeed in understanding, in noting that
> nothing of all that is *from him*, is *him. He*, physically and
> mentally, is the multitude of others.
>
> This "multitude of others" includes the material elements
> —the ground, one might say—which he owes to his heredity,
> to his atavism, then those which he has ingested, which he
> has inhaled from before his birth, by the help of which his
> body was formed, and which, assimilated by him, have be-
> come with the complex forces inherent in them constituent
> parts of his being.
>
> On the mental plane, this "multitude of others" includes
> many beings who are his contemporaries: people he consorts
> with, with whom he chats, whose actions he watches. Thus a
> continual inhibition is at work while the individual absorbs
> a part of the various energies given off by those with whom
> he is in contact, and these incongruous energies, installing
> themselves in that which he considers his "I," form there a
> swarming throng.
>
> This actually includes a considerable number of beings
> belonging to what we call the Past. . . . personalities with
> which [he] might have been in contact in the course of his
> reading and during his education. (32)

This is no other than a description of the organism, the
body, as inseparable from a system of physical relations,

and of the ego as G. H. Mead's "generalized other," the individual's feeling or conception of himself arising from social intercourse. As to reincarnation, she continues:

> When the student becomes aware of this crowd in himself, he should avoid imagining, as some do, that it represents memories of his preceding lives. There is no lack of those who state and are convinced that such and such a personage, who lived in the past, is reincarnated in them. Stories depicting reincarnations are innumerable in Asia where they keep alive the childish thirst for the marvellous among the masses. (33)

In other words, reincarnation is not understood literally as the successive re-embodiment of an individual ego, or even of an individual "chain of *karma*" or causally connected behavior pattern.[4] The individual's multitude of lives is interpreted as the multitude of his physical and social relations.

I do not wish to dwell tediously on the theme of understanding reincarnation symbolically rather than physically,

---

[4] The hypothesis of the individual chain of *karma* as distinct from the soul-entity (*jivatman*) was invoked by Nagasena and many others to preserve physical and literal reincarnation as a Buddhist doctrine. But what *other* hypotheses does this require to account for connections between a *karma*-chain running from, say, 1600 to 1650 and the same chain's next incarnation between 1910 and 1975? Through what system of relations does the chain maintain its identity in the interim? I do not deny that such a system *may* exist. The point is only that whether it exists is irrelevant to a correct understanding of Buddhism. According to the Madhyamika philosophy of Nagarjuna, the linear, catenary causal chain between "things" is purely conceptual (*vikalpa*) and descriptive. Murti (34), in trying too hard to assimilate the Madhyamika to Kantian ideas, makes the strange confusion of saying that Nagarjuna intended this critique of causality to apply to the noumenal world and not to the phenomenal. But which of these two is the physical? Surely, both are the physical—but the phenomenal world, in which causality applies, is the physical world described *as phenomena*, as if it were separate things and events. But how much confusion could be avoided if it were kept clear that things or phenomena are units of description, not of what we are describing.

but it is somewhat crucial for realizing that *maya* lies in the social sphere of description and thought, and not in the larger sphere of natural and physical relations. Something should, however, be said as to the Buddha's own attitude to the problem, insofar as it can be recovered. It is clear from the canonical texts that he denied the reality of any substantial ego, but that he neither denied nor affirmed the possibility of past or future "lives." He considered it irrelevant because he was concerned with man's liberation not from the physical world but from the egocentric style of consciousness. Whether such liberation did or did not terminate the continuity of individual existence as a physical organism, upon this plane of being or any other, was quite beside the point.

> Of such a brother, Ananda, whose heart is thus set free, if any one should say: "His creed is that an Arahant [liberated one] goes on after death," that were absurd. Or: "His creed is that an Arahant does not go on . . . does, and yet does not, go on . . . neither goes on nor goes not on after death," all that were absurd. (35)

In the Buddha's original doctrine all metaphysical speculations and all interest in miraculous controls of the physical world are considered not only as beside the point but also as positive hindrances to liberation. It should also be added that the idea of physical reincarnation is no part of Taoism, and that, according to A. K. Coomaraswamy (36), the proper interpretation of the Vedanta is that "the one and only transmigrant" is the Supreme Self, the Atman-Brahman, and never an individual soul. By such insights the whole reincarnation cosmology of ancient India dissolved either into a myth or into a mere possibility

with which one need no longer be concerned. The night-
mare of the same individual's repeatedly enduring poverty,
disease, and death for aeons of time, or imprisonment for
centuries in the torture chambers of demons, came to an
end in the realization that there is *no one* to endure it.

What of the claim that liberation confers supernormal
powers over the world (*siddhi*)? Where this is not a trick
or device (*upaya*) to challenge the student's false assumptions, the interpretation must again be symbolic. The *guru*
evades any direct request for miracles by saying that even
when one has such powers, they are not to be used to
satisfy idle curiosity, and, moreover, that concern with
them is a serious obstacle to the attainment of liberation.
It should be noted that when anyone has a reputation for
extraordinary power or skill of any kind, people will go
out of their way to discover it in the ordinary coincidences
of the life that goes on around him, and to interpret perfectly normal events in a supernormal way. The comedian
is often one who can so beguile an audience into *expecting*
him to be witty that he can set them to bursting their
sides with quite ordinary remarks. The philosopher, too,
can create a situation in which platitudes or sheer nonsense
strike listeners as the greatest profundities, and this may
also happen quite without his intention. In the same way,
people are positively eager to confirm a particular psychiatrist's reputation for reading their characters like a book,
and the whole skill of the fortune-teller is in exploiting the
information which his clients let slip in their eagerness to
have him read their past and foretell their future. Under
such circumstances it is quite useless for the "man of
power" to deny his magic, his sanctity, his wit, or his profundity, for a denial will simply be taken as modesty.

The genuine *guru* uses this situation not to make fools of his students, but to increase their zeal to dominate the physical world or their own feelings, to act consistently on the false premise that there is a contest between the ego and its experience. For situations of this kind are simply special instances of the double-bind which society puts upon the individual: he *knows* that there are separate events and things, and that he and others are independent agents, just as he *knows* that the comedian's casual remarks are howlingly funny. This is the whole technique of hypnosis, of the judo by which the operator persuades the subject that he cannot disobey him (37), and in Buddhism liberation is called awakening (*bodhi*) just because it is release from social hypnosis. To be hypnotized is to pretend unconsciously that, say, the hypnotist is invisible, or, comparably, that a game is serious or that "I" am inside my skin and that my field of vision is outside.

But for the symbolic interpretation of supernormal powers let us take, for example, the claim to omnipotence. "I am God, and therefore *everything* that happens is my doing." There is, of course, no way of disproving such an assertion. If I can persuade anyone to believe it, I will have him in a double-bind because he will take me to be willing what would ordinarily be against my will. The only way to escape from the bind is to comment on it, to make a meta-statement, as that such an assertion cannot possibly be verified, or that "I do *everything*" is logically equivalent to "I do *nothing*." But the point of ascribing everything that happens to a single agent is to call into question the idea of agency, and at the same time to modify the consciousness of "oneself." In other words, the realization that the ego agent, apart from the act or the choice, is a fiction is equivalent to the feeling that all actions of which you are aware are your own. This feeling is "omnipotence," but it is not actually an awareness of the ego's doing everything. It is awareness of action happening in a unified field, in which it is still possible to observe the conventional difference between "my" deeds and "yours" because they happen at different places in the field. It would mean something to say that I, the ego agent, make choices, perform actions, or think thoughts if it could make any demonstrable difference to what choices and actions occur. But it is *never* demonstrable either that what is done *could* have been done otherwise, or that what is done *must* be done— except by confining one's attention to very small fields, by cutting out variables, or, in other words, taking events out of the context in which they happened. Only by ignoring the full context of an action can it be said either that I did it freely or that I could not help it. I can try the same action again; if it comes out differently, I say that I could have done it otherwise, but if the same, that I could not. But in the meantime the context has of course changed. Because of this the same action can never be repeated.

Now to ignore the context of events is exactly the Buddhist *avidya,* ignorance or ignore-ance, which liberation dispels. In one way the repeatable experiments of science are based on ignore-ance, for they are performed in artificially closed fields. But these experiments add to our knowledge just because the scientist *knows* that he is ignoring. By rigorous isolation of the field he gets more and more detailed knowledge of the way in which fields are, in practice, related to each other. He does not ignore ignore-ance. In the same way the Buddhist discipline overcomes unconscious ignorance—the habitual selective acts of consciousness which screen out "separate" things from their context—by intense concentration. This is *judo* applied to ignore-ance. The fiction of the ego agent is dispelled by the closest awareness of what actually happens in intending, choosing, deciding, or being spontaneous. One thus comes to understand that consciousness, or attention, *is* ignore-ance and cannot be otherwise. But now one knows it, and thus the *siddhi* of omniscience is not to know everything but to understand the whole process of knowing, to see that all "knowns" are distinguished by ignore-ance. When ignore-ance is unconscious, we take its isolates for realities, and thus the habitual and conventional way of classifying things and events is taken for the natural.

The Buddhist principle that "form is void *[sunya]*" does not therefore mean that there are no forms. It means that forms are inseparable from their context—that the form of a figure is also the form of its background, that the form of a boundary is determined as much by what is outside as by what is inside. The doctrine of *sunyata*, or voidness, asserts only that there are no self-existent forms, for the more one concentrates upon any individual thing, the more it turns out to involve the whole universe. The final Buddhist vision of the world as the *dharmadhatu*—loosely translatable as the "field of related functions"—is not so different from the world view of Western science, except that the vision is experiential rather than theoretical. Poetically, it is symbolized as a vast network of jewels, like drops of dew upon a multidimensional spider web. Looking closely at any single jewel, one beholds in it the reflections of all the others. The relationship between the jewels is technically called "thing/thing no obstacle" (*shih shih wu ai*), which is to say that any one form is inseparable from all other forms.

In sum, then, the Buddhist discipline is to realize that anguish or conflict (*duhkha*) arises from the grasping (*trishna*) of entities singled out from the world by ignoreance (*avidya*)—grasping in the sense of acting or feeling toward them as if they were actually independent of context. This sets in motion the *samsara* or vicious circle of trying to solve the false problem of wresting life from death, pleasure from pain, good from evil, and self from not-self—in short, to get one's ego permanently "one up" on life. But through the meditation discipline the student finds out that he cannot stop this grasping so long as he thinks of himself as the ego which can either act or refrain from action. The attempt *not* to grasp rests upon the same false premise as the grasping: that thinking and doing, intending and choosing, are caused by an ego, that physical events flow from a social fiction. The unreality of the ego is discovered in finding out that there is nothing which it can either do or not do to stop grasping. This insight (*prajna*) brings about *nirvana*, release from the false problem. But *nirvana* is a radical transformation of how it feels to be alive: it feels as if everything were myself, or as if everything—including "my" thoughts and actions—were happening of itself. There are still efforts, choices, and decisions, but not the sense that "I *make* them"; they arise of themselves in relation to circumstances. This is therefore to feel life, not as an encounter between subject and object, but as a polarized field where the contest of opposites has become the play of opposites.

It is for this reason that Buddhism pairs insight (*prajna*) with compassion (*karuna*), which is the appropriate attitude of the organism to its social and natural environment when it is discovered that the shifting boundary between the individual and the world, which we call the individual's behavior, is common to both. My outline, which is not just the outline of my skin but of every organ and cell in my body, is also the inline of the world. The movements of this outline are my movements, but they are also movements of the world—of its inline. "According to relativity theory, space is not regarded as a container but as a constituent of the material universe" (38). Seeing this, I *feel with* the world. By seeing through the social institution of the separate ego and finding out that my apparent independence was a social convention, I feel all the more one with society. Corresponding, then, to the final vision of the world as a unified field (*dharmadhatu*), Buddhism sees the fully liberated man as a Bodhisattva, as one completely free to take part in the cosmic and social game. When it is said that he is in the world but not of it, that he returns to join in all its activities without attachment, this means that he no longer confuses his identity with his social role— that he plays his role instead of taking it seriously. He is a Joker or "wild" man who can play any card in the pack.

His position is thus the same as that of the Atman-Brahman in Vedanta, of the unclassifiable and unidentifiable Self which plays all the various parts in the cosmic and social drama. As, on a lower level, one is never quite sure who an actor is, since, even when off stage, he may still be acting, so also the Bodhisattva has no identity that can be pinned down. "His door stands closed, and the wise ones do not know him. His inner life is hidden, and he moves outside the ruts of the recognized virtues" (39). It is in the same sense that "the foxes have holes and the

birds of the air have nests, but the Son of Man has nowhere to lay his head," for the real sense of the homeless
life, of being a "forest dweller" (*vanaprastha*) outside
caste, is that the role of one's ego is only being played. One's
life is an act with no actor, and thus it has always been
recognized that the insane man who has lost his mind is a
parody of the sage who has transcended his ego. If one is
paranoid, the other is metanoid. The sphere of the Bodhisattva is thus what Gerald Heard calls "meta-comedy,"
a jargonesque and up-to-date equivalent of the Divine
Comedy, the viewpoint from which the tragedy of life is
seen as comedy because the protagonists are really players.
So, too, the lower outcaste, whether criminal or lunatic
who cannot be trusted, is always the mirror image of the
upper outcaste, the impartial one who takes no sides and
cannot be pinned down. But the former retreats from the
tragedy of the double-bind because it appears to him to be
an insoluble problem. The latter laughs at it because he
knows it to be nonsense. When society cannot distinguish
between these two outcastes, it treats both alike.

The relation of liberation to social convention becomes
clearer still when we pass from India to China. Taoism, the
way of liberation, is often described as being fundamentally opposed to Confucianism, the system of social norms,
but it is a serious mistake to regard them as mutually
exclusive points of view like determinism and free will.
Basic to Confucianism is the idea that the proper ordering
of society depends upon the "rectification of names," that
is by common agreement as to the definition of roles and
their relationships. The Taoist position is that no such
definition can be undertaken seriously. Names or words
have to be defined with other words, and with what words

will these be defined? Therefore the celebrated classic
attributed to Lao-tzu begins:

The Tao [Way of Nature] that can be told of
  Is not the Absolute Tao;
The Names that can be given
  Are not Absolute Names.
The Nameless is the origin of Heaven and Earth;
The Named [or, Naming] is the Mother of All Things. (40)

For things, as we have seen, are units of description, and
it is therefore naming and describing which makes nature
seem to consist of separate units. But

Tao was always nameless. . . .
Inasmuch as names are given, one should also
  know where to stop.
Knowing where to stop one can become imperishable. (41)

This "knowing where to stop" is more generally called *wu-
wei,* a term whose literal meaning is nonaction or noninterference, but which must more correctly be understood as
not acting in conflict with the Tao, the Way or Course of
nature. It is therefore against the Tao to try, exhaustively,
to pin its unceasing transformations to names, because
this will make it appear that the structure of nature is the
same as the structure of language: that it is a multitude of
distinct things instead of a multitude of changing relations.
Because it is the latter, there is actually no way of standing
outside nature as to interfere with it. The organism of man
does not confront the world but is in the world.

Language *seems* to be a system of fixed terms standing
over against the physical events to which they refer. That
it is not so, appears in the impossibility of keeping a living
language stable. Thinking and knowing seem to be con-

fronting the world as an ego in the same way that words seem to stand over against events; the two illusions stand or fall together. Speaking and thinking are events in and of the physical world, but they are carried on *as if* they were outside it, as if they were an independent and fixed measure with which life could be compared. Hence the notion that the ego can interfere with the world from outside, and can also separate things and events from one another as one can apparently separate "right" (*shih*) from "wrong" (*fei*). Thus Chuang-tzu says:

> How can Tao be so obscured that there should be a distinction of true and false? How can speech be so obscured that there should be a distinction of right [*shih*] and wrong [*fei*]? ... There is nothing which is not *this*; there is nothing which is not *that*. What cannot be seen by *that* [the other person] can be known by myself. Hence I say, *this* emanates from *that*; *that* also derives from *this*. This is the theory of the interdependence of *this* and *that*. Nevertheless, life arises from death, and *vice versa*. Possibility arises from impossibility, and *vice versa*. Affirmation is based upon denial, and *vice versa*. Which being the case, the true sage rejects all distinctions and takes his refuge in Heaven [*i.e.*, in the basic unity of the world]. (42)

Taoism, especially in the philosophy of Chuang-tzu, constantly makes fun of Confucian solemnity, of the seriousness with which it is supposed that the right and the wrong can be defined and society put in permanent order. Chuang-tzu related the following (apocryphal) interview between Lao-tzu and Confucius:

> Confucius began to expound the doctrines of his twelve canons, in order to convince Lao-tzu.

"This is all nonsense," cried Lao-tzu, interrupting him. "Tell me what are your criteria."

"Charity," replied Confucius, "and duty towards one's neighbor." . . .

"Tell me," said Lao-tzu, "in what consist charity and duty to one's neighbor?"

"They consist," answered Confucius, "in a capacity for rejoicing in all things; in universal love, without the element of self. These are the characteristics of charity and duty to one's neighbor."

"What stuff!" cried Lao-tzu. "Does not universal love contradict itself? Is not your elimination of self a positive manifestation of self? Sir, if you would cause the empire not to lose its source of nourishment,—there is the universe, its regularity is unceasing; there are the sun and moon, their brightness is unceasing; there are the stars, their groupings never change; there are birds and beasts, they flock together without varying; there are trees and shrubs, they grow upwards without exception. Be like these; follow Tao; and you will be perfect. Why then these vain struggles after charity and duty to one's neighbor, as though beating a drum in search of a fugitive [who will thus hear you coming and make his escape]. Alas! Sir, you have brought much confusion into the mind of man." (43)

The philosophy of *wu-wei* or noninterference implies, then, the apparently dangerous counsel that people must accept themselves as they are. This will disturb the social order far less than splitting themselves apart to strive after impossible ideals.

This talk of charity and duty to one's neighbor drives me nearly crazy. Sir, strive to keep the world to its own original simplicity. And as the wind bloweth where it listeth, so let

virtue establish itself. . . . The heron is white without a daily
bath. The raven is black without daily coloring itself. (44)

Human nature could be trusted enough to leave itself
alone because it was felt to be embedded in the Tao, and
the Tao was in turn felt to be a perfectly self-consistent
order of nature, manifesting itself in the polarity of *yang*
(the positive) and *yin* (the negative). Their polar relationship made it impossible for one to exist without the other,
and thus there was no real reason to be for *yang* and
against *yin*. If, on the other hand, men do not trust their
own nature or the universe of which it is a part, how can
they trust their mistrust? Going deeper, what does it mean
either to trust or mistrust, accept or reject oneself, if one
cannot actually stand apart from oneself as, say, thinker
and thoughts? Will the thinker correct wrong thoughts?
But what if the thinker needs to correct the thinker? Is it
not simpler to suppose that thoughts may correct themselves?[5]

Chuang-tzu's gentle twitting of Confucian solemnity
rises to a genuine humor, almost unique in literature of
this kind, because he also makes fun of his own point of
view. To do this he employs, in the purest spirit of "meta-
comedy," all the analogies between the sage, on the one
hand, and the fool, idiot, drunkard, and wastrel, on the
other. As an example of liberation from the dangers of
social convention, he idealizes a hideous hunchback who
is the first to be rejected by conscription officers and the
first to be given a free handout by social service agencies
(45). The sage is as "useless" as a fantastic tree which grew

[5] Which indeed they do, by thoughts about thoughts, or language about
language, now known as meta-language. Thought is corrected not by a
thinker, but rather by further thinking on a higher level.

to immense proportions because its fruit was bitter, its leaves inedible, and its trunk and branches so twisted that no one could make planks of it (46). The way of liberation is "the way down and out"; it is taking, like water, the course of least resistance; it is by following the natural bent of one's own feelings; it is by becoming stupid and rejecting the refinements of learning; it is by becoming inert and drifting like a leaf on the wind. What is really being said is that intelligence solves problems by seeking the greatest simplicity and the least expenditure of effort, and it is thus that Taoism eventually inspired the Japanese to work out the technique of *judo*—the easy or gentle Tao (*do*).

There is an obvious parallel here with the philosophy of Carl Rogers' nondirective therapy, in which the therapist simply draws out the logical conclusions of his client's thinking and feeling by doing no more than rephrasing it in what seems to be the clearest form. The responses of the therapist are confined to expressions of his own understanding of what the client says to him. He trusts in the wisdom of the "positive growth potential" of every human being to work out the solution of the problem if only it can be clearly and consistently stated. The therapist himself is therefore "stupid" and "passive" like a Taoist in that he has no theory of what is wrong with his client or what he ought to become in order to be cured. If the client feels that he has a problem, then he has a problem. If he feels that he has no problem, he stops coming for therapy. And the therapist is content in the faith that if the problem is *really* unsolved, the client will eventually return. This is exactly the attitude of a Taoist sage to any would-be student, but its success would seem to depend on whether the therapist is applying a mechanical technique or whether he is genuinely at peace within himself.

The Taoist's position, like Wittgenstein's, is that while there may be logical problems there are no natural, physical problems, Nature or Tao is not pursuing any purpose, and therefore is not meeting any difficulties.

> He who replies to one asking about Tao, does not know Tao. Although one may hear about Tao, he does not really hear about Tao. There is no such thing as asking about Tao. There is no such thing as answering such questions. To ask a question which cannot be answered is vain. To answer a question which cannot be answered is unreal. And one who thus meets the vain with the unreal is one who has no physical perception of the universe, and no mental perception of the origin of existence. (47)

This is not because the Tao is inherently mysterious but because the problems of human society are artificial.

> *When the great Tao is lost, spring forth benevolence and righteousness.*
> *When wisdom and sagacity arise, there are great hypocrites.*
> *When family relations are no longer harmonious, we have filial children and devoted parents.*
> *When a nation is in confusion and disorder, patriots are recognized.* (48)

Chuang-tzu therefore compares the liberated man to the "pure men of old" who are supposed to have lived before the artificial aims of society were invented.

> The pure men of old acted without calculation, not seeking to secure results. They laid no plans. Therefore, failing, they had no cause for regret; succeeding, no cause for congratulation. And thus they could scale heights without fear.

. . . They did not know what it was to love life and hate death. They did not rejoice in birth, nor strive to put off dissolution. Quickly come, and quickly go;—no more. . . . This is what is called not to lead the heart astray from Tao, nor to let the human seek to supplement the divine. (49)

Now one might suppose that the Taoists were advocating a romantic primitivism, like the idealization of the Noble Savage in eighteenth-century Europe. This would be a natural conclusion if the passages quoted are taken entirely out of their social context. But Needham (50) has made a very convincing case for the idea that the artificiality and "technology" to which the Taoists were opposed were those of a feudal system in which the laws were a protection of exploitation, and technology the manufacture of weapons. Still more important is the fact that Confucianism, despite its undoubted merits, was a scholastic, ritualistic, and purely theoretical conception of the social order without the slightest interest in the order of nature. The whole literature of Taoism shows a deep and intelligent interest in the patterns and processes of the natural world and a desire to model human life upon the observable principles of nature as distinct from the arbitrary principles of a social order resting upon violence.

A violent wind cannot last a whole morning; pelting rain cannot last a whole day. What achieves these things but heaven and earth? Inasmuch as heaven and earth cannot keep up such activity, how much less can man? (51)

In other words, social conventions in direct contradiction with physical patterns cannot support an enduring society. If this is romantic primitivism, psychotherapy is no less so in our own age in advocating ways of life that are consistent with human biology rather than social tradition. In Confucianism the source of authority was a traditional literature; in Taoism it was the observation of the natural universe, and, as Needham has suggested, there is a close parallel here with the break between Western science, reading the book of nature, and Western scholasticism, reading only the Bible, Aristotle, and St. Thomas Aquinas.

Under any civilized conditions it is, of course, impossible for anyone to act without laying plans, or to refuse absolutely to participate in an economy of waste and violence, whether its ideological sponsorship be capitalist or communist. It is, however, possible to see that this competitive "rat race" need not be taken seriously, or rather, that if we are to persist in it at all it *must* not be taken seriously unless "nervous breakdowns" are to become as common as colds. Bear it in mind that Chuang-tzu's descriptions of the pure men of old and of the life of noninterference are always somewhat exaggerated; they are humorous, like Liang K'ai's paintings of Zen masters (52).

> The man of character lives at home without exercising his mind and performs actions without worry. . . . Appearing stupid, he goes about like one who has lost his way. He has plenty of money to spend, but does not know where it comes from. (53)

Just as *wu-wei* is not literally doing nothing, liberation is not literally quitting the social game, but treating it as the old man treats the cataract in the following anecdote:

> Confucius was looking at the cataract at Lüliang. It fell from a height of two hundred feet, and its foam reached fifteen miles away. No scaly, finny creature could enter therein. Yet Confucius saw an old man go in, and thinking

that he was suffering from some trouble and desirous of ending his life, bade a disciple run along the side to try and save him. The old man emerged about a hundred paces off, and with flowing hair went carolling along the bank. Confucius followed him and said, "I had thought, sir, you were a spirit, but now I see you are a man. Kindly tell me, is there any way to deal thus with water?"

"No," replied the old man, "I have no way. . . . Plunging in with the whirl, I come out with the swirl. I accommodate myself to the water, not the water to me. And so I am able to deal with it after this fashion." (54)

Between A.D. 400 and 900 there arose out of the interplay of Taoism and Mahayana Buddhism the school of Ch'an or Zen, with its astonishing technique (of which more will be said later) of teaching liberation by "direct pointing" instead of discussion. The fundamental position of Zen is that it has nothing to say, or, again, that nature is not a problem.

> The blue hills are simply blue hills;
> The white clouds are simply white clouds.

That is the whole of Zen, and therefore when the student approaches the master with some such artificial question as, "How do I enter the path to liberation?" the master replies, "Do you hear the stream?" "Yes." "There is the way to enter." Or, simpler still, to the question "What is the meaning of Buddhism?" he answers, "Three pounds of flax!" The difficulty of Zen is the almost overwhelming problem of getting anyone to see that life-and-death is *not* a problem. The Zen master tackles this by asking the student to find out *for whom* the world is a problem, for whom is pleasure desirable and pain undesirable, thus turning con-

sciousness back upon itself to discover the ego. But of
course it turns out that this mythical "I" that seems to confront experience or to be trapped in the world is nowhere
to be found. One day the old master Sekito found his
(very advanced) student Yakusan sitting on a rock. "What
are you doing here?" asked Sekito.

"Not one thing," replied Yakusan.

"If so, you are sitting idly."

"Even the sitting idly is doing something."

"You say, 'doing nothing,' but pray what is that which
is doing nothing?"

"Even when you call up thousands of wise men, they
cannot tell you that" (55).

With their differing methods, Vedanta, Buddhism, and
Taoism all involve the realization that life ceases to seem
problematic when it is understood that the ego is a social
fiction. Sickness and death may be painful, indeed, but
what makes them problematic is that they are shameful
to the ego. This is the same shame that we feel when
caught out of role, as when a bishop is discovered picking
his nose or a policeman weeping. For the ego is the role,
the "act," that one's inmost self is permanent, that it is in
control of the organism, and that while it "has" experiences
it is not involved in them. Pain and death expose this pretense, and this is why suffering is almost always attended
by a feeling of guilt, a feeling that is all the more difficult
to explain when the pretense is unconscious. Hence the
obscure but powerful feeling that one *ought* not to suffer
or die.

> *You no longer feel quite human.*
> *You're suddenly reduced to the status of an object—*
> *A living object, but no longer a person. . . .*

When you've dressed for a party
And are going downstairs, with everything about you
Arranged to support you in the role you have chosen,
Then sometimes, when you come to the bottom step
There is one step more than your feet expected
And you come down with a jolt. Just for a moment
You have the experience of being an object
At the mercy of a malevolent staircase. (56)

The state of consciousness which follows upon liberation from the ego fiction is quite easily intelligible in neuropsychiatric terms. One of the important physical facts that socialization represses is that all our sensory experiences are states of the nervous system. The field of vision, which we take to be outside the organism, is in fact inside it because it is a translation of the external world into the form of the eye and the optical nerves. What we see is therefore a state of the organism, a state of ourselves. Yet to say even this is to say too much. There is not the external world, and then the state of the nervous system, and then something which sees that state. The seeing is precisely that particular state of the nervous system, a state which for that moment *is* an integral part of the organism. Similarly, one does not hear a sound. The sound is the hearing, apart from which it is simply a vibration in the air. The states of the nervous system need not, as we suppose, be watched by something else, by a little man inside the head who registers them all. Wouldn't he have to have *another* nervous system, and another little man inside *his* head, and so ad infinitum? When we get an infinite regression of this kind we should always suspect that we have made an unnecessary step in our reasoning. It is the same kind of oscillation that happens when the earpiece of a telephone is placed against the mouthpiece. It "howls."

So, too, when we posit what is in effect a second nervous system watching the first, we are turning the nervous system back upon itself, and thereupon our thoughts oscillate. We become an infinite series of echoes, of selves behind selves behind selves. Now indeed there is a sense in which the cortex is a second nervous system over and above the primary system of the thalamus. Oversimplifying things considerably, we could say that the cortex works as an elaborate feedback system for the thalamus by means of which the organism can to some extent be aware of itself. Because of the cortex, the nervous system can know that it knows; it can *re*cord and *re*cognize its own states. But this is just one "echo," not an infinite series. Furthermore, the cortex is just another neural pattern, and its states are neural patterns; it is not something other than neural pattern as the ego agent is supposed to be, in the organism but not of it.

How can the cortex observe and control the cortex? Perhaps there will come a day when the human brain will fold back on itself again and develop a higher cortex, but until then the only feedback which the cortex has about its own states comes through other people. (I am speaking here of the cortex as a whole. One can of course remember remembering.) Thus the ego which observes and controls the cortex is a complex of social information relayed back into the cortex—Mead's "generalized other." But this is social misinformation when it is made to appear that the information of which the ego consists is something other than states of the cortex itself, and therefore ought to be controlling the cortex. The ego is the unconscious pretense that the organism contains a higher system than the cortex; it is the confusion of a system of interpersonal information with a new, and imaginary, fold in the brain—or with something quite other than a neural pattern, a mind, soul, or self. When, therefore, I feel that "I" am knowing or controlling myself—my cortex—I should recognize that I am actually being controlled by other people's words and gestures masquerading as my inner or better self. Not to see this brings about utter confusion, as when I try to force myself to stop feeling in ways that are socially objectionable.

If all this is true, it becomes obvious that the ego feeling is pure hypnosis. Society is persuading the individual to do what it wants by making it appear that its commands are the individual's inmost self. What we want is what you want. And this is a double-bind, as when a mother says to her child, who is longing to slush around in a mud puddle, "Now darling, you don't *want* to get into that mud!" This is misinformation, and this—if anything—is the "Great Social Lie."

Let us suppose, then, that the false reflex of "I seeing my sights" or "I feeling my feelings" is stopped, by such methods as the ways of liberation employ. Will it not thereupon become clear that all our perceptions of the external world are states of the organism? The division between "I" and "my sights" is projected outwardly into the sharp division between the organism and what it sees. Just such a change of perception as this would explain the feeling, so usual at the moment of liberation (*satori*), that the external world is oneself and that external actions are one's own doing. Perception will then be known for what it is, a field relationship as distinct from an encounter.[6] It

[6] I am reasonably satisfied that something approximating this change of perception, the realization that sensations are states of the organism itself, is brought about by lysergic acid (LSD-25). Many drugs suspend inhibitions that are useful, but it seems that LSD suspends an inhibition

is hardly too much to say that such a change of perception would give far better ground for social solidarity than the normal trick of misinformation and hypnosis.

There is one further question which should be raised at this point, a question that repeatedly comes up in any discussion of the usefulness of the ways of liberation to the psychotherapist. Despite Freud's own basic prudishness, the whole history of psychotherapy is bound up with a movement toward sexual freedom in western culture. This seems to be in sharp conflict with the fact that the ways of liberation so largely enjoin celibacy and the monastic or eremitic life upon their followers. Many texts could be cited to show that sexual passion is held to be a major obstacle to liberation.

To understand this, we must first go back to the social context of liberation in ancient India. In the normal course of things, no one entered upon these disciplines until the latter part of his life. In the various *ashramas* or stages of life the liberative stage of "forest dweller" (*vanaprastha*) came only after completion of the stage of "householder" (*grihastha*). No one was expected to seek liberation until he had raised a family and handed over his occupation to his sons. It was assumed that liberation was not only freedom from social convention but also from social responsibility. Mahayana Buddhism was to modify this idea radically, and we shall see that the answer to our problem lies here rather than in the disciplines that remain inseparable from Hindu culture—Vedanta and Yoga. But it is significant that Jung, too, regards the individuation

which is of very doubtful value, and thus its use as a therapeutic might be explored further on the hypothesis that this is the main feature of its action. Elsewhere (57) I have discussed more fully the partial resemblances between the LSD experience and "cosmic consciousness."

process of his psychotherapy as a task for the second half of life, as a preparation for death.

In all ancient precontraceptive societies sexual activity is obviously inseparable from procreation, and thus from several points of view it seemed unsuitable for a man in the stage of *vanaprastha* to become a father. In an age when life expectancy was far shorter than it is today, there was slight chance that he would live to raise his children to maturity. Furthermore, there was a potential conflict between the duty of socializing the children and liberating himself. It must also be remembered that primitive physiology associates the seminal emission with a "loss" of vital fluid comparable to a loss of blood, confusing the relaxation of detumescence with impaired vitality. Hence the widespread but quite fallacious notion that "Every animal is sad after intercourse [*Omne animal triste post coitum*]." But, apart from all these considerations, the main reason for insisting upon the repression of sexual desire was that this offered a major challenge to the reality of the ego, as if to say, "If you can thwart your biological nature, you really do exist!"

This is such a drastic method of challenging the ego that, as with certain potent drugs, one is justified in using them only if fairly certain that they will work. Indeed, all the methods of liberation were supposed to work and therefore to be *temporary* disciplines. The Buddhist discipline is often likened to a raft for crossing from the shore of *samsara* to the shore of *nirvana*, and the texts say again and again that when the farther shore is reached the raft should be left behind. In Mahayana Buddhism, as we have seen, the liberated Bodhisattva returns from the forest or hermitage into society and the world. But the practical difficulty is that in Asia the ways of liberation are, with some exceptions, as inefficient and as theoretically confused as psychotherapy in the West. Indeed, the whole point of comparing them with psychotherapy is to effect a mutual clarification. Chronic Buddhism is perhaps even more common than chronic psychotherapy—twice a week for twenty years or more.

For, as things actually work out, followers of the ways in modern Asia seem to have lost their nerve to such an extent that one rarely hears of anyone actually being liberated outside the particular discipline of Zen Buddhism. (Perhaps other schools are more modest, and, indeed, there is a certain contradiction in saying "*I* am liberated" if the ego is unreal. But there is also the false modesty of so imitating humility that it becomes more important to be humble than to be liberated. Golden chains are as binding as chains of iron. There are also followers of the ways who remain anonymous and unorganized—Taoists, for example, who simply mind their own business and lay no claim to anything at all save, with a certain humor, stupidity.) But the general loss of nerve is due in part to what might be called the distance of excessive reverence. Whenever a tradition becomes venerable with the passage of time, the ancient masters and sages are elevated to pedestals of sanctity and wisdom which lift them far above the human level. The way of liberation becomes confused with a popular cult; the ancient teachers become gods and supermen, and thus the ideal of liberation or Buddha-hood becomes ever more remote. No one believes that it can be reached except by the most unusually gifted and heroic prodigies. Consequently the medicine of the discipline becomes a diet, the cure an addiction, and the raft a houseboat. In this manner, a way of liberation turns into just another social institution and dies of respectability.

Outside the sphere of influence of Mahayana Buddhism this has happened so widely that being on the way to liberation is the most that anyone expects. The few liberated ones to be recognized are freaks of birth, like Sri Ramakrishna or Sri Ramana Maharshi, or very old men like the late Sri Aurobindo. But under these circumstances what was intended as a swift remedy, the effort to repress sexuality, becomes chronic prudery, and it is thus forgotten or simply hushed up that the Bodhisattva is not expected to be celibate. Nor, on the other hand, is he likely to be a libertine since he does not need to use sexual release as an escape from the "problem" of life. It is important, too, to remember that, outside the supposedly temporary discipline of liberation, the sexual mores of Asian cultures are in many ways far more liberal than ours and the association of sexuality with sin is rare indeed. Thus the sexual expression of the Bodhisattva is limited only by his own sense of good taste and by the customs of whatever secular society may be his home. The "graduate" of a Zen community may therefore become a married priest or simply return into lay life.[7]

[7] This is not the place to enter into the very special problem of the Tantric use of sexuality in the actual discipline of liberation. The reader is referred to Dasgupta (58), Eliade (59), and Woodroffe (60) for highly reliable accounts, and to my own more conjectural interpretation (61). But as to the permissibility of sexuality for the Bodhisattva or liberated man, many texts are perfectly explicit. E.g., *Chandogya Upanishad*, 8. 12. 3., "Man issues forth from bodily identification to assume his real form upon attainment of the great illumination. Such a man is best among men. He lives like a king—eating, playing, and enjoying women, possessions, and family, without identification with the body." *Subhashita-samgraha*, 47, "Foolish people think of liberation as something entirely different from the enjoyment of the world; but whatever there is sublime and great

There is good reason to believe that liberated sexuality might be something like a mature form of what Freud so inappropriately called the "polymorphous perverse" sexuality of the infant, that is, an erotic relationship of organism and environment that is not restricted to the genital system (65). The eyes and the ears, the nose and the skin, all become avenues of erotic communion, not just with other people, but with the whole realm of nature, for genital eroticism is simply a special canalization of the basic love which is the polarity of *yang* and *yin*. The texts say repeatedly that the Bodhisattva is free to enter into the relationship of love because he is unattached. This does *not* mean that he enters into it mechanically, with feelings as cold as ice. Nor is this the sort of subterfuge whereby some religious libertines have justified anything that they do by explaining that all physical states are illusory, or that their "spirit" is really above it all. The point is rather that such sexuality is completely genuine and spontaneous (*sahaja*); its pleasure is detached in the sense that it is not compulsively sought out to assuage anxiety, to prove one's manliness, or to serve as a substitute for liberation. "Sahaja," wrote Coomaraswamy, "has nothing to do with the cult of pleasure. It is a doctrine of the Tao, and a path of non-pursuit. All that is best for us comes of itself into our hands—but if we strive to overtake it, it perpetually eludes us" (66).

---

which is heard, seen, smelt, eaten, known, and touched, is good all round. . . . The whole drama of the world is to be known as perfectly pure by nature" (62). *Saraha-pada*, 19, "Without meditating, without renouncing the world, / One may stay at home in the company of one's wife. / Can that be called perfect knowledge, Saraha says, / If one is not released while enjoying the pleasures of sense? (63)" Modern Indian spirituality, especially among the classes affected by Western-style education, is heavily tinged with (presumably) British puritanism, but the best discussion of this whole problem is that by A. K. Coomaraswamy (64).

IV

Through a Glass Darkly

It is perfectly natural that man himself should be the most unintelligible part of the universe. The way his organism looks to an outside observer, such as a neurosurgeon, is so astonishingly different from the way it feels from the inside. The way in which human behavior is described by the biologist or the sociologist is so unlike what is seen by the ordinary individual that he can hardly recognize himself. But the disparity is no different in principle from the shock of hearing for the first time a recording of one's own voice, and from getting a frank description of one's character from a shrewd observer. These descriptions, like the whole external world itself, seem so foreign, so *other*. Yet the time may come when the shock of strangeness turns into the shock of recognition, when looking at the external world as a mirror we may exclaim with amazement, "Why, that's *me!*"

Collectively, we are still a long way from this recognition. The world beyond us is an alien and unfathomable unknown, and we look into its glass very darkly indeed, confronting it as though we did not belong.

> *I, a stranger, and afraid,*
> *In a world I never made.*

Only slowly does it dawn upon us that there is something fundamentally wrong with this feeling; simple logic, if nothing else, forces us to see that however separated self and other may be there is no self without this other. But standing in the way of this recognition is the fear of finding out that this external world may be *only* oneself, and that the answer to one's voice is only an endless reverberation of echoes. This is, of course, because our conception of self is confined to a very small and mainly fictitious part of our being, and to discover that the world were a belt of mirrors round *that* taper's flame would indeed be a horrifying solipsism. Yet if it turns out that self and other are one, it will also turn out that self and surprise are one.

We have been seeing all along that although Western science started out by trying to gain the greatest objectivity, the greatest lack of involvement between the observer and the observed, the more diligently this isolation is pressed, the more impossible it is found to be. From physics to psychology, every department of science is realizing more and more that to observe the world is to participate in it, and that, frustrating as this may first seem to be, it is the most important clue of all to further knowledge. At the same time, it is often pointed out that there is an ever-widening gap of communication between the scientific specialist and the lay public because his language is incomprehensible and his models of the world ever more remote from the images of common sense. Another aspect of this gap is that the world as we are coming to know it theoretically bears little resemblance to the world that we feel: we have sixteenth-century personalities in the world of twentieth-century concepts because social conventions lag far behind the flight of theoretical knowledge.

Is it possible, however, that science will become Western man's way of liberation? Such an idea is about as repugnant as anything can be to most exponents of the traditional Eastern ways, who are apt to regard science as the very nadir of Western materialism. Thus one of the most gifted interpreters of the Vedanta, René Guénon, writes:

> The domain of every science is always dependent upon experimentation, in one or other of its various modalities, whereas the domain of metaphysic [i.e., liberation] is essentially constituted by that of which no external investigation is possible: being "beyond physics" we are also, by that very fact, beyond experiment. Consequently, the field of every separate science can, if it is capable of it, be extended indefinitely without ever finding the slightest point of contact with the metaphysical sphere. (67)

But the world of knowledge may, like the earth, be round —so that an immersion in material particulars may quite unexpectedly lead back to the universal and the transcendent. Blake's idea that "the fool who persists in his folly will become wise" is the same as Spinoza's "the more we know of particular things, the more we know of God." For this, as we have seen, was the essential technique of liberation: to encourage the student to explore his false premises consistently—to the end. Unhappily, most Western devotees of the Eastern ways know little or nothing of what has happened in science during the last fifty years, and think of it still as the reduction of the world to the "objects" of Newtonian mechanics.[1]

It is true that the historical origins of applied science lay in Western man's exaggerated feeling of estrangement from nature, and that in many ways his technology is still

[1] It would not be fair to say so without admitting that I myself have labored under the same ignorance, as any informed reader of *The Supreme Identity* will see.

an attack upon the world. Psychoanalysts galore have pointed out the degree to which the objective, rigorous, analytical, and parsimonious spirit of science is an expression of hostility, an attempt to render the physical world perfectly sterile. No one but us objects around here! Everything is scrubbed clean of mystery until it is quite dead, and the universe is explained away as "nothing but" mechanism and fortuitous arrangements of blind energy. But one cannot persist in such hostility without discovering that something is wrong, just as a social group cannot annihilate its enemy without discovering that it has lost a friend. As Norman Brown puts it:

> Whitehead and Needham are protesting against the inhuman attitude of modern science; in psychoanalytical terms, they are calling for a science based on an erotic sense of reality, rather than an aggressive dominating attitude toward reality. . . . The mentality which was able to reduce nature to "a dull affair, soundless, scentless, colourless; merely the hurrying of material endlessly, meaninglessly"—Whitehead's description—is lethal. It is an awe-inspiring attack on the life of the universe; in more technical psychoanalytical terms, its anal-sadistic intent is plain. (68)

But he goes on to quote the psychoanalytically oriented historian of science, Gaston Bachelard, in a passage which curiously misinterprets the twentieth-century revolution in scientific description:

> It does indeed seem that with the twentieth century there begins a kind of scientific thought in opposition to the senses, and that it is necessary to construct a theory of objectivity *in opposition to* the object. . . . It follows that the entire use of the brain is being called into question. From now on the

brain is strictly no longer adequate as an instrument for scientific thought; that is to say, the brain is the *obstacle* to scientific thought. It is an obstacle in the sense that it is the coordinating center for human movements and appetites. It is necessary to think *in opposition to* the brain. (69)

At a time when the electronic computer is taking over so much of the burden of thought and when, as we have said, physical models of the universe appear to be sensuously inconceivable, Bachelard's words are persuasive. This is the more so when the practical outcome of modern physics might be the actual destruction of life upon this planet. But Bachelard does not see that what science is now overcoming is a type of sense perception and a whole image of the world that was itself in opposition to the senses and the organism. Newton's mechanical universe was far more inhuman than Einstein's relative universe. Descartes's firm dichotomy of subject and object, ego and world, was far more anti-organic than modern field theory. And what about the still earlier conceptions of the body and the physical world as the domain of corruption and evil? Indeed, when we look through the microscope, as when we look at the art of Picasso, Klee, or Pollock, the human body is not there in its familiar form. Kepes' *New Landscape* (70) and similar works present both the macroscopic and microscopic forms of nature revealed by scientific instruments as objects for aesthetic contemplation, and who can deny their incomparable beauty?

But this is not necessarily, in Berdyaev's phrase, "the destruction of the human image." It is certainly not the image of man as it was seen by painters of the Renaissance and, still less, of *l'art officiel* of the nineteenth century. For this was an image which stressed above all the separation of man from his surroundings, an art in which man was defined and bounded by his skin, and in which conventional perspective stressed the distance of the subject from the object. But when we compare Kepes' photographs with the Islamic arabesque, with Chinese calligraphy, or with the fantastic border ornaments of Celtic manuscripts is the resemblance quite fortuitous? Indeed, this new landscape is unfamiliar, but with one more turn of the screw on the microscope we shall again see ourselves. We shall look a little longer at the photographs from Palomar, and the shape of the cosmos will be seen, perhaps quite suddenly, to be the shape of man: it will make *sense*. It will not, however, be the shape of the ego, of the purely abstract and conceptual man who is locked up inside his skin.

We might say that the more unfamiliar, the more *other* the form in which man learns to recognize himself, the deeper his knowledge of himself becomes—reversing the Delphic aphorism into "Know the universe and the gods, and thou shalt know thyself." If, then, man is to rediscover his own image in the macroscopic and microscopic worlds which science reveals, this will be the "own image" in which God is said to have created him—that is, the universal man, the Adam-Kadmon, the Son of Man, or the universe considered as the Body of Buddha (*buddhakaya*). These are mythological symbols, and however poetic and anthropomorphic they may seem to be, their meaning is the fact upon which exact science has now stumbled: that the part and the whole, the individual and the cosmos, are what they are only in relation to one another. The hitherto unconscious or socially ignored form of man is the form of the world. As Whitehead puts it:

Appearances are finally controlled by the functionings of the animal body. These functionings and the happenings within the contemporary regions [i.e., environments of the body] are both derived from a common past, highly relevant to both. It is thereby pertinent to ask, whether the animal body and the external regions are not attuned together, so that under normal circumstances, the appearances conform to natures within the regions. The attainment of such conformation would belong to the perfection of nature in respect to the higher types of animal life. . . . We have to ask whether nature does not contain within itself a tendency to be in tune, an Eros urging towards perfection. (71)

Is not this at least the beginning of an answer to the hope which Freud expresses at the end of *Civilization and Its Discontents?*

Men have brought their powers of subduing the forces of nature to such a pitch that by using them they could now very easily exterminate one another to the last man. They know this—hence arises a great part of their current unrest, their dejection, their mood of apprehension. And now it may be expected that the other of the two "heavenly forces," eternal Eros, will put forth his strength so as to maintain himself alongside of his equally immortal adversary. (72)

"And," adds Norman Brown, "perhaps our children will live to live a full life, and to see what Freud could not see—in the old adversary [Thanatos], a friend" (73).

But if science is actually to become our way of liberation its theoretical view must be translated into feeling, not only for laymen but for scientists themselves. Shortly after I had read one of the most fascinating accounts of this new unitary view of man-in-the-world, *The Next Development in Man* (74) by the British biophysicist L. L.

Whyte, I put this very problem to the author. He replied that it had never occurred to him and, that so far as he was concerned, the feeling should naturally follow from a thorough comprehension of the theory. I was asking, in other words, whether science should not comprise a *yoga* —a discipline for realizing its view as what psychologists call *insight*, over and above verbal understanding. There may be some truth in what Whyte said. After all, when it has been pointed out to us that the following two-dimensional figure is a cube, we really feel it to be so.

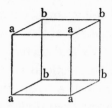

But it is extremely difficult to point out insights which go against common sense and social standards of sanity, just as it is difficult for the convention of perspective to suggest depth to a member of a culture in which it is not used. By what effort can *we* see at a single glance that the above figure is two cubes, one of which has the square with corners *a* in front, and the other the square with corners *b*? Can we see two different facts as one? (75) To be truly liberative Western science must have its own *yoga*, and some outgrowth of psychotherapy is the natural candidate for the task. The question is whether the kind of psychotherapy that we know is in any position to fulfill it, even for the small minority that can be reached by its consultative method.

There are, indeed, a number of ways in which science

and psychotherapy have already been liberative, in the strict sense of enabling people to see the contradictory or fictitious character of some social institutions. With a somewhat different approach, science has done to the Christian cosmology of Dante and St. Thomas what Buddhism did to the reincarnation cosmology of ancient India: it has exorcised its terrors, and also made it thoroughly implausible. It is not by any means that science has disproved the existence of God the Father, Heaven and Hell, the hosts of angels, and the resurrection of the body. On the one hand, modern astronomical, physical, and biological knowledge makes this cosmology simply inappropriate. In comparison with the new image of the universe, the traditional Christian image is naïve, and theologians can save it only by tortuous feats of sophistication. On the other hand, historical research makes evident that its origins were something very different from divine revelation. The concept of God the Father was, as Whitehead says, "a sublimation from its barbaric origin. He stood in the same relation to the whole World as early Egyptian or Mesopotamian kings stood to their subject populations. Also the moral characters were very analogous" (76).

Science and psychotherapy have also done much already to liberate us from the prison of isolation from nature in which we were supposed to renounce Eros, despise the physical organism, and rest all our hopes in a supernatural world—to come later. But that this liberation is by no means complete is clear from the fact that nineteenth-century naturalism was the basis for a technological assault on nature without precedent in history. This liberation is, in other words, a very partial affair even for the small minority which has fully understood and accepted it. It leaves us still as strangers in the cosmos—without the judgment of God but without his love, without the terrors of Hell but without the hope of Heaven, without many of the physical agonies of prescientific times but without the sense that human life has any meaning. The Christian cosmos has vanished, but the Christian ego remains—with no resort but to try to forget its loneliness in some sort of collectivism, of huddling together in the dark.

Can psychotherapy complete the job? In almost all its forms it has one enormous asset: the realization that escape is no answer, that the shudders, horrors, and depressions in which "the problem of life" is manifested must be explored and their roots felt out. We must get rid of the idea that we ought not to have such feelings, and the relatively new Existential school goes so far as to say that anxiety and guilt are inseparable from human life; to be, consciously, is to know that being is relative to nonbeing, and that the possibility of ceasing to be is present at every moment and certain in the end. Here is the root of *angst*, the basic anguish of being alive which is approximately the Buddhist *duhkha*, the chronic suffering from which the Buddha proposed deliverance. To be or not to be is *not* the question; to be *is* not to be. Because of anxiety man is never fully possessed of what Tillich calls "the courage to be," and for this he always feels guilt; he has never been completely true to himself.[2] This is one example of the fact

[2] I am not sure whether the Existentialists' complete acceptance of *angst* is intended, by indirection, to annul it—overcoming it by *allowing* it to be. Rollo May (77) states that the aim of existential therapy is to enable the patient to experience his own existence, his being-in-the-world, fully and authentically. When one's existence is not confronted with the constant possibility of nonexistence, it is taken for granted—i.e., it is not taken seriously. Is not this the old Christian principle of "Live every day as if thy last"? But this is still something different from the serenity of the one who is "already dead," who is completely willing not to be. Unfortunately May does not discuss this—and he is one of the very few representatives of the school whose writing begins to be readable!

that the strength of our psychotherapies lies in their attitudes rather than their theories and techniques. Or, as George Mora has put it:

> We find increasing acknowledgement of the fact that psychotherapeutic results are strikingly similar regardless of the theoretical framework followed by each therapist, that the personality of the therapist is more important than his adherence to a particular school of thought. (78)

The logical counterpart of the attitude that escape is no answer is the attitude of the acceptance of all "psychological reality" by the therapist and, in turn, by the patient, whether it be aesthetically or morally objectionable or contrary to sane ideas of what reality is. Perhaps this has been most eloquently expressed by Jung, speaking before a group of ministers back in 1932:

> We cannot change anything unless we accept it. Condemnation does not liberate, it oppresses. . . . If a doctor wishes to help a human being he must be able to accept him as he is. And he can do this in reality only when he has already seen and accepted himself as he is. Perhaps this sounds very simple, but simple things are always the most difficult. In actual life it requires the greatest art to be simple, and so acceptance of oneself is the essence of the moral problem and the acid test of one's whole outlook on life. That I feed the beggar, that I forgive an insult, that I love my enemy in the name of Christ—all these are undoubtedly great virtues. What I do unto the least of my brethren, that I do unto Christ. But what if I should discover that the least amongst them all, the poorest of all beggars, the most impudent of all offenders, yea the very fiend himself—that these are within me, and that I myself stand in need of the alms of my own kindness, that I myself am the enemy who must be loved—

what then? . . . Had it been God himself who drew near
to us in this despicable form, we should have denied him a
thousand times before a single cock had crowed. (79)

To have "seen and accepted himself as he is" appears,
then, to be that essential quality of personality which, as
Mora says, is more important for the therapist than his
theory or school. Though it sounds simple, and not very
heroic, its implications are tremendous and its difficulties
extraordinary—for what constitutes "myself" and who is
it that accepts me? This is no mere matter of bringing
about a reconciliation between the ego and a number of
repressed experiences, shameful or painful but always
contents of one's own subjectivity. It is the much larger
problem of integrating the split which has come about
between the individual and the world, and, as we have
seen, this has little to do with adjusting him to society.

Speaking quite generally, this is the point at which
psychotherapy falls short of being a way of liberation,
even when it is recognized that therapy is far more than
adjustment. The weakness lies not so much in the theoretical differences and confusions of the various schools as in
certain tacit agreements—in particular the continued acceptance of the dualistic view of man: ego and unconscious, psyche and soma, subject and object, reality principle and pleasure principle, reason and instinct. Therapy
is healing, making whole, and any system which leaves
the individual upon one horn of the dualistic dilemma is
at best the achievement of courageous despair. This is
just what Freud himself came to; his later writings reflect
the deep pessimism of a very brave man, for he felt that
the conflict between the pleasure principle, Eros, and the
demands of the reality principle, of the necessities of

civilization, was irreconcilable. For its own survival Eros must be regulated, civilized, and repressed, but

> the repressed instinct never ceases to strive for complete satisfaction, which would consist in the repetition of a primary experience of satisfaction. No substitutive or reactive formations and no sublimations will suffice to remove the repressed instinct's persisting tension. (80)

As the social obligations of the individual grow larger and civilized life requires more and more discipline, the situation gets worse.

> If civilization is an inevitable course of development from the group of the family to the group of humanity as a whole, then an intensification of the sense of guilt . . . will be inextricably bound up with it, until perhaps the sense of guilt may swell to a magnitude that individuals can hardly support. (81)

But the problem is insoluble because of the way in which it is posed. The great irreconcilables, pleasure principle and reality principle, Eros and Thanatos, rest upon the deeper duality of the knower and the known which Freud took for granted because it was the primary assumption of his culture—even though he saw so clearly that the ego is not master in its own house. He saw that the ego arises out of the tension between the libido and culture; he knew, in other words, that the ego is a social artifact. But he regarded it as essential to consciousness; there could be no knowing, no control of human affairs, no science or art, without the opposition of the knower to the known—that is, of civilized order to nature and of the ego to the unconscious. Thus all that is distinctively human is against nature even though—and here is the conflict

THROUGH A GLASS DARKLY

—inseparable from it. Eros *cannot* be put down but it *must* be. Nature is boundless lust and rapacity, and man has evolved from it through the ruthless struggle of natural selection. Although it was now clear from biology that consciousness had grown out of the unconscious, the ego from the id, this must be regarded as a natural accident. Left to itself, the unconscious evolution of the ego could not be expected to go any further, because nature was inherently unintelligent. Nature's accident, man, must be seized from inevitable dissolution by proceeding to act as if reason were opposed to nature. In practice, then, to regard man as a natural accident, whose survival is thenceforth inconsistent with nature, amounts to the same thing as regarding him as an intelligence outside nature. This is why nineteenth-century naturalism, in the assumptions of which Freud shared, simply intensified the traditional split between spirit and nature.

Yet, as L. L. Whyte has shown in his critique of Freud, all this is bad biology.

In biological development dualism or conflict is always superimposed on a prior unity. The existence of an organism capable of survival implies integration and unity is therefore always prior to inner conflict. Conflict may arise as the result of an inappropriate adaptation, and it may prove fatal or it may be overcome. But the recovery of organic health never involves the synthesis of fundamentally opposed principles, since these cannot co-exist in an organism. It only seems to do so because the actual condition of the organism has been misinterpreted in using a dualistic language. The historical process does not involve the synthesis of pre-existing logical opposites, though it may appear to in the confused language of immature dialectical theories. (82)

In other words, Freud did not see that the ego was an in-appropriate adaptation. He saw that, as a social convention, it was self-contradictory, but he did not see that it was unnecessary. He could not conceive of consciousness without the duality of subject and object.[3]

With all his knowledge of Eastern thought, Jung seems to be in no better position.

> The Eastern mind, however, has no difficulty in conceiving of a consciousness without an ego. Consciousness is deemed capable of transcending its ego condition; indeed, in its "higher" forms, the ego disappears altogether. Such an ego-less mental condition can only be unconscious to us, for the simple reason that there would be nobody to witness it. . . . I cannot imagine a conscious mental state that does not refer to a subject, that is, to an ego. The ego may be depotentiated —divested, for instance, of its awareness of the body—but so long as there is awareness of something, there must be somebody who is aware. (84)

How a mere convention of syntax, that the verb must have a subject, can force itself upon perception and seem to be the logic of reality! Under these circumstances Jung's understanding of the "ego-less" state of consciousness as the Eastern texts describe it leaves much to be desired.

---

[3] Yet how often he came so close to the point! One thinks, in particular, of his remarkable little essay on "The Antithetical Sense of Primal Words" (83), where he reviews Karl Abel's studies of the polarity of such words as the ancient Egyptian *ken*, meaning both strong and weak. Freud had noticed a similar ambivalence or polarity in the symbolism of dreams. "Dreams," he wrote in the same essay, "show a special tendency to reduce two opposites to a unity or to represent them as one thing." He goes on to quote Abel, "It is clear that everything on this planet is relative and has independent existence only in so far as it is distinguished in its relations to and from other things. . . . Man has not been able to acquire even his oldest and simplest conceptions otherwise than in contrast with their opposite; he only gradually learnt to separate the two sides of the antithesis and think of the one without conscious comparison with the other."

To put it rather briefly, he believes that it is not ego-less at all (85). It is only that the ego is temporarily forgotten in descending to a more primitive level of awareness, to the undifferentiated awareness that is supposed to have been characteristic of man's precivilized mentality—Lévy-Bruhl's *participation mystique*. However, he does not confuse it with an actual reversion to primitivity. His point is that members of the ancient Eastern cultures can afford this relapse into undifferentiated awareness just because of their maturity, just because their cultures have given them very strong ego structures and have at the same time provided for the ordered fulfillment of all their instinctual urges (86). This is why he strongly discourages the use of Eastern techniques, such as *yoga*, by Westerners. For us there is the danger of "inflation," of being swamped and possessed by the unconscious just because we have repressed it so strongly and have not yet come to terms with our less respectable instincts. The Westerner who lowers the level of consciousness and relaxes the vigilance of the ego, without all the safeguards of the analytic situation, is therefore liable to lose self-control in the uprush of repressed forces. One thinks immediately of the "beat" variety of Zen in America's bohemias, and the delusions of spiritual and occult grandeur among some of those who take up Theosophy or Vedanta.

There are so many points upon which Jung has such excellent intuitive judgment that one hates to take issue with his premises. In East and West alike there is always a danger of disorder when social institutions are called in question, and it is the same whether the institution be the ego or the subjugation of women. When authority is questioned at one point, it tends to become unstable at others.

East and West alike have fostered the ego as such an institution, though with differing ideas of its roles and duties. If Eastern cultures were less ego-conscious than Western, Buddhist and Taoist texts would be relatively silent as to the illusory nature of the ego. Jung is therefore perfectly right in sounding a warning—but for the wrong reason. He assumes that a strong ego structure, a struggle against nature, is the necessary condition of civilization, and is thus in danger of reaching the same despair as Freud. But it is one thing to note that civilization as we know it *has* depended upon the ego concept; it is quite another to assert that it *must*, as if this convention were somehow in the nature of things. Freud and Jung are both fully alive to the interdependence of life's great opposites, but for both they constitute a finally insoluble problem. Freud fears that the tension between them must at least become unbearable; Jung seems prepared to walk the tightrope between them forever.

> The serious problems of life, however, are never fully solved. If it should for once appear that they are, this is the sign that something has been lost. The meaning and design of a problem seem not to lie in its solution but in our working at it incessantly. This alone preserves us from stultification and petrifaction. (87)

Is not this, after all, the voice of the Protestant conscience? Man is inherently lazy; by nature, by original sin, he will always slide back into dissolution unless there is something to goad him, and thus there must never, never be anything but quite temporary rest from the task of working out his salvation with fear and trembling.

Maslow (88) has amassed a most impressive series of

quotations from American psychologists, one and all aver-
ring the identity of problem solving, or "coping," and mental health, and to read them thus lumped into a chorus is
downright funny.

> Western culture generally [writes Maslow] rests on the
> Judaic-Christian theology. The United States particularly is
> dominated by the Puritan and pragmatic spirit which
> stresses work, struggle and striving, soberness and earnest-
> ness, and above all, purposefulness. Like any other social
> institution, science in general and psychology in particular is
> not exempt from these cultural climate and atmosphere
> effects. American psychology, by participation, is overprag-
> matic, over-Puritan, and overpurposeful. . . . No textbooks
> have chapters on fun and gaiety, on leisure and meditation,
> on loafing and puttering, on aimless, useless, and purposeless
> activity. . . . American psychology is busily occupying itself
> with only half of life to the neglect of the other—and per-
> haps more important—half. (89)

In all directions we use the means of life to justify the
ends: we read or go to concerts to improve our minds; we
relax to improve our work; we worship God to improve our
morals; we even get drunk *in order to* forget our worries.
Everything that is done playfully, without ulterior motive
and second thought, makes us feel guilty, and it is even
widely believed that such unmotivated action is impossible. You *must* have a reason for what you do! But the
statement is more of a command than an observation. As
soon as the ego is divided from the world, like the effect
from its cause, it seems to be the puppet of "motivations"
which are really the disowned parts of ourselves. If we
could see ourselves whole, as differing positions in the unified field of the world, we should see that we are unmoti-

vated—for the whole floats freely and does not rest upon
something beyond itself.

Jung and his students have shown such a deep interest
in Asian philosophy and mythology that their defective
understanding of liberation cannot be passed over lightly.
They come so close to the point, and yet miss it, and there
may be something here which is symptomatic of the whole
situation of Western psychotherapy vis-à-vis the Eastern
ways. The difficulty seems to arise from three interconnected factors: (1) the Christian and more particularly
Protestant view of man; (2) anthropological theories of
the nineteenth century; and (3) "psychologism."

As we have seen, our Western and Christian social
institutions define man in a way that is not only paradoxical but also self-contradictory. Man is seen as an embodied
conflict between reason and instinct, spirit and nature,
such that to be healthy or to be saved he must always mistrust himself. Jung does not show this contradiction as
acutely as Freud because he holds that the unconscious is
at root creative and intelligent, and thus *ultimately* trustworthy.[4] The mythologies, dreams, and fantasies which
represent unconscious activity are regarded as sources of
healing and wisdom, and are comparable to the processes
of growth and homoeostasis in the physical organism.
Nevertheless, Jungian writings abound in such passages as
the following from M. E. Harding:

> Beneath the decent façade of consciousness with its dis-
> ciplined, moral order and its good intentions, lurk the crude

[4] In differing ways, Groddeck (90), Reich (91), Marcuse (92), and
N. O. Brown (93) show the interesting results of being more Freudian
than Freud, of going the whole way and trusting the id. Groddeck's
work seems to have fallen into obscurity, and it is strange that Brown
does not mention him.

instinctive forces of life, like monsters of the deep—devouring, begetting, warring endlessly. They are for the most part unseen, yet on their urge and energy life itself depends: without them living beings would be as inert as stones. But were they left to function unchecked, life would lose its meaning, being reduced once more to mere birth and death, as in the teeming world of primordial swamps. (94)

We are never allowed to forget, in the Jungian philosophy, that not only consciousness but also psychic integration, the goal of therapy, is *precarious*. It echoes the Biblical warning, "Brethren be sober, be vigilant, for your adversary the Devil walketh about as a roaring lion, seeking whom he may devour!" The unconscious can be creative, it seems, only if skillfully pacified by the conscious, which must act all the while like the wary trainer of a performing lion. Therefore unless the lion is first tamed, the "invasion" of the conscious by unconscious contents which is said to occur in mystical experience will unleash the demons instead of the gods.

The conception of man as an angel riding a wild animal is also basic to the anthropological theories which arose out of Darwin's doctrine of evolution by natural selection. Consciousness and reason are precarious because they are the fragile "epiphenomena" of the blind and bestial process of physical evolution. They are the freakish products of the famous "primordial swamp," so freakish that there is really no common measure between the two. Outside man's skin there is really nothing corresponding to the intelligence inside it. Our survival must therefore be the cautious and rigidly controlled exploitation of a natural fluke. At the same time, anthropologists made an equation between primordial and near-animal man, on the one hand, with the child and the primitive, on the other. Was it altogether by chance that "primitives" turned out to be just those peoples upon whom the Western Europeans wanted to confer the benefits of their more "evolved" civilization?

In the nineteenth century our actual information about early man was negligible; our position is not much better even now. But, in differing ways, both Freud and Jung constructed a theory of primordial man for which there is no historical evidence. Its assumptions are: (1) that intelligence rests precariously on a biological and instinctual basis which is "animal" in the worst sense; (2) that existing cultures differing from ours in not having developed certain scientific and literary skills are survivals of primordial man, and are thus dubbed "primitive"; and (3) that by analogy with the repetition of evolutionary changes in the growth of the human foetus, the first years of infancy rehearse man's primordial mentality (95). Take these assumptions hand-in-hand with the fact that psychotherapy was at first preoccupied with the study of deranged personalities, and what happens? It is assumed that irrational behavior is *historical* regression, that the disturbed individual is having difficulty in coping with traits which he inherits from the primordial swamp. In other words, what is repressed in the unconscious is the historical and prehistorical past, and consequently psychoanalysis becomes a tool for investigating the earliest history of man. In default of real evidence about primordial man, such a theory can only be self-validating.

All that has been said before, by others. I raise it here because it is the basis of Jung's theory of the evolution of consciousness and the ego. It leads him to regard the egocentric mode of consciousness as a universal and historically necessary step in the development of mankind. It is the problematic but essential mechanism for regulating the primordial instincts of the swamp and the cave, for raising mankind from the merely animal level. But we should consider another alternative: that man's peculiar bestiality has little to do with beasts; that his irrationalities, inordinate appetites, mass hysterias, and deeds of shocking violence and cruelty are not historically regressive at all; they are protests against just this mode of consciousness, against the double-bind of a self-contradictory social institution. Does not the practice, as distinct from the theory, of psychotherapy confirm this again and again? The disturbed individual is not so much the historical throwback in whom sufficient ego strength somehow failed to develop; he is the victim of too much ego, too much individual isolation. Furthermore, one should not assume that the development of an ego is the universally necessary basis for consciousness and intelligence. The neural structures of that "enchanted loom," the brain, upon which intelligence depends are certainly not the deliberate creations of any conscious ego, and they do not dissolve into pulp when the ego is seen to be fictitious—by an act of intelligence. It would follow, then, that when the ego is dispelled there is not an "invasion" of consciousness by primordial contents from the swamp and the jungle. There is instead insight: the perception of a whole new pattern of relationships comparable to scientific or artistic discovery.

Jung has often been accused of "psychologism," but I am not, like Buber, using this word to criticize his neglect of the metaphysical or supernatural grounds of spiritual experience. The point is rather that his view of "the unconscious" on the one hand and of the content of the liberation experience on the other is too narrowly psychological. Of course, one can say that all experience is psychological experience because it happens in the psyche. But aside from the question of whether there really is a psyche, doesn't the equation of all experience with psychological experience make the latter term meaningless? As we have seen, the unconscious which needs to be examined for man's liberation contains physical, biological, and social relationships which are repressed not so much by a "psychological organ," such as the ego, as by defective communication and language. Nor is the content of the liberation experience—*satori, nirvana,* "cosmic consciousness," etc.—something psychological in the sense of a flash of subjective light.[5] Its content is the physical world, seen in a new way.

> While Rikko, a high government official of the T'ang dynasty, had a talk with his Zen master Nansen, the official quoted a saying of Sojo, a noted monk-scholar of an earlier dynasty:
>
> > *Heaven and earth and I are of the same root,*
> > *The ten-thousand things and I are of one substance,*
>
> and continued, "Is not this a most remarkable statement?"
> Nansen called the attention of the visitor to the flowering plant in the garden and said, "People of the world look at these flowers as if they were in a dream." (97)

The event of seeing the world in a new way is perhaps psychological in that it is an event of perception and intelligence. But its content is not psychological in the sense of

---

[5] I have discussed the "subjective phenomena" of this experience elsewhere (96), showing that they are quite incidental to its content—like the feeling of relief that comes with solving a difficult problem.

an "archetype" or visionary form seen in a dream or trance. When Nansen pointed to the flowers, he was not using them as a symbol of something psychological. If anything, he was pointing away from the psychological, from the private and enclosed world of the "subject." He was pointing at the flowers.

Considering the general character of Western assumptions about Buddhism and Taoism—according to which they are religions—Jung is hardly to be blamed for a wrong classification of the domain in which their experiences happen. We think of religious and spiritual experiences as events of the "inner life," but this is all because of the false severance of the subject from the object. The Eastern ways direct their students to "look within," to find out the self, only to dispel the illusion that it is inside as distinct from outside. As the Chinese Zen master Lin-chi put it: "Make no mistake: there is nothing on the outside and, likewise, nothing on the inside that you can grasp" (98).

We cannot leave Freud and Jung, the great masters of "depth psychology," without asking whether there is any connection between liberation and the analysis of dreams, as well as the whole process of free association. Psychotherapists are often surprised to find that the ways of liberation seem almost entirely unconcerned with dreams, and this is just because their orientation is not exactly psychological in our sense. It is sometimes assumed that liberation is a work only to be undertaken by those who have gone beyond the need for anything that dream analysis can achieve, but this would be to put it on too remote a pedestal. My own hypothesis is that dream analysis is a "gimmick" (*upaya*) useful in therapy but not essential to it. Free association, or unblocked communication, is more fundamental, but this is a technique which can be related to other matters than dreams—Rorschach pictures, stories, everyday events, lists of words, and, indeed, almost anything. Its use will be discussed in the next chapter.

The theory that dreams are important goes hand in hand with the idea that the unconscious is primarily psychological and subjective, in which case dreams would seem to be the royal road to finding out what goes on in the "hidden night life" of the patient. Needless to say, psychoanalysis has been much criticized for its tendency to speak of *the* unconscious as if it were a psychological organ with a mind of its own. The permanent value of Freud's hypothesis is in the way in which it directed attention to unconscious*ness*, to the fact that we are not aware of how we are conditioned to think and act as we do. L. L. Whyte (99) has suggested that it would be far more accurate to speak of man's life as "unconscious process with conscious aspects," and obviously "unconscious process" in this sense goes far beyond the psychological domain. "Unconsciousness" would correspond exactly with the Buddhist term *avidya* (ignore-ance), but there is no real equivalent of "the unconscious" in Indian or Chinese terms.[6]

To some extent the postulates of Existential analysis are more consistent with the ways of liberation than those of either Freud or Jung. Rollo May (100) explains that this movement has arisen out of the dissatisfaction of many

[6] The nearest equivalent is perhaps the Mahayana Buddhist expression *alaya-vijnana,* or "store consciousness," which really designates the totality of *samskaras* or habitual patterns of psychophysical activity. The common criticism, often made by Coomaraswamy and others, that Western psychologists fail to distinguish between the subconscious and the superconscious does not seem very helpful. There would be some point in making a contrast between unconsciousness and expanded consciousness.

psychiatrists with such traditional concepts as the libido, the censor, the unconscious, and indeed the whole psycho-analytical theory of man. In particular Ludwig Binswanger, one of its main exponents, attacks "the cancer of all psychology up to now . . . the cancer of the doctrine of subject-object cleavage of the world" (101). Man is an "I am" not as a detached ego but as *being-in-the-world*, with emphasis on the dynamic, process character of *being* and on the fact that this *being* is necessarily in relation to a world. The world with which every subject is polarized is threefold: the *Umwelt* of our biological and physical foundations, the *Mitwelt* of social relations, and the *Eigenwelt* of one's own inner life and self-consciousness. No therapy can be adequate which does not take account of all three realms of relation. May (102) notes that the likeness between Existential analysis and such Eastern philosophies as Taoism and Zen goes

> much deeper than the chance similarity of words. Both are concerned with ontology, the study of being. Both seek a relation to reality which cuts below the cleavage between subject and object. Both would insist that the Western absorption in conquering and gaining power over nature has resulted not only in the estrangement of man from nature but also indirectly in estrangement of man from himself. The basic reason for these similarities is that Eastern thought never suffered the radical split between subject and object that has characterized Western thought, and this dichotomy is exactly what existentialism seeks to over-come.

So far so good. But we have seen that the Existential school takes anxiety, Kierkegaard's *angst*, and its concomitant guilt as inseparable from *being* since "to be" implies "not to be," and since to know fully that one exists will necessarily involve the dread of not existing. Perhaps this is a therapeutic gambit, for one is a great deal less anxious if one feels perfectly free to be anxious, and the same may be said of guilt. Or it may be that there would be no joy in being alive save in relation to the awesome prospect of death. Yet the Existentialists give, rather, the impression that to live without anxiety is to live without seriousness. Being and nonbeing are not so much a polarity as a "dialectic of crisis," an oscillation, a wobbling on the brink, which is precisely Kierkegaard's "fear and trembling."[7] Not to be thus anxious, not to take one's own and other people's being-in-the-world seriously, is to disregard the whole dignity of being a person, to fail in being fully human.

Here we run straight into an ancient quarrel between West and East, since the former has always alleged that the latter does not take human personality seriously. Slavery, downtrodden women, starvation, a million dead of cholera—such is life! Is not this the Buddhist formula *sarva samskara duhkha, sarva samskara anatma, sarva samskara anitya,* all compounds (including people) are in anguish, all compounds are without self, all compounds are impermanent? If this be true, does it not make liberation the art of learning not to care? The stereotyped atti-

[7] Gregory Bateson (103) has explored, at least tentatively, the possibility of a connection between such oscillatory emotional states as anxiety (trembling), sobbing, and laughing and life situations in which there is a logical paradox. An electric bell oscillates because its armature is so arranged that when the current is turned on, it switches itself off, but this in turn switches it on. Yes implies no, and no implies yes. He points out a similar property in the statement "I am lying," which is false if true, etc., and in the whole mechanism of the double-bind. But if this goes right to the root of life, should we tremble or laugh?

tudes of a culture are of course always a parody of the insights of its more gifted members. Not caring is the parody of serenity, just as worrying is the parody of concern. We shall gain more understanding if we compare East and West at a higher level, and the comparison is often best seen as projected into superb works of art. Thus if we compare the faces of Christ and the Madonna of Michelangelo's Pietà in St. Peter's, Rome, with that astonishing statue of the Buddha-to-come, Maitreya, at Horyu-ji in Nara, what do we find? Anxiety? Anguish? On the contrary, there is in all three faces an incredible mixture of tenderness, wise sadness, serene—and somehow utterly confident—resignation, all with the slightest hint of a smile. Each face is young and unwrinkled and yet immeasurably old—in the sense that these are the faces of immortal archetypes who have seen everything, understood everything, and endured everything without the least bitterness, at one extreme, or sentimentality, at the other. None are without concern or sorrow, and yet there is not the faintest trace of guilt or apprehension.

Are the attitudes expressed on these divine faces humanly possible? This is, as a matter of fact, the face that many people wear in death and which accounts for the extraordinary nobility of so many death masks. Here, of course, we are all out of our depth and there is nothing in the way of statistics or scientific information to help us. But I think I may hazard the suggestion that in the moment of death many people undergo the curious sensation not only of accepting but of having willed everything that has happened to them. This is not willing in the imperious sense; it is the unexpected discovery of an identity between the willed and the inevitable.

It is to this that the recognition of the inseparability of being and nonbeing should lead us. This is the whole meaning of polarity, of life implying death, of subject implying object, of man implying world, and of Yes implying No. The ways of liberation propose that what many, perhaps, discover in death may also be discovered in the midst of life. Just as liberation involves the recognition of oneself in what is most other, it involves the recognition of life in death—and this is why so many rites of initiation take the neophyte through a symbolic death. He accepts the certainty of death so completely that, in effect, he is dead already—and thus beyond anxiety. In the words of the Zen master Bunan:

> *While living, be a dead man, thoroughly dead;*
> *Whatever you do, then, as you will, is always good.* (104)

This is where Freud and Jung seem in some ways to be wiser than the Existentialists: they see that death is the goal of life. Nonbeing fulfills being; it does not negate being, just as space does not negate what is solid. Each is the condition for the reality of the other. This is why Norman Brown is so right in saying that it is just death which gives the organism its individual uniqueness.

> The precious ontological uniqueness which the human individual claims is conferred on him not by possession of an immortal soul but by possession of a mortal body. . . . At the simplest organic level, any particular animal or plant has uniqueness and individuality because it lives its own life and no other—that is to say, because it dies. . . . If death gives life individuality and if man is the organism which represses death, then man is the organism which represses his own individuality. Then our proud views of humanity

as a species endowed with an individuality denied to lower animals turns out to be wrong. The lilies of the field have it because they take no thought of the morrow, and we do not. Lower organisms live the life proper to their species; their individuality consists in their being concrete embodiments of the essence of their species in a particular life which ends in death. (105)

Thus the Existentialists are right in saying that nonbeing and death give being, a being, its authenticity. But anxiety is the repression of death, for whatever is repressed does not simply vanish from sight; it lurks in the corner of one's eye as a perpetual distraction, and the center of vision and attention trembles because it cannot fully look away from it. If at the popular, parodied level the East has no concern for the person, it is not because of liberation; it is because of the popular doctrine of reincarnation, which implies that the individual, the ego, is unable to die. To be released from reincarnation is to be able to die, and thus to be able to live.

The Nirvana-principle [says Norman Brown, using the term, unlike Freud, in its proper sense] regulates an individual life which enjoys full satisfaction and concretely embodies the full essence of the species, and in which life and death are simultaneously affirmed, because life and death together constitute individuality, and ripeness is all. (106)

What amounts in Existentialism to an idealization of anxiety is surely no more than a survival of the Protestant notion that it is *good* to feel guilty, anxious, and serious. This is quite a different matter from admitting honestly that that is how one feels, thereby breaking the vicious circle of anxiety by ceasing to be anxious about being anxious. Allowed anxiety ceases to be anxiety, for the whole nature of anxiety is that it *is* a vicious circle. It is the frustration of not being able to have life without death, that is, of not being able to solve a nonsensical problem. As Freud saw, the ego is constituted by a repression of Eros and Thanatos, of life and death, and for this reason it is a parody of authentic individuality. And as Norman Brown goes on to show, repressed Thanatos turns itself outward as the desire to kill, as aggression; and, on the other hand, repressed Eros becomes a fixation to the past, to the search for satisfaction in the repetition of some primary experience of satisfaction.

> Under conditions of repression, the repetition-compulsion establishes a fixation to the past, which alienates the neurotic from the present and commits him to the unconscious quest for the past in the future. (107)

It is thus that the Western equivalent of reincarnation is our obsession with history, "a forward-moving *recherche du temps perdu*" (108), the fruitless attempt to move forward to a satisfactory future by the logic of an impoverished past. For history is the record of frustration, and its earliest sources are the monuments in which men began, in Unamuno's phrase, to store up their dead. History is the refusal to "let the dead bury their dead." History, or better, historicism is a chronic hoarding of trash in the hope that it will someday "come in useful." It is the state of mind in which the record of what is done becomes more important than what is done, in which there is less and less room for action because of more and more room given over to results. This is why the *Bhagavad-Gita* describes liberation as action without clinging to the fruits of action, for when life and death are lived completely they proceed without trace in an eternal present.

Life is renewed by death because it is again and again set free from what would otherwise become an insufferable burden of memory and monotony. Genuine reincarnation lies in the fact that whenever a child is born "I"—or human awareness—arises into the world again with memory wiped clean and the wonder of life restored. Everlasting annihilation is as nonsensical as everlasting individuality. And who can doubt that if human life has arisen in this tiny area of one immense galaxy, it must be happening again and again, on grounds of sheer probability, throughout the whole diffusion of nebulae that surrounds us. For where the organism is intelligent the environment also must be intelligent.

Like so much of our psychotherapy, Existentialism does not actually take full account of death. Indeed, in the whole literature of psychotherapy there is the barest mention of suitable treatment for the patient facing death, and this is not, I fear, from the recognition that the problem of death is not a problem at all. It is rather from the feeling that it is an *insoluble* problem, a hard, inevitable fact which is "just too bad." Yet, again, the Existentialists are on the right track. If death makes the individual authentic, the authentic psychotherapy will be the first one to take death in its stride. When a patient is about to die, or is struck in mid-life with the dread of death, this is not the moment to hand him over to the *consoling* ministrations of some religious fantast who will try to explain death away. No one, I believe, has made any serious and rigorous study of the degree to which the fear of death is involved in the psychoses and neuroses. To ignore it or explain it away is to pass up the major opportunity of psychotherapy, for what death negates is not the individual, not the organism /environment, but the ego, and therefore liberation from the ego is synonymous with the full acceptance of death. For the ego is not a vital function of the organism; it is abstracted by social influence from memories; it is the hypothetical substance upon which memory is recorded, the constant which endures through all the changes of experience. To identify with the ego is to confuse the organism with its history, to make its guiding principle a narrowly selected and incomplete record of what it has been and done. This abstraction from memory thereupon seems to be a concrete and effective agent. But it is just this which is lost in death. Oneself as a *story* comes to an end, which shows that the ego is in every sense a story.

Apart from Existentialism, it seems to me that one of the most fruitful approaches to psychotherapy must lie among the lines begun by H. S. Sullivan and Frieda Fromm-Reichmann, for it is here that the social context of personality begins to be taken with full seriousness, and, as Sullivan himself said, the self-system (ego) as we know it today is "the principal stumbling block to favorable changes in personality" (109).

> The general science of psychiatry seems to me to cover much the same field as that which is studied by social psychology, because scientific psychiatry has to be defined as the study of interpersonal relations, and this in the end calls for the use of the kind of conceptual framework that we now call *field theory*. From such a standpoint, personality is taken to be hypothetical. That which can be studied is the pattern of processes which characterize the inter-

action of personalities in particular recurrent situations or fields which "include" the observer. (110)

On one side, this line of thought has spread out into the whole work of the Washington School with its highly intelligent interest in the ways of liberation, and, on another, to the study of psychotherapy as a problem of communication, "the social matrix of psychiatry," as explored in varying ways by Jurgen Ruesch (111), Gregory Bateson (112), Anatol Rapoport (113), Jay Haley (114), and others. This latter development seems to be gaining rather slow recognition, especially in Europe, because of the false impression that it represents a complete dehumanization of psychiatry in which man is studied by analogy with electronic computers and systems of mathematical logic. Yet it is just from here that we get such concepts as the double-bind which, quite apart from its merits in identifying the causes of schizophrenia, may well prove to be one of the very great ideas in the whole history of psychology. After all, if mathematical thinking has given us such deep understanding of physics and astronomy without in any way destroying the glory of the stars, why should it not someday prove as useful in understanding ourselves without in any way destroying the dignity of man? In any case, mathematics has long ceased to mean mere mechanics, and what is feared is that a mathematical description of man's behavior will reduce him to a machine without poetry. It is a serious mistake to oppose poetry to mathematics as the living flesh to the driest bones. The problem is merely that mathematics as taught begins in the arid wastes of arithmetic, elementary algebra, and Euclid— screening out poets from the start. The living flesh is substance and stuff only to those whose eyes are so dull that they cannot see the beauty of its patterns. Taken to its full possibilities, mathematical thinking can reveal the physical world to be something astonishingly akin to music.

It is feared, too, that when methods of this kind are pursued too far in the study of man and of his world, all their sublime unities may be disintegrated into digital, discontinuous bits, and that, again, the "human image" may vanish into mere arrangements of point-units. Those who think mathematically and analytically have gone some way in this direction, but this is why they are the first to discover its. limits. In the words of Jurgen Ruesch:

> The peculiarities of language introduce a number of distortions into psychiatric research. When words are employed to refer to behavior, action and movement, which are continuous functions, are sliced into discrete elements, as if they were replaceable parts of a machine. The continuity of existence thus is split into arbitrary entities which are not so much a function of actual behavior as the result of language structure. (115)

And while I know of no one who has thought more analytically and mathematically of human behavior than Gregory Bateson, he has this to say:

> The old Berkeleyan motto, *esse est percipi*—to be is to be perceived—leads on the one hand to such philosophical toys as the question, Is the tree there in the wood when I am not there to see it? But on the other hand it leads to a very profound and irresistible discovery that the laws and processes of our perception are a bridge which joins us inseparably to that which we perceive—a bridge which unites subject and object. . . . To increase awareness of one's scientific universe is to face unpredictable increases in

one's awareness of the self. And I wish to stress the fact that such increases are always in the very nature of the case unpredictable in nature. . . . No one knows the end of that progress which starts from uniting the perceiver and the perceived—the subject and the object—into a single universe. (116)

To lose the reality of the isolated ego is not, as Erich Fromm (117) seems to fear, to lose the integrity of the individual.[8] To find that the organism is inseparable from its environment is neither to lose the clarity of its form nor the uniqueness of its position. Furthermore, to remove the particular type of repression which ego-consciousness involves is not to throw the gates open to the unrestrained rapacity of the id. For it is not the ego which makes man different from serpents, lions, sharks, and apes; it is his organic structure, and the type of environment in which this structure can appear. It is not romantic and sentimental to blame the peculiar violence and cruelty of man upon social institutions rather than nature. It is true that men have invented these institutions, but is it not obvious that what may start out as a small and unnoticed mistake may turn into a catastrophe as one rolling pebble may start an avalanche? Who could have known that the mistake of regarding men as separate egos would have had such disastrous consequences? But it is easy to be wise in retrospect.

As the Chinese Taoists have seen, there is really no alternative to trusting man's nature. This is not wishful

[8] Fromm's disagreements with Sullivan as to the reality of the "self" are surely based on the semantic confusion whereby the terms "I," "ego," "self," "person," "individual," etc., are used indiscriminately and interchangeably. Were it otherwise, Fromm's deep interest in Zen Buddhism (118) would be inconceivable.

thinking or sentimentality; it is the most practical of practical politics. For every system of mistrust and authoritarian control is *also* human. The will of the would-be saint can be as corrupt as his passions, and the intellect can be as misguided as the instincts. The authority and effectiveness of the police is only as sound as public morale. Faith in our own nature works if it only works fifty-one per cent of the time. The alternative, as Freud saw, is the swelling of guilt "to a magnitude that individuals can hardly support."

V

The Counter-Game

THE social psychologist is always in danger of being a determinist, seeing individual behavior as subordinate to social behavior, the organism as responding willy-nilly to the conditions of its environment. If we define the organism by a complex boundary—the external skin, the skins of internal organs as well, down to the very surfaces of cells and molecules—its behavior will consist in the movements of this boundary. But the boundary of the organism is *also* the boundary of its environment, and thus its movements can be ascribed to the environment as well. Systems of description ascribe these movements now to one side and now to the other, and these changes of viewpoint are mutually corrective. Philosophical fashions swing between voluntarism and determinism, idealism and positivism, realism and nominalism, and there is never any clear issue between these alternatives when one regards them as opposed. The point I have been trying to make all along is that we gain better understanding by describing this boundary and its movements as belonging to both the organism and its environment, but that we do not ascribe the origin of movement to either side. The question as to which side of a curved surface moves first is always unanswerable, unless we restrict our observations to limited areas and ignore some of the factors involved.

We have seen that the social game is based on conventional rules, and that these define the significant areas to be observed and the ways in which the origin of action is to be ascribed to one side of the boundary or another. Thus all social games regard the boundary between organism and environment, the epidermis, as significant, and almost all regard the inside of this boundary as an independent source of action. They tend to ignore the fact that its movements can also be ascribed to the environment, but this "ignore-ance" is one of the rules of the game. But when the philosopher, the psychologist, or the psychiatrist begins to observe human behavior more carefully he starts to question the rules and to notice the discrepancies between social definitions and physical events. To quote Bateson again:

> There seems to be a sort of progress in awareness, through the stages of which every man—and especially every psychiatrist and every patient—must move, some persons progressing further through these stages than others. One starts by blaming the identified patient for his idiosyncrasies and symptoms. Then one discovers that these symptoms are a response to—or an effect of—what others have done; and the blame shifts from the identified patient to the etiological figure. Then, one discovers perhaps that these figures feel a guilt for the pain which they have caused, and one realizes that when they claim this guilt they are identifying themselves with God. After all, they did not, in general, know what they were doing, and to claim guilt for their acts would be to claim omniscience. At this point one reaches a more general anger, that what happens to people should not happen to dogs, and that what people do to each other the lower animals could never devise. Beyond this, there is, I think, a stage which I can only dimly en-

visage, where pessimism and anger are replaced by something else—perhaps humility. And from this stage onward
to whatever other stages there may be, there is loneliness.
(119)

This is the loneliness of liberation, of no longer finding
security by taking sides with the crowd, of no longer believing that the rules of the game are the laws of nature.
It is thus that transcending the ego leads to great individuality.

Who, then, wants to follow this path? Liberation begins
from the point where anxiety or guilt becomes insupport-
able, where the individual feels that he can no longer
tolerate his situation as an ego in opposition to an alien
society, to a universe in which pain and death deny him,
or to negative emotions which overwhelm him. Ordinarily,
he is quite unaware of the fact that his distress arises from
a contradiction in the rules of the social game. He blames
God, or other people, or even himself—but none of these
are responsible. There has simply been a mistake whose
consequences no one could have foreseen—a wrong step
in biological adaptation which, presumably, seemed at first
to be very promising. L. L. Whyte (120), in his marvellous
account of the way in which the duality of the human
nervous system became the conflicting dualism of reason
against instinct, writes:

> Intellectual man had no choice but to follow the path
> which facilitated the development of his faculty of thought,
> and thought could only clarify itself by separating out
> static concepts which, in becoming static, ceased to con-
> form to their organic matrix or to the forms of nature. . . .
> European languages in general begin with a subject-noun
> whose action is expressed in an active verb. Some apparently

permanent element is separated from the general process, treated as an entity, and endowed with active responsibility for a given occurrence. This procedure is so paradoxical that only long acquaintance with it conceals its absurdity.

It is thus, then, that the ego is separated out as the static entity responsible for action, and from this mistake the trouble begins.

In quest of liberation from this problem the individual therefore goes to the *guru* or to the psychotherapist with such questions as: "How can *I* escape from birth-and-death (*samsara*)?" "What shall *I do* to be saved?" "How can *I* get out of these extreme depressions?" "How can *I* stop *myself* drinking so much?" "I am terrified of getting cancer, and how am *I* to stop worrying?" All these questions take as real the very illusion which constitutes the actual problem, but what is the *guru* or therapist to do? He cannot say, "Stop worrying," because the ego is not in control, and just that seems to be the problem. He cannot say, "Accept your fears," without implying that the ego is an effective agent which can actively accept. He cannot say, "There's nothing you can do about it," without leaving the impression that the ego is the helpless victim of fate. He cannot say, "Your trouble is that you think you're an ego," because the inquirer genuinely feels that he is, or, if he doubts it, will come back with the question "Well, how am *I* to stop thinking so?" There is no direct answer to an irrational question, which was why one Zen master replied, none too helpfully, "When you know the answer you won't ask the question!" As we have seen, almost the only thing that the *guru* or therapist can do is to persuade the individual to act upon his false premise in certain consistent directions until he sees his mistake. To do this the individual must be drawn into a game, playing *as if* his ego were real, but not along the wandering or circular paths of ordinary life which do not involve the experiments necessary for the denouement. The *guru* therefore initiates a "counter-game," a game countering the contradictions in the social game.

The genesis of this idea came to me from J. Haley's delightful and ostensibly satirical comparison of psychoanalysis with the "ploys" or techniques of the British humorist Stephen Potter for getting socially "one-up" on other people—the art of "One-upmanship" (121). I am afraid that Haley's article was none too well received by the many therapists who missed its point and felt themselves accused of conducting a very artful racket, or worse, of being therapists because of an unconscious need to be one-up on other people. I am sure Haley did not miss the humor of this misunderstanding, but his article was in fact intended as a serious contribution to psychoanalytic theory. I shall defer going into the details of Haley's view of psychoanalysis until later. It is enough to say here that if the neurotic or ego-ridden individual is one who insists upon being one-up on his own feelings or on life as a whole, the analyst engages him in a game of one-upmanship in which he cannot win. As the game proceeds, it becomes apparent that the patient's contest with the analyst is one and the same as his contest with life, or with the alienated aspects of his own feelings. The game ends with the insight that the patient could not win because the very premises of the game were absurd: he was trying to make the subject one-up on the object, the organism one-up on the environment, himself one-up on himself. He had failed to see that every explicit duality is an implicit unity. Haley came to this clarification by trying to see whether psychoanalysis could be better understood by disregarding its theoretical postulates and simply describing what happens in analysis by way of communication and interpersonal exchange.

At first sight, Haley's hypothesis seems to be a tremendous oversimplification, and I was indeed inclined to this view until I began to try it out upon what I knew of the ways of liberation—to find that it was a simplification capable of almost endlessly complex expressions. The way of liberation to which Haley's view is most clearly applicable is Zen Buddhism, which, with Taoist humor, is regarded by its own masters as something of a racket. But the "ploys" of one-upmanship are just what the Zen masters refer to as their "old tricks," their "traps" for unwary students, or, in other words, the *upaya*—the "skillful means" which the compassionate Bodhisattva employs to bring about the liberation of others.

The basic position of the Zen master is that he has nothing to teach, no doctrine, no method, no attainment or insight of any kind. In words attributed to the Buddha himself, "I obtained not the least thing from unexcelled, complete awakening, and for this very reason it is called 'unexcelled, complete awakening'" (122). On one occasion a Zen master ascended the rostrum and gave a lecture consisting of total silence. When asked the meaning, he replied, "The scriptures are explained by the preachers, the commentaries by the commentators." What, then, does a Zen master explain? There is nothing to say because there is no problem. All that there is in Zen is said to be perfectly obvious from the beginning, and if there is anything to say at all it is just that "the water flows blue and the mountain towers green." This is not "beautiful" nature mysticism. When asked, "What is the Buddha?" another master replied, "Dried excrement!" Nor is it pantheism; it is no "ism" or doctrine of any kind. When asked, "What is the Way [Tao]?" Nansen answered, "Your everyday mind is the Way." "How, then, does one get into accord with it?" "If you try to accord, you deviate." Life, he is saying, is not a problem, so why are you asking for a solution?

Nevertheless, Zen is a discipline and a rugged one. Though there is nothing to teach, its masters accept students and establish seminaries for their training. Yet all this, said Lin-chi, "is like using an empty fist or yellow leaves to beguile a little child.[1] How can you find any juice from thorns and dried branches? There is nothing to be grasped outside the mind [everyday consciousness], and nothing inside. What is it that you seek? You say on all sides that the Tao is to be practiced and put to the proof. Do not be mistaken! If there is anyone who can practice it, he is just involving himself in *samsara*" (123). Or again, "It is said everywhere that there is a Way which must be followed and a method which must be practiced. What method do you say must be practiced, and what Way followed? What do you lack in what you are using right now? What will you add to where you are? Not understanding this, raw young students put faith in the spells of some wild fox, promising to help them attain liberation by some strange doctrine which just puts people in bondage" (124). Ma-tsu, an early master of the T'ang dynasty, put the problem succinctly as follows:

[1] The child is crying for gold and thus is beguiled with yellow leaves.

The Tao has nothing to do with discipline. If you say that it is attained by discipline, finishing the discipline turns out to be losing the Tao. . . . If you say there is no discipline, this is to be the same as ordinary [unliberated] people. (125)

But just because the Zen masters are so devastatingly frank, no one believes them. They do not appear to have any problem that seriously troubles them. The would-be student, however, has—and is therefore convinced that there must be some way, some method, of becoming as much at peace with the world and with oneself as the masters. For the masters seem to take the world and its sufferings as if it were just a dream, and the aspirant to Zen imagines that *he* could feel that way too if only he could find the right method for transforming his consciousness. Yet it is not possible to be accepted for Zen training without considerable persistence; all kinds of barriers are put in the applicant's way, but the more the barriers, the more his eagerness, the more he becomes sure that the master is guarding some deeply occult secret and testing his fitness and sincerity for admission to an elite. But by these means the assertion that he has a problem is put squarely on the applicant's own shoulders. As we say, "Anyone who goes to a psychiatrist ought to have his head examined!" In other words, his problem is his question, his belief that the question he is asking makes sense.

When at last the applicant gains admission to the master, he finds himself confronted by a very formidable figure— usually a much older man, superbly self-confident and at ease, completely present and undistracted, and with the kind of twinkle in his eyes which indicates that he sees through the student like glass. In Chinese and Japanese culture the Zen master is, furthermore, a great authority figure, far more so than father or grandfather, and the student meets with him in the most formal circumstances —the master enthroned in his inner sanctum, and the student bowing most humbly before him. Everything is done, in short, to impress the student that in being admitted he has received the greatest condescension from a personage who has attained heights of wisdom far beyond his ken. This is no mere pretense; or rather, it is very great mastery of a certain kind of bluff in which the master has the same confidence as a highly accomplished player of poker or chess.

Having, then, indicated his great earnestness to attain "awakening," the liberation which Zen promises, the student is given a *koan* or Zen question and told to return some time later with an answer. The preliminary *koan* is in fact a concealed form of the question which the student has asked the master, "How can *I* attain liberation?" Though worded in many different ways, the *koan* is actually asking, "Who asks the question? Who wants to be liberated?" But the student is told that a merely verbal answer is not enough; he must *demonstrate* or in some way actually show this "who" in action. The master is saying, in effect, "You say *you* want to be liberated. Show me this *you!*" What this amounts to is a request for completely unpremeditated or spontaneous action which is also entirely sincere, but in circumstances so powerfully suggestive of the authority of his culture, this is about the last thing that a Chinese or Japanese student can do. By such means the student is, as we say in current slang, totally "bugged." How, in such formal circumstances, can he do something without first intending to do it? How can he conceal his prior intention from such an apparent mind reader? The formality of presenting an answer to the *koan* involves much preliminary ritual, and when the student is finally seated before the master he has to repeat the *koan* and then present his answer. The more he tries to be sincere and spontaneous, the more he is aware of contriving an answer. It is like being told that a wish will come true if you make it without thinking of a green elephant.

But this is not all. Between his interviews with the master the Zen student spends many hours in meditation, sitting cross-legged with his fellow students in the *zendo* or "meditation hall," watched by alert monks with "warning sticks" to beat the backs of those who fall asleep or go into trance. Meditation in Zen is, first, an attempt to attain perfect concentration and control of thought by counting one's breaths, and, second, a period for devoting one's whole attention to the *koan* in quest of a solution. Students are urged to devote their minds exclusively to the *koan,* holding its question before them with all their energy, but rather looking at it than thinking about it since the solution is not to be found in an intellectual answer.

Looking at this "from the outside," we can see that the master has "tricked" the student into putting himself, voluntarily, into an extreme double-bind. In the first place, he is asked to show his naked and genuine self in the presence of one who represents the full authority of the culture, and is felt to be the most acute judge of character. In the second place, he is asked to be spontaneous in circumstances where he can hardly be anything but deliberate. In the third place, he is asked to concentrate on something without thinking about it. In the fourth place, he cannot comment on the bind, not only because thinking about the *koan* is not the answer, but also because the master will, even forcibly, reject all verbal comments. In the fifth place, he is not allowed to escape the dilemma by going into trance. And all this calls for the most powerful exertion of his will or ego, though he is free at any time to quit the field.

In a wonderfully concealed way, the master has encouraged the student to commit himself to the solution of a self-contradictory problem. (E.g., the *koan*, "What is the sound of one hand?") The student comes to feel that he *must* find the answer, but is at the same time made to realize that there is no way of finding it—because everything that *he does* acting, as he thinks, as an ego is rejected as wrong. The *koan* can be answered, but you—the ego—must not answer it. You—the ego—must first meditate to get rid of the ego. As Eugen Herrigel discovered when studying with a Zen archery master, he was expected to release the bowstring without doing it himself, on purpose (126). But let us remember that the self-contradictory problem to which all the student's energies are directed is the *same* problem which he originally brought to the master, which he went out of his way to insist upon and raise: How can my ego liberate itself? By asking this question the student engages himself in a game with the master in which the student can never win; he can never get one-up on the master because he can never get one-up on himself. The one hand cannot clap itself.

The individual has therefore been engaged in an intense struggle in which all his energy—misconceived as his ego strength—has been defeated. It seems that absolutely nothing that he can do is right, spontaneous, or genuine; he can act neither independently (self-fully) nor unselfishly. But in the moment of defeat he sees what this means: that he, the agent, cannot act, does not act, and never did act. There is just action—Tao. It is happening, but neither to anyone nor from anyone. At once, therefore, he ceases to block action by trying to make it (for there is no ego) do itself, force itself to be spontaneous, or right, or unselfish. Because, now, he has nothing to prove and nothing to lose, he can go back to the master and call his bluff.

Yet the ego is a very deeply ingrained habit of feeling, and such insights (*satori*), intense and convincing as they may be at the moment, have a way of wearing off. Knowing this, the master has many more tricks up his sleeve, and says, "Now you have reached a most important understanding, but as yet you have only entered the gate. To get the real understanding, you must practice still more diligently." This is, of course, a "come on" to test the student and see if he will fall for it, as, indeed, he will if there is still even the ghost of a notion that there is something in Zen to get. On the other hand, the student may go away, feeling no need for further study. But because the master has sown a doubt in his mind, it may not be long before he most apologetically returns, for so long as any doubt remains to be played upon the job is not finished. In this way the game proceeds, ploy by ploy, until at last the student reaches the same unassailable position as the master. For the master cannot lose the game because he does not care in the least whether he wins or loses. He has nothing to prove and nothing to defend.

Must this be taken to be true of his whole relation to life, and not just to the particular game of Zen, so that he actually does not care whether he lives or dies? In a way this is true, but only because he has not the least ambition to be courageous, and therefore puts up no resistance to his natural feelings. He does not create anxiety by trying to be one-up on anxiety. No aspect of experience, of emotion or feeling, remains alien—nor does he hold this state of affairs up to himself as an ideal. He has seen quite clearly that the idea of a controlling agent behind acts, thinker behind thoughts, and feeler behind feelings is an illusion. More correctly, it is seen, not by him, but *in* the acting, thinking, and feeling.

It is, of course, one of the most familiar problems in psychotherapy that the free flow of a patient's thought or action is "blocked." In Zen this is called "doubt" or "hesitation" and is regarded as the chief symptom of ego, in contrast with "going directly ahead" (*mo chih ch'u*). Blocking is not thinking a problem out; it is *stopping* to think—a kind of anxious going blank through eagerness to win or fear to lose. Blocking is thus the typical response to a double-bind, and in the ordinary course of life it is the brief hesitation before thought or action which we confuse with an actual sensation of the ego. It is the feedback process, say, the cortex, trying to get feedback about itself and going blank because it is unable to do so. Thus part of the Zen master's game is to do everything possible to make the student block, until he ceases to care whether he blocks or not. This is well illustrated in the following incident:

> Nansen found the students of the eastern and western dormitories quarrelling over the ownership of a cat. Grasping hold of the cat, he exclaimed: "If anyone can say a true word, the cat can be saved!" There was no reply, whereupon Nansen immediately cut the cat in two. The same evening when Joshu returned, Nansen put the incident to

him, and at once Joshu put his sandals on his head and walked out. "If only you had been here," said Nansen, "the cat could have been saved." (127)

The students blocked, not only because they were stumped by such a sudden request for the "true word" about Zen, but also because they were horrified at the thought of a Buddhist monk's slaying an animal. But nothing stopped Joshu.[2]

Westerners often ask whether it is absolutely necessary to go through such a disciplinary mill as Zen in order to attain liberation, or whether there might be some more efficient and less arduous way. The question really answers itself: the more you believe that liberation is something which *you* can get, the harder you will have to work. Liberation is attractive to the degree that one's ego seems to be a problem.

Another important example of the counter-game is the Buddha's own dialectic of the "middle way," as it has recently been clarified by A. J. Bahm (131). It appears that in the Buddha's own time and region of India the way of liberation was largely confused with an attempt to destroy the ego and its appetites by extreme measures of asceticism, which the Buddha himself tried and found useless. Instead, he proclaimed a middle way between asceticism and hedonism, but this was something much more than a counsel of moderation. The middle way is ultimately the implicit unity of contraries, something like Jung's "reconciling principle."

---

[2] Zen anecdotes of this kind, called "question-answer" (*mondo*), could be cited indefinitely, and those interested in studying the actual performance of the game should consult Reps (128), Suzuki (129), and Watts (130).

As always, the problem is posed by the aspirant, and here it is the desire to find release from anguish (*duhkha*). The Buddha's counter is that desire (*trishna*) is the cause of anguish, and so the dialectic continues:

A: Then how do I get rid of desire?

B: Do you really want to get rid of it?

A: Yes and no. I want to get rid of the desire that causes anguish; but I do not want to get rid of the desire to get rid of it.

B: Anguish consists in not getting what one desires. Therefore, do not desire more than you have or will be able to get.

A: But I shall still have anguish if I do not succeed in desiring only as much as I have or will get.

B: Do not then desire to succeed in any greater measure than you can or will.

A: But there is still anguish if I fail to accomplish *that!*

B: Do not then desire to accomplish more of *that* than you can or will.

Etc.

This is not a straight conversation. At every step the aspirant has been experimenting with the Buddha's advice, trying in meditation to discover the degree to which he can stop desire, desiring to stop desire, and so on. But notice that the design of the dialectic is not circular but convergent, and that each step is a meta-step with respect to the one before. On each higher level, the aspirant is learning to halve the distance between his excessive, and anguish-causing, desire and what can actually be done. In this manner he is being brought to accept things as they are, but, at each step, things as they are include more and more the way he feels about them, and the way he feels about his feelings, etc. As Bahm shows, the various steps correspond to the stages of meditation (*jhana*) described in the early Buddhist records.

> The *jhanas* may be interpreted as degrees of shifting from concern about means to enjoyment of ends. Each new increase in generality of acceptance entails an increase in what is included in that which is experienced as an end. *Jhanas* are degrees of freedom from anxiety. *Jhanas* constitute levels of clarification or enlightenment relative to the extensiveness of the generality embodied in present enjoyment. *Jhanas* are successive degrees of diminution of one's desire to interfere wilfully in the natural course of events. *Jhanas* are shifts of interest increasingly from what ought to be to what is. (132)

In other words, as with each *jhana*-stage the acceptance of what is includes more and more one's feelings about what is, there is going to come a point when the sphere of what is (the world) and the sphere of one's feeling or desire about it (the ego) are identical. The aspirant began by seeking release from anguish, from the world of birth-and-death (*samsara*) as a trap. But at the end there is *only* the trap, and thus no one caught in it!

Another form of the dialectic of the middle way in Buddhism is the celebrated Madhyamika system of Nagarjuna (*c*. A.D. 200). At first sight this seems to be a purely philosophical and intellectual tour de force, the object of which is simply to refute any point of view that may be proposed. Taken in a purely logical and academic way, the Madhyamika is the systematic refutation of any philosophical opinion that may be classified under what Indian logic calls the "four propositions": (a) is, (b) is not, (c) both is and is not, and (d) neither is nor is not;

or (a) being, (b) nonbeing, (c) both being and nonbeing, and (d) neither being nor nonbeing. Thus, for example, *a* would assert Being or Substance as the ultimate reality in the manner of St. Thomas Aquinas; *b* in Humean fashion would dismiss this as the mere reification of a concept; *c* in the synthetic style of Hegel would affirm both sides, stressing their mutuality; and *d* would be some form of agnosticism or nihilism. But because language is dualistic or relational, any affirmation or denial whatsoever can have meaning only in relation to its own opposite. Every statement, every definition, sets up a boundary or limit; it classifies something, and thus it can always be shown that what is inside the boundary must coexist with what is outside. Even the idea of the boundless is meaningless without the contrast of the bounded. The Madhyamika dialectic uses this as an infallible method for pointing out the relativity of any metaphysical premise, and thus to engage such a dialectician in argument is inevitably to play a losing game.

But the intention of the Madhyamika is not to create an infallible system for winning arguments. It is quite definitely a therapy, a liberative counter-game, and is one of the historical antecedents of the technique of Zen. Like the therapist or the Zen master, the Madhyamika dialectician makes no proposition and raises no problem. He waits for one to come to him, and of course the problem posed may not at first seem to be anything like a metaphysical proposition. The system assumes, however, that almost everyone, however unlearned, has some metaphysical premise, some usually unconscious opinion to which he clings very dearly, and which lies at the root of his psychological security. By careful questioning the dialectician finds out what this opinion is, and then challenges the student to propose and defend it. Naturally, the defense fails and, to the degree that the student is emotionally dependent upon his opinion, he begins to feel insecure, not just intellectually but psychologically and even physically. He therefore looks about for some other premise to which he can hold, but as he takes up such alternatives the dialectician disposes of them one after another. At this point the student begins to feel a kind of vertigo because it seems that he has no basis from which to think and act, a situation which is obviously equivalent to the inability to find an ego agent. Because there is nowhere for him to take his stand there is also nowhere for him to be. Left to himself in this predicament he might well go out of his mind, but there is always the presence of the *guru* to reassure him, not by argument but by personality, that it is possible to have passed through this crisis with gain rather than loss of sanity. The "contest" of these counter-games is always conducted under the supposition that the players are not equal, that the *guru* is the master, and that therefore this is a learning game rather than a real battle. This is presupposed by the student in the initial act of seeking the *guru's* instruction.

Another form of the counter-game, often used in Yoga and of which there is also a rather full account in connection with the Taoist sage Lieh-tzu (133), centers around the task of attempting to gain perfect control of one's mind. The *guru* gives the student to understand that his problem lies not in the external world but in his own thoughts, feelings, and motivations. Pain and death will take care of themselves if only the student will take care of his own mind, and therefore he is encouraged to block his mental activity completely. At the same time, the student is given the impression that the *guru* can read his mind so that there is no chance of concealing its vagaries from the ever-watchful master.

This is an obvious double-bind, not only because the mind that needs to be controlled is the same as that which is trying to control it, but also because the student is "bugged" and made painfully self-conscious by knowing that he is watched. The disadvantage of this method, accounting for the fact that Yoga is so often a cul-de-sac, is that it can easily degenerate into nothing more than a deep hypnotic trance. This is why the early Zen texts repeatedly discourage attempts to block mental activity completely, saying that if this be liberation, then blocks of wood and stone are already Buddhas (134). However, the skillful *guru* will always lead the student's attempts at mind control into a vicious circle, reminding him, for example, that he is not really concentrating but thinking about trying to concentrate, or actually directing him to concentrate on concentration, to be aware of awareness, or urging him to concentrate upon some object without first, or subconsciously, intending to do so. The premise which the *guru* is challenging is the student's assumption that there really is a knower of his knowledge and a controller or thinker of his thoughts. While this assumption remains there is never perfect concentration because one is always "in two minds"—the knower and knowledge.

When at last the student discovers that "he" cannot really control his mind at all, and that however much he exerts himself his concentration is always "with intention," and that the *guru* knows it, he gives up and, in Lieh-tzu's words, "lets his mind think whatever it likes"—

because there is simply no alternative. Whereupon he realizes that the mind is *always* concentrated; the thinker is always completely one with and absorbed in its thought because there is nothing else than the succession of thoughts![3] Willing concentration merely introduces an oscillation effect into the succession of thoughts, because it is an attempt to make thought think itself. We can think about thinking by meta-thinking, by commenting on our thoughts at a higher level; but we cannot think thinking on one and the same level. When the confusion of this oscillation effect no longer arises, when, in other words, the yogi no longer tries to think with a thinker, his natural powers of concentration become enormously enhanced. There is no further "interference," in the electronic sense, from the supposed thinker.

A comparable technique is to encourage the student to stop his mind from wandering by thinking only about the events of the immediate present. Thought seems to be detached from time because memory images enable us to review events in succession and to project their future course. Because of this seeming ability to look now at the present, now at the past, and now at the future, the sensation of there being a constant thinker separate from the flow of events is all the more plausible. It therefore seems possible and reasonable to make an effort to attend to the present alone. But as the student perseveres, he discovers

---

[3] Cf., the Zen master Ma-tsu: "A *sutra* says, 'It is only a group of elements which come together to make this body.' When it arises, only these elements arise. When it ceases, only these elements cease. But when these elements arise, they do not say, 'I am arising,' and when they cease they do not say, 'I am ceasing.' So, too, with our former thoughts, later thoughts, and intervening thoughts: the thoughts follow one another without being linked together. Each one is absolutely tranquil" (135).

that the actual present is astonishingly elusive. In the very microsecond that he observes a present event it has already become a memory image, and it seems that without time for events to impress themselves upon memory there is no way of knowing anything at all. But if knowing must involve this lapse of time, is not all knowledge knowledge of the past, and what we call present knowledge just knowledge of the immediate past? The task assigned appears to be impossible, for the present reduces itself to an infinitesimal nothing. Yet in the moment when the experiment fails it also succeeds, but in an unexpected way. For it strikes the student that the memory images themselves are present events, and, if this is so, there is no knowledge *except* knowledge of the present. He had therefore been tricked into trying to do what happens in any case. But now the illusion which made it possible for him to fall for the trick is dissolved: if all knowledge is knowledge of the present, there is no observer separate from the flow of events.

The common design of all these methods is now clear: they challenge the student to demonstrate the power and independence of his presumed ego, and to the extent that he believes this possible he falls into a trap. As the trap closes, his feeling of helplessness becomes more and more critical, just because his habitual sense of being able to act from his own center has been so completely challenged. While the least identification with the observing ego remains, he seems to be being reduced more and more to an inert and passive witness. His thoughts, feelings, and experiences appear to be a mutually conditioning series of events in which he cannot genuinely intervene, since it always turns out that intervention was motivated, not by the ego, but by one or more of the observed events. Thoughts and feelings are conditioned by other thoughts and feelings, and the ego is cut down to a mute observer. Finally, as in the exercise of trying to concentrate only on the present, even its power to observe is challenged. Or perhaps its very passivity is challenged by the invitation to *be* passive, or simply to watch and accept what happens. But then, how is one to accept what happens when, among the things that are happening, there are feelings of resistance to life, of nonacceptance; or if it turns out that one is really accepting life in order to be one-up on it?

This is the point where, in the imagery of Zen, the student is likened to a mosquito biting an iron bull, or to a man who has swallowed a ball of red-hot iron which he can neither spit out nor gulp down. Press the point, and there is suddenly a "flip" of consciousness. There is no ego left with which one can identify. As a result the sense of self shifts from the independent observer to everything that is "observed." It feels that one *is* all that one knows, that one is doing all that is seen to happen, for the conflict of subject and object has entirely disappeared. This may at first be disconcerting and confusing, because there seems to be no independent point from which to act upon events and control them. It is like the moment in which one first learns to ride a bicycle or to swim: the new skill seems to be happening by itself. "Look, Mama, no hands!" But as the shock of unfamiliarity wears off, it becomes possible to conduct one's affairs in this new dimension of consciousness without the least difficulty.

In the language of psychotherapy, what we have here is the end of alienation, both of the individual from himself and of the individual from nature. The new state of affairs could also be described as self-acceptance or as psychological integration. However unscientific his terminology, and whatever his presuppositions about the biology of reason and instinct, this is certainly what Jung has in mind as the outcome of therapy.

> One must be able to let things happen. I have learnt from the East what is meant by the phrase *Wu-wei*: namely, "not-doing, letting be," which is quite different from doing nothing. . . . The region of darkness into which one falls is not empty; it is the "lavishing mother" of Lao-tzu, the "images" and the "seed." When the surface has been cleared, things can grow out of the depths. People always suppose that they have lost their way when they come up against these depths of experience. But if they do not know how to go on, the only answer, the only advice, that makes any sense is "Wait for what the unconscious has to say about the situation." A way is only *the* way when one finds it and follows it oneself. There is no general prescription for "how one should do it." (136)

"The region of darkness" and "the unconscious" are of course this unfamiliar world of polarity where we live as organism/environment instead of subject at war with alien objects, and it is dark and unconscious only because it has been repressed by our conventional way of seeing things. This is quite clearly, too, the mode of consciousness which both Norman Brown and Herbert Marcuse see as the logical outcome of psychoanalysis—if one follows it with a consistency which Freud himself seemed to lack.

> Freud describes the "ideational content" of the surviving primary ego-feeling as "limitless extension and oneness with the universe" (oceanic feeling). . . . He suggests that the

oceanic feeling seeks to reinstate "limitless narcissism." The striking paradox that narcissism, usually understood as egotistic withdrawal from reality, here is connected with oneness with the universe, reveals the new depth of the conception: beyond all immature autoeroticism, narcissism denotes a fundamental relatedness to reality which may generate a comprehensive existential order. In other words, narcissism may contain the germ of a different reality principle: the libidinal cathexis of the ego (one's own body) may become the source and reservoir for a new libidinal cathexis of the objective world—transforming this world into a new mode of being. (137)

Wherever something of this kind emerges from the Freudian tradition, it is assumed that the new relationship of man to his world will be *erotic*—not the specialized eroticism of the genital apparatus, but the diffused eroticism of primary narcissism and of the "polymorphous perverse" body of the infant. Psychoanalysts of what I must call the hard-boiled variety regard all this dabbling with mysticism and oceanic feelings as pure regression, as an expression of the infant's global *egotism* which completely disregards any real problems of divergent interests between oneself and others. But narcissism is necessarily egotism only if it can be assumed that conflict between the organism and its environment is biologically prior to the mutual development of the two, and in the present state of our knowledge this simply cannot be maintained. In discussing man's "earliest encounters of his trustful past" in infancy, even so ego-oriented an analyst as Erik Erikson can say:

Finally, the glass shows the pure self itself, the unborn core of creation, the—as it were, preparental—center where

God is pure nothing: *ein lauter Nichts,* in the words of Angelus Silesius. God is so designated in many ways in Eastern mysticism. This pure self is the self no longer sick with a conflict between right and wrong, not dependent on providers, and not dependent on guides to reason and reality. . . . But must we call it regression if man thus seeks again the earliest encounters of his trustful past in his efforts to reach a hoped-for and eternal future? . . . If this is partial regression, it is a regression which, in retracing firmly established pathways, returns to the present amplified and clarified. (138)

And earlier he has said:

From the oldest Zen poem to the most recent psychological formulation, it is clear that "the conflict between right and wrong is the sickness of the mind." (139)

In the stress upon the erotic and delightful character of this new feeling for the world, Westerners inclined to oriental mysticism will also demur out of the feeling that liberation is a purely "spiritual" condition. They join hands with Freud and the hard-boiled psychoanalysts in basic mistrust of the physical world, that is, in alienation from the organism, forgetting that when India and Tibet looked for the supreme symbol of the reconciliation of opposites they chose *shakta* and *shakti,* the god and the goddess, the figure and the ground, the Yes and the No, in eternal intercourse—using the most erotic image imaginable.

But I have tried to show that everything ascetic, spiritual, and other-worldly in the ways of liberation is a challenge to the ego—a "come on" or *judo* inciting the student to prove that his central self is an independent soul-agent which can make itself one-up on the world. The hard discipline of the ways is the total defeat of this ambition, leading to a new identification of one's life and being, not with the skin-encapsulated "I," but with the organism/environment field. The essential hostility of the ego to the physical organism and world is dissolved by a *reductio ad absurdum*, in which the most skillful means are employed to beguile the egocentric consciousness into consistent action upon its own premises. To what extent, then, are various forms of psychotherapy doing the same thing, however much their avowed objectives may have something else in mind?[4]

Haley's hypothesis can, I think, be used to show that many forms of psychotherapy with wide theoretical differences are using the same pattern of strategy as between the *guru* and his student. Yet it seems that, in many instances, the use of this strategy in psychotherapy is on a different level, perhaps less radical, and often with the object of fortifying the ego rather than dissolving it. However, there are exceptions to this, and the confusion of terminology leaves some doubt as to the precise difference between a strong and responsible ego, on the one hand, and a unique and integrated individual, on the other.

[4] The problem is outside the scope of this book, but if there is a discrepancy between psychotherapeutic theories and the way in which they actually work, may there not be at least the potentiality of a similarly unconscious effectiveness in Christianity, such that it could become a way of liberation? Jesus' commandment, apparently addressed to the ego, "Thou *shalt* love the Lord thy God with all thy heart and with all thy soul and with all thy mind," is emphatically a double-bind. "You *must* be sincere." If taken as skillful means (*upaya*) rather than as a positive precept, these words could also be understood as a challenge to the ego and all its counsels of perfection. Jesus was certainly challenging the self-righteousness of the Pharisees, but we seem to have missed the humor of his equal challenge to Christians.

Haley begins (140) with the assumption that psychopathological symptoms must be studied in the light of their function in any social context. How, in other words, do apparently involuntary symptoms of, say, anxiety, migraine, depression, alcoholism, phobia, or lethargy enable their victim to relate to other people? He suggests that such symptoms are strategic: they enable the person to control others without accepting responsibility for doing so, as when a mother prevents a daughter from marrying by becoming helplessly dependent on her undivided attention by some sort of invalidism. She is saying, in effect, that *she* is not requiring the daughter's attentions; her sickness requires them. The daughter cannot then refuse the bind without defining herself as inhumanly callous and undutiful, and she cannot accept it without denying her independence and her love for a man. Furthermore, the daughter cannot say, "But you are using this sickness to control me," without either insulting her mother or baffling her, for the mother simply cannot feel any responsibility for her symptoms. Thus the bind on the daughter is double. From Freud on it has seemed sound policy to look for the function or purpose of psychopathological symptoms, whether in the interpersonal context of social relations, or in the intrapersonal context of superego, ego, and id. The highly conjectural nature of the latter constellation gives greater probability to the former, in the sense of making it a more promising field of study.

Haley goes on to point out that in any social situation where one individual is putting double-binds upon others, the others respond with the same type of behavior. In the example cited, the mother wants the daughter's love—but the daughter cannot say, "I am staying home because I love you and because I want to." She has to say that she is acting involuntarily, because her mother is sick. In effect, the daughter is saying that she is loving her mother because she cannot help it, and does not want to—and now the mother is in a double-bind. She cannot get love from her daughter without realizing that it is not really love; and yet she cannot say, "Well, after all, you do not really love me," without the daughter's countering, "Then why do you think I am looking after you?" Furthermore, she cannot say, "You are just looking after me because you would feel ashamed to do otherwise"; she would not only be denying outright what she wants, love; she would also be giving away her own game. In this way, her symptoms are perpetuated. Because she has to be sick involuntarily, the daughter has to love her involuntarily, and therefore she has to be sick involuntarily. To get what they want, they are both doing what they don't want. They are in conflict and in misery, feeling themselves in the vicious circle of an insoluble problem.

It is worth pausing here to note a still deeper level of paradox. What do we mean when we ask to be loved voluntarily? We are *not* asking to be loved out of a sense of duty, which is what is ordinarily meant by a sense of responsibility. Willed, or forced, love—the ego trying to dominate emotion—is just what we don't want. Surely, what we are asking is that the other person love us because he cannot help it, that he love *in*voluntarily, but that the ego does not resist the emotion. We want the individual to enjoy his involuntary feeling for us. Confusion would be avoided by calling such love not voluntary, but spontaneous. Now the spontaneous is what happens of itself, the Taoist *tzu-jan* or "of itself so," what happens without forced effort. Spontaneity is not an ego action at all; on the contrary, it is action which the social control mechanism of the ego does not block. If anyone says, "With all my heart I love you," it is not the ego that speaks. He means that it is delightful to love spontaneously without blocking from and conflict with socially implanted notions of one's role, identity, and duty. When someone loves *first* out of a sense of duty, and later begins to like it, we may often suspect that what he has actually come to enjoy is the security of being obedient, of feeling again the warmth of parental approval.[5]

Herein lies the profound confusion of so many of our ethical and marital conventions. Society may well be within its rights to require controls of the expression of spontaneity, to say, "On such occasions and in such ways you must *not* be spontaneous." But to say, "You *must* be spontaneous," is the flat contradiction at the root of every double-bind. Hypnosis alone can produce an apparently obedient spontaneity, and this is perhaps why "cures" based on simple hypnotherapy are so superficial and short-lived.

If, as Haley supposes, the task of the therapist is to break the double-binds imposed upon the patient and so stop him from imposing them on others, his basic objective must be to make the patient see the nonsense of demanding spontaneity. To this end he knowingly or unknowingly engages the patient in a therapeutic double-bind. It is therapeutic because the therapist does not really want to dominate the patient for his own ends, and because it is going to be directed in such a way as to reveal

[5] In which case the object of love becomes a father or mother substitute, and the relationship therefore implicitly incestuous; hence guilt and hence the genesis of a vicious circle.

its own contradiction. In short, the patient becomes involved in a relationship which he cannot define or control however hard he may try.

From the very start the patient has to come as the suppliant. He has to define himself as in need of help; he has to pay for the privilege of consultation; he has to humiliate himself in saying that he cannot refrain from doing things that he does not want to do, that he is not in control of his own behavior. Every sound therapy resorts at this point to *judo*. The therapist does not deny the symptoms by saying, "Stop being nervous!" Nor does he deny the patient's feeling that he ought to be in control by saying, "Well, there's nothing you can do about it." Either response would end the relationship then and there. Instead, the therapist takes the side of the patient's ego against the symptoms; he accepts the patient's definition of the problem, and *allows* him, as perhaps other people do not, to be out of control. By having the therapist's permission to be sick, the patient is at once reassured and brought under the therapist's authority.

Let us suppose, now, that the therapist's method is one of the forms of psychoanalysis. He will then suggest that there are unconscious reasons for the difficulty. It matters little whether these be described as repressed traumas of infancy or concealed factors in interpersonal relationships. The point is to say either, "You are in difficulty because you do not understand yourself," or, "You do not really want to control your symptoms." In either case the competence of the ego is challenged, but at a new and higher level, for while the therapist has agreed that the ego is not in control he has questioned whether it "really" wants to be in control or whether it has defined the problem correctly. The patient may either accept or reject this suggestion, but if the latter, the therapist will not argue. He will simply ask, "I wonder why you seem so anxious to deny that possibility?" He will imply, then, that the patient is resisting treatment, indirectly reinforcing the suggestion that he does not "really" want to get well. More indirectly still, he may suggest that the patient's desire to retain his symptoms is unconscious, or that "the unconscious" is producing them, acting as a sort of second self, more powerful than the ego.

The idea of "the unconscious" enables the patient to express and talk about himself without assuming responsibility for what he says. This pattern of communication is, of course, the same as using one's symptoms to control relationships. "It is happening, but I am not doing it and so cannot be blamed." By assuming an unconscious mind, the therapist accepts and encourages this behavior pattern, but at the same time prevents the patient from using it to control *him*. On the one hand, the therapist takes authority for interpreting this indirect communication. Whether the therapist actually makes interpretations or not, the patient is given to understand that his dreams and free associations are intelligible to the therapist in a way that they are not intelligible to himself. On the other hand, the patient is apparently put in charge of the situation by being told to do the talking himself, to initiate the topics of discussion, and to bring up whatever "unconscious material" he pleases. But just because this is what the therapist has told him to do, his controlling the conversation is obedience to the therapist, and by this *judo* the patient is put in a double-bind. Try as he may to control the situation and to use communication from "the unconscious" to shield himself from unpleasant discoveries, he is always doing so at the therapist's direction. In other words, try as he may to shift responsibility to the therapist—"*You* tell me what to do; *you* cure me, tell me what is wrong with me, etc."—the fact is that this behavior is being commanded without being accommodated. In the transference, for example, the analyst becomes a parental figure upon whom the patient depends without being able to make him actually take responsibility. But a blunt refusal to take responsibility is never made, for this would no longer challenge the patient to try to control the therapist. He therefore avoids taking responsibility indirectly by saying, "I must help you to find out what *you* really want to do," or, "Let us wait and see what comes up from your own unconscious." In short, the therapist is directing the patient to try to control the relationship, but making it appear that he is not being directive at all and that everything is happening on the patient's own initiative.

However the patient tries to control the therapist, he is at once countered with a *judo* "ploy" which simultaneously frustrates the attempt and provokes a further effort. He is, furthermore, being allowed and encouraged to make the attempt in his characteristic way—unconsciously and irresponsibly, as by describing his dreams or free associations, which thus become extensions of his involuntary symptoms—an enlarged and enriched description of all behaviors which he does not claim as *his*. Naturally, he describes all this "unconscious material" in the hope that the therapist will tell him what it means, or that it will lead to a diagnosis for which the therapist can simply prescribe a remedy. But the therapist never refuses to do so directly. Instead he encourages more dreams and more free associations, as if these would elucidate what has gone before, or lead down into deeper and deeper regions of the unconscious. At the same time he is directing the patient to take charge of the situation by such questions as "Well, what do *you* think the dream means?"

In due course the double-bind on the patient becomes critical. He cannot get out of it by quitting the relationship, because the therapist has defined this as unconscious resistance to treatment, or as admitting that he does not really want to get well. He cannot force the therapist to make decisions for him, because the relationship is always being defined by the therapist as supportive but nondirective. He cannot break out of the situation by aggression, by abusing the therapist, because the latter can never be fazed: he simply accepts the attack by going limp or by questioning its motivation, e.g., "I wonder if you don't like me because I remind you of someone else?" According to Haley, at this critical point of frustration the patient has to give up, but he cannot give up by quitting. He can only give up by behaving in a different way; but what can he do?

Haley suggests that because the patient has in fact been offering his symptoms at the therapist's direction, he can only escape from the therapeutic bind, from the therapist's control, by losing interest in his symptoms and by ceasing to offer them. Alternatively, he can acknowledge that he has been trying unsuccessfully to control the therapist, and other people as well, by offering these symptoms—but in this case he has to claim them as his own behavior, to accept responsibility for them. The therapist's *judo* has provoked the patient to behave consistently in his symp-

tomatic way, to the point of discovering that it is completely inappropriate and unsuccessful.

But I feel that something more needs to be said.
Throughout all this the therapist has been testing two
premises which the patient assumed from the outset. The
first is that some of his actions are his own, and that they
proceed freely from his ego. The second is that some of his
actions are not his own, and that they happen spontaneously against his will. The therapist challenges the
first premise by asking whether behavior which the patient
believes to be voluntary is really so. "Do you really want
to get well?" "I wonder what you really mean when you
say that you don't like me?" He challenges the second
premise by attributing intent to involuntary behavior,
suggesting that dreams express hidden wishes or questioning the significance of the patient's automatic gestures or
nervous movements. This, too, is a double-bind because
it implies that however the patient behaves, voluntarily
or involuntarily, he reveals himself and that all his defenses are transparent to the therapist. Again, if he leaves
the field he is resisting. If he goes blank and tries to
frustrate this maneuver by blocking himself, the therapist
may gently imply that this, too, is revealing and that there
must be something that he is extremely anxious to conceal
from himself.

The other side of the fact that the patient is trying to
control the therapist is that he is trying to get help without
having to be aware of himself. What he actually is, is so
inconsistent with his image of himself that he dare not
find out, and yet he would not be coming for treatment at
all unless he were dimly aware of the discrepancy. The
therapist "bugs" the patient by suggesting that he cannot

really conceal himself, but at the same time indicates that his own attitude is one of complete acceptance and friendliness. Obviously, this situation is not established in a single consultation; it develops through the interaction of the two persons over a period of time. As the relationship proceeds, the patient discovers that all his attempts at blocking and self-concealment are absurd, that he is locked in a situation from which the only escape is simply to be what he is without restraint. The compliant patient may of course imitate spontaneity and positively gush with free associations, but the perceptive therapist detects and challenges every artifice until the patient can no longer be blocked or fazed.

At this point the patient simply stops pretending. He does not learn to "be himself" as if that were something which one can *do;* he learns rather that there is nothing he can do *not* to be himself. But this is just another way of saying that he has ceased to identify himself with his ego, with the image of himself which society has forced upon him. As a result of the therapist's challenge to his two premises, his voluntary behavior and his involuntary behavior come together as one, and he finds out that his total behavior, his organism, is both and neither: it is spontaneous. One may call this integration of the "personality," actualization of the "self," or even the development of a new "ego structure"; but it does not correspond at all to the normal sense of ego or self as the directive agent behind action.

Whenever this is the outcome of therapy, it is, at least in principle, the same as liberation. It has integrated the individual with his own "external" world, that is, with his involuntary and spontaneous aspects. But it still does not fully challenge the presumed split between the organism as a whole and its environment. It does not, like the Eastern ways, challenge the conventions of perception, whereby sights and sounds are taken to be outside the organism, and whereby movements of the organism/environment boundary are taken to be initiated by the organism. One of the few approaches to something of this kind in the West is the relatively little-known school of Gestalt Therapy. In a work of this title by Perls, Hefferline, and Goodman, the authors state:

> It is meaningless to define a breather without air, a walker without gravity and ground, an irascible without obstacles, and so on for every animal function. The definition of an organism is the definition of an organism/environment field; and the contact-boundary is, so to speak, the specific organ of awareness of the novel situation in the field. . . . In the case of a stationary plant . . . the osmotic membrane is the *organ of the interaction* of organism and environment, both parts being obviously active. In the case of a mobile complicated animal it is the same, but certain illusions of perception make it more difficult to conceive. The illusions, to repeat them, are simply that the mobile wins attention against the stationary background, and the more tightly complicated wins attention against the relatively simpler. But at the boundary, the interaction is proceeding from both parts. (141)

One might prefer Bentley's "transaction" to "interaction," but otherwise this is a perfect description of the illusion-creating factor of the Buddhist *avidya*—"ignore-ance." The theoretical work of these authors is magnificent, but when it comes to therapy itself the technique rests too much upon trying deliberately to feel relationship. Experimental challenging of the illusions of separateness is far more convincing, because the final experience of the organism/environment field is a revelation and not an artificial construction. In general, however, it is the one-sidedly psychological emphasis of Western therapies which obstructs this further extension of liberation.

If, then, the essential technique of therapy is to challenge the patient's false and neurotic assumptions so that the more he holds to them, the more he finds himself in a double-bind, it seems to make little difference whether the theory be Freudian, Jungian, Rogerian, Existential, Interpersonal, or simply eclectic. The extreme nondirective theory of Carl Rogers is just as much a *judo* imposing double-binds as the more directive theory of, say, John Rosen (142). Once two people enter into a relationship it is simply impossible for one of them, the therapist, to be so passive that he serves as nothing more than a mirror to the patient. As Haley points out, just to accept what the patient says or does is already to permit his behavior and thus take control of it.

> Whatever a therapist says or does not say in response to a patient will circumscribe the patient's behavior. Even if a therapist says, "I'm not going to tell you what to do," when a patient asks for direction, he is still directing the patient not to ask him what to do. If a patient complains to a therapist and the therapist is silent, this silence is inevitably a comment on the patient's behavior. (143)

What, then, is more of a double-bind than a situation in which the therapist is directing the patient by being completely nondirective? Rosen's directive *judo* is simply a different application of the same principle. For example, by commanding the patient to produce his symptoms, or even exaggerate them, he takes control of what the patient does even if the patient does not produce them—for the context of the situation is therapeutic and thus the therapist's aim is to get rid of the symptoms. He wins either way!

All this may seem to be a tremendous oversimplification of therapy, but it is of the utmost importance to understand that the principle cannot be *used* in the simplified form in which it has been *described*. For one thing, the patient would see through it too easily and refuse the challenge. For another, applying it as a counter to the specific maneuvers of particular patients requires great versatility, practice, and judgment of character—though more in the way that a novelist or shrewd salesman judges character than a theoretical psychologist. We saw that the ways of liberation make much use of *upaya*, of skillful or "tricky" means to challenge their students. The description of dreams, the production of fantasies and free associations, and the discussion of their symbolism is, I believe, *upaya*. It is necessary and therapeutic hocus-pocus, but it would be of very great help to the therapist to realize it. The difficulty of such theoretical systems as the Freudian and Jungian is that patients come away from therapy believing in them as religions. "Getting religion" may sometimes be effective therapy, if not liberation, but when the attention of therapists is set exclusively upon, say, dream symbolism they lose sight not only of the essential technique of therapy but also of the social context of psychopathology.

This is not, of course, to say that the Freudian and Jungian theoretical systems are *pure* hocus-pocus without the least scientific value. Naturally, hypotheses which have had scientific value in the past may have less today, but the point is that, to a very great extent, these theories *function* as hocus-pocus in therapy. We saw, for instance, that telling a patient that he has an "unconscious mind" enables him to communicate with the therapist indirectly, without having to feel that *he* is responsible for what he says: it is the unconscious. This may not be acceptable to hard-core Freudians and Jungians, but if such individuals are to represent themselves in any sense as scientists nothing could be more inappropriate than a rigid theoretical party line. It is a great disadvantage to any therapist to have an ax to grind, because this gives him a personal interest in winning the counter-game with his patient. But we saw, in reference to the Zen master, that he can play the game effectively just because winning or losing makes no difference to him. In the absence of this essential qualification, psychotherapy degenerates into a power game in which the therapist double-binds unfortunate patients for years and years for nothing but his own satisfaction.

This whole view of psychotherapy retains certain elements of these classical theories. It still seems quite proper to describe the ego as a construct of the reality principle (social convention) exercising repression upon life processes which thereby become more or less unconscious. It still seems valid to suppose that in the formation of the ego feeling the effects of training in infancy and childhood are of immense importance, even if it may not be necessary to recall them in therapy. As a result, it is surely true that the child's attitude to father or mother influences his attitudes to other people in later life, making him give and receive demands for forced spontaneity. It still seems to be true that, for Western cultures at least, the repression of sexuality is a major source of psychopathological behavior. Furthermore, Jung's constant insistence upon therapy as a reconciliation of opposites and upon the acceptance and assimilation of the Shadow, the dark and repressed aspect of one's nature, is quite central to this view of liberation. The problem is always that acceptance of oneself can never be a deliberate act; it is as paradoxical as kissing one's own lips. But the counter-game challenges the actual possibility of rejecting oneself, and in the end does not construct but *reveals* the wholeness of man as an inescapable fact.

From this point of view we can also see a new significance in Freud's attribution of a sexual character to unconscious motivation—that is, if we take it as therapeutic strategy rather than psychological fact. In any culture which is sexually squeamish, the suggestion that one's real motivations are sexual is a peculiarly effective challenge to the ego. Just because the culture regards sexuality as evil or degrading, the suggestion implies that one's true motivations are the *opposite* of one's conscious intention and thus that the ego is not really in charge of things at all. When the individual is strongly identified with his ego, such a suggestion is at once resisted, and then the therapist has only to point out that the patient would have no reason to deny the suggestion so energetically if it were not true. He is thereby put in the position of denying his ego by the very act of affirming it, and the double-bind thus imposed is all the more effective because he cannot honestly deny the existence of sexual feeling and its inevitable attraction. If the therapist's intention were to attack and accuse the patient, we might feel that this strategy gave him a very unfair advantage. But in fact the imposition of this particular bind simply exposes the bind which has already been imposed upon the patient by society. He would never have fallen into the therapist's "trap" if he had not first been tricked into disowning himself and his own feelings by accepting the fiction that *he* is his ego or soul, and not his entire organism.

To escape from the therapist's trap, the patient can only stop defending himself against himself, and in dropping this defense he ceases, at the same time, to identify himself with the ego. But this can happen only as it becomes clear to the patient that the therapist is not attacking him, which in turn depends upon the therapist's having genuinely accepted himself. This means, however, that the therapist represents a philosophy other than that of society and stands, as it were, for the authority of nature rather than the authority of men. But this becomes the superior authority only as it can be shown that social authority contains a self-contradiction from which natural authority is free, and a self-contradiction so basic that its perpetuation must destroy society and drive men to madness.

VI

Invitation to the Dance

THE saying "By their fruits ye shall know them" is generally taken to mean that men are finally to be judged by their moral behavior, and philosophies of life by their moral consequences. But the only definition of morality which can today command any general assent is: conduct which furthers the survival of society. We understand the fruits of thought and action as their nutritive utility; that fruits may be lovely in taste and texture is quite incidental. The question is only whether they contain the proper vitamins, and taste is important only insofar as it facilitates digestibility. In such a morality the function of play is to make work tolerable, and work is a burden, not because it requires more effort than play, but because it is a contest with death. Work as we know it is contaminated with the fear of death, for work is what *must* be done in order to survive, and to survive, to go on, is the ultimate and irreducible necessity. Why is it not obvious that to make survival necessary is to make it a burden? Life is above all a spontaneous process, and, as we have seen, to command spontaneity, to say that one *must* live, is the basic contradiction imposing the double-bind on us all.

To take sides is always the first step in a *game*, and to choose life as against death, being as against nonbeing, is only to pretend that they are separable. Yet it is repre-

sented to us as the ultimately serious choice. The proto-
types of being and nonbeing are doubtless matter and
space, form and emptiness, and it was perhaps inevitable
that we should have thought of matter as enjoying a precarious and transitory existence in the midst of infinite and
eternal nothingness. But it seems almost certain that
modern astronomy and cosmology are coming close to a
vision of the universe where space is no longer the inert
container of the galaxies but an integral part of their form.
Form encloses space just as much as space encloses form.
Speaking metaphorically, it is as if space and form lay
together upon the surface of a sphere in such a way that
the choice as to which is figure and which background
is quite arbitrary. Life, or formative process, is not therefore happening within some alien continuum that is not
life.

In the sleep of "ignore-ance," of narrowed attention
which does not see things whole, our gaze is captured by
the convenient figure rather than its ground, or counter-
figure. But the awakening of liberation is to realize that all
choices between "opposites" are the separation of in-
separables. In the words of the Zen master Seng-ts'an:

> The perfect Way [Tao] is without difficulty,
> Save that it avoids picking and choosing. . . .
> If you want to get the plain truth,
> Be not concerned with right and wrong.
> The conflict between right and wrong
> Is the sickness of the mind. (144)

The point is not that one stops choosing, but that one
chooses in the knowledge that there is really no choice.
Eastern philosophy is full of such seeming paradoxes—to

act without action, to think without thought, to love without attachment. It is simply that in a universe of relativity all choosing, all taking of sides, is playful. But this is not that one feels no urgency. To know the relativity of light and darkness is not to be able to gaze unblinkingly into the sun; to know the relativity of up and down is not to be able to fall upward. To feel urgency without compulsion is the seemingly paradoxical way of describing what it is like for a feeling to arise spontaneously without its happening to a feeler.

What, then, are the fruits of liberation if it sets one free from the morality of survival and flight from death? It is only natural that we should be disturbed at the thought that people live among us who do not take the social game seriously. How will they behave if they do not ultimately believe in our rules? The question applies also to psychotherapy, and has been asked again and again ever since Freud connected neurosis with repression. Freud and the psychoanalysts have not really faced the question because they have never seriously considered doing away with repression. On the whole, they have taken the side of the reality principle, of the superego and the ego against the id. But at the same time they have softened the conflict, and the social effect of Freud's doctrine has been tremendous, not only in bringing about a greater degree of sexual freedom, but also in changing our ideas of individual responsibility. The whole recognition that deviants, delinquents, and criminals are sick rather than sinful and need psychotherapy rather than punishment stems directly from Freud, and has become characteristic of all liberal and "progressive" social reform. Nevertheless, there are many who fear that the Freudian ethic is seriously undermining our society, for as a result of it there are more and more people who do not accept full responsibility for their actions. The blame for one's behavior can be shifted indefinitely, and without a good old-fashioned sense of guilt we seem to lose not only an effective deterrent to evil but also a sense of human dignity.

Freud, it must be remembered, remained a dualist in his view of human nature, and so long as there seems to be a basic incompatibility between instinct and reason, Eros and civilization, there must remain an insoluble moral problem—to which repression only *seems* to be a workable answer. Thus in defining the problem of education Freud said:

> The child has to learn to control its instincts. To grant it complete freedom, so that it obeys all its impulses without any restriction, is impossible. It would be a very instructive experiment for child-psychologists, but it would make life impossible for the parents and would do serious damage to the children themselves. . . . Education has therefore to steer its way between the Scylla of giving the instincts free play and the Charybdis of frustrating them. (145)

It may be necessary to divide the child against itself for the purpose of learning certain patterns of social behavior, but if the child does not later in life discover that this division was, like the myth of Santa Claus, a trick, it turns into a permanently alienated personality. When such personalities, in their turn, bring up children they impose the division upon them without knowing that it is a trick, and thus their admonitions are given without humor and often without essential kindness. For when the child is recalcitrant, the self-alienated adult is genuinely furious;

he does not realize that bringing up children is playing a game with them.

The practical problem of repression as a human disease does not, therefore, require that we stop disciplining our children. It is more simply a question of realizing that when we teach them to think of themselves as the duality of ego and instinct, controller and controlled, this is nothing but strategy. The practical problem is for adults, and it is the problem which Norman Brown has stated so masterfully in his *Life Against Death*: is it not time that we carried Freud's thought to its full conclusion and learned to live without repression? The question is at first sight outrageous, which is just what makes Brown's sophisticated and scholarly book all the more impressive. Yet if the question could be answered affirmatively, the fruits of liberation would really be fruits. The results which the practical moralist demands from any change in consciousness, from the mystical vision, are not really fruits at all. He wants self-sacrifice, courage, and dedication as a means to the continuation of social life. But there is absolutely no point in clothing the naked, feeding the hungry, and healing the sick if it is just that they may live to be naked, hungry, and sick again, or live merely to be able to do the same for others. Practical morality, whether Judaic or Christian, capitalist or communist, is provision for a future—a perpetual renunciation or postponement. This is a future which no one is ever going to be able to enjoy because, by the time it arrives, everyone has lost the ability to live in the present. Thus the test of liberation is not whether it issues in good works; the test of good works is whether they issue in liberation—in the capacity to *be* all that one is without repression or alienation. On the principle that "the sabbath is made for man, and not man for the sabbath," the function of moral behavior is always secondary and subordinate.

But to what? One has the impression that the ways of liberation, like Catholic Christianity, conceive the *summum bonum,* the true end of man, to be eternal contemplation and enjoyment of the bodiless and spiritual Godhead in a future life beyond death. Yet when the Eastern ways are understood more deeply, it appears that *nirvana* is not after, beyond, or away from birth-and-death (*samsara*), but that, in the Zen master Hakuin's words:

> *This very earth is the Lotus Land of purity,*
> *And this very body the Body of Buddha.* (146)

Eternity is now, and in the light of unrepressed vision the physical organism and the physical world turn out to be the divine world. But so long as life is work-against-death this cannot be seen. As Brown says:

> This incapacity to die, ironically but inevitably, throws mankind out of the actuality of living, which for all normal animals is at the same time dying; the result is denial of life (repression). . . . The distraction of human life to the war against death, by the same inevitable irony, results in death's dominion over life. The war against death takes the form of a preoccupation with the past and the future, and the present tense, the tense of life, is lost. (147)

Thereupon the business of life is guided by the neurotic repetition-compulsion, the quest for survival, for more and more time in which we hope by some miracle to grasp what always eludes us in the present. It is thus that, starting from Freud, Brown can come to the same conclusion as Hakuin:

If we connect—as Freud did not—the repetition-compulsion with Freud's reiterated theorem that the instinctual processes of the id are timeless, then only repressed life is in time, and unrepressed life would be timeless or in eternity. Thus again psychoanalysis, carried to its logical conclusion and transformed into a theory of history, gathers to itself ageless religious aspirations. The Sabbath of Eternity, that time when time no more shall be, is an image of that state which is the ultimate goal of the repetition-compulsion in the timeless id. . . . Psychoanalysis comes to remind us that we are bodies, that repression is of the body, and that perfection would be the realm of Absolute Body; eternity is the mode of unrepressed bodies. (148)

The final aim of psychoanalysis must therefore be a veritable Resurrection of the Body as distinct from some future reanimation of the corpse.

The aim of psychoanalysis—still unfulfilled, and still only half-conscious—is to return our souls to our bodies, to return ourselves to ourselves, and thus to overcome the human state of self-alienation. . . . What orthodox psychoanalysis has in fact done is to reintroduce the soul-body dualism in its own new lingo, by hypostatizing the "ego" into a substantial essence which by means of "defence mechanisms" continues to do battle against the "id." Sublimation is disposed of by listing it as a "successful" defense mechanism. In substantializing the ego, orthodox psychoanalysis follows the authority of Freud, who compared the relation of the ego to the id to that of a rider to his horse—a metaphor going back to Plato's *Phaedrus* and perpetuating the Platonic dualism. (149)

Orthodox psychoanalysis has thus allied itself with the reality principle and the ethics of survival. Its issue is not "a union with others and with the world around us based not on anxiety and aggression but on narcissism and erotic exuberance" (150); it is the dull thud, the anemic anticlimax of what Philip Rieff has called "psychological man."

> The psychological ideal of normality has a rather unheroic aspect. Think of a whole society dominated by psychotherapeutic ideals. Considered not from the individual's but from a sociological point of view, psychoanalysis is an expression of a popular tyranny such as not even de Tocqueville adequately imagined. . . . In the emergent democracy of the sick, everyone can to some extent play doctor to others, and none is allowed the temerity to claim that he can definitively cure or be cured. The hospital is succeeding the church and the parliament as the archetypal institution of Western culture. (151)

For this is the tame and insipid consequence of a middle way in which the opposites are not transcended but compromised, where there is no more than a cautious treaty between the rider and the horse, the soul and the body, the ego and the id.

As we have seen, the failure of orthodox psychoanalysis is the result of Freud's dualism, and thus of the fear that the unrepressed human body will turn out to be a wild animal rutting and snarling in the squalor of its own excrement. Biologically and morphologically man may be an animal, but he is *not* a horse, a tiger, or a baboon. The unique structure of his organism and brain enables him to discipline himself, but it is simply pretense that this self-control is based upon an actual dualism of soul and body, ego and id. The pretense may be useful as a temporary measure, as a pedagogical gambit; but when it becomes the permanent cast of human feeling it is nothing more than an artificial prolongation of childhood tutelage, a failure to grow up which makes all the disciplines of culture abortive. For when the pretense remains unconscious and is taken to be real the soul thus abstracted from the body is abstracted from the organ of enjoyment. It becomes chronically afraid to be physical and to participate completely in physical spontaneity. As a result, the man identified with the soul is always frustrated and always needs more time. Because he knows that the body will die, its corruptible form becomes his enemy. The disciplines of art and science are therefore pressed into service in the war against death, against the body, and against spontaneity. Morality, too, becomes the servant of the discarnate soul.

But everything that fights against the body and death becomes death, that is, becomes incapable of spontaneity and therefore of genuine delight. The quest for future satisfaction is consequently a vicious circle, and cultural progress becomes the course of its ever more frantic attempts to solve the self-contradictory problem. It is no answer to abandon the disciplines of art, science, and morality in the current style of "beat-ism." The real problem is to put these disciplines at the disposal of spontaneity. For when we have Eros dominated by reason instead of Eros expressing itself with reason, we create a culture that is simply against life, in which the human organism has to submit more and more to the needs of mechanical organization, to postpone enjoyment in the name of an ever more futile utility.

When cultural disciplines are in the service of Eros, ethics are transformed from the rules of repression into the technique of expression, and morality becomes the aesthetics of behavior.

The discipline of aesthetics installs the *order of sensuousness* as against the *order of reason*. Introduced into the philosophy of culture, this notion aims at a liberation of the senses which, far from destroying civilization, would give it a firmer basis and would greatly enhance its potentialities. Operating through a basic impulse—namely, the play impulse—the aesthetic function would "abolish compulsion, and place man, both morally and physically, in freedom." It would harmonize the feelings and affections with the ideas of reason, deprive the "laws of reason of their moral compulsion," and "reconcile them with the interest of the senses." (152)

Marcuse, here quoting Schiller, seems to be reviving the "discredited" idealism of the eighteenth-century romantics, the naturalistic optimism which the two world wars are supposed to have demonstrated to be a false philosophy. But in no sense are the wars and revolutions of modern times examples of what happens when civilized repression is removed. They are the outbursts of sadistic rage for which the civilization of repression must always provide; they are its price, but a technological civilization can no longer afford the price. But for the same reason—as Marcuse argues—it does not need to pay it. For the technology which makes these outbursts insanely destructive also makes the culture of repression unnecessary because, in principle, it abolishes the need for drudgery and labor. Yet technology is not permitted to abolish labor because

of all things, hard work has become a virtue instead of the curse which it was always advertized to be by our remote ancestors. . . . Our children should be prepared to bring

their children up so they won't have to work as a neurotic
necessity. The necessity to work is a neurotic symptom. It
is a crutch. It is an attempt to make oneself feel valuable
even though there is no particular need for one's working. (153)

When technology is used—quite absurdly—to increase
employment rather than get rid of it, work becomes "busy-
work"—an artificial creation of ever more meaningless
routines, an interminable production of things that are not
so much luxuries for physical gratification as pretentious
trash. Technology then works against Eros and, as a result,
labor is all the more alienated and the necessity for violent
outbursts increased. As Marcuse says, "to link performances on assembly lines, in offices and shops with instinctual needs is to glorify dehumanization as pleasure"
(154). The type of human being who submits to this culture is, almost literally, a zombie. He is docile and "mature" in the style of our drab and dismal bourgeoisie; he
is quite incapable of gaiety or exuberance; he believes
that he is dancing when he is shuffling around a room; he
thinks he is being entertained when he is passively watching a couple of muscle-bound thugs in a wrestling match;
he thinks he is being scholarly and intellectual when he is
learning to speak with modesty and "all due reservations"
about some minor Elizabethan playwright; worse still, he
thinks he is rebelling against all this when he grows a
beard and gets himself a dingy pad in the slums. This is
the *only* major movement of dissent, apart from the protest against racial segregation, now current in the United
States!

This is not, of course, a balanced and considered opinion;
it is an expression of feeling, but not without very evident

grounds. The tragedy is that both the ways of liberation in the East and psychotherapy in the West have, to so large an extent, been sidetracked into the war against death and therefore into alienation from the body and from spontaneity. While the swami and the monk are poisoned with addiction to their own medicine and, out of false humility simply do not dare to be liberated, the "psychological man" —be he therapist or graduate patient—walks with solemn balance along his tightrope between too much Logos and too much Eros. As Rieff says:

> Being essentially negative, normality is an ever-retreating ideal. An attitude of stoic calm is required for its pursuit. No one catches the normal; everyone must act as if it can be caught. Nor can the psychological man forget himself in pursuit of the normal, for his normality consists of a certain kind of self-awareness. (155)

As the run-of-the-mill yogi is permanently *on the way* to liberation, so there is a tendency for the analyst and the analysand alike to be permanently "bugged," to be always suspicious of themselves, and thus to avoid any behavior —outside the consulting room—which might be taken to be unconscious. The absence of spontaneity at almost any gathering of psychotherapists is one of the sorriest sights in the world.

The question as to what a society of liberated people would be like is perhaps academic. What would happen if everyone in Manhattan decided to catch the same train for New Haven? Yet as the ideas of Freud, however twisted, have had the most far-reaching social influence, it is not impossible that ideas derived from the ways of liberation and from such revolutionary interpreters of psychoanalysis as Norman Brown may stir up something far more disturbing and energetic and exuberant than the Beat Generation. Some of their popular perversions are going to be devastating, but, even so, far preferable to anything foreshadowed in Huxley's *Brave New World*, Orwell's *1984*, and even to much of the dreary sobriety that already surrounds us. It is still far from certain, as Richard LaPiere (156) and others contend, that the Freudian ethic itself has actually increased social irresponsibility, for there was never a moralist at any time who was not certain that things were going from bad to worse.

> Delinquency has been with us from the time man began trying to civilize himself by establishing certain social codes of behavior. John Locke, the great English educator, three hundred years ago deplored delinquency in the same vein as we do today. Six thousand years ago an Egyptian priest carved on a stone, "Our earth is degenerate. . . . Children no longer obey their parents." (157)

LaPiere's case for the "subversion of American character," of the enterprising Protestant ethic, by the Freudian view of human nature simply recoils upon itself. In urging the ever-growing need for men of idealism and enterprise to cope with the problems which technological civilization is piling up for us, it is by no means beside the point to note that men of idealism and enterprise, busily at war with death, created the problem in the first place. Certainly, the problem cannot be abandoned, but it would be insane to go on wrestling with it in the same spirit that created it—the spirit of alienation from nature and ecological blindness.

If the Freudian ethic is demoralizing, it is not because it

has revealed the unconscious springs of action beyond control of the ego. It is because it has retained the ego as the subjective experient and puppet of the instincts and of social conditioning alike, and this has, if anything, increased the isolation of man-as-ego from his organic life on the one hand and from his fellow men on the other. For an impotent ego is more alienated than one which feels itself fully in control. The position of psychoanalysis is paradoxical because it is a step in the right direction which has not gone nearly far enough. It is attacked for the poverty of its results, and yet it has uncovered so many facts which can hardly be denied.

But the ethical problem is completely relevant if it is put in its proper place. Liberation is not the release of the soul from the body; it is recovery from the tactical split between the soul and the body which seems to be necessary for the social discipline of the young. It therefore sets reason and culture not against Eros but at the disposal of Eros, of the "polymorphous perverse" body which always retains the potentiality of a fully erotic relationship with the world—not just through the genital system but through the whole sensory capacity. Liberation restores the "primary narcissism" not just of the organism by itself, but of the organism/environment field. It is thus quite pertinent to ask how this "narcissism" might express itself ethically, or what, in other words, might be the ethics of Eros and of spontaneity as distinct from the ethics of survival.

It simplifies things to think of ethical behavior as a language, for like language proper, like art and music, it is a form of communication. But among all moralists, religious and otherwise, there is a tendency to treat ethics as a dead language, and to use it as Latin is used in the

Catholic church. In other words, authority shows a far greater resistance to ethical innovation and change than to comparable changes in language and the arts. Yet, in spite of this, the forms of ethical expression do in fact change, but the official versions tend to recognize these changes only by rather reluctant reinterpretation of such ancient standards and formulations as the Ten Commandments. There is obviously no guarantee that the ethics of Eros would be expressed in any such bronze-age terms.

It has almost always been man's custom to look for the authority for ethical standards outside ethics, to the laws of nature or the laws of God. We have never felt fully free to base our ethical principles simply upon what we would like to do and have done to us, for fear that such experimental conduct might injure us in unforeseen ways. There is obvious sense, up to a point, in sticking to what has worked in the past (if, indeed, it has), but equally obvious nonsense in attributing past formulations to a wisdom greater than ours. It is all very well to believe that "Mother is always right" until you yourself are a mother, but the constant attribution of a mysterious wisdom to antiquity is all bound up with our failure to recover from being children. We forget that we are being unnecessarily impressed by ancestors who also failed to recover from childhood and who, for that reason, revered authorities in the same predicament as themselves.

Nevertheless, tradition in ethics has the same sort of importance as tradition in language: it is simply the way in which people get to know what the rules are. One must therefore respect ethical tradition in the same way that one must respect linguistic or artistic tradition: not because it is sacrosanct, but because it is the only way of being in communication with others. If I wish to make an innovation in language acceptable, I must point out its meaning in the terms and the context of language as it already exists, for a completely abrupt change will not be understood. In Western culture, for example, the rules of painting and music have changed far more rapidly than the rules of speech, so that time after time the public has been shocked by paintings and compositions which seem incomprehensible. The early Beethoven symphonies provoked as much dismay at first hearing as the work of any of the great moderns, and the first reaction to such communications is not generally that they are difficult but that they are *bad*. The public feels that the artist has lost control of his technique. But later, if we try to understand what he is doing, we find that he has greatly enriched our experience. The artist's problem is to avoid changing the rules so radically that no bridge remains over which the public can follow him.

Now there are always purists and conservatives who will insist that there are absolute standards of correct speech and aesthetic technique. They will maintain, for example, that the ear has a fixed structure to which only one set of musical rules is appropriate, and anyone who claims to enjoy music composed by other rules will be accused of having perverse ears, or of deceiving himself. There are even those who would like to freeze the English language into the form in which it was spoken, say, in upper-class London in 1900—though why not 1800 or even 1600? One will not deny that dead languages, like Sanskrit and Church Latin, have certain technical uses, but spoken languages in daily usage change whether one likes it or not. The task of the grammarian and lexicographer is to maintain orderly change—not to lay down the law, but to stabilize linguistic change by keeping all members of a society informed as to what rules are being used.

Our culture inherits from both Jerusalem and Rome an ethical philosophy analogous to code law rather than common law. For wherever we ask what we *ought* to do, and seek authority for ethical standards either in the will of God or the laws of nature, we assume a pre-existing pattern, like a legal code or like roads and rails, to which human behavior is supposed to conform. This is much more than asking only that human behavior proceed in a pattern that is consistent with its own past—that it refrain from unintelligible jumps. Common law, on the other hand, makes itself up as it goes along; it sets precedents but they are never unalterable, because they are derived ultimately, not from a book of rules, but from a judge's intuitive feeling for equity and fair play—from a man rather than a machine. Code law assumes a pattern laid down once and for all; common law assumes a freely developing pattern which is nevertheless consistent with itself, like the development of a living language.

Now if liberation brings about the subordination of reason to Eros, as distinct from the subordination of Eros to reason, it is obviously allied to common law rather than code law. The ultimate authority for behavior does not, then, lie in any verbal formulation of oughts and ought-nots; it lies in the order of the organism/environment, an order which can never be fully or finally formulated in any stated laws of nature. Expecting scientific description to discover the pattern to which nature conforms is really assuming that law, or verbal formulation, precedes physical behavior—following the ancient notion that God *told* the universe what to do. But if we see that nature, instead of *conforming to* a pattern, *is* a pattern, we can get rid of a redundant and confusing step in our thinking. To say that reason is subordinate to Eros is simply to say that it is feedback, that it serves Eros by feeding back a description of spontaneous action. In just the same way, scientific description follows the pattern of nature; it does not lay down, like rails, the rules which nature *must* follow, for the pattern itself is developing freely. The feedback, the description, simply helps the human pattern to develop in a more orderly fashion. What reason and science are thus serving, and what always remains therefore the authority for action, is the body, and the order of the body is not mechanical but organic.[1]

We saw that common law rests ultimately upon the judge's intuitive feeling for equity. Every case is unique, and no code or set of fixed principles can provide for every eventuality. The deciding factor is therefore something far more subtle and complex than any formulation of rules can be—the judge's brain, *assisted* by precedents and rules. Code law, as well as authoritarian and traditionalist ethics, subverts the hierarchy of nature. It gives greater trust and authority to the relatively crude and rigid structure of verbal rules than to the infinitely more fluid and complex structure of the brain, the organism, and the field in which they live. Liberation returns us to the natural hierarchy, and I say "hierarchy" because it is a pattern in which reason and verbal rules are subordinated but not obliterated.

[1] For a fuller discussion of the difference between mechanical and organic order see Watts (158), and also the brilliant discussion by Needham (159) of the relation of Chinese ideas of natural order to Chinese law.

There are, then, two main reasons for comparing ethics with language and art. The first is to stress their aesthetic character, to say that they must work as a technique for expressing Eros or what Marcuse calls "the order of sensuousness," and thus put them in their proper place in the hierarchy. Ethics are then subordinate to spontaneity as in Lao-tzu's description of the ascending levels of natural order:

> The model [or, law] of man is the earth;
> The model of the earth is heaven;
> The model of heaven is the Tao;
> The model of the Tao is spontaneity. (160)

From this follows the second reason: to show that the function of ethics is not directive, but advisory and suggestive. Their creative use can no more be prescribed than we can write down simple instructions for making masterpieces of poetry or painting. But just as the inspired use of language is impossible without knowledge of the language, there can be no ethical expression of Eros to a repressed society without tact, that is, without a familiarity with the conventions of the society, with the channels open to communication and the blocks in its way.

For the joyous task which confronts an ethic of spontaneity, however difficult it may be, is quite literally to woo people out of their armed shells. But where in either East or West has this been seriously proposed? The forces working for social change never seem to think of summoning Eros to their aid. The tyranny of civilized masochism (of which the exploiters themselves are victims) cannot, as communism supposes, be overthrown by armed revolution. What is gained by force must be held by force, and for this reason the communist culture is, if anything, still more against life than the capitalist, and still more committed to the ethics of survival. On the other hand, the social idealism of Gandhi or of the Quakers is *also* a way of violence, of spiritual violence against the body, making its appeal to the masochism of "self-sacrifice." Admirable, devoted, and sincere as its followers are, the love which they are expressing is a blend of duty and pity, a soul-love in which there is no erotic warmth or gaiety, and which therefore fails to express the whole man. The idealisms which civilization produces are strivings of the alienated soul against death, and because their appeal is to hostility to fear, to pity (which is also fear), or to duty, they can never arouse the energy of life itself—Eros—which alone has the power to put reason into practice.

If there is anything to be learned from history, it is that scoldings, warnings, and preachings are a complete ethical failure. They may serve as part of the mummery with which children are hurried into learning adult conven- tions, but as the general means of inducing social change they only confirm and ingrain the attitudes which keep us at war. Psychoanalysis in the West and the ways of liberation in the East should enable us to see that the only effective way is to appeal to Eros, without which Logos— the sense of duty and reason—has no life. The problem is that civilized man has learned to be so deeply afraid of Eros that he scorns any suggestion that social love must be erotic; it conjures images of something slimy, lustful, fawning, and obscene which he wants to crush like a loath- some insect. As we have seen, this is in part because the erotic as he knows it is restricted to the genital and does not irradiate the whole sensory field, and thus he imagines that erotic fellowship with others would be a collective sexual orgy. At a deeper level, the fear of the erotic is the dissociated soul's resentment of its mortal body—failing to see that death is a problem, not for the organism, but for the soul. It is thus that so much of the organism's spontaneous behavior is shameful: it denies the ego's claim to be master.

But to appeal to Eros, psychoanalysis must overcome the remnants of antagonism in its own attitude to culture, and its use of a jargon which still carries the implication that the erotic is disgusting. So often the psychoanalytic interpretation of culture seems to be nothing more than debunking. It finds erotic symbolism in all the deliberate creations of art, science, and religion as if to say, "What dirty animals you are after all!" But Freud's detection of the erotic in everything supposedly spiritual and sublime is really a marvellous revelation. It shows that, try as we may, spontaneity cannot be prevented, and the fact that man is a living organism cannot be concealed. There is no reason for shame in the recognition that our most lofty images and conceptions have an erotic symbolism. Psychotherapy and liberation are completed in the moment when shame and guilt collapse, when the organism is no longer compelled to defend itself for being an organism, and when the individual is ready to own his unconscious behavior. But psychoanalysis does not, in practice, make it clear that the erotic is deeper than the genital. Beyond the play of the penis in the vagina lies the play of the organism in its environment—the polymorphous eroticism of man's original body as it comes from the womb.

"Polymorphous eroticism" is by no means a fancy term

for hedonism, for the mere pursuit of pleasure on all fronts. As Coomaraswamy said, spontaneity (*sahaja*) is "a path of non-pursuit," whereas the *pursuit* of pleasure implies an organism's assaulting its environment to "get something out of it" as if the environment were not part and parcel of the organism. Like the complete sexual orgasm, the delight of this eroticism must "come" unforced. There is no self-conscious exercise in deliberately relaxing or opening the senses that can bring it about, save as an *upaya*, a technique to show that it cannot be commanded. Polymorphous eroticism can neither be cultivated nor made into a cult; it can only develop of itself when the soul has been returned to the body and the individual is no longer identified with the ego. It is thus that the adult recovers what in Zen is called the "natural endowment" which he had as a child, and this is why the Taoists see in the body of the child a model for the body of the sage. In the words of Chuang-tzu:

> Can you be like a newborn child? The baby cries all day and yet his voice never becomes hoarse; that is because he has not lost nature's harmony. . . . The baby looks at things all day without winking; that is because his eyes are not focussed on any particular object. He goes without knowing where he is going, and stops without knowing what he is doing. He merges himself with the surroundings and moves along with it. These are the principles of mental hygiene. (161)

This is Freud's "primal narcissism," and as Norman Brown says:

> Freud says not only that the human ego-feeling once embraced the whole world, but also that Eros drives the ego to recover that feeling: "The development of the ego

consists in a departure from primal narcissism and results in a vigorous attempt to recover it." In primal narcissism the self is at one with a world of love and pleasure; hence the ultimate aim of the human ego is to reinstate what Freud calls "limitless narcissism" and find itself once more at one with the whole world in love and pleasure. (162)

The adult or mature version of primal narcissism is, of course, "cosmic consciousness," or the shift from ego-centric awareness to the feeling that one's identity is the whole field of the organism in its environment. But if this is not to remain a purely contemplative state, if, in other words, the liberated man is to return into the world like the Bodhisattva, he will seek the means for expressing his sense of being "at one with the whole world in love and pleasure." Because the means are aesthetic his approach to the world is, as Marcuse suggests, that of Orpheus "the priest, the mouthpiece of the gods," who tames both men and beasts by the allure and magic of his harp. His method is not that of the preacher or the politician but that, in its widest sense, of the artist. For in the value system of civilization, of compulsive survival, the artist is irrelevant. He is seen as a mere decorator who entertains us while we labor. As strolling minstrel, player, clown, or poet he can pass everywhere because no one takes him seriously. "His language," says Marcuse, "is *song*, and his work is *play*."

Totalitarian states, however, know the danger of the artist. Correctly, if for the wrong reasons, they know that all art is propaganda, and that art which does not support their system must be against it. They know intuitively that the artist is not a harmless eccentric but one who under the guise of irrelevance creates and reveals a new reality.

If, then, he is not to be torn to pieces like Orpheus in the myth, the liberative artist must be able to play the counter-game and keep it as well hidden as the *judo* of Taoism and Zen. He must be able to be "all things to all men," for as one sees from the history of Zen any discipline whatsoever can be used as a way of liberation—making pots, designing gardens, arranging flowers, building houses, serving tea, and even using the sword; one does not have to advertise oneself as a psychotherapist or *guru*. He is the artist in whatever he does, not just in the sense of doing it beautifully, but in the sense of *playing* it. In the expressive lingo of the jazz world, whatever the scene, he makes it. Whatever he does, he *dances* it—like a Negro bootblack shining shoes. He swings.

It is not by chance that one thinks of the American Negro, his music and his language, in this connection. He retains the vestiges of a truly erotic culture, and it is this rather than his color and features which the Anglo-Saxon subculture so strongly resents. It is quite miraculous to listen to a Negro preacher and congregation convert the most unattractive Bible religion of the South into a swinging dance of superb nonsense. It is something of an exception to Jacob Boehme's feeling that

> no people understands any more the sensual language, and the birds in the air and the beasts in the forest do understand it according to their species. Therefore man may reflect what he has been robbed of, and what he is to recover in the second birth. For in the sensual language all spirits speak with each other, they need no other language, for it is the language of nature. (163)

I am not idealizing the Negro because, under the circumstances, his culture is no more than a vague glimmer of what I am trying to suggest, and survives through over-whelming poverty and squalor. I am suggesting that it is possible to stop taking the universe and human life seri-ously by telling it that it *must* play, as if it were in course to some future ideal which it must reach at all costs. To feel this way is indeed, to use the jazz lingo again, "a very far-out scene"—a way of being so intensely alienated that recovery will present an astonishing contrast.

The ways of liberation make it very clear that life is not going anywhere, because it is already *there*. In other words, it is playing, and those who do not play with it have simply missed the point. As Lewis Mumford puts it:

> Beauty, for example, has played as large a part in evolu-tion as use and cannot be explained, as Darwin sought to, merely as a practical device for courtship or fertilization. In short, it is just as permissible to conceive nature, mytho-logically, as a poet, working in metaphors and rhythms, as to think of nature as a cunning mechanic, trying to save material, make both ends meet, do the job efficiently and cheaply. (164)

The two views may be equally permissible in the sense that there is no reason why we may not play either, though to play that we are not playing leads to the vicious circles, frustrations, and contradictions of the double-bind—and *that* game is not worth the candle. It is to the degree that children play that they are not playing that "cops and rob-bers" leads to bloody noses and hurt feelings, and thus to the end of the game. Music, dancing, rhythm—all these are art forms which have no goal other than themselves, and to participate in them fully is to lay aside all thought of a *necessary* future; to say "must" to rhythm is to stop it

INVITATION TO THE DANCE

dead. In the moment when he is anxious to play the correct
notes, the musician is blocked. In both senses, he stops
playing. He can only perfect his art by continuing to play,
practicing without *trying* until the moment comes when
he finds that the correct rhythm plays itself.

All perfect accomplishment in art or life is accompanied
by the curious sensation that it is happening of itself—
that it is not forced, studied, or contrived. This is not to
say that everything which is felt to happen of itself is a
perfect accomplishment; the marvel of human spontaneity
is that it has developed the means of self-discipline—which
becomes repressive only when it is felt that the controlling
agent is separate from the action. But the sensation that
the action is happening of itself, neither *from* an agent
nor *to* a witness, is the authentic sensation of life as pure
process in which there is neither mover nor moved. Process
without source or destination, verb without subject or
object—this is not deprivation, as the word "without" suggests, but the "musical" sensation of arriving at every moment in which the melody and rhythm unfold.

Music is our nearest approximation to Boehme's "sensual
language," for, unlike ordinary language, it does not refer
to anything beyond itself, and though it has phrases and
patterns, it is without sentences which separate subject
from object, and parts of speech which separate things
from events. "Abstract" as they may at first seem to be,
music and pure mathematics are closer to life than are
useful languages which point to meanings beyond themselves. Ordinary language refers to life, but music is living.
But life itself is made to behave as ordinary language when
it is lived for a purpose beyond itself, when the present
serves the future, or when the body is exploited for the

purposes of the soul. Such a way of life is therefore "beside itself"—insane—and because it is being made to behave as language and words it becomes as empty as "mere words." It has no recourse except to go on and on to the future to which the present apparently refers, only to find that here, too, the meaning is still beyond.

The liberative artist plays the part of Orpheus by living in the mode of music instead of the mode of language. His entire activity is dancing, rhythm for its own sake, and in this way he becomes a vortex which draws others into its pattern. He charms their attention from then to now, absorbing them into a rhythm in which survival ceases to be the criterion of value. It is by this attraction, and not by direction or commandment, that he is sought out as a teacher in the way of liberation. It is easy enough to become a martyr by throwing open challenges and judgments at the ways of the world. It is all too simple to indulge the sense of being in the right by flaunting one's lack of inhibition and scandalizing a repressed society. But the high art, the *upaya*, of a true Bodhisattva is possible only for him who has gone beyond all need for self-justification, for so long as there is something to prove, some ax to grind, there is no dance.

From the standpoint of genuine liberation there are no inferior people. Because the ego never actually exists, those who are most captivated by its illusion are still playing. That they take it seriously and do not know that they are playing is honored by the Bodhisattva as an extremely abandoned and risky game. For if the world *is* play there is no way of going against it. The most outright contradictions, the most firm assertions that the game is serious, the most absurd attempts to command spontaneity, and the most involved vicious circles can never be anything but extremely "far-out" forms of play. When it comes down to it, civilized repression simply builds up the power of Eros like water accumulating behind a dam. The game of hide-and-seek goes on because Eros continues to conceal and reveal itself in every rationalization, in the most deliberately spiritual and other-worldly images. Seeing this, the Bodhisattva can never feel that he is condescending or that his liberation, his knowledge that the world is play, makes him superior to others. That he works for their liberation at all is only because of his compassion for them in the agony they feel when the game is unconscious, when seriousness is being played to an extreme. It is not so much the Bodhisattva himself as the very extremity of the situation which generates compassion, for the most intense darkness is itself the seed of light, and all explicit warfare is implicit love.

Bibliographical References

1 A. W. Watts, *The Way of Zen*, Pantheon, New York, 1957.
2 P. Teilhard de Chardin, *The Phenomenon of Man*, Harper, New York, 1959, pp. 43–44.
3 J. Needham, *Science and Civilization in China*, Vol. 2, Cambridge University Press, 1956. See secs. 10, 13, 16, and 18.
4 *Cheng-tao ke*, 11, tr. D. T. Suzuki, *Manual of Zen Buddhism*, Kyoto, 1935, p. 108.
5 C. G. Jung, *Psychology and Religion: West and East*, Collected Works, Vol. 11, Bollingen Series 20, Pantheon, New York, 1958, p. 476.
6 N. O. Brown, *Life Against Death: The Psychoanalytical Meaning of History*, Wesleyan University, 1959, pp. 170–171.
7 R. Wilhelm and C. G. Jung, *The Secret of the Golden Flower*, Routledge, London, 1931, p. 83.
8 G. Murphy, *Personality: A Biosocial Approach to Origins and Structure*, Harper, New York, 1947.
9 A. F. Bentley, *Inquiry into Inquiries*, Beacon, Boston, 1954, p. 4.
10 L. Wittgenstein, *Tractatus Logico-Philosophicus*, Routledge, London, 1960, Sec. 6.37.
11 See reference 10, 6.371.
12 See reference 10, 6.5, 6.51, 6.52, 6.521.
13 J. Dewey and A. F. Bentley, *Knowing and the Known*, Beacon, Boston, 1949.
14 A. Angyal, *Foundations for a Science of Personality*, Commonwealth Fund, New York, 1941.

15 E. Brunswik, "Organismic Achievement and Environmental Probability," *Psychological Review*, Vol. 50, 1943.

16 See reference 8, p. 891.

17 See reference 10, 6.35.

18 *Tao Te Ching*, 2.

19 A. Strauss, ed., *The Social Psychology of George Herbert Mead*, Phoenix, Chicago, 1956.

20 See reference 19, pp. 257–258.

21 See reference 19, pp. 258–259.

22 See reference 19, p. 257n.

23 G. Bateson, with D. D. Jackson, J. Haley, and J. H. Weakland, "Towards a Theory of Schizophrenia," *Behavioral Science*, Vol. 1, 4, October, 1956, pp. 251–264.

24 S. Radhakrishnan, *The Bhagavadgita*, Harper, New York, 1948, p. 177.

25 W. James, *A Pluralistic Universe*, New York, 1909, p. 380.

26 From *Freud: The Mind of the Moralist* by Philip Rieff. Copyright © 1959 by Philip Rieff. Reprinted by permission of The Viking Press, Inc. Pp. 153–154.

27 E. Cassirer, *Substance and Function and Einstein's Theory of Relativity*, Dover, New York, 1953, p. 398.

28 G. Murphy, *Human Potentialities*, Basic Books, New York, 1958, p. viii.

29 T. R. V. Murti, *The Central Philosophy of Buddhism* Allen and Unwin, London, 1955, p. 141.

30 See reference 10, 6.44, 6.522.

31 *Wu-men Kwan*, 49. P. Reps, *Zen Flesh, Zen Bones*, Tuttle Rutland and Tokyo, 1957, p. 161.

32 A. David-Neel, *Secret Oral Teachings in the Tibetan Buddhist Sects*, Maha-Bodhi Society, Calcutta, n.d., pp 99–101.

33 See reference 32, pp. 101–102.

34 See reference 29, p. 167.

35 T. W. and C. A. F. Rhys Davids, trs., *Dialogues of the Buddha*, Luzac, London, 1951, Part II, p. 65.

36 A. K. Coomaraswamy, "Recollection Indian and Platonic, and The One and Only Transmigrant," Supplement to *Journal of the American Oriental Society*, Vol. 64, 2, 1937.

37 M. H. Erickson, J. Haley, and J. H. Weakland, "A Transcript of a Trance Induction with Commentary," *American Journal of Clinical Hypnosis*, Vol. 2, 2, 1959.

38 R. O. Kapp, *Towards a Unified Cosmology*, Basic Books, New York, 1960, pp. 57–58.

39 *Shih Niu T'ou*, 10.

40 Lin Yutang, *The Wisdom of Laotse*, Random House, New York, 1948, p. 41.

41 Ch'u Ta-kao tr., *Tao Te Ching*, Buddhist Society, London, 1937, p. 44.

42 *Chuang-tzu*, 2. See reference 40, pp. 48–49.

43 *Chuang-tzu*, 13. H. A. Giles, tr., *Chuang Tzu*, Shanghai, 1926, pp. 166–167.

44 *Chuang-tzu*, 14. See reference 43, pp. 184–185.

45 *Chuang-tzu*, 4.

46 *Chuang-tzu*, 4.

47 *Chuang-tzu*, 22. See reference 43, p. 289.

48 *Tao Te Ching*, 18. See reference 41, p. 28.

49 *Chuang-tzu*, 6. See reference 43, pp. 69–70.

50 See reference 3, sec. 10, *f* and *g*.

51 *Tao Te Ching*, 23. See reference 41, p. 33, adjuv. auct.

52 Cf. D. T. Suzuki, *Zen and Japanese Culture*, Bollingen Series 64, Pantheon, New York, 1959, Plates 1, 16, 58, 60, 63.

53 *Chuang-tzu*, 12. See reference 40, p. 129.

54 *Chuang-tzu*, 19. See reference 43, pp. 238–239.

55 D. T. Suzuki, *Living by Zen*, Rider, London, 1950, p. 137.

56 From *The Cocktail Party*, copyright, 1950, by T. S. Eliot. Reprinted by permission of Harcourt, Brace & World, Inc., New York, 1952, p. 307.

57 A. W. Watts, *This Is It*, Pantheon, New York, 1960, final essay.

58 S. B. Dasgupta, *Introduction to Tantric Buddhism*, University of Calcutta, 1950.

59 M. Eliade, *Yoga: Immortality and Freedom*, Bollingen Series 58, Pantheon, New York, 1958, esp. pp. 264–265.

60 J. Woodroffe, *Shakti and Shakta*, Luzac, London, 1929.

61 A. W. Watts, *Nature, Man, and Woman*, Pantheon, New York, 1958, pp. 190–195.

62 See reference 58, p. 203.

63 D. Snellgrove, tr., in E. Conze, ed., *Buddhist Texts*, Cassirer, Oxford, 1954, p. 226.

64 A. K. Coomaraswamy, *The Dance of Shiva*, Noonday, New York, 1957, pp. 124–134.

65 See reference 6.

66 See reference 64, p. 131.

67 R. Guénon, *Introduction to the Study of the Hindu Doctrines*, Luzac, London, 1945, p. 112.

68 See reference 6, p. 316.

69 G. Bachelard, *La Formation de l'esprit scientifique*, Paris, 1947, pp. 250–251.

70 G. Kepes, *The New Landscape*, Theobald, Chicago, 1956.

71 A. N. Whitehead, *Adventures of Ideas*, Mentor, New York, 1955, pp. 250–251.

72 S. Freud, *Civilization and Its Discontents*, Hogarth, London, 1930, p. 144.

73 See reference 6, p. 322.

74 L. L. Whyte, *The Next Development in Man*, Holt, New York, 1948.

75 See reference 10, 5.5423.

76 See reference 71, p. 172.

77 R. May, *Existence*, Basic Books, New York, 1958, pp. 86–90.

78 G. Mora, "Recent American Psychiatric Developments," *American Handbook of Psychiatry*, 2 vols., Basic Books, New York, 1960, p. 32.

79 See reference 5, p. 339.

80 S. Freud, *Beyond the Pleasure Principle*, Hogarth, London, 1955, p. 56.

81 See reference 72, pp. 121–122.

82 See reference 74, pp. 238–239.

83 S. Freud, *On Creativity and the Unconscious*, Harper, New York, 1958, pp. 55–62.

84 See reference 5, p. 484.

85 See reference 5, pp. 504–505.

86 See reference 7, p. 80.

87 C. G. Jung, *Modern Man in Search of a Soul*, Routledge, London, 1936, pp. 118–119.

88 A. H. Maslow, *Motivation and Personality*, Harper, New York, 1954, pp. 292–293.

89 See reference 88, pp. 291–292.

90 G. Groddeck, *The Book of the It* and *The World of Man*, C. W. Daniel, London, 1935 and 1934.

91 W. Reich, *The Sexual Revolution*, Orgone, New York, 1945. Also, *Character Analysis*, Orgone, New York, 1949.

92 H. Marcuse, *Eros and Civilization*, Beacon, Boston, 1955.

93 See reference 6.

94 M. E. Harding, *Psychic Energy*, Bollingen Series 10, Pantheon, New York, 1947, p. 1.

95 C. G. Jung, *The Development of Personality*, Collected Works, Vol. 17, Bollingen Series 20, Pantheon, New York, 1954, p. 53.

96 See reference 57, Chap. 1.

97 See reference 52, p. 353.

98 *Lin-chi lü.*

99 Personal communication.

100 R. May, "The Existential Approach," *American Handbook of Psychiatry*, 2 vols., Basic Books, New York, 1959, Vol. 2, p. 1349.

101 L. Binswanger, *Ausgewählte Vorträge und Aufsätze*, Bern, 1947. Quoted in reference 100.

102 See reference 77, pp. 18–19.

103 J. Ruesch and G. Bateson, *Communication: The Social Matrix of Psychiatry*, Norton, New York, 1951, Chap. 8.

104 See reference 55, p. 124.

105 See reference 6, pp. 104–105.

106 See reference 6, p. 106.

107 See reference 6, p. 92.

108 See reference 6, p. 93.

109 H. S. Sullivan, *The Interpersonal Theory of Psychiatry*, Norton, New York, 1953, p. 169.

110 H. S. Sullivan, "Tensions Interperson and International," in H. Cantril, ed., *Tensions that Cause War*, University of Illinois, 1950, p. 92.

111 J. Ruesch, *Disturbed Communication*, Norton, New York, 1957. J. Ruesch and W. Kees, *Nonverbal Communication*, University of California, 1956. See also reference 103.

112 G. Bateson, "The New Conceptual Frames for Behavioral Research," *Proceedings of the Sixth Annual Psychiatric Institute, Princeton, 1958*, pp. 54–71. See also reference 23.

113 A. Rapoport, "Mathematics and Cybernetics," *American Handbook of Psychiatry*, 2 vols., Basic Books, New York, 1959, Vol. 2, p. 1743.

114 J. Haley, "The Art of Psychoanalysis," *ETC.*, Vol. 15, 1958, pp. 190–200. Also, "Control in Psychoanalytic Psychotherapy," in *Progress in Psychotherapy*, Grune and Stratton, New York, 1959.

115 J. Ruesch, "The Trouble with Psychiatric Research," *AMA Archives of Neurology and Psychiatry*, Vol. 77, 1957, p. 96.

116 G. Bateson, "Language and Psychotherapy," *Psychiatry*, Vol. 21, pp. 96 and 100.

117 E. Fromm, *The Sane Society*, Rinehart, New York, 1955, p. 143.

118 E. Fromm and D. T. Suzuki, *Zen Buddhism and Psycho-analysis*, Harper, New York, 1960.

119 See reference 116, pp. 99–100.

120 See reference 74, pp. 57 and 67.

121 See reference 114, "The Art of Psychoanalysis."

122 *Vajracchedika*, 22.

123 *Lin-chi lü*.

124 *Lin-chi lü*.

125 *Ku-tsun-hsü Yü-lu*, 1. 6.

126 E. Herrigel, *Zen in the Art of Archery*, Pantheon, New York, 1953.

127 *Wu-men kwan*, 14.

128 P. Reps, *Zen Flesh, Zen Bones*, Tuttle, Rutland and Tokyo, 1957.

129 D. T. Suzuki, *Essays in Zen Buddhism*, 3 vols., Rider, London, 1949, 1950, 1951.

130 See reference 1.

131 A. J. Bahm, *The Philosophy of Buddha*, Harper, New York, 1958.

132 See reference 131, p. 98.

133 L. Giles, *Taoist Teachings*, Murray, London, 1925, pp. 40–42. Also in reference 1, p. 22.

134 See reference 1, pp. 93–94.

135 See reference 125, 1.2.4.

136 C. G. Jung, *The Integration of Personality*, Rinehart, New York, 1939, pp. 31–32.

137 See reference 92, pp. 168–169.

138 E. Erikson, *Young Man Luther*, Norton, New York, 1958, p. 264.

139 See reference 138, p. 263.

140 J. Haley, "Control in Psychoanalytic Psychotherapy," in *Progress in Psychotherapy*, Grune and Stratton, New York, 1959, pp. 48–65.

141 F. S. Perls, R. F. Hefferline, and P. Goodman, *Gestalt Therapy*, Julian Press, New York, 1951, p. 259 and n.

142 J. Rosen, *Direct Analysis*, Grune and Stratton, New York, 1953.

143 See reference 140, p. 59.

144 *Hsin-hsin ming*. See reference 1, p. 115.

145 S. Freud, *New Introductory Lectures on Psychoanalysis*, Norton, New York, 1933, pp. 203–204.

146 Hakuin, *Zazen Wasan*. Cf. D. T. Suzuki in reference 4, p. 184.

147 See reference 6, p. 284.

148 See reference 6, p. 93.

149 See reference 6, pp. 158–159.

150 See reference 6, p. 307.

151 See reference 26, p. 355.

152 See reference 92, pp. 181–182.

153 C. B. Chisholm, in "The Psychiatry of Enduring Peace and Social Progress," *Psychiatry*, Vol. 9, 1, 1946, p. 31.

154 See reference 92, p. 221.

155 See reference 26, p. 355.

156 R. LaPiere, *The Freudian Ethic*, Duell, Sloan and Pierce, New York, 1959.

157 A. M. Johnson, "Juvenile Delinquency," *American Handbook of Psychiatry*, 2 vols., Basic Books, New York, 1959, Vol. 1, p. 840.

158 See reference 61, pp. 51–69.

159 See reference 3, sec. 18.

160 *Tao Te Ching*, 25.

161 *Chuang-tzu*, 23. In reference 40, pp. 85–86.

162 See reference 6, p. 46.

163 J. Boehme, *Mysterium Magnum*, Chap. 35, 59–60.

164 L. Mumford, *The Conduct of Life*, Harcourt, Brace, New York, 1951, p. 35.